Wissenschaftliche Untersuchungen zum Neuen Testament · 2. Reihe

Herausgeber/Editor
Jörg Frey

Mitherausgeber / Associate Editors
Friedrich Avemarie · Judith Gundry-Volf
Martin Hengel · Otfried Hofius · Hans-Josef Klauck

192

Aquila H. I. Lee

From Messiah to Preexistent Son

Jesus' Self-Consciousness and Early Christian
Exegesis of Messianic Psalms

Mohr Siebeck

Aquila H. I. Lee, born 1963; BA at National University of Buenos Aires; M.Div. at Biblical Graduate School of Theology (Singapore); 2003 Ph.D. at University of Aberdeen; Lecturer of New Testament and Greek at Biblical Graduate School of Theology (Singapore).

BT
198
.L425
2005

ISBN 3-16-148616-1
ISSN 0340-9570 (Wissenschaftliche Untersuchungen zum Neuen Testament 2. Reihe)

Die Deutsche Bibliothek lists this publication in the Deutsche Nationalbibliographie; detailed bibliographic data is available in the Internet at *http://dnb.ddb.de*.

The book was printed by Druckpartner Rübelmann GmbH in Hemsbach on non-aging paper and bound by Buchbinderei Schaumann in Darmstadt.

Printed in Germany.

Preface

This book is a slightly revised version of my doctoral thesis submitted to the Department of Divinity and Religious Studies at the University of Aberdeen in 2003.

The present study would not have come to fruition without the guidance and encouragement of many people. To each one of them I am extremely grateful. First and foremost, I would like to express my heartfelt gratitude to Professor I. Howard Marshall, my *Doktorvater*, for his patient supervision and constant encouragement throughout the course of research. His constructive criticisms and perceptive comments have stimulated and encouraged clearer thinking and writing during the production of the thesis. I am especially thankful to him for his example of rigorous scholarship combined with warm Christian friendship. My thanks must also go to Dr Simon Gathercole (Aberdeen) and Dr Peter Head (Cambridge), the examiners of the thesis, for their helpful and incisive criticisms. Acknowledgement must also made of the way in which I was challenged and stimulated by my fellow postgraduate students. Their friendship, questions and comments have been received with much appreciation. Our time in Scotland would not have been possible without the financial and prayer support from many people. Special thanks go to my father, my parents-in-law and Rev Dr Quek Swee Hwa and friends from Zion B-P Church (Singapore). My special thanks are also due to Prof. Jörg Frey, editor of *WUNT 2*, who was extremely efficient, helpful and supportive in reading and commenting on the manuscript after a few weeks of receiving it. I am also grateful to the Council and colleagues at Biblical Graduate School of Theology for their support and kind generosity in reducing my teaching responsibilities in order for me to work with the revision of the manuscript.

Finally and on a more personal note, I wish to thank my wife Soo-Yon who has willingly come along for this long journey of writing a PhD thesis and helped create a nurturing home for me and our son, Abraham. Without her selfless commitment, sacrificial support and constant encouragement, this project would not have been completed with a happy ending.

1 March 2005   Aquila Lee

Table of Contents

THE FOUNDATION FOR PRE-EXISTENT SON CHRISTOLOGY

THE CATALYST FOR PRE-EXISTENT SON CHRISTOLOGY

Chapter 1

Introduction

In recent times an area which has attracted a great deal of scholarly attention is the development and origin of the early Christian view of Jesus as a divine and pre-existent being. The early Christian conviction that Jesus of Nazareth, who suffered a shameful death on the cross, is divine and pre-existent alongside one God is indeed a very remarkable development.[1] If the late nineteenth century and early decades of the twentieth was mainly dominated by the history-of-religions school's attempts to find precedents from Hellenistic and Eastern religions,[2] the last quarter of a century has seen a growing emphasis on Jewish backgrounds to early christology from the Second Temple period. This new trend in the discussion of the formative period of Christianity – labelled in some quarters as a new *religionsgeschichtliche Schule*[3] – does not only see the development of early christology as having taken place within Jewish soils, but it also locates the emergence of high christology within the first two or three decades after Jesus' death and resurrection.

Such a renewal of interest in the parallel motifs to early christology from Second Temple Judaism has led some scholars to re-evaluate the true character of the first century Jewish monotheism. In fact, NT scholars have long been puzzled by a seemingly enigmatic relationship between Jewish monotheistic belief of one God of Israel and the divine/pre-existent status given to Jesus in the early church. What prompted the earliest Christians to regard Jesus as divine and pre-existent alongside one God? How was it possible for the pious Jews of the first century, who had been brought up with a strong monotheistic belief in one God, to be able to accord such a

---

[1] That the early church came to a fuller understanding of who Jesus really is from the resurrection onwards seems to be beyond question.

[2] They insisted that the divine status of Jesus in early Christianity was the result of syncretistic influence from "pagan" religions of the Roman era on "Hellenistic" Christians supposedly more susceptible to such influence than were "Palestinian" Jewish Christians.

[3] The term was first coined by M. Hengel in his comment on the back cover of American edition of L. W. Hurtado, *One God, One Lord: Early Christian Devotion and Ancient Jewish Monotheism* (London: SCM, 1988, 1998). See now L. W. Hurtado, *Lord Jesus Christ: Devotion to Jesus in Earliest Christianity* (Grand Rapids: Eerdmans, 2003), 5-18, for a quick comparison between the old school of Göttingen and the new.

unique status to a man whose life came to an abrupt end on a Roman cross as a criminal?

1.1. The Development and Origin of Jesus' Pre-existence

Contemporary scholarship has proposed a number of different theories about the development and origin of the early Christian understanding of Jesus as a divine/pre-existent being.[4] Although any attempts to categorize the views of others may run the risk of oversimplification, it is nonetheless necessary to group them into categories if we are to present and evaluate them effectively. We may thus for convenience group the different theories into the following categories: (1) Paul's wisdom christology; (2) John's pre-existence christology; (3) divine agent or divine identity christology; and (4) angelic/angelomorphic christology.

1.1.1. Paul's Wisdom Christology

That Paul was indebted to the Jewish wisdom tradition is widely recognized among NT scholars today, although to what extent it was influential to his understanding of Jesus is still debated.

Hans Windisch was the first scholar who argued that Paul's christology was decisively influenced by the Jewish wisdom tradition, where the figure of the Messiah had already become merged with that of Wisdom, and that Paul identified the pre-existent Christ with divine Wisdom.[5] Windisch found the identification of the Messiah and Wisdom from two Jewish sources: (1) the description of the Son of Man in terms of Wisdom in *1 Enoch* (48:2,6; 49:3; 92:1; 49:4; 42:1); (2) the LXX translation of Mic 5:1 and Ps 110:3. He claimed that behind Paul's descriptions of Jesus as the Wisdom of God (1 Cor 1-3), the following rock (1 Cor 10:4), the firstborn

---

[4] Although some studies do not deal with the issue of the origin of Jesus' pre-existence specifically, they assume that the concept of Jesus' divinity is closely related to that of his pre-existence, and this assumption will be confirmed during the course of our study.

[5] H. Windisch, "Die göttliche Weisheit der Juden und die paulinische Christologie" in *Neutestamentliche Studien: Georg Heinrici zu seinem 70. Geburtstag* (ed. A. Deissmann; Leipzig: Hinrichs, 1914), 220-34. In 1966, about 50 years later his hypothesis is developed in greater detail by A. Feuillet, *Le Christ, sagesse de Dieu: d'apres les épitres pauliniennes* (Paris: Lecoffre, 1966). Recently, W. Horbury, *Jewish Messianism and the Cult of Christ* (London: SCM, 1998) and J. Schaper, *Eschatology in the Greek Psalter* (WUNT 2/76; Tübingen: Mohr Siebeck, 1995), have postulated that there was a tradition about a pre-existent messianic figure in Second Temple Judaism. They find evidence of such a tradition primarily from the interpretative translation of the LXX.

of creation (Col 1:15-20), the head of the church (Eph 1:19-21), and the word of righteousness that is near (Rom 10:6-9) lies the figure of Lady Wisdom familiar from Prov 8, Sir 24, and Wis 9.

W. L. Knox popularized Windisch's view with further appeal to apocryphal literature, Philo and rabbinic tradition. Rather than claiming any direct literary influence of Sirach, Wisdom, or Philo on Paul's letters, Knox argued that a common tradition of interpretation lies behind all these different speculations about divine Wisdom.[6]

Later W. D. Davies revised Windisch's theory by locating the supposed source of the Paul's wisdom christology in the Apostle's identification of Jesus with the Torah, which itself was already understood as the pre-existent σοφία of God active in creation and redemption. Davies argued that Paul regarded Jesus as the "new Torah" by ascribing to him all the attributes of Wisdom (e.g., pre-existence and mediation in creation).[7] He strengthened his case by bringing in a number of Jewish ideas (such as Wisdom, Torah and Messiah) that to a certain degree could be regarded as identifiable to one another. Once Paul has replaced the law with Christ, all the attributes inherent to Wisdom, says Davies, must have automatically transferred to Jesus.

E. Schweizer argued that the two clauses "God sent his Son" and "in order to redeem . . ." in Gal 4:4 (cf. Rom 8:3, John 3:17, and 1 Jn 4:9) were the basis of a pre-Pauline "sending formula" which originated from the Torah-Wisdom-Logos speculations of Alexandrian Judaism and was taken over by Hellenistic Christians to speak about Jesus as the pre-existent Son of God.[8] To support his hypothesis, Schweizer emphasizes the parallels between Wis 9:10-17 and Gal 4:4-7 where the verb used for the sending of both Wisdom and the Son, ἐξαποστέλλειν, is a Pauline *hapax legomenon* and the sending of Wisdom/Son in both passages is followed by the sending of the Holy Spirit. He also finds parallels from Philo.

In his 1964 essay "Der vorpaulinische Hymnus Phil 2,6-11," D. Georgi discerned behind this pre-Pauline hymn the myth of the humiliation and exaltation of the wise man in Wis 2-3, a theme which itself already

---

[6] W. L. Knox, *St Paul and the Church of the Gentiles* (Cambridge: CUP, 1939), 55-89, 111-24.

[7] W. D. Davies, *Paul and Rabbinic Judaism: Some Rabbinic Elements in Pauline Theology* (London: SPCK, 1948, 1970), 147-76.

[8] E. Schweizer, "Zum religionsgeschichtlichen Hintergrund der 'Sendungsformel' Gal. 4,4f., Rö. 8,3f., Jn 3,16f., 1Jn 4,9" *ZNW* 57 (1966), 199-210; Schweizer, "υἱός," *TDNT* 8.354-57; E. Schweizer, "Paul's Christology and Gnosticism" in *Paul and Paulinism: Essays in Honour of C. K. Barrett* (eds. M. D. Hooker *et al.*; London: SPCK, 1982), esp. 118-19.

4 _Chapter 1: Introduction_

interprets the Suffering Servant of Isaiah as one in whom pre-existent Wisdom dwells.[9]

M. Hengel attempted in 1975 to explain all of early Christian language about Jesus – and especially Paul's – from Jewish wisdom traditions.[10] Taking as his point of departure the title Son of God, Hengel examines the historical antecedents to what he calls "the thought-patterns involved with [the title Son of God]: pre-existence, mediation at creation and sending into the world."[11] Hengel builds on Schweizer's theory that the formula "God sent his Son" reflects Hellenistic Torah-Wisdom-Logos speculations[12] by adding his own explanation of the religio-historical background of other christological titles and confessional statements. His conclusion that "the question of the relationship of Jesus to other intermediary figures" was prompted by "the confession of the exaltation of Jesus as Son of Man and Son of God" and once the idea of pre-existence had been introduced, the attributes of Wisdom was automatically transferred to Jesus" was however essentially a revision of Davies' explanation.[13]

S. Kim located the root of the identification of Jesus and wisdom in Paul's own experience of the Damascus Christophany where he became convinced that Jesus is the "image of God" and the Son of God.[14] While Hengel argued that Jewish identification of Wisdom and Torah led early Christians to identify Jesus with Wisdom and then with Torah, Kim reversed the chronological order of that identification by postulating the identification of Jesus with Torah first and then with Wisdom.

While accepting the influence of the Jewish wisdom tradition on Paul's christology, J. D. G. Dunn challenged the majority view[15] by arguing that

---

[9] D. Georgi, "Der vorpaulinische Hymnus Phil 2,6-11" in _Zeit und Geschichte: Dankesgabe an Rudolf Bultmann zum 80. Geburtstag_ (eds. E. Dinkler _et al._; Tübingen: Mohr Siebeck, 1964), 263-93.

[10] M. Hengel, _The Son of God: the Origin of Christology and the History of Jewish-Hellenistic Religion_ (London: SCM, 1976), originally published as _Der Sohn Gottes: Die Entstehung der Christologie und die jüdische-hellenistische Religionsgeschichte_ (Tübingen: Mohr Siebeck, 1975; rev. 1977).

[11] Hengel, _Son of God_, 57.

[12] On Schweizer's hypothesis see §8.2.1.

[13] Hengel, _Son of God_, 67, 72.

[14] S. Kim, _The Origin of Paul's Gospel_ (WUNT 2/4; Tübingen: Mohr Siebeck, 1981), 114-31, 257-60.

[15] Those who discern the idea of Jesus' pre-existence in Paul's letters are among others: E. Schweizer, "Zur Herkunft der Präexistenzvorstellung bei Paulus" in _Neotestamentica_ (Zürich: Zwingli Verlag, 1963), 105-9; R. Hamerton-Kelly, _Pre-Existence, Wisdom, and the Son of Man_, 192 and passim; Hengel, _Son of God_, 48-51, 66-76; R. Riesner, "Präexistenz und Jungfrauengeburt" _TBei_ 12 (1981), 185-86; Kim, _Origin_, 114-31, 257-60.

Paul's wisdom passages were not "intended to assert the pre-existence of Christ, or to affirm that Jesus was a divine being personally active in creation" but to speak about him as full embodiment of the creative and saving activity of God.[16]

However, some recent scholars seem to readily accept the majority view about wisdom influence on Paul's thought and build their own study into a possible relationship of wisdom with another particular tradition or motif in Jewish literature and Paul's letters. For example, while J. Davis examines the relationship between wisdom and the spirit in 1 Cor 1:18-3:20, E. J. Schnabel investigates the relationship between wisdom and the law in the writings of Ben Sira and Paul and draws his conclusion about Paul's ethical teaching.[17] C. M. Pate, on the other hand, takes the same subject as Schnabel's monograph, but investigates how Paul employs the wisdom motif for the purpose of reversing the Deuteronomic curses and blessings.[18]

Despite such a strong appeal to the Jewish wisdom tradition lying behind Paul's theology or more specifically his christology, other scholars expressed their scepticism whether wisdom influence on Paul was as strong or single an influence, or whether it had direct influence on Paul's understanding of Christ as a personal being.

L. Cerfaux was the first scholar who expressed some reservations about the possibility of finding clear evidence of wisdom influence on Paul's christology. While accepting that Paul made allusions to wisdom texts and traditions, Cerfaux could find in each passage alternative interpretations to the one previously argued for. In his view, Paul nowhere specifically equates Jesus with the mythological figure of Wisdom, although he was certainly familiar with Jewish wisdom traditions and made use of those traditions to explain the nature of Christ.[19]

Approaching the issue from the argument of 1 Cor 2-3 itself rather than from the general question of christology U. Wilckens suggested on the basis of Gnostic references to the myth of Sophia that Paul's wisdom language does not derive directly from Jewish tradition about personified Wisdom, but indirectly from the Valentinian Gnostic language of the

---

[16] J. D. G. Dunn, *Christology in the Making: a New Testament Inquiry into the Origins of the Doctrine of the Incarnation* (London: SCM, 1980, 1989), 176-96.

[17] J. A. Davis, Wisdom and Spirit: an Investigation of 1 Corinthians 1.18-3.20 Against the Background of Jewish Sapiential Traditions in the Greco-Roman Period (Lanham; London: University Press of America, 1984); E. J. Schnabel, Law and Wisdom From Ben Sira to Paul (WUNT 2/16; Tübingen: Mohr Siebeck, 1985).

[18] C. M. Pate, *The Reverse of the Curse: Paul, Wisdom, and the Law* (WUNT 2/114; Tübingen: Mohr Siebeck, 2000).

[19] L. Cerfaux, *Christ in the Theology of St. Paul* (New York: Herder, 1959), 271, originally published as *Le Christ dans la théologie de Saint Paul* (Paris: du Cerf, 1952).

Corinthians, who *mis*used σοφία as a title for Christ.[20] According to Wilckens, Paul responded to the Corinthians' faulty christology not by rejecting it altogether but redefining it. In other words, Paul is saying that Christ is the Wisdom of God, the Lord of Glory, but he is above all the Crucified (1 Cor 2:2).

About fifty years after Windisch's proposal, H. Conzelmann readdressed the question of Paul's relationship to the Jewish wisdom tradition from a completely different perspective, and suggested that in 1 Cor 2-3 Paul is using the vocabulary of the Corinthians and that his reworking of wisdom theology and wisdom traditions should be located within a school of Paul, located probably in Ephesus, where "wisdom" was methodically taught and discussed.[21] In his discussion Conzelmann drew a distinction between wisdom and apocalyptic speculations.

In contrast to Conzelmann, R. Scroggs fused both wisdom and apocalyptic speculations into what he repeatedly referred to as "Jewish and Christian apocalyptic-wisdom theology," without providing any clear definition for that term.[22]

R. G. Hamerton-Kelly, in his monograph on the concepts of pre-existence in the NT, examined all the passages formerly invoked in support of wisdom christology and a number of others and concluded that personified Wisdom did contribute to the early Christian understanding of Jesus, but it was Paul who modified that traditional christology substantially by means of Jewish apocalyptic categories.[23]

Thus, the notion of pre-existence that Windisch and others had found in wisdom traditions Hamerton-Kelly discerns in apocalyptic literature as well.[24] In his view, those "entities" regarded as pre-existent in apocalyptic literature, such as The Son of Man in 4 Ezra, the law, the heavenly Jerusalem, and personified Wisdom, play a part in Paul's theology.[25] For Hamerton-Kelly, Paul does not see the wisdom of God primarily as Christ,

---

[20] U. Wilckens, *Weisheit und Torheit: eine exegetisch-religionsgeschichtliche Untersuchung zu 1. Kor. 1 und 2* (BHT 26; Tübingen: Mohr Siebeck, 1959); see also his "σοφία" in *TDNT* 7.517-22; on criticisms of Wilckens's view, see E. E. Ellis, "'Wisdom' and 'Knowledge' in 1 Corinthians" in *Prophecy and Hermeneutic in Early Christianity* (Grand Rapids: Eerdmans, 1978), 45-62; R. Scroggs, "Paul: ΣΟΦΟΣ and ΠΝΕΥΜΑΤΙΚΟΣ" *NTS* 14 (1967-1968), 33-35; Hamerton-Kelly, *Pre-Existence*, 112-19.

[21] H. Conzelmann, "Paulus und die Weisheit" *NTS* 12 (1965-1966), 231-44.

[22] Scroggs, "ΣΟΦΟΣ," 33-55.

[23] Hamerton-Kelly, *Pre-Existence*, 195.

[24] Hamerton-Kelly, *Pre-Existence*, 105: "the earliest Christian theology used the Jewish apocalyptic scheme of things existing in heaven before their eschatological manifestation."

[25] Hamerton-Kelly, *Pre-Existence*, 106-7.

but as the whole apocalyptic plan of God for salvation.[26] Unlike Windisch, he sees wisdom and apocalyptic categories as working together in Paul's theology. Thus, the σοφία θεοῦ, far from being a christological title, is Paul's description of God's apocalyptic plan of salvation and his "identification" of Christ with the Wisdom of God (1 Cor 1:24, 30) is simply his synecdochic shorthand (meaning "the whole is taken to signify its parts") for all the salvific blessings present and yet to be revealed (2:9).[27]

In his 1974 essay A. van Roon presented a sharp criticism of any sort of wisdom christology in Paul and offered alternative religio-historical sources for Paul's language.[28] His examination of these wisdom passages led him to conclude that in his letters Paul is using "divine attributes for Christ and considers him equal to God. This opinion is consistent with his christology."[29] So for example, the phrase "and the rock was Christ" in 1 Cor 10:4 is not parallel to Wis 10:17 but is "a reapplication of the identification between God and the rock to Christ."[30] He also conjectured that behind those passages where attributes of God are applied by Paul to Christ lies Paul's "idea of the pre-existence of the Messianic Son of God" derived from Ps 110:3 and Mic 5:2.[31]

Convinced of the fact that Jewish apocalyptic language and thought play a substantial role in Paul's letters, E. E. Johnson examined how the different wisdom and apocalyptic elements function together in the largely apocalyptic argument of Romans 9-11.[32] After an examination of the function of confluent apocalyptic and wisdom traditions in Jewish literature roughly contemporary to Paul (the Wisdom of Solomon, 1 Enoch, 4 Ezra, the Qumran documents, and 2 Baruch) she concluded that "although each of these documents is fundamentally either apocalyptic or sapiential in character, each makes use of material from both traditions."[33] In her view, the wisdom traditions in Rom 9-11 are not so prominent as the apocalyptic, and influence from wisdom texts and traditions are discernible

---

[26] Hamerton-Kelly, *Pre-Existence*, 117.

[27] Hamerton-Kelly, *Pre-Existence*, 115-17. Against Wilckens, he suggests that neither does Paul adopt any allegedly Gnostic terminology from the Corinthians nor are they themselves Gnostics; instead, they are influenced by a type of Philonic anthropology and mysticism (pp.114-23).

[28] A. van Roon, "The Relationship between Christ and the Wisdom of God according to Paul" *NovT* 16 (1974), 207-39.

[29] van Roon, "Relationship," 233.

[30] van Roon, "Relationship," 230.

[31] van Roon, "Relationship," 234.

[32] E. E. Johnson, *The Function of Apocalyptic and Wisdom Traditions in Romans 9-11* (SBLDS 109; Atlanta: Scholars Press, 1989).

[33] Johnson, *Function*, 55-109 (quotation from p.207).

in two passages (9:20-23; 10:6-8) and in the concluding wisdom hymn to God (11:33-36). Having established through the exegesis of the two chapters that Paul's argument in these chapters is substantially influenced not only by apocalyptic thought but by wisdom traditions as well, and that Paul modified the largely apocalyptic argument with elements from wisdom texts and traditions, Johnson draws the conclusion of her study in the following words:

> this Pauline "modification" of apocalyptic thought is itself somewhat traditional. Even among some of the Jewish documents that define what it means to be apocalyptic, wisdom traditions in varying measures contribute to "modifications" of the ideal apocalyptic perspective. The use of sapiential traditions is obviously not the only variable in the diversity of Jewish and Christian apocalyptic literature . . . But it is clear that wisdom language and motifs are one of the means available for expressing one's particular sense of apocalyptic reality.[34]

Our survey of research into Paul's wisdom christology suggests that, while a great number of scholars today recognize that the Jewish wisdom tradition has exerted great influence upon Paul's presentation of his christology, the question whether his wisdom christology is to be understood as an explicit identification of Jesus with personified Wisdom or as speaking of Jesus in terms of Lady Wisdom is by no means settled.

1.1.2. John's Pre-existence Christology

Another area which has attracted a great deal of scholarly attention in recent decades is the relationship between early christology and Jewish monotheism and the concept of "divine agency" or "intermediary figures" in Second Temple Judaism.

As early as the beginning of the 20th century W. Bousset postulated the view that early Christianity was influenced by the Greco-Roman pagan religions.[35] He contended that Jewish monotheism had already been considerably compromised during the post-exilic period by the current speculations about chief angels and hypostatic beings. He believed that the erosion of Jewish monotheistic belief took place even before the flux of Gentile converts into Christianity which, at the same time, accelerated the same process by elevating Jesus into a divine status and by placing him alongside God as another object of faith.[36]

---

[34] Johnson, *Function*, 211.

[35] W. Bousset, *Kyrios Christos: Geschichte des Christusglaubens von den Anfängen des Christentums bis Irenaeus* (Göttingen: Vandenhoeck & Ruprecht, 1913).

[36] W. Bousset, *Die Religion des Judentums im späthellenistischen Zeitalter* (HNT 21; Tübingen: Mohr Siebeck, 1926), 302-357; also *idem, Kyrios Christos*.

The same issue was reviewed by J. D. G. Dunn, who asks "whether Christianity began as a departure from Jewish monotheism" or "was in fact a monotheistic faith from the beginning."[37] Having examined pre-Christian Jewish documents to see whether there was any concept or heavenly figure which could have constituted some kind of threat or compromise to Jewish monotheism, he comes to the conclusion that the language of personified divine attributes or any other "speculation about a being other than God" did not exercise any real threat to Jewish monotheism.[38]

Dunn argues that the personifications of divine attributes such as Wisdom and Logos are "ways of speaking about *God* in his relation to the world" and "serve to express his immanence without compromising his transcendence."[39] In pre-Christian Judaism, Wisdom and Logos did not become a hypostasis or a being who existed independently apart from God, but remained a vivid metaphor for God's own attributes and activity.[40] He insists that even with growing speculations about exalted patriarchs or principal angels during the inter-testamental period Jewish monotheism was not in danger. On the contrary; the great number and majesty of the angelic hosts in Jewish apocalyptic speculations did not threaten God's sovereign authority, but rather enhanced it.[41] In short, Dunn finds no clear evidence that pre-Christian Jewish monotheism was in any degree influenced or affected by speculations about divine attributes, exalted patriarchs or principal angels.

In Dunn's view, Paul applied the Wisdom category to Jesus (as in 1 Cor 1:24, 30; 8:6; 10:1-4; Rom 10:6-10; Col 1:15-20) and described the risen Christ as the full embodiment of God's Wisdom. Although it may be regarded as a significant step, it is still within the Jewish metaphorical usage. Paul and other early Christians cannot be said to have worshiped Jesus as God, since the development from Christian devotion of the exalted Christ towards "full-scale worship" was still on its way until the crisis came with the Fourth Gospel where the evangelist pushes the developing

---

[37] J. D. G. Dunn, "Was Christianity a Monotheistic Faith From the Beginning?" *SJT* 35 (1982), 303.

[38] Dunn, "Was Christianity," 321-22. Dunn observed one exception in "one strand of esoteric mysticism – a speculation involving the ancient idea of an angel in whom Yahweh had put his name, the man-like figure and the empty throne(s) of Daniel's vision, and the translated Enoch" (322).

[39] Dunn, "Was Christianity," 319.

[40] Dunn, *Christology*, 167, who acknowledges that the "tradition of (pre-existent) Wisdom has been influential at many points in NT christology."

[41] Dunn, "Was Christianity," 309-13. Neither does he find any threat to Jewish monotheism in Philo or Josephus.

Wisdom speculation of early Christianity to a totally new dimension.[42] In adapting what may have been a hymn on Logos/Wisdom within the bounds of Jewish metaphorical usage, the writer combines Wisdom christology and Son of God christology into one explicit christology of pre-existence and incarnation. Dunn concludes that a full-blown idea of pre-existence and incarnation of Jesus was limited to John's writings and that "for John Jesus was the incarnation *not* of the Son of God, but of *God* – God's self-revelation become flesh and blood."[43]

M. Casey stands in basic agreement with Dunn that Jewish monotheism was not breached before Paul. He argues that Jesus' exaltation to divine status occurred after AD 70 when Jews in the Johannine community were expelled from the synagogue. Casey regards the repeated description of the people with whom Jesus disagrees as "the Jews" as clear evidence that the author of the Fourth Gospel and his community reflected a Gentile self-identification.[44] According to Casey, "John uses the term more than 60 times, and in the majority of cases it denotes opponents of Jesus, despite the fact that all Jesus' disciples at this stage were Jewish."[45] The continuous elevation of Jesus' status and functions during the first century was only limited by monotheism, one of the most important identity factors of the Jewish community. With Gentile self-identification the Johannine community removed the restraint of Jewish monotheism, and declared the deity and incarnation of Jesus. In this way, a "Jewish prophet" became a "Gentile God."[46]

Without specifically linking to the question of Jewish monotheism J.-A. Bühner argues that the "sending" concept in John, the basis for his pre-

---

[42] J. D. G. Dunn, *The Partings of the Ways: Between Christianity and Judaism, and Their Significance for the Character of Christianity* (London: SCM, 1991), 205-206, 228-229.

[43] Dunn, *Partings*, 229.

[44] M. Casey, *From Jewish Prophet to Gentile God: the Origins and Development of New Testament Christology* (Cambridge: CUP, 1991), 27. In general terms, Casey denies the historical accuracy of the Johannine account and argues that the christology of the Fourth Gospel is the product of Johannine community; cf. also M. Casey, *Is John's Gospel True?* (London; New York: Routledge, 1996).

[45] Casey, *Jewish Prophet*, 27. For other interpretations, see R. E. Brown, *The Gospel According to John* (AB; London: Chapman, 1971), lxx-lxxiii; J. D. G. Dunn, "The Making of Christology: Evolution or Unfolding?" in *Jesus of Nazareth: Lord and Christ: Essays on the Historical Jesus and New Testament Christology* (J. B. Green *et al.*; Grand Rapids: Eerdmans, 1994), 442-43; N. N. Hingle, *Jesus, a Divine Agent: Three Christological Comparisons Between the Gospels of Matthew and John* (Aberdeen Univ. Ph.D. dissertation, 1995), 15.

[46] Casey, *Jewish Prophet*. In his list of the eight identity factors "monotheism" becomes the controlling difference between acceptable and unacceptable christological claims.

existence christology, is indebted to the fusion of prophet and angel traditions. He finds behind the ἐγώ εἰμι and the ἦλθον statements Ancient Near Eastern assumptions concerning the role and practice of a messenger, conceptions which also reflect Jewish angelology.[47] Bühner attempts to demonstrate how much of John's "sending christology" can be explained against the background of the Jewish concept of the שליח acting in the place of the one who sent him.[48] Bühner also contends that John's christology developed from a fusion of the concept of the Danielic Son of Man as an angel (i.e., messenger from heaven) with the concept of a prophet as one with a heavenly commission (received in a visionary ascent to heaven).[49]

In his critique of Casey, Dunn correctly observes two significant jumps in Casey's argumentation:

> From observing that a subgroup can be hypothesized behind each of the figures of Enoch and Wisdom, the deduction is made that the figures indicate or embody (two significantly different claims) the identity of these subgroups, and then the further jump is taken to the claim that the developments in these figures were *caused* by the *needs* of these subgroups.[50]

Although Dunn agrees with Casey that Jewish monotheism of this period was strict and thereby the high christology occurred in the late part of New Testament period,[51] he questions whether "the deity of Jesus is a belief which could have developed only in a predominantly Gentile church," and whether "the deity of Jesus is . . . *inherently* unJewish."[52]

Despite these differences, both Casey and Dunn agree that high christology was a product of late development (after AD 70). What led them to agree on this point? Casey and Dunn are similar in their reasoning that if the New Testament writers did not make something explicit it is because they did not know about it or believe in it. If Paul, for example, did not make Jesus' pre-existence and/or incarnation explicit, does this necessarily mean that he was not aware of it or firmly believe in it? In fact, it is entirely possible, if not more plausible, that the conviction about Jesus' incarnation was so central to Paul that he did not need to belabour

---

[47] J.-A. Bühner, *Der Gesandte und sein Weg im 4. Evangelium: die kultur- und religionsgeschichtlichen Grundlagen der johanneischen Sendungschristologie sowie ihre traditionsgeschichtliche Entwicklung* (WUNT 2/2; Tübingen: Mohr Siebeck, 1977).

[48] Bühner, *Gesandte*, 181-267. Similarly, he attempts to explain the Johannine understanding of the Son's pre-existence on the same basis (cf. pp.234, 426).

[49] Bühner's position appears to follow that of M. Werner, *Die Entstehung des christlichen Dogmas: problemgeschichtlich dargestellt* (Bern-Leipzig: Haupt, 1941).

[50] Dunn, "Making of Christology," 444.

[51] Dunn, *Partings*.

[52] Dunn, "Making of Christology," 447 (quotations from Casey, *Jewish Prophet*, 169, 176).

the point. In addition, Casey and Dunn are to be criticized for undermining the distinctiveness or enigmatic nature of early Christianity.

Moreover, Dunn sees the development of high christology in a straight line, beginning from the earliest Christians, later Paul and then John. He seems to ignore that Paul, the earliest NT writer, had as developed a christology as any other writer in the New Testament. Moreover, Dunn's attempt to explain high christology mainly in terms of its background seems to undermine a radical novelty brought by Christians themselves after the resurrection of Jesus. We need to allow a room for the possibility that what the NT writers meant was something different from what their Jewish contemporaries said or believed even when they make use of concepts or motifs already known to pre-Christian Judaism.[53]

1.1.3. Divine Agent or Divine Identity Christology

Despite his agreement with Dunn and Casey that Jewish monotheism was not weakened or compromised prior to Christianity by Jewish speculations about intermediary beings, L. W. Hurtado stresses the importance of these speculations for the understanding of the origin of the New Testament christology.[54] Hurtado argues that Jewish interest in intermediary beings has provided the formative framework for early christology. Hurtado finds "interesting linguistic parallels" to the way the exalted Christ is described in the NT from the way the personified divine attributes, the exalted patriarchs and the principal angels were depicted in ancient Judaism. All these three categories do not only form the Jewish background of the early Christian understanding of the exalted Jesus, but also "point to the more fundamental conceptual background from which the language was borrowed."[55]

For Hurtado, the worship of Jesus by the early Christians was not a product of syncretistic tendencies from Hellenism, but "a significant mutation or innovation in Jewish monotheistic tradition" as a result of drawing upon important resources in ancient Judaism by the earliest Christians.[56] As to when the redefinition of Jewish monotheism took place in early Christianity, Hurtado comes to a different conclusion from Dunn and Casey. He contends that the process of innovation had already taken

---

[53] We have in mind what Dunn has to say about Wisdom: "This language would almost certainly have been understood by Paul and his readers as ascribing to Christ the role in relation to the cosmos which pre-Christian Judaism ascribed to Wisdom" (*Christology*, pp.209-10).

[54] Hurtado, *One God*.

[55] Hurtado, *One God*, 50.

[56] Hurtado, *One God*, 2, 99. By 'mutation' he means "a direct outgrowth from, and indeed a variety of, the ancient Jewish tradition."

place before Paul because the way he exalted and revered Jesus is evidence that Paul regarded him as divine and his view about Jesus was not something unique to him but in agreement with that of his predecessors.[57] In other words, Hurtado emphasizes that worship is the real test of monotheistic faith in religious practice.[58] Hurtado insists that Paul and early Christians did think of Jesus as God and "apparently felt thoroughly justified in giving Jesus reverence in terms of divinity *and* at the same time thought of themselves as worshiping *one* God."[59] In short, the veneration of Jesus stems from the divine agency concept of Second Temple Judaism and the religious experiences of the early Christians.

While Hurtado stresses an emphasis on a distinctive "mutation" or innovation in the Jewish monotheistic tradition, R. Bauckham insists that the traditional Jewish way of understanding the one God of Israel is the key to unlock the seemingly enigmatic development of New Testament christology. He pointed out that "early Judaism had clear and consistent ways of characterizing the unique identity of the one God and thus distinguishing the one God absolutely from all other reality."[60] Ancient Jews did not think of God in terms of divine essence or nature, which is concerned with what divinity is, but rather in terms of divine identity, which is concerned with who God is. He stresses that Second Temple Jewish literature insists on the absolute distinction between God and all other beings, and accused recent scholarship of blurring this distinction.[61] In this way Bauckham challenges the view that Jewish intermediary figures are a crucial category for the study of early christology.

Drawing a sharp distinction between personifications or hypostases of God's attributes on the one hand, and principal angels and exalted patriarchs on the other, Bauckham insists that the former are unequivocally included within the unique identity of God, while the latter are unequivocally excluded from the unique identity of God.[62]

Bauckham argues that the early Christians developed this novel idea by doing creative exegesis of the Old Testament passages such as Psalm 110:1 and Deutero-Isaiah 40-55.[63] With a twofold emphasis on the unique

---

[57] Hurtado, *One God*, 3-5.

[58] Hurtado, *One God*, 38.

[59] Hurtado, *One God*, 2 (emphasis his).

[60] R. Bauckham, *God Crucified: Monotheism and Christology in the New Testament* (Didsbury Lectures 1996; Carlisle: Paternoster, 1998), vii.

[61] R. Bauckham, "The Throne of God and the Worship of Jesus" in The Jewish Roots of Christological Monotheism: Papers From the St. Andrews Conference on the Historical Origins of the Worship of Jesus (eds. C. C. Newman et al.; Leiden: Brill, 1999), 43-69 .

[62] Bauckham, *God Crucified*, 17.

[63] Bauckham, *God Crucified*, 31.

identity of God and the early Christian creative exegesis of the OT, Bauckham insists that "the earliest Christology was already the highest Christology."[64]

A detailed criticism of Hurtado came from P. A. Rainbow, who, while accepting the main thrust of his position, finds the explanation concerning the relationship between Jewish monotheism and early christology in terms of divine agency traditions problematic. If the concept of divine agency did not modify monotheism within Judaism itself, he asks, how could the same concept be said to have helped Jewish Christians to solve the precise problem stated at the beginning of his book: to make sense of the cultic veneration of Jesus beside God.[65]

Similarly, T. Eskola has recently pointed out the weaknesses of the divine agents theory espoused by Hurtado. He criticizes the way Hurtado handled his theory of Jewish divine agents tradition and the idea of Christian mutation:

When divine agents are made some kind of prototypes for the exalted Christ, there should be a useful parallelism and sufficient identity between the two. Hurtado is, however, obliged to refrain from making detailed comparisons in the end. Actually, he doesn't even mean that Jesus is merely God's chief agent, even though he explicitly stated so. This may be seen in some of Hurtado's most crucial statements.[66]

Eskola goes on to point out that

Apparently Hurtado has not been able to complete his theory without taking the idea of transformation into account. Therefore he made a distinction between the presentation of the exalted Christ in the New Testament and the presentation of divine agents in Jewish writings. He calls the difference a Christian mutation that has taken place in such tradition. . . . What use is it to refer to such figures if they are not in fact exploited in the interpretation?[67]

1.1.4. Angelic/Angelomorphic Christology

Recent scholarship has, however, stressed the significance of Jewish speculations about the nature and function of angelic/angelomorphic beings and other intermediary figures for the development of early

---

[64] Bauckham, *God Crucified*, viii.

[65] P. A. Rainbow, "Jewish Monotheism As the Matrix for New Testament Christology, a Review Article" *NovT* 33 (1991), 86-87.

[66] For a fuller criticism of Hurtado see T. Eskola, *Messiah and the Throne: Jewish Merkabah Mysticism and Early Christian Exaltation Discourse* (WUNT 2/142; Tübingen: Mohr Siebeck, 2001), 323-25.

[67] Eskola, *Messiah*, 324, also points out that Hurtado did not bring out sufficiently the significance of the enthronement scene itself. His rhetorical question is surely significant.

christology. Thus, in the last two or three decades the relationship between Jewish "angelology" and early christology came to the fore of the scholarly discussion. An emphasis on the exalted angels and other intermediary beings led some scholars to question whether Jewish monotheism of the first century AD was really as strict as was assumed in the past. Those who stand in this side of scholarship have argued that before the emergence of Christianity an increasing interest in angels, exalted human figures, and "hypostatic" beings led to a bifurcation of the conception of God within Second Temple Judaism, thus opening the way for an understanding of Jesus as divine and even pre-existent.

C. Rowland, for example, argues in his broad study of Apocalyptic writings in Judaism and early Christianity that some visions of glorious angels in Jewish apocalyptic literature are evidence of a bifurcation in the conception of God in pre-Christian Judaism. Such development in the conception of God, he argues, helped early Christians to understand Jesus as a divine being next to God.[68] He claims that Ezek 1:26-28, 8:2-4, and Dan 10:5-6 disclose a tendency whereby the human form of God (Ezek 1:26-8) is separated from the divine throne-chariot and functions as "a quasi-angelic mediator" (Ezek 8:2-4) similar to the angel in Daniel 10:5-6. While the description of the angel in Daniel 10:5-6 seems to have been influenced by the theophany of Ezek 1:26-28, the figure in Ezek 8:2-4 is comparable with "one like a son of man" in Dan 7:13, where both heavenly figures are described in "quasi-divine terms."[69]

Observing that in the LXX version of Dan 7:13 the divine status of the human figure is even more apparent and his coming is spoken of "as the Ancient of Days" instead of "unto the Ancient Days" Rowland argues that the LXX variant was responsible for the portrayal of the risen Jesus in Rev 1:14 similar to that of the Ancient of Days in Dan 7. Thus Rowland claims to have found "the beginning of a hypostatic development similar to that connected with divine attributes like God's word and wisdom."[70]

Rowland also observes another development which is related to the divine throne but taking a somewhat different form. He finds this development particularly in the *Similitudes of Enoch* and the *Testament of Abraham*. He notes that "instead of the splitting of the human figure from the throne, there would appear to be an attempt to reinterpret the throne-

---

[68] C. Rowland, *The Open Heaven: a Study of Apocalyptic in Judaism and Early Christianity* (London: SPCK, 1982), 84-113.

[69] C. Rowland, "The Vision of the Risen Christ in Rev. 1.13ff: the Debt of an Early Christology to an Aspect of Jewish Angelology" *JTS* 31 (1980), 1-5; Rowland, *Open Heaven*, 94-101.

[70] Rowland, *Open Heaven*, 100. Rowland finds a similar explanation for the background to the glorious angel Yahoel in *Apoc. Ab.* 10-11.

theophany by identifying the figure on the throne, not with God but with a *man* exalted to heaven by God."[71]

Some scholars have even gone further to postulate the view that ancient Judaism has *never* been strictly monotheistic. M. Barker and P. Hayman have independently argued that, except for a small minority of Jews, strict monotheism was something unknown in ancient Judaism. They claim that ancient Jews believed in a High God (*'El 'Elyon*) who had several Sons of God, of whom Yahweh was one, to whom Israel was given as his heritage (cf. Deut 32:8-9 LXX), and this ancient belief lies behind subsequent talk in particular of a supreme angel. Throughout the First and Second Temple Judaism, they argue, the influence of the ancient dualism between El and Yahweh continued.[72]

In his search for the origins of the Gnostic demiurge, J. E. Fossum attempts to demonstrate that Jewish ideas about the creative agency of the hypostatized divine Name and of the Angel of the Lord were the forerunner of the Gnostic demiurge.[73] He cites Yahoel as an example of such agency.[74] According to Fossum, a named angel, now with "a distinct personality and permanent existence," represents a shift from the stage when the Angel of the Lord was more or less indistinguishable from God.

In his examination of rabbinic literature of the second century AD and later Alan Segal has shown that some Jewish "heretics" were accused of giving too much reverence to principal angels and hypostatic manifestations in heaven.[75] From his argument that elements within NT Christianity represent one of the earliest examples of the "Two Powers heresy," which was developed from Jewish interests in figures other than God on the throne in Jewish apocalyptic literature, Segal concludes that early Christians identified a number of human figures in heaven and

---

[71] Rowland, *Open Heaven*, 104 (emphasis mine).

[72] M. Barker, *The Great Angel: a Study of Israel's Second God* (London: SPCK, 1992), 3; and P. Hayman, "Monotheism: A Missued Word in Jewish Studies?" *JJS* 42 (1991), 1-15. Now see also M. Barker, "The High Priest and the Worship of Jesus" in *The Jewish Roots of Christological Monotheism: Papers From the St. Andrews Conference on the Historical Origins of the Worship of Jesus* (eds. C. C. Newman *et al.*; Leiden: Brill, 1999), 93-111, who proposes that the worship of Jesus is to be explained by alleged traditions of the real apotheosis of divine kings and priests in ancient Israel, who were worshiped by Israelites as human embodiments of the God of Israel.

[73] J. E. Fossum, *The Name of God and the Angel of the Lord: Samaritan and Jewish Concepts of Intermediation and the Origin of Gnosticism* (WUNT 36; Tübingen: Mohr Siebeck, 1985), iii.

[74] Fossum, *Name of God*, 319-21, 333.

[75] A. F. Segal, *Two Powers in Heaven: Early Rabbinic Reports About Christianity and Gnosticism* (SJLA 25; Leiden: Brill, 1977).

angelic intermediaries with Jesus.[76] It is also noticeable that he emphasizes the use of the "Son of Man" title in both Jewish apocalyptic literature and the Gospel tradition.[77]

C. A. Gieschen, a student of Fossum, sets forth his thesis based mainly on the work of Segal, Rowland and his teacher that:

> Angelomorphic traditions, especially those growing from the Angel of the Lord traditions, had a significant impact on the early expressions of Christology to the extent that evidence of an Angelomorphic Christology is discernible in several documents dated between 50 and 150 CE.[78]

Gieschen boldly argues that Jewish traditions about Wisdom, Spirit, Name, Glory, Son of Man, Image, and Anthropos and the christology of the early church are ultimately rooted in the angelomorphic tradition in which "the Angel of the Lord is God appearing in the form of a man."[79]

Not all scholars who engage in research on the development of early christology and its debts to Jewish angelology come to the same conclusion that Jewish monotheism has been already compromised by speculations about exalted angelic/angelomorphic figures and other intermediary beings during the Second Temple period, thus paving the way for early Christians to accommodate Jesus in this category. There are those who, while accepting the importance or relevance of Jewish angelology for our understanding of the origins of early christology, do not go as far as to uphold the view that strong monotheism was broken or modified in pre-Christian Judaism.[80]

C. Fletcher-Louis, a student of Rowland, applies Jewish angelomorphic traditions for an understanding of the christology and soteriology in Luke-Acts and argued for the angelomorphic depiction of the earthly Jesus.[81] Since he holds that no angels were worshiped in pre-Christian Judaism, he

---

[76] Segal, *Two Powers*, 208. Dating the opposition of the rabbis to this heresy to the second century AD Segal contends that "the rabbis' second-century opponents had first-century forebears," such as Philo's talk of a "second god" and Paul's polemic against angelic veneration.

[77] Segal, *Two Powers*, 205-10.

[78] C. A. Gieschen, *Angelomorphic Christology: Antecedents and Early Evidence* (AGAJU 42; Leiden: Brill, 1998), 6.

[79] Gieschen, *Angelomorphic*, 5-6.

[80] L. T. Stuckenbruck, *Angel Veneration and Christology: a Study in Early Judaism and in the Christology of the Apocalypse of John* (WUNT 2/70; Tübingen: Mohr Siebeck, 1995); P. R. Carrell, *Jesus and the Angels: Angelology and the Christology of the Apocalypse of John* (SNTSMS; Cambridge: CUP, 1997); C. H. T. Fletcher-Louis, *Luke-Acts: Angels, Christology and Soteriology* (WUNT 2/94; Tübingen: Mohr Siebeck, 1997); D. D. Hannah, *Michael and Christ: Michael Traditions and Angel Christology in Early Christianity* (WUNT 2/109; Tübingen: Mohr Siebeck, 1999).

[81] Fletcher-Louis, *Luke-Acts*.

sets out to examine traditions about angel-like human beings, cases "where a figure who is both angelic but also human and fully Divine, receives worship" as a "fruitful context for the elucidation of the worship of Jesus."[82] After a survey of all the evidence from Jewish sources for angel-like human beings,[83] Fletcher-Louis argues that some of these beings were actually worshipped (i.e., Adam, Moses, the High Priest who came out to greet Alexander the Great, and the Son of Man) and that some of them were not only like angels but actually angels (cf. the priest in Mal 2:6-7; Jacob in Prayer of Joseph cited by Origen and his commentary on John's Gospel).[84]

Building on recent discussions on Jewish angelology, L. T. Stuckenbruck investigates the phenomenon of the veneration of angels in Revelation and other literature based on a form-critical study of the "refusal tradition" in which angels refuse the worship of humans.[85] He then examines whether this tradition served as "the backdrop of formative traditions" commonly shared by the author and his readers and whether it is a source for the christology found in Revelation. He concludes that, while Jesus "as an object of worship alongside God was not intended as a breach of monotheism," angel veneration in early Judaism "may ultimately have provided a significant underlying model behind the author's way of placing this religious outlook alongside the indispensable primacy in devotion to the one unique and transcendent God 'who sits upon the throne.'"[86]

Similarly, in his examination of angelomorphic christology in Revelation P. R. Carrell argues that Jewish angelomorphic traditions did not lead to a bifurcation in the conception of God, but rather to an understanding of the exalted Christ as the chief divine agent with a sort of mutation in Christianity.[87] Having examined angelomorphic traditions from a variety of Jewish sources he concludes that even if there are angels that represent God and occupy roles as junior partners to God, and even if the descriptions of glorious angels or exalted humans include theophanic

---

[82] Fletcher-Louis, *Luke-Acts*, 7.

[83] E.g., kings, priests, and prophets; Adam, Enoch, Noah, Abraham, Jacob/Israel, Joseph, Moses, David, and Elijah; and all the angel-like Jewish communities.

[84] Fletcher-Louis, *Luke-Acts*, 127, 159-61.

[85] Stuckenbruck, *Angel Veneration*; also L. T. Stuckenbruck, "An Angelic Refusal of Worship: the Tradition and its Function in the Apocalypse of John" in *SBLSP 33* (ed. E. H. Lovering; Atlanta: Scholars Press, 1994), 679-96.

[86] Stuckenbruck, *Angel Veneration*, 272-73.

[87] Carrell, *Jesus*, 1-13. He summarizes his thesis that, "Angelology has influenced the christology of the Apocalypse in such a way that one of its important strands is an angelomorphic christology which upholds monotheism while providing a means for Jesus to be presented in visible, glorious form to his church" (p.226).

imagery, the boundaries of monotheism did not break before the end of the first century AD.[88] Until that time neither a consistent identity for the chief angel nor a significant dualism can be observed. Behind the angelomorphic christology in Revelation Carrell sees both pastoral and christological motives working at the same time, the close connection of Jesus to his church and the prevention of his identification as an angel.[89]

In light of the recent scholarship on early christology and its debts to Jewish angelology D. D. Hannah sets out to examine Michael traditions in Jewish apocalyptic and related literature, the sectarian works from Qumran, Philo, Rabbinic and Hekhalot literature, the NT, and the Christian literary remains of the second and third centuries with the hope of making contribution to the understanding of the origins and development of early christology.[90] Hannah argues that Michael traditions were found useful for early Christian writers (such as John's Revelation, Justin Martyr, the author of Hebrews and possibly Luke) in elucidating the significance of Christ, while carefully distinguishing Christ from Michael.[91]

1.1.5. Some Critical Observations

Despite many differences, the one common denominator between Dunn, Casey, Hurtado, and Bauckham is that first century Jewish monotheism showed a strong commitment to the one God of Israel and that it was not weakened or modified before the rise of Christianity.[92] The focal point of disagreement between one group (Hurtado and Bauckham) and the other (Dunn and Casey), however, lies in that the former group locates the innovation/modification of Jewish monotheistic belief within the early stage of development of early christology, whereas the latter thinks that it did not happen before AD 70 or John's Gospel was written. As will become clear during the course of our study, we agree with these "traditionalists" about the strict nature of Jewish monotheism, while our

---

[88] Carrell, *Jesus*, 24-97.

[89] Carrell, *Jesus*, 128.

[90] Hannah, *Michael*.

[91] Hannah, *Michael*, 216-17.

[92] In addition to Dunn, Hurtado, Casey and Bauckham included in this category are: N. A. Dahl, "Sources of Christological Language" in *The Crucified Messiah: and Other Essays* (Minneapolis: Augsburg, 1974), 113-36, esp. 121, 131; R. T. France, "The Worship of Jesus: A neglected factor in Christological Debate?" in *Christ the Lord: Studies in Christology Presented to Donald Guthrie* (ed. H. H. Rowdon; Leicester: Inter-Varsity, 1982), 24-25; N. T. Wright, *The Climax of the Covenant: Christ and the Law in Pauline Theology* (Edinburgh: T & T Clark, 1991); N. T. Wright, *The New Testament and the People of God* (London: SPCK, 1992); Rainbow, "Jewish Monotheism," 78-91; Carrell, *Jesus*.

position on the "timing" of innovation is in basic agreement with Hurtado
and Bauckham as opposed to Dunn and Casey. Moreover, Bauckham's and
Rainbow's appeals to the OT scriptures as a key to unlock the enigmatic
development of early christology are to be welcomed as commendable.

With regard to the so-called "angelomorphic" traditions, it is interesting
to note that, while discussing topics and sources very similar to Rowland's,
Carrell arrives at a very different conclusion from Rowland concerning the
nature of Jewish angelology and the state of the first century Jewish
monotheism.

The monographs by Gieschen and Fletcher-Louis in their own ways are
to be criticized for putting almost everything into one basket. By making
broader the category from angelic to angelomorphic, they find a category
broad enough to include as many concepts or beings as they wish. With
such an all-embracing category one could prove any thesis![93] Moreover,
some scholars, such as Fossum and Gieschen, could be seen as committing
the fallacy of reading later developments into earlier stages of religious
traditions without sufficient caution.

The recent tendency to find Jewish precedents for early christology by
the so-called "New *Religionsgeschichtliche Schule*" is in fact
commendable in that it has brought the roots of christological thinking of
the early church to the right place by rejecting completely the obsolete
view of the Hellenistic pagan roots for the divine status of Jesus.[94] An
overemphasis by this new school upon Jewish roots for early christology
and continuity between early Judaism and early Christianity, however,
needs some correction; some "members" of this school seem to be working
with an assumption – if not a conviction – that the origin and development
of early christology cannot be properly explained unless one could
establish that something similar to it already existed in pre-Christian
Judaism. If the recent trend is placed within the wider movements of
thought before and after the Second World War, what is happening today
in the discussion of early christology and in NT scholarship in general is
quite understandable. Ever since the Holocaust, scholars have been
encouraged to look more positively at Jewish influences on Christianity
rather than seeing them as antithetical to one another. In fact, there is
nothing wrong with such a positive attitude towards Judaism. On the

---

[93] J. C. O'Neill, Review of Fletcher-Louis's *Luke-Acts: Angels, Christology and Soteriology*, *JTS* 50 (1999), 229, correctly points out, "Because there is this clear and consistent difference between God and his creatures, whether angelic and human" and because "Jesus was worshipped and could only have been worshipped if he were a human being who was not created," Fletcher-Louis's attempt to examine "the traditions about created human beings who were like angels is doomed to failure."

[94] See now Hurtado, *Lord Jesus Christ*, 11-18, for a sketch of this newer scholarly trend.

contrary, recent contributions of Jewish studies to our understanding of early Christianity can hardly be overestimated. Nevertheless, too much emphasis on Jewish precedents in recent studies of Christian origins has led to a somewhat distorted understanding of it as a result of neglecting – or paying no sufficient attention to – the importance of early Christian contributions in the development of early christological thinking (e.g., the impact made by Jesus to his followers through his teaching and deeds, his resurrection/exaltation, their own exegesis of OT scriptures, etc.). A more recent tendency in giving a more refined treatment of the influence from Jewish angelology on early christology is to be seen as a healthy reminder that an one-sided approach to christology should be avoided. Thus, the present study seeks to offer a more balanced and cogent explanation of the origins and development of early christology by paying sufficient attention not only to the Jewish precedents but to specific contributions made by members of early Christian communities.

1.1.6. Our View of First Century Jewish Monotheism

Our review of recent scholarship on the relationship between Jewish monotheism and early christology made clear that the nature or character of Jewish monotheism of the first century is quite controversial and calls for a clear definition.[95] As a careful reader might have already noticed, we are by no means convinced by recent attempts to revise or redefine Jewish monotheism; on the contrary, the following considerations are overwhelmingly in favour of the view that first century Jewish monotheism was essentially a strong commitment to the one God of Israel as their creator and sovereign Lord, and this was demonstrated by their refusal to give worship to anyone other than himself. Monotheism in this sense was the religion of Second Temple Judaism.

As far as the extreme views of Barker and Hayman are concerned, it should be observed that a strong commitment to the one God of Israel from the exile onward remained at the heart of Judaism. Clear evidence can be seen not only from the *Shema* (Deut 6:4-5; cf. 10:12; 11:13)[96] and Deutero-Isaiah (esp. 45:20-25), but also from the Jesus tradition (cf. Mk 12:29-30

---

[95] See the useful discussion in Stuckenbruck, *Angel Veneration*, 15-21; also Hurtado, *One God*, 17-39; and his "What Do We Mean," 348-68; Rainbow, "Jewish Monotheism," 78-91; Dunn, *Partings*, 19-21; Bauckham, "Throne," 43-48. See also M. Hengel, *Judaism and Hellenism: Studies in Their Encounter in Palestine During the Early Hellenistic Period* (London: SCM, 1974), 264; J. M. G. Barclay, *Jews in the Meditteranean Diaspora. From Alexander to Trajan (323 BCE-117 CE* (Edinburgh: T & T Clark, 1996), 99-100, 312-13; Hurtado, *Lord Jesus Christ*, 29-53.

[96] Josephus, *Ant.* 4.212; *Pseudo-Aristeas* 160; 1QS 10:10. Bauckham, "Throne," 43.

par.) and writings from Jews (Philo and Josephus) as well as outside
Judaism (Celsus):[97]

Philo *Decal.* 65: "Let us, then, engrave deep in our hearts this as the first and most sacred
of commandments, to acknowledge and honour one God who is above all, and let the
idea that gods are many never even reach the ears of the man whose rule of life is to seek
for truth in purity and goodness"

Josephus, *Ant.* 5.112: "to recognize God as one is common to all the Hebrews."

Celsus, *Contra Celsum* 1:23-24: "The goatherds and shepherds who followed Moses as
their leader were deluded by clumsy deceit into thinking that there was only one God . . .
(and) abandoned the worship of many gods. . . . The goatherds and shepherds thought
that there was one God called the Most High, or Adonai, or the Heavenly One, or
Sabbaoth, or however they like to call this word; and they acknowledged nothing more."

C. A. Gieschen has recently proposed the following five criteria for
"measuring" the divinity of an intermediary figure alongside God in
support of his argument that the line between God and intermediary beings
was blurred by growing speculations about these beings in Second Temple
Judaism. He asks the following five questions: (1) *divine position*: is the
intermediary being positioned with or near God or his throne? (2) *divine
appearance*: does he have the physical characteristics of God's visible
form as depicted in various theophanies? (3) *divine functions*: does he
carry out an act, or actions, typically ascribed to God? (4) *divine name*:
does he possess the Name of God or is he seen as an hypostasis of the
Divine Name? (5) *divine veneration*: is he the object of some form of
veneration? On the basis of his answers to these questions he then claims
that "the presence of one or more of these five criteria in a text may
indicate that the angelomorphic mediator figure was understood to share
God's status, authority, and nature."[98]

His "maximalist" view about the five criteria of divinity for
intermediary beings is, however, far from convincing. On the contrary, the
clear distinction between God and these intermediaries has never been
blurred or compromised but firmly maintained, despite growing
speculations about intermediary beings in Second Temple Judaism.[99]

First, Gieschen claims that the mediator's position in relation to God or
his throne is important. However, as a rule of thumb, in heaven God alone
sits, while the angels who attend him (service and worship) are regularly

---

[97] Since Philo, Josephus and Celsus were capable of highly sophisticated thought and
nuanced expression, their words should be given full weight.

[98] Gieschen, *Angelomorphic*, 30-34: "the Jewish understanding of God during this
period was certainly more complex than the issue of worshiping one God."

[99] See our fuller discussion in Chapters 2 and 3.

described as standing next to God. Even Michael, the great archangel, is never described as seated before God. The descriptions of human beings who sit before God seem to represent honour and reward for faithfulness rather than attribution of divinity as a vice regent. As Bock rightly observed, "God's presence is such that only a few are contemplated as being able to approach him directly. Such figures are great luminaries of the past or anticipated luminaries of the future. Those who sit in his presence constitute an even smaller group. They are directed to do so by God and often sit for a short time."[100]

We have, however, a few intermediary figures who are described as *sharing* God's throne in Second Temple Jewish literature that call for our special attention; such a privilege is given only to Wisdom, Moses and the Son of Man.[101]

In the case of Wisdom, she is portrayed as sharing God's throne (Wis 9:4, 10; *1 Enoch* 84:2-3).[102] However, as we will see in our detailed discussion in Chapter 2, such a description of Wisdom was not in the least tension with the monotheistic emphasis on God's oneness and sovereignty because she was not an entity distinguishable from God but a personification of God's own wisdom.[103] Wisdom language did not breach the monotheistic boundary at all but provided Second Temple Jews a useful way of speaking about God's presence and action in this world without compromising or calling into question his transcendence or oneness.

In Ezekiel the Tragedian, Moses is enthroned with great authority, but his exalted role is best understood merely as a metaphorical picture of his authority in establishing the nation (*Eze. Trag.* 68-69). The reference to his "deification" seems to be explained by his function as God's powerful agent, so he is "like a god before Pharaoh" (Exod 7:1; Philo, *Mos.* 1.155-62; *Det.* 160-62; *Sac.* 9-10). Thus, on closer examination such a highly

---

[100] See full discussion of exalted figures in Judaism in D. L. Bock, Blasphemy and Exaltation in Judaism and the Final Examination of Jesus: a Philological-Historical Study of the Key Jewish Themes Impacting Mark 14:61-64 (WUNT 2/106; Tübingen: Mohr Siebeck, 1998),113-83.

[101] Cf. Bock, *Blasphemy*, 112-83: "God's presence is such that only a few are contemplated as being able to approach him directly. Such figures are great luminaries of the past or anticipated luminaries of the future. Those who sit in his presence constitute an even smaller group. They are directed to do so by God and often sit for a short time" (p.234).

[102] *1 Enoch* 84:3 presents a textual difficulty. While E. Isaac, "1 (Ethiopic Apocalypse of) Enoch" in *The Old Testament Pseudepigrapha* (ed. J. H. Charlesworth; London: Darton, Longman & Todd, 1983), 62, translates: "Your throne has not retreated from her station nor from before your presence," he notes that another manuscript reads: "Wisdom does not depart from the place of our throne, nor turn away from your presence."

[103] Cf. Bauckham, "Throne," 54.

exalted depiction of Moses turns out to be less exceptional than it first appears.[104]

The Son of Man in the *Parables of Enoch* is unique among exalted human or angelic figures depicted in Second Temple Jewish literature in two respects: he sits on the divine throne (62:2, 5; 69:27, 29; cf. 51:3) and he receives worship (46:5; 48:5; 62:6, 9). What Ezekiel the Tragedian attributes only figuratively to Moses, the Parables of Enoch attribute literally to the Son of Man, although only in the eschatological future.[105] Therefore, only Wisdom and the Enochic Son of Man can be said to provide real – but limited – precedents for the Christian claim that the exalted Jesus shares the heavenly throne of God. This significant point will be taken into consideration in our subsequent discussion about Jesus' exaltation/enthronement to the right hand of God.

Second, Gieschen emphasizes the physical resemblance between God and the exalted angels, but the fact that "some angelophanies are reminiscent of theophanies" and apocalyptic writers seem to be working "from a 'limited stock of imagery' . . . in a variety of epiphanic contexts, while clearly distinguishing between God and the glorious angels" strongly suggests that the resemblance of imagery between them should not be stressed.[106]

Third, Gieschen stresses the divine functions ascribed to intermediary beings. It is true that intermediary beings often carry out divine functions typically ascribed to God, but these divine functions are only delegated to them rather than shared with them. Exalted angels act on God's behalf; they act merely as representatives or servants of God. Divine attributes such as Wisdom and Word are also described as acting on God's behalf, but because they are personifications of God's own attributes they need to be seen as none other than God himself. They must be regarded as one of different ways of speaking about God's presence and action in this world. In order for intermediary figures to be qualified as divine in this category they need to be shown to share those divine functions exclusively reserved for God. A good example would be an angel or any intermediary beings taking part in the creation, but so far we have not come across any Jewish texts with such information (except with personified divine attributes!).

Fourth, Gieschen also claims that the possession of the Name of God by several principal angels is "the key attribute that bestows divine authority, and in a qualified manner, a sharing in divine substance,"[107] but, as we will demonstrate in greater detail later in Chapter 3, his arguments for the

---

[104] Bock, *Blasphemy*, 133-45.
[105] Bauckham, "Throne," 59.
[106] Carrell, *Jesus*, 61, 75; cf. Dunn, *Christology*, xxiv.
[107] Gieschen, *Angelomorphic*, 151.

hypostatization of the Name of God as a particular angel are not convincing. However exalted an angel is said to be, or however clearly he is described as possessing the Divine Name, he cannot be seen as having a divine identity, let alone as sharing in divine substance.

Finally, God alone is to be worshiped.[108] The worship due to God alone is contrasted not only with the worship of pagan gods but also with the worship of creaturely servants of God (Josephus *Ant.* 1.155-56). Angels were not an object of worship. The motif is found in some apocalypses, when an angel rejects the worship offered him by the seer on the grounds that they are both fellow-servants of God (*Ascen. Is.* 8:5; Rev 19:10; 22:9; cf. also Tob 12:18).[109] One of the crucial differences between an angel and Jesus is that in the NT Jesus is never described as a heavenly figure who worships God before the throne of Glory. In this regard, there is no exact identification of Jesus with the angels even as regards their heavenly functions.

In the light of the above discussion, we have serious doubt about the five criteria of divinity proposed by Gieschen and his attempt to show that the clear distinction between God and the intermediary beings has been blurred by increasing speculations about them.[110] We therefore strongly uphold the view that the first century Jewish monotheism was not broken or compromised by growing speculations about intermediary figures but firmly maintained with a strong commitment to the one God of Israel as ever before. Moreover, our view of the first century Jewish monotheism will receive further confirmation from our detailed discussion of Jewish speculations about the personified divine attributes and other intermediary beings during the OT and the Second Temple period (see Chapters 2 & 3).

1.2. Jesus' Self-Consciousness of Divine Sonship

One of the most important titles given to Jesus in the New Testament is certainly the title "Son of God." According to the Synoptic Gospels, Jesus spoke of God as his Father and of himself as his Son. In other words, Jesus understood himself and his mission primarily according to his divine sonship. Unfortunately, the discussion of early christology has been mostly dominated by the presupposition that Jesus did not conceived himself to be

---

[108] See now Hurtado, *Lord Jesus Christ*, 29-48, for his interaction with those who disgree with his emphasis on the devotion to one God of Israel as the main character of Jewish monotheism.

[109] R. Bauckham, *The Climax of Prophecy: Studies on the Book of Revelation* (Edinburgh: T & T Clark, 1993), 120-48; Stuckenbruck, *Angel Veneration*, 75-103.

[110] See also Eskola, *Messiah*, 145.

the Son of God which led to different attempts to show that the title was applied to him by early Christians on other grounds than his self-consciousness of divine sonship.

The history-of-religions school of the early 20th century attempted to explain the title "Son of God" in terms of the Hellenistic concept of the divine man (*theios anēr*) with influence from the Gnostic myth. Although the expression *theios anēr* does not occur in the Gospels, or for that matter in the NT, the title "Son of God" was seen as its equivalent. R. Bultmann, following W. Bousset,[111] claimed that the application of the title "Son of God" can be traced back neither to Jesus himself, nor to the original Palestinian church, but only to Hellenistic Christianity, which accepted the general meaning of the concept in the Hellenistic environment.[112]

This understanding of the origin of the title is, however, generally rejected on the following grounds: (1) the Hellenistic concept stands in tension with the NT emphasis on the uniqueness of Jesus' divine sonship as well as with the NT insistence that the divine sonship of Jesus involves primarily suffering and death rather than the performance of miracles;[113] (2) the notion of *theios anēr* was not as pervasive or uniform as once thought;[114] and (3) there is no explicit connection in Hellenistic sources between *theios anēr* and persons held to be "sons of the gods."[115]

Although the post-war discussions on christology were largely dominated by the Bultmann circle, other scholars in various ways tried to establish some kind of starting point in the teaching of Jesus for the later development of the title in the early church. Approaching the development of early christology by means of a study of the christological titles applied to Jesus O. Cullmann attempted to establish a link between the early Christian use of the title "Son of God" and Jesus' own consciousness of the Father-Son relationship to God.[116] Cullmann insisted that Jesus was conscious of his divine sonship, although he used the title with deliberate

---

[111] W. Bousset, *Kyrios Christos: a History of the Belief in Christ From the Beginnings of Christianity to Irenaeus* (Nashville: Abingdon, 1970), 91-98 (originally published in German in 1913).

[112] Bultmann, *Theology*, 1.128-33, but he also recognized that at first "Son of God" was used as a royal title for the Messiah (p.50).

[113] O. Cullmann, *The Christology of the New Testament* (London: SCM, 1963), 275-78; F. Hahn, *The Titles of Jesus in Christology* (London: Lutterworth, 1969), 284-88; and R. H. Fuller, *The Foundations of New Testament Christology* (London: Lutterworth, 1965), 164-67.

[114] W. von Martitz, *TDNT* 8.335-40.

[115] Von Martitz, *TDNT* 8.338 n.23, points out that *theios* was used predicatively, not as an attribute.

[116] Cullmann, *Christology*, 270-305; B. M. F. van Iersel, *'Der Sohn' in den synoptischen Jesusworten* (Leiden: Brill, 1961).

reserve. His view was supported by the evidence that the early church did not derive the Son of God designation for Jesus from his messianic calling.[117]

Attempts have also been made from a traditio-historical perspective to account for all the uses of the title within the developing theology of the early church. Using the titular approach pioneered by Cullmann, both F. Hahn and R. H. Fuller argued that the title was first applied to Jesus in the early Palestinian church with reference to his future work as Messiah and only at a later stage – in Hellenistic Jewish Christianity – was it applied to him with reference to his exalted position after the resurrection.[118] The basic assumption underlying their arguments is the distinction between the Palestinian Jewish church, the Hellenistic Jewish church and the Hellenistic Gentile church.[119] The criterion employed for distinguishing one area from another is the degree of Jewish or non-Jewish influence. However, the validity of such a rigid scheme for establishing the geographical origin of the literature or concepts in question has been severely criticized by leading scholars such as W. G. Kümmel, O. Cullmann, and M. Hengel. Kümmel stressed that it is virtually impossible to distinguish between the theology of the Hellenistic Jewish and Gentile churches with the resources at our disposal; nor does he find it easy to distinguish between the thought of the earliest church and the Hellenistic church.[120] Hengel has demonstrated how Palestine itself had been subject to Hellenistic influences in the period up to 150 BC, with a strong indication that the whole of Judaism during the NT period should be seen as Hellenistic Judaism.[121]

Surely, one of the crucial implications of Hahn's and Fuller's view is that Jesus' divine sonship was linked with his resurrection, thereby suggesting that Jesus became Son of God from this point onward. As one

---

[117] Cullmann, *Christology*, 278-83. He pointed out that the fact that Jesus was recognized by others as the Son of God only in exceptional cases (by Peter: Mt 16:17; by Satan: Mt 4:3, 6; by demons: Mk 3:11; 5:7; at his baptism and transfiguration) suggests that the Synoptic writes did "in fact preserve the recollection that it is the *Son of God* concept more than any other understanding of Jesus which goes back to Jesus himself and to its attestation during his earthly life" (p.279).

[118] Hahn, *Titles of Jesus*, 284-88; and Fuller, *Foundations*, 164-67. Hahn postulated a distinction between the two titles "the Son" and "the Son of God," which in the later NT documents they were assimilated to one another.

[119] Hahn refined Bousset's claim that between Jesus and Paul there stood not only the Palestinian Jewish church but also the Gentile communities.

[120] W. G. Kümmel, *The Theology of the New Testament: According to Its Major Witnesses, Jesus, Paul, John* (Nashville: Abingdon, 1973), 105-6, 118-19; cf. Cullmann, *Christology*, 323.

[121] Hengel, *Judaism and Hellenism*. See further I. H. Marshall, "Palestinian and Hellenistic Christianity: Some Critical Comments" *NTS* 19 (1972-1973), 271-87.

of the representatives of current scholarship, J. D. G. Dunn maintains that the application of the title to Jesus was a late development and Jesus' consciousness of his divine sonship cannot be traced back to him. While the title "Son of God" was originally understood simply as a means of expressing the close relationship of the royal Messiah to God, the early church applied it to Jesus because his resurrection was understood as the moment of his becoming the Son of God.[122] Subsequently, the early church gradually pushed the inauguration of Jesus' status as Son of God back to the Transfiguration (Mk 9:7), then to baptism (Mk 1:11) and finally either to his virginal conception or pre-existence.[123]

I. H. Marshall, on the other hand, argued that the use of the title by the early church was originally connected with Jesus' self-consciousness "as it was confirmed by the resurrection and illuminated by Old Testament prophecy and contemporary Jewish thought about the figure of wisdom." He interpreted both Rom 1:3-4 and Acts 13:33 as confirming "an already-existent status rather than as the conferring of a new status."[124] For Marshall, "it is highly unlikely that one who was regarded as 'Son of David' (a Messianic title) before his death should have been adopted by God as his Son at a subsequent stage" or that Ps 2:7 "was read as an allusion to the resurrection and then applied to Jesus. . . . [rather] it is much more likely that the mention of the Lord's anointed and his Son led to the application to Jesus and then to his resurrection."[125]

Denying the authenticity of Mt 11:25-27 and Mk 13:32, Maurice Casey argued that the origin of the use of the term "Son of God" for Jesus goes back to the period of Jesus' earthly ministry, whereas its development into a title as a means of conveying his unique status should be located within the needs of the early church. He argued that Jesus could have been called a son of God because he was thought to be a righteous person, as the demon's designation "son of God Most High" demonstrates (Mk 5:7), and the application of the title fits well with one of the main needs of the early church: "the belief that Christians rather than Jews formed the covenant community."[126]

With regard to Jesus' view of God as his Father, J. Jeremias has succeeded in bringing back the question of Jesus' divine sonship to the centre of the debate by showing that the use of *abba* in his address to God

---

[122] Dunn, *Christology*, 35-36. For instance, Dunn argued that "primitive Christian preaching seems to have regarded Jesus' resurrection as the day of his appointment to divine sonship, as the event by which he became God's son."

[123] Schweizer, *TDNT* 8.366-74.

[124] I. H. Marshall, *The Origins of New Testament Christology* (Downers Grove: Inter-Varsity, 1976, 1990), 120.

[125] Marshall, *Origins*, 120.

[126] Casey, *Jewish Prophet*, 46.

was a characteristic and distinctive feature of Jesus' prayer-life.[127] Although there have been attempts to undermine some of his arguments, his treatment of the subject was so widely accepted by NT scholarship that it was considered "one of the assured results of modern scholarship."[128] However, in recent decades there have been some attempts to reconsider the significance of Jesus' divine sonship based on a fresh assessment of his own estimate of God as his Father.[129]

With a more sympathetic view of early Judaism and the consequent willingness to see continuity between early Judaism and early Christianity, N. T. Wright suggested that "Jesus' language about, and address to, Israel's god as 'father' belongs in the first instance with the basic aim and belief [of Jesus] that . . . evokes the memory of *Israel's designation as god's son*, with overtones of the exodus in particular."[130] He also finds behind Jesus' divine sonship the idea of "the Messiah as the special son, the one whom Israel's sonship is focused."[131]

Wright's suggestion about Jesus' view of God was taken up and developed by M. M. Thompson in her recent study of Father language in the OT, early Judaism and early Christianity.[132] As we shall see in more detail later, she attempts to demonstrate the continuity between the early Jewish view of God as Father of Israel and Jesus' understanding of God as his Father and of himself as his Son. Moreover, there is a more frontal criticism of Jeremias's view by scholars of a certain feminist persuasion like M. R. D'Angelo who categorically denies that "the Gospels do not and cannot support the claim that Jesus always addressed God as 'Father.'"[133] On the other hand, offering a counterargument against recent challenges B. Witherington and L. M. Ice defend the basic line of Jeremias' argument that Jesus' address to God as *abba* shows his self-consciousness of a unique and intimate relationship to God as his Father.[134]

---

[127] See §4.2 for a summary of his arguments and our critical discussion of recent criticisms against his view.

[128] R. Hamerton-Kelly, "God the Father in the Bible" in *God As Father?* (eds. J. B. Metz *et al.*; Edinburgh: T. & T. Clark; New York: Seabury Press, 1981), 101.

[129] There has been in recent decades a resurgence of theological debate about the viability and propriety of speaking and thinking of God as Father fuelled by challenge posed by feminist theologians of diverse stances. For a brief survey of "the feminist challenge" see M. M. Thompson, *The Promise of the Father: Jesus and God in the New Testament* (Louisville: Westminster/John Knox, 2000), 3-13.

[130] N. T. Wright, *Jesus and the Victory of God* (London: SPCK, 1996), 649 (emphasis ours).

[131] Wright, *Victory of God*, 649.

[132] Thompson, *Promise*.

[133] M. R. D'Angelo, "Abba and Father: Imperial Theology and the Jesus Traditions" *JBL* 111 (1992), 611-30 (quotation from p.618).

[134] Witherington and Ice, *The Shadow of the Almighty*.

Our review of the subject shows that there have been two broadly opposing positions on Jesus' self-consciousness of his divine sonship. While some scholars maintain that Jesus regarded himself as the Son who was aware of his unique and intimate relationship to the Father, the majority of scholars question in various ways whether Jesus did in fact think of himself as God's Son and whether the earliest church thought of him in this way. There is also a growing criticism against Jesus' unique sonship to God in recent times with willingness to recognize continuity between early Jewish view of God as Father and Jesus' own view.

This recent scholarly trend thus suggests that there is a need to re-examine older arguments in order to see whether evidence for Jesus' self-consciousness of divine sonship – understood as standing in a unique and intimate relationship to God – can be sustained in the light of recent scholarship (especially, Jesus' view of God as his Father). Our review of previous approaches to the subject also suggests that, although it is beyond question that the christological title was given to Jesus in the early church, the discussion concerning Jesus' divine sonship would be much more profitable if we approach the problem with the questions *whether* and in *what* sense Jesus conceived himself to be the Son of God and *how* such self-consciousness of his sonship to God made an impact to the understanding of him in the early church, and not the other ways around.

1.3. Early Christian Exegesis of the OT

The influence of the Old Testament on New Testament and other early Christian thought and literature is hard to overestimate. Early Christians often used quotations from the OT scriptures to demonstrate the continuity between these sacred writings and their faith centered on Jesus Christ.[135] They also used the OT allusively and implicitly. Such use of the OT provided early Christians models and patterns which were used to describe and reveal the significance of Jesus and the emerging Christian church. Early Christian use of the OT can rightly be seen as the "sub-structure" of New Testament theology, as the subtitle of C. H. Dodd's the well-known book suggests.[136]

The observation that the OT texts were not read randomly, but early Christians quoted or alluded to certain passages or sections of the OT

---

[135] The Gospel of Matthew, for example, has fifty-four scriptural quotations, while Paul has sixty quotations in his letter to the Romans alone. Quotation and allusion statistics are taken from the indices of the UBSGNT 4th ed.

[136] C. H. Dodd, *According to the Scriptures: the Sub-Structure of New Testament Theology* (London: Nisbet, 1952).

scriptures more than others prompted some scholars to ask precisely which scriptural passages and patterns were of fundamental importance for early Christians and just how and why these passages and patterns were so chosen.

J. R. Harris conjectured that before the writing of the New Testament a "testimony book" was already compiled under the authority of the apostle Matthew.[137] According to Harris, this "book" consisted of topically arranged scriptural proof-texts that fell into two major categories: proofs of christological beliefs (e.g., that Jesus, the messiah, had to suffer) and anti-Jewish proofs (God had rejected the Jews as his people and had instead chosen the Christians).[138]

C. H. Dodd followed Harris in isolating a central core of scriptural "testimonia" used by NT writers and argued that these "testimonia" made a pervasive influence on earliest Christian thought.[139] Dodd, however, rejected Harris's proposal of a "testimony book" and attributed these "testimonia" to Christian oral tradition in which certain larger sections of scripture were regarded as "testimonia" blocks.[140] For Dodd, the quotation of a single verse from any one of these "testimonia" blocks was sufficient to evoke the whole passage.

B. Lindars accepted the main line of Dodd's argument, but developed it into a more sophisticated model for uncovering the scriptural roots of NT theology.[141] While his study was a "growth" from the discussion of the testimonia theories, he made a valuable contribution to the NT discussion of the early Christian exegesis of the OT through his detailed discussion of the life-setting in which these testimonia were used. According to Lindars, early Christians made use of the OT primarily for an apologetic purpose: to provide an exegetical response to Jewish objections against Christian beliefs.[142] With Dodd, Lindars posited a close relationship between OT

---

[137] J. R. Harris, *Testimonies* (Cambridge: CUP, 1916-20).

[138] Harris was led to this conjecture by two major pieces of evidence: (1) extant patristic writings in which scriptural *testimonia* are indeed topically arranged (especially Cyprian's *To Quirinus* [248 AD] and Ps.-Gregory of Nyssa's *Against the Jews* [ca. 400 AD], and (2) peculiarities in early Christian quotations of scripture (use of non-standard [i.e., non-MT and non-LXX] texts, conflated quotations, false attributions, the same series of quotations in independent authors) which suggested that the Christians were not quoting directly from scriptural manuscripts, but rather from collections of proof-texts. Harris held that the Testimony Book was developed and employed in a context of early Christian-Jewish debate and conflict.

[139] Dodd, *According*.

[140] Dodd recognized three major groups of "testimonia": apocalyptic-eschatological scriptures (e.g., Joel 2-3; Zech 9-14); scriptures of the New Israel (Hos; Jer 31); and scriptures of the Servant of the Lord and the righteous sufferer (Ps 22; Isa 53).

[141] Lindars, *Apologetic*.

[142] Lindars, *Apologetic*, 13.

passages and the early Christian kerygma; presumably the original scriptural apologetic "answers some objection to the primitive kerygma."[143]

A valuable contribution to the study of early Christian exegesis of the OT comes from D. M. Hay.[144] His classic work on the early Christian interpretation of Psalm 110 begins with a survey of Jewish and early Christian interpretations of the psalm, followed by a functional analysis of early Christian use of the psalm in expressing Jesus' exaltation, supporting christological titles, affirming the subjection of powers to Jesus as well as the intercession and priesthood of Jesus. An important aspect of Hay's study on Psalm 110 is his discussion of "intermediary" sources. Hay argues that early Christian references to Jesus' sitting at God's right hand may not indicate direct use of Ps 110:1, but simply use of indirect sources in the form of a hymn or confession which incorporated the verse. Unlike Lindars, however, Hay concludes that no simple line of development can be traced in the psalm's interpretation.[145]

While disagreeing with Lindars about the purpose of the use of the OT, D. Juel recognized the importance of scriptural reflection in the development of the early Christian understanding of Jesus.[146] His main thesis that the understanding of Jesus as the royal Davidic messiah who was crucified and rose again was of fundamental importance for early Christians in their "search of the scriptures." He contended that early Christians would have first used royal messianic testimonia (e.g., 2 Sam 7:10-14; Gen 49:10-12; Num 24:17; Ps 2; Isa 11; Zech 6:12; Jer 33) in developing their christology.[147] One of his major objectives was to demonstrate from Qumran and from later rabbinic literature that the abovementioned texts were in fact interpreted messianically in late Second Temple Judaism.[148] In view of the fact that direct messianic quotations are few,[149] Juel argued that early Christians used Jewish midrashic techniques to combine messianic texts with other related scriptural texts to expand

---

[143] Lindars, *Apologetic*, 9, 23-24. Here Lindars explicitly agreed with Harris in emphasizing the anti-Judaic character of much of the primitive testimonia.

[144] D. M. Hay, *Glory at the Right Hand: Psalm 110 in Early Christianity* (SBLMS 18; Nashville: Abingdon, 1973).

[145] Hay, *Glory*, 156.

[146] D. H. Juel, *Messianic Exegesis: Christological Interpretation of the Old Testament in Early Christianity* (Philadelphia: Fortress, 1988).

[147] Juel, *Messianic*, 11.

[148] Juel, *Messianic*, 61-75 and 105-7.

[149] One example is the quotation of Ps 2:7 and 2 Sam 7:14 in Heb 1:5 to show that Jesus is God's Son.

their understanding of Jesus and his significance.[150] His study thus suggests that discussions of early Christian use of scripture should be given more attention to the messianic background.

An extensive study of the opening verse of Psalm 110 comes from M. Hengel's Strasburg colloquium lecture in 1990.[151] He explores the significance of this text for the development of christology until the third century AD. According to Hengel, Psalm 110:1 is not only of central importance for the interpretation of the earliest passages which speak of the resurrection but also an important starting point for early christology. His main contribution to the study of early Christian exegesis of the OT is his detailed study of the early Christian use of the Psalm 110:1 throughout the NT and the significance of the fusion of Ps 110:1 and Ps 8:6. By isolating a confession-like formula from NT references to Ps 110:1 he was able to trace back the influence of this psalm to the earliest period of the early church.

Martin C. Albl, in a recent attempt to draw out implications of earlier scholars, stood against the current scholarly tendency to attribute this exegetical work to the creativity of NT writers. Having *re*-examined in detail the form, function and original life-setting of the earliest Christian "testimonia" and other scriptural excerpt collections, Albl comes to the conclusion that "authoritative Christian exegetical traditions, often in the form of written *testimonia* collections and exegetical comments, were established even before the earliest NT compositions."[152]

In contemporary NT scholarship, research into early Christian exegesis of the OT has been vastly conducted with a specific aim to clarify the forms and functions of certain "testimonia" collections, and the question of the influence certain OT texts in the NT – in the form of quotations or allusions – might have exerted for the development of early christology

---

[150] See Juel, *Messianic*, 31-56, on the "rules of the game" for scriptural interpretation in the first century. He notes that "the greatest difference between early Christian exegesis and other forms of Jewish scriptural interpretation is the impact made by Jesus" (p.57).

[151] The written paper underlying the lecture appeared in the 1991 *Festschrift* in honour of F. Hahn's 65th birthday in C. Breytenbach *et al.*, eds., *Anfänge der Christologie: Festschrift für Ferdinand Hahn zum 65. Geburtstag* (Göttingen: Vandenhoeck & Ruprecht, 1991), 43-73; considerably expanded in M. Philonenko, *Le Trône de Dieu* (WUNT 69; Tübingen: Mohr Siebeck, 1993), 108-94, and then translated into English in M. Hengel, "'Sit at My Right Hand!' The Enthronement of Christ at the Right Hand of God and Psalm 110:1" in *Studies in Early Christology* (Edinburgh: T & T Clark, 1995), 119-225.

[152] M. C. Albl, *'And Scripture Cannot Be Broken': the Form and Function of the Early Christian Testimonia Collections* (NovTSup 96; Leiden: Brill, 1999), 6.

has been relatively neglected. We hope to contribute to filling this gap in NT scholarship.

While Dodd and Lindars chose to begin their reconstructions of the early Christian exegesis from the narrative of Acts, Juel began with the confessional tradition behind 1 Cor 15:3-7, convinced that Acts does not give us direct access to the earliest stages of Christian interpretation but represents "a rather developed stage of sophisticated scriptural argumentation."[153] One of our concerns, however, is not so much with the reconstruction or the possible starting point of early interpretation of the scriptures but rather as to how quotations or allusions to certain OT texts were used by early Christians in their endeavour to develop and clarify their understanding of Jesus. More specifically, we will concentrate on how early Christian exegetes used and interpreted two messianic psalms (Ps 110:1 and Ps 2:7) in order to illuminate how this early Christian exegesis affected their understanding of Jesus.

Furthermore, our unique contribution to the study of the origin and development of early christology is to present a cogent explanation of the emergence of pre-existent Son christology by combining insights from Jesus' own teaching about his self-understanding and the early Christian exegesis of Ps 110:1 and Ps2:7 in the light of their *re*-interpretation of the former.

1.4. Aim and Plans of the Study

The study seeks to clarify the origin and development of early Christian understanding of Jesus as the pre-existent Son of God. We will attempt to argue for the thesis that at the root of the pre-existent Son christology lies the early Christian exegesis of Ps 110:1 and Ps 2:7 (the catalyst) in the light of Jesus' self-consciousness of divine sonship and divine mission (the foundation). The tremendous impact left by his resurrection and the picture of Jesus being "literally"[154] enthroned to the right hand of God led to their understanding of him as the pre-existent Son of God.

We will demonstrate that Jesus' self-consciousness of his divine sonship – understood as standing in a unique and intimate relationship to God – did

---

[153] Juel, *Messianic*, quotation from p.140.

[154] His enthronement in the "literal" sense should be distinguished from the "metaphorical" sense. Both Jews and early Christians alike no doubt envisaged the heavenly sphere in which God is in the same way as the earthly sphere, so that for them it would not be unfair to say that he *literally* sits on a throne. By contrast, when a human being (e.g., a king) is said to share God's throne, this is metaphorical language for God giving him dominion and victory. See further §7.3.1.

not only play the most significant part in the development of an early Christian understanding of him as the Son of God but served also as laying the *foundation* for their conviction that he is the pre-existent Son of God. However, such a fuller understanding of him was only possible with the help of another crucial factor which I would call the *catalyst*, understood in the sense of speeding up a certain process to help reach its final goal. In other words, the full conviction about Jesus as the *pre-existent* Son was crystallized as they came to term with the full significance of what the prophetic words of God recorded in Ps 110:1 and Ps 2:7 really meant. However, such an understanding was not possible without one or the other. It was only possible through the early Christian exegesis of these two messianic psalms as it was done in the light of the very foundation Jesus himself laid for his disciples: his teaching about his self-understanding of him as *the* Son of God. In other words, early Christian exegetes were able to build upon Jesus' self-understanding of himself as the Son of God their fuller understanding of him as the pre-existent Son of God "literally" enthroned at his Father's right hand. Such a powerful picture of him was only possible through their christological exegesis of their two most important and cherished messianic psalms which served as the catalyst to help reach the full conviction about Jesus.

In Chapters 2 and 3 (Part II) we will look at the different sets of Jewish traditions about personified divine attributes (i.e., Wisdom of God, the Word of God, and the Name of God), exalted angels and a pre-existent messiah. The aim of these chapters will be twofold: (1) to argue that the personification of various attributes of God in Jewish traditions never led to the development of divine hypostases separate from God prior to Christianity nor speculations about principal angels and a pre-existent messianic figure ever provided a ready-made category for viewing Jesus as a divine and pre-existent being alongside God; and thereby (2) to strengthen our view that a strong monotheistic belief of Second Temple Judaism remained intact despite such speculations; rather than weakening their commitment to one God, they provided the first century Jews to speak meaningfully and vividly about the one God of Israel in his presence, manifestation, and action in the world without calling into question his transcendence and uniqueness.

In Chapters 4 and 5 (Part III) we will examine evidence from the Synoptic Gospels for Jesus' self-consciousness of divine sonship and divine mission. In Chapter 4 we will discuss whether and in what sense Jesus conceived himself to be the Son of God. The discussion will be focussed on Jesus' use of *abba* and his other sayings that might suggest his self-consciousness of a unique and personal relationship to God as his Father and of himself as his Son (Mt 11:27; Mk 13:32; Mt 16:17; Lk

22:29; Mk 12:1-12; Mk 1:9-11). Similarly, in Chapter 5 we will discuss whether and in what sense he was conscious of having come from and been sent by God. The discussion will be focussed on those sayings that can be categorized as "I have come" sayings (Mk 2:17 pars.; Mk 10:45 par.; Lk 19:10; 12:49, 51 par.) and "I was sent" sayings (Mt 15:24 par.; Mk 9:37 pars.). At the end of the chapter we will draw some christological implications of Jesus' self-understanding and see whether his self-understanding was open to interpretation in terms of pre-existence.

In Chapters 6 and 7 (Part IV) we will discuss how early Christians employed Ps 110:1 and Ps 2:7 for their understanding of Jesus and how the 'gap' – for some a seemingly irreconcilable one – between what Jesus claimed to be and what his early followers came to believe was successfully 'filled' through their exegesis of the two messianic psalms most cherished in the early church. We will argue that Jesus' self-consciousness of divine sonship and divine mission and the early Christian exegesis of these messianic psalms should be considered the foundation and the catalyst for the pre-existent Son christology.

In Chapter 8 we will argue that crucial evidence for the early Christian conviction about Jesus' pre-existence is found in the so-called "pre-Pauline 'sending' formula" (Gal 4:4; Rom 8:3; Jn 3:17; 1 Jn 4:9, 10, 14). Once Jesus' divinity and pre-existence were confirmed through the exegesis of the psalms, Jewish wisdom traditions were helpful in drawing out the full significance of his pre-existence in terms of his being active in creation and co-eternal with God the Father. The early Christian conviction about Jesus as the pre-existent Son sent by the Father as is found in the "sending" formula should be regarded as the culmination of the early church's desire to know more about their master – the one who was crucified but risen again and exalted at God's right hand – through their exegesis of two most cherished messianic psalms in the light of Jesus' self-revelatory statements.

Chapter 2

Personified Divine Attributes

As our survey of current scholarship on the origins of early "divine" christology suggests, we now turn to discuss the extent to which personified divine attributes in early Jewish tradition played a significant role in the understanding of God in Second Temple Judaism and early Christianity. Our discussion will be particularly focused on the question whether these personified attributes of God set the real precedent for viewing Jesus as a divine and pre-existent being next to God in the early church. For this purpose, we will take a close look at how Wisdom, Word and the Name of God were understood in the Old Testament and Second Temple Judaism.[1]

2.1. Problem of Definition

In biblical scholarship the term "divine hypostasis" has long been used to denote "a quasi-personification of certain attributes proper to God, occupying an intermediate position between personalities and abstract beings."[2] G. Pfeifer attempted to redefine the term as "eine Grösse, die teilhat am Wesen einer Gottheit, die durch sie handelnd in die Welt eingreift, ohne dass sich ihr Wesen im Wirken dieser Hypostase

---

[1] We are aware of other divine attributes, such as Glory, Power, Spirit, Face/Presence of God, that have been the focus of scholarly discussion, but, due to the constraints of space, our discussion will have to be confined to Wisdom, Word and Name. Such limitation, however, will not affect the outcome of our discussion as all these concepts can be gathered into one broad category of personified divine attributes.

[2] The definition given by W. O. E. Oesterley and G. H. Box, *The Religion and Worship of the Synagogue: an Introduction to the Study of Judaism From the New Testament Period* (London: I. Pitman, 1911), 195, and endorsed by H. Ringgren, *Word and Wisdom: Studies in the Hypostatization of Divine Qualities and Functions in the Ancient Near East* (Lund: Ohlsson, 1947), 8; see also W. Schencke, *Die Chokma (Sophia) in der jüdischen Hypostasenspekulation: ein Beitrag zur Geschichte der religiösen Ideen im Zeitalter des Hellenismus* (Kristiania: Utgit, 1913).

erschöpft."[3] S. D. McBride gave his own definition of the term as "a quality, epithet, attribute, manifestation or the like of a deity which through a process of personification and differentiation has become a distinct (if not fully independent) divine being in its own right."[4] Leon D. Muñoz used the terms "hypostasis" and "hypostatization" to refer to "a figurative way of speaking in which a divine attribute in a certain way becomes personalized, without giving too much attention to the practical consequences of this way of speaking. It is in this sense that the Bible speaks of 'Wisdom' and the terms such as Shekinah, Name, etc. are thus worthy of being studied."[5] S. Olyan has avoided the use of the terms "hypostasis" and "hypostatization," introducing the term "special figurative treatment" to describe the same phenomenon.[6] Recently C. A. Gieschen has come up with yet another definition: "an aspect of God that has a degree of independent personhood."[7]

---

[3] G. Pfeifer, *Ursprung und Wesen der Hypostasenvorstellungen im Judentum* (ArbT 1/31; Stuttgart: Calwer, 1967), 15: "a magnitude/greatness which participates in the Person of a deity, who intervenes in the world through it, without his Person being exhausted in the working of this hypostasis" (my translation).

[4] S. D. McBride, *The Deuteronomic Name Theology* (Cambridge: CUP, 1969), 5.

[5] D. Muñoz Leon, *Dios-Palabra: Memrá en los Targumim del Pentateuco* (Granada: Institutión San Jerónomo, 1974), 99, n.6, my translation of his definition: "una manera de hablar figurada en la que un atributo divino en cierta manera se personaliza, sin atender demasiado a las consecuencias prácticas de esta manera de hablar. En este sentido la Biblia habla de la 'Sabiduria' y son dignos de estudiarse los términos Shekiná, Nombre, etc."

[6] S. M. Olyan, *A Thousand Thousands Served Him: Exegesis and the Naming of Angels in Ancient Judaism* (TSAJ 36; Tübingen: Mohr Siebeck, 1993), 89-90, give three reasons for this change: (1) such terminology emphasizes the figurative nature of the language used; (2) it avoids unwarranted associations with "the rather ill-conceived notion of an increasingly distant and inaccessible God emerging during the period of the Second Temple, and a resulting need for intermediary figures between God and Israel," a notion which has been already rejected by many contemporary scholars; (3) it is a more general and inclusive term. For the critique of the distant God hypostasis see G. F. Moore, "Christian Writers on Judaism" *HTR* 14 (1921), 241-48; G. F. Moore, *Judaism in the First Centuries of the Christian Era: the Age of the Tannaim* (Cambridge: CUP, 1930), 404-05; for the alternative theses see H. B. Kuhn, "The Angelology of the Non-Canonical Jewish Apocalypses" *JBL* 67 (1947), 228-30: "a naïve way of imagining the mediation of God's word and will in the universe by personal agents"; E. P. Sanders, *Paul and Palestinian Judaism: a Comparison of Patterns of Religion* (London: SCM, 1977), 212-17; L. W. Hurtado, *One God, One Lord: Early Christian Devotion and Ancient Jewish Monotheism* (London: SCM, 1988, 1998), 22-27. For a critique of Bousset *et. al.* on "hypostases" see A. Goldberg, *Untersuchungen über die Vorstellung von der Schekhinah in der frühen rabbinischen Literatur (Talmud und Midrasch)* (Berlin: Walter de Gruyter, 1969), 1-7.

[7] C. A. Gieschen, *Angelomorphic Christology: Antecedents and Early Evidence* (AGAJU 42; Leiden: Brill, 1998), 90.

Such a variety of definitions for "divine hypostases" suggests that there is no scholarly agreement on the basic understanding of the term and a clarification of the term is needed. While there seems to be no clear distinction between "divine hypostases" and "personified divine attributes," if the discussion is to be fruitful, there ought to be a clear distinction between the two. We therefore suggest two distinct definitions for "divine hypostases" and "personified divine attributes."

By "personified divine attribute"[8] we mean "a quality, epithet, attribute, manifestation or the like of a deity which, having been subjected to a literary personification, behaves *as though* it is a distinct (if not fully independent) divine being in its own right, but still remains within the literary realm." By "divine hypostasis" we mean "a quality, epithet, attribute, manifestation or the like of a deity, which through a process of personification, concretization, or differentiation, *has become* a distinct (if not fully independent) divine being in its own right." While the former still remains within the literary realm, the latter has already crossed over the boundary of the literary world to encompass a concrete, actual, divine being alongside a deity.

Unfortunately, many biblical scholars still use the term "divine hypostasis" in reference to certain attributes of God which are nothing more than literary personifications and spoken merely in a figurative language.[9] However, rather than just a misuse of the term, it is the misunderstanding of the linguistic phenomenon involved in a vivid description of divine attributes in ancient Jewish sources which is more problematic.

A. Gibson has made a strong criticism of those critics who have taken linguistic hypostatization (personification) as though it were attributive hypostatization. Gibson pointed out that "this conflation can act as a

---

[8] The expression "personified divine attribute" is used by Hurtado, *One God*, 42, *passim*. See Olyan, *A Thousand*, 89-91, for the benefits of replacing the terms "hypostasis" and "hypostatization."

[9] Some scholars use the term "hypostasis," even without subscribing to the common definition of the term. See for example, P. A. Rainbow, *Monotheism and Christology in I Corinthians 8. 4-6* (D.Phil. Dissertation, Oxford University, 1987), 86, who defines a divine hypostasis as "a title, attribute, function, or activity of God which at the level of linguistic discourse is abstracted from the person of God in such a way as to be treated as a conceptual entity in its own right." See Hurtado, *One God*, 36-37, for the critique of the use of "hypostasis" and Pfeifer, *Ursprung*, 69, who concluded that the items referred to as hypostases seem to have played no important role in Jewish theology of postexilic period, with the possible exception of Philo.

generating point for confusing personification with hypostatization and *falsely introducing a referent* for personification."[10] He explained:

> This comes about because what is actually a linguistic (literary) device has been taken to be equivalent to attributive hypostatization, as a scholar in confusion sees it; the latter, which is actually a different phenomenon involving ontological commitment, is unwittingly (in the scholar's hypothesis) taken to imply a referent for personificatory expressions.[11]

In this chapter, we will attempt to demonstrate that the term "personified divine attributes" best explains the language used by ancient Jews to talk about God. In other words, the language used to speak about God using different divine attributes is none other than a literary device called "personification." In this regard, any attempts to explain the special literary device used to talk about God in terms of "divine hypostasis" should be regarded as a failure to understand the character of ancient Jewish religious language. One of the aims of the present chapter is therefore to see whether a vivid description of various divine attributes by ancient and Second Temple Jews remained within the literary realm or led them to conceptualize the phenomenon as "semi-divine beings" and something like "a quasi-personification of certain attributes proper to God, occupying an intermediate position between personalities and abstract beings."[12]

S. M. Olyan argued that the personification of divine attributes is a very common phenomenon in the OT.[13] He provided the Name of God as an example, but also pointed out that other divine attributes such as Wisdom, Word, Presence/Face, and Glory should be treated similarly.

N. T. Wright is also in agreement with our view when he asserts that:

> Language about supernatural agencies other than the one god had to do, rather, with the theological problem of how to hold together providence (with covenant as a special case of providence) and a belief in a transcendent god. Unless this god is to collapse back into being a mere absentee landlord, in which case providence and covenant go by the board, or unless he ceases to be in any meaningful sense transcendent, moving instead towards pantheism or paganism, one is bound to develop, and second-temple Jews did develop, ways of speaking about *the divine action in the world* which attempt to do justice to these different poles of belief. Thus it is that language about angels, about the Shekinah or

---

[10] A. Gibson, *Biblical Semantic Logic: a Preliminary Analysis* (Oxford: Blackwell, 1981), 96 (emphasis ours); cf. J. Barr, "Hypostatization of Linguistic Phenomena in Modern Theological Interpretation" *JSS* 7 (1962), 85-94.

[11] Gibson, *Biblical Semantic Logic*, 96.

[12] The definition given by Oesterley and Box, *Religion and Worship*, 195, and endorsed by Ringgren, *Word and Wisdom*, 8, but I must confess that it is very difficult to conceptualize. See also Schencke, *Chokma*.

[13] Olyan, *A Thousand*, 92-97.

'presence' of Israel's god, about Torah, about Wisdom, about the Logos – all of these make their appearances, not as mere fantasy or speculative metaphysics, but as varied (and not always equally successful) attempts to perform a necessary theological task. At one level this task was purely linguistic: speaking of the divine 'presence' or 'word' enabled one to speak of the one god active in his world without committing the solecism of suggesting that this god was somehow contained within this action, or indeed within the world.[14]

We can concur also with J. D. G. Dunn, who concludes his study on Wisdom with the following statement:

it is very unlikely that pre-Christian Judaism ever understood Wisdom as a divine being in any sense independent of Yahweh. The language may be the language of the wider speculation of the time, but within Jewish monotheism and Hebraic literary idiom Wisdom never really becomes more than a *personification* – a personification not so much of a divine attribute (I doubt whether the Hebrews thought much in terms of 'attributes'), a personification rather of a *function* of Yahweh, *a way of speaking about God himself, of expressing God's active involvement with his world and his people without compromising his transcendence.*[15]

He also states:

Our conclusion here is borne out by what we learned above concerning the Spirit of God and the Wisdom of God in pre-Christian Judaism. As they were ways of speaking about *Yahweh acting toward and in his creation,* so too with the Word of God. As they enabled the Jewish writers to speak of the immanence of God without threatening his transcendence, so with the Word.[16]

One of the recent scholars who ably defends the language of the personification of divine attributes, levelling criticism at those who use the term "hypostasis," is L. W. Hurtado. He comments:

Finally, in reference to hypostases, I find the attempts to define or justify the use of this term as a description of personified attributes of God in Jewish tradition neither very clear nor compelling. For example, just what are we to make of something defined as "a quasi-personification of certain attributes proper to God, occupying an intermediate position between personalities and abstract being"? The use of descriptions of such items as divine Wisdom for evidence of a belief in actual quasi-divine entities distinct from God is a failure to understand the language used by ancient Jews to describe *God's activities and powers,* taking literally what is in fact best understood as a vivid idiom of ancient Jewish religious expression.[17]

---

[14] N. T. Wright, *The New Testament and the People of God* (London: SPCK, 1992), 258-59.

[15] J. D. G. Dunn, *Christology in the Making: a New Testament Inquiry into the Origins of the Doctrine of the Incarnation* (London: SCM, 1980, 1989), 176.

[16] Dunn, *Christology*, 219 (italics ours).

[17] Hurtado, *One God*, 37 (italics ours).

If these scholars are right, to see a figurative way of speaking about God as a hypostasis is a serious failure to understand the true character of ancient Jewish religious language. L. W. Hurtado rightly asserts that:

> That the divine Name, divine Wisdom or Word, and other divine attributes are referred to in ancient texts in language of personification is not sufficient reason to conclude that these items were understood by ancient Jews as personal beings or as things somewhere in "between personalities and abstract beings" (e.g., hypostases). While personified divine attributes behave in the linguistic world of ancient Jewish texts as personal beings, this is not necessarily indicative of the *function* of divine attributes in the conceptual world and religious life of the people who created the texts.[18]

If our definition is correct, it is entirely possible for Wisdom to speak in the first person and refer to God in the third person (Prov 8:22-29) and still be *the object of a literary personification to speak about God himself working in this world.* In what follows we will discuss in detail the development of the concepts such as Wisdom of God, the Word of God and the Name of God in Jewish tradition to see whether they *became* "divine hypostases" in the eyes of Second Temple Jews and set the real precedent for viewing Jesus as a divine and pre-existent figure alongside God.

2.2. Wisdom of God

It is widely recognized that the figure of Wisdom played an important role in the development of early christology. Wisdom christology is claimed to have been the main bridge between the earliest belief in the exalted Christ and the belief that he also pre-existed with God prior to his incarnation. The language used of the figure of Wisdom in the Old Testament and inter-testamental literature can be traced in the New Testament passages where references to Christ's pre-existence are commonly detected (Jn 1:1-18, 1 Cor 8:5-6, Col 1:15-20; Heb 1:1-3, etc.).[19] The influence of Jewish Wisdom traditions upon the christology of the New Testament is indisputable. In fact it is widely accepted that some NT writers have identified the exalted Christ with the figure of Wisdom.

Despite such an identification in the New Testament there has been no scholarly consensus on the true nature or identity of this highly mysterious figure with whom/which Christ has been identified. In the past this figure

---

[18] Hurtado, *One God*, 47 (italics ours).

[19] While acknowledging references to Wisdom in these passages, Dunn, *Christology*, 176-212, does not see in them a reference to Christ's pre-existence, except in John.

of Wisdom has been variously understood as (1) a divine being;[20] as (2) a hypostasis;[21] as (3) a personification of a divine attribute;[22] or as (4) the personification of cosmic order.[23] In recent scholarship, at least among the NT scholars who study the origins of early christology, the opinion seems to be narrowed down to the options (2) and (3).[24] In short, it has become a matter of viewing Jewish Wisdom speculations either in a figurative way or in a fairly literal sense.

Personification of divine attributes as a literary device is not unknown in the Old Testament and inter-testamental literature (Pss 85:10-11; 96:6; 43:3; 57:3b). It is also interesting to note that God's arm and his hand were personified as independent entities (Isa 51:9; Wis 11:17). Not only divine attributes or parts of the body of God but human characteristics were also subject to such personification in the OT (Job 11:14; Ps 107:42; Isa 35:10).

In the case of Wisdom, however, the extent of the literary personification is so great that many scholars have questioned whether the term "personification" does justice to the figure of Wisdom. This problem of definition has led some in recent scholarship to the inclusion of wisdom

---

[20] As an independent deity, similar to Egyptian and Mesopotamian gods/goddess. Cf. U. Wilckens, *Weisheit und Torheit: eine exegetisch-religionsgeschichtliche Untersuchung zu 1. Kor. 1 und 2* (BHT 26; Tübingen: Mohr Siebeck, 1959), 190-7; also *TDNT* 7.508-9; H. Conzelmann, "The mother of wisdom" in *The Future of Our Religious Past: Essays in Honour of Rudolf Bultmann* (ed. J. M. Robinson; London: SCM, 1971), 232ff.

[21] Ringgren, *Word and Wisdom*, 8; see also Schencke, *Chokma*; O. S. Rankin, *Israel's Wisdom Literature: Its Bearing on Theology and the History of Religion* (Edinburgh: T & T Clark, 1936), ch.9, especially p. 224; Pfeifer, *Ursprung*, 24, 26-28, 30f., 43f., 45f., 60f. (definition of "hypostasis" on pp.14f.); M. Hengel, *Judaism and Hellenism: Studies in Their Encounter in Palestine During the Early Hellenistic Period* (London: SCM, 1974), 1.153ff., 171; Gieschen, *Angelomorphic*, 89-103.

[22] E.g. Marcus, "Hypostases," 167ff.; R. B. Y. Scott, "Wisdom in Creation: the 'Amon of Proverbs 8.30" *VT* 10 (1960), 223; R. N. Whybray, *Wisdom in Proverbs: the Concept of Wisdom in Proverbs 1-9* (SBT 45; London: SCM, 1965), 103; C. Larcher, *Études sur le livre de la Sagesse* (EBib; Paris: Lecoffre, 1969), ch.5, particularly 402-10; R. E. Murphy, *The Tree of Life: an Exploration of Biblical Wisdom Literature* (New York: Doubleday, 1996), 133, defines wisdom as "a communication of God."

[23] G. von Rad, *Wisdom in Israel* (Nashville: Abingdon, 1972), 144-76.

[24] Among the advocates of Wisdom as a hypostasis are A. F. Segal, *Two Powers in Heaven: Early Rabbinic Reports About Christianity and Gnosticism* (SJLA 25; Leiden: Brill, 1977); C. Rowland, *The Open Heaven: a Study of Apocalyptic in Judaism and Early Christianity* (London: SPCK, 1982); J. E. Fossum, *The Name of God and the Angel of the Lord: Samaritan and Jewish Concepts of Intermediation and the Origin of Gnosticism* (WUNT 36; Tübingen: Mohr Siebeck, 1985); Gieschen, *Angelomorphic*. For them, not only Wisdom but other divine attributes such as Word, Glory, Name, are also hypostases of God.

traditions in a broader category called "angelomorphic traditions."[25] The latter category includes not only Wisdom and other personified divine attributes but also traditions about exalted patriarchs and principal angels. Angelomorphic traditions are said to take the figure of Wisdom as a divine hypostasis, something more than just a personification of a divine attribute.[26]

If we want to discern how Second Temple Jews and early Christians would have understood the figure of Wisdom we need not only to look closely at those texts where the personification of Wisdom occurs, but also to set this type of language in a wider context of Hebrew thought. We have seen above that the use of the literary device of figurative language to speak about God with the use of different divine attributes was not a strange phenomenon in the OT. This gives us only a partial answer. Now we will turn to the texts in question: Job 28, Prov 8:22-31, Sir 24, Bar 3:9-4:4, Wis 6:12-11:1, *1 Enoch* 42, and various references to Wisdom in Philo.

2.2.1. Job 28

It is well recognized that this chapter is an independent poem on wisdom, skilfully constructed in three sections with a refrain in vv.12 and 20. In this poem "wisdom" [חכמה] stands in synonymous parallelism with "understanding" [בינה] (vv.12; 20) just as in the book of Proverbs.[27] This shows that the author is not interested in an exact definition of terms, which in turn indicates that wisdom is not referred to as a divine attribute but as wisdom in this world. Unlike other wisdom passages, wisdom here is not personified as a female figure. Rather, wisdom is something hidden from the creatures (v.21) and only God knows its whereabouts (v.23). According to v.27, however, God did something with it when creating the world (vv.25-26): "he saw it and declared it; he established it, and searched it out." G. von Rad interprets wisdom simply as "the order given to the world by God,"[28] a mystery that human beings cannot reach. However, the idea of wisdom as a gift from God is found in 1 Kings 3:5-12, where Solomon prayed to God asking not for long life or wealth but only for wisdom, and God granted him wisdom as a gift. The double question "But where shall wisdom be found? And where is the place of understanding?" (v.12, 20) and the answer "God understands the way to it, and he knows its place" (v.23) suggest the desire of the writer to receive

---

[25] Gieschen, *Angelomorphic*.
[26] Cf. Gieschen, *Angelomorphic*, 89-103.
[27] Prov 2:2; 2:6; 3:13; 3:19; 5:1; 7:4; 8:1; 9:10; 10:13; 16:16; 19:8; 24:3.
[28] von Rad, *Wisdom in Israel*, 148; also Dunn, *Christology*, 168.

wisdom, which only comes to him as God's gift. It is likely that the writer of Job wanted to assert "how impossible it is for men to acquire wisdom by their own efforts, but it can be acquired only as God's gift."[29] Therefore, in the wisdom poem of Job we do not yet encounter the personification of Wisdom as a divine attribute, but the reification of wisdom as God's gift to men. Wisdom is in fact more like a hidden treasure to be found!

2.2.2. Proverbs 1-9

While it may be possible to argue that the personification of Wisdom can be seen in Job 28,[30] the first clear example of wisdom being personified appears in Proverbs 1-9, particularly in 1:20-33; 3:13-18; and 8:1-9:12. In these passages Wisdom is depicted as an attractive woman speaking in public places.[31] However, the most vivid personification of Wisdom, with Wisdom speaking of herself as present at the creation of the world as God's companion, is found in 8:22-31. Here lies the focal point of controversy. What do we make of this highly enigmatic figure?

H. Ringgren asserts that 8:22-31 is "the most obvious evidence in Prov. for the hypostatization of Wisdom."[32] He also argues that it is "obvious that Wisdom is here not an abstraction or a purely poetic personification but a concrete being, self-existent beside God."[33] One of the recent strong advocates of Wisdom as a divine hypostasis which forms part of the background of early christology is C. A. Gieschen. In a study to trace the antecedents and early evidence for the angelomorphic christology, Gieschen argues that, unlike other personifications of Wisdom in Proverbs, in Prov 8:22-31 Wisdom is portrayed as "an aspect of God that has a degree of independent personhood."[34] He supports his argument in the following manner:

---

[29] S. Sandmel, *Philo of Alexandria: an Introduction* (New York; Oxford: OUP, 1979), 98.

[30] Some scholars have been inclined to find an allusion to Prov 8:22f. in Job 15:7f. See Ringgren, *Word and Wisdom*, 89-90.

[31] Like in Job 28, throughout chapters 1-9 "wisdom" is used interchangeably with "understanding" (2:2; 2:6; 3:13; 3:19; 5:1; 8:1). This shows that the author of Proverbs is not interested in an exact definition of the terms.

[32] Ringgren, *Word and Wisdom*, 99.

[33] Ringgren, *Word and Wisdom*, 104. His conclusion about the hypostatization of Wisdom and Word of God, however, was vitiated by the view advanced about the word by L. Dürr, *Die Wertung des göttlichen Wortes im Alten Testament und im antiken Orient: zugleich ein Beitrag zur Vorgeschichte des neutestamentlichen Logosbegriffes* (Leipzig: J. C. Hinrichs Verlag, 1938), whose view has been severely criticized by A. C. Thiselton, "The Supposed Power of Words" *JTS* 25 (1974), 283-99. See also below section B. The Word of God.

[34] Gieschen, *Angelomorphic*, 90.

Wisdom speaks in the first person and refers to God in the third person several times (8.22-29). A distinction exists between the origins of Wisdom and those of God; Wisdom is also distinct from the rest of creation (8.22). She is God's companion, even a participant ("master craftsman" [MT: אמון; LXX: ἁρμόζουσα]), in the creation. Furthermore, the position of Wisdom in relation to God also indicates a degree of independent personhood: Wisdom is "beside him" and "in his presence" (8.30). The latter position is typical of descriptions of angels standing before God (e.g., Dan 7.10).[35]

Then he presses his argument further by noting that the preposition "beside him" [אצלו] in Prov 8:30a, a phrase normally used in Jewish and Christian literature of someone next to, or on, the throne of God,[36] suggests a position higher than that of a typical angel (cf. Sir 1:8-9).[37] According to Gieschen, the verb נסך ("pour out, anoint, install")[38] in Prov 8:23 indicates Wisdom's enthronement.[39]

However, if we demonstrate that Prov 8:22-31 uses figurative language for Wisdom to speak usefully about God himself no single argument put forward for Wisdom as a divine hypostasis would stand. If we isolate this particular text from the broad context of Prov 1-9 we may be in danger of misrepresenting the real significance of the passage. Therefore it is crucial to place the passage in question within the broader context of Prov 1-9.

According to L. Perdue, Prov 1-9 can be described as "an elegantly crafted collection consisting of a general introduction, ten instructions, five related poems on Woman Wisdom, and a variety of short wisdom sayings scattered throughout the collection, and the poems on Woman Wisdom are strategically inserted at the beginning and end of the collection (1:20-33; 8:1-11, 12-21, 22-31; and 9:1-18) to form a literary inclusio.[40] Prov 8 can

---

[35] Gieschen, *Angelomorphic*, 90-91

[36] Gieschen, *Angelomorphic*, 93-97, sees that Wisdom's position relative to God's throne is made explicit in Wis 9:4, 11 and notes that Sir 24:4 mentions that Wisdom's throne is in a "pillar of cloud."

[37] Gieschen, *Angelomorphic*, 91.

[38] Cf. Psalm 2:6.

[39] Gieschen, *Angelomorphic*, 91.

[40] L. G. Perdue, *Wisdom and Creation: the Theology of Wisdom Literature* (Nashville: Abingdon, 1994), 78. See C. Kayatz, *Studien zu Proverbien 1-9: Eine form- und motivgeschichtliche Untersuchung unter Einbeziehung ägyptischen Vergleichsmaterials* (WMANT 22; Neukirchen-Vluyn: Neukirchener Verlag, 1966). Perdue finds in Prov 1-9 a "rhetorical structure [which] stimulates the imagination to find behind the voice of the teacher in Proverbs 1-9 a second, even more authoritative and revelatory voice, that of Woman Wisdom, who is teacher, sage, Queen of Heaven, the child of God, and the mediator between heaven and earth. And behind her, more distant, but still audible, the voice of God, who addresses through the teacher and Woman Wisdom those who take up sapiential instruction" (78). See C. A. Newsom, "Woman and the Discourse of Patriarchal Wisdom: A Study of Proverbs 1-9" in *Gender and Difference in Ancient Israel* (ed. P. L. Day; Minneapolis: Fortress, 1989), 142-60.

in turn be seen as a well-crafted section on Woman Wisdom, consisting of five related parts: 8:1-3 ("The Sage's Introduction to Woman Wisdom"), 8:4-11 ("Wisdom's Call"), 8:12-21 ("Wisdom's Providential Rule"), 8:22-31 ("Wisdom's Place in Creation"), and 8:32-36 ("Wisdom's Instruction of Life").[41] Perdue explains that "Wisdom as a teacher begins (8:1-11) and concludes (8:32-36) the section, providing an inclusio that enfolds two poems on Wisdom's roles in providence (8:12-21) and creation (8:22-31)."[42] Going through section by section, Perdue clearly shows that Wisdom is personified in a variety of roles in this chapter.[43] Wisdom is personified as a peripatetic teacher who goes in search of students, inviting them to take up her course of study and learn from her (8:1-11; cf. 1:20-33), as a royal goddess, the Queen of Heaven, who possesses both fertility and wisdom (8:12-21), and as the firstborn of God or the master worker for God,[44] who serves as mediator between Yahweh and the inhabited world (8:22-31). In the final section (8:32-36), "Wisdom, the firstborn of creation, perhaps active in the shaping of the cosmos, and the providential ruler of history, now issues once more the call to life that she had offered in the first section of the poem (8:1-11)," giving the invitation of Woman Wisdom even greater authority.[45] Perdue also notes that Woman Folly in Prov 9 is the exact opposite of Woman Wisdom. Of course, it is most likely that the sage wanted to "counteract the influence of the Astarte cult, by representing Wisdom as much more attractive than the 'strange woman' against whom he warns in chs. 2, 5, 6, and 7."[46] The depiction of Wisdom as a goddess in chapters 3 and 8 must have had a similar effect. H. Ringgren also points out that Prov 1-9 was intended as "a conscious

---

[41] Perdue, *Wisdom and Creation*, 84.

[42] Perdue, *Wisdom and Creation*, 84.

[43] Perdue, *Wisdom and Creation*, 84-94.

[44] This depends on how one translates the word "אָמוֹן" in v.30a. A variety of translations have been proposed, but two are most probable: a master worker (NRSV) or a little child.

[45] Perdue, *Wisdom and Creation*, 91.

[46] Whybray, *Wisdom in Proverbs*, 87-92. Some scholars have pointed out the cult of Isis as the background for Prov 8:22-31, and more clearly in Sir 24. Wisdom is comparable also to Isis in that she also proclaims herself as the divine agent who created and sustains the universe, as the teacher who has revealed to men the principles of morality and the laws and arts of civilization. For Isis influences, see W. L. Knox, "The Divine Wisdom" *JTS* 38 (1937), 230-7; also W. L. Knox, *St Paul and the Church of the Gentiles* (Cambridge: CUP, 1939), ch. 3; A. J. Festugiere, "A propos des Arétalogies d'Isis" *HTR* 42 (1949), 209-34; Conzelmann, "Mother of Wisdom," 230-43; Kayatz, *Studien*, ch.2; Hengel, *Judaism and Hellenism*, 1.157ff.; J. Marböck, *Weisheit im Wandel: Untersuchungen zur Weisheitstheologie bei Ben Sira* (BBB 37; Bonn: Hanstein, 1971), 49-54; B. L. Mack, *Logos und Sophia: Untersuchungen zur Weisheitstheologie im hellenistischen Judentum* (Göttingen: Vandenhoeck & Ruprecht, 1973), 38-42.

contrast to a cult, hostile towards Yahweh."[47] He further explains the relationship between the foreign goddess and the figure of Wisdom thus:

> Behind the 'foreign women' the goddess, whom they represent in the cult, is visible. Wisdom is [deliberately] described with traits reminding one of the foreign goddess. She is presented as a contrast to Astarte and her pernicious cult. Wisdom is a *substitute* for the love goddess and her cult and a protection against them, and we have here 'one of the roots of the figure of Wisdom',[48] since the hypostatized wisdom of Yahweh has been given features borrowed from the mother goddess.[49]

It is important to note at this point the criticism of H. Ringgren by Dunn. Dunn rightly criticizes the conclusion drawn by Ringgren from words like *Maat* (truth, righteousness, order and regularity in the cosmos) and *Mēšaru* (righteousness) which came to denote independent deities.[50] Dunn points out that words like *Maat* and *Mēšaru* are rightly seen by Ringgren as more than merely poetic personifications because *Maat* had many priests and *Mēšaru* had its own image in the temple and was the object of worship. But we know of no such things with Wisdom.[51]

Placed in the context of Prov 1-9 the highly enigmatic poem of Wisdom in 8:22-31 becomes just one example of the multi-faceted personification of Wisdom. Thus it is entirely possible for Wisdom to speak in the first person and refer to God in the third person (8:22-29). However highly Wisdom was exalted and closely related to God, an attempt to see Wisdom in Prov 8:22-31 as a divine hypostasis not only ignores the character of ancient Jewish religious language of the time, but also, more specifically,

---

[47] Ringgren, *Word and Wisdom*, 134.

[48] G. Boström, *Proverbiastudien: die Weisheit und das fremde Weib in Spr. 1-9* (Lund: Gleerup, 1935), 174.

[49] Ringgren, *Word and Wisdom*, 134 (italics ours). However, I do not endorse his use of the term "hypostatized wisdom"; For a critique of Ringgren, see Dunn, *Christology*, 169-70. While Dunn agrees with Ringgren that "however deeply rooted in Palestinian soil and Jewish faith was the late Israelite talk of Wisdom, *many of the images and words used to describe her were drawn from wider religious thought and worship* – the aim being to present the worshippers of Yahweh with as attractive as possible an alternative to the cults and speculations more widely prevalent in their time," he is not in agreement with Ringgren when he concludes that "*language which denoted a hypostasis or independent deity in polytheism would certainly have a different connotation within a monotheistic religion*" (italics his).

[50] Ringgren, *Word and Wisdom*, 45-59. For *Maat* as a source of Jewish Wisdom tradition see Mack, *Logos und Sophia*, 34-9.

[51] Dunn, *Christology*, 170. Similarly, Perdue, *Wisdom and Creation*, 99, is certainly right when he states that "Since normative Israelite religion did not provide a divine consort for Yahweh, the personification of Wisdom as a goddess was, to the imagination, a metaphorical alternative."

the metaphorical language used by the author/editor of the book of Proverbs. L. W. Hurtado is certainly right when he asserts that:

While personified divine attributes behave in the linguistic world of ancient Jewish texts as personal beings, this is not necessarily indicative of the *function* of divine attributes in the conceptual world and religious life of the people who created the texts.[52]

Therefore, the wisdom poem of 8:22-31, simply reinforces, in the most vivid and poetical way possible, what is said earlier about divine origin of Wisdom ("For the Lord gives wisdom; from his mouth come knowledge and understanding" [2:6]), God's creative activities ("The LORD by wisdom founded the earth; by understanding he established the heavens" [3:19]),[53] and the incomparable value of Wisdom ("She is more precious than jewels, and nothing you desire can compare with her" [3:15; cf. 8:11]).

Perdue finds in Prov 1-9 a "rhetorical structure [which] stimulates the imagination to find behind the voice of the teacher in Proverbs 1-9 a second, even more authoritative and revelatory voice, that of Woman Wisdom, who is teacher, sage, Queen of Heaven, the child of God, and the mediator between heaven and earth. And behind her, more distant, but still audible, the voice of God, who addresses through the teacher and Woman Wisdom those who take up sapiential instruction."[54] It is not surprising, therefore, to get the impression in 1:20-33 and 8:1-21, for instance, that God himself is acting and urging the reader through or in the disguise of the figure of Wisdom. Although Wisdom is not explicitly identified with the Torah just as in Sirach and Baruch, in the book of Proverbs we can find many references pointing in such a direction.[55] When Wisdom cries out in the street "How long, O simple ones, will you love being simple?" (1:20-22) or when she says "Then they will call upon me, but I will not answer; they will seek me diligently, but will not find me," her speech reminds us not only of God's desire for his people to know him and to obey his commandments, but also of God's manner of responding to his disobedient people in other books of the Old Testament. Now in 8:22-31 Wisdom is speaking of herself as having been with God at the beginning of creation.

---

[52] Hurtado, *One God*, 47 (italics ours); See also Wright, *People of God*, 258.

[53] This verse speaks in a metaphorical language about God as the builder/architect who lays the foundations of a building prior to the erection of the columns and the walls (cf. Job 38:4-7; Ps. 104:5). In this image of the divine architect, wisdom is the skill, plan, and knowledge God uses to secure and order the cosmos. See Perdue, *Wisdom and Creation*, 83;

[54] Perdue, *Wisdom and Creation*, 78. See Newsom, "Woman and the Discourse," 142-60.

[55] E.g., 1:7 "The fear of the LORD is the beginning of knowledge; fools despise wisdom and instruction."

For the author of this hymn Wisdom was not meant to be taken as a divine being distinct from God or an aspect of God that has a degree of independent personhood, but as God's own attribute through which the world was created (3:19).[56] It is another way of saying the same thing in a more poetical and vivid way that in the very beginning God himself created the world in perfection. In conclusion, the writer who, with the help of a literary device available to him, could personify Wisdom so vividly as a woman crying out in the street and raising her voice in the squares (1:20-33; 8:1-11) and as a goddess offering life and wealth (3:16-18; 8:12-21) is certainly not guilty of going beyond vivid personification when he depicts Wisdom as a master worker who has been with God at creation (8:22-31).

Now although in the book of Proverbs Wisdom is most likely to be seen as the personification of a divine attribute, rather than a divine hypostasis, it does not necessarily follow, as some scholars would like to argue, that subsequent readers understood it in the same way as the writer intended. Thus now we will turn to examine how these Jewish wisdom traditions were understood in the Hellenistic period.

2.2.3. Sirach

In the whole book of Sirach we find five poems about Wisdom.[57] Unlike the other four (1:1-10; 4:11-19; 6:18-37; 14:20-15:10),[58] the poem in 24:1-23 has Wisdom speaking in the first person (vv.3-22).

In this wisdom poem she describes herself as a member of God's heavenly council (v.2) and as a figure with eternal existence (v.9), who appeals to the readers in intimate terms to learn from her (vv.19-22). In her self-praise Wisdom reinforces her *divine origin* in vv.3-4. Wisdom declares that she was looking for a resting-place (v.7) and God gave her a command to dwell in Jerusalem (vv.8-11). She then goes on to speak about her life on earth using a series of striking metaphors of trees and plants,

---

[56] See G. B. Caird, "The Development of the Doctrine of Christ in the New Testament" in *Christ for Us Today* (ed. W. N. Pittenger; London: SCM, 1968), 76: "there is all the difference in the world between personification and a person. . . . The personified Wisdom of Jewish literature remains from start to finish an activity or attribute of God."

[57] The book is known as Sirach (the name found in the Greek mss) or Ecclesiasticus (the Latin title). It is generally recognized that the book was originally composed in Jerusalem during the early 2nd century BC.

[58] Ben Sira's understanding of wisdom is thematized in the series of wisdom poems that punctuate the book. See A. A. Di Lella, "The Meaning of Wisdom in Ben Sira" in *In Search of Wisdom* (eds. L. G. Perdue *et al.*; Louisville: Westminster/John Knox, 1993), 133-48.

and other exotic elements characteristic of Palestine (vv.13-17). Then, making use of the imageries of eating and drinking and obeying and working she makes an exhortation to commune with her and to follow her instructions (v.19-22).

Here we need to ask the question once again: Was the description of Wisdom herself meant to be understood as a divine hypostasis, or was the language used here a poetic personification? Before attempting to suggest an answer to this question, however, it would be helpful to review how the book of Sirach is related to the book of Proverbs.

In his prologue, the grandson writes that Ben Sira spent a lifetime studying the Scriptures of Israel. Although Ben Sira tried to make the Scriptures relevant to the Jews of the new Hellenistic age,[59] the work that he mostly commented on was Proverbs, the book most like his own.[60] From the book of Proverbs he attempted to explain and develop its implications for his own day and world. In fact, his dependence on the book of Proverbs is not difficult to detect.[61]

In addition, the primary theme of the book and his main thesis (Sir 19:20) correspond to that of Proverbs.[62] Significantly, the description of Wisdom in the poem, though somewhat more vivid and explicit, is also reminiscent of the figure of Wisdom in Proverbs. As we have seen, Wisdom in Proverbs was also personified as a peripatetic teacher making an exhortation to learn from her (cf. Prov 1:20-33; 8:1-11 with vv.19-22) and as the firstborn of God or the master worker for God in creation (cf. Prov 8:22-31 with vv.3-6).

Having in mind the close relationship between Proverbs and Sirach, what appears to be a reference to a divine hypostasis (24:3-4) becomes nothing more than a restatement of what he asserts in the very beginning of his book (1:1). Again, God's command to "make your dwelling in Jacob, and in Israel receive your inheritance" (v.8) should be understood as nothing but a reference to the giving of the Torah through Moses at Sinai, which is confirmed by an explicit identification of Wisdom and the Torah in v.23.[63] The self-praise and the exhortation of Wisdom to the readers

---

[59] Compare with e.g., Deut 6:5 and Sir 7:29-30; Job 29:21 and Sir 13:23; Isa 51:3 and Sir 15:6.

[60] Di Lella, "Wisdom of Ben-Sira," *ABD* 6.939-40.

[61] Compare, e.g., Prov 8:22 with Sir 1:4; Prov 1:7 with Sir 1:14; Prov 8:18-19 with Sir 1:16-17; Prov 17:3 with Sir 2:5; and Prov 3:34 with Sir 3:18.

[62] Di Lella, *ABD* 6.940. The expression "fear of the Lord," or its equivalent, occurs fifty-five to sixty times in Ben Sira and the noun "wisdom" (Gk *sophia*), 55 times in the Greek translation.

[63] On the identification of Wisdom with the Torah see J. T. Sanders, *Ben Sira and Demotic Wisdom* (SBLMS 28; Chico: Scholars Press, 1983), 16-26. This verse is an echo of Exodus 24:7 and a word-for-word quotation of LXX Deut. 33:4.

(vv.1-22) is only the prelude for the climactic identification of her with the Torah, the main purpose of the poem. Such a striking claim is not found in any part of earlier wisdom tradition. While in Job the stress is on the inaccessibility of wisdom, in Prov 8 there are no specific links with Israel's own traditions. It is then possible to suggest that the question of the inaccessibility (Job 28) and divine origin of Wisdom (Prov 8) took a further development in Sirah. However, since similar ideas are also found in Baruch, it seems more likely that such a mode of thinking was developing more widely in the Judaism of ben Sira's day.[64] Now Wisdom is commanded to dwell in Jerusalem in the guise of the Torah.

Some scholars have noted that the description of Wisdom speaking in the first person (vv.3-22) may have been drawn from the aretalogies of the Egyptian goddess Isis.[65] H. Conzelmann found in Sirach not only formal resemblance but also thematic parallels to Isis aretalogies.[66] However, it is equally plausible to argue that our writer was dependent on the Wisdom poem in Prov 8:22-31.[67] While it is quite probable that ben Sira's language was indebted to some extent to Isis aretalogies, the fact that he draws heavily on biblical language also points to the likelihood that he adapts Isis hymns for his own purpose.[68] It is quite clear from Sir 24: 23, 25 that his own purpose was to identify Wisdom with the Torah.[69] Ben Sira wanted to demonstrate that "true wisdom is to be found primarily in Jerusalem and not in Athens, more in the inspired literature of Israel than in the clever writings of Hellenistic humanism."[70] Dunn rightly suggests that both the Jews of Alexandria as well as the Jews of Palestine well adapted such a polytheistic speculation to their own faith and posed to Wisdom (one of Isis's many names) worshipped as a divine being "the alternative of Wisdom identified as the law given to Israel by (the one) God."[71]

---

[64] R. J. Coggins, *Sirach* (Guides to Apocrypha and Pseudepigrapha; Sheffield: Sheffield Academic Press, 1998), 77. The date for Baruch is disputed.

[65] See Marböck, *Weisheit im Wandel*, 47-54; J. Blenkinsopp, *Wisdom and Law in the Old Testament: the Ordering of Life in Israel and Early Judaism* (New York: OUP, 1995),143-44.

[66] Conzelmann, "Mother of Wisdom," 230-43.

[67] It has been also argued that this wisdom poem itself was also influenced by the Egyptian cult. Cf. Kayatz, *Studien*, 76-119.

[68] See G. T. Sheppard, *Wisdom as a Hermeneutical Construct: a Study in the Sapientializing of the Old Testament* (BZAW 151; Berlin: Walter de Gruyter, 1980), 19-71.

[69] Dunn, *Christology*, 170; Kayatz, *Studien*, 138-139; J. J. Collins, *Jewish Wisdom in the Hellenistic Age* (Edinburgh: T & T Clark, 1998), 54; Murphy, *Tree of Life*, 140.

[70] Di Lella, *ABD* 6.933. See further A. A. Di Lella, "Conservative and Progressive Theology: Sirach and Wisdom" *CBQ* 28 (1966), 140-42.

[71] Dunn, *Christology*, 172 (his emphasis removed).

It then becomes clear that, following the tradition of the book of Proverbs, ben Sira made use of the same literary device as his predecessor to serve his own purpose: to encourage his readers, whose faith was swayed by the questions and doubts that arose from Greek philosophy, religion, and lifestyle, and to study the Torah diligently as the way to ensure a life ordered by divine wisdom.[72] This view is confirmed by the fact that in at least two other passages ben Sira speaks of creation as God's act without any reference to Wisdom (16:26; 18:1, 2, 4).[73] Given his deep commitment to the one God of Israel, what becomes clear from all this is that, like the author(s) of Proverbs, ben Sira did not see Wisdom as a divine hypostasis alongside God, but placed emphasis on the divine origin and the great importance of Torah for his people. In fact, Wisdom is to be understood as what God wills for his people, primarily through the Torah. In our author's mind Wisdom was simply a poetic personification of the divine will, a literary device made available for him to speak about "the fear of the Lord" as the way of life.[74] But in the end, when we acknowledge that the call of Wisdom to her readers is in fact the voice of God speaking through his wisdom, then we can safely conclude that she is none other than the revelation of God himself.[75]

2.2.4. Baruch

The wisdom poem in Bar 3:9-4:4, like that of Sir 24, also identifies Wisdom with the Torah: "She is the book of the commandment of God, the law that endures for ever" (4:1).[76] This poem explains Israel's exilic punishment as the result of forsaking wisdom (3:10-12) and makes an exhortation not to forsake her again (4:1-4). Baruch ingeniously takes up the words of Deut 30:12-13 to indicate that the way to Wisdom is not known to human beings but only to God (3:29-32). While Job 28 does not

---

[72] Dunn, *Christology*, 172; Di Lella, *ABD* 6.933.

[73] Dunn, *Christology*, 172.

[74] See also Marböck, *Weisheit im Wandel*, 65f., 129f.: "It cannot be the aim of the self-praise to mark out a clearly outlined person or hypostasis, but to indicate through the presentation of the activity and attributes of Wisdom where and how *God's nearness*, his presence and his activity may be experienced . . ." ". . . The Wisdom of God, the 'Wisdom from above' . . . is in ben Sira not to be conceived as an intermediary being between God and creation or as a hypostasis. Wisdom in accordance with the kaleidoscope of metaphors is to be taken rather as a poetic personification for God's nearness and God's activity and for God's personal summons" (translated by Dunn, *Christology*, 327 n.37; Dunn, *Christology*, 172: "For ben Sira then, Wisdom is just a way of speaking about God's ordering of creation and design for man in the law."

[75] Murphy, *Tree of Life*, 115-18.

[76] It is difficult to date the poem, but it gives the impression that the identification has already made some time earlier.

tell us clearly what God did with Wisdom, Baruch tells us that she has been given to Israel in the form of the Torah. Indeed, this is a conclusion that the reader of Job 28 and Prov 1-9 would not have predicted. It is likely that "an older connection between the goals of Torah and the wisdom literature is fully exploited" by the writers of Sir and Bar.[77] In that sense, Baruch does not go beyond Sirach in revealing the true nature of Wisdom in Jewish wisdom literature.

2.2.5. Wisdom of Solomon

We have seen so far that the figure of Wisdom in Proverbs, Sirach, and Baruch is to be seen as a poetic personification rather than a divine hypostasis. Now we turn to the description of Wisdom in Wis 7:22-8:1, which seems at first sight to give support to those who view Wisdom as a divine hypostasis.[78]

Wisdom is described as the fashioner of all things who possesses a spirit of multiple characteristics (vv.22-23). In vv.25-26 a fivefold succession of metaphors (a breath [ἀτμίς], a pure emanation [ἀπόρροια], a reflection [ἀπαύγασμα], a spotless mirror [ἔσοπτρον ἀκηλίδωτον], and an image [εἰκών]) portrays Wisdom as an emanation or a reflection from God's power, glory, light, or goodness. She is compared with the sun, constellation of the stars, and the light (vv.29-30). She is also pictured as an almighty being (7:27, 8:1).

It is generally recognized that the description of Wisdom in 7:22b-23 consists of a series of twenty one epithets (7x3) borrowed largely from Greek philosophy.[79] This shows that the author was to some extent familiar with Greek philosophy.[80] D. Winston insists that the background of the Wisdom of Solomon should not be sought in classical Platonism or Stoicism, but in "the philosophical sphere of Middle Platonism, whose

---

[77] Sheppard, *Wisdom*, 99.

[78] The date for the book of Wisdom of Solomon is placed by scholars anywhere between 220 BC and AD 50; see the discussion about the date in D. Winston, *The Wisdom of Solomon: a New Translation With Introduction and Commentary* (AB 43; New York: Doubleday, 1979), 20-25 and W. Horbury, "The Christian use and the Jewish origins of the Wisdom of Solomon " in *Wisdom in Ancient Israel: Essays in Honour of J. A. Emerton* (eds. H. G. M. Williamson *et al.*; Cambridge: CUP, 1995), 183-85.

[79] See Winston, *Wisdom*, 178-83.

[80] There is no scholarly consensus on the extent of his familiarity with Greek philosophical thinking. Winston, *Wisdom*, 33, holds that his philosophical orientation was Middle Platonist.

boundaries stretch from ca. 80 B.C.E. to ca. 200 C.E."[81] He further argues that "the remarkable similarity of its teaching on many points with that of Philo of Alexandria . . . only reinforces the view that its philosophical orientation is Middle Platonist."[82] His familiarity with Middle Platonism, however, does not necessarily mean that his basic thought is rooted in Greek philosophy. In fact, if we are to understand properly how Pseudo-Solomon understood Wisdom we should turn to the strong Jewish heritage he must have received from his ancestors. We cannot by any means overlook his Jewish background at the expense of his familiarity with Greek philosophy. In fact, his meditations on Wisdom are most probably motivated by his Jewish faith. His firm commitment to the one God and the special election of Israel can be clearly seen in Wis 12:12-19:22. Although, unlike in Sirach and Baruch, Wisdom is not explicitly identified with the Torah, she is most emphatically and explicitly connected with the God of Israel and with the revelation of God and his will in the Jewish scriptures. The writer places a strong emphasis on the revelation of God as the character of Wisdom, for example, when Wisdom is described in a fivefold metaphor as "a breath of the power of God," "a pure emanation of the glory of the Almighty," "a reflection of eternal light," "a spotless mirror of the working of God," and "an image of his goodness" (7:25-26). This seems to suggest that these descriptions of Wisdom are to be understood as the revelation of God *himself*, rather than a being distinct from God, a divine hypostasis. Moreover, the close link between Wisdom and the God of Israel can be seen in Wisdom's involvement in the sacred history of Israel, beginning with the creation of Adam (10:1-2) and extending through Abraham (10:5), Lot and Sodom (10:6-8), Jacob (10:9-12), Joseph (10:13-14), and the exodus/wilderness/conquest story (10:15-12:11). Furthermore, it is generally accepted that the book of Wisdom was intended to preach to those Jews who, being sympathetic to Greek culture and thought, were in danger of falling away.[83] Scholars rightly emphasize

---

[81] Winston, *Wisdom*, 33; cf. Collins, *Jewish Wisdom*, 201. Contrast Larcher, *Études*, 235-36, contends, on the basis of the diversity of philosophical doctrines of the writer, that the author of the Wisdom of Solomon has read a little of everything but has failed to grasp the totality of any philosophical system or to understand the differences between the various philosophical schools.

[82] Winston, *Wisdom*, 34. For a detailed listing of parallels, see 59-63. The ideas commonly shared between Wisdom and Philo can be seen in their virtually identical theory of creation, the prominent role given to the doctrine of immortality, their similar ethical theory, and striking linguistic parallels.

[83] J. S. Kloppenborg, "Isis and Sophia in the Book of Wisdom" *HTR* 75 (1982), 63; J. M. Reese, *Hellenistic Influence on the Book of Wisdom and Its Consequences* (AnBib 41; Rome: Biblical Institute Press, 1970), 117-21, 151-52; Winston, *Wisdom*, 18-20.

the preaching of the superiority of the Jewish religion over paganism as the primary aim of the book.[84]

Middle Platonism believed in the existence of a transcendent deity and an intermediate realm between the highest deity and the visible world.[85] But as a committed Jew our writer must have also believed that God *himself* created the world. Although Pseudo-Solomon borrows expressions from Greek philosophy when he meditates on Wisdom, his basic understanding of Wisdom still remains Jewish. In his description of Wisdom our writer draws characteristics and imageries from early wisdom traditions. Our author ascribes the role of creating the world to Wisdom as the author of Proverbs did (Wis 7:22; 8:6; Prov 3:19; 8:30).[86] The imagery of Wisdom sitting by (or sharing) God's throne (Wis 9:4, 10) is reminiscent of her being next to God (Prov 8:27-31) and her throne located "in a pillar of cloud" (Sir 24:4). The fivefold metaphor describing Wisdom (Wis 7:25-26) is paralleled with the self-praise of Wisdom "I came forth from the mouth of the Most High" (Sir 24:3). Wisdom's pervading all creation (Wis 7:24) recalls ben Sira's picture of Wisdom as covering "the earth like a mist" (24:3).

The synonymous use of "word" and "wisdom" in 9:1-2, which alludes to Ps 33:6 and Prov 3:19, is an indication that the author was familiar with the literary personification of these words to speak about God's creative activities. It also implies that his understanding of Wisdom is rooted in the Jewish scriptures.

It should be noted that in the Wisdom of Solomon Wisdom is identified with God himself. In 7:15-22 the writer seems to identify Wisdom with God when he first states that it is God who provided him with knowledge of philosophy, physics, history, astronomy, zoology, religion, botany, and medicine (vv.15-21), but finally he confesses that Wisdom was the one who taught him (v.22).

Some critics draw attention to the mythological influences in shaping the figure of Wisdom by pointing to its parallels to the cult of the Egyptian goddess Isis.[87] J. M. Reese has strongly argued that the presentation of

---

[84] Winston, *Wisdom*, 63; idem, "Wisdom of Solomon" *ABD*, 6.120-127; Kloppenborg, "Isis and Sophia," 63-64.

[85] T. H. Tobin, *The Creation of Man: Philo and the History of Interpretation* (CBQMS 14; Washington, DC: Catholic Biblical Association of America, 1983), 10-19; J. M. Dillon, *The Middle Platonists: a Study of Platonism, 80 B.C. to A.D. 220* (London: Duckworth, 1977), 136-37.

[86] The expression "the fashioner of all things" can be paralleled with the term אמון "a master worker."

[87] Reese, *Hellenistic Influence*, 40-52; Mack, *Logos und Sophia*; B. L. Mack, "Wisdom Myth and Mythology" *Int* 24 (1970), 46-60; Kloppenborg, "Isis and Sophia," 57-84.

Sophia, especially with regard to the motif of union with Sophia, "is a conscious effort to offset the appeal of the literature of the revived Isis cult."[88] Similarly, in a detailed study on the Logos and Sophia in Hellenistic Judaism, B. L. Mack concluded that mythic language from the cult of Isis had influenced Pseudo-Solomon.[89] However, although Reese and Mack attempt to demonstrate parallels between Wisdom and Isis, some of the common epithets and characteristics are not peculiar to them alone. The motif of ordering the universe was more strongly associated with the Stoic Logos, and the imagery of light had a central role in the Platonic tradition.[90] Thus J. J. Collins rightly regards these influences merely as "the tacit allusions to Isis," which were "taken up into the complex picture of Wisdom to enrich it and make it more attractive and satisfying to a hellenized Jewish readership."[91] In his view, "the allusions to Isis are not essentially different in function from the more overt allusions to Greek philosophy: they make the figure of Wisdom intelligible by depicting it in terms that were familiar and well respected in the Hellenistic world."[92] Thus, while mythological influences from the Isis cult seem to be indisputable, they are no more than just the "borrowing" of characteristics and imageries.

What becomes clear from the foregoing discussion is that, although it is undeniable that Pseudo-Solomon is surely aware of the challenge posed by the Isis cult that leads him to use some of her imageries to counteract the challenge, it is very unlikely that in his mind he conceived Wisdom as a goddess or a divine being distinct from God. His strong commitment to the one God of Israel would have most probably prevented him from doing so. Therefore, we can safely conclude that neither philosophical (Middle Platonism) nor mythological (the cult of Isis) input exercised any significant influence on our author so as to make radical changes to his understanding of Wisdom inherited from his predecessors. In short, it is

---

[88] Reese, *Hellenistic Influence*, 36-50, quotation from p.40. For the criticism of Reese see Kloppenborg, "Isis and Sophia,", 59-61. Kloppenborg argues that "the peculiar configuration of Sophia's characteristics is a result of and a response to the immediate and powerful challenge to Judaism presented by another feminine figure, savior and revealer, a goddess linked to the pursuit of wisdom and one associated with the throne: Isis" (p.67).

[89] Mack, *Logos und Sophia*, 63-107. For Mack, however, the use of mythic language was not part of apologetics, but rather a truly reflective and theological enterprise: to understand Yahwism afresh in the midst of hostility, persecution and death.

[90] Collins, *Jewish Wisdom*, 203. There are also other motifs which are generally attributed to both Wisdom and Isis: the description of Wisdom as a female figure; Wis. Sol. as an address to the king of the earth; and Wisdom as saviour (Wis 10).

[91] Collins, *Jewish Wisdom*, 204.

[92] Collins, *Jewish Wisdom*, 204.

hardly possible to find any clear evidence for the shift from the literary personification to the hypostatization.[93]

Gieschen has recently argued that the characteristics of Wisdom in Proverbs as a divine hypostasis "were developed in an even more pronounced way" by Pseudo-Solomon.[94] He provides as evidence for viewing Wisdom as a divine hypostasis the cosmogenic role of Wisdom (7:22; cf. 8:6), the depiction of Wisdom as sharing the divine throne of God (9:4, 10), and Wisdom's involvement in the lives of the patriarchs and Moses in the retelling of Israel's history (10:1-21). However, as we have already seen, the first two pieces of evidence point to Wisdom as a poetic personification rather than a divine hypostasis. However highly Wisdom is depicted in these texts, there is no warrant to believe that she is more than a personified figure.

With regard to the appearance of Wisdom replacing the angel of the Lord in the retelling of the history of Israel we suggest that the divine action was ascribed to Wisdom because the angel of the Lord in the Pentateuch and the Book of Judges was an expression of God's own action, manifestation or presence among his people, rather than a distinct figure from God. It is thus a clear indication that he understood Wisdom as the divine presence/action in the lives of his people, following not only his Jewish ancestors in their understanding of "the angel of the Lord" as God's presence/action, but also wisdom writers before him in their use of literary personification to speak about Wisdom as the action of God himself. What the author of the Wisdom was trying to do was simply to say that God himself was with the patriarchs and Moses protecting them and guiding them. Thus the author's replacement of God by Wisdom becomes fully intelligible.

However, as we shall see in Chapter 3, the concept of the angel of the Lord has undergone a profound development from the pre-monarchic period to the post-exilic period. The angel of the Lord concept itself has shifted from an expression of divine manifestation to a mere reference to an individual angel. We should recognize, however, that this change does not necessarily mean that the references to the angel of the Lord in the Pentateuch and the Book of Judges were automatically understood in later period (i.e., in the time of the Wisdom of Solomon) as an individual angel distinct from God. Although the conception of an individual angel distinct from God was drawn out from the earlier references to the angel of the Lord, it is most likely that the original interpretation of the passages in question had not entirely faded away but still remained.[95]

---

[93] Cf. Hurtado, *One God*, 43-44; Dunn, *Christology*, 163-76.

[94] Gieschen, *Angelomorphic*, 92-103.

[95] Cf. Hurtado, *One God*, 43.

In the light of the above discussion we may conclude that it is most likely that the figure of Wisdom as portrayed in the Wisdom of Solomon should be seen as a highly poetic personification of Wisdom as God himself working in the creation and with his chosen people, along the same line as the earlier wisdom traditions, this time with the aid of the philosophical and mythological language of the day.[96]

2.2.6. 1 Enoch 42

This passage is most probably another variation of the theme expressed in Sir 24:5-11.[97] It is at the same time "characteristic of the pessimistic view of the apocalyptic writers regarding the wickedness of this world."[98] C. H. Talbert has argued that "the identification of wisdom and angel is made already in *1 Enoch* 42:1-2 where it is said that when heavenly wisdom came down, found no dwelling place, and returned to heaven, she took her seat among the angels."[99] This interpretation implies that wisdom was already understood as a divine hypostasis. However, we do not agree with Talbert's interpretation. Although Wisdom is described as an angel, Wisdom is not an angel. We understand that Wisdom is here personified as an angel, in the same way as Iniquity is. Both Wisdom and Iniquity are personified as angels trying to dwell among the people of Israel. The writer seems to choose Wisdom as the opposite to Iniquity or Unrighteousness in order to talk about the wickedness of the time. In view of Iniquity [or Unrighteousness] being personified in a similar way to Wisdom, and having not encountered any instances of Iniquity being the object of a vivid personification as Wisdom was in other passages, we can fairly conclude that Wisdom here is not hypostatized but personified in the same way as Iniquity is.

2.2.7. Philo

Now we turn to the writings of Philo to examine his understanding about Wisdom. In Philo, Wisdom is depicted as a city and dwelling (πόλις καὶ οἶκος; *Leg. All.* 3.3) or a turtle dove (τρυγών; *Heres* 127), is identified with the tent of meeting (σκηνή; *Leg. All.* 3.46) and the tree of life (τὸ τῆς ξύλον

---

[96] See also H. J. Wicks, *The Doctrine of God in the Jewish Apocryphal and Apocalyptic Literature* (London: Hunter & Longhurst, 1915), 85.

[97] Ringgren, *Word and Wisdom*, 122.

[98] Ringgren, *Word and Wisdom*, 122.

[99] C. H. Talbert, "The Myth of a Descending-Ascending Redeemer in Mediterranean Antiquity" *NTS* 22 (1976), 426. Cf. G. Dix, "The Heavenly Wisdom and the Divine Logos in Jewish Apocalyptic" *JTS* 26 (1925), 5.

ζωῆς; *Leg. All.* 52), or is likened in a favourite metaphor to a fountain (πηγή; *Leg. All.* 2.86f.; *Det.* 117; *Post.* 136-8; *Som.* 2.242; *Spec. Leg.* 4.75; *Prob.* 13, 117; cf. *Leg. All.* 1.64f.). The many-fold metaphorical designation of Wisdom serves as a warning against any literal interpretations about Wisdom in Philo.

In Philo, Wisdom is identified with the *Logos* in several places.[100] In his allegorical exposition of Gen 2:10-14 Philo writes that "River" is generic virtue, goodness (*Leg. All.* 1.65) and explains that "this issues forth out of Eden, the wisdom of God (τῆς τοῦ θεοῦ σοφίας), and this is the Reason of God (ὁ θεοῦ λόγος)." In *Fug.* 97 Philo states that the Divine Word is the fountain of Wisdom (λόγον θεῖον, ὅς σοφίας ἐστὶ πηγή). Also in *Som.* 2.242 Philo writes that "the Divine Word descends from the fountain of wisdom like a river to lave and water the heaven-sent celestial shoots and plants of virtue-loving souls." Although in the last two passages there is no exact identification of Wisdom and the *Logos*, it is quite obvious from the fact that what comes out of the fountain of Wisdom is nothing but the *Logos* that the identification of these two was in Philo's mind. Such identification between the *Logos* and Wisdom is possible for Philo because in his understanding Scripture ascribes to Wisdom attributes and functions assigned to the *Logos*. This is the case with the statement about creation (Ps 104:24; Prov 3:19; Jer 10:12) and about "wisdom" coming out of the mouth of God (Prov 8:1ff.). Moreover, in Wis 9:1-2 Wisdom is identified with the *Logos*.[101]

Philo also uses the mother imagery for Wisdom (particularly Sarah; *Leg. All.* 2.82; *Det.* 124; *Cong.* 12f.). However, we need to bear in mind that Wisdom's picture as a mother should not be separated from his consistent allegorization, as though the mother imagery meant that Wisdom was a divine being or goddess for him.[102] Dunn clearly states that:

It is certainly very unlikely that he intended to evoke the Isis-Osiris myth when he spoke of God as 'the husband of Wisdom' (*Cher.* 49), any more than he expected to be taken literally when he spoke of God impregnating Sarah, Rebekah, Leah and Zipporah (*Cher.* 44-7). And though he depicts Wisdom as the mother of the Logos in *Fuga* 108f., he also depicts the Logos as the fountain of Wisdom (*Fuga* 97), which indicates that no specific mythological formulation is in mind but *simply a kaleidescope of imagery none of which may be pressed too hard in isolation from the wider context of his thought*.[103]

---

[100] See L. K. K. Dey, *The Intermediary World and Patterns of Perfection in Philo and Hebrews* (SBLDS 25; Missoula: Scholars Press, 1975), 8.

[101] R. Williamson, *Jews in the Hellenistic World: Philo* (Cambridge: CUP, 1989), 105. For a full discussion of Philo's doctrine of the Logos, see section B. *Logos* in Philo.

[102] Dunn, *Christology*, 173.

[103] Dunn, *Christology*, 173-74.

Although we must wait for the full discussion of Philo's doctrine of the Logos in the next section, so far we are unable to find any real indication that Philo conceives Wisdom as a personal being or as a divine hypostasis. Nor do we find any convincing evidence that his monotheistic faith in the one God of Israel is in any way challenged by such talk about Wisdom. On the contrary, we find him affirming that God is "the fountain of Wisdom ... the only wise (being)" (*Sac.* 64), that "the maker of this whole universe was and is God" (*Leg. All.* 3.99).[104]

2.2.8. Summary

We have argued that the use of Wisdom in a figurative manner to speak about God is found in the OT (Proverbs), OT Apocrypha (Sirach, Baruch, and the Wisdom of Solomon), OT Pseudepigrapha (*1 Enoch* 42), and Philo. We have seen that in Job 28 Wisdom is not personified as a divine attribute, but reified as God's gift to men. In Proverbs Wisdom appears personified in a variety of ways, such as a peripatetic teacher, a royal goddess, and, in the highly enigmatic poem of 8:22-31, as the firstborn of God or the master worker for God. We have pointed out, however, that such multi-faceted metaphors of Wisdom all point in one direction: to speak about God himself, rather than Wisdom herself. In Sir 24 Wisdom is described as a member of God's heavenly council, who in turn is identified with the Torah. For this writer, however, Wisdom was nothing but what God wills for his people, a personified divine will. The book of Baruch does not give us any more information about Wisdom than ben Sira. The Wisdom of Solomon shows traces of influences from Greek philosophy and the Isis cult, but we did not find any evidence that these influences were strong enough to make the writer modify his strong commitment to the one God of Israel and to conceptualize Wisdom as a divine being distinct from God. Following his predecessors, his language remained within the realm of vivid personification. In *1 Enoch* 42 Wisdom and its counterpart Iniquity are both personified as angels trying to dwell among the people of Israel. Philo portrays Wisdom using a variety of metaphors, such as a city, a turtle dove, the tent of meeting, the tree of life, and a fountain. He also identifies Wisdom with the *Logos*. We have suggested that the language describing Wisdom's picture as a mother should not be interpreted literally but figuratively, although we should await for the fuller discussion of the doctrine of Philo's *Logos* in the next section. Our examination of relevant texts has allowed us to conclude that Wisdom is most likely to be understood as *a literary device of poetic personification* employed by different wisdom writers to speak about *God himself*, about

---

[104] Dunn, *Christology*, 174.

his revelation to his people and his action in his world, rather than as a divine hypostasis. We have also noted that to view Wisdom as a divine hypostasis is a serious failure to understand the character of ancient Jewish religious language. Thus we fully agree with Dunn that:

> Wisdom as a divine hypostasis . . . involves the importation of a concept whose appropriateness here is a consequence of the technical meaning it acquired in the much later Trinitarian controversies of the early church. It has *not* been demonstrated that Hebrew thought was already contemplating such distinctions within its talk of God.[105]

Having said that Jewish wisdom language was no more than a literary personification of God's presence and action for his people in this world without compromising his transcendence and uniqueness, we cannot rule out the possibility that Jewish wisdom speculation still might have exercised some influence upon early christology. In fact, the majority of scholars today maintain that the Jewish wisdom tradition has been influential to the early Christian understanding of Jesus, attested primarily in Paul's letters. The discussion about the influence of Jewish wisdom tradition upon the thinking of early Christians, however, will have to wait until Chapter 8.

2.3. Word of God

Now we shall examine how the Word of God is understood in the OT and the Second Temple period, paying special attention to Philo. Our enquiry will attempt to answer the question whether there is evidence for a tendency to hypostatize the Word of God in the OT and thereafter before the rise of Christianity. It will involve the study of the OT use of the Word in reference to God, in particular the expression דבר יהוה, followed by the study of the term *logos* in the Wisdom of Solomon, Philo's doctrine of the *Logos*, and the *Memra* in the Targums. But before going into a detailed study of the OT usage, we shall review certain misconceptions about the spoken word in ancient Israel that have been prominent in the study of the word of God in the OT.

2.3.1. Misconceptions about the Spoken Word

According to a number of biblical scholars the spoken word in ancient Israel was believed to possess an autonomous power, even a quasi-material identity, "whose action cannot be hindered once it has been

---

[105] Dunn, *Christology*, 174.

pronounced."[106] Thus W. Eichrodt insists that words have "what is virtually a life of their own; they are like independent beings waiting their opportunity to invade reality."[107] E. Jacob speaks of "a projectile shot into the enemy camp whose explosion must sometimes be awaited but which is always inevitable."[108] Such an understanding of the spoken word goes back to the two classic studies by Grether (1934) and Dürr (1938), with additional reference to Hamp (1938).[109] Ringgren, for example, closely follows these writers in his *Word and Wisdom*, and similar conclusions are either repeated or taken for granted by other writers.[110] However, this popular understanding of the words has been convincingly criticized by Thiselton as an argument without a proper theological basis but rooted in a particular view of language, a view about how words relate to things.[111]

According to Thiselton, the advocates of the popular view tend to emphasize the fact that the Hebrew word דבר means both "word" and "thing."[112] Thus Knight, for example, asserts that "Once a word, *dabhar*, is uttered with intent . . . it becomes a thing."[113] Such an argument, however, as Barr properly suggests, simply rests on a misunderstanding of the nature of polysemy in language.[114] Barr concludes that "the senses 'word' and 'matter' are alternative. . . . We cannot therefore agree that the ancient speaker meant both."[115] Thiselton explains:

We do not argue, for example, that because 'taste' in English, *goût* in French, *Geschmack* in German, and *gusto* in Italian, all mean either 'taste' in tasting food, or else 'taste' in

---

[106] E. Jacob, *Theology of the Old Testament* (London: Hodder and Stoughton, 1958), 127.

[107] W. Eichrodt, *Theology of the Old Testament* (OTL; London: SCM, 1967), 69.

[108] Jacob, *Theology*, 131; Procksch, *TDNT* 4.93; G. von Rad, *Old Testament Theology* (Edinburgh: Oliver & Boyd, 1965), 2.85, understands the word to be "an objective reality endowed with mysterious power."

[109] O. Grether, *Name und Wort Gottes im Alten Testament* (ZAW 64; Giessen: A. Topelmann, 1934), 59-158; Dürr, *Die Wertung*, 22-77, 92-114; V. Hamp, *Der Begriff 'Wort' in den aramäischen Bibelübersetzungen: Ein exegetischer Beitrag zur Hypostasen-Frage und zur Geschichte der Logos-Spekulation* (München: Filser, 1938).

[110] Ringgren, *Word and Wisdom*, esp. 157-64; cf. Eichrodt, *Theology*, 69-78; Procksch, *TDNT* 4.91-100; Jacob, *Theology*, 127-34; von Rad, *Theology*, 2.80-98.

[111] Thiselton, "Power of Words," 286.

[112] Thiselton, "Power of Words," 286. Our summary is heavily indebted to this article.

[113] G. A. F. Knight, *A Christian Theology of the Old Testament* (London: SCM, 1959), 59, offers an analogy of the words in a children's comic: "there the words . . . are ringed around and connected by a line to the speaker's mouth. Their words . . . have become an object, a thing, and are now separate from the person who uttered them. . . . It has now become impossible to push the words back into the speaker's mouth. They are . . . potent in themselves."

[114] J. Barr, *The Semantics of Biblical Language* (London: OUP, 1961), 133-38.

[115] Barr, *Semantics of Biblical Language*, 133.

aesthetic appreciation, Englishmen, Frenchmen, Germans, and Italians all believe that good taste in society is connected with taste in the dining room, and are perhaps less able than other nations to distinguish the one from the other. In practice, the phenomenon of polysemy, which is very frequent in most languages, may arise from any one of several sources which, as has been pointed out in modern semantics, often depend on historical accidents.[116]

Another problem with this traditional view of the words has been observed by Thiselton. He points out that their "arguments are put forward about the nature of *words in general* on the basis of passages which speak not about words as such but about words which have been uttered usually *by a god*, or sometimes by a king or a prophet."[117] However, "such arguments break down if words which have been spoken by Yahweh, or by Marduk, or by Atum or Khnum, are in practice regarded as 'power-laden' not because of the supposed nature of words in general, but precisely because *these* words proceed from the mouth of a god."[118] In fact, most of the chapters in Dürr's book are not concerned with human words but exclusively with the divine word, as the title of his book *Die Wertung des göttlichen Wortes* suggests.[119]

Moreover, the advocates of the traditional view have commonly put forward an argument on the basis of etymology. They argue that etymologically דבר is linked with "back," "background," "projection of what lies behind."[120] Procksch, for example, contends that "In דָּבָר one is thus to seek the 'back' or 'background' of a matter . . . It is easy to see that in speech the meaning or concept stands for the thing, so that the thing . . . has in its דָּבָר its historical element, and history is thus enclosed in the דְּבָרִים as the background of things."[121] However, this commonly-held hypothesis has been persuasively criticized by J. Barr.[122]

The critical discussions advanced by Barr and Thiselton clearly show that the study of the word of God in the OT has been vitiated by the confusion between the supposed power of words in general and the powerful word of God. Barr and Thiselton certainly give us a warning against a tendency to ascribe undue independence to words in general when discussing the Word of God in the OT.

---

[116] Thiselton, "Power of Words," 290.
[117] Thiselton, "Power of Words," 289-90.
[118] Thiselton, "Power of Words," 290-91.
[119] Dürr, *Die Wertung.*
[120] cf. Grether, *Name und Wort,* 59-62; Jacob, *Theology,* 128; Procksch, *TDNT* 4.92.
[121] Procksch, *TDNT* 4.92.
[122] Barr, *Semantics of Biblical Language,* 129-40, and more broadly 107-60.

2.3.2. The Word of God in the OT

There are nearly 400 references to the word of God in the OT. Of these references the phrase דבר יהוה "the word of the Lord" occurs predominantly (over 240 times),[123] and over 90% of these are words of prophecy.[124] In other words, דבר יהוה is used in the OT almost as a technical term for the divine communication and revelation of God's will spoken by a prophet in a particular situation.[125] It is thus not surprising to encounter the expression "the word of the Lord came . . ." over and over again in the OT. In fact, this expression occurs more than one hundred times, and is found, for example, in Gen 15:1, 4; 1 Sam 15:10; 2 Sam 7:4; 24:11; 1 Kgs 6:11; 13:20, quite often in the story of Elijah in 1 Kgs, and most frequently in the prophetic books of Jer and Ezek (23 and 50 times respectively).[126] From this we learn that Israel's God is a God who speaks to the world, unlike idols "who have mouths but do not speak" (Pss 115:5; 135:16; Jer 10:5). Thus the "coming" of the word of the Lord to a prophet probably means nothing more than that "the word became an active reality in the life of the prophet from a source other than the prophet's own mind."[127] The OT understanding of the word of God is therefore closely related to the conviction that the God of Israel "revealed his will immediately and directly to his people through prophetic inspiration and vision."[128]

Nevertheless, we find other references to the word of God that at first sight seem to have an independent existence of its own apart from God himself. The word of God is usually described using metaphor such as weapon (Hos 6:5; Isa 9:7[8]; cf. Zech 9:1), fire (Jer 5:14; 20:9), hammer (Jer 23:29), messenger (Pss 107:20; 147:15, 18), and rain and snow (Isa 55:10-11). It is also described as an instrument of creation (Ps 33:6).

- Word of God as weapon:

Hos 6:5   Therefore I have hewn them by the prophets, I have killed them by the words of my mouth, and my judgment goes forth as the light.

Isa 9:7[8]   The Lord sent a word (ἀπέστειλεν) against Jacob, and it fell on Israel.

---

[123] Fretheim, "Word of God," *ABD* 6.961.

[124] Dunn, *Christology*, 217.

[125] Grether, *Name und Wort*, 77; for an extensive discussion on the OT background, see 59-158.

[126] See further W. H. Schmidt, *TDOT* 3:111-14.

[127] Fretheim, *ABD* 6.962.

[128] Dunn, *Christology*, 217.

- Word of God as fire:

Jer 5:14   Therefore thus says the LORD, the God of hosts: Because they have
              spoken this word, I am now making my words in your mouth a fire, and
              this people wood, and the fire shall devour them.

Jer 20:9   If I say, "I will not mention him, or speak any more in his name," then
              within me there is something like a burning fire shut up in my bones; I
              am weary with holding it in, and I cannot.

- Word of God as a hammer:

Jer 23:29   Is not my word like *fire*, says the LORD, and like *a hammer* that breaks
              a rock in pieces?

- Word of God as a messenger:

Ps 107:20   he sent out (ἀπέστειλεν) his word and healed them,
              and delivered them from destruction.

Ps 147:15,18 He sends out (ἀποστέλλων) his command to the earth;
              his word runs swiftly. . . .
              He sends out his word (ἀποστελεῖ τὸν λόγον αὐτοῦ), and melts them;
              he makes his wind (τὸ πνεῦμα αὐτοῦ) blow, and the waters flow.

- Word of God as the rain and the snow:

Isa 55:10-11 For as the rain and the snow come down from heaven, and do not return
              there until they have watered the earth, making it bring forth and sprout,
              giving seed to the sower and bread to the eater, so shall my word be that
              goes out from my mouth; it shall not return to me empty, but it shall
              accomplish that which I purpose, and succeed in the thing for which I
              sent it.

- Word of God as the instrument of creation:

Ps 33:6   By the word of the LORD the heavens were made (ἐστερεώθησαν),
              and all their host by the breath of his mouth.

Some critics have seen in these passages hypostatization of the word of
God. As early as 1938 L. Dürr contended that

. . . steht auch hier am Ende der Entwicklung bereits im A.T. das von der Gottheit
ausgehende, aber selbständig wirkende, ruhig und sicher seine Bahn ziehende 'göttliche
Wort', ein Stück von der Gottheit, als Träger göttlicher Kraft, deutlich von ihr
geschieden und doch wieder zu ihr gehörig, Hypostase im eigentlichsten Sinne des
Wortes.[129]

---

[129] Dürr, *Die Wertung*, 123.

Following closely Dürr's work, Ringgren also interprets the word of God in the above cited passages (e.g., Isa. 9:7; 55:10-11; Pss. 107:20; 147:15) as a reference to "a concrete substance charged with the divine power, emanating from the deity, and acting so to speak mechanically and reaching its goal irresistibly."[130]

However, a close examination of the texts indicates that, rather than the word itself as acting independently from God, it is Yahweh himself who speaks the word who should be treated as the main subject; God and his will must indeed be emphasized. Thus for example, in Isa. 55:10-11 the whole emphasis of vv. 6-11 is on God himself. T. Boman properly insists that "It is no hypostasis or remnant of a hypostasis that stands in the foreground but it is Jahveh personally. . . . The word that proceeds from Jahveh's mouth is no . . . substance, but is an effective and spoken word."[131] Thiselton correctly observes that this view is in complete agreement both with the main point in 55:6-11 and the theology of God in chapters 40-55. He states:

The admonition in 55:6 is to seek Yahweh himself, whose ways are entirely different from those of men (v.8). While all flesh is grass, and the grass withers and passes away, Yahweh's word will stand forever (40:6-8; cf. 44:26). From the mouth of God goes forth 'a word that shall not return' because 'there is none besides me . . . I am God and there is no other' (45:21-23).[132]

Moreover, the metaphorical language used in describing the word of God must be understood simply as "striking ways in which the swift and powerful effect of the word of God can be made more vivid."[133] Using vivid poetical language biblical writers are able to speak about *God* in his creative (Ps 33:6), salvific or restoring (Ps 107:20), providential (Ps 147:15, 18),[134] judging (Isa 9:8), and all-powerful (Isa 55:10-11) work or action towards this world. Although these passages describe the word of God as though it were independent from God, if we take into account the nature of the language used, there is no warrant to interpret them as something more than literary reifications or personifications of the word of God. A rather literal interpretation of such language, therefore, must be

---

[130] Ringgren, *Word and Wisdom*, 157-64; cf. Pfeifer, *Ursprung*, 34-35, 44, 72-73; Gieschen, *Angelomorphic*, 103-107.

[131] T. Boman, *Hebrew Thought Compared With Greek* (London: SCM, 1960), 61-62.

[132] Thiselton, "Power of Words," 291-92.

[133] Fretheim, *ABD* 6.962. However, he sees that the word in Wis 18:15-16 can be viewed as an extension of this use of language, which can be treated as a later tendency to view the word of God as an hypostasis, but without any substantiation.

[134] Cf. Fretheim, *ABD* 6.965, who interprets the word of God in this passage as "a way of personalizing the active will of God at work in the world."

considered a failure to do justice to the vivid and poetic language used by biblical writers to speak about God himself acting in this world.[135] In short, their language simply represents just one of many useful ways of speaking about the immanence of God, without compromising his transcendence and uniqueness.[136]

2.3.3. The Logos in the Wisdom of Solomon

Some scholars find evidence for the word of God being depicted as a divine hypostasis in the description of the *Logos* in Wis 18:14-16.[137] They argue that in this retelling of the story of the killing of the Egyptian first-born the *Logos* does not only refer to the destroying angel (משחית) of Ex 12:23 but also resembles both in appearance and function the angel of the Lord in 1 Chr 21:15-16. According to this view, the *Logos* is to be identified with this angel. In 1 Chr 21 this angel, who is described as both the "destroying angel" (מלאך המשחית) and the "angel of the Lord" (יהוה מלאך), is sent to destroy Jerusalem, is said to be "standing between earth and heaven," and has a sword in his hand. However, even if the claim that the *Logos* is described similarly to this angel is granted, the identification of the *Logos* with this angel is doubtful. First, while in Exod 12 the LORD and the "destroyer" – same as the angel of the LORD – are virtually indistinguishable, in 1 Chron 21 the destroying angel is clearly distinguishable from the LORD, since he is subordinate to God. Second, the *Logos* belongs to the "royal (i.e. divine) throne" and is not commanded to come down to earth but leaps down spontaneously from the throne.[138]

These observations lead us to conclude that the *Logos* is not understood as a figure distinct from God but God himself in action. Although the depiction of the *Logos* comes from an angelic story, it does not necessarily follow that it must be understood to be an angel, a figure clearly distinguishable from God. However, even if we accept the identification of the *Logos* with the angel, we are not obliged to conclude that Pseudo-Solomon saw the *Logos* as a divine hypostasis. Given the identification of

---

[135] Contrast a recent attempt to see "the word of God" as a divine hypostasis in the early portion of the OT by Gieschen, *Angelomorphic*, 103-107.

[136] Note a slightly different interpretation by Dunn, *Christology*, 218: the word of God is *"the word of Yahweh, the utterance of Yahweh, Yahweh himself speaking."*

[137] Ringgren, *Word and Wisdom*, 158-159; J. E. Fossum, *The Image of the Invisible God: Essays on the Influence of Jewish Mysticism on Early Christology* (Göttingen: Vandenhoeck & Ruprecht, 1995), 50-51. For the merger of Wisdom with the figure of the Logos and the principal angel – as well as other intermediaries – in different Hellenistic Jewish quarters, see Talbert, "Redeemer," 426-29.

[138] P. R. Carrell, *Jesus and the Angels: Angelology and the Christology of the Apocalypse of John* (SNTSMS; Cambridge: CUP, 1997), 91-92.

the *Logos* with Wisdom (Wis 9:1-2), and the latter being a literary personification of a divine attribute rather than an assertion of hypostatic existence in the Wisdom of Solomon, the *Logos* is to be understood as "an angelomorphic figure without the implication that the Logos is an angel."[139] In short, like the word of God in the OT, the *Logos* here is nothing but a literary personification of divine action![140]

2.3.4. The Logos in Philo

As we have seen, throughout the OT and the inter-testamental period "the word of God" was understood as a divine action in the world rather than a divine hypostasis. Now we turn to examine evidence from Philo, in particular, from his doctrine of the *Logos*.

Like the author of the Wisdom of Solomon, Philo also uses language which seems to imply that the *Logos* is a personal being distinct from God, an intermediary being between God and the world. For example, Philo calls the *Logos* an angel (*Leg. All.* 3.177; *Deus* 182; *Mut.* 87; *Som.* 1.239-40) or the archangel (*Conf.* 146; *Her.* 205), the son or firstborn of God (*Agr.* 51; *Conf.* 63, 146),[141] governor and administrator of all things (*Qu. Gen.* 4.110-11), and even θεός (*Som.* 1.227-30) and ὁ δεύτερος θεός (*Qu. Gen.* 2.62). Such descriptions for the *Logos* raises a question of a great significance for our thesis: "Does Philo regard the Logos as a reality, as a distinct entity having real existence, or is the Logos no more than an abstract construct, convenient to Philo's philosophy, but without true existence?"[142]

Recent scholarship on Philo has inclined to interpret him primarily as an exegete of the Hebrew scripture, rather than a philosopher or systematic theologian.[143] It is not advisable, therefore, to be too concerned about

---

[139] Carrell, *Jesus*, 92. Dunn, *Christology*, 219, contends that Wis 18:14-16 must be understood as a dramatic interpretation of the story of Exod 11-12.

[140] See J. C. Rylaarsdam, *Exodus* (New York: Abingdon, 1952) 923: "The judgment upon Egypt is God's work, but his activity is personified as the destroyer"; W. C. Kaiser, *Exodus* (Grand Rapids: Regency Reference, 1990) 376.

[141] Cf. also *Ling. All.* 3:175; *Det.* 118; *Mig.* 6; *Her.* 205; *Som.* 1.230, in each of which the *Logos* is described, explicitly or implicitly, as the "eldest" of all created things.

[142] Sandmel, *Philo of Alexandria*, 98, raises this question, but he does not give an answer to the question.

[143] Sandmel, *Philo of Alexandria*, 4, 78; P. Borgen, "Philo of Alexandria," 138-42; the introduction chapter of P. Borgen, *Philo of Alexandria: an Exegete for His Time* (NovTSup 86; Leiden: Brill, 1997); D. T. Runia, *Philo of Alexandria and the Timaeus of Plato* (Leiden: Brill, 1986), 17-20; V. Nikiprowetzky, *Le commentaire de l'Ecriture chez Philon d'Alexandrie, son caractere et sa portee: observations philologiques* (ALGHJ 11; Leiden: Brill, 1977), 170-80. Contrast D. Winston, *Logos and Mystical Theology in Philo of Alexandria* (Cincinnati; Hoboken, N.J: Hebrew Union College Press, 1985), 13-14.

certain inconsistencies or even contradictions in his thought. Indeed, previous scholarship attempting to over-systematize Philo's expositions has been criticized. The major target of criticism has been directed towards Wolfson's two-volume work, in which he makes great efforts to portray Philo as the most significant philosopher between Aristotle and Spinoza.[144] Wolfson is criticized for picturing Philo as much more systematic than he ever was.[145] However, we should also beware of going to the other extreme and pointing out inconsistencies and contradictions in every page of his writings. Therefore, we need to admit that what often "looks like an inconsistency or a contradiction does so because of the intellectual and religious viewpoint of the (usually non-Jewish) reader of works."[146]

Philo's thought can be catalogued as a synthesis of Hellenistic philosophy and Judaism. On the one hand, as his writings clearly attest, he was deeply influenced by contemporary currents in Greek philosophy, especially Middle Platonism,[147] and to a lesser extent Stoicism and Pythagoreanism as well.[148] On the other hand, as a Jew, Philo was strongly committed to the Torah and the Jewish traditions. Indeed, his writings show his strong monotheistic stand. Although Philo uses very exalted language to describe the *Logos*, the divine powers, and even certain heroes from the history of Israel (e.g., Moses), not only did he firmly hold his monotheistic belief but also strongly rejected any idea that suggests a plurality of deities.[149] Thus, Philo could emphatically assert that μόνος δὲ καὶ καθ' αὑτὸν εἷς ὢν ὁ θεός, οὐδὲν δὲ ὅμοιον θεῷ "but God, being One, is alone and unique, and like God there is nothing" (*Leg. All.* 2.1).[150] For Philo only God has absolute existence and other lesser beings derive their existence from Him (*Det.* 160). God's absolute existence can also be seen

---

[144] H. A. Wolfson, *Philo: Foundations of Religious Philosophy in Judaism, Christianity, and Islam* (Cambridge: CUP, 1947).

[145] For criticism of Wolfson's work see Borgen, "Philo of Alexandria: a Critical and Synthetical Survey," 142.

[146] Williamson, *Philo*, 103.

[147] Dillon, *Middle Platonists*, 45-46, 86, 252; Winston, *Logos and Mystical Theology*, 15.

[148] P. Borgen, "Philo of Alexandria" in *Jewish Writings of the Second Temple Period: Apocrypha, Pseudepigrapha, Qumran, Sectarian Writings, Philo, Josephus* (ed. M. E. Stone; Philadelphia: Fortress, 1984), 256.

[149] Williamson, *Philo*, 28-31: "Philo was not merely a theologian or a philosopher. He was an ardent believer, a devout worshipper, a charismatic exegete, and he wrote with the fervour of a mystic" (p.28); Wolfson, *Philo*, 1.171-173; Runia, *Philo and Timaeus*, 433: "Starting point for Philo's doctrine of God is to be sought nowhere else than in the God of the Pentateuch, the God who tolerates no other gods beside him, the God of Israel who revealed himself to the Patriarchs and above all to the prophet and nomothete Moses."

[150] The texts and translations are from F. H. Colson and G. H. Whitaker, *Philo: in Ten Volumes and Two Supplementary Volumes* (LCL; London: Heinemann, 1929-53).

in the phrases reserved by Philo for God alone such as "He that IS" (ὁ ὤν) and "the Being One" (τὸ ὄν).[151] We can also witness his deeply committed monotheism in his exposition of the first commandment:

> Let us, then, engrave deep in our hearts this as the first and most sacred of commandments, to acknowledge and honour one God Who is above all, and let the idea that gods are many never even reach the ears of the man whose rule of life is to seek for truth in purity and guilelessness (*Dec.* 65).

It is true that Philo ascribes to the *Logos* highly exalted terms like ὁ θεῖος λόγος "the divine Logos,"[152] θεός "God,"[153] or even ὁ δεύτερος θεός "the second God,"[154] but we should not overlook that he always makes a careful distinction between God and His *Logos*. Commenting on Gen 31:13 Philo clearly distinguishes God from His *Logos* (*Som.* 1.228-230):

> Surely a right noble cause of vaunting it is for a soul, that God deigns to shew Himself to and converse with it. And do not fail to mark the language used, but carefully inquire whether there are two Gods; for we read "I and the God that appeared to thee," not "in my place" but "in the place of God," as though it were another's. What, then, are we to say? He that is truly God is One, but those that are improperly so called are more than one. Accordingly the holy word in the present instance has indicated Him Who is truly God (τὸν μὲν ἀληθείᾳ), by means of the articles saying "I am the God," while it omits the article when mentioning him who is improperly (τὸν δ' ἐν καταχρήσει) so called, saying "Who appeared to thee in the place" not "of the God," but simply "of God." Here it gives the title of "God' to His chief Word, not from any superstitious nicety in applying names, but with one aim before him, to use words to express facts. Thus in another place, when he had inquired whether He that Is has any name, he came to know full well that He has no proper name, and that whatever name anyone may use of Him he will use by licence of language; for it is not the nature of Him that Is to be spoken of, but simply to be.

In this passage Philo tells the reader that ὁ θεός refers to "Him Who is truly God" whereas the anarthrous θεός refers to the *Logos*, who is "improperly" called God. In Philo's view, the biblical writer employs the title θεός for the *Logos* "not from any superstitious nicety in applying names, but with one aim before him, to use words to express facts." While Philo wants to defend the use of θεός for the *Logos*, he carefully distinguishes the *Logos* from God himself.[155]

---

[151] Wolfson, *Philo*, 1.210.

[152] *Som.* 1.62.

[153] *Som.* 1.227-230.

[154] *Qu. Gen.* 2.62. The phrase ὁ δεύτερος θεός occurs here only in his voluminous writings, but some, such as Segal, *Two Powers*, 159-81; and M. Barker, *The Great Angel: a Study of Israel's Second God* (London: SPCK, 1992), 114-33, seem to regard it as Philo's favourite phrase.

[155] Williamson, *Philo*, 123-24.

How then should we understand Philo's concept of the *Logos*? What is
its relation to God in his thought? Being a committed monotheist, why
does he use such honorific language for the *Logos*? Can his understanding
of the *Logos* serve as a good testimony that he conceived of the *Logos* as a
personal being distinct from God? Indeed, scholarly opinions on this issue
are sharply divided. While some see the *Logos* as a divine hypostasis,[156]
others regard it as an abstract concept.[157] Despite such a disagreement
among critics, we submit that the *Logos* in Philo's thought was nothing
more than metaphorical language, a useful way of expressing God's action
in the world without compromising his transcendence and uniqueness.[158]

J. D. G. Dunn has most persuasively argued for an understanding of the
Logos as an abstract concept rather than a divine hypostasis.[159] Philo's
thought can be categorized as "a unique synthesis of Platonic and Stoic
world-views with Jewish monotheism."[160] From the Platonic theory of
ideas, as expressed in the *Timaeus* of Plato,[161] Philo derives the conviction
that there is not only the world in which we live, but also the "world of
ideas" or the "intelligible world" (ὁ κόσμος νοητὸς), as Philo calls it (cf.
Op. 36; *Ebr.* 132; *Her.* 280).[162] Philo also derives his idea about the *Logos*
from the Stoic concept of divine reason (λόγος) immanent in the world,
permeating all things (cf. *Her.* 119).[163] However, Philo does not simply
take over ideas from Platonism and Stoicism but modifies them for his
own purpose. Thus in Philo the Platonic ideas are understood as thoughts
in the mind of *God*, the plan in the mind of the divine architect (*Op.* 16-
25). The Stoic *Logos* is something material, in a system which tends
towards pantheism, whereas in Philo the *Logos* is immaterial; in Stoicism
the divine reason is God, while in Philo beyond the *Logos* there is always
God (*Som.* 1.66).[164]

---

[156] E.g., Runia, *Philo and Timaeus*, 450; Wolfson, *Philo*, 1.231-252; cf. also Fossum,
Name of God; Gieschen, *Angelomorphic*, 107-12.

[157] E.g., Williamson, *Philo*, 107; Dunn, *Christology*, 220-28; Hurtado, *One God*, 44-
48.

[158] Dunn, *Christology*, 222-23; Runia, *Philo and Timaeus*, 450.

[159] Dunn, *Christology*, 220-28. We shall follow his argument closely here.

[160] Dunn, *Christology*, 221.

[161] Cf. Runia, *Philo and Timaeus*, 158-74; Wolfson, *Philo*, 1.200-207.

[162] "The incorporeal world (ὁ ἀσώματος κόσμος) was now finished and firmly settled
in the divine reason (ἐν τῷ θείῳ λόγῳ), and the world patent to sense (ὁ δ' αἰσθητός)
was ripe for birth after the pattern of the incorporeal" (*Op.* 36); ". . . the archetypal ideas
which, invisible and intelligible *there*, are the patterns (παραδείγματα) of things visible
and sensible *here*" (*Her.* 280).

[163] "He that opens the womb of each of these, of mind to mental apprehension, of
speech to the activities of the voice, of the senses to receive the pictures presented to it
by objects . . . is the invisible, seminal artificer, the divine Word . . ." (*Her.* 119).

[164] Dunn, *Christology*, 223.

For his argument Dunn draws attention to the Stoic distinction between two types of *logos*: (1) λόγος ἐνδιάθετος "the unexpressed thought, the thought within the mind" and (2) λόγος προφορικός "the uttered thought, the thought expressed in speech."[165] Philo was thoroughly familiar with this distinction and thus made considerable use of it in his writings.[166] Significantly however, in Philo these two meanings ("thought" and "speech") are not always clearly distinguished but run into one another (*Sac.* 80-3; *Ebr.* 157; *Som.* 1.102-14). This observation suggests that *logos* in Philo can be basically defined as *"thought coming to expression in speech."*[167] For Philo, the relation between thought and speech in the individual is also the relation between the world of ideas (= the divine *Logos*) and the world of sense perception (the material world). The parallel is explicitly stated in *Mos.* 2.127-29:

. . . the rational principle (λόγος) is twofold as well in the universe as in human nature. In the universe (τὸ πᾶν) we find it in one form dealing with the incorporeal and archetypal ideas from which the intelligible world was framed, and in another with the visible objects which are the copies and likeness of these ideas and out of which this sensible world was produced. With man, in one form it resides within, in the other it passes out from him in utterance. The former is like a spring, and is the source from which the latter, the spoken, flows . . .

From this parallel we can draw the conclusion that *"the divine Logos is for Philo in effect the thought of God coming to expression,* first in the world of ideas and then in the world of sense of perception."[168] Philo illustrates this idea using the example of an architect who, in the service of his monarch, first plans the city in his mind and then constructs it in accordance with the image, the blueprint in his mind (*Op.* 16-44). As the plan or blueprint is not to be considered something separate from the architect, there is no intermediate state between the plan in the mind and the actual construction of the city. In the same way, when God created the physical world, he first created the world of ideas, which had "no other location than the Divine Reason (ὁ θεῖος λόγος; *Op.* 20).

---

[165] Cf. *Det.* 39-40, 126-32; *Mut.* 208.

[166] *Migr.* 70-85; *Abr.* 83.

[167] Dunn, *Christology*, 224 (emphasis his). Cf. E. R. Goodenough, *An Introduction to Philo Judaeus* (Oxford: Blackwell, 1962), 103: "Logos means primarily the formulation and expression of thought in speech"; Wolfson, *Philo*, 1.233: *Logos* "is not only a mind capable of thinking; it is also a mind always in the act of thinking"; C. H. Dodd, *The Johannine Epistles* (MNTC; London: Hodder & Stoughton, 1946), 4: "*Logos* as 'word' is not mere speech, but rational speech; not mere utterance, but the utterance of a meaning; and *logos* as 'reason' is not the reasoning faculty, but a rational content of thought, articulate and fit for utterance; the meaning which a word expresses."

[168] Dunn, *Christology*, 224 (emphasis his).

The goal of philosophy, so to speak, is to know this invisible world of ideas, but this intelligible world is not accessible to the senses but only to the mind. For Philo, however, beyond the world of ideas, beyond the *Logos*, is God himself (τὸ ὄν), the highest Being unknowable even to the purest intellect.[169] Thus in Philo the *Logos* is as close as one can approach to God (*Fug.* 101; *Conf.* 96f.; *Mut.* 15; *Spec. Leg.* 1.32-50). The clearest expression of this thought comes from his exposition of Gen 28:11 ("he [Jacob] met a place"[170]) by means of Gen 22:3f. ("He [Abraham] came to the place of which God had told him: and lifting up his eyes he saw the place from afar").[171] Philo writes:

Tell me, pray, did he who had come to the place see it from afar? Nay, it would seem that one and the same word is used of two different things: one of these is a divine Word, the other God who was before the Word. One who has come from abroad under Wisdom's guidance arrives at the former place, thus attaining in the divine word the sum and consummation of service. But when he has his place in the divine Word he does not actually reach him who is in very essence God (τὸν κατὰ εἶναι θεόν), but sees him from afar: or rather, not even from a distance is he capable of contemplating him; all he sees is the bare fact that God is far away from all creation, and that the apprehension of him is removed to a very great distance from all human power of thought . . . The 'place' on which he 'lights' is . . . the Word of God . . . For God, not deeming it meet that sense should perceive him, sends forth his Words (λόγους) to succour the lovers of virtue . . . Jacob . . . meets not now God but a word of God [λόγῳ θεοῦ], even as did Abraham, the grandfather of his wisdom. (*Som.* 1.65-66, 68-70; similarly *Post* 16-20).

In short, "the Logos is what is knowable of God, . . . God insofar as he may be apprehended and experienced."[172]

So far we have argued that the *Logos* in Philo is what is knowable of God. Philo uses as an illustration his favourite sun and light example (cf. *Som.* 1.239; *Ebr.* 44; *Praem.* 45; *Qu. Ex.* 2.67), where "the Logos is to God as the corona is to the sun, the sun's halo which man can look upon when he cannot look directly on the sun itself. That is not to say that the Logos is God as such, any more than the corona is the sun as such, but the Logos is that alone which may be seen of God."[173] Moreover, the reason why Philo can call the *Logos* the "eldest of created things" and Wisdom the "first" of all God's works, but also the world as "the first and the greatest and the most perfect of God's works" is because the *Logos* as creator and created, and Wisdom as "mother of all" and created, simply refer to God in his

---

[169] Cf. *Leg. All.* 1.36-37; *Post.* 15, 168f.; *Immut.* 62; *Mut.* 9; *Praem.* 40, 44; *Leg.* 6; *Qu. Ex.* 2.67.

[170] "ἀπήντησε τόπῳ" (*Som.* 1.61).

[171] "ἦλθεν εἰς τὸν τόπον ὃν εἶπεν αὐτῷ ὁ θεός· καὶ ἀναβλέψας τοῖς ὀφθαλμοῖς εἶδε τὸν τόπον μακρόθεν" (*Som.* 1.64).

[172] Dunn, *Christology*, 226 (emphasis removed).

[173] Dunn, *Christology*, 226-27.

highest approach to his creation.[174] Now we are ready to answer the question posed at the beginning as to why Philo could ascribe highly exalted terms like ἄγγελος "angel" or ἀρχάγγελος "archangel," ὁ θεῖος λόγος "the divine *Logos*," θεός "God," or even ὁ δεύτερος θεός "the second God" to the *Logos*. These expressions are not meant to convey the idea that the *Logos* was a divine hypostasis, a real intermediary being between God and the world. Rather, these highly exalted terms are appropriated by Philo in support of his doctrine of the *Logos*, an abstract construct helpful in expressing the involvement of God in this world without compromising his wholly otherness.[175] In fact, the phrase ὁ δεύτερος θεός occurs only once in his voluminous writings (*Qu. Gen.* 2.62).[176] Moreover, while Philo ascribes the term ὁ ἀρχάγγελος to the *Logos* twice (*Conf.* 146-147; *Her.* 205-206), he also uses the same term for God himself (*Som.* 1.157). Some still might want to argue that in *Som.* 1.157 it similarly refers to the *Logos*,[177] but the phrase τὸ ὄν "The One that IS," which immediately follows, and the context in general lead us to conclude that Yahweh is the referent.[178]

Could the foregoing observations about the *Logos* in Philo properly explain why he spoke of the *Logos* as an intermediary between God and the world, between God and human beings, and why he chose to use highly exalted terms for his *Logos*? We can answer these questions affirmatively because, as Dunn properly insists, "for Philo it is in and through the Logos that God reaches out to his creation, and it is by responding to the Logos that man comes as near as he can to God."[179] In short, the *Logos* is for Philo nothing but God's self-revelation or his "face" turned towards his creation.

2.3.5. The Memra of God

In the Targums, the word of God, *memra*, is often substituted where the text of the Bible speaks of God anthropomorphically. In some cases the *memra* appears to be more than a mere circumlocution and represents a

---

[174] Dunn, *Christology*, 228.

[175] Note Hannah, *Michael*, who agrees with us on the point that the *Logos* was "for Philo a way of expressing the immanence of God, which also allowed Philo to affirm the Divine transcendence" (p.79), but, influenced by Runia, *Philo and Timaeus*, 450-51, he is cautious enough to conclude that "Philo understood the Logos as the Mind of God and, at times, as a hypostasis" (p.90).

[176] However, some scholars seem to regard ὁ δεύτερος θεός as Philo's favourite phrase; cf. Segal, *Two Powers*, 159-81; and Barker, *Great Angel*, 114-33.

[177] Cf. Wolfson, *Philo*, 1.377-78; Segal, *Two Powers*, 170.

[178] Hannah, *Michael*, 86.

[179] Dunn, *Christology*, 227.

personified abstraction of the divine presence and power.[180] To quote Moses ben Nachman, the *memra* is "God himself in certain modes of self-manifestation."[181]

Having surveyed the various uses of *memra* in the Targums on the Pentateuch and the Prophets, G. F. Moore states that, while it is sometimes used as the expression of God's will, the revelation of his purpose or the resolution of a metaphor for his power, in many cases "it is clearly introduced as a verbal buffer . . . to keep God from seeming to come to too close quarters with men and things; but it is always a buffer-*word*, not a buffer-idea; still less a buffer-person."[182] He thus categorically denies that *memra* is "a 'being' of any kind or in any sense, whether conceived personally as an angel employed in communication with men, or as a philosophically impersonal created potency . . . or God himself in certain modes of self-manifestation."[183] For Moore, *memra* in the Targums is no more or less than a buffer-word for the sake of God's transcendence.

Hayward is in agreement with Moore that *memra* is not an hypostasis or a simple replacement for the Name Yahweh. He defines *memra* as "an exegetical term representing a theology of the Name *'HYH.*"[184] We can therefore conclude with Moore and Hayward that the *memra* in the Targums is used as no more than a "buffer-word" for safeguarding God's transcendence or as a circumlocution for God himself.[185]

2.3.6. Summary

We have argued that the word of God in the OT, the *logos* in the Wisdom of Solomon, and the Logos in Philo does not go beyond the poetic personification of divine action in the world. We have also reviewed the discussions about the use of the *memra* in the Targums and concluded that *memra* is used as no more than a "buffer-word" or as a circumlocution for God himself. We have also observed certain misunderstandings about the supposed power of words in general which would probably have

---

[180] Cf. Barker, *Great Angel*, 146-48, who has revived the old thesis that Philo's understanding of the Word was probably influenced by the targumic traditions concerning *memra*.

[181] Quoted by G. H. Box, "The Idea of Intermediation in Jewish Theology: A Note on Memra and Shekinah" *JQR* 23 (1933), 118.

[182] G. F. Moore, "Intermediaries in Jewish Theology: Memra, Shekinah, Metatron" *HTR* 15 (1922), 52-53. For more recent discussion on *memra* in the Targums on the Pentateuch see Muñoz Leon, *Dios-Palabra*.

[183] Moore, "Intermediaries," 52-53.

[184] R. Hayward, *Divine Name and Presence: the Memra* (Totowa: Allanheld, 1981), preface. Cf. Hurtado, *One God*, 143, n.73.

[185] Moore, "Intermediaries," 58-59.

influenced the study of the word of God in the OT in a direction which sees it as something separate from God.

2.4. Name of God

In this section we will examine whether the name of God was understood as a divine hypostasis in the OT and the Second Temple period.

2.4.1. The Name of God in OT

An examination of OT texts referring to the name of God tells us that his Name is commonly used as a simple appellation for God himself. Thus we find phrase doublets such as "praise the Lord" and "praise the name of the Lord [שם יהוה]" (Pss 113:1; 135:1; cf. 148:5, 113; 149:3; Joel 2:26); "sing praises to the Lord" (Isa 12:5; Pss 9:12; 30:5; 98:5), "sing praises to his Name" (Pss 68:5; 135:3) and "sing praises to the glory of his Name" (Ps 66:2); "to give thanks to the Lord" (Ps 92:2; 1 Chr 16:7; 2 Chr 5:13; 7:6), "to give thanks to the name of the Lord" (Ps 122:4; cf. Pss 54:8; 138:2; 140:14; 142:8), "to give thanks to his holy name" (Ps 106:47; 1 Chr 16:35) and "Let them give thanks (to) your great and terrible name, for it is holy" (Ps 99:3); "they will fear the Lord" (2 Kgs 17:28; cf. Ps 33:8) and "(they) will fear the name of the Lord" (Isa 59:19; Ps 102:16); "trust in the Lord" (Isa 26:4; Pss 4:6; 115:11), "Let him trust in the name of the Lord" (Isa 50:10; cf. Zeph 3:12) and "we trust in his holy name" (Ps 33:21); "to love the Lord your God" (Deut 11:13, 22; 19:9; 30:6, 16, 20; Josh 22:5; 23:11) and "to love the name of the Lord" (Isa 56:6).[186]

There is no doubt that the above references demonstrate that the name of God can be used as a synonym for God because his name can be taken to express and represent the person himself. In fact, in 1 Kgs 8:13, 20, 27, and 29 God's name is interchangeably used with God himself.

8:13	"I have built . . .a place for *you* to dwell"
8:20	"[I] have built the house for *the name of the Lord, the God of Israel* [לשם יהוה אלהי ישראל]"
8:27	"Even heaven and the highest heaven cannot contain *you*, much less this house that I have built."
8:30	"the place of which you said, 'My name shall be there'"

---

[186] Huffmon, "Name," *DDD* 1149-50.

The name of God is commonly combined with the preposition ב, which always denotes a connection, a special link or contact.[187] The phrase יהוה בשמ (usually translated as "in/on/by the name of the Lord") is connected with a variety of verbs, but these verbs can be classified broadly as (1) verbs of utterance such as קרא "to call, to invoke, or to proclaim" (Gen 4:26; 12:8; 13:4; 21:33; 26:25; Exod 33:19; 34:5; 1 Kgs 18:24; 2 Kgs 5:11; Isa 48:1; Joel 3:5; and Zeph 3:9), דבר "to speak" (Deut 18:22; 1 Kgs 22:16; 1 Chr 21:19; 2 Chr 18:15; 33:18; Jer 26:16; 44:16), ברך "to bless" (Deut 21:5; 2 Sam 6:18; 1Chr 16:2; Ps 129:8), קלל "to curse" (2 Kgs 2:24) נבא "to prophesy" (Jer 11:21; 26:9, 20), and שבע "to swear"(1 Sam 20:42; Isa 48:1); or (2) verbs of different actions such as שרת "to minister" (Deut 18:5, 7; 21:5), בוא "to come" (1 Sam 17:45; Ps 118:26), הלך "to walk" (Mic 4:5), ירא "to trust, to fear" (Isa 50:10), מיל "to cut off" (Ps 118:10, 11, 12), and בנה "to build" an altar (1 Kgs 18:32). Both types of usage belong to the language of devotion to God rather than to the name itself. Expressions like "to invoke or call on the name of the Lord" and "to build an altar in the name of the Lord" are generally used in the context of worshipping God.[188] "To speak, to bless, to curse, to prophesy, in the name of the Lord" means to utter such words on behalf of God or on his commission. Actions like "to minister" or "to come" in the name of the Lord means doing something on his behalf. Expression like "to trust in the name of the Lord" signifies trusting in God himself. We can conclude, therefore, that with the expression בשמ יהוה we remain within the literary realm of personification rather than hypostatization of God's name.

Some scholars find God's name as a hypostasis in some references where his name is variously described as an acting subject, an object of thanksgiving, a place to hide, or a means or instrument in the hand of God: "You (O Lord) are great, and your name is great in might" (Jer 10:6); "We give thanks; your name is near" (Ps 75:1); "See, the name of the Lord comes from far away" (Isa 30:27); "The Lord answer you in the day of trouble! The name of the God of Jacob protect you!" (Ps 20:1) "Glorify the Lord . . . , (even) the name of the Lord" (Isa 24:15); "I will give thanks to your name, O Lord" (Ps 54:6); "Let them praise the name of the Lord, for

---

[187] The expression בשמ יהוה occurs 43 times in the OT: Gen 4:26; 12:8; 13:4; 21:33; 26:25; Exod 33:19; 34:5; Deut 18:5, 7, 22; 21:5; 1 Sam 17:45; 20:42; 2 Sam 6:18; 1 Kgs 18:24, 32; 22:16; 2 Kgs 2:24; 5:11; 1 Chr 16:2; 21:19; 2 Chr 18:15; 33:18; Pss 20:8; 118:10, 11, 12, 26; 124:8; 129:8; Isa 48:1; 50:10; Jer 11:21; 26:9, 16, 20; 44:16; Joel 3:5; Amos 6:10; Mic 4:5; Zeph 3:9, 12; 13:3.

[188] C. J. Davis, *The Name and Way of the Lord* (JSOTSS 129; Sheffield: Sheffield Academic Press, 1996), 110, understands that the Niphal of בשמ יהוה + קרא denotes God's ownership, and suggests that "'calling on the name of the Lord' could refer to an appeal simply to God and not an appeal to 'the name' as somehow distinct from God."

his name alone is exalted" (Ps 148:13); and "the name of the Lord is a strong tower" (Prov 18:10); and "Save me, O God, by your name, and vindicate me by your might" (Ps 54:1). However, it is most likely the case that the name of God or his name is here used to show the writer's strong feeling towards God in a vivid or poetical way rather than implying its independence of God himself. As van der Woude puts it, his name refers to "Jahwe in Person" or "Jahwe in seiner Herrlichkeit."[189] It has to do with the language rather than the actual concept.[190] Although in the ancient Near East we frequently find aspects or epithets of particular deities becoming separate divine entities with separate cults,[191] we do not find such evidence in these references.

However, some scholars understand the name of God as "a transcendent entity at work in the world, or an instrument by which Yahweh works," and see a connection with "the general post-exilic tendency to heighten the transcendence of God and increasingly to transfer His immanent working to intermediary beings."[192] To evaluate this assertion we now turn to the Name theology in Deuteronomy.

2.4.2. The Name Theology in Deuteronomy

Deuteronomy refers to the name of God twenty-one times. Although God's name as a means of revealing himself was not unique to Deuteronomy, OT scholarship has commonly found in this characteristic emphasis of the book a theological corrective to earlier and cruder concepts that God himself was somehow actually present in Israel's shrines.[193] Deuteronomy is seen as in some way "demythologizing" the divine presence, viz., what is present is *not* God himself (for he dwells in heaven), but his *name*.[194]

The classic formulation of Name Theology comes from G. von Rad's oft-quoted assertions that well summarize its main idea:

The Deuteronomic theologumenon of the name of Jahweh clearly holds a polemic element, or, to put it better, is a theological corrective. It is not Jahweh himself who is

---

[189] van der Woude, "Name," *THAT* 2.957.

[190] So Davis, *Name*, 110-11: "only linguistic."

[191] Ringgren, *Word and Wisdom*.

[192] Bietenhard, *TDNT* 5.258; cf. Grether, *Name und Wort*, 44ff.; A. R. Johnson, *The One and the Many in the Israelite Conception of God* (Cardiff: University of Wales Press, 1961), 17ff.; Pfeifer, *Ursprung*, 11-16; Fossum, *Name of God*, 87; Gieschen, *Angelomorphic*, 70-78.

[193] This idea was made popular by G. von Rad, *Studies in Deuteronomy* (SBT 9; London: SCM, 1953), 37-38.

[194] von Rad, *Studies*, 40. M. Weinfeld, *Deuteronomy and the Deuteronomic School* (Oxford: Clarendon, 1972), 190, describes this process as "the collapse of an entire system of concepts which for centuries had been regarded as sacrosanct."

present at the shrine, but only his name as the guarantee of his will to save. . . .
Deuteronomy is replacing the old crude idea of Jahweh's presence and dwelling at the
shrine by a theologically sublimated idea.[195]

The Name theology is derived primarily from two sets of texts: (1) texts
referring to Yahweh's *Name* dwelling or being present at the sanctuary
(e.g. in Deut 12-26 and throughout the Deuteronomistic History) and (2)
those referring to Yahweh *himself* dwelling or being in heaven (e.g. Deut
4:36; 26:15 and 1 Kgs 8, in Solomon's prayer at the dedication of the
temple).[196] Von Rad then asserts that the name of God achieved "a
constant and almost material presence," so that the conception of it "verges
closely on a hypostasis."[197]

It is widely recognized that several OT traditions regarded as earlier
than the book of Deuteronomy depict God as being in some sense present
on the earth or, in certain contexts, present with the people of Israel. Many
scholars hold that the Yahwistic and Elohist sources, for example, in their
accounts of the law-giving at Sinai in the book of Exodus portray God as
either descending to (J) or dwelling on (E) the mountain,[198] while the Zion
tradition, which is found in some of the Psalms and in the pre-exilic
Prophets, represents him as abiding in the city of Jerusalem.[199] The Zion
tradition saw Yahweh's dwelling in Mount Zion in the sense of the
Canaanite-mythological idea of the god's cosmic abode.[200] God was
conceived in a corporeal way. Within the tabernacle "sits the Deity
ensconced between the two cherubim, and at his feet rests the ark, his
footstool."[201] The priestly duties served to satisfy God's physical needs,
and were carried out in his very presence (לפני יהוה).[202] Israel's right to
dwell in the land was regarded as cultic and it was guaranteed by
Yahweh's dwelling on Zion.[203] In this view, this had the effect of
evacuating Israel's religion of ethical content, and led to the opposition of

---

[195] von Rad, *Studies*, 38-39; cf. T. N. D. Mettinger, *The Dethronement of Sabaoth: Studies in the Shem and Kabod Theologies* (Lund: Gleerup, 1982), 48-51; R. E. Clements, *God and Temple: the Idea of the Divine Presence in Ancient Israel* (Oxford: Blackwell, 1965), 35, 68-69, 96; Weinfeld, *Deuteronomy*, 36-37, 208-209.

[196] I. Wilson, *Out of the Midst of the Fire: Divine Presence in Deuteronomy* (SBLDS 151; Atlanta: Scholars Press, 1995), 3.

[197] von Rad, *Studies*, 38.

[198] Jeremias, "Theophany in the OT," *Theophany* 897; J. P. Hyatt, *Commentary on Exodus* (NCBC; London: Oliphants, 1971), 23, 196, 202.

[199] Mettinger, *Dethronement*, 19-37, esp. 24-28, 36-37; Clements, *God and Temple*, 40-78

[200] Clements, *God and Temple*, 94, cf. 51ff.

[201] Weinfeld, *Deuteronomy*, 191.

[202] Weinfeld, *Deuteronomy*, 192.

[203] Clements, *God and Temple*, 86-87.

the prophets; but the most systematic "demythologization" of the Jerusalem theology is said to be found in Deuteronomy.

Various suggestions have been made to explain such a change of belief. Some scholars hold that the belief in a personal dwelling of Yahweh at the sanctuary could be perceived as limiting his presence to that particular place as well as his freedom of action.[204] Others find the rationale for the Name theology in different historical events: the centralization of the cult,[205] the loss of the ark from the northern kingdom,[206] or the destruction of the temple.[207]

However, this widely-held theory has not gone unchallenged. On the one hand, J. G. McConville rightly criticized von Rad's emphasis on Deuteronomy's Name theology over against the Glory theology of Priestly traditions. He cogently argued that the contexts in which God's name is invoked are ordinarily ones of personal devotion and covenantal relationship, in contrast to God's presence in his glory, a more universal and dramatic denotation.[208] This is the reason why the name of God occurs frequently in the legal part of Deuteronomy, the section which deals with what is to be the routine of worship in the new land, whereas the use of "glory" is more appropriate in the narrative of the exodus, where dramatic, exceptional divine manifestations take place. He concluded that "the use of the two terms is determined, not by the appropriateness of each to one or the other theological movement, but rather by their *separate functions*, which appear to be recognized throughout the Old Testament."[209]

On the other hand, by pointing out the inadequacy of the twofold biblical foundation (references to the divine name at the sanctuary and references to heaven as Yahweh's abode) upon which the traditional Name theology has been argued, I. Wilson examined a number of possible references to divine presence in Deuteronomy.[210] He convincingly argued against the scholarly consensus that the *earthly* presence of Yahweh is also represented in the book of Deuteronomy. He argued for the literal interpretation of לפני יהוה in Deut 12-26 as a reference to "the localized Presence of the Deity at the 'chosen place,'" and suggested that "God is

---

[204] Clements, *God and Temple*, 100, 104; G. E. Wright, "God Amidst His People: the Story of the Temple" in *The Rule of God: Essays in Biblical Theology* (New York: Doubleday, 1960), 72.

[205] Grether, *Name und Wort*, 35.

[206] E. W. Nicholson, *Deuteronomy and Tradition* (Oxford: Blackwell, 1967), 72-73.

[207] Mettinger, *Dethronement*, 50, 59-62, 78-79, 133, postulates that the Name theology was developed to interpret the invasion by the Babylonians which brought the disastrous destruction of the temple in 586 BC.

[208] J. G. McConville, "God's 'Name' and God's 'Glory'" *TynBul* 30 (1979), 149-63.

[209] McConville, "Name and Glory," 161 (emphasis ours).

[210] Wilson, *Out of the Midst*.

represented as being present on the earth not only in the context of the Wilderness wanderings and Holy War but also in that of the cult, and at the very place at which the divine Name is known to be present."[211]

From his study Wilson draws the following conclusions:[212] (1) the examination of comparable passages in Deuteronomy and the Tetrateuch shows that "the affirmation of divine Presence is a clear feature of some at least of the historical sections of Deuteronomy;" (2) it also shows that references to Yahweh's earthly Presence have been "neither eliminated nor systematically reduced;" (3) "this affirmation of divine Presence in the historical sections of Deuteronomy finds support in the legal section of the book;" and (4) "there is no evidence of any weakening in Deuteronomy of the way in which the divine Presence is expressed."

In the light of the critical assessment of the Name theology we conclude that "the existence in Deuteronomy of a thoroughgoing Name Theology as traditionally defined begins to look unlikely."[213] The evidence suggests that the traditional understanding of the Deuteronomistic Name theology seems to have led many scholars to see a non-existing hypostatization of the divine name not only within Deuteronomy and the related works but also in the rest of the OT.[214] They must also have been influenced by the ill-founded nineteenth-century view of a distant God and the need for intermediaries such as angels or hypostases.[215]

2.4.3. The Divine Name as a Hypostasis?

One of the most outspoken advocates of divine name as a divine hypostasis is J. E. Fossum. He finds the concept of the name of God as a divine hypostasis in passages where the divine name "appears as the acting subject without standing in parallelism to the Tetragrammaton" (Ps 54:6-7; 148:13; Joel 2:26; Prov 18:10; Mal 1:11).[216]

With regard to Isa 30:27 Fosssum asserts that "the Name must here be understood as a divine hypostasis," because "what is normally said of YHWH is here said of his Name, which seems to be conceived of as an

---

[211] Wilson, *Out of the Midst*, 204-205.

[212] Wilson, *Out of the Midst*, 210.

[213] Wilson, *Out of the Midst*, 217.

[214] Cf. van der Woude, *THAT* 2.954-58; W. Zimmerli, *Gottes Offenbarung: gesammelte Aufsatze zum Alten Testament* (TBü 19; München: Kaiser, 1963)126.

[215] For a detailed discussion of this view see Moore, "Christian," 227-254; cf. also J. Abelson, *The Immanence of God in Rabbinical Literature* (London: Macmillan, 1912), 12-16; Moore, *Judaism*, 1.405, 423-42; Goldberg, *Untersuchungen*, 1-2; Sanders, *Paul*, 215.

[216] Fossum, *Name of God*, 84-85.

entity of its own at work in the world."[217] However, as we have seen, his interpretation does not do justice to vivid and poetical expressions employed by biblical writers to show their strong feelings and deep devotion to God.

Fossum also attempts to link the name of God with the portrayal of the word of God in Wis 18:15-16, which in turn was based on the description of the destroying angel of Exodus and that of the angel of the Lord in 1Chr 21:16.[218] Moreover, he finds the idea of the name of God as a hypostasis in Deuteronomy where, in his view, God dwells in heaven (e.g., 4:36; 26:36), whereas he has chosen a place on earth as the abode for his name (e.g., 12:5, 11; 14:23-24; 16:11 et al.). Thus he contends that "YHWH certainly inhabits the earthly temple, but not in person; he is present through the agency of his Name."[219] Others claim that the tendency towards hypostatization of a divine "name" in the world surrounding Israel can support their argument.[220] Regarding Fossum's first point we have already rejected the idea that the word of God in *Wisdom* might be understood as a hypostasis. The second point has also been considered in our demonstration that the Name theology is to be seriously questioned. Concerning the last point, we should point out, from what we have seen in the discussion of the Wisdom of God, that while Israel was not completely isolated from the neighbouring religious world, Jews were very capable of adapting many of the concepts, images, and words from their neighbours without compromising their own religious convictions (i.e., monotheistic belief).[221] Therefore, we conclude that in the OT the name of God was a way of speaking about the divine presence among his people but never succeeded in becoming separate from God.

2.4.4. Summary

An examination of the use of the name of God in the OT and the Name Theology in Deuteronomy leads us to conclude that the name of God was not understood as a hypostasis by OT writers in general or the author(s) of Deuteronomy, but as none other than a poetic personification of divine presence in the world. Against the widely-held Name Theology in Deuteronomy and its related writings, in which God's name (but not Yahweh) was thought to be present at the sanctuary, we have shown that

---

[217] Fossum, *Name of God*, 85.

[218] Fossum, *Name of God*, 86.

[219] Fossum, *Name of God*, 87, refers to the work of Mettinger, *Dethronement*.

[220] To support his argument Mettinger, *Dethronement*, 131, refers to the work of McBride, *Name Theology*, 130-141.

[221] See § 2.2; also Dunn, *Christology*, 169

the *earthly* presence of Yahweh is also represented in the book of Deuteronomy. We have also pointed out the distorted influence which has been exercised by the ill-founded nineteenth-century view of a distant God and the need for intermediaries on the now-questionable theory of Deuteronomistic Name Theology.

2.5. Conclusion

In the light of a detailed examination of Jewish speculations about Wisdom of God, the Word of God and the Name of God we come to the conclusion that these personified divine attributes have never led to the development of divine hypostases separate from God. The vivid descriptions of these divine attributes – whether it be Wisdom, the Word or the Name of God – offered the Second Temple Jews a variety of religious language to speak meaningfully and powerfully about God's presence, manifestation and action in the world without calling into question his transcendence and uniqueness.

However, we cannot rule out the possibility that the language used to speak about God's wisdom in Second Temple Judaism might have been influential to early christology. In fact, the majority of scholars today recognize that the Jewish wisdom tradition was influential to the early Christian understanding of Jesus, especially Paul's christology. Our discussion about such influence upon Paul's wisdom passages, however, will have to wait until Chapter 8.

Chapter 3

Exalted Angels and Pre-Existent Messiah

Having examined personified divine attributes we now turn to investigate whether Jewish speculations about exalted angels and a pre-existent messiah ever provided the real precedent for viewing Jesus as a divine and pre-existent being alongside God. It will be argued that exalted angels and a pre-existent messianic figure did not blur the clear distinction between God and the intermediary beings, but in a similar way to the personified divine attributes offered the Second Temple Jews a variety of religious language to speak about God's presence, manifestation, and action in the world without calling into question his transcendence and uniqueness.

3.1. Exalted Angels

The angel of the Lord is one of the most enigmatic and most prominent angelic figures in the OT. The aim of this section is to examine whether an old understanding of this angel as an expression of God's presence and action for his people had completely faded by the end of the OT period and led to an understanding of him as a prominent member of the heavenly host. Before undertaking this task, we will do a broad survey of the OT understanding about angels and different theories proposed for the relationship between this angelic figure and God himself.

3.1.1. OT Understanding about Angels

The most common Hebrew word in the OT for "angel" is מלאך, which also can be rendered as "messenger." Alongside the term מלאך, however, a rich variety of expressions are used in the OT for such beings. While some expressions such as בני־האלהים "sons of God," בני אלים "sons of gods, divine beings," and אלהים "gods" denote their divine status, the phrase קדשים "holy ones" indicates their special sanctity.[1] Among functional terms we find

---

[1] Gen 6:2, 4; Job 1:6; 2:1; 38:7; Ps 29:1; 89:6; Ps 82:1; Ps 89:5, 7.

משרתים "ministers," שׂר "commander or prince," צבאוֹת "hosts, army," and the most common one מלאך "messenger, envoy."[2]

The term מלאך derives from the root לאך, which is not found in the OT or later Hebrew literature but in Arabic, Ethiopic and Phoenician writings with the meaning "to send."[3] The Arabic, Ethiopic, and Ugaritic languages all have a noun for "messenger" built on the consonants "mlk."[4] Thus, מלאך means "one who is sent" or "messenger."[5] However, מלאך, being primarily a functional term, can refer both to human and heavenly beings.[6] Thus, angels were understood to be heavenly beings sent by God to accomplish his will in the world.

In Israel, as in the ancient Near East in general, the underlying conception of the heavenly world was that of a royal court. Yahweh was envisioned as a king, and at his service were angelic beings who served as counsellors, political subordinates, warriors, and general agents. Thus we find different representations of these angelic beings which fit well to the pattern of the royal court. Often these angelic beings are described as a group,[7] and are understood to form a heavenly council or a heavenly army.[8] While these angelic beings are given various roles to play as a group, in many other texts the term מלאך "messenger" or מלאך יהוה/אלהים "the messenger of Yahweh/God" is used to describe the action of a single angelic being.[9]

3.1.2. The Angel of the Lord

The expression מלאך יהוה "angel of the Lord" is mentioned fifty-eight times and מלאך אלהים "angel of God" eleven times in the OT.[10] In contrast to the messenger deities of the ancient Near East, the angel of the Lord is never

---

[2] Ps 103:21; Josh 5:14; Dan 10:13; Ps 89:8.

[3] BDB, 521; V. Hirth, *Gottes Boten im Alten Testament: die alttestamentliche Mal'ak-Vorstellung unter besonderer Berücksichtigung des Mal'ak-Jahwe-Problems* (ThA 32; Berlin: Evang. Verlagsanst, 1975), 23.

[4] M. Mach, *Entwicklungsstadien des jüdischen Engelglaubens in vorrabbinischer Zeit* (TSAJ 34; Tübingen: Mohr Siebeck, 1992), 39-40.

[5] von Rad, *TDNT* 1.76. Note the LXX's standard translation of מלאך, ἄγγελος, which also means "messenger."

[6] Mach, *Entwicklungsstadien*, 37-43, 47-51. Cf. also Newsom, "Angels," *ABD* 1.248-49.

[7] Gen 28:12; 33:1-2; Pss 29:1; 89:6-9.

[8] Ps 82:1; Jer 23:18; Job 15:8; Ps 89:6, 9; Ps 148:2; 1 Kgs 22:19. See further Newsom, *ABD* 1.249. The most extensive description of the council and its tasks in the OT is found in 1 Kgs 22:19-22.

[9] Newsom, *ABD* 1.249.

[10] G. J. Wenham, *Genesis 16-50* (WBC 2; Dallas: Word Books, 1994), 9.

given a name in the OT.[11] The מלאך יהוה or the מלאך אלהים appears most frequently in Genesis and Judges but rarely in the writings of later periods. On occasions when this angel appears in these books we find a curious oscillation between this angel and God. Frequently this angel speaks and acts as a messenger of God and further along the line he speaks and acts as God himself (e.g., Gen 16:7-16, 21:8-19; 22:9-18; 32:22-32; Judg 6:11-24, 13:1-23). Within the same portion of a narrative not only is he clearly distinguishable from God but also appears as if he and God are one and the same. Moreover, the angel of God speaks to Jacob in a dream that he is "the God of Bethel" (31:10-13), while later in 48:15-16 both האלהים and המלאך are, standing in a poetic parallelism, clearly distinguishable from each other.

3.1.2.1. Relationship between God and the Angel of the Lord

Puzzled by such a phenomenon, some scholars have attempted to explain the relationship between this enigmatic figure and God and have proposed a number of different theories:[12]

(1) The *logos theory* asserts that the מלאך יהוה is God's means of communication with the world. This angel, like Philo's Logos, manifests himself in many different forms and circumstances.[13]

(2) The *representation theory* asserts that מלאך יהוה is a messenger spirit who represents God as his ambassador. Thus this angel speaks and acts for God, but is not God.[14]

(3) The *identity theory* asserts that the מלאך יהוה is a manifestation of God himself. This view defines the angel of the Lord as "the visible or

---

[11] Meier, "Angel of Yahweh," *DDD* 97.

[12] For a survey of scholarship, H. Röttger, *Mal'ak Jahwe, Bote von Gott: die Vorstellung von Gottes Boten im hebräischen Alten Testament* (Frankfurt: Lang, 1978), i-xxii, 12-32. For a treatment of the Angel of the Lord in the context of Jewish angelology, see Mach, *Entwicklungsstadien*. For a review of the various theories of interpretation, see, W. G. Heidt, *Angelology of the Old Testament: a Study in Biblical Theology* (Washington: The Catholic University of America Press, 1949), 69-101; Ficker, "מלאך," *THAT* 1.900-908; A. S. van der Woude, "De *Mal'ak Jahweh*: Een Godsbode" *NedTTs* 18 (1963-1964), 1-13; Hirth, *Gottes Boten*, 13-21; C. A. Gieschen, *Angelomorphic Christology: Antecedents and Early Evidence* (AGAJU 42; Leiden: Brill, 1998), 53-56.

[13] G. Fr. Oehler, *Theologie des Alten Testaments* (Stuttgart: J. F. Steinkopf, 1882), 203-4; P. Heinisch, *Personifikationen und Hypostasen im Alten Testament und im Alten Orient* (BZ 9.10/12; Münster: Aschendorff, 1921), 24-25; see also Heidt, *Angelology*, 96-97. W. Eichrodt, *Theology of the Old Testament* (OTL; London: SCM, 1967), 2.28, believes that this view has been abandoned.

[14] A. Rohling, "Über den Jehovaengel des AT" *TQ* 48 (1866), 431; cf. Heidt, *Angelology*, 97-99.

audible phenomenon through which God manifests himself and communicates with the person or persons concerned."[15]

(4) The *hypostasis theory* asserts that the יהוה מלאך is a personification of an aspect of God that has taken on a distinct, but not separate, identity.[16] According to Ringgren, the יהוה מלאך shares God's nature and can speak or act as God himself.[17]

(5) The *l'âme extérieure theory* asserts that elements of a personality can detach themselves without ceasing to be connected with the person (i.e., an exterior or external soul).[18]

(6) The *interpolation theory* asserts that the יהוה מלאך figure was a later addition by redactors to soften the bold anthropomorphisms of very old textual traditions that portrayed God as appearing in the form of a man.[19]

(7) The *messenger theory* asserts that the best conceptual background for interpreting these texts is the idea of the union between the sender and the messenger in the Near East.[20]

We cannot here examine all the issues raised, nor can we discuss in detail the theories above mentioned. Although all the above theories endeavour to figure out the identity of the יהוה מלאך and his relation to God himself, they seem to focus primarily on those passages where there is an oscillation between this angel and Yahweh or a virtual identification between them. As we shall see, however, we find in the later sources a clear evidence of a certain development in the identity of this angelic figure. We need to leave open therefore the possibility that one single

---

[15] Heidt, *Angelology*, 70. See Eichrodt, *Theology*, 2.27-29, who argues that the angel of the Lord safeguards God's transcendent nature while also maintaining his immanent presence through temporary incarnations. However, Gieschen, *Angelomorphic*, 55, points out that "the earliest Angel of the Lord traditions have little to do with God's transcendence." Referring to J. Barr, "Theophany and anthropomorphism in the Old Testament" in *Congress Volume: Oxford, 1959* (International Organization of Old Testament Scholars; Leiden: Brill, 1960), 31-38, Gieschen argues that "The answer must center on the holiness of God which makes his normal visible form something that brings death to the viewer. Therefore, when God manifests himself in these ancient Angel of the Lord traditions, he visibly appears as an angel (in the form of man, fire, or a cloud) so as not to destroy those who see him."

[16] Ringgren, "Geister, Dämonen, Engel," *RGG* 2.1301-2. Ringgren, "Hypostasen," *RGG* 3.503-6.

[17] Gieschen, *Angelomorphic*, 55, also favours this view.

[18] A. Lods, "L'Ange de Yahvé et l'âme extérieure" *BZAW* (1913), 265-78.

[19] G. von Rad, *Genesis* (OTL; London: SCM, 1972), 193-94. This view was criticized by Barr, "Theophany," 33-34; and Eichrodt, *Theology*, 2.25-26, but has been endorsed recently by Meier, *DDD* 96-108.

[20] van der Woude, "Mal'ak Jahweh," 6-13, contends that the angel in these accounts should not be understood as a being distinct from God, but rather as an extension of God himself who speaks, protects, and punishes.

theory would not do justice to the entire period of its development. It is also important to note that not all these theories are necessarily mutually exclusive. The messenger theory is, for example, quite different from the earlier ones in that it explains how a person can stand in for another. So this theory is not an alternative to the rest of the theories, but should be taken into account when attempting to account for the enigmatic phenomenon of the angel of the Lord.

Having examined different theories and the passages in question, we think that the identity theory would best explain the relationship between the מלאך יהוה and Yahweh in the earliest period because the indistinguishability between them is most prominent feature in this period. Nevertheless, we have to admit, as Eichrodt also does, that "the borderline between the *mal'āk* as a specific medium of divine revelation and as the created messenger of God cannot always be sharply drawn."[21] The customary interchange between the מלאך יהוה and God in various texts seems to have originated from the theological paradox which attempted to express both the presence of God and the impossibility of human beings having an unmediated encounter with God.[22] It appears that the מלאך יהוה was an expression of the divine presence or the manifestation of God himself.[23] Given a certain development in the later period, however, we think that the representation theory would be most adequate to explain the angel of the Lord as a figure quite clearly distinct from God. And since the messenger theory seems to be also correct, the representation theory complemented with the messenger theory would best explain the relationship between this enigmatic figure and Yahweh. The angel of the Lord is a messenger of God who represents God; he is the one who speaks and acts for God, but is not God himself. However, the מלאך יהוה, as we shall argue, still remains in some sense an expression of the divine presence or the manifestation of God himself, although he is not "the visible and audible" manifestation of God himself as such, as the identity theory asserts.

---

[21] Eichrodt, *Theology*, 2.29.

[22] Newsom, *ABD* 1.250; cf. Freedman and Willoughby, "מלאך," *TWAT* 4.901; Hirth, *Gottes Boten*, 83-84; Westermann, *Genesis 12-36*, 2.242-43; Barr, "Theophany," 34: the מלאך יהוה should be understood "not so much that the deity is invisible as that it is deadly for man to see him."

[23] J. I. Durham, *Exodus* (WBC 3; Dallas: Word Books, 1986), 335; cf. J. D. G. Dunn, *Christology in the Making: a New Testament Inquiry into the Origins of the Doctrine of the Incarnation* (London: SCM, 1980, 1989), 151.

3.1.2.2. Development in the Identity of "the Angel of the Lord"

Some critics have suggested that the concept of the מלאך יהוה belongs to the earliest period of Israel's history, and differs largely from later Jewish ideas about angels. While the term continued to be used, the concept underwent a profound development in the later period.[24] The enigmatic oscillation between Yahweh and his angel, which was frequently attested in the earliest period, is no longer found in the later sources. Thus it has been suggested that the מלאך יהוה as an expression of the divine presence or the manifestation of God was confined only to the period before the monarchy.[25] From the time of the monarchy, however, the term began to be used for an individual angel, and the concept of the divine presence among his people was more often indicated in terms of cultic expressions and the prophetic movement.[26] When the term מלאך יהוה reoccurred it was no longer used to express the presence or manifestation of God, but as a means of referring to individual angels, although speculations about these angels were not as fully developed as in the apocalyptic writings in Second Temple Judaism.

In tracing such a development, some scholars suggested that the Exodus angel was the starting point of a lengthy process in which the מלאך יהוה concept underwent a certain development "away from an extension or manifestation of the divine presence and toward an individual existence."[27] According to this view, this angel appears several times in Exodus and other places, and the designations given to this angel[28] and the usual interchange between him and God suggest that this angel and the angel of the Lord are to be identified.[29] The Exodus angel does not only carry the divine Name (Exod 23:20-21), a particular way of affirming divine presence, but is also a substitute for God (Exod 33:1-3). Moreover, unlike in the patriarchal narratives, this angel is spoken of by God in the third person (23:20-21, 32:34 and 33:2-3). Such evidence leads Hannah to

---

[24] Westermann, *Genesis 12-36*, 2.243; cf. G. von Rad, *Old Testament Theology* (Edinburgh: Oliver & Boyd, 1965), 1.286.

[25] Hannah, *Michael*, 22.

[26] Hannah, *Michael*, 22; cf. Eichrodt, *Theology*, 2.29.

[27] Hannah, *Michael*, 21. Cf. Exod 14:19; 23:20-33; 32:34; 33:2-3; Num 20:16; Judg 2:1-5; Num 22:21-35 and Josh 5:13-15. See also Gieschen, *Angelomorphic*, 57-69.

[28] Cf. מלאך יהוה in Judg 2:1-5, מלאך האלהים in Exod 14:19 and מלאכי in Exod 23:23 and 32:34. Hannah notes the textual tradition showing a tendency "to make the identification with the angel of the Lord specific in those passages where it is not. Thus the Samaritan Pentateuch, the LXX, and the Vulgate all presuppose at Ex 23:20 and the LXX again at Ex 33:2. Only Num 20:16 has no textual witness supporting such a reading."

[29] Note Exod 23:23, 32:2, and esp. Judg 2:1-5. Note also the parallels between Josh 5:13-15 and Exod 3:1-6.

conclude that "the angel of the Exodus is beginning to have a quasi-individual existence."[30]

According to Hannah, although the oscillation between God and his angel still appears in Judg (6:11-24, 13:1-23) it is only from the narratives of Samuel and Kings onwards that the interchange between the יהוה מלאך and יהוה begins to disappear, and the מלאך יהוה appears as God's agent.[31] This development towards an individual angel continued in the exilic and post-exilic periods. The מלאך יהוה of 2 Kgs 19:35 is portrayed merely as an angel *sent* by God in 2 Chr 32:21. By the post-exilic period, the notion of the מלאך יהוה as a figure indistinguishable from God, a feature so prominent in the patriarchal narratives, has completely faded. This lengthy process of development comes to its end when in Zech 1-8 the מלאך יהוה is clearly an individual angel, and in Daniel angels have their own names (e.g., Michael and Gabriel).

3.1.2.3. Continuity of the Underlying Concept

The account given above by Hannah, however, seems to misinterpret a very important point. While he attempts to offer an account of the development of the concept of this angelic figure, his account appears more to do with the *identity* (or the designation) attributed to this figure at different points in time rather than the *concept* itself. The identity and the concept attributed to this figure might be closely related to each other, but they are not necessarily the same thing. It is imperative at this juncture therefore to make a distinction between what we regard as the *identity* assigned to this figure and what we see as the *concept* lying behind this figure. While it is certainly correct to claim that the identity or the designation assigned to "the angel of the Lord" underwent a profound development away from a figure indistinguishable from God to an individual angel clearly distinguishable from God, there is no clear indication that the *concept* too developed in the same way as the identity. Put differently, while there seems to have been a development in the identity attributed to this figure, who performed God's action or expressed God's presence among his people, there is no indication of any profound development, as some have suggested, in the concept intended for such a figure in the later passages. The only development which we are able to detect in later sources is a development in his identity away from the one indistinguishable from God (a feature so prominent in the earliest writings) to an individual figure who (despite his description as clearly distinct from God) still represents God as his ambassador and speaks and acts on God's

---

[30] Hannah, *Michael*, 21.

[31] Cf. 2 Sam 24; 1 Kgs 19:7; 2 Kgs 1:3, 15; 19:35.

behalf. In other words, what has remained unchanged throughout our period is the purpose of introducing the angelic figure by different biblical writers in their narratives. By introducing this angelic figure, they in different points in time intended to express how God acts himself and manifests his presence and his concern for his people. The table below shows concisely what we have stated:

Identity given to the angelic figure	An angelic figure indistinguishable from God →	An individual angel clearly distinct from God
Concept lying behind the figure	Presence and action of God remained constant	
Theory	Identity theory →	Representation theory complemented with Messenger theory

We have already seen that in the earliest narratives the angel of the Lord (or the Name Angel) appears as a way of expressing God's presence or action in the world. Such an underlying concept can be seen from various OT passages (e.g., Exod 23:20-21; Judg 2:1-5; 2 Sam 24:15-17; 1 Kgs 19:7-9; 2 Kgs 1:3, 15; 2 Kgs 19:35; 2 Chr 32:21; Zech 3:1-5).

Although the identity of the angel in 2 Sam 24 appears as a figure distinct from God, since there is no longer the usual interchange between the angel of the Lord and Yahweh, it is clear that this angel acts on God's behalf. It is the Lord who sends a pestilence, but the angel of the Lord does the destroying. While David can see the angel, he still speaks to God rather than to the angel. Although the angel of the Lord is here described as a figure distinct from God, he represents God because he acts on God's behalf and makes his appearance in the place of God himself. In this respect, the concept of this angel as indicating God's presence and action towards his people still remains unchanged.

In the story of Elijah in 2 Kgs 19 the angel of the Lord appears to Elijah twice and touches him and speaks to him. This angel described as a figure distinct from God also represents God in his acting and speaking to his chosen people. This angel gives encouragement to Elijah on God's behalf.

It is certainly possible to stress the significance of the slight change introduced to 2 Kgs 19:35 by the Chronicler (from the angel of the Lord acting on behalf of God to the angel sent by God), but it is difficult to deny that the same concept underlies the two accounts of the same event. God's presence and action in this world through this angel is emphasized in both passages. It seems therefore highly doubtful whether the change was motivated by a change in the writer's theological perception. It seems rather a matter of preference or style of the writer than anything else. Both passages are more concerned about the way God deals with his people than what the angel does. This can be seen from the statement that it is God who "saved Hezekiah and the inhabitants of Jerusalem from the hand of King Sennacherib of Assyria and from the hand of all his enemies" (2 Chr 32:21). In both passages each writer is more concerned to tell the readers that it is *God* who saved Israel than that it is *through* the angel of the Lord sent by God that Israel was saved. The emphasis is on God rather than the angel. It thus becomes clear that the presence and action of *God* is the main focus of the story in both passages.

The angel of the Lord in Zechariah is clearly distinct from God, yet nevertheless invested with power and authority to represent God. He represents God as judge and presider in the divine council (3:1-10). He is "a figure akin to the vizier – the powerful official to whom the supreme ruler delegates rule, authority, and power."[32] He is not a manifestation of God himself as such, as in the earliest period, but the underlying concept of him still expresses God's presence and action in this world.

If our interpretation of the passages is correct, what has undergone a certain development was not the underlying concept attached to this angelic figure but the way of asserting God's presence and action towards his people in the world. The concept of divine presence and action inherent in "the angel of the Lord" has not completely faded in the later texts; rather the same underlying concept began to be expressed by portraying God as a king in majesty and splendour ruling over his kingdom and his people through his royal servants, i.e., innumerable number of angels under his authority.[33] Thus, although it is plausible that the idea of an individual angel in later texts was first derived from the Exodus angel, it does not necessarily mean that the underlying concept of God's presence and action was replaced by the concept of an individual angel. The message that later biblical writers were trying to convey to their readers was still the presence and action of God himself.

An analogy might help to understand what we mean. For example, when drawing a picture, one painter may choose to draw an antique chair by using only a black pencil, and yet another painter may want to draw the same chair in a more colourful way by using a set of crayons, paints, or whatsoever. In other words, the same picture can be reproduced in different ways. Similarly, we might say that later biblical writers wished to

---

[32] P. R. Carrell, *Jesus and the Angels: Angelology and the Christology of the Apocalypse of John* (SNTSMS; Cambridge: CUP, 1997), 26; cf. F. Stier, *Gott und sein Engel im alten Testament* (Münster: Aschendorff, 1934), 79; Newsom, *ABD* 1.251.

[33] For a concise survey on the growing interest in the heavenly world and its inhabitants see S. M. Olyan, *A Thousand Thousands Served Him: Exegesis and the Naming of Angels in Ancient Judaism* (TSAJ 36; Tübingen: Mohr Siebeck, 1993), 1-13.

describe in a much more vivid way how God acts and manifests his presence in his world (i.e., through his glorious angels). As P. G. Davis puts it, "mediators were not significant in themselves but because of what they mediated, namely, the covenant relationship with God."[34] Olyan also showed that the process of generating the names of angelic divisions and individual angels came from a careful study of the biblical texts about theophanies and angelophanies.[35]

A slightly different approach to the Exodus angel is found in Gieschen's recent work. According to Gieschen, unlike other מלאך יהוה texts which depict him as a figure indistinguishable from God, the angel of Exod 23:20-21 is "a personal being clearly distinguishable from God" and yet "remains closely associated with God through the possession of the Divine Name."[36] He finds in this passage "important evidence that a divine attribute of God, nothing less than his powerful Name, was hypostatized as a particular angel."[37] Gieschen also argues that Exod 23:20-21 was very influential in the development of later angelology in which the exalted status of the principal angels was "determined by virtue of their possession of the Name of God."[38] However, several points of criticism are in order.

First, our exegesis of the text does not allow us to take this angel as a figure clearly distinct from God. The angel of Exod 23 is best understood as an expression of God's presence among his people in the same way as in other מלאך יהוה passages before the time of the monarchy. Durham interprets the angel as "the equivalent of Yahweh himself, thus another way of indicating Yahweh's Presence."[39] In his view, "the reference to the messenger whom Yahweh is to send out . . . is in fact a restatement of the promise and proof of Presence motif that dominates the narrative of Exod 1-20."[40] Indeed, the oscillation between Yahweh and the מלאך יהוה is best

---

[34] P. G. Davis, "Divine Agents, Mediators, and New Testament Christology" *JTS* 45 (1994), 501-02.

[35] Olyan, *A Thousand*, 14-120.

[36] Gieschen, *Angelomorphic*, 67 (emphasis mine).

[37] Gieschen, *Angelomorphic*, 67.

[38] Gieschen, *Angelomorphic*, 67 n.45, refers to Yahoel in the *Apoc. Ab.* 10-11, with his twice-theophoric name (YHWH+EL), Metatron in *3 Enoch* 10:9, and the angel Israel in *Pr. Jos.* 9. Gieschen identifies the angel of the Lord in Judg 13:18 with the angel who bears the Name of God.

[39] Durham, *Exodus*, 335. von Rad, *TDNT* 1.77-78, understands the מלאך יהוה as "the personification of Yahweh's assistance to Israel," and notes that Yahweh and his מלאך are "obviously one and the same," the מלאך being "an important literary theologization" introduced to soften "primitive tradition" regarding Yahweh's theophanic Presence; see also von Rad, *Theology*, 1.285-89. For the critique of von Rad's view, see Barr, "Theophany," 33-34. For recent endorsement of von Rad's view, see Meier, *DDD* 96-108.

[40] Durham, *Exodus*, 335.

understood as "the expression of a tension or paradox between an affirmation of God's presence and the impossibility of an unmediated encounter of man with God."[41] We have seen in the previous chapter that Deuteronomistic Name theology uses the similar concept for the Name of God to describe the way in which God is present in the Jerusalem temple (1 Kgs 8:16, 29; 9:3; cf. Jer 7:12).[42]

Second, our research on the Name of God as a personification of God's attributes has demonstrated that it never led to the development of a divine hypostasis separate from God himself prior to Christianity.[43]

Third, Gieschen's argument relies almost entirely on an artificial distinction between some OT texts which describe the angel as a figure indistinguishable from God and other texts in which the angel appears to be a figure distinct from God. As Gieschen also admits, however, with only one exception (Exod 23:20-21), the rest of the angel of the Lord texts depict him as a manifestation of God who is indistinguishable from God.[44] His sharp distinction between the indistinguishability and the distinguishability between the angel of the Lord and God himself misinterprets the OT evidence and must thus be abandoned. That later exegetes saw in Exod 23:21 an angel distinct from God does not necessarily mean that they understood this angel as a divine hypostasis. In fact, even granted that the idea of an individual angel was drawn from this passage, it is more likely that the concept of divine presence and action towards his people still remained unchanged, as the book of Wisdom clearly attests (Wis 10).[45] Thus, however glorious the language that was used for the principal angel, an attempt to view this individual angel in post-exilic writings (i.e., Divine Name Angel) as sharing divine authority and "in a qualified manner . . . divine substance"[46] is seriously misleading.

P. R. Carrell rightly observes that while "some angelophanies are reminiscent of theophanies," the depiction of these angels with the "power, majesty, and closeness to God . . . probably did not result in any of them being worshipped or acclaimed as a second power in heaven before the end

---

[41] Newsom, *ABD* 1.250; cf. also Barr, "Theophany," 34; Freedman and Willoughby, *TWAT* 4.901; Hirth, *Gottes Boten*, 83-84.

[42] See §2.4.2.

[43] See §2.4.

[44] Gieschen, *Angelomorphic*, 67.

[45] See §2.2.

[46] Gieschen, *Angelomorphic*, 67-68, 77, 151; cf. also J. E. Fossum, *The Name of God and the Angel of the Lord: Samaritan and Jewish Concepts of Intermediation and the Origin of Gnosticism* (WUNT 36; Tübingen: Mohr Siebeck, 1985), 307-21, claims that a principal angel was often seen as the personification of the name (*Yahweh*) and glory of God. He also claims that this figure shares in "the divine nature," or the divine "mode of being," without defining clearly what he means (p.310, 333).

of the first century C.E."[47] He also notes that since there is no consistent identity for the principal angel, "the significance of an apparent dualism between God and one outstanding angel should not be exaggerated."[48] Given the above evidence, we seriously doubt whether Gieschen's attempt to argue for the hypostatization of the Name of God as a particular angel was successful.[49]

3.1.2.4. Summary

We have examined the identity of the angel of the Lord and its development in the OT and argued that, although the identity of this angel underwent a remarkable development towards an understanding of him as an individual angel distinct from God, the underlying concept of him as an expression of God's presence and action towards his people still remained unchanged. We find therefore the concept of the divine presence and action in this world in the angel of the Lord tradition from start to the end.

3.1.3. Principal Angels

In the this section we will examine the increasing speculations about angelic beings and the heavenly realm in Second Temple Judaism and see whether such speculations blurred the clear distinction between angels and God in the OT.

3.1.3.1. Jewish Angelology in Second Temple Judaism

Although references to angels were found from the earliest stage of the OT, the evidence shows that speculations about the heavenly world and its inhabitants became fully developed in the late Second Temple period. The new developments include the emergence of named angels, classes of heavenly beings, angelic hierarchy, archangels, heavenly temples and cults, conflict between good and bad angels, expanding roles of angels in the human world, and characterization of angels. In many cases, however,

---

[47] Carrell, *Jesus*, 75.

[48] Carrell, *Jesus*, 75.

[49] Meier, *DDD* 108, referring to the works of Rowland, Gieschen and Segal, comments that "It is true that one may trace in Jewish apocalyptic the development of a single exalted angel that some have tried to derive from the earlier *mal'ak YHWH*, but the connection between the two remains undemonstrated and the terminology is different. Quite the contrary, a vigorous element in early Judaism resisted sectarians who believed that a certain principal angel was a special mediator between God and man. Developing descriptions about the highest-ranking angels tend to avoid the phrase 'angel of the Lord' in favour of more elaborate titles."

these new ideas were not really new but expansions and concretizations of old ideas of Israelite popular religion.[50] While the old notion of the divine council continued to be important for descriptions of the heavenly world, graphic depictions of the heavenly court and the splendour and magnitude of the scene were introduced. The heavenly realm as a place of deliberations became a place of judgment (Dan 7:10-14; *1 Enoch* 60:2-6), of revelatory pronouncements (Dan 7:13-14), and of praise (*1 Enoch* 61:9-13; *2 Enoch* 20:4-21:1; *Apoc. Ab.* 10:8; 18:11-14; *Ps.-Philo* 18:6).[51] In addition, the temple imagery, together with descriptions of the angels as priests who serve in the heavenly temple, was added to the royal court imagery.[52]

With regard to the functions of angels, angels are given the general function of carrying out the will of God. Their specific functions include: (1) to help and protect the pious and to bring their prayers before God; (2) to decree and execute punishment in accordance with God's will; (3) to keep records at the time of judgment; and (4) to be teacher and mediator of revelation in non-apocalyptic settings; and (5) to reveal, guide, and interpret mysteries and visions in apocalyptic writings.

The Second Temple Jewish understanding about angels shows the following characteristics: (1) their appearance is described in terms of light, fire, shining metals, or precious stones; (2) their garments are white linen or white with golden sashes; (3) they are assumed to be spiritual beings; and (4) they are created beings.

There have been much scholarly speculations as to why there was such a growing interest in the heavenly realm and its inhabitants, and a considerable number of explanations have been suggested:[53] (1) a mystery; (2) foreign influence, particularly the influence exerted by Babylonian and Persian cultures; (3) the influence of magic; (4) the inaccessible God and the resulting need for intermediaries; (5) the influence of gnostic ideas; (6) internal developments in the religion of Israel such as the avoidance of anthropomorphism, the elaboration of God's activities in relation to Israel and the world, and the role played by changing ideas about God; and (7) the close word-by-word exegesis and rewritings of biblical texts.[54]

---

[50] J. J. Collins, *The Apocalyptic Vision of the Book of Daniel* (Missoula: Scholars Press, 1977), 101-4.

[51] For a concise overview of angels from the OT to the Second Temple period and relevant biblical and extra-biblical passages see, Newsom, *ABD* 1.248-53.

[52] Newsom, *ABD* 1.253.

[53] For a variety of theories and the brief evaluation and bibliographies see Olyan, *A Thousand*, 3-13.

[54] The last option is argued by Olyan, *A Thousand*, 10.

3.1.3.2. Principal Angels as God's Servants

Although speculations about angels played a greater role in the Jewish apocalyptic literature, there was one thing which remained unchanged. Even in these apocalyptic writings the main focus of the texts or narratives was God himself rather than a particular angel, who – however exalted he was – was no more than just a servant of God carrying out the tasks he had been commanded to do. A particular function or feature ascribed to an angel, therefore, should not be overemphasized at the expense undermining the primary intention of the texts or narratives. Even in these writings the writer's main concern is to convey the message of God's action and concern for his chosen people in whatever circumstances they are placed. Angels are merely God's servants and play the role of enhancing the greatness of God as he is in control of every single affair of his people's life. However gloriously principal angels are depicted in these texts, however highly they are ranked in the angelic hierarchy, and however closely they are linked to the way God rules over his world and his people, one thing should remain absolutely clear: they are creatures of God and belong to the category of the innumerable angels in the service of God, far from competing with God. It is, therefore, possible to contend that Jewish apocalyptic literature was written to show how God works or acts towards his creation and his chosen people, rather than how much these angelic beings participate in the sovereign rule of God. The main focus must be placed on God's presence and action, rather than his medium or instrumentality, i.e., his angels.

It is also important to note that, although there is some continuity between individual angels of later period and the early tradition about the angel of the Lord, later angelology continued to use the same language about God's action, presence, and manifestation in this world. Jewish apocalyptic angelology must be interpreted in terms of God's action in this world rather than angelology as such. It is an undeniable fact that there were growing speculations about angelic beings and the heavenly realm in the Jewish apocalyptic literature of the Second Temple period. However, we need to take heed of what Bauckham has to say about recent scholarship that seems to give too much emphasis to what was meant to be of secondary importance:

The evidence that Jews of this period could easily and were in the habit of drawing a firm line of clear distinction between the one God and all other reality is far more considerable than the small amount of evidence adduced by those who argue that so-called intermediary figures blur this distinction."[55]

---

[55] R. Bauckham, *God Crucified: Monotheism and Christology in the New Testament* (Didsbury Lectures 1996; Carlisle: Paternoster, 1998), 16.

Angels are not meant to compete with "the Mighty One" or "the Eternal One." For the Second Temple Jews angels were no more than God's creatures ready to serve him.[56] The angelology of this period portrays God carrying out his will *through* his angels, and his principal angels are often given the function of carrying out more specific tasks.

3.1.3.3. A Sharp Distinction between God and Exalted Angels

To support his argument that angelology in the Second Temple period blurred the line between God and exalted angels, Gieschen proposes the five criteria of divinity in terms of divine position, divine appearance, divine functions, divine name, and divine veneration. However, our critical review of his criteria of divinity in Chapter 1 and the discussion in this chapter made clear that his attempt to show that a clear dividing line between God and the intermediary beings has been blurred by increasing speculations in exalted angels and other intermediaries is far from convincing.

3.1.3.4. Summary

We have argued so far that an increasing interest in principal angels in Second Temple Judaism did not blur the clear line between God and the created beings.

We conclude that principal angels were another way of speaking about God's presence and/or action in the world. While principal angels – such as Michael, Gabriel, and Yahoel, to name but a few – are depicted as highly exalted figures in the heavenly world, they are in fact none other than God's servants in carrying out his will for his people on his behalf. Their "active" involvement in this world thus shows God's concern for his chosen people. Their presence and action in this world expresses God's presence and action in this world. It is not the presence and action of principal angels but the action and presence of *God* himself which is to be emphasized.

3.2. A Pre-existent Messiah

In his book *Christology in the Making* James D. G. Dunn claims that we cannot find in pre-Christian Judaism any antecedents for the Christian doctrine of incarnation. He conducted a detailed survey of various possible

---

[56] For angels as created beings, see *Jub.* 2:2; *Bib. Ant.* 60:2; 2 Bar 21:6; *2 Enoch* 29:3; 33:7.

backgrounds for the emergence of the Christian belief in Jesus' pre-existence, dealing with different categories such as the Son of God, the Son of man, the last Adam, Spirit or angel, the Wisdom of God and the Word of God. It is interesting to note, however, that among the list of possible antecedents the category of the Messiah is missing. Dunn declares that *"there was no conception of a pre-existent Messiah current in pre-Christian Judaism prior to the Similitudes of Enoch."*[57] Dunn dismisses possible evidence from the LXX translation of Ps 110:3 and Micah 5:2 by stating that:

> Although Ps. 110.1 and 110.4 were important proof texts in earliest Christian apologetic . . . Ps. 110.3 is never explicitly cited in the NT period. It was not until Justin took it up in the middle of the second century AD (*Dial.* 63.3; 76.7) that it began to be used as a prophecy of Christ's pre-existence. Similarly with Micah 5.2, though often cited by the ante-Nicene fathers, the citation only rarely extends to the last line, and then without any implication of pre-existence being drawn from it. This would certainly be a most odd feature if these LXX renderings were already understood as speaking of the Messiah's pre-existence. The silence of the first century AD points rather in the other direction: viz. that such an interpretation only became current after the pre-existence of Christ was already taken for granted.[58]

However, in his recent book Horbury argues that it is possible to find the idea of a pre-existent messiah in Second Temple Judaism.[59] He claims that "the messianic king, a human figure endued with heavenly virtue and might, can be regarded as the manifestation and embodiment of a spirit sent by God."[60] Horbury urges that the depictions of a spiritual and superhuman messiah were not incompatible with his humanity or inconsistent with the depictions of the messiah as a conquering king. These portrayals took up the exalted characteristics of many messianic passages in the Hebrew scriptures and were widely attested in biblical interpretation from the time of the LXX Pentateuch onwards, and continued to be

---

[57] Dunn, *Christology*, 72. Dunn also states that "we lack any sort of firm evidence that the 'one like a son of man' in Dan. 7 was understood within pre-Christian Judaism as the Messiah, pre-existent or otherwise." However, see W. Horbury, "The Messianic Associations of 'the Son of Man'" *JTS* 36 (1985), 34-55 for its possible messianic associations.

[58] Dunn, *Christology*, 71.

[59] W. Horbury, *Jewish Messianism and the Cult of Christ* (London: SCM, 1998), 86-108.

[60] Horbury, *Jewish Messianism*, 90. Horbury comes to the conclusion that "Ancient Jewish presentation of the messiah as a glorious mortal king with spiritual and superhuman aspects is then not necessarily far removed from the contemporary New Testament and early Christian depictions of a crucified but spiritual and glorious 'Christ'" (108).

influential in rabbinic tradition.[61] He insists that these portrayals of a spiritual messiah "assumed the importance of the spirit in the human make-up, and continued the notion of a foreordained spiritual messiah known to God."[62] Horbury finds a common background for the view of God among the ancient Jews and early Christians: the conception of God as lord of godlike angels and spirits (Num 16:22 LXX [θεὸς τῶν πνευμάτων]; Ps 80 [79]:5 LXX [θεὸς τῶν δυνάμεων]; Esther 4:17r LXX = Rest of Esther 14:12 [βασιλεῦ τῶν θεῶν]; and 4Q400 2, 5 [King of the "gods"]; Heb 12:9 [πατρὶ τῶν πνευμάτων]; Exod. R. 15.6, on 12:2).[63] He also thinks that the relative independence of souls or spirits and beliefs in the pre-existence and transmigration of souls have left an impression on ancient Judaism. Horbury then suggests that biblical oracles such as Isa 9:5(6) and Micah 5:1(2) might include the idea of pre-existence, which characterizes the glorious messianic figures depicted with traits of the Danielic Son of man in the Parables of Enoch, 2 Esdras and the Fifth Sibylline book; but he disagrees with the common view that identifies the conception of an angelic messiah almost exclusively with the Jewish apocalypses. Rather, he argues, "the apocalyptic sources themselves show that the Danielic figure of the Son of man coming with the clouds of heaven had come to be associated closely with the series of messianic oracles in the Pentateuch, Prophets and Psalms."[64]

Here we have two rather opposite views on the possible attestation of an idea about a pre-existent messiah in pre-Christian Judaism, regardless of its possible influence upon the Christian belief about Jesus' pre-existence. Since Horbury has provided evidence for the existence of this idea in pre-Christian Judaism, a critical review of his argument will be in order. This exercise will help us not only to explore an area that Dunn might have overlooked, but also to be able to assess the environment in which the early Christians would have been immersed when they were doing messianic exegesis of the OT.

Horbury's argument is an inference from a number of texts, which he regards as reflecting the same broad understanding of the messiah. His case is primarily based on a number of Septuagintal texts from the

---

[61] Horbury, *Jewish Messianism*, 87.

[62] Horbury, *Jewish Messianism*, 87-88.

[63] Horbury, *Jewish Messianism*, 87, 89. Cf. Mach, *Entwicklungsstadien*, 65-278, for the angelology of the LXX and extra-biblical writings, without special reference to divine titles.

[64] Horbury, *Jewish Messianism*, 90. See further Horbury, "Messianic Associations," 40-8; for the Parables of Enoch, a similar conclusion is reached in the fresh review of biblical allusions by J. C. VanderKam, "Righteous One, Messiah, Chosen One, and Son of Man in 1 Enoch 3-71" in *The Messiah: Developments in Earliest Judaism and Christianity* (ed. J. H. Charlesworth; Minneapolis: Fortress, 1992), 169-91.

Pentateuch, Prophets, and Psalms, but it is also corroborated by convergence of these texts with a number of different sources.[65]

(I) Septuagintal texts from the Pentateuch, Prophets, and Psalms, which are associated with:

    (a) light: Isa 9:1(2); 9:5(6);

    (b) divinely sent spirit: Amos 4:13; Lam 4:20;

    (c) angelic character, star: Num 24:17 (regularly linked with Isa 11:1-2);

    (d) the title *anatolé*: Zech 6:12;

    (e) existence prior to the creation of heavenly bodies: Ps 72 (71):5, 17; Ps 110 (109):3

(II) Others:

    (a) The Psalms of Solomon;

    (b) Apocalypses of the late Herodian period;

    (c) The Fifth Sibylline book;

    (d) Rabbinic material

3.2.1. Isaiah 9:5(6) LXX

Horbury argues that the phrase μεγάλης βουλῆς ἄγγελος "angel of great counsel," the Greek translation of the Hebrew גבור אל יועץ פלא "wonderful counsellor, mighty god," "gains pictorial force from the possibility of identifying the child with the 'great light' (φῶς μέγα) announced at the beginning of the oracle," and "forms part of a broader Septuagintal interpretation of Isaianic messianic oracles, displaying a consistent emphasis on spiritual gifts."[66] He suggests that within this broader interpretation the title "angel" of Isa 9:5 LXX is "consistent with"[67] other messianic oracles in 11:2-4 LXX, ἀναπαύσεται ἐπ' αὐτὸν πνεῦμα τοῦ θεοῦ . . . ἐμπλήσει αὐτὸν πνεῦμα φόβου θεοῦ "a spirit of God shall rest upon him . . . a spirit of the fear of God shall fill him," and 61:1, πνεῦμα κυρίου ἐπ' ἐμέ οὗ εἵνεκεν ἔχρισέν με "the spirit of the Lord is upon me, because he has anointed me."[68]

Despite Horbury's attempt to link the various messianic oracles in the LXX version of Isaiah to show that a spiritual messiah was in view, he has

---

[65] Horbury, *Jewish Messianism*, 90.

[66] Horbury, *Jewish Messianism*, 90.

[67] I wonder what the precise meaning of this expression is; see also n.81 below.

[68] Horbury, *Jewish Messianism*, 91, adds that this depiction has probably been influenced by the angelic and spirit-inspired biblical image of David himself. However, the link between these messianic depictions and the image of David in 2 Kgdms 23 seems to be quite speculative.

not shown that these oracles testify to anything more than just a "spirit-inspired" messiah, far from being a pre-existent messiah. Being inspired or anointed by a/the spirit does not make someone pre-existent.

3.2.2. Amos 4:13 LXX; Lam 4:20 LXX

Horbury also claims that in the LXX translations from the prophetic books elsewhere the messianic king has been associated with the divinely-sent spirit.[69] Amos 4:13 LXX speaks of God as κτίζων πνεῦμα καὶ ἀπαγγέλλων εἰς ἀνθρώπους τὸν χριστὸν αὐτοῦ "creating spirit, and announcing to men his Christ."[70] It is pointed out that the messiah appears in a passage on creation, where he "is announced from the time of creation, and is mentioned just after the thunder and the "wind" or "spirit", which in this context recalls the spirit upon the face of the waters in Gen 1:2."[71]

Another example is Lam 4:20 LXX, where the king is spoken of as "the breath of our nostrils," the breath of national life. It is also noted that here the Hebrew רוח can also be rendered as "spirit," and the messiah is "associated once again with creation and the breathing of life into newly created humanity . . ."[72] Horbury claims that Amos 4:13 LXX and Lam 4:20 LXX can be taken to show that "the messianic king was associated with creation and divinely sent spirit(s), and could himself be understood as a spiritual messiah, in touch with or embodying a spirit sent from God."[73]

Once again, the fact that a messianic figure is "associated with the divinely-sent spirit" or with creation does not necessarily mean that he was pre-existent or a heavenly being. The evidence cannot be pressed to imply anything more than a "divine inspiration" of the messiah or God's foreknowledge of him. We find therefore no hint of the pre-existence of the messiah in these texts.

---

[69] Horbury, *Jewish Messianism*, 91. I have reservations about his often-used phrase "be associated with." The precise meaning of this slippery expression when examining the sources is not clear.

[70] The reference to "his Christ" can be explained by the messianic development of the "tabernacle of David" in Amos 9:11 and a reference to the messianic adversary "king Gog" in Amos 7:1 LXX (Γωγ ὁ βασιλεύς).

[71] Horbury, *Jewish Messianism*, 91. Compare the third century rabbinic interpretations of this as "the spirit of the messiah."

[72] Horbury, *Jewish Messianism*, 91-92. Note again the slippery term "associated with."

[73] Horbury, *Jewish Messianism*, 92.

3.2.3. Num 24:17 LXX

In Num 24:17 LXX the prophecy of Balaam כוכב מיעקב וקם שבט מישראל
דרך "a star shall march forth from Jacob, and a sceptre shall arise out of
Israel" is rendered as ἀνατελεῖ ἄστρον ἐξ Ιακωβ καὶ ἀναστήσεται
ἄνθρωπος ἐξ Ισραηλ "a star shall spring out of Jacob, and a man shall rise
up out of Israel." Horbury urges that a link between a star and a man by
this oracle suggests the angelic character of the messiah, since the stars
belonged to the angelic "host of heaven" (צבא השמים Deut 4:19; cf.
1Kings 22:19).[74] Further evidence was drawn from the nickname Bar
Kokhba, "son of the star" (*Barchochebas*, Justin Martyr, *1 Apol.* 31), a
Jewish leader of the Hadrianic period who claimed to be a "luminary come
down from heaven to shine upon those in distress" (Eusebius, *HE* 4, 6, 2)
and a later midrash speaking of an angel- or star-like messiah as standing
radiant on the temple-roof and proclaiming "Meek ones (cf. Isa 61:1), the
time for your redemption has come; and if you do not believe in me, look
at my light which shines upon you" (Pes. R. 36.12, with reference to Isa
60:1-3, "your light").[75] Horbury also notes that the later influence of the
star-prophecy (Num 24:17) with its combination with the Jesse-oracle (Isa
11:1-2) in both Christian and Jewish circles[76] suggests "a long-standing
association" of these two prophecies, already current in the Second-
Temple period, as is suggested by its emergence in *Ps. Sol.* 17; 1QSb =
1Q28b, col. v;[77] *T. Judah* 24; and Rev 22:16.[78]

However, while it is true that stars were counted among the angelic
"host of heaven" in Jewish thinking, in Num 24:17 the star is not linked
with angelic beings but is said to spring out from Jacob (i.e., Israel). A star
among the people of Israel will most probably refer to one among them,
rather than one of another kind. Moreover, the two lines "ἀνατελεῖ ἄστρον
. . . ἐξ Ισραηλ" belong to a Hebrew parallelism that expresses the same

---

[74] However, note that the LXX renders צבא השמים "host of heaven' variously as κόσμος
τοῦ οὐρανοῦ "heavenly world/bodies' (Deut 4:19; 17:3; στρατιὰ τοῦ οὐρανοῦ 1Ki 22:19;
2Chr 33:3, 5[//2Ki 21:3, 5: it means that στρατιὰ and δύναμις are synonyms]; δύναμις
τοῦ οὐρανοῦ 2Ki 17:16; 21:3, 5; 23:4, 5; 2Chr 18:18//1Ki 22:19.

[75] A. Goldberg, *Erlösung durch Leiden. Drei rabbinische Homilien über die
Trauernden Zions und den leidenden Messias Ephraim, PesR 34. 36. 37* (FJS 4;
Frankfurt: Lang, 1978), 154-5.

[76] Justin Martyr, *1 Apol.* 32.12-13; cf. Commodian, *Carm. apol.* 291; Test. Judah 24;
Targ. Isa. 11.1; Targ. Num. 24.17.

[77] According to Horbury, *Ps. Sol.* 17 draws on both Num 24:17 and Isa 11:4 in its
evocation of the longed-for son of David (see vv.23-24, 27 [21-22, 24]); and the blessing
of the Prince of the Congregation (1QSb = 1Q28b, col. v) follows Isa 11, but then echoes
Num 24:17 as well as Gen 49:10, as J. T. Milik has shown. Cf. D. Barthélemy and J. T.
Milik, *Qumran Cave I* (DJD 1; Oxford: Clarendon, 1955), 128-9.

[78] Horbury, *Jewish Messianism*, 92-3.

thought in two different ways; then "star" should be taken as synonymous with "sceptre" or "man." The occurrence of "star" and "man" in the same verse, therefore, does not testify to the angelic character of the messiah, let alone his pre-existence. Rather, the prophecy in Numbers 24 speaks about the appearance of the messianic king in highly poetical terms.[79] The evidence adduced from the later Jewish and Christian sources then loses its weight or becomes irrelevant if the "star-prophecy" does not contain implications for the angelic character of the messiah.

3.2.4. Jer 23:5; Zech 3:9; 6:12 LXX

Observing the translation of the Davidic royal title צמח "shoot" or "branch" into ἀνατολή in the LXX version of Jer 23:5; Zech 3:9(8); 6:12, and the rendering of the Hebrew verb דרך "march forth" into ἀνατέλλω "spring up" in Num 24:17 LXX, Horbury conjectures that the title ἀνατολή was already understood as "dayspring" by the time of the LXX translation.[80] He gives as evidence (1) the use of ἀνατολή in the sense of sun-rise in the canticle *Benedictus* (Luke 1:78-79); (2) the sequential quotation of Num 24:17 (star and man) and Zech 6:12 (man called ἀνατολή) by Justin Martyr (*Dial.* 106.4); and (3) Philo's discussion about the angelic implications of the title ἀνατολή (*Conf.* 60-3; *Qu. Gen.* 1.4; *Conf.* 146).[81] Horbury then comes to the conclusion that ἀνατολή is "another of the Septuagintal titles which were associated with an understanding of the messianic figure as a luminary and a heavenly being."[82]

Although Horbury claims to find angelic implications of the title ἀνατολή in the LXX prophetic texts, his argument is less than convincing. The LXX rendering of ἀνατέλλω in Num 24:17 for the Hebrew verb דרך can be nothing more than a natural or non-literal translation when a star or another heavenly body is the subject of the verb (cf. Mal 3:20 LXX; Isa

---

[79] "Star" and "sceptre" can be taken as metonymy for a king.

[80] Horbury, *Jewish Messianism*, 94.

[81] In *Conf.* 60-3 Philo discusses "rising' (ἀνατολή) in connection with the move ἀπὸ ἀνατολῶν "from the sunrising' (Gen 11:2 LXX). Horbury states: "Quoting 'Behold, a man whose name is *anatolé*' (Zech. 6.12), Philo says that *anatolé* would be a strange name for a 'man' of body and soul, and rather denotes the 'man' as the incorporeal first-born who fully conforms to the divine image the eldest son whom the Father of all 'raised up' (ἀνέτειλε). This is the figure whom Philo later in this treatise calls 'the Man according to the image' – the heavenly man from the double creation of heavenly and earthly man indicated by the pair of verses Gen. 1.27; 2.7 (*Qu. Gen.* 1.4) – the Logos, 'the eldest of the angels, as it were Archangel' (Philo, *Conf.* 146)." However, if this speculation belongs to purely Philonic allegories, Philo cannot be adduced for evidence.

[82] Horbury, *Jewish Messianism*, 94.

58:10 LXX). This makes it unlikely that the choice of ἀνατέλλω had any special significance for the translators (e.g., that the title ἀνατολή was already understood as "dayspring"). While the rendering of צמח as ἀνατολή can be significant, we need to take into consideration that ἀνατολή was not only used for sunrise or star-rise but also for growth or sprout, as Horbury himself admits.[83] The choice of this particular word, in a context where the referent is most likely to be a human figure, does not provide sufficient evidence in favour of an understanding of the messiah as a heavenly being. Thus, ἀνατολή can have become a messianic title in the LXX, but it is very unlikely that ἀνατολή did amount to an expression of the heavenly character of the messiah or his pre-existence. Moreover, bearing in mind that the LXX was not done by one group of translators all at one time, but developed over a period, attempts to make "associations" between different sections of the LXX corpus and to argue that "the LXX translators" had a common view on a particular matter become less than persuasive.

On the other hand, the precise meaning of ἀνατολή in Luke 1:78-79 is also debatable. Here ἀνατολή could have been associated with the Isaianic "great light" and thus understood as a messianic title.[84] It is possible, however, to be understood without an explicit reference to the messiah, since there is no evidence for ἀνατολή being connected with the imagery of the casting of light as is the case in this canticle.[85] The "star" of Num 24:17 is so developed in *T. Levi* 18.3-4, but the field of imagery involved in the LXX use of ἀνατολή seems to be that of brightness representing (royal) glory (cf. Isa 14:12; Dan 12:3; Judg 5:31; *1 Enoch* 104.1; Matt 13:43).[86] A fresh development is always possible, but is not positively evidenced. Such a development would in any case only be possible in a Greek text, not in a Hebrew one using צמח. So if ἀνατολή is not derived from צמח, then the messianic uses of ἀνατολή lose their relevance. The background for Luke 1:78b-79a could well be found in the cluster of Isaianic texts 9:1; 58:8, 10; 60:1-3 (and cf. Mal 3:20 [MT 4:2]; Isa

---

[83] See I. H. Marshall, *The Gospel of Luke: a Commentary on the Greek Text* (NIGTC; Grand Rapids: Eerdmans, 1978), 94, for two different uses of the same word.

[84] Cf. the ἄστρον of Num 24:17 and the φῶς which the servant of Isa 42:6 is; Marshall, *Luke*, 94-95: "The double meaning of the word . . . allowed it to be applied to both the shoot and the star, so that in effect two messianic images are brought together here. . . . The imagery is thus that of the Davidic Messiah, the Shoot from Jesse (Is. 11:1ff.) and the star from Jacob (Nu. 24:17) who is to visit men from on high, i.e., from the dwelling place of God (2 Sa. 22:17; *et al.*)."

[85] J. Nolland, *Luke* (WBC 35; Dallas: Word Books, 1993), 90.

[86] Cf. Isa 14:12; Dan 12:3; Judg 5:31; *1 Enoch* 104.1; Mt 13:43.

30:26).[87] The Hebrew זרח "rising" in Isa 60:3 could well be translated as
ἀνατολή and is best understood of the light which rises to shine upon
God's people (cf. v.2 and Isa 58:8, 10). The cognate verb זרח "to rise" is
found in Isa 58:10; 60:2; Mal 3:20 [MT 4:2]). The passage is thus not so
much about the *identity* of the messiah as the *ministry* of the messiah.[88]
Horbury appears to be too confident in working back to an idea in early
sources from the same or similar idea attested in later sources, assuming
far too greater probability of influence between different texts of same
corpus as well as from early writings to later sources, regardless of the
language and/or their provenance. He seems to be falling into the fallacy of
assuming that what is true for one occurrence of a word/idea is true for all
or most other occurrences as well, when he argues from the presence of a
motif in one text that it is also present in other texts from the same corpus,
where its presence is much less obvious.

3.2.5. Psalm 72 LXX

Horbury argues for the attestation of a similar understanding about a pre-
existent messiah in the LXX Psalter, adducing evidence from some
Christian writings of the second century, where proofs of Christ's glorious
pre-existence are quoted from Pss 72 (71) and 110 (109) LXX. He refers to
Justin Martyr's *Dial.* 45, 4 and 76.7.[89] According to Horbury, these
Christian testimonies had some contact with Jewish interpretations
regarding the existence of the messiah's name "before the sun" (*Bar.* in
Pesah. 54a; *Tg.* Ps 72:17). The widely attested application of v.17 in both
Christian and Jewish circles leads Horbury to suggest that by the end of the
Second Temple period "before the moon" (v.5) and "before the sun" (v.17)
were interpreted temporally.[90] He also suggests that the temporal
interpretation of Ps 72:5, 17 might have been responsible for the pre-
existence of the messiah's name in *1 Enoch* 48:3.[91]

Horbury's suggestion here is nothing new. Ps 72:17 LXX has already
been taken by some scholars as an early example of the belief in the pre-
existence of the messiah's name. It is said that the pre-existence of the

---

[87] Nolland, *Luke*, 90.

[88] The same principle applies to "a great light" in Mt 4:16.

[89] *Dial.* 45, 4 (Christ was "before daystar and moon"), with allusion to Ps 110:3 and
Ps 72:5, and *Dial.* 76.7 ('David proclaimed that "before sun and moon" he should be
"begotten of the womb" according to the "counsel" of the Father'), with allusion to Ps
72:17 LXX, "before the sun" and Isa 9:6 (5) LXX "angel of great counsel."

[90] Horbury, *Jewish Messianism*, 95.

[91] Cf. A. Goldberg, "Die Namen des Messias in der rabbinischen Traditionsliteratur.
Ein Beitrag zur Messiaslehre des rabbinischen Judentums" *Frankfurter Judaistische
Beiträge* 7 (1979), 77.

messiah's name is another way of expressing the religious idea that the messiah was prior to creation. Observing many examples of this idea in later Judaism P. Volz claimed that:

Ebenso weicht die Angabe in Ps 71 = 72 17 . . . ein wenig vom Original ab, indem sie die Ewigkeit des Messiasnamens, die der hebräische Text von der Zukunft behauptet, auch auf die Vorzeit ausdehnt, wahrscheinlich auf Grund der bereits bestehenden Theorie von der Präexistenz des Messiasnamens.[92]

Volz's claim has been recently defended by J. Schaper.[93] While Schaper does not insist that only a temporal interpretation is possible with πρὸ τοῦ ἡλίου "before the sun," he attempts to highlight the increased importance of the *name* of the king in the LXX. Schaper observes that, due to an insertion of εὐλογημένον into the Greek text the concept of the *name* has received a greater emphasis. In addition, while the Hebrew text makes a distinction between the king's name and God's name in vv.17 and 19,[94] in the Greek version *both* names are "blessed," thereby

the name of the (messianic) king has virtually been equated in importance with that of God himself. This indicates the increased significance of the king in the Greek version of the psalm. It seems to point towards an even more enriched concept of kingship. The (messianic) king is regarded as a bringer of salvation.[95]

Schaper finds a similar understanding in the Targumic interpretation on Ps 72:17, which is rendered as follows:[96]

יהי שמיה מדכר לעלם וקדם מהוי שמשא מזומן
הוה שמיה ויתברכון בזכותיה כל עמיא ויימרון טב ליה:

---

[92] P. Volz, Die Eschatologie der jüdischen Gemeinde im neutestamentlichen Zeitalter nach den Quellen der rabbinischen, apokalyptischen und apokryphen Literatur (Tübingen: Mohr Siebeck, 1934), 205. However, W. Bousset, Die Religion des Judentums im späthellenistischen Zeitalter (HNT 21; Tübingen: Mohr Siebeck, 1926), 263, n.1, being more cautious, just refers to obvious texts from the Targums and 1 Enoch as secure evidence for the existence of such an idea.

[93] J. Schaper, *Eschatology in the Greek Psalter* (WUNT 2/76; Tübingen: Mohr Siebeck, 1995), 93-96; 101-107.

[94] Cf. v.17 יהי שמו לעולם with v.19 וברוך שם כבודו לעולם (the king's name is to last forever and God's name is to be "blessed").

[95] Schaper, *Eschatology*, 94. Cf. εὐλογητόν in v.19 and εὐλογημένον in v.17. See also G. Schimanowski, *Weisheit und Messias: die jüdischen Voraussetzungen der urchristlichen Präexistenzchristologie* (WUNT 2/17; Tübingen: Mohr Siebeck, 1985) 146ff., who interprets the LXX as a further approximation towards the wording of the divine promise to Abraham in Genesis (12:3; 18:18; 28:14), although he misses the newly established parallel between vv.17 and 19.

[96] Text from P. A. de Lagarde, *Hagiographa Chaldaice* (Leipzig: Teubner, 1973).

A translation of this verse would run as follows:

His name will be remembered forever, and before the sun was, his name was appointed.
And all nations will be blessed through his righteousness and will praise him.

According to Schaper, in this Targumic version the ambiguity of the LXX translation concerning the preposition πρό disappears:

By means of the interpretative insertion מהוי the ambiguity of קדם has been resolved. As קדם, just like its Greek equivalent, has spatial *and* temporal connotations, the *meturgeman* (or the final redactors), intent upon resolving difficulties and making the text accessible, clarified its understanding by employing this particular insertion. Nevertheless, the Greek text allows for both interpretations; possibly the translator consciously opted for this hermeneutical ambiguity.

Then, a much clearer example of the pre-existence of the messiah's name is attested in *1 Enoch* 48:2-3, a document probably dated pre-70 AD.

And at that time the Son of Man was named in the presence of the Lord of Spirits
And his name before the Chief of Days;
And before the sun and the "signs" were created,
Before the stars of the heavens were made,
His name was named before the Lord of spirits.[97]

Schaper then is able to conclude that both LXX and the Targum show a certain tendency towards an interpretation of Ps 72:17 in terms of the pre-existence of the messiah's name and it is further supported by a later text from *1 Enoch*.[98] While it is true that the Targum attests the pre-existence of the messiah's name, it seems incorrect to assume that the pre-existence of his name can be equated with the messiah being existed before creation.[99] It is merely the *idea* about the messiah that was in God's mind prior to creation.[100] As Schimanowski rightly insists, the Targum written as a

---

[97] The translation is taken from M. Black, ed., *The Book of Enoch or I Enoch: a New English Edition* (SVTP 7; Leiden: Brill, 1985), 49.

[98] Schaper, *Eschatology*, 95.

[99] See Schimanowski, *Weisheit*, 150-52, for the interpretation of the Aramaic word זמן as "to predetermine" or "to arrange" as opposed to "to exist."

[100] Cf. J. Klausner, *The Messianic Idea in Israel* (London: Allen and Unwin, 1956), 460: "That the Messiah himself existed before creation is nowhere stated in Tannaitic literature . . . 'the name of the Messiah' is the *idea* of the Messiah, or, more exactly, *the idea of redemption through the Messiah*. This idea did precede creation"; also S. Mowinckel, *He That Cometh* (Nashville: Abingdon, 1956), 334; G. Vermes, *Jesus the Jew: a Historian's Reading of the Gospels* (London: Collins, 1973), 138-39; Dunn, *Christology*, 71.

paraphrase brings out the election of the promised messiah in a special way by tracing back the point of the election to the very beginning.[101]

As far as the LXX is concerned the evidence is more than doubtful. For example, the second line of v.17 "before the sun his name *will* remain" is stated in the future, in contrast to the Targum's "before the sun *was*, his name *was* appointed." A temporal interpretation of πρό makes less sense with the statement in the future. Moreover, Schaper's discussion of the LXX does not carry further Volz's claim. The increased significance of the messiah's name does not amount to his supernatural character or pre-existence. As far as the Targum and *1 Enoch* are concerned, it is questionable to assume that what is found in the Greek LXX is the view of Hebrew/Aramaic speaking Jews as well. Bearing in mind that *1 Enoch* was probably written originally in Aramaic,[102] it seems less likely that Hebrew/Aramaic speaking Jews would have been influenced by the Greek LXX. Thus, even if Schaper is right that *1 Enoch* 48:2-3 and the Targum on Ps 72:17 attest the doctrine of the pre-existence of the messiah's name (and hence the pre-existence of the messiah), the evidence cannot be used with any confidence to support a possible attestation of the same idea in the LXX. Horbury's conclusion that the LXX version of Ps 72 "had come to be taken temporally" is going too far beyond the evidence. Even Schaper's conclusion that "there definitely is a tendency in the Septuagint passage to assign a heightened importance to the Messiah's name"[103] cannot be pressed too far in support of the idea about a pre-existent messiah in the LXX Psalter.[104] Our conclusion coheres with Schimanowski's judgment:

Sowohl im MT wie auch in Septuaginta und Peschitta geht es um eine Verheißung für den zukünftigen Herrscher (Messias); überall dort wird das Bild von Sonne und Mond verwendet, um die ewige beständige Dauer von Dynastie, Namen und königlicher Herrschaft herauszustellen. Im Gesamten erfleht das Gebet von Gott für den König göttliche Qualitäten, damit dieser als Mandatar und Stellvertreter Gottes in rechter Weise sein Amt wahrnehmen kann. Bleibender Segen auf dem Königshaus ist dabei ein Zeichen der göttlichen Erwählung. Diese Erwählung hat die Septuaginta besonders durch die enge Verknüpfung mit der Väterverheißung (Gen 12.18 und 28) verstärkt.[105]

---

[101] Schimanowski, *Weisheit*, 148-53.

[102] Cf. *ABD* 2.508.

[103] Schaper, *Eschatology*, 96. Goldberg, "Die Namen des Messias," 77, holds that the temporal interpretation of Ps 72:5, 17 LXX on the king and his name has influenced *1 Enoch* on the royal Son of man.

[104] It is therefore not surprising that Ps 72 is never quoted in the NT.

[105] Schimanowski, *Weisheit*, 152-53.

3.2.6. Psalm 110:3 LXX

Another passage that is said to yield a similar interpretation about the pre-existence of the messiah is Ps 110 (109):3 LXX. Horbury cites P. Volz and J. Schaper,[106] who argue that this verse speaks about an eschatological saviour figure, whose pre-existence is expressed in the phrase πρὸ ἑωσφόρου ἐξεγέννησά σε and comparable with the messianic figure of *1 Enoch* (46:1; 48:6; 62:7).

Because the meaning of the Hebrew text is obscure, an attempt to rearrange and to make sense out of it can be detected from the Greek version:

עמך נדבת ביום חילך
בהדרי-קדש מרחם משחר לך טל ילדתיך

μετὰ σοῦ ἡ ἀρχὴ ἐν ἡμέρᾳ τῆς δυνάμεώς σου
ἐν ταῖς λαμπρότησιν τῶν ἁγίων
ἐκ γαστρὸς πρὸ ἑωσφόρου ἐξεγέννησά σε

When the two texts are set side by side it becomes quite obvious that עמך was read as עמְּךָ (μετὰ σοῦ) and נדבת was behind ἡ ἀρχὴ.[107] The following expression ἐν ἡμέρᾳ τῆς δυνάμεώς σου "in the day of your power" is the result of a literal translation of the Hebrew ביום חילך. However, the meaning of the rest of the verse in Hebrew is almost unintelligible: "in sacred splendours, from (or: from the time of) the womb of the dawn . . . to you the dew of your youth" (NJB). In contrast, the LXX rendering, which is much more coherent than the original Hebrew, distinctly describes the birth of a divine child.[108]

---

[106] Volz, *Eschatologie*, 204-05: "Auch die Septuaginta unterstreicht den übernatürlichen Charakter des eschatologischen Heilandes, seine himmlische Herkunft und Präexistenz. Nach Ps 109 = 110 ist er von Gott gezeugt, älter als der Morgenstern." Cf. also Bousset, *Die Religion*, 265: "Hier scheint auch den Uebersetzern der Messias als ein engelgleiches präexistentes Wesen vorzuschweben . . . ." Schaper, *Eschatology*, 101-7, makes a criticism against the exclusion of a temporal interpretation of πρὸ by Schimanowski, *Weisheit*, 139-41.

[107] Cf. R. J. Tournay, *Voir et entendre Dieu avec les Psaumes ou La liturgie prophétique du Second Temple à Jerusalem* (CRB 24; Paris: Gabalda, 1988), 168.

[108] Mowinckel, *He That Cometh*, 67, and many other OT scholars think that the LXX is close to the sense of the original Hebrew text, arguing that the corruption of the present Hebrew text may have resulted from deliberate efforts by scribes to conceal the meaning. Cf. A. Bentzen, *Introduction to the Old Testament* (Copenhagen: Gad, 1952), 100. From the absence of any allusion to v.3 in the NT, H.-J. Kraus, *Psalmen* (BKAT 15/1; Neukirchen-Vluyn: Neukirchener Verlag, 1960), 2.764, concluded that probably its meaning was unknown.

With you [will] the dominion [rest] on the day of your power
in the radiance [or: brightness] of the saints
from the womb I have begotten you before the morning star.

Schaper points out that translating ἑωσφόρος merely as "dawn" misses the
point as it has the very specific meaning of "the Morning-star."[109] While
Schaper admits that behind the Greek term ἑωσφόρος may have been a
reading of the *hapax legomenon* מִשְׁחָר as מִשַּׁחַר "from dawn,"[110] he is
convinced that it does not fully explain the translators' choice of ἑωσφόρος
rather than ἕως. The translators opted for a much more specific vocabulary
than the mere Greek equivalent for the Hebrew word שׁחר.[111] Like Volz,
Schaper is convinced that in the words of πρὸ ἑωσφόρου ἐξεγέννησά σε the
pre-existence of the messiah is expressed.

To strengthen his argument Schaper places this peculiar interpretation
within the psalm as a whole. He finds in the words of λαμπρότησιν τῶν
ἁγίων the idea of likening saints or wise men to the radiance of heavenly
bodies (Dan 12:3; 1En 39:7; 16:7; 104:2; Matt 13:43).[112] Schaper finds in
the Greek version a very different context from that of the Hebrew text.
The Greek Psalm provides "a context that relates primaeval (πρὸ ἑωσφόρου
ἐξεγέννησά σε) to future events (ῥάβδον δυνάμεώς σου ἐξαποστελεῖ
κύριος), thereby qualifying the ἡμέρᾳ τῆς δυνάμεώς σου. On this day, the
saviour's *potential* might (cp. v.1) will finally be actualized (cp. v.2:
ἐξαποστελεῖ), and he will exercise his powers in communion with the saints
in their heavenly splendour."[113]

Schaper goes on to comment on the importance of the relation between
the saviour figure and the saints in an eschatological context:

The 'brilliance' (λαμπρότης) of the saints is not just a piece of literary imagery. It refers
us to a body of beliefs elevating the saints to a *heavenly* existence, either in terms of their
pre-existence, or as a consequence of the last judgement. These two aspects are
inextricably linked, since the eschatological action is generally expected to be a *restitutio
in integrum* of primaeval perfection. This relation between primaeval and eschatological
events finds its expression in a number of ways. It may be called an early example of the
employment of analogies in religious thought.[114]

---

[109] LSJ, 752. Cf. the references to its occurrences in Greek literature. See also its
occurrences in the LXX (Job 11:17; 38:12; 41:9; 1Kgs 30:17; Isa 14:12). NJB has "from
the womb before the dawn I begot you."

[110] This is the suggestion of BHS.

[111] Schaper, *Eschatology*, 102.

[112] The LXX in its proto-Theodotionic version renders the Hebrew יזהרו כזהר הרקיע
והמשכלים as follows: καὶ οἱ συνιέντες ἐκλάμψουσιν ὡς ἡ λαμπρότης τοῦ στερεώματος.

[113] Schaper, *Eschatology*, 106.

[114] Schaper, *Eschatology*, 104.

According to Schaper, this analogy is seen in our psalm's correlation between the saviour figure's coming into existence prior to creation and his eschatological action in judgement. He finds striking parallels in other Jewish writings dealing with messianic saviour figures (cf. the "Son of Man" in 1En 48:3).[115]

Schaper contends that Ps 110 (109) LXX, which is firmly rooted in a set of beliefs about the heavenly existence of the saints, is not just about a messianic king, but about messianic judgement. He also claims that Ps 110 LXX shows a new usage of δυ□ναμις in a Hellenistic Jewish context. By the time of the Greek Psalter the significance of the word δυ□ναμις had already undergone "a shift from its original semantic field, the depiction of demonstrations of divine power in a given historical situation, to a new one, that of eschatological speculation."[116] Thus he contends that in the context of Ps 110 LXX "the saviour's ἡμέρᾳ τῆς δυνάμεώς is the day of the *manifestation* of his power, the outward symbol of which is his sceptre, the ῥάβδος δυνάμεως."[117]

However, we doubt whether Schaper's attempt to argue for the interpretation of the messiah as a pre-existent figure in Ps 110 LXX by recreating an eschatological context for the psalm is successful. His argument is too speculative and the difference in context is too subtle to press further. While it is very unlikely that the LXX translators were conscious of doing what Schaper proposes that they have done, we admit that the final rendering of v.3 becomes capable of being understood by later readers (e.g., early Christians?) as implying the pre-existence of the messiah.

After having surveyed the relevant texts from the LXX Horbury comes to the conclusion that in these texts:

the messianic king was envisaged, variously yet consistently, as *an angel-like spirit waiting to appear and be embodied*; the shining of a 'great light' corresponds to the birth of a child who is 'angel of great counsel', and the rising of a 'star' to the coming of a 'man', the man whose very name is 'dayspring', and who was before sun, moon and daystar.[118]

---

[115] For an attempt to dismiss a temporal understanding of the expression πρὸ ἑωσφόρου see Schimanowski, *Weisheit*, 139ff.

[116] Schaper, *Eschatology*, 107.

[117] Schaper, *Eschatology*, 107.

[118] Horbury, *Jewish Messianism*, 96 (emphasis mine), finds similar expectations with the heavenly sanctuary which waits above to be revealed, the "ready dwelling" in the LXX, and the depiction of the great enemy of the messianic king as the embodiment of an evil spirit, the archdemon Beliar (96-97).

Horbury also adduces evidence for "traces of a concept of pre-existence" from the ideas about God's foreknowledge of the messianic king in the Psalms of Solomon (17:23[21], 47[42]) and the "Messianic Rule" (1QSa) from Qumran, as well as two further messianic themes from rabbinic Jewish literature (the messiah as light and the soul of the messiah linking with the, or a, spirit of God).[119]

3.2.7. Concluding Remarks

Our review of Horbury and Schaper does not allow us to be as confident as they are as to whether we do witness a pre-existent messiah in Judaism by the time of the LXX translation for the following reasons:

First, as we have pointed out, the individual texts adduced by Horbury do not state or imply as much as he wants to see from them. For example, a spirit-inspired messiah is not necessarily a pre-existent messiah or a heavenly being.

Second, Horbury argues from the presence of a motif in one text that it is also present in other texts from the same corpus, where its presence is much less obvious, committing the fallacy of assuming that what is true for one occurrence of a word/idea is true for all or most other occurrences as well.

Third, one wonders whether what we find in the Greek LXX can be rightly assumed to be the view of Hebrew/Aramaic speaking Jews as well, especially if the apocalypses and Qumran documents testify to the same ideas. As most scholars agree, the messianic figure in *Ps. Sol.* 17 is portrayed as an earthly messiah. A connection that Horbury endeavours to find between the star-oracle in Numbers and the Jesse-oracle in Isaiah in later sources does not imply anything more than that these two messianic images were often brought together because they were already interpreted as messianic prophecies.

Fourth, although speculations about the pre-existence of the messiah's name cannot be equated with the pre-existence of the messiah himself, it encouraged some Jewish writers to think about the idea of the messiah as

---

[119] Horbury, *Jewish Messianism*, 97-108. However, J. J. Collins criticizes that, while Horbury is right to emphasize the heavenly character of the messiah in several Jewish texts from the first century AD, his argument seems to press too far in an attempt to harmonize various kinds of messiahs in the Jewish literature. Instead of admitting that various kinds of messiahs were envisaged he argues that even clearly earthly messiahs in the Messianic Rule (1QSa) from Qumran and the Psalms of Solomon show "traces of a concept of pre-existence." The reading in 1QSa is notoriously disputed, and in the Psalms of Solomon, the trace is a statement that God has knowledge of the beauty of the messianic king. Moreover, the diversity suggested by expectation of a priestly as well as a kingly messiah in the Dead Sea Scrolls is not considered adequately.

having existed in God's mind from the beginning, prior to the creation of the world. This might have created an atmosphere in which the messiah is not to be thought of only in terms of his human character, but also of his heavenly character. The most we can say is that there appears to be an atmosphere in pre-Christian Judaism leading *towards* an understanding of the messiah as a pre-existent figure.

Finally, it is therefore most likely that there was not a coherent concept of a pre-existent messiah before Christianity for the early church to readily apply it to Jesus. This assessment, however, does not completely rule out the possibility that some of the LXX texts (especially Ps 110:3) might have been interpreted as entailing the pre-existence of the messiah at a later stage by early Christians. The evidence thus strongly suggests that it would be more profitable for us to focus our attention to how the early church made use of these OT messianic texts in such a way that led to an understanding of Jesus' pre-existence than finding a ready-made category of pre-existence in pre-Christian Judaism into which Jesus could be placed. If we bear in mind that the Greek version of Ps 110:3 was to some extent capable of being interpreted in terms of the messiah's pre-existence by pre-Christian Jews, we cannot rule out the same possibility when early Christians read this text in the light of their exegesis of two most important messianic texts in the early church, two psalms speaking about the messiah being exalted to the right hand of God (Ps 110: 1) and being addressed as his Son (Ps 2:7).

3.3. Conclusion to Part II

Our discussion of Jewish traditions about various personified divine attributes, exalted angels and a pre-existent Messiah suggests that there was no ready-made category of pre-existent "beings" into which Jesus could be placed. Although our discussion was not meant to be a comprehensive criticism of recent scholarship, it certainly weakens their view that these traditions served as the real precedent for viewing Jesus as a divine and pre-existent being alongside God. Rather, the concepts of divine attributes and principal angels offered the Second Temple Jews a variety of religious language to speak about God's presence and/or action in the world without calling into question his transcendence and uniqueness.

In the following two chapters we will examine Jesus' self-consciousness of divine sonship and divine mission as the foundation for the early Christian understanding of him as the pre-existent Son of God. In Chapter 4 we will discuss whether and in what sense Jesus conceived himself to be the Son of God. The discussion here will be focused on his use of *abba* and other Synoptic texts that suggest his self-consciousness of being uniquely related to God as his Father and conceiving himself as God's Son (Mt 11:27; Mk 13:32; Mt 16:17; Lk 22:29; Mk 1:11 Mk 12:1-12). In Chapter 5 we will investigate whether and in what sense he was conscious of having come from and being sent by God. Here the discussion will be concentrated on those sayings that can be broadly grouped as "I have come" sayings (Mk 2:17 pars.; Mk 10:45 par.; Lk 19:19; 12:49, 51 par.) and "I was sent" sayings (Mt 15:24; Mk 9:37 pars.). At the end of the chapter we will evaluate the implications drawn from these dominical sayings and see if his self-consciousness of divine sonship and divine origin does amount to his divinity and if it is indeed compatible with a consciousness of pre-existence. To this task we now turn in the next two chapters.

Chapter 4

Jesus' Self-Consciousness of Divine Sonship

One of the most important titles given to Jesus in the NT is undoubtedly the title "Son of God." The four Gospels unanimously present a portrayal of Jesus speaking of God as his Father and of himself as his Son. One of the most common views about Jesus' divine sonship today, however, asserts that the application of this title to Jesus in the NT documents was a late development and it cannot be traced back to his self-consciousness of his divine sonship. While the "Son of God" was originally understood simply as a means of expressing the close relationship of the royal Messiah to God, the early church applied it to Jesus because his resurrection was seen as the moment when he became the Son of God.[1] Subsequently, the early church gradually pushed the inauguration of Jesus' status as Son of God back to the Transfiguration (Mk 9:7), then to his baptism (Mk 1:11) and finally either to his virginal conception or pre-existence.[2] However, if it can be shown that Jesus conceived himself to be the Son of God – understood as one who stands in a unique personal relationship to God as his Father – and conveyed this self-understanding to his first disciples, this common view would collapse.

In this chapter we will argue that Jesus' self-consciousness of his divine sonship – understood as standing in a unique and intimate relationship to God – did not only play the most significant part in the development of an early Christian understanding of him as the Son of God but served as the *foundation* for their conviction that he is also the pre-existent Son of God.

---

[1] J. D. G. Dunn, *Christology in the Making: a New Testament Inquiry into the Origins of the Doctrine of the Incarnation* (London: SCM, 1980, 1989), 35-36. For instance, Dunn argued that "primitive Christian preaching seems to have regarded Jesus' resurrection as the day of his appointment to divine sonship, as the event by which he became God's son." He supports his case with Rom 1:3-4 and Acts 13:33, "the earliest (traceable) Christian use of Ps. 2.7." See also B. Lindars, *New Testament Apologetic: the Doctrinal Significance of the Old Testament Quotations* (London: SCM, 1961), 140-43; E. Lövestam, *Son and Saviour: A Study of Acts 13, 32-37* (Lund: Gleerup, 1961), 23-48; B. M. F. van Iersel, *'Der Sohn' in den synoptischen Jesusworten* (Leiden: Brill, 1961), 66-73, 83, 174-75; Schweizer, "υἱός," *TDNT* 8.367; R. E. Brown, *The Birth of the Messiah: a Commentary on the Infancy Narratives in the Gospels of Matthew and Luke* (New York: Doubleday, 1993), 29-30, 136.

[2] Schweizer, *TDNT* 8.366-74.

In an anticipation of our fuller arguments to come later in this study, such an understanding of him, however, was only possible with the aid of their scriptural exegesis of the two most important messianic psalms, which I would call the *catalyst*, understood in the sense of a means of speeding up a certain process to help reach its final goal. In other words, an understanding of Jesus as the *pre-existent* Son was crystallized as they brought out the full significance of God's words written down in Ps 110:1 and Ps 2:7 in the light of Jesus' self-consciousness of divine sonship as it is reflected in his self-revelatory statements. It is important to recognize that this process was an interactive process and it was not possible without one or the other. Early Christian conviction about Jesus' pre-existence was only possible through their christological exegesis of Ps 110:1 and Ps 2:7 as it was done in the light of the very foundation Jesus himself laid for his followers. Early Christian exegetes were able to reflect upon Jesus' self-consciousness of divine sonship and build upon this foundation their fuller understanding of him as the pre-existent Son of God who is "literally" enthroned at his Father's right hand. It is therefore vitally important for us to investigate whether Jesus was conscious of his divine sonship and, if so, in what sense he referred to God as his Father and saw himself as his Son.

4.1. Methodological Remarks

4.1.1. Criteria for the Authenticity of Jesus' Sayings

Intrinsic to research on the quest for the historical Jesus is a very important tool for ascertaining whether or not a certain saying or action is authentic. In recent years the various criteria have been carefully sorted out and some dubious criteria have been dismissed.

One of the best presentations of the criteria of authenticity has been set out by J. P. Meier, who lists five primary criteria for authenticity:[3]

(1) *the criterion of embarrassment*: it focuses on actions or sayings of Jesus would have embarrassed or created difficulty for the early church;

---

[3] J. P. Meier, *A Marginal Jew: Rethinking the Historical Jesus* (New York: Doubleday, 1991-2001), 1.168-84. He also set out four secondary or dubious criteria: (1) the criterion of traces of Aramaic; (2) the criterion of Palestinian environment; (3) the criterion of vividness of narration; and (4) the criterion of the tendencies of the developing Synoptic tradition. For further discussion, with more detail and more examples, see R. H. Stein, "The 'Criteria' for Authenticity" in *Studies of History and Tradition in the Four Gospels* (eds. R. T. France *et al.*; Sheffield: JSOT Press, 1980), 225-63; C. A. Evans, "Recent Development in Jesus Research: Presuppositions, Criteria, and Sources" in *Jesus and His Contemporaries: Comparative Studies* (Leiden: Brill, 1995), 13-26.

(2) *the criterion of dissimilarity*: also labelled criterion of discontinuity, originality, or plausibility it focuses on words or deeds of Jesus that cannot be derived either from Judaism at the time of Jesus or from the early church after him;

(3) *the criterion of multiple attestation*: it focuses on those sayings or deeds of Jesus that are attested in more than one independent literary source (e.g., Mark, Q, Paul, John) and/or in more than one literary form or genre (e.g., parable, dispute story, miracle story, prophecy, aphorism);

(4) *the criterion of coherence*: also labelled criterion of consistency it holds that other sayings and actions of Jesus that fit in well with the preliminary data established by the above three criteria have a good chance of being historical;

(5) *the criterion of rejection and execution*: it gives great significance to the historical fact that Jesus met a violent end at the hands of Jewish and Roman officials and then asks us what historical words and deeds of Jesus can explain his trial and crucifixion.

(6) To the above five criteria we would add the sixth one, *the criterion of Semitisms and Palestinian background*: materials which reflect Semitic ways of expression and Palestinian background (especially those which are most plausibly explained as literal translations from Aramaic) clearly go back at least to the earliest days of the church when it was still an Aramaic-speaking or bilingual group in Jerusalem.[4]

In the past, great importance has been assigned to the criterion of double dissimilarity as the key tool for assessment.[5] With this criterion, critical scholars isolated a pool of authentic traditions of Jesus on which to work and then used them as a basis for ascertaining other traditions which may be authentic (the criterion of coherence).[6] The results obtained by the

---

[4] Although Meier regards this criterion as secondary or dubious, we would certainly give more weight to this criterion than Meier does. Moreover, it is important to note that this criterion cannot be used to rule out materials which are more Greek or Hellenistic in character, since we know that Judaea and especially Galilee were subject to Hellenistic influences, and since people can have translated what Jesus said with greater or less literalism.

[5] So E. Käsemann, "The Problem of the Historical Jesus" in *Essays on New Testament Themes* (London: SCM, 1964), 37; J. M. Robinson, *A New Quest of the Historical Jesus* (Studies in Biblical Theology 25; London: SCM, 1959), 116-19; R. H. Fuller, *The Foundations of New Testament Christology* (London: Lutterworth, 1965), 18; N. Perrin, *Rediscovering the Teaching of Jesus* (New Testament Library; London: SCM, 1967) 89; D. L. Mealand, "Dissimilarity Test" *SJT* 31 (1978), 41-50.

[6] So N. Perrin, *What Is Redaction Criticism?* (Guides to Biblical Scholarship; Philadelphia: Fortress Press, 1969), 71; D. Polkow, "Method and criteria for historical Jesus research" in *Society of Biblical Literature Seminar Papers* (ed. D. J. Lull; Atlanta: Scholars Press, 1987), 347.

use of this criterion are often considered more assured than those obtained from other criteria formulated (e.g., the criterion of multiple attestation).

It is becoming increasingly recognized that the negative use of this criterion is, however, untenable. Its primary weaknesses of this criterion are the following. First, by its very nature, it goes in search of a peculiar Jesus and not a characteristic one.[7] What may be characteristic of Jesus is not necessarily unique. And by focusing only on the unique aspects, a skewed picture of Jesus is obtained. Second, it presupposes that Jesus must be divorced from his Jewish environment.[8] Third, it assumes that Jesus made no influence on the post-Easter community whatsoever.[9] Fourth, for this criterion to be viable, complete knowledge on our part of first-century Judaism and the theology of the early church is required.[10]

We propose that this criterion should not be the key tool and that it should be used positively and not negatively. In other words, any material from the Jesus tradition which passes the test of this criterion should be judged authentic, but even if it does not meet the requirements of this criterion it should not be judged automatically as inauthentic. Instead, other criteria should be brought into service to ascertain the possibility of its authenticity.

In the light of the danger of misuse and abuse we are not committed to any single criterion in particular, but we will make use all of them as appropriate and recognize, at the same time, their limitations. In our arguments for the authenticity of a particular saying we shall attempt to show how past arguments against its authenticity are mistaken and provide arguments to show why we consider the contrary to be correct.[11] As the question of authenticity is a very important issue for our arguments for Jesus' self-consciousness of divine sonship and divine origin, much attention will be given to it in our study.

---

[7] M. D. Hooker, "On Using the Wrong Tool" *Theology* 75 (1972), 574.

[8] More recent scholars have replaced it with a criterion of "plausibility" which asks: "what is plausible in the Jewish context and makes the rise of Christianity understandable"? See G. Theissen and A. Merz, *The Historical Jesus: a Comprehensive Guide* (London: SCM, 1998), 116-18.

[9] If the first two assumptions were correct, it would make Jesus a man without parallel in history since he neither depended on his predecessors nor influenced his followers at any point. See S. C. Goetz and C. L. Blomberg, "The Burden of Proof" *JSNT* 11 (1981), 43.

[10] Hooker, "On Using the Wrong Tool," 575.

[11] Cf. S. Westerholm, *Jesus and Scribal Authority* (Coniectanea Biblica: New Testament Series 10; Lund: Gleerup, 1978), 8-10.

4.1.2. Handing Down of the Gospel Tradition

Related to the question of authenticity is the question of the handing down of the Gospel tradition, which can be approached from two different perspectives.

It has been commonly assumed that the traditions about Jesus were handed down in the form of isolated units and that the chronological framework in which they have been placed in the Gospels is secondary and largely historically worthless. This theory was defended by K. L. Schmidt in 1919 and it has been accepted uncritically by scholars ever since.[12] However, it has now been subjected to a thorough criticism by D. R. Hall who demonstrated just how much it is based on arbitrary assumptions.[13]

The next question is about the reliability of the Gospel tradition. It asks how the actual material was handed down and whether it was handed down reliably. There are two main contrasting positions.

On the one hand, we have the position of the dominant school in study of the Q document; it argues for a series of separate stages in which the material was radically developed, giving rather different impressions of Jesus at each stage. This suggests very active creativity that was linked to the situation and needs of a specific community.

On the other hand, we have the sort of view espoused by R. Riesner and B. Gerhardsson which emphasizes the role of Jesus as a teacher and the faithful handing down of his teaching by responsible people.[14] This picture has received strong backing from K. E. Bailey with his theory of controlled tradition.[15] Bailey distinguishes between what he calls informal uncontrolled oral tradition, formal controlled oral tradition and informal controlled oral tradition. The first of these categories is what Bultmann envisaged: oral transmission that was in no way controlled by the community and so was allowed to run riot. Over against this view was that of Gerhardsson which stressed the place of special persons, the apostles

---

[12] K. L. Schmidt, *Der Rahmen der Geschichte Jesu: literarkritische Untersuchungen zur ältesten Jesusüberlieferung* (Berlin: Trowitzsch, 1919).

[13] D. R. Hall, *The Gospel Framework: Fiction or Fact?: a Critical Evaluation of Der Rahmen der Geschichte Jesu by Karl Ludwig Schmidt* (Carlisle: Paternoster, 1998).

[14] R. Riesner, *Jesus als Lehrer: eine Untersuchung zum Ursprung der Evangelien-Überlieferung* (WUNT 2/7; Tübingen: Mohr Siebeck, 1981); B. Gerhardsson, *The Reliability of the Gospel Tradition* (Peabody: Hendrickson, 2001). We happily align ourselves with this approach. Cf. B. F. Meyer, "Some Consequences of Birger Gerhardsson's Account of the Origins of the Gospel Tradition," *Jesus and the Oral Gospel Tradition* (JSNTSup 4; ed. H. Wansbrough; Sheffield: Sheffield Academic Press, 1991), 424-40.

[15] K. E. Bailey, "Middle Eastern Oral Tradition and the Synoptic Gospels" *ExpTim* 106 (1995), 363-67; K. E. Bailey, "Informal Controlled Oral Tradition and the Synoptic Gospels" *Themelios* 20.2 (1995), 4-11.

and others, in the preservation and memorization of the 'holy word' concerning Jesus. Bailey advocates a third model, where traditions can be handed down flexibly – the wording is not sacrosanct – but nevertheless there is control exercised by the audience who know whether the stories they are hearing are faithful in substance to what they have heard previously. Bailey argues that this mechanism, which he has personally observed in the Middle East, gives us the clue to what went on in the early church. The implication for our study is that, if this second approach is compelling, then it will also broadly affect one's approach to the question of authenticity of the Jesus tradition!

4.2. Contemporary Debate on Jesus' Use of Abba

It was Joachim Jeremias who championed the view that Jesus' use of *abba* as an address to God in his prayers is completely novel and unique and expresses the heart of Jesus relationship to God.[16] Jeremias's position can be set forth in his own words:

> In the literature of Palestinian Judaism *no evidence has yet been found* of "my Father" being used by an individual as an address to God. . . . It is quite unusual that Jesus should have addressed God as "my Father"; it is even more so that he should have used the Aramaic form *Abba.* . . . We do not have a single example of God being addressed as *abba* in Judaism, but Jesus *always* addressed God in this way in his prayers.[17]

Jeremias stressed the fact that as an individual Jesus addressed God as *abba* in his prayers. Jeremias's basic claim was not that Jesus' *view of God* was entirely novel, but his *mode of address* to God was novel because his relationship to God was distinctive. In other words, some texts that expressed a corporate relationship to God (e.g., later rabbinic prayers addressing God as "father") or the general use of Father imagery to describe some activity of God – rather than the actual addressing of God as Father – (e.g., *b.Ta'an* 34b) were not true parallels to Jesus' usage.

4.2.1. Evidence for Jewish Precedents

James Barr argued in his article "'Abba' Isn't 'Daddy'" that the available evidence favours the view that children used the adult term rather than

---

[16] J. Jeremias, *New Testament Theology* (London: SCM, 1971), 67. See also his *Prayers of Jesus*, 57-65.

[17] Jeremias, *Theology*, 64-66 (emphasis his).

Jesus using a childish term.[18] It is true that Jeremias, in his earlier argument, had postulated that Jesus used the language of a small child addressing his father (e.g., as if *abba* meant something like "daddy"), but, to his credit, he later changed his mind because he saw that *abba* was a form of address used even by an adult of his father.[19] Thus, although J. Barr was quite right to emphasize that *abba* does not mean "daddy," this must not be taken as an adequate criticism of Jeremias's mature form of argument. "The term *abba* is clearly enough an intimate way of addressing God using family language, whether by a small child or an adult, and as such is surely less formal than addressing God simply as God or Lord."[20]

G. Vermes claimed that Jeremias was wrong when he concluded that "*we do not have a single example* of God being addressed as *Abba* in Judaism."[21] Vermes provided the following Jewish texts as the basis of his criticism: *b.Ta'an.* 23b; *Tg. Mal.* 2:10; and *Tg. Ps.* 89:27. Let us see whether Vermes's criticism is valid.

First, *b.Ta'an.* 23b recounts a story related to Hanin ha Nehba, a grandson of Onias the Circle-maker, who lived at the end of the first century B.C. The text reads: "Hanin ha-Nehba was the son of the daughter of Onias the Circle-maker. When the world needed rain, our teachers used to send schoolchildren to him, who seized the hem of his coat and implored him: '*Abba, abba habh lan mitra*," ("Father, father give us rain"). He said to Him (God): 'Master of the world, grant it (the rain) for the sake of these who are not yet able to distinguish between an *abba* who has the power to give rain and an *abba* who has not.'"[22] Jeremias rightly noted that Hanin is not addressing God as *abba* in prayer, but simply repeating what the children say. In fact, what we have here is a play on words, so typical of Jewish teachers and *hasids* of that time.[23] God is addressed with the proper phrase "Master of the world." What this text does prove, however, is that *abba* was used by small children of their elders, in this case a revered teacher, although it was more commonly used of one's father.

Second, *Tg. Mal.* 2:10 (הלא אבא חד לכולנא) uses *abba* for God because the Hebrew original makes the rendering *abba* necessary. However, it is important to make a distinction between merely applying *abba* to God and

---

[18] See J. Barr, "'Abba' Isn't 'Daddy'" *JTS* 39 (1988), 28-47; also his "Abba, Father," 173-79. Barr recognizes that Jeremias did not maintain that Jesus called God "Daddy."

[19] See Jeremias's self correction in his *Theology*, 67.

[20] B. Witherington and L. M. Ice, *The Shadow of the Almighty* (Grand Rapids: Eerdmans, 2002), 22.

[21] Jeremias, *Theology*, 66 (emphasis his).

[22] This text was first pointed out by J. Leipoldt, *Jesu Verhältnis zu Juden und Griechen* (Leipzig, 1941), 136-37.

[23] J. Jeremias, *The Prayers of Jesus* (SBT 2/6; London: SCM, 1967), 61.

actually invoking him by using it.[24] The latter case is the only true parallel to Jesus' use.

Third, *Tg. Ps.* 89:27 (אחי אבא לי יקרא) is most likely to be taken as evidence that Jesus saw himself as the Davidic messiah rather than supporting the view that some people in Jesus' time addressed God as *abba*.[25]

Another attempt to undermine Jeremias's argument comes from Dunn, who provided as evidence the following Second Temple Jewish texts: Wis 14:3; Sir 23:1, 4; 51:10; and 3 Macc 6:3, 8.[26] Examples from Wisdom and 3 Maccabees, however, are not useful because they were most likely composed in Greek and do not go back to a Semitic original. If so, it is fruitless to cite such evidence to show that *abba* may have been used by Jews before or during Jesus' day. The book of Sirach was probably composed in Hebrew by Sirach around 180 BC and translated into Greek a generation or two later by his grandson.[27] In Sir 51:10 God is addressed in Hebrew as *abi*, not as *abba*, the Aramaic term of endearment, and in the Greek version of Sir 23:4 God is called *kurie pater*. Thus, the evidence from all these texts only suggests that there was a growing use of the term "Father" for God, even in prayer during the Second Temple period (cf. Wis 14:3).[28]

In relation to evidence from Jewish texts which might be taken as against Jesus' distinctive or unique use of *abba*, J. Barr cites, in addition to other arguments (e.g., *abba* is not "daddy"), evidence from Targums, especially the Targum of Isaiah.[29] His case, however, is not likely to stand up to close scrutiny, for the Targumic texts that he cites are representative of later Aramaic. It is important to note that in later Aramaic there was a tendency to drop the initial consonant *aleph* on words.[30] As Fitzmyer suggested, both the Qumran Aramaic and the Aramaic words and substratum in the NT do not fit into the grammar and style of late Aramaic (post- 200 AD), but middle Aramaic (200 BC to AD 200).[31] Qumran Aramaic makes clear that the emphatic state had not yet become weak

---

[24] Jeremias, *Prayers*, 60-61.

[25] B. Witherington, *The Christology of Jesus* (Minneapolis: Fortress, 1990), 216-17.

[26] Dunn, *Christology*, 27. See also M. R. D'Angelo, "Abba and Father: Imperial Theology and the Jesus Traditions" *JBL* 111 (1992), 619-22.

[27] Cf. Di Lella, "Wisdom of Ben-Sira," *ABD* 6.931.

[28] Witherington, *Christology*, 217.

[29] Barr, "'Abba' Isn't 'Daddy'," 28-47 and *idem*, "Abba, Father," 173-79.

[30] J. A. Fitzmyer, "Methodology in the Study of the Aramaic Substratum of Jesus' Sayings in the New Testament" in *Jesus aux origines de la Christologie* (ed. J. Dupont; Gembloux: Leuven University Press, 1975), 92-93.

[31] Fitzmyer, "Methodology," 84-85.

during and before the New Testament period.[32] With Jesus' use of *abba* we are dealing with words that have the emphatic ending in -a, and this makes Barr's criticism less compelling.

As recently as 1990 a text from Qumran (4Q372 1) was published by E. H. Schuller, who claims that it provides evidence for the use of *abi* as an address to God.[33] Named as the Psalm of Joseph, it includes a prayer in which Joseph addresses God as אבי ואלהי "my father and my God" (4Q372 1.16). In light of this evidence some scholars contended that Jeremias's conclusion that "there is as yet no evidence in the literature of ancient Palestinian Judaism that 'my father' is used as a personal address to God"[34] is no longer true.[35] The new Qumran text can thus nullify Jeremias's conclusion on this specific point, but it still does not provide us with examples of the use of *abba* at all, much less *abba* in prayer language. The word *ab* with the possessive suffix *i* means 'my father,' not simply Father or the Father.

To sum up, the evidence we have suggests that Jeremias's earlier view that Jesus was using a childish term is an overstatement, as he himself admitted. However, Barr's attempt to deny that the term belongs to family language is equally inappropriate. Moreover, many attempts to criticize Jeremias' use of Jewish evidence for his claim that *abba* is a unique feature of Jesus' prayer language are not compelling enough to overthrow his claim.

4.2.2. Linguistic Evidence for the Origin of "Abba"

In addition to the debate over Jewish precedents for Jesus' use of *abba* as an address to God, there have been various attempts to account for the possible origin of this Aramaic term from a linguistic point of view.[36]

First, it is often explained as *a child's word*, a baby's babbling sound with a special familiar connotation, much like English "papa" or

---

[32] Cf. J. A. Fitzmyer, *The Genesis Apocryphon of Cave 1: a Commentary* (Rome: Biblical Institute Press, 1971), 220.

[33] E. M. Schuller, "4Q372 1: a Text about Joseph" *RQ* 14/55 (1990), 343-76. She also refers to another prayer text from Qumran (4Q460) in connection with 4Q372, and concludes that "4Q372 and 4Q460 suggest that this manner of addressing God may have been more common in Palestinian Judaism than hithertoward suspected (p.363); see also E. M. Schuller, "The Psalm of 4Q372.1 Within the Context of 2nd Temple Prayer: Genre and Prosody of Jewish and Christian Piety in Psalmody" *CBQ* 54 (1992), 67-79.

[34] Jeremias, *Prayers*, 29.

[35] Cf. D'Angelo, "Abba and Father," 618.

[36] Here we are indebted to J. A. Fitzmyer, "Abba and Jesus' Relation to God" in *A cause de l'Evangile: études sur les Synoptiques et les Actes* (ed. F. Refoule; Paris: Cerf, 1985), 15-38.

"daddy."[37] The doubling of the *b* in the form of *'ab* "father" (from Protosemitic *'abū*) may have been influenced by its female counterpart *'immā'*, "mother," where the doubling of *m* is original (from Protosemitic *'immū'*).

Second, Aramaic *'abbā'* reflects *the emphatic state* of the noun *'ab*, basically meaning "the father."[38]

Third, rather than the emphatic state the Aramaic *'abbā'* is a special form developed by the addition of an (originally Protosemitic) adverbial ending *-ā'* to become *a vocative*.[39]

However, Fitzmyer proposed a slightly different view. While he accepts that the Aramaic *'abbā'* can be used as a vocative, he insists that it is still an emphatic state: "There is no reason to invoke the survival of an ancient ending *-ā'* to explain what otherwise appears to be an emphatic state."[40] Rejecting the view that the Greek translation added to the Aramaic *'abbā'* (Mk 14:36) was not correct Greek usage,[41] Fitzmyer insists that the Greek translation regarded the Aramaic form as an emphatic state, since it uses ὁ πατήρ. Fitzmyer gives examples from classical and Hellenistic sources as well as the LXX and the NT where the nominative case was used at times as a substitute for the vocative. Fitzmyer thus concludes that "when the Greek translation was added to *abba* the articular nominative not only reflected the emphatic state of the original but also made use of a not-too-common, but certainly correct Greek usage to do so."[42]

---

[37] Jeremias, *Prayers*, 58. It is important to add that Jeremias retracted an earlier view that *abba* was the language of a tiny child, "baby-talk" or babble, a position that he himself had once advanced.

[38] Fitzmyer, "Abba and Jesus' Relation to God," 17: "One would normally expect the emphatic state to be *'ᵃbā'* or possibly *'ᵃbāh*, with a reduced vowel in the pretonic syllable, as it is in some other forms of Aramaic. The Greek *abba'*, however, with the doubled *beta* clearly reflects the Aramaic form *'abbā'* that is attested in vocalized texts from antiquity." See also G. H. Dalman, *The Words of Jesus: Considered in the Light of Post-Biblical Jewish Writings and the Aramaic Language* (Edinburgh: T & T Clark, 1902), 192.

[39] Proponents of this view are T. Nöldeke, E. Littmann, G. Kittel, J. Barr, and J. Jeremias among others.

[40] Fitzmyer, "Abba and Jesus' Relation to God," 18.

[41] This view is supported by the fact that the Greek language has a vocative for addressing a person and could have rendered *'abbā'* properly as *pater*, the very form used in Lk 22:42, where the evangelist avoids the foreign word because of his predominantly Gentile Greek-speaking readers.

[42] Fitzmyer, "Abba and Jesus' Relation to God," 19-20.

4.2.3. Jesus' View of God as Father

Criticisms of Jeremias were not confined to Jewish evidence or linguistic evidence. Instead of merely focusing on whether Jesus really used *abba* in his prayer to God or the origin and the significance of the term, the contemporary debate about Jesus' use of *abba* revolves around whether Jesus held decidedly new convictions about God or his understanding falls in with the views of his contemporaries. In other words, some scholars stress the continuity between Jesus' convictions about God and those of the Jewish matrix from which he came,[43] while others uphold that Jesus' use of Father for God was new and distinct, surpassing all previous characterization of God of Israel.[44] Nevertheless, most scholars share the assumption that Jesus did indeed call God Father and the term that he probably used for God was *abba*, although there is a bald denial that Jesus used the designation Father for God at all.[45]

4.2.3.1. Did Jesus Speak of God as Father?

One of the main criticisms against Jeremias's contention that Jesus addressed God as *abba* is that there is insufficient evidence for the actual

---

[43] This group includes B. S. Childs, *Biblical Theology of the Old and New Testaments* (Minneapolis: Fortress, 1992), 358: "Jesus brought no new concept of God, but he demonstrated in action the full extent of God's redemptive will for the world which was from the beginning." Similarly, N. T. Wright, *Jesus and the Victory of God* (London: SPCK, 1996), 130, interprets Jesus' distinctive vision of a loving and forgiving God manifested in the parable of the prodigal son: "For Israel's god to act in this way is not an innovation; it is consistent with his character as revealed throughout Israel's long and chequered history. This is who he is, who he will be." For Wright it was the appropriation of these beliefs to his own mission and vocation that distinguished Jesus. M. M. Thompson, *The Promise of the Father: Jesus and God in the New Testament* (Louisville: Westminster/John Knox, 2000).

[44] Cf. W. Bousset, *Jesu Predigt in ihrem Gegensatz zum Judentum: Ein religionschichtlicher Vergleich* (Göttingen: Vandenhoeck & Ruprecht, 1892), 41, 43, cited and translated in G. F. Moore, "Christian Writers on Judaism" *HTR* 14 (1921), 242: "What is most completely original and truly creative in the preaching of Jesus comes out most strongly and purely when he proclaims God the heavenly Father. . . . The [Judaism of Jesus' time] had neither in name nor in fact the faith of the Father-God; it could not possibly rise to it." Also R. Bultmann, *Theology of the New Testament* (London: SCM, 1952), 1.23-25; G. Kittel, *TDNT* 1.6: "Jesus' term for God . . . shows how this Father-child relationship to God far surpasses any possibilities of intimacy assumed in Judaism, introducing indeed something which is wholly new"; Jeremias, *Prayers*, 11-65; Witherington and Ice, *Shadow*, 28: "the prevalence of the use of Father language for God in the early church comes from Jesus' own use of such language, and more to the point, comes from Jesus' own intimate and special relationship with the Father, which set him apart from other and early Jews in important ways."

[45] Most notably, D'Angelo, "Abba and Father," 611-30.

references of the term *abba*. The very word *abba* occurs only three times in the entire NT, and only once in the gospels, at Mark 14:36, and it is urged that this is not enough evidence on which to base the conclusion that *abba* was Jesus' preferred, indeed exclusive, name for God.

Mary Rose D'Angelo categorically denies that "the Gospels do not and cannot support the claim that Jesus always addressed God as 'Father.' The most the NT enables us to conclude is that 'father' is seen by the NT authors as an appropriate address for God, and that 'father' is more important to John, Matthew, and Luke than to Mark and Q."[46] Her argument can be set forth in her own words:

> *Abba* cannot be attributed to Jesus with any certainty. It was certainly of significance in the early Greek-speaking Christian communities of Paul and Mark, where it expressed empowerment through the spirit. It may have originated or been of special importance in the Syrian communities, where Paul began his career and which many scholars see as the venue of Mark. . . . *"Father" as an address to God cannot be shown to originate with Jesus*, to be particularly important to his teaching, or even to have been used by him.[47]

Her contention is, however, far from convincing in the light of evidence available before us. First, whenever Jesus directly addresses God in the Gospels he always speaks to God as Father except for the so-called cry of dereliction from the cross (Mk 15:34, "My God, my God, why have you forsaken me?") which is a quotation of the opening line of Psalm 22.[48] To put matters the other way around, Jesus never addresses God as King or Master or by other terms familiar to early Jews, including landowner, farmer, master, king, and judge, etc. This phenomenon is significant and needs explanation.

Second, Jesus alone is portrayed in the Gospels as speaking of God as "my Father," and outside the Gospels the phrase "my Father" appears only

---

[46] D'Angelo, "Abba and Father," 618. D'Angelo makes criticism of Jeremias on a number of points: (1) the evidence for the use of the word *abba* in the NT is extremely slender (three times in the entire NT, and only once in the Gospels). (2) Nor can *abba* be credited to Jesus on the grounds that it is distinct from the usage of the early church. (3) Although Jeremias retreated from the claim that *abba* had the same connotations as "daddy" and acknowledged that the word was in common use by adults and was used as a mark of respect for old men and for teachers, he continued to stress the origins in babytalk and the consequent intimacy as a distinctive feature of Jesus' use of *abba*.

[47] D'Angelo, "Abba and Father," 630 (emphasis ours). Approaching the matter slightly differently, Thompson, *Promise*, 30, also argues that "even if Jesus' use of the vernacular in prayer were the decisive issue, it is still curious that no one is ever shown as objecting to Jesus' use of *abba* because of its startling connotations." However, this argument is problematic because, besides the fact that it is an argument from silence, when we are dealing with *abba* as an address to God we are talking about Jesus' prayer language rather than his form of public discourse with anyone other than his disciples.

[48] Thompson, *Promise*, 28.

on Jesus' lips (Rev 2:27; 3:5; 3:21). Jesus does not pray *with* his disciples "Our Father!" but rather he teaches his disciples to do so as part of *their* corporate prayer life (cf. Mt 6:9; Lk 11:2). Moreover, evidence from the earliest NT documents suggests that early Christians only began to pray to God as *abba* as a result of having received the Holy Spirit who prompts such prayer (cf. Rom 8:15-16; Gal 4:6). In other words, there is a distinction between the prayer life of Jesus and that of the disciples during Jesus' ministry. This demonstrates that only Jesus actually addressed God as *abba* during his ministry and the disciples were able and prompted to do so when they received the eschatological Spirit.[49] Thus, it is highly unlikely that the sonship of Jesus was qualitatively identical with that of early Christians, and as such it suggests that Jesus had a consciousness of a unique personal relationship to God as his Father.[50]

Third, when Jesus was in the garden of Gethsemane praying for guidance, Jesus addressed God as *abba* (Mk 14:36).[51] The setting suggests an earnest pleading with God in the most intimate of terms.[52]

And finally, "Father" for God is found in multiple sources in the Gospels (Mark, Q, M, and L).[53] In some of this material, especially the Q saying attested in Mt 11:25-27/Lk 10:21-22, the intimate relationship between the Father and the Son is strongly emphasized.[54] They share knowledge that others do not have unless the Son dispenses it.

In the light of the above evidence it is fair to conclude that Jesus addressed God as Father and he taught his disciples to do so, but at the same time he made a clear distinction between his own relationship to the Father and that of his followers.

---

[49] Thompson, *Promise*, 65, is right when she writes: "a more plausible hypothesis, in light of the restricted use of Father in Paul and its virtual disappearance in Acts [only in Acts 1:5, 8 and 2:33] and other New Testament books, is that the usage was deemed characteristic of Jesus and thus was taken over in continuity with Jesus' own usage. Hence, the persistent use of 'our Father' and the absence of 'my Father' from the rest of the New Testament may suggest that both could be traced back to Jesus, with 'our Father' as a form of address commended to his followers and 'my Father' limited to Jesus himself."

[50] I. H. Marshall, "The Divine Sonship of Jesus" in *Jesus the Saviour: Studies in New Testament Theology* (Downers Grove: Inter-Varsity, 1990), 137.

[51] Thompson, *Promise*, 29, is right to point out that "Jeremias's contention that Jesus 'always addressed God as *abba*' is a deduction drawn from the whole gospel tradition rather than merely a descriptive summary of the evidence in that tradition."

[52] The fact that Luke and Matthew in the parallels to this text omit the term *abba* while retaining its translation as "Father" probably tells us more about their audience's (or their own?) lack of knowledge of Aramaic, than of the authors' reluctance to characterize Jesus' prayer language in these terms.

[53] See Thompson, *Promise*, 59-61.

[54] We will discuss this text in detail below §4.3.1.

4.2.3.2. Proliferation of Father Language in the NT

The extreme scepticism of D'Angelo about Jesus' use of "Father" or *abba* for God is, however, primarily based on her own explanation about the increasing frequency of Father language for God in the early church. She claims that "development of Christology was the most significant factor in the importance of 'father' in Christian theology."[55] In her frontal criticism against Jeremias, D'Angelo concludes that the application of Father to God became increasingly important in early Christianity, being placed on the lips of Jesus in Matthew and Luke significantly more frequently than in Mark and Q. She attributes the increase of the title of Father for God in the NT to the development of christology. In other words, the development of christological thought goes hand in hand with an increased attribution to God of the role or title of Father. The "higher" the christology, the more one finds God called upon as Father.

As a response to D'Angelo on this point, Thompson points out a number of interesting points against the theory that the christological speculation and the increase in Father language belong together: (1) "while Matthew and Luke do show an increase in the *frequency* of the use of Father for God, especially, vis-à-vis Mark, the distinctive material in Matthew and Luke is not uniformly more christological, in the sense of always serving the articulation of a 'higher' Christology"; (2) Unlike Mark, Matthew and Luke "contain a lot of material with a decidedly *communal* and *ethical*, rather than a more narrowly christological, focus, which elaborates the significance of God's Fatherhood for the community of disciples";[56] and (3) the span of time between the Gospels does not account adequately for the striking difference between Mark's scant evidence that Jesus spoke of God as Father and Matthew and Luke's material that Jesus did so regularly. Rather, she suggests that "It seems from the beginning there were different emphases with respect to God's Fatherhood in the traditions about Jesus and that these have been used and developed in varied ways."[57]

4.2.3.3. The Impact of Jesus' Use of Abba

In a study of Jesus' use of "Father" for God Witherington and Ice undertook a different approach to deal with the question about the astonishing proliferation of Father language for God in the NT

---

[55] D'Angelo, "Abba and Father," 622.

[56] Thompson, *Promise*, 63.

[57] Thompson, *Promise*, 64.

documents.[58] Having re-examined Jeremias's arguments and discussed recent critiques of Jesus' use of *abba* and its significance they arrived at the conclusion that explanations of the increasing frequency of Father language for God in the NT "from the influence of the OT or early Jewish usage or as a residue of the general patriarchal culture or of pagan practices, for instance, in the emperor cult" can hardly be supported by evidence from the NT.[59] Instead, they argued that "It is Jesus himself that places the emphasis on God as Father, and this explains why the usage in the NT is so much more prevalent than in the OT."[60] More importantly, it is the new perspective of seeing the Father through the eyes of the Son and on the basis of the Son's relationship to the Father that explains what we find in the NT.[61] They pointed out that "God the Father is most often referred to as Jesus' Father or the Son's Father, and only in a derivative sense, through discipleship to Jesus, as the believer's Father. On rare occasions the term 'Father' is used to refer to God as creator of all creation and creatures."[62]

In support of their argument Witherington and Ice pointed out that, although there is some precedent for the use of father language of God in early Judaism, the following items are lacking from this literature:[63] (1) the use of *abba* as an address for God in prayer; (2) the regular use of "Father" or *abba* by a particular historical individual to indicate his personal relationship to God; (3) any adequate historical explanation for the increasing frequency of Father language for God in the NT; (4) any adequate explanation for why the use of Father language in early

---

[58] Witherington and Ice, *Shadow*. Interestingly enough, while Thompson begins from the OT and early Jewish view of God, Witherington and Ice begins with the NT evidence for Jesus' and early Christian view of God.

[59] Witherington and Ice, *Shadow*, 59. *Contra* D'Angelo, "Abba and Father," 623-30.

[60] Witherington and Ice, *Shadow*, 5. They draw an analogy with "the enormous meteor crater in Arizona, in which there are only small traces of the meteor itself. The size of the crater, however, clearly bears witness to the original size of the meteor. Though the evidence for Jesus' use of *abba* in particular in the Gospels is not plentiful, nevertheless its importance can be judged by its impact on his earliest followers. Paul was certainly one of those earliest followers, converted within a few years of Jesus' death" (p.25 n.14).

[61] See C. R. Seitz, *Word Without End: the Old Testament As Abiding Theological Witness* (Grand Rapids: Eerdmans, 1998), 258, who suggests an interesting point that in the older testament things are seen from the Father's point of view, whereas the Father is largely viewed from the Son's point of view in the NT. In other words, the "change . . . has less to do with matter of culture *or even something more personal or psychological*, and more to do with the appearance of the man Jesus and a change in perspective: from the Son to YHWH who is referred to from that filial point of standing as 'Heavenly Father.'"

[62] Witherington and Ice, *Shadow*, 59.

[63] Thompson, *Promise*, 19-64.

Christianity seems to have increased from the time of the writing of the earliest Gospel to the time of the writing of the later Gospels (particularly Matthew and John, with some 30 and 120 references to God as Father respectively).

The foregoing evidence therefore leads us to conclude that the best explanation for the nature and frequency of Father language in the NT is that this phenomenon reflects the impact of Jesus' God language, Jesus' relationship with God, and the way Jesus instructed his disciples to speak about and relate to God. Moreover, as we shall see below, this evidence is indeed one of the important deciding factors for the question whether Jesus' use of Father for God is to be seen as novel and unique or an appropriation of "the biblical imagery for himself and his community in order to articulate his vocation within Israel as the heir of the kingdom and Son of the Father through whose mission God was effecting the restoration of Israel."[64]

4.2.3.4. Is Jesus' God Father of Israel?

In an examination of the significance of Jesus' address of God as "Father" Marianne M. Thompson argues that the use of Father language in the NT is basically grounded in OT and early Jewish usage, particularly in places where God is referred to as the Father of Israel.[65] She argues that "Jesus understood God first as father of the people of Israel, and his own relationship to God in and from that framework . . ."[66] and "to trust God as Father is thus not to come to a new intimacy with God but, rather, to renew one's trust in the God of Israel."[67] However, the problem with this view is that it does not seem to grasp fully the radicality of Jesus' own ministry and mission.[68] It is important to note that Jesus was not merely renewing an already extant relationship between God and his people. To the contrary, Jesus held the view that Israel was basically lost and needed to be redeemed (cf. Lk 19:10; Mk 2:17). Jesus, like John the Baptist, called for radical repentance and categorically denied that the new eschatological covenant was merely a renewing of the old one. Such radicality of Jesus' own ministry and mission is eloquently brought out by Witherington and Ice:

---

[64] This is one of the main conclusions of Thompson, *Promise*, 19.

[65] Thompson, *Promise*, 40-53; see her conclusions, 156-62. D'Angelo, "Abba and Father," 613 (emphasis hers), also agrees with those who see a continuity between early Jewish view of God and Jesus' use of *abba* that "if Jesus indeed used the title 'father' for God, he did so *with* rather than against the stream of Jewish piety."

[66] Thompson, *Promise*, 79.

[67] Thompson, *Promise*, 84.

[68] Witherington and Ice, *Shadow*, 21 n.3.

Jesus wishes to call Israel forward into a new relationship with a God who can be addressed as *abba* if one will become a disciple of the one who has a unique relationship with that *abba*. "Father" is the only mode of address for God in the Gospels with good reason, and this fact cannot be explained on the basis of the rare instances where Father language is predicated of God in the OT and in early Judaism. The only adequate explanation for this phenomenon is the Christological one, both at the level of Jesus' own belief and practices, and at the level of the Christological beliefs and practices of the early church. The father remained, in Christian thought throughout the NT era, in the first instance the Father of Jesus, and then through Jesus the Father of Jesus' disciples.[69]

Moreover, a rather striking contrast between OT and early Jewish usage and NT usage needs to be noted: (1) The address of God in *intimate* terms using Father language is exceedingly rare in the OT and early Judaism, and it is as though there were mainly special individuals who had what one would call a personal relationship with God, if such a relationship entails addressing God as Father or in equivalent terms. (2) Even in those rare references, the uses were in most cases analogies rather than the naming of God as Father in prayer or any other sort of direct address. (3) It was never linked to a particular relationship with one particular historical individual, with one telling exception: David or his descendant (2 Sam 7; Ps 2). However, even this Father-Son language for the Davidic figure provides little precedent for the NT Father-Son relationship between Jesus and God. This is not an insignificant point. It strongly suggests that the dominant category underlying Jesus' self-understanding was probably not messiahship but sonship to God, and from this "his other basic convictions about himself and his mission arose."[70] (4) Last, but not least, there is still no clear evidence in the early Jewish literature for praying to God as *abba* prior to the time of Jesus. As we have seen earlier, addressing God as "my Father" is a more formal sort of address than *abba*.

As far as Paul's letters are concerned, he sometimes speaks of God, as in some OT references to God as Father, as a compassionate Father (see 2 Cor 1:3), but "the story that undergirds the references to the Fatherhood of God in Paul's letters is the story of Jesus, and the Father's relationship to him, not the story of Israel as a nation and God's relationship to Israel" (cf. Rom 6:4; 1 Cor 15:24).[71] In this regard it is quite revealing that God is not referred to as Father when Paul actually speaks at length about the future of Israel in Rom 9-11 nor is God's Fatherhood related to the forefatherhood of Abraham in Rom 4.

---

[69] Witherington and Ice, *Shadow*, 63.

[70] J. D. G. Dunn, Jesus and the Spirit: a Study of the Religious and Charismatic Experience of Jesus and the First Christians as Reflected in the New Testament (London: SCM, 1975), 39.

[71] Witherington and Ice, *Shadow*, 34. *Pace* Thompson, *Promise*, 132.

Another important contribution of Jeremias was his emphasis on reading Jesus' God language in the eschatological context of Jesus' general theological discourse: "the expressions of God's fatherly goodness are eschatological events."[72] In other words, Jesus' conviction was that God was acting as Father and redeemer of his children in a final and definitive way through Jesus' own ministry. As Jeremias puts it, "In Jesus' eyes, being a child of God is not a gift of creation, but an eschatological gift of salvation."[73] Jesus was not simply upholding the earlier Jewish usage of Father language for God. He believed that such a relationship with God comes through a positive response to Jesus' ministry in the form of discipleship to Jesus.

However, Thompson interprets Jeremias differently. She reads Jeremias's emphasis on the eschatological reading of Jesus' God language as supporting evidence for the continuity between Jesus' convictions about God and those of his Jewish contemporaries and concludes that "It was not a new conception of God that prompted Jesus' use of Father. Instead Jesus' conviction that God's eschatological salvation was now proffered through his own person and work led him, conscious of this distinctive role and of his unique relationship to God, to address God, personally and directly, as *abba*."[74] Here we need to remember that in Jer 31:9 ("I am Israel's father, and Ephraim is my firstborn son") God is lamenting the broken relationship between Israel and God, a relationship which, if healthy, should have led them to call God Father. Jeremias then grounded the *abba* language in Jesus' unique filial consciousness, and the passing on of that language to his followers was grounded in the eschatological situation that Jesus believed he himself was inaugurating. In our opinion, this is an important distinction that Thompson does not seem to fully grasp. As Witherington and Ice put it,

Jesus did not see himself as one of those God was now redeeming, thus warranting his own use of *abba* language. Rather, he saw himself as the one who stood on God's side doing the redeeming. Thus *abba* for him reflects an intimate relationship intact throughout the ministry, at least until the cross, while *abba* for his followers indicates they have been redeemed through the eschatological ministry of Jesus and were now able to appropriately address God as *abba*, as Jesus always could.[75]

---

[72] Jeremias, *Prayers*, 43; cf. Mt 7:11 par.; Lk 12:32.

[73] Jeremias, *Theology*, 181.

[74] Thompson, *Promise*, 32-33.

[75] Witherington and Ice, *Shadow*, 24 n.13.

4.2.3.5. Inability to Know about Jesus' Experience

Marianne M. Thompson is also critical about Jeremias's contention that Jesus' use of *abba* articulates his experience of God and that this experience of God provides the clue to his own self-consciousness or sense of identity.[76] Citing L. T. Johnson's view that "Experience is inaccessible except through subjective consciousness and the communication of that consciousness"[77] Thompson argues that we do not have direct access to Jesus' experience of God nor do we know whether Jesus considered his understanding of God as Father an aspect of his inner experience because the Gospels tell us nothing that purports to be a "report" from Jesus of his "experience" or "subjective consciousness."[78]

However, the problem with her scepticism seems to lie in her inability to distinguish between a relationship Jesus had with God, which has some public dimensions, and his subjective experiences.[79] One's relationship with God is certainly something more comprehensive than one's subjective impressions or experiences acquired while in that relationship. It is true that we may not be able to talk about Jesus' *subjective* experience of God, for example, in Schleiermacherian terms that he had a "feeling of absolute dependency on God," since Jesus does not usually discourse on his feelings or his subjective religious experiences. And yet a case could be made that the temptation narrative in Q and the baptismal narrative in Mark reflect Jesus' relating of visionary experiences to his disciples, as might the saying "I saw Satan fall like lighting from the sky." It is hardly deniable that we learn from the Gethsemane narrative that Jesus had an intimate *relationship* with God (Mk 14:36), so intimate that he could ask God to let him bypass the cross! Moreover, Jesus' statement in the Q saying (Mt 11:25-27/Lk 10:21-22) suggests that he, as the Son, enjoyed an intimate and unique relationship with God the Father.

4.2.4. Conclusion

Now we may draw a number of conclusions from the foregoing discussion. First, we conclude that there is overwhelming evidence that Jesus himself

---

[76] Thompson, *Promise*, 31.

[77] L. T. Johnson, *Religious Experience in Earliest Christianity* (Minneapolis: Fortress, 1998), 48.

[78] Thompson, *Promise*, 31.

[79] Witherington and Ice, *Shadow*, 25. See also S. McKnight, *A New Vision for Israel: the Teachings of Jesus in National Context* (Studying the Historical Jesus; Grand Rapids: Eerdmans, 1999), 61: "Jesus did not come to teach about God; he came to experience God, to dwell in that experience with God, and out of that experience to point others to the kingdom."

prayed to God and addressed God as *abba* or Father. This seems to have reflected the intimacy of his relationship with God.

Second, while the fact that the very word *abba* that Jesus himself used was also used by the early church might suggest that Jesus' use of it as an address to God is nothing unique in itself, we have suggested several reasons to think otherwise and concluded that it provides support to his unique sonship to God.

Third, we also conclude that, although we may not be able to talk about Jesus' *subjective* experience of God in Schleiermacherian terms, it is clear from the Gethsemane narrative and Jesus' prayer of praise preserved in Mt 11:25-27 and Lk 10:21-22 that Jesus had an intimate and special *relationship* with God, so much so that he was not only able to ask God to let him bypass the cross but also to claim for himself exclusive mutuality with God.

Fourth, we also conclude that the best explanation for the nature and frequency of Father language in the NT is that this phenomenon reflects the impact of Jesus' God language, Jesus' relationship with God, and the way Jesus instructed his disciples to speak about and relate to God.

Fifth, it is therefore fully warranted to conclude that the prevalence of the use of Father language for God in the early church can only be adequately explained from Jesus' own use of such language[80] and, more importantly, from Jesus' own intimate and special relationship with the Father, which set him apart from other and early Jews in important ways.[81] Thus, while an attempt to place Jesus' view of God and his relationship to him within the framework of the OT and early Judaism is understandable, we are not convinced by the view that "Jesus understood God first as father of the people of Israel, and his own relationship to God in and from that framework."[82]

4.3. Exegesis of Jesus' Self-Revelatory Statements

Having re-examined the main arguments of Jeremias and interacted with recent criticisms of his arguments, we know turn to a detailed discussion of individual sayings of Jesus in the Gospels, together with the narrative relating his experience of the baptismal theophany recorded in our earliest Gospel. In the light of the foregoing discussion it should be stressed that the primary context out of which one ought to read Jesus' statements about

---

[80] *Contra* D'Angelo.

[81] *Contra* Thompson.

[82] Cf. Thompson, *Promise*, 79.

the Father is not just the degree of intimacy with the Father that set him apart, but the unique relational role he played as the Father's only Son.

4.3.1. Mt 11:25-27/Lk 10:21-22

Jesus' thanksgiving for the unique revelation of the Father through the Son found in the gospels of Matthew (11:25-27) and Luke (10:21-22) offers valuable data for our study.

The logia in both gospels exhibit considerable verbatim agreement which leads to the conclusion that the original source of Matthew and Luke is almost certainly Q. After considerable difference in the introduction Matthew and Luke follow fairly closely the wording of their source, though the Matthean form is generally considered to have a better claim to originality.

Jesus addresses the Father in a prayerful expression of rejoicing and praise because it has been the Father's will to reveal things hidden from the wise to the disciples (Q10:21). What has been revealed to the disciples, however, has come from the Father through the Son who possesses all power and knowledge and who alone can reveal the Father (Q10:22).

While the authenticity of the former logion is generally accepted (Q 10:21), the authenticity of the latter one (Q 10:22) has been the focus of much debate, with mixed results. Its authenticity is often denied for the following reasons: (1) form critically, it should be understood as a commentary on the previous saying; (2) its content, expressing too high a christology, cannot be attributed to Jesus; (3) it was originally uttered in a generic sense; and (4) it reflects Q's wisdom christology.

Many form critics have detected originally two different sayings with two different forms between Q 10:21 (a thanksgiving prayer) and Q 10:22 (a revelation utterance),[83] which led them to regard the latter saying as a later addition in the form of a commentary.

Proponents of this view point to the *Stichworte* common to both sayings (ἀπεκάλυψας/ἀποκαλύψαι) as the main reason for the juxtaposition.[84] While some critics suggest that the two sayings were placed together by Q or the

---

[83] So Bultmann, *Synoptic Tradition*, 159-60, who argued that the first saying has an Aramaic background, whereas the second reflects Hellenistic mysticism. Jeremias, *Theology*, 1.190, pointed out a close parallel to the first saying in 1QH 7:26, which shows similarity in both form and content and, thus, helps to confirm that the thought is fully explicable in Jewish terms.

[84] W. D. Davies and D. C. Allison, *A Critical and Exegetical Commentary on the Gospel According to Saint Matthew* (ICC; Edinburgh: T & T Clark, 1988, 1991, 1997), 279.

redactor of Q,[85] others hold that the latter saying was composed by the early church as a commentary on the first one in order to remove its obscurity.[86] While the former option does not necessarily amount to an argument against the authenticity of either sayings, the latter does.

One of the major criticisms the latter approach must face is, however, that it magnifies the difference between the two sayings.[87] We need to bear in mind that the difference in form does not necessarily indicate the separate origin of the two logia. Instead, the presence of the same motifs in both sayings favours their common origin. For example, both sayings speak about the revelation of the hidden things. Moreover, the explicit contrast of the Father and the Son in the latter saying is already implicit in the former saying.[88] We conclude with Marshall that

> it is much more probable that the second saying represents a development of the thought in the first saying by the same author, especially since the same motifs in fact appear in both sayings. The fact that the two sayings are assigned to different form-critical categories will be found a difficulty only by those who impose a rigid schematisation on the Gospel tradition.[89]

Linguistic evidence also favours the authenticity. The pervasive character of the Semitisms in the logia, which suggests an early date for the material, renders the view that the latter saying was a commentary to the former unlikely:[90] (1) the un-Greek οὐδείς . . . εἰ μή and οὐδέ . . . εἰ μή, which correspond to the Aramaic אילולא . . . לית, a paraphrase for "only" (but see

---

[85] D. Lührmann, *Die Redaktion der Logienquelle* (WMANT 33; Neukirchen-Vluyn: Neukirchener Verlag, 1969), 65; see also Bultmann, *Synoptic Tradition*, 159f.; Klostermann, *Matthäusevangelium*, 102; van Iersel, *Sohn*, 148; J. S. Kloppenborg, "Wisdom Christology in Q" *LTP* 34 (1978), 137; C. Deutsch, *Hidden Wisdom and the Easy Yoke: Wisdom, Torah and Discipleship in Matthew 11.25-30* (JSNTSup 18; Sheffield: JSOT Press, 1987), 49.

[86] S. Schulz, *Q: die Spruchquelle der Evangelisten* (Zürich: Theologischer Verlag, 1972), 215; U. Luz, *Matthew 8-20* (Hermeneia; Minneapolis: Fortress, 2001), 158, 164, states: "The post-Easter church now adds a commentary to this saying of Jesus. It explains ταῦτα ("these things") and holds fast to the place where God's revelation takes place for it." Luz, *Matthew 8-20*, 158, contends that v.27 is a creation by the early church, even though vv.25-26 go back to Jesus. He gives the following reasons: (1) there is a transition between v.27a and v.27b from the first to the third person; (2) the evidence from a Semitic linguistic background is somewhat ambiguous; (3) the logion cannot stand alone; πάντα in v.27a presupposes something. He thus concludes that v.27 is best understood as a commentary on vv.25-26.

[87] Marshall, *Luke*, 431.

[88] Fitzmyer, *Luke*, 866.

[89] Marshall, *Luke*, 431.

[90] Jeremias, *Theology*, 1.57-59.

the comments on 15:24)[91]; (2) the un-Greek use of ἀπεκάλυψας in the sense "you have revealed"; (3) parallelism in statements of theme (vv.25b, 27a), in elaborations of theme (vv.26cd, 27bc), and in emphatic conclusions (vv.26, 27d); (4) asyndeton at the beginning of v.27; (5) the un-Greek repetition of ἐπιγινώσκει; (6) repetition in v.27bc because of the lack of a reciprocal pronoun in Semitic languages; and (7) the resting of πάτερ and ὁ πατήρ on אבא. Gundry adds another point: (8) "gracious will . . . before you," a periphrastic avoidance of anthropomorphism.[92]

To sum up, it would be much easier to accept the authenticity of the present logion than to reject it as the early church's attempt to frame a saying as if it genuinely goes back to Jesus himself.

Some scholars have argued that the absolute use of "the Son" reflects the post-Easter understanding about him and cannot be attributed to Jesus.[93] With regard to the title "the Son," we have already demonstrated that Jesus' use of *abba* as an address to God gives fairly strong support to the view that Jesus was conscious of a unique personal relationship to God as his special Son. Furthermore, evidence from Qumran suggests that the saying may be authentic even with its reference to "the Son." The title "Son of God" has been demonstrated to be as much at home in a Palestinian Jewish context (cf. 4QFlor. 1:10-14) as in the Hellenistic world.[94] Thus, the absolute use of "Son" cannot be dismissed as impossible on Jesus' lips as being too Hellenistic.[95] Neither can the saying be dismissed as inauthentic due to its similarity in tone to the Fourth

---

[91] R. H. Gundry, *Matthew: a Commentary on his Handbook for a Mixed Church under Persecution* (Grand Rapids: Eerdmans, 1994), 313, takes it as a Matthean insertion.

[92] Gundry, *Matthew*, 218. See e.g., *Tg. Isa* 53:6, 10; *b. Ber.* 17a; 19a; 28b; 29b; *b. Ta'an.* 24b; cf. Matt 18:14. Though 4QFlor 10-14 applies 2 Sam 7:14 to the Messiah as a son of God, there the mutuality of knowledge that gives the present passage its special flavour is lacking.

[93] Cf. Bultmann, *Synoptic Tradition*, 160; Norden, *Agnostos Theos*, 277-308; T. Arvedson, *Das Mysterium Christi: eine Studie zu Mt 11:25-30* (Uppsala: Wretmans Boktryckeri, 1937), 229-30. Among recent commentators, Luz, *Matthew 8-20*, 158, dismisses Jeremias' arguments about the original Semitic structure of the saying without justification; and Davies and Allison, *Matthew*, 2.282-83, acknowledge that they could not make up their mind on this specific issue. Their position is, while they see no certain signs of a post-Easter creation, neither do they find "any truly telling signs of an origin with Jesus." For them, the only possible pointer in this direction is "no one knows the Son except the Father," but they think that these words give too much attention on the Father and stand in tension with the Christian formulations in Jn 14:7; 17:3; 2 Cor 5:16; Phil 3:10; 2 Tim 1:12; and 1 Jn 2:3. These reasons, however, are not compelling as will be shown in our discussion.

[94] Fitzmyer, *Luke*, 206-7.

[95] See Marshall, "Divine Sonship," 134-35, for his critique of F. Hahn's attempt to distinguish between "the Son" and "the Son of God."

Gospel "unless we are prepared to lay down as a canon of criticism that no saying in the Synoptics which has a parallel in the Fourth Gospel can be a genuine utterance of Jesus."[96] It is also doubtful whether a Q saying may have been taken from the Fourth Gospel that probably dates from the last decade or two of the first century.[97] Thus, all attempts to dismiss the saying as inauthentic on the basis of its content cannot stand close scrutiny.[98]

Jeremias claimed that Q 10:22 was originally a parable. He suggested that in Aramaic the definite articles were generic ("a son," "a father"), and Jesus was simply illustrating his situation by calling to mind a common feature of everyday life:[99]

All things have been given to me by my Father.
Just as no one (really) knows a son except his father,
so no one (really) knows a father except his son,
and anyone to whom the son chooses to make him known.

Several features of the passage, however, militate against this view: (1) the immediately preceding address to God as "Father" (Q 10:21, bis); (2) the preceding designation of God as "my father" (10:22a); and (3) the immediately following designation of Jesus as "the Son" (10:22d, where "a son" very doubtfully would fit "chooses . . . to reveal").[100] Moreover, a generic use requires that we separate the two clauses in the middle (10:22b-c) from the first and last clauses (10:22a and d), but they are integrally related to the first one.[101] As Marshall well pointed out, "if Jesus could have uttered Matthew 11.27 in the form suggested by Jeremias, there

---

[96] Manson, *Teaching of Jesus*, 110.

[97] Dunn, *Spirit*, 28.

[98] An attempt by F. Hahn, *Christologische Hoheitstitel* (Göttingen: Vandenhoeck & Ruprecht, 1964), 321-6, to reject the authenticity of this saying by arguing that the reference in "all things have been delivered to me" is to the kind of authority and might mentioned in Matthew 28:18 has been rightly countered by J. Jeremias, *Abba: Studien zur neutestamentlichen Theologie und Zeitgeschichte* (Göttingen: Vandenhoeck & Ruprecht, 1966), 51, who pointed out that the whole context of the saying is governed by the thought of revelation rather than of authority and might, and that the use of the technical term παραδίδωμι requires this understanding of the phrase.

[99] Jeremias, *Prayers*, 45-52; C. H. Dodd, "A Hidden Parable in the Fourth Gospel" in *More New Testament Studies* (Manchester: Manchester University Press, 1968), 30-40; R. Bauckham, "The Sonship of the Historical Jesus in Christology" *SJT* 31 (1978), 251-52. For criticisms see Marshall, "Divine Sonship," 137-39; Dunn, *Spirit*, 32; Gundry, *Matthew*, 217.

[100] Gundry, *Matthew*, 217.

[101] Witherington, *Christology*, 226.

is no reason in principle to deny that he could have spoken it in the form actually preserved in the Gospels."[102]

It is sometimes urged that our saying cannot be authentic because it reflects Q's wisdom christology. The argument is based on several Q sayings with wisdom motifs (Mt 11:16-19/Lk 7:31-35; Mt 12:42/Lk 11:31; Mt 23:34-36/Lk 13:34-35; Mt 11:27/Lk 10:22) which are evidence that the Q community was concerned either to portray Jesus as Wisdom or to incorporate wisdom motifs into their christological portrait of him.[103] However, the major problem with this theory is that there is little evidence that a Q community ever existed. It is "based on silence because it is methodologically unsound to base conclusions on this matter purely on sayings from the Synoptics."[104] Moreover, even if real evidence for the existence of Q community is found, scholarly opinions are against the view that a consistent wisdom christology can be found in Q.[105] Witherington points out another shortcoming of this theory in the following words:

Because these [Q] sayings collections were being compiled well before the fall of Jerusalem and the dispersion or death of a significant group of eyewitnesses to the life and teachings of Jesus, the burden of proof lies with those who insist that certain themes in Q do not go back to Jesus but only to early Palestinian Christianity (e.g., the Wisdom theme). We are looking at a span of only two or, at the most, three decades before such collections were available in relatively fixed forms. It is unlikely that early Palestinian Christianity deviated significantly from Jesus in its handling of such major themes as the Jewish wisdom motif in Q.[106]

To sum up, even if wisdom christology is present in Q 10:22, it cannot be used as evidence against the authenticity of the saying.[107]

---

[102] Marshall, "Divine Sonship," 138.

[103] Suggs, *Wisdom*, argued that the wisdom motifs in Matthew are due to the redaction of the evangelist, but his argument met a criticism from M. D. Johnson, "Reflections on a Wisdom Approach to Matthew's Christology" *CBQ* 36 (1974), 44-64, who shows that it does not blend in with the overall Christology of the First Gospel.

[104] Witherington, *Christology*, 223.

[105] Cf. Suggs, *Wisdom*, 96; G. N. Stanton, "On the Christology of Q" in *Christ and Spirit in the New Testament* (eds. S. S. Smalley et al.; Cambridge: CUP, 1973), 37. That there is a wisdom theme in Q is undeniable, but that it amounts to a consistent wisdom Christology is another matter.

[106] Witherington, *Christology*, 224. Cf. Gerhardsson, *Reliability*; Bailey, "Middle Eastern Oral Tradition," 363-67; Bailey, "Informal Controlled Oral Tradition," 4-11.

[107] Since D. F. Strauss first argued for wisdom christology in Mt 11:25-30, many scholars have followed his step. However, in Mt 11:25-27 Jesus is described principally as God's Son, while Wisdom is always portrayed as a woman in Jewish literature. Moreover, we do not find such close parallels to Wisdom revealing and electing in the way that the Son does.

Our evaluation of different proposals that seek to undermine the authenticity of the present saying leads us to conclude with Fitzmyer that

> Even when one considers the parallels to the sayings in Lk 10, 21-22 in ancient extrabiblical literature or in the Johannine tradition and makes allowance for obvious redactional modifications of the evangelists, it is difficult to be apodictic and deny to Jesus himself the *revelatory* contents of these verses. For he must have said or insinuated something similar to what is recorded here to give rise to the rapid conclusion that surfaced not long after his death, that he was indeed the Son of God (even if that were not yet meant with the full nuances of Nicaea). Though I am inclined to regard the substance of these sayings as authentic, that substance may have to be traced only to an implicit formulation in Jesus' own words and deeds.[108]

If we are correct to argue that Q 10:21-22 probably go back to Jesus as his authentic sayings, what does it convey for our purpose? The latter saying makes explicit what is implicit in the former saying: the revelation of the hidden things from the Father to νηπίοις has come through the Son. While πάντα refers firstly to the ταῦτα, it goes beyond that to include the whole revelation of God in Jesus.[109]

In the first saying Jesus addresses God first as πάτερ, the Greek equivalent of the Aramaic *abba*. While this form is found in Greek prayers (3 Macc. 6:3, 8), its use in a Palestinian context appears to be found uniquely in the prayers of Jesus and in the way in which he taught his disciples to pray (Lk 11:2). The address to God as "Father" may reflect an original use of the intimate term *abba*, which is found in Mk 14:36, but is less striking in its intimacy here than in that text because of the following "Lord of heaven and earth," and, therefore, cannot be said necessarily to transcend contemporary Jewish sensitivities. However, the second address to God as Father stands alone and is thus more intimate, and the exclusive correlation of Father and Son suggests that it should be understood as an expression of Jesus' distinctively intimate relationship with God.[110]

In the second saying the first clause states that all has been handed over to Jesus by the Father. The verb παραδίδωμι can be used of the handing down of knowledge, especially of a tradition handed on from a teacher to a pupil (cf. Mk 7:13; 1 Cor 11:2, 23); it can also be used of the transfer of power or authority (Lk 4:6). The πάντα can also be understood in both

---

[108] Fitzmyer, "Abba and Jesus' Relation to God," 37-38.

[109] So Marshall, *Luke*, 431. We disagree with those who interpret v.27 in the light of Dan 7:13-14 and Mt 28:18. Hunter, "Crux," 246, gives the reasons: "(a) Jesus proceeds to speak, and to speak exclusively, of the knowledge of God' (b) since Jesus was not yet 'glorified', the idea of universal power is not yet relevant; (c) the verb παρεδόθη suggests a contrast with the *paradosis* of the Scribes (Mark vii. 3, 9) who are clearly in view in the first and last strophes."

[110] J. Nolland, *Luke* (WBC 35; Dallas: Word Books, 1993), 571-72.

senses. Such ambiguity has led to considerable debate over whether the handing over all things to Jesus should be taken as concerned with the transmission of knowledge, as the continuing development of the verse might suggest, or whether the transmission of full authority to Jesus is in view, for which appeal is made to Dan 7:14 and 2:37-38, but which seems less contextually appropriate. However, this seems to be to some extent a false antithesis. Nolland rightly pointed out that the emphasis lies on "on the privileged status of the one who has received from God all that which it is his to dispose" and the basis of this handing over is "the intimacy of relationship."[111] Witherington rightly explained the intimate relationship between the Father and the Son:

> They share knowledge that others do not have unless the Son dispenses it. Mt 11:25-27 suggests that God shares with his Son certain intimate knowledge, and indeed this saying suggests that the way to know the Father is through receiving the revelation of who the Father is from the Son. Jesus is portrayed as the one who meditates the knowledge of God and the blessings of God. He himself is not the recipient of the OT promises of God, especially the promise that God can be known by his people, but rather the one who fulfills them or bestows them.[112]

Not only does the saying stress the intimacy of relationship, but it is also described in divine terms, sharing the identity of God: (1) there is an exclusive mutuality between Father and Son; (2) such a mutuality is extended even to the Son's possession of πάντα; (3) like the Father, the Son is unknowable; (4) the Son is not only elect one, but also the *electing* one for the benefits of others: "no one knows the Father except the Son *and those to whom the Son chooses to reveal him.*" Here we are not far from Jn 1:18 ("No one has ever seen God; God the only Son, who is in the bosom of the Father, he has made him known") and Jn 14:9 ("He that has seen me has seen the Father").

From Jesus' sayings recorded in Q 10:21-22 we come to the conclusion that Jesus was conscious of being God's unique agent who alone mediated the final revelation of God, and thus as God's unique Son. While the idea of pre-existence is not explicit in our saying, it strongly suggests that Jesus' sonship entails his self-consciousness of a unique and intimate relationship to God as his Father.

---

[111] Nolland, *Luke*, 573, rightly suggests that John 13:3 may well be dependent on this tradition.

[112] Witherington and Ice, *Shadow*, 26.

4.3.2. Mk 13:32

Scholarly discussions of this saying of Jesus have come up with three basic positions. Either it is wholly authentic as it stands, or it is wholly a product of the early church, or it is a distorted saying of Jesus, especially by adding the reference to "the Son."[113]

While scholars like R. Bultmann regarded the present saying as belonging to a Jewish saying with the last six words being added by a Christian redactor,[114] few scholars today would reject the whole saying as inauthentic, since it is difficult to imagine that the early church would have invented such a "hard saying" in which the Son is made to confess his ignorance on such a highly important matter.[115] It can be countered that the creation of such a saying was necessary in the early church due to some apocalyptic enthusiasts who insisted that they knew the exact date of the parousia.

However, it is difficult to accept this conjecture, since it is still extremely unlikely that the early church would have invented such a saying at the expense of producing such serious damage as attributing ignorance to their exalted Lord (criterion of embarrassment). In fact, there is some evidence on textual critical grounds that the present saying led the church into some doctrinal difficulty. The majority of the witnesses of Matthew omit the phrase οὐδὲ ὁ υἱός, including the later Byzantine text, while it is included by the best witnesses of the Alexandrian, Western, and Caesarean text types. The saying is omitted by Luke altogether, and John makes clear that Jesus knew everything (cf. 5:6; 6:6; 8:14; 9:3; 11:11-15; 13:1-3, 11).[116] It is therefore likely that, while the phrase οὐδὲ ὁ υἱός was originally present in Matthew, as it certainly was in Mark, it was later removed from the original saying for similar reasons.[117] About the present saying Dunn rightly pointed out that

The earlier we postulate its origin the less need was there to attribute ignorance to Jesus, since Jesus' generation did not die out for decades (cf. Mk. 13.30); but the later we postulate its origin, to explain the delay of the parousia, the more exalted Jesus had

---

[113] The saying is accepted as authentic by van Iersel, *Sohn*, 117-23; Witherington, *Christology*, 228-33; and regarded as a distorted saying by Dalman, *The Words of Jesus*, 194; Kümmel, *Promise*, 40-42; Bornkamm, *Jesus of Nazareth*, 226; and Jeremias, *Abba*, 40.

[114] Cf. Bultmann, *Synoptic Tradition*, 130; Hahn, *Hoheitstitel*, 327.

[115] van Iersel, *Sohn*, 117-23.

[116] Meier, *Marginal Jew*, 169.

[117] Cf. B. M. Metzger, *A Textual Commentary on the Greek New Testament: a Companion Volume to the United Bible Societies' Greek New Testament* (London: UBS, 1975), 62.

become in the thought of the Christian communities and the less likely the ascription of ignorance to Jesus would be permitted.[118]

The view that the phrase οὐδὲ ὁ υἱός is not genuine but an addition by the early church has been argued from three different angles: (1) the early church's desire to account for Jesus' prophetic error or the delay of the parousia; (2) the absence of Jewish precedent for the title "the Son"; and (3) it entails too high a christology. These arguments, however, are hardly convincing.

First, it is extremely unlikely that Jesus foretold "the immediacy of his parousia and that in consequence the early Church soon felt disillusioned and had to reframe its theology."[119] Rather, it must be stressed that "if a saying existed which made no reference to the ignorance of the Son, it is hard, if not impossible, to conceive of the early Church's proceeding to transform an unexceptionable saying into a 'hard' one."[120]

Second, against the lack of Jewish evidence for the title "the Son"[121] it has been shown that such Jewish use of "the Son" is attested both in the Qumran literature (4QFlor 1:10-14; 4Q246) as well as in the OT texts (Ps 2:7; 2 Sam 7).[122]

---

[118] Dunn, *Spirit*, 35.

[119] Marshall, "Divine Sonship," 140.

[120] Marshall, "Divine Sonship," 139.

[121] Cf. Kümmel, *Promise*, 42.

[122] For 4QFlor. see Fitzmyer, *Luke*, 206-7; G. J. Brooke, *Exegesis at Qumran: 4Q Florilegium in its Jewish Context* (JSOTSS 29; Sheffield: JSOT Press, 1985); for a recent discussion of 4Q246 see J. A. Fitzmyer, "The Contribution of Qumran Aramaic to the Study of the New Testament" in *A Wandering Aramean: Collected Aramaic Essays* (Missoula: Scholars Press, 1979), 85-113; F. García Martínez, "The Eschatological Figure of 4Q246" in *Qumran and Apocalyptic: Studies on the Aramaic Texts From Qumran* (Leiden: Brill, 1992), 162-79; É. Puech, "Fragment d'une apocalypse en araméen (4Q246=ps Dan d) et le 'royaume de Dieu'" *RB* 99 (1992), 98-131; J. J. Collins, "The *Son of God* Text from Qumran" in *From Jesus to John: Essays on Jesus and New Testament Christology in Honour of Marinus de Jonge* (ed. M. C. de Boer; Sheffield: Sheffield Academic Press, 1993), 65-82; J. A. Fitzmyer, "4Q246: The 'Son of God' Document From Qumran" *Bib* 74 (1993), 153-74; J. J. Collins, "The Background of the 'Son of God' Text" *BBR* 7 (1997), 51-62; C. A. Evans, "Jesus and the Messianic Texts from Qumran: A Preliminary Assessment of the Recently Published Materials" in *Jesus and His Contemporaries: Comparative Studies* (Leiden: Brill, 1995), 107-11. Evans rightly defends a probable messianic reading of this Qumran text, comparing parallels between this text, Isa 10:20-11:16, and Ps 89:27-28 (Eng. 26-27). See also J. Zimmermann, "Observations on 4Q246: the 'Son of God'" in *Qumran-Messianism: Studies on the Messianic Expectations in the Dead Sea Scrolls* (eds. J. H. Charlesworth et al.; Tübingen: Mohr Siebeck, 1998), 175-90. For the OT texts see G. R. Beasley-Murray, *Jesus and the Kingdom of God* (Grand Rapids: Eerdmans, 1986), 336 and notes.

Third, those who find it difficult to accept the title "the Son" on Jesus' lips have also suggested that the phrase οὐδὲ ὁ υἱός is a Christian addition to the text, or that it is a Christian interpretation of an original οὐδὲ ὁ υἱός τοῦ ἀνθρώπου "nor the Son of man."[123] The logic of the former view is that once the phrase οὐδὲ ὁ υἱός is removed the phrase "the Father" can be read as "my Father" (an alternative rendering of the Aramaic *abba*),[124] but against such a linguistic argument it must be emphasized that the present saying, like the saying in Mt 11:27, belongs most likely to the esoteric teaching of Jesus to his disciples.[125] The latter view may sound plausible from the apocalyptic context of the saying, but lack of evidence from any other occurrences of the same phenomenon and the very close link in meaning between "Son" and "Son of man" lead us to conclude with R. Schnackenburg that "there are no grounds for striking out the final words ("nor the Son but the Father") as long as we accept the genuineness of Matthew 11.27 – Luke 10.22."[126]

The idea that God knows everything, including the future is found in the OT and Jewish literature (e.g., Isa 46:10; Zech 14:7; 4 Ezra 4:51-52; *2 Bar* 21:8). There are also traditions that declare that human beings, or even angels, do not and cannot know the future (4 Ezra 4:44-52; *Pss. Sol.* 17:21; *2 Bar* 21:8; *b. Sanh.* 99a; *Mek.* on Exod 16:28-36).[127] In this saying, however, Jesus mentions "nor the Son." The reference to the Son after the angels in heaven suggests that his proximity to the Father is even closer to the angels; in fact it suggests that he is the closest to God in heaven. However, the coming of "that day" has been so secretly guarded that it was not revealed by God even to the closest one. Such a close proximity of the Son to the Father goes beyond a messianic sonship and implies a divine sonship of a unique personal relationship to the Father. This implication is enforced if one accepts the authenticity of Mt 11:27/Lk 10:22, where Jesus' self-consciousness of such a relationship is more evident.

We can therefore conclude that Jesus' saying in Mk 13:32 goes back to a *Sitz im Leben Jesu*, and provides cumulative evidence for Jesus' self-consciousness of divine sonship.

---

[123] Cf. Fuller, *Foundations*, 114. The latter view is suggested by E. Lohmeyer, *Das Evangelium des Markus* (Göttingen: Vandenhoeck & Ruprecht, 1951), 283, but he unquestionably accepted the saying as authentic.

[124] This view is argued by Jeremias, *Abba*, 52-54.

[125] Marshall, "Divine Sonship," 140.

[126] R. Schnackenburg, *God's Rule and Kingdom* (Freiburg: Herder, 1963), 210.

[127] C. A. Evans, *Mark 8:27-16:20* (WBC 34B; Dallas: Word Books, 2001), 336-37.

4.3.3. Mt 16:17

There are basically three different approaches to the tradition-history of Mt 16:13-20, which undermine the authenticity of our present saying.[128]

First, the text as it stands represents a more primitive tradition than the Markan and Lukan parallels. According to Bultmann, Mt 16:17-19 contains the original conclusion to Peter's confession but was formulated in the early church as words of the risen Lord; it was replaced in Mark's tradition by a passion prediction and the rebuke of Peter (Mk 8:31-33).[129]

Second, 16:17-19 contain pre-Matthean tradition/s which originally belonged to some other contexts or preserve two or more isolated sayings, which originally belonged to post-resurrection contexts.[130]

Lastly, all three verses are a Matthean composition as they exhibit triads, parallelism and redactional vocabulary.[131]

The last option is regarded by Davies and Allison as the least likely on the basis of the following points: (a) vv.17-19 contain non-Matthean words and expressions (Βαριωνᾶ, σὰρξ καὶ αἷμα, πύλαι ᾅδου, κατισχύω, κλείς); (b) a high number of Semitisms (Βαριωνᾶ as 'son of Jonah'; σὰρξ καὶ αἷμα with the sense of 'earthly'; ὁ πατήρ μου ὁ ἐν τοῖς οὐρανοῖς; πύλαι ᾅδου; δῆσαι . . . λῦσαι; asyndeton in v.19; and a possible wordplay in Aramaic *Kephā'/kephā*); (c) there are partial parallels to the content of vv.17-19 in several NT texts (e.g., Mk 3:16; Jn 1:42; 20:23; and Gal 1:15-18); and (d) "although Matthew loves parallelism and triads, nowhere else does he manufacture a triad consisting of three units with the form of thesis statement + antithetical couplet."[132]

---

[128] Davies and Allison, *Matthew*, 2.604-15, provide the most comprehensive treatment of the issue.

[129] Bultmann, *Synoptic Tradition*, 258-59. Cf. M.-J. Lagrange, *Évangile selon saint Matthieu* (EBib; Paris: Gabalda, 1948), 321; G. W. E. Nickelsburg, "Enoch, Levi, and Peter: Recipients of Revelation in Upper Galilee" *JBL* 100 (1981), 575-600, regarded Mt 16:13-19 as a commissioning story with formal similarities to the epiphanic commissioning stories in 1 En 12-16 and T. Levi 2-7.

[130] Cf. E. Stauffer, "Zur Vor - und Frühgeschichte des Primatus Petri" *ZKG* 62 (1943), 3-34 (part of a resurrection story); R. E. Brown, *The Gospel According to John* (AB; London: Chapman, 1971), 2.1088-89 (a composite of sayings which originally belonged to post-resurrection contexts); B. P. Robinson, "Peter and his Successors: Tradition and Redaction in Matthew 16.17-19" *JSNT* 21 (1984), 85-104 (three separate sayings with three different origins). See also O. Cullmann, "L'apôtre Pierre instrument du diable et instrument de Dieu" in *New Testament Essays* (ed. A. J. B. Higgins; Manchester: Manchester University Press, 1959), 94-105 (in the context of the Last Supper).

[131] Cf. M. D. Goulder, *Midrash and Lection in Matthew* (London: SPCK, 1974), 383-93; Gundry, *Matthew*, 330-6.

[132] Davies, *Matthew*, 2.605.

The second option too received negative criticisms from Davies and Allison on the basis of the following points: (1) the unity of the section is probable; (2) arguments for connecting 16:17-19 with a resurrection appearance have little substance; and (3) the interesting conjecture by Cullmann is less than probable.[133]

With regard to the first option, after assessing both sides of the argument, Davies and Allison provide reasons why they are not convinced by Bultmann's suggestion that Mt 16:13-20 should be labelled an Easter story.[134] But most importantly, they raise the possibility that the Matthean account rests upon an event in the life of Jesus. They provide evidence for this possibility from the following categories:[135] (1) the evidence of Paul; (2) Semitisms; (3) the Dead Sea Scrolls; (4) the criterion of consistency; (5) the criterion of dissimilarity; (5) the geographical setting; and (6) the response to objections. Davies and Allison conclude the whole discussion by stating that Mt 16:17-19 "*may* preserve the original conclusion to the incident at Caesarea Philippi, and the text *may* give us an important glimpse into the life of Jesus."[136] While their concern not to be dogmatic on this issue is understandable, our assessment of evidence they provided leads us to conclude that the pericope as a whole is most likely to be authentic.[137]

With regard to Mt 16:17, one may contend that the phrase ὁ πατήρ μου ὁ ἐν τοῖς οὐρανοῖς may be a Matthean redaction. However, while that may be true, it is much more likely that the phrase ὁ ἐν τοῖς οὐρανοῖς only redactional if Jeremias's detailed study is correct. He concluded that "the *considerable increase in the use of the title 'Father' for God* in the tradition of the words of Jesus *had already begun in the stratum which was available to Matthew.*"[138] Then, we can count Mt 16:17 as another authentic saying of Jesus in which he referred to God as his Father, the revealer of his own identity to Peter. This saying is reminiscent of another authentic saying of Jesus preserved in Q ("No one knows the Son except the Father" Mt 11:27/Lk 10:22). Thus, this saying provides cumulative evidence that Jesus regarded God as his Father and saw himself as his Son

---

[133] See Davies, *Matthew*, for detailed explanations, including a refutation of Cullmann's view.

[134] Davies, *Matthew*, 2.606-9.

[135] See Davies, *Matthew*, 2.609-15, for a detailed analysis of each category.

[136] Davies, *Matthew*, 2.615.

[137] Cf. Marshall, "Divine Sonship," 141, 148 n.39; R. H. Gundry, "The Narrative Framework of Matthew XVI.17-19" *NovT* 7 (1964), 1-9, who convincingly argued that the Caesarean Philippi setting is the most likely context for our saying.

[138] Jeremias, *Prayers*, 30-32, concludes that "the *considerable increase in the use of the title 'Father' for God* in the tradition of the words of Jesus *had already begun in the stratum which was available to Matthew*" (p.32, emphasis his).

and that he was conscious of standing in a unique Father-Son relationship with God.

4.3.4. Lk 22:29

There has been considerable debate regarding which form of wording stands nearest to the original saying because the saying recorded in Lk 22:28-30 is completely different from a similar saying in Mt 19:28.

While there is a variety of opinion among scholars on this rather complex issue, the majority of scholars regard the Matthean wording as standing closer to the original.[139] However, the originality of the Lukan form is argued by some scholars.[140] H. Schürmann, for example, argued that the Lukan version, based on Luke's special source, is more likely to be original and the phrase ὁ πατήρ μου is not a Lukan addition but belongs to his source.[141]

A close examination of the Matthean and Lukan texts reveals that there is nothing corresponding to vv.29-30a in Matthew.[142] The idea that the disciples are promised a share in the rule of Jesus is in effect replaced by Matthew with a reference to the eschatological regeneration, when the Son of man will sit on the throne of his glory, and the reward promised to the disciples is that of sitting on thrones, as in Lk 22:30b.[143] Again, the phrase ἐν τῇ παλιγγενεσίᾳ in Mt 19:28 probably corresponds to ἐν τῇ βασιλείᾳ

---

[139] Bultmann, 170-71; E. Klostermann, *Das Lukasevangelium* (HNT; Tübingen: Mohr Siebeck, 1929), 209; Kümmel, *Promise*, 47; P. Vielhauer, "Erwägungen zur Christologie des Markusevangeliums" in *Aufsätze zum Neuen Testament* (Munich: Kaiser, 1965), 67-68; Schulz, *Q*, 330-32.

[140] E. Schweizer, *Das Evangelium nach Matthäus* (Göttingen: Vandenhoeck & Ruprecht, 1973), 251-52; H. Schürmann, *Quellenkritische Untersuchung des lukanischen Abendmahlsberichtes Lk. 22,7-38* (Münster: Aschendorff, 1953-1957), 3.37-54; Marshall, *Luke*, 815, with some hesitation, while acknowledging that to some extent Luke has edited the saying.

[141] Schürmann, *Quellenkritische Untersuchung*, 3.37-54. Davies and Allison, *Matthew*, 3.55, reject the suggestion that Lk 22:29 + 30a preserves an independent, pre-Lukan logion. Certainly, the phrase is not especially characteristic of Luke. Cf. Marshall, "Divine Sonship," 141 and n.41: "In Luke 2.49 the phrase is essential to the story. Only in Luke 24.49 does the possibility of redactional addition arise, but against this should be set the avoidance of the title in Luke 9.26; 22.42 in contrast with Mark 8.38 and 14.36 respectively." See also Marshall, *Luke*, 816.

[142] Cf. 2 Tim 2:12; Rev 2:26-27; 3:21.

[143] It seems likely that the reference to the Son of man is a Matthean addition (cf. Mt 25:31) to explain the meaning of the unusual phrase παλιγγενεσία, which will then have stood in Matthew's source. Cf. Schürmann, *Quellenkritische Untersuchung*, 3.43-44. So arguments by Schulz, *Q*, 331 n.62, to the effect that Matthew would not have replaced this concept for that found in Luke are beside the point.

μου in Lk 22:30a.[144] Hence, it is possible that Matthew himself or his source omitted this verse, or Luke added vv.29-30a to the present saying, which was not known to Matthew but which was handed down in Luke's tradition as an authentic saying of Jesus.[145] This is more likely, since Luke may be dependent on a different source from Matthew at this point. And since vv.29-30a are unlikely to be due to Lukan redaction, it is likely that both Matthew and Luke were dependent on different sources or, more probably, on two different recensions of Q.[146] In addition, there is evidence that in v.29 Luke seems to be reflecting tradition. Guillet, drawing on the analysis made by O. de Dinechin of the Johannine pattern,[147] has noted the frequent occurrences in the Gospel of John of variants of the pattern here: "as the father . . . to me, so I . . . to you."[148]

The authenticity of the saying is often questioned in terms of its content.[149] It has been urged that the following ideas or words seem to reflect a late development: (a) the statement that the disciples share in the temptations of Jesus could be a way of venerating the disciples; (b) the use of διατίθεμαι which should mean "to bequeath"; and (c) the reference by Jesus to "my table" and "my kingdom" is too high a christology for the earthly Jesus. However, each of these three points has been rightly rejected:[150] (a) the use of πειρασμός is pre-Lukan and Luke is unlikely to have invented a saying in praise of the disciples and inserted it in this context; (b) the verb διατίθεμαι has the sense of ordaining freely or disposing authoritatively rather than conveying the idea of making a will

---

[144] Schürmann, *Quellenkritische Untersuchung*, 3.50-51. Matthew's phrase could be original here, and altered by Luke to an easier expression.

[145] Marshall, *Luke*, 817. However, Nolland, *Luke*, 1063, disputes this point. While he agrees that v.29 preserves early tradition, he insists that it is much more likely that this verse was already an integral part of what Luke received in vv.28-30. His reason for taking this position is that "Matthew's attribution of thrones to both the Son of Man and to the disciples has its analogue in Luke's attribution of a kingdom to each." The evidence, however, seems to favour the view that the correspondence Nolland points out is to be found in Lk 22:30b and thereby there is nothing corresponding to v.29 in Matthew.

[146] So Marshall, *Luke*, 815; cf. Manson, *Sayings*, 216, who ascribes the two forms to M and L respectively.

[147] O. de Dinechin, "καθώς: La similitude dans l'évangile selon saint Jean" *RSR* 58 (1970), 195-236.

[148] J. Guillet, "Luc 22,29: Une formule johannique dans l'évangile de Luc" *RSR* 69 (1981), 113-22. The same pattern is found in Rev 2:26-27; cf. 3:21.

[149] Cf. F. W. Beare, *The Earliest Records of Jesus* (Oxford: Blackwell, 1962), 227f.

[150] Cf. Marshall, "Divine Sonship," 141.

as it is used of the Father as well as of Jesus;[151] and (c) there is no reason to deny such authority to Jesus in his reference to "my table" and "my kingdom," and the thought of his kingly authority is not a late development.[152]

If we are correct that the saying, including the phrase ὁ πατήρ μου, is more likely to go back to Jesus, then this saying provides support for Jesus' self-consciousness of divine sonship without explicitly using the term "Son." In this saying Jesus is the only heir of the Father who conferred his kingdom on him, and as the only heir he can ordain freely or dispose authoritatively with the kingdom conferred on him. The idea of Jesus as the only heir of the Father, coupled with διατίθεμαι in the sense of ordaining freely or disposing authoritatively, suggests that his divine sonship here is not simply a messianic sonship, but implies a unique personal relationship with God as his Father.

We can therefore conclude that the saying is more likely to go back to Jesus, and as such it can be taken as another piece of cumulative evidence that Jesus regarded God as his Father and conceived himself as his Son.

4.3.5. Mk 12:1-12

The parable of Jesus attested in Mk 12:1-12 and pars., also known as the parable of the wicked tenants, has been the focus of considerable debate among scholars in relation to (1) its original form, (2) its authenticity, (2) its socio-cultural background, (4) the coherence of its OT references, (5) the role and significance of the "Son," and (6) the real meaning of the parable itself. With the examination of these important questions surrounding the parable we hope to give answer to the twin question whether the parable as is recorded in Mk 12:1-12 or any other parallel sources goes back to Jesus himself and what christological implications we can draw out for Jesus' self-consciousness of divine sonship.

4.3.5.1. Different Versions of the Parable

It is generally agreed that the version preserved by Mark is closest to the original source of the synoptic tradition, with Matthew and Luke being

---

[151] Since God is the subject, the idea of a will or testament is excluded, and the meaning must be "to assign." Cf. Schürmann, *Quellenkritische Untersuchung*, 3.41 n.145; similarly, M.-J. Lagrange, *Évangile selon St Luc* (EBib; Paris: Gabalda, 1941), 551; Klostermann, *Lukasevangelium*, 212.

[152] Cf. Schürmann, *Quellenkritische Untersuchung*, 3.44.

literarily dependent on Mark.[153] However, there are three other proposals:
(1) A. T. Cadoux suggested that, in addition to Mark's version, a Q version
stands behind the other two Synoptic accounts.[154] (2) K. R. Snodgrass
contended that the earliest of all versions was preserved in the special
Matthean tradition, which Matthew conflated with materials from Mark
and Q.[155] (3) T. Schramm held that a version of the parable existed in the
special Lukan tradition, which Luke combined with material from Mark.[156]

The parable appears not only in the three Synoptic Gospels but also in
the *Gos. Thom.* The question of whether the parable in the *Gos. Thom.* is
dependent on one or more of the Synoptic versions is very much debated.
While some scholars have contended that the version in *Gos. Thom.* is
altogether independent of the other three versions and preserves the
earliest account of the parable, others have concluded that it is dependent
on at least one of the Synoptic Gospels. There are two reasons for viewing
the account in *Gos. Thom.* as the earliest account of the parable: (1) it does
not contain the allusion to Isaiah 5, the christological hints, or the final
question; and (2) it has only the simple threefold sending, which is

---

[153] J. A. T. Robinson, "The Parable of the Wicked Husbandmen: A Test of Synoptic
Relationships" *NTS* 21 (1975), 443-61; J. Gnilka, *Das Evangelium nach Markus*
(EKKNT 2/2; Einsiedeln: Benziger Verlag, 1979), 2.142-43; D. Stern, "Jesus' Parables
from the Perspective of Rabbinic Literature: The Example of the Wicked Husbandmen"
in *Parable and Story in Judaism and Christianity* (eds. C. Thoma *et al.*; New York:
Paulist, 1989), 51.

[154] A. T. Cadoux, *The Parables of Jesus: Their Art and Use* (New York: Macmillan,
1931), 40-41. The main argument is that there are similarities between Matthew 21:39,
44//Luke 20:15, 18 over against Mark. But the first of these verses can be accounted for
as an easy, even obvious, step in allegorizing (in both cases) of material taken from Mark
12:8; and the second collapses on the basis of textual criticism, since it is missing from
Matthew in some highly regarded Greek mss (D, 33) as well as in most Old Latin texts,
Syriac Sinaiticus, and texts cited by Origen and Eusebius. UBS has it in brackets, but
Metzger, *Textual Commentary*, says they thought it was an addition.

[155] K. R. Snodgrass, *The Parable of the Wicked Tenants: an Inquiry into Parable
Interpretation* (WUNT 27; Tübingen: Mohr Siebeck, 1983), 56-71. However, Gundry,
Matthew, 424-32, counters that agreements between Matthew and Luke against Mark,
like similar ones found elsewhere, may derive from the secondary influence of Matthew
on Luke, and in his judgment it is more probable that Matthew smoothes out the
roughness in Mk 12:5b and creates an allusion to the former and latter prophets than that
Mark adds v. 5b to compensate for his earlier scaling down of the plurality represented in
Matthew. See also J. S. Sibinga, Review of Snodgrass's *The Parable of the Wicked
Tenants: an Inquiry into Parable Interpretation, NovT* 26 (1984), 383-84.

[156] T. Schramm, *Der Markus-Stoff bei Lukas: eine literarkritische und
redaktionsgeschichtliche Untersuchung* (SNTSMS 14; Cambridge: CUP, 1971), 154-67.

common to folk stories.[157] However, there is stronger evidence for the *Gos. Thom.* account being dependent on the Synoptic versions:[158] (1) the underlying presupposition in *Thomas* that the owner of the vineyard is away;[159] (2) verbal similarities with the Lukan version (δώσουσιν in Lk 20:10 and ἴσως in 20:13);[160] (3) the Synoptic-like sequence of logia 65 and 66 with the attachment of Ps 118:22 as the next logion in *Thomas*;[161] and

---

[157] Cf. J. Jeremias, *The Parables of Jesus* (Göttingen: Vandenhoeck & Ruprecht, 1972), 24, 70-72; Crossan, "Parable," 461; C. S. Mann, *Mark: A New Translation With Introduction and Commentary* (AB 27; New York: Doubleday, 1986), 461; W. G. Morrice, "The Parable of the Tenants and the Gospel of Thomas" *ExpTim* 98 (1987), 104-7; Fitzmyer, *Luke*, 1280-81; J. Marcus, *The Way of the Lord: Christological Exegesis of the Old Testament in the Gospel of Mark* (Louisville: Westminster/John Knox, 1992), 112; Davies and Allison, *Matthew*, 3.187. Note, however, that B. B. Scott, *Hear Then the Parable: a Commentary on the Parables of Jesus* (Minneapolis: Fortress, 1989), 245, pointed out that even if *Gos. Thom.* is independent, it is not obvious that it is superior, for its simplicity may result from its wisdom ideology.

[158] Among the advocates of this view are H. F. Bayer, *Jesus' Predictions of Vindication and Resurrection: the Provenance, Meaning, and Correlation of the Synoptic Predictions* (WUNT 2/20; Tübingen: Mohr Siebeck, 1986), 96-97; Gnilka, *Markus*, 2.142-43; M. Fieger, *Das Thomasevangelium: Einleitung Kommentar und Systematik* (Münster: Aschendorff, 1991), 188-94; R. H. Gundry, *Mark: A Commentary on His Apology for the Cross* (Grand Rapids: Eerdmans, 1993), 683; D. A. Hagner, *Matthew 14-28* (WBC 33; Dallas: Word Books, 1995), 620; J. Lambrecht, *Out of the Treasure: the Parables in the Gospel of Matthew* (Louvain: Peeters, 1992), 107; Nolland, *Luke*, 3.948; J.-M. Sevrin, "Un groupement de trois paraboles contre les richesses dans L'Evangile selon Thomas: EvTh 63, 64, 65" in *Les paraboles évangéliques: perspectives nouvelles* (ed. J. Delorme; Paris: Editions du Cerf, 1989), 425-39; N. T. Wright, *The New Testament and the People of God* (London: SPCK, 1992), 443; G. J. Brooke, "4Q500 1 and the Use of the Scripture in the Parable of the Vineyard" *DSD* 2 (1995), 268-294, esp. 280.

[159] Cf. A. J. Hultgren, *The Parables of Jesus: a Commentary* (Grand Rapids: Eerdmans, 2000), 365.

[160] W. Schrage, *Das Verhältnis des Thomas-Evangeliums zur synoptischen Tradition und zu den koptischen Evangelien-übersetzungen* (BZNWKAK 29; Berlin: A. Töpelmann, 1964), 140; Hultgren, *Parables*, 365: "The expression 'that the tenants might give him [the slave] the produce of the vineyard' appears to be dependent on Luke 20:10 ('that they [the tenants] should give him some of the fruit of the vineyard'), in contrast to the wording of Mark and Matthew; and the clause 'perhaps they will show respect to my son' in the *Gospel of Thomas* 65 appears to be dependent on Luke 20:13 ('perhaps they will respect him [= my son]'). The Greek word ('perhaps') appears only here in the entire NT (and only once in the LXX, 1 Sam 25:21); its equivalent in the *Gospel of Thomas* 65 has the appearance of dependence on Luke."

[161] Hultgren, *Parables*, 366. The fact that "logion 66 is the only passage in the *Gospel of Thomas* composed of OT material" suggests the likelihood that it has been composed out of the Synoptic materials at hand. *Contra* S. J. Patterson, *The Gospel of Thomas and Jesus* (Sonoma: Polebridge, 1993), 60-61, who suggests that the present position of this logion in *Gos. Thom.* may not be original.

(4) the evidence from the old Syriac Gospels that *Gos. Thom.* represents a harmonizing tendency in Syria.[162]

Moreover, Hultgren detects a Gnostic influence in *Gos. Thom.*:

> the son represents the living Jesus (the light, cf. logion 77), who comes into the material world to gather the fruits of the vineyard, thereby rekindling within Gnostics remembrance of their belonging to the realm of light and being rejected by the people of the world (the tenants).[163]

Furthermore, J.-M. Sevrin demonstrated in his analysis of the grouping of the three parables in logia 63-65 (the Rich Fool, the Great Banquet, and the Wicked Tenants) that *Gos. Thom.* is very likely to be a reinterpretation of the Synoptic tradition. He argued that the purpose of such grouping by the author was to show the futility of any attempt to accumulate wealth since riches are an impediment to salvation. He also contended that the author has significantly modified the parable of the wicked tenants by focusing on the servant's lack of knowledge ("perhaps *he* did not know *them*") and the tenants' possession of knowledge.[164] By placing emphasis on knowledge the author of *Gos. Thom.* portrayed the servants as negative characters and the tenants as positive ones. Sevrin further suggested that the first line of the parable should be reconstructed as a "lender" or "usurer" (*chrēstēs*) rather than a "good" (*chrēstos*) man.[165] If this reading is correct, the person in question does not represent God but a man of wealth whose riches lead to destruction, thus enhancing the case that the version in *Thomas* is secondary.[166] It is therefore much more likely that the Synoptic accounts of the parable are closer to the original form, with the *Gos. Thom.* being dependent on one or more of them.

---

[162] K. R. Snodgrass, "The Gospel of Thomas: A Secondary Gospel" *SecCent* 7 (1989), 28-31; Snodgrass, *Parable*, 52-54; see also J. H. Charlesworth and C. A. Evans, "Jesus in the Agrapha and Apocryphal Gospels" in *Studying the Historical Jesus: Evaluation of the State of Current Research* (eds. B. D. Chilton *et al.*; Leiden: Brill, 1994), 479-533. See Morrice, "Parable of the Tenants," 106, for the suggestion that the Syriac Gospels have been shaped by *Gos. Thom.* Also Patterson, *Gospel of Thomas*, 60 n.16, who argues that in a context of a lively oral tradition, agreement on a few details does not indicate literary dependence. However, as K. R. Snodgrass, "Recent Research on the Parable of the Wicked Tenants" *BBR* 8 (1998), 194, notes, "The issue is not literary dependence . . . but whether *Thomas* preserves an account unaffected by the Synoptic accounts in any way."

[163] Hultgren, *Parables*, 366. Cf. Fieger, *Thomasevangelium*, 193-94.

[164] Sevrin, "Un groupement," 425-39.

[165] Only the first three letters and the last letter remain in the text.

[166] Sevrin, "Un groupement," 437. However, even if the reading "good" were original, Sevrin's explanation of the grouping of the three parables and of the intent of the cryptic ending of *Gos. Thom.* is still convincing. The point could be that even a good person focusing on wealth ends up in destruction.

4.3.5.2. Authenticity of the Parable

As we have already pointed out, if this parable is authentic, it could give us a vital clue about not only his self-consciousness of divine sonship but also his self-consciousness of divine origin.[167] However, the existence of allegorical features and the inclusion of an OT quotation and several OT allusions in the parable has led some scholars to reject its original form and authenticity.

As early as 1899 A. Jülicher questioned the authenticity of the parable by claiming that the parables of Jesus are simple comparisons which are self-evident and do not contain allegorical features. Thus he catalogued the parable as an early Christian "allegorical presentation of the history of salvation," with the death of Jesus in retrospect, and treated any allegorical traits as belonging to the evangelists' own creation.[168]

A number of scholars, notably C. H. Dodd and J. Jeremias who were influenced by the presuppositions of Jülicher and of classical form criticism, argued that a genuine parable uttered by Jesus himself lies at the basis of the gospel tradition, which has been subsequently allegorized and expanded.[169] In an attempt to find its original meaning, they stripped off the allegorical traits and the OT references (Isa 5:2; Ps 118:22-23), although they still ended up giving allegorical interpretations. They tried to show that this simplified form of the parable has historical verisimilitude in first-century Palestine, where economic unrest often caused landlords to live elsewhere and to lease their farms to tenant farmers. However, an attempt to safeguard the authenticity of such a "reduced" form of the parable meant a rejection of many important elements embedded in the parable for a proper understanding of the meaning intended by the original teller.

W. G. Kümmel rejected any attempts to de-allegorize, to peel off the secondary elements, and to explain unrealistic features of the parable. He believed that the parable in its allegorical form should not be rejected on a priori grounds because Jesus' parables have series of metaphors and

---

[167] Cf. Dunn, *Christology*, 28, tries to dismiss the significance of sending the beloved son: ". . . the distinction between 'servants' and '(beloved) son' in Mark 12.2-6 provides no sure foundation since the contrast can be fully explained as part of the dramatic climax of the parable."

[168] A. Jülicher, *Die Gleichnisreden Jesu* (Tübingen: Mohr Siebeck, 1899), 1.65-85; 2.385-406. Similarly, Bultmann, *Synoptic Tradition*, 177, 205, who regarded it as "a community product."

[169] See C. H. Dodd, *The Parables of the Kingdom* (Welwyn: James Nisbet, 1961), 96-102; Jeremias, *Parables*, 70-77. Cf. van Iersel, *Sohn*, 124-45; Lindars, *Apologetic*, 173-74, who contended that the OT elements were added for apologetic purposes. Witherington, *Christology*, 213, also defends the simplified form as it is attested in *Gos. Thom.* as the closest to the original.

sometimes contain unlikely features.[170] He found, however, two major objections to the authenticity of the parable on other grounds: (1) "the transference of the promise from the Jews who reject the son to a new people of God is here described as a punishment for the *murder* of the son, whilst in other cases Jesus lets this punishment follow on the rejection of his person without mentioning his death"[171] and (2) while Judaism did not know the messianic title "Son of God," the parable presupposes that the hearers would recognize the son as the bringer of eschatological salvation.

Thus, reasons for assessing the parable as a post-Easter creation can be summarized as follows: (1) Jesus could not have made use of allegory; (2) Judaism did not know the messianic title "Son of God"; (3) various features of the parable are unrealistic; and (4) the use of a quotation and allusions from the OT is a later addition by the early church.

The first objection to authenticity, however, would not stand if the version preserved by Mark is shown to be closest to the original form of the parable, as we have already demonstrated when we discussed the relationship between the different version of the parable.

The second objection that no Jew would recognize "son" as a messianic claim is not convincing "since it is by no means obvious that Jesus did mean to speak directly about himself and his status to the people through this parable." Furthermore, the primary reason for telling the parable was not to make a christological claim but to issue an accusation against the Jewish religious leaders, the audience only perceive that the reference was to a godly person who enjoyed intimacy with God. As Jeremias rightly observed, it is therefore important "to distinguish between what Jesus himself meant, and the way in which his audience understood him."[172] Moreover, the contention has been shown to be incorrect especially since the discovery of the Qumran scrolls.[173] James H. Charlesworth provided fifteen examples from early Judaism that Jews roughly contemporaneous

---

[170] Kümmel, *Promise*, 82-83.

[171] Kümmel, *Promise*, 83.

[172] Jeremias, *Parables*, 72.

[173] This was one of the four reasons why U. U. Mell, *Die 'anderen' Winzer: eine exegetische Studie zur Vollmacht Jesu Christi nach Markus 11,27-12,34* (WUNT 77; Tübingen: Mohr Siebeck, 1994), regarded our parable as a Hellenistic Jewish Christian creation. The other three reasons are: (1) the use of the LXX; (2) the rejection of Israel implied in 12:9; and (3) his scepticism about a prediction of death by Jesus. However, these objections can be satisfactorily answered: (1) it is to be expected that the wording would be assimilated to the LXX in the course of translation and transmission; (2) As we have seen above, this passage is not about the rejection of Israel but a condemnation of Jewish religious leaders; (3) it is entirely possible or more probable that Jesus might have predicted his untimely death, given the death of John the Baptist and the opposition he often encountered. See the discussion in Bayer, *Jesus' Predictions*.

with Jesus did use the technical term "son" or "Son of God" for "paradigmatic holy individuals, including the long-waited Messiah, in God's drama of salvation."[174]

The last two objections to the authenticity of our parable will lead us into a more detailed discussion of the issues about the socio-cultural background and the significance of OT references in the parable.

4.3.5.3. Socio-Cultural Background of the Parable

The authenticity of the parable has often been questioned on the basis of its unrealistic features.[175] Those who deny its authenticity tend to focus on the incomprehensible actions of the owner of the vineyard (i.e., his extraordinary slowness to act and his sending his own son despite his servants' ill-treatment) and the unrealistic expectation of the tenants to gain the inheritance by killing the son.[176] Thus the reasoning behind this objection is: the more improbable the parable appears to be, the more likely it is going to be seen as an artificial creation by the early church. However, J. D. M. Derrett and M. Hengel demonstrated that the story was conceivable in the context of first-century Palestine, by reconstructing the events of the parable in light of rabbinic law (Derrett) and by providing additional parallels from the Zenon papyri and from the rabbinic parallels (Hengel).[177] They both argued that while Mark's account is obviously

---

[174] J. H. Charlesworth, "Jesus' Concept of God and his Self-Understanding" in *Jesus Within Judaism: New Light From Exciting Archaeological Discoveries* (London: SPCK, 1989), 149-52.

[175] For a summary of the objections against the realism and authenticity of the parable, see Kümmel, *Promise*, 82-83; W. G. Kümmel, "Das Gleichnis von den bösen Weingärtnern (Mk 12:1-9)" in *Heilsgeschehen und Geschichte: Gesammelte Aufsätze 1933-64* (Marburg: N. G. Elwert Verlag, 1965), 207-17; C. E. Carlston, *The Parables of the Triple Tradition* (Philadelphia: Fortress, 1975), 178-90.

[176] Jülicher, *Gleichnisreden*, 2.406; E. Haenchen, *Der Weg Jesu: Eine Erklärung des Markus-Evangeliums und der kanonischen Parallelen* (Berlin: Topelmann, 1966), 399-403; Kümmel, "Gleichnis," *passim*. Recently, Mell, *Winzer*, 107, 121-26; and Scott, *Hear Then*, 247-53. See also S. R. Llewelyn, "Self-Help and Legal Redress: The Parable of the Wicked Tenants" in *New Documents Illustrating Early Christianity* (eds. R. A. Kearsley et al.; North Ryde: Macquarie University, 1992), 86-105, who argues, on the basis of a four-year lease contract from 44 CE, that it is unlikely that a new vineyard would be leased immediately after construction, since it would not be commercially viable for a few years (cf. *Jub.* 7:1). See Snodgrass, "Recent Research," 196-97, for criticism of this view.

[177] J. D. M. Derrett, "Fresh Light on the Parable of the Wicked Vinedressers" *Revue internationale des droits de l'Antiquité* 10 (1963), 11-42; J. D. M. Derrett, "Allegory and the Wicked Vinedressers" *JTS* 25 (1974), 426-32; M. Hengel, "Das Gleichnis von den Weingärtnern Mc 12,1-12 im Lichte der Zenonpapyri und der rabbinischen Gleichnisse" *ZNW* 59 (1968), 1-39.

overloaded with the multiple sendings in 12:5b, the basic story reflects well the tensions between owners and tenants in the ancient world. Furthermore, building on their previous work K. Snodgrass was able to refute in detail the eight charges against the lack of realism brought by some scholars.[178]

More recently, U. Mell argued against the authenticity by contending on the basis of Heb 1:1-4 that the parable focuses on the son as heir and on his inheritance and this concept comes from a late stage of redaction.[179]

An der auf christlichen Traditionen beruhenden Ouvertüre des Hebräerbriefes, Hebr 1,1-4, läßt sich exemplarisch nachvollziehen, daß erstens die Eschatologisierung der Geschichte (Mk 12,5cd.6aα.bβ), zweitens das soteriologische Erbe-Konzept (V.7b.d) und drittens dieses in Kraft setzende sühnetheologische Heilsverständnis des Todes Jesu Christi (V. 8b) an die (erweiterte) Winzerallegorie redaktionell herangetragen wurde.[180]

However, this argument is again refuted by Snodgrass who interprets the word κληρονομία as possession rather than a reference to legal inheritance:

The stumbling block is that people read the word κληρονομία ("inheritance") as a reference to legal inheritance. However, the word often means "possession" and is used elsewhere of people usurping property. The most significant instances are of Ahab's seizure of Naboth's vineyard (3 Kgs 20 [21]:15-16; Josephus *Ant.* 8.359-60; *J.W.* 2.249), but see also Sir 24:20 and 1 Macc 6:24. The issue is not legal inheritance, but possession by whatever means.[181]

A far more important contribution comes from C. A. Evans, who builds on the work of Hengel and collects information from several early papyri to confirm that the parable is entirely realistic in its description of landowners and those who leased from them. Evans shows that the language detailing the lease agreement, development of the vineyard, disputes over debts, rejection of emissaries, and redress of wrongs is all closely paralleled in the papyri.[182] He makes an important observation that tenants were not always poor farmers, but often fairly well-to-do individuals. Furthermore,

---

[178] Snodgrass, *Parable*, 31-40. More briefly E. Bammel, "Das Gleichnis von bösen Winzern (Mk 12,1-9) und das jüdische Erbrecht" *Revue internationale des droits de l'Antiquité* 3 (1959), 11-17.

[179] Mell, *Winzer*, 130-31 and 162-65. Cf. R. Dormandy, "Hebrews 1:1-2 and the Parable of the Wicked Husbandmen" *ExpTim* 100 (1989), 371-75, also links the parable to Heb 1:1-2.

[180] Mell, *Winzer*, 162.

[181] Snodgrass, "Recent Research," 196.

[182] C. A. Evans, "God's Vineyard and Its Caretakers" in *Jesus and His Contemporaries: Comparative Studies* (Leiden: Brill, 1995), 381-406. For a detailed discussion of issues surrounding this parable see also his *Mark 8:27-16:20* (WBC 34B; Nashville: Nelson, 2001), 216-39, esp. 224-31.

it is shown from a form-critical point of view that the features of the story are paralleled in various rabbinic parables, while from a tradition-critical standpoint the parable is seen as Jesus' critique of the Temple establishment.

The above discussion of the socio-cultural background of our parable has shown that the objection to its authenticity in the light of seemingly unrealistic features cannot stand. However, it is important to pay attention to what Snodgrass has to say about the purpose of discussing the socio-cultural background:

In arguing that the story is culturally understandable, no one is suggesting that it tells of an everyday occurrence. Stories are told because something unusual happens; in this case it is a reprehensible murder. Nor is there any thought that the details of a cultural understanding provide an unknown key to explain the purpose of the parable. The discussion about cultural factors is merely to determine whether the parable constructs a believable narrative world or whether it would have required so much of first-century hearers that it would have sounded like science fiction. The story would have been unexpected, possibly even shocking, but it fits in the first-century Palestinian narrative world. Conflict over farming agreements were an all-too-common occurrence.[183]

4.3.5.4. Coherence of the OT References with the Parable

The purpose and the meaning of the parable will be made clear when we evaluate the place of OT references in our parable. This task will also serve as an answer to the last objection to its authenticity.

As we have already seen, attempts to find the original form of the parable by de-allegorizing it led some scholars to peel off the allegorical features and the OT references from the parable itself. Recent studies, however, have come to appreciate the significance of these OT references as an integral part of the parable told by Jesus on the ground that the parable seems to presuppose Aramaic interpretative tradition.

G. J. Brooke, in his analysis of 4Q500 1 and some other Qumran texts in connection with the use of scripture in our parable, urged that "the allegorical character of the parable should not be downplayed as secondary and insignificant" because "the vineyard should not be understood solely in terms of real life situations in first-century Palestine, but in light of the

---

[183] Snodgrass, "Recent Research," 197. There are others who take the socio-cultural issues in an entirely different direction: J. D. Hester, "Socio-Rhetorical Criticism and the Parable of the Wicked Tenants" *JSNT* 45 (1992), 27-57 and W. R. Herzog, *Parables As Subversive Speech: Jesus As Pedagogue of the Oppressed* (Louisville: Westminster/John Knox, 1994), argue that the parable originally was told to express the plight of Jewish tenant farmers who originally owned the land but now were forced to work as tenants. See also Patterson, *Gospel of Thomas*, 238-39, for a similar reading of the parable in the *Gos. Thom.*

scriptural allusion which rests behind its use as that was understood in contemporary Jewish texts, such as 4Q500."[184] He concluded that "4Q500 and its Qumran counterparts do not provide the sources which Jesus or others used, but they show what exegetical traditions were current in Palestine at the time of Jesus."[185] As far as the quotation from Ps 118 is concerned, he asserted that

> The prooftext from Psalm 118 is remarkably coherent with the opening parts of the parable, so much so that it can be deemed an integral part of the pericope (as the use of בנה in 4Q500 helps us see). The literary context of the parable is thoroughly suitable to its use of scripture . . . . Indeed the historical context portrayed suggests that the use of scripture in the pericope as a whole is not the result of the creative work of the early church, but goes back to Jesus himself."[186]

Similarly, Evans contended that, when the complexity and coherence in the interpretation of passages from the OT are fully appreciated, it becomes more likely that allusions to Isa 5:1-7 and the quotation from Ps 118:22-23 derive from Jesus rather than from the Greek-speaking church. He made an important observation that, while the prophetic criticism of Isaiah 5 was originally directed against the people as a whole, in the targumic version of Isa 5:1-7 the focus is narrowed down to the temple cult.[187] According to Evans, the Aramaic version contains three very important elements as compared to the original version in Hebrew:[188] (1) Isaiah's Song of the Vineyard is introduced in explicitly parabolic terms; (2) in place of the

---

[184] Brooke, "4Q500," 268-94 (quotation from p.294); see also J. M. Baumgarten, "4Q500 and the Ancient Conception of the Lord's Vineyard" *JJS* 40 (1989), 1-6.

[185] Brooke, "4Q500," 291.

[186] Brooke, "4Q500," 294.

[187] C. A. Evans, "Jesus' Parable of the Tenant Farmers in Light of Lease Agreements in Antiquity" *JSP* 14 (1996), 70. For a detailed discussion, see B. D. Chilton, *A Galilean Rabbi and His Bible: Jesus' Use of the Interpreted Scripture of His Time* (Wilmington: Michael Glazier, 1984), 111-14; and more recently B. D. Chilton and C. A. Evans, "Jesus and Israel's Scriptures" in *Studying the Historical Jesus: Evaluation of the State of Current Research* (eds. B. D. Chilton *et al.*; Leiden: Brill, 1994), 299-309.

[188] The Isaiah Targum post-dates the New Testament by three or four centuries, but many of its interpretative traditions may well date to the time of Jesus or earlier. On this question, see B. D. Chilton, *The Glory of Israel: the Theology and Provenience of the Isaiah Targum* (JSOTSup 23; Sheffield: JSOT Press, 1982). Evans notes that "The discovery of targums at Qumran (e.g., 4QtgLev, 4QtgJob, and 11QtgJob) proves that written targums existed in the time of Jesus, but no early targum of Isaiah to date has been discovered. It needs to be emphasized that the language and style of the extant Isaiah Targum are late; one cannot assume that it necessarily retains the actual wording of Aramaic paraphrases and interpretations of Scripture from the time of Jesus. What it apparently does retain in a few instances are themes, interpretations, and manners of speaking that derive from antiquity."

various words that speak of building and digging, there are references to a "high" hill (i.e., the Temple Mount), a "sanctuary," and an "altar" for making atonement; and (3) it introduces into the passage the language of "heritage" or "inheritance," an important element of thematic and dictional coherence with our parable (cf. κληρονομία Mark 12:7).[189] The introduction of Temple imagery in the targumic version is therefore taken as evidence for the shift of divine judgment more specifically against the religious establishment.[190]

Furthermore, *Tg.* Ps 118:19-27 also shows some thematic and exegetical coherence with our parable. Verse 22 of the Targum has the Aramaic טליא ("boy") instead of the Hebrew אבן ("stone"), which suggests that the former word probably derives from a word play involving האבן ("the stone") and הבן ("the son").[191] This observation led Evans to conclude that

Such a word play in Hebrew, reflected in the targumic tradition, but not preserved in the LXX, suggests that the quotation derives from Jesus and not from the Greek-speaking Church . . . . The linkage between the quotation and the parable, which tells of a rejected son, becomes much closer.[192]

Moreover, as Snodgrass pointed out, the key in determining whether the quotation from Ps 118 was originally attached to the parable should be the quotation itself because without the quotation (which functions as an application or explanation to the parable) the identity of the tenants and the intention of the parable would not have been known to the hearers, just as the intention of Nathan's parable would have been unintelligible to David if there was not explanatory *nimshal* (2 Sam 12:1-7).[193]

In a study of the targumic background of Mark 12:1-12, J. C. de Moor also came to a similar conclusion that every element in Mark's version of the parable "can be interpreted in accordance with attested Targumic exegesis" and "the audience may have been acquainted with the story, or at least with the standard interpretation of its main metaphors in the Targumic exposition of Scripture in the synagogue."[194]

---

[189] Evans, "Jesus' Parable," 70-71.

[190] Evans, "Vineyard," 401; Evans, "Jesus' Parable," 71.

[191] Evans, "Vineyard," 403.

[192] Evans, "Vineyard," 403, also suggests that the Aramaic version shows that the Psalm was understood in a messianic sense prior to the rise of Christianity. See B. Gärtner, "טליא als Messiasbezeichnung" *SEÅ* 18-19 (1953-1954), 98-108.

[193] Snodgrass, *Parable*, 96-97; Snodgrass, "Recent Research," 203-05.

[194] J. C. de Moor, "The Targumic Background of Mark 12:1-12: The Parable of the Wicked Tenants" *JSJ* 29 (1998), 66-79 (quotation from p.79), has a detailed discussion of metaphors used in the parable.

However, J. Kloppenborg Verbin has recently challenged the contention that Isa 5:1-7 is integral to the fabric of the parable on the grounds that "Isaian elements in Mark 12:1, 9 are Septuagintal" and that "Mark agrees with the LXX, but never with the MT *against* the LXX."[195] He carefully compares the MT of Isa 5:1-7 with the version in the LXX and argues that in various ways the LXX has reconceived the scenario of Isaiah's vineyard and that Egyptian viticultural practices have exerted influence on the LXX's rendering. (1) As a part of his response to this challenge Evans notes two important points: (1) the Semitic character of the elements drawn from Isa 5:1-7 does not necessarily prove their originality to the parable; (2) nor does the appearance of some Septuagintalisms prove that Isa 5:1-7 was not present in the parable from the very beginning, "for Septuagintalizing inevitably took place as the Gospel tradition evolved from Aramaic into Greek."[196] While he concedes that a degree of Septuagintalism cannot be denied, he correctly pointed out that (1) at points Isa 5:1-7 in Mk does agree with the MT against the LXX; (2) as several scholars have already noted, there are important points of coherence between the exegetical backdrop of Isa 5:1-7 and the interpretative tendency of Aramaic Isaiah; and (3) like many rabbinic parables, "stock images and common themes, complete with allusions to and sometimes formal quotations of Scripture, are the building blocks out of which Jewish parables of late antiquity were constructed."[197] We agree with Evans that

Kloppenborg Verbin may have succeeded in finding closer correspondence between LXX Isa. 5:1-7 and Mark 12:1-9 than has been recognized before, but the Semitic flavor of the parable as a whole and the Semitic coherence of the Markan context and framework throughout and not simply in 12:1, where the words from Isaiah 5 actually appear, also argue against the claim that the allusions to Isa. 5:1-7 in the text of Mark "are purely Septuagintal."[198]

To sum up, if the above contention that our parable presupposes Aramaic interpretative tradition is correct, it should caution us against any attempts to strip off the OT references from the parable or to argue that the parable was either created by the Greek-speaking church or that the allusions to Isa

---

[195] J. S. Kloppenborg Verbin, "Egyptian Viticultural Practices and the Citation of Isa 5:1-7 in Mark 12:1-9" *NovT* 44 (2002), 134-59 (quotations are from pp.137 and 159 and emphasis his).

[196] C. A. Evans, "How Septuagintal Is Isa 5:1-7 in Mark 12:1-9?" *NovT* 45 (2003), 106.

[197] Evans, "How Septuagintal," 110.

[198] Evans, "How Septuagintal," 110.

5:1-7 and the quotation of Ps 118:22-23 originated in the Greek-speaking, LXX-reading church.

4.3.5.5. Role and Significance of the "Son"

Having adequately refuted all criticisms against the authenticity of our parable we now turn to the question of the role and significance of the son in the parable. According to the survey by Snodgrass, however, a quite number of different possibilities for the referent of the son has been proposed:[199] (a) a self-reference by Jesus, (b) without referent at all, (c) a symbol of forgiveness and goodness, (d) a christological allegorizing by the early church, (e) a reference to John the Baptist, (f) an allusion to the conflict between Ishmael and Isaac, or (g) a reference even to Isaiah.

---

[199] Snodgrass, "Recent Research," 199-200, offers criticisms against some of these arguments. Scholars holding different views on the role of the son in the parable are:

(a) a self-reference by Jesus: Bayer, *Jesus' Predictions*, 109; C. Blomberg, *Interpreting the Parables* (Downers Grove: Inter-Varsity, 1990), 250-51; Charlesworth, "Concept of God," 131-64; R. Feldmeier, "Heil im Unheil: Das Bild Gottes nach der Parabel von den bösen Winzern (Mk. 12,1-12 par)" *TBei* 25 (1994), 7-9; Gundry, *Mark*, 686, 691; C. A. Kimball, "Jesus' Exposition of Scripture in Luke (20:9-19): An Inquiry in Light of Jewish Hermeneutics" *BBR* 3 (1993), 77-92; J. D. Kingsbury, "The Parable of the Wicked Husbandmen and the Secret of Jesus' Divine Sonship in Matthew: Some Literary-Critical Observations" *JBL* 105 (1986), 643-55; Lambrecht, *Treasure*, 114-15; R. H. Stein, *Luke* (NAC 24; Nashville: Broadman, 1992), 491-92; Wright, *Victory of God*, 178-79, 497, 501, 565-66; B. H. Young, *Jesus the Jewish Theologian* (Peabody: Hendrickson Publishers, 1995), 215-22.

(b) without referent at all: A. Milavec, "Mark's Parable of the Wicked Husbandmen As Reaffirming God's Predilection for Israel" *JES* 26 (1989), 100-104; A. Milavec, "A Fresh Analysis of the Parable of the Wicked Husbandmen in the Light of Jewish-Christian Dialogue" in *Parable and Story in Judaism and Christianity* (eds. C. Thoma *et al.*; New York: Paulist, 1989), 301-04; A. Milavec, "The Identity of 'The Son' and 'The Others': Mark's Parable of the Wicked Husbandmen Reconsidered" *BTB* 20 (1990), 32-33.

(c) a symbol of forgiveness and goodness: M. Petzoldt, *Gleichnisse Jesu und christliche Dogmatik* (Göttingen: Vandenhoeck & Ruprecht, 1984), 41, 44.

(d) a christological allegorizing by the early church: Mell, *Winzer*, 114-15.

(e) a reference to John the Baptist: Stern, "Jesus' Parables," 57-65; D. Stern, *Parables in Midrash: Narrative and Exegesis in Rabbinic Literature* (Cambridge: CUP, 1991), 192-96; M. Lowe, "From the Parable of the Vineyard to a Pre-Synoptic Source" *NTS* 28 (1982), 257-63.

(f) an allusion to the conflict between Ishmael and Isaac: J. D. Levenson, *The Death and Resurrection of the Beloved Son: the Transformation of Child Sacrifice in Judaism and Christianity* (New Haven: Yale University Press, 1993), 228.

(g) a reference to Isaiah: R. Aus, *The Wicked Tenants and Gethsemane: Isaiah in the Wicked Tenants' Vineyard, and Moses and the High Priest in Gethsemane* (Atlanta: Scholars Press, 1996).

While one may be perplexed by such a variety of opinions about the role the son plays in the story, downplaying or even dismissing the real significance of the son in the story is most likely to be blamed.

B. van Iersel argued that the introduction of the son in the parable is incidental to the story and its absence would have made no important changes.[200] Similarly, Dunn contended that the contrast between the owner's slaves and son can be "fully explained from the dramatic climax of the parable," with the result that "nothing [christological] can be made of the distinction."[201] However, these arguments are not convincing.

While the presence of a son or sons in other parables of Jesus usually carries no specific metaphorical significance,[202] our parable shows three different features that enhance the significance of the son. First, unlike other parables of Jesus, our parable is undoubtedly an allegory. Allegories are not self-evident and require interpretation. Second, as Dunn also admits, the son is the turning-point of the parable and some emphasis on this part is wholly expected.[203] If the son was not significant, Jesus might have skipped directly from the sending of the slaves to the coming of the owner because the tenants' ill-treatment of the slaves would well have justified the owner's coming. Third, as Evans and others have emphasized, if the stone quotation is likely to be part of the original parable, the significance of the son's being sent and then murdered is very much enhanced because Jesus then represents the rejected son/stone sent by God (i.e., the final envoy from God).[204] Thus the view that the "son" in the parable is an implicit self-reference by Jesus is to be preferred.

4.3.5.6. Meaning and Christological Implications of the Parable

In a survey on recent research on our parable Snodgrass lists sixteen different possibilities for understanding the meaning of the parable.[205] In his opinion three factors are responsible for such a disparate set of opinions: (a) ignoring its OT and Jewish context; (b) the desire to avoid any thought of judgement; and (c) the desire to avoid any connection with

---

[200] van Iersel, *Sohn*, 144.

[201] Dunn, *Spirit*, 36.

[202] This observation led Schramm, *Markus-Stoff*, 168, to claim that there is no reference to Jesus in the parable.

[203] Snodgrass, *Parable*, 81: "It is only natural that some emphasis is placed on this part of the story. None of the rabbinic parables ignores the significance of the climax of its plot. Even if the identity of the son was not immediately perceived, special importance would have to be accorded to his coming."

[204] Evans, "Vineyard," 403-4; also Snodgrass, *Parable*, 63-65, who suggested that the quotation of Ps 118 probably derives from the wordplay between בן and אבן.

[205] Snodgrass, "Recent Research," 206-8.

Jesus. However, as we have already seen, recent studies that defend the view that the stone quotation is an integral part of the original form of the parable have clarified the meaning of the parable as a condemnation of the Temple leadership for "their insensitivity to what God intended for Israel and what he intended with the ministry of Jesus."[206]

Having established that Jesus told the parable to issue a warning against the Temple leadership, with the son as a reference to himself, we now turn to draw some christological implications from our discussion of the parable.

Some scholars have found in the parable an implicit messianic claim by Jesus.[207] Others, considering that the intention of telling the parable was not christological but pronouncing judgement against the Jewish religious leadership, conclude that the parable in itself does not provide any significant clues about Jesus himself or his self-consciousness of divine sonship.[208] However, even if christology was not the point of the parable, the facts that the "son" was used as an indirect self-reference by Jesus and that the *sending* of the son takes place at the climactic point of the story both increase the likelihood that in telling the parable Jesus used a term which arose from his self-consciousness of being God's only son and of being sent by God. Moreover, it coheres with other passages which reflect his self-consciousness of divine sonship and divine mission. That is, when we consider that the parable is told by someone who, in the light of other passages, showed a self-consciousness of being uniquely related to God as his Father and of coming from God, it is entirely legitimate to interpret the christological significance attached to the parable in the whole context of his self-consciousness. Then it becomes highly likely that in telling this parable Jesus implicitly revealed his self-consciousness of divine sonship and of divine mission, although this was not his primary intention.

Furthermore, there may be strong grounds for connecting the parable with the development of the early Christian understanding of Jesus as the pre-existent Son *sent* by the Father. Given that Jesus' dominant category of self-understanding was his self-consciousness of divine sonship, the bigger the impact of the parable made upon the early Christian understanding of Jesus, the higher the probability that the so-called "pre-Pauline 'sending' formula" in the NT ("God sent his Son"; cf. Gal 4:4; Rom 8:3; Jn 3:17; 1

---

[206] Snodgrass, "Recent Research," 209.

[207] Cf. Witherington, *Christology*, 215.

[208] Cf. Snodgrass, "Recent Research," 208-9: "The parable and quotation imply the importance of Jesus' own role, but the specifics of that role and what content should be assigned to an image such as 'son' will have to be determined by other texts. The primary concern of the parable is its accusation against the Jewish *leaders* for their insensitivity to what God intended for Israel and what he intended with the ministry of Jesus."

Jn 4:9, 10, 14) derived from Jesus, who also spoke of himself as having been "sent" by God (although we still need to discuss in what sense he spoke in this way).[209] If, as we have already shown, our parable was not a creation by the early church but goes back to Jesus, then the fact that all three Synoptic evangelists – including the author of *Gos. Thom.* – preserved and made use of the parable strongly suggests that it had left a big impact upon the earliest early Christians.

4.3.6. Mk 1:9-11

Unlike other Synoptic texts discussed so far, the present text is not a saying of Jesus but a divine declaration coming from heaven at his baptism.

In the past, when attempting to locate the place of the theophany at Jesus' baptism in the developments of early christology, scholars' attention tended to focus mainly on the divine voice heard from heaven. But in recent years the discussion has been broadened to include not only the question of the historicity of the theophany but also the baptismal event as a whole – i.e., the baptism, the theophany and the timing of the two.[210] However, our attention will be focused on the theophany experienced by Jesus, which includes the descent of the Spirit and the voice from heaven addressing Jesus as ὁ υἱός μου ὁ ἀγαπητός "my beloved Son."

4.3.6.1. Authenticity of the Baptismal Account

The view that Jesus was baptized by John is generally accepted.[211] However, the authenticity of the theophany in the baptismal narrative has been variously questioned.

It has been argued that the portrayal of Jesus as endowed with the Spirit and identified as God's Son fits too well with the developing christology of the early church (i.e., against the criterion of dissimilarity).[212] Several pieces of evidence, however, can be put forward in favour of its authenticity.[213]

---

[209] Further discussion of this last point will have to await until Chapter 8.

[210] See R. L. Webb, "Jesus' Baptism: Its Historicity and Implications" *BBR* 10 (2000), 261-309. However, the question of the historicity of Jesus' baptism lies beyond our scope.

[211] Cf. Webb, "Baptism," 261; Meier, *Marginal Jew*, 2.105.

[212] Dibelius, *Tradition*, 271-72, contended that the early church created the tradition to set Jesus' sonship and messianic role at the beginning of his ministry.

[213] Webb, "Baptism," 275-77.

First, according to the criterion of coherence,[214] the two components of the theophany (i.e., the endowment of the Spirit and the heavenly revelation of Jesus' divine sonship) could well derive from Jesus' own experience. The Gospel traditions suggest that Jesus attributed his power in ministry to a special endowment of the Spirit (Mt 12:27-28/Lk 11:19-20; Mt 12:31-32/Mk 3:28-29/Lk 12:10; cf. Lk 4:16-21) and was conscious of a special relationship with God as his Father (Mt 26:39/Mk 14:36/Lk 22:42; Mt 11:25-27/Lk 10:21-22).[215]

Second, it is legitimate to say that "if Jesus was perceived by himself and others as a prophet, then it is reasonable to assume that at some point he experienced a prophetic call-vision."[216]

Third, according to the criterion of dissimilarity, the lack of a convincing or obvious background for the origins and significance of the "like a dove" imagery in the theophany narrative renders its authenticity more likely.[217]

It has also been argued that the theophany serves well the early Christian apologetic purpose of dealing with the problems of Jesus' baptism by John.[218] More recently Meier has conjectured that the theophany is the result of a Christian "midrash" of a number of OT texts (e.g., Ps 2:7 and Isa 42:1) which was inserted into the baptismal narrative in order to provide a first interpretation of who Jesus is:

The theophany does not mirror some inner experience Jesus had at the time; it mirrors the desire of the first-generation Christian church to define Jesus as soon as the primitive Gospel story begins – all the more so because this definition was needed to counter the impression of Jesus' subordination to John, implicit in the tradition of the former being baptized by the latter. Indeed, Christian embarrassment over the *fact* of Jesus' baptism

---

[214] Cf. Meier, *Marginal Jew*, 1.176-77, for a description of this criterion.

[215] On this point Dunn, *Spirit*, 63, also concurs: "It is certain that Jesus believed himself to be empowered by the Spirit and thought of himself as God's son. These convictions must have crystallized at some point in his life. Why should the traditions unanimously fasten on this episode in Jesus' life if they had no reason for making the link and many reasons against it."

[216] Webb, "Baptism," 276.

[217] See bibliography on this issue in Webb, "Baptism," 276 n.38, and the survey of alternatives in Davies and Allison, *Matthew*, 1.331-34. One cannot, however, apply this criterion in an excluding manner to argue that, if something attributed to Jesus agrees with the thinking of his followers, then it must have been original to them rather than Jesus.

[218] A. Vögtle, *Offenbarungsgeschehen und Wirkungsgeschichte: Neutestamentliche Beiträge* (Freiburg: Herder, 1985), 134-39, argues that it was created to counter the question of why the Greater One, the Messiah, submitted to John's baptism. Haenchen, *Der Weg Jesu*, 62, contends from a pragmatic perspective that it was intended as the prototype for Christian baptism.

was probably a major factor in the creation of the *story* of Jesus' baptism, complete with interpretative theophany.[219]

It is true that there is some evidence pointing towards the existence of an apologetic purpose behind some gospel writers. It cannot, however, be pressed so far as to contend that the supernatural components associated with Jesus' baptism are wholly a creation of the early church. To the contrary, several pieces of evidence, such as the lack of a comparison between Jesus and John (contrast with vv.7-8), the seeing of the Spirit's descent only by Jesus, and the addressing of God's voice only to Jesus, seem to render the suggestion unlikely.[220] In other words, if early Christians were to create a story which encompasses their high estimate of Jesus they would have made the theophany to be seen by the crowd or at least by someone else (as the Fourth evangelist did in Jn 1:32-34) and the heavenly voice heard by others (as the First and the Fourth Gospel writers did in Mt 3:17 and in Jn 1:32-34).[221] Moreover, the criterion of multiple attestation seems to tip the balance towards the authenticity of both the baptism and the theophany.[222]

Our examination of evidence for both sides of the argument leads us to conclude that it is much more likely that Jesus experienced at some point a prophetic call-vision, if not the baptismal theophany, which included the elements of divine sonship and spirit anointing.[223]

4.3.6.2. Background and Meaning of the Theophany

Having argued for the authenticity of the baptismal theophany, we will now focus more specifically on the possible background for the heavenly voice in order to draw out its christological significance.

The divine declaration from heaven as recorded in Mk 1:11 addresses Jesus as his beloved Son (Σὺ εἶ ὁ υἱός μου ὁ ἀγαπητός, ἐν σοὶ εὐδόκησα). The wording of this heavenly voice seems to recall the language of Ps 2:7 (Υἱός μου εἶ σύ, ἐγὼ σήμερον γεγέννηκά σε) and Isa 42:1 (Ιακωβ ὁ παῖς

---

[219] Meier, *Marginal Jew*, 2.107.

[220] Gundry, *Mark*, 53.

[221] Cf. Mk 9:2-8 pars.

[222] The probability of its authenticity will increase even more if Webb, "Baptism," 262-74, is right to argue that there are three or probably four independent accounts behind this tradition: Q 3:21-22 (probable); Mk 1:9-11; Jn 1:29-34; *GHeb* §2.

[223] Webb, "Baptism," 277, thinks it is possible that a prophetic call-vision may have taken place at Jesus' baptism, although he admits that there are problems in linking these two events.

μου ἀντιλήμψομαι αὐτοῦ Ισραηλ ὁ ἐκλεκτός μου προσεδέξατο αὐτὸν ἡ ψυχή μου).[224]

A number of different interpretations of the heavenly voice have been advanced by scholars depending on different OT allusions proposed.

(1) Some who see in the baptismal saying an original allusion only to Isa 42:1 claim that behind the identification of Jesus as the Son one should find a trace of christological development from a "servant" christology to a "son" christology.[225]

(2) Those who see an allusion to Gen 22:2, where God commands Abraham to sacrifice Isaac, interpret the divine declaration to imply that Jesus as the Son of God fulfils the typology of Isaac.[226]

(3) Those who find an allusion to Exod 4:22-23, where Israel is referred to as God's firstborn son, interpret the heavenly voice as affirming that the role of Israel as God's son is being fulfilled by Jesus.[227]

(4) Those who see John 1:34 as reflecting an independent form of the baptismal tradition with the third person form of address as original find a christological development from a "chosen one" christology to a "son" christology.[228]

(5) Finally, those who find an allusion to Ps 2:7 commonly argue that an understanding of Jesus as the Messiah is the most probable meaning of the text.

However, a close analysis of the saying and the OT passages mentioned above seems to indicate that a single text does not account adequately for the heavenly voice as a whole.[229]

J. Jeremias championed the view that the original form of the heavenly voice was based purely upon Isa 42:1 and thus did not refer to Jesus as the Son.[230] According to his view, παῖς stood originally in the saying but was later changed to υἱός by Hellenistic Christians, making the first step in a

---

[224] V. Taylor, *The Gospel According to St. Mark: the Greek Text* (London: Macmillan, 1952), 162.

[225] Jeremias, "παῖς θεοῦ," *TDNT* 5.701-2.

[226] G. Vermes, *Scripture and Tradition in Judaism: Haggadic Studies* (Leiden: Brill, 1961, 1973), 222-23, states, "Instead of recognizing that the Gospel tradition transmits a composite citation of Genesis 22 and Isaiah 42, most commentators make an entirely useless and inconclusive effort to show that the Mark formula is either based on Psalm 2.7 and Isaiah 42.1, or that Isaiah 42 alone underlies the quotation but translated differently from the Septuagint"; and E. Best, *The Temptation and the Passion* (Cambridge: CUP, 1965), 169-70.

[227] P. Bretscher, "Exodus 4:22-23 and the Voice from Heaven" *JBL* 87 (1968), 301-11, contends that πρωτότοκος stands behind uses of ἀγαπητός, μονογενής, and ἐκλεκτός.

[228] Marcus, *The Way*, 54-55.

[229] R. A. Guelich, *Mark 1-8:26* (WBC 34A; Dallas: Word Books, 1989), 33.

[230] Jeremias, *TDNT* 5.701-2; Jeremias, *Theology*, 1.53-55. For a concise summary of Jeremias's view see I. H. Marshall, "Son of God or Servant of Yahweh," 122.

process which led to the complete assimilation of the saying to Psalm 2:7 as attested in the Codex Bezae (D) reading of Lk 3:22.

The view represented by Jeremias has enjoyed a widespread recognition in the past.[231] Although the explanation for the exchange between παῖς and υἱός has received much criticism, the basic thrust of the argument (i.e., the absence of the "son" motif in the original tradition) is still accepted by many scholars today.[232]

Convinced by most of Jeremias' arguments, but somewhat suspicious about the suggestion that an original παῖς was replaced by υἱός in Hellenistic Christianity Davies and Allison made a slight modification to Jeremias' theory.[233] In their opinion, Jeremias failed to explain the precise form of the first line of Mk 1:11. The address to Jesus in the second person form (σὺ εἶ) is not from Isa 42:1, but recalls the statement of Ps 2:7. They see the baptismal saying as a conflation of texts, with the entire first line having been taken over from Ps 2:7 with some contextual modification. They come to the conclusion that "at some time in the history of the tradition, a quotation of Isa 42.1 was altered in order to gain an allusion to Ps 2.7."

It is true that Isa 42:1 has some advantages over other texts as a possible background for Mk 1:11. In terms of the context, Isa 42:1 has the advantage of providing a better parallel than any other texts to the descent of the Spirit. In terms of verbal similarities, it has also advantage over Ps 2:7, and the final part of the saying (ἐν σοὶ εὐδόκησα) most likely renders רצתה in Isa 42:1.[234] However, to contend that Isa 42:1 is the only background for the heavenly voice is somewhat problematic for the following reasons:

(1) Isa 42:1 does not have a direct address to the "servant."

(2) Even if the possibility of a change from the ambiguous παῖς το υἱός is granted, two more difficulties still need to be overcome: (a) the absence of evidence for an earlier παῖς christology in the baptismal setting; and (b) the difficulty of explaining the change of παῖς το υἱός in the early church,

---

[231] It has won acceptance from O. Cullmann, *The Christology of the New Testament* (London: SCM, 1963), 66; Fuller, *Foundations*, 169-70; Hahn, *Hoheitstitel*, 338, 340; and J. Gnilka, *Das Evangelium nach Markus* (EKKNT 2; Einsiedeln: Benziger Verlag, 1978-1979), 1.50. However, it is important to recognize that this view is too much indebted to a presupposition widespread among NT scholars that high christology cannot be attributed to Jesus himself or to the earliest period of the early church.

[232] Cf. Davies and Allison, *Matthew*, 1.337-38. For a similar view, see Lindars, *Apologetic*, 139-40, who holds that the reference to Psalm 2:7 was consciously added to the original text by the early church. Marcus, *The Way*, 48-56; idem, *Mark*, 158-67.

[233] Davies and Allison, *Matthew*, 1.337-38.

[234] MT has "my soul is well pleased"; LXX has προσεδέξατο αὐτόν ἡ ψυχή μου; cf. εὐδοκεῖν in A Θ Σ and Mt 12:18; *Tg. Isa.* has 'my word is well pleased.'

where παῖς consistently connoted "servant" when used as a title (e.g., Mt 12:18; Lk 1:54, 69; Acts 4:25, 27, 30; cf. 3:13, 26; *Did.* 9.2-3).[235]

(3) There is no textual evidence that υἱός replaced παῖς in this account.[236]

(4) It is heavily dependent upon an alleged tradition of a loose translation between ἀγαπητός and ἐκλεκτός. What we have in Lk 9:35 and Jn 1:34[237] is "a variant for ἀγαπητός and not for υἱός; they cannot, therefore, be used as part of a proof that υἱός was not an original part of the text." Moreover, "the fact that ἀγαπητός *may* be drawn from Isaiah 42.1 is no argument that the preceding phrase must come from the same place."[238]

The evidence therefore suggests that an influence from Isa 42:1 does not necessarily exclude the possibility that other OT passages such as Ps 2:7 have also influenced the saying. The following evidence supports the possibility that υἱός was an original part of the saying.

(1) It accounts best for the direct address to the son, σὺ εἶ ὁ υἱός μου ("you are my son"),[239] as opposed to the third person form in the other suggested texts (Isa 42:1; Gen 22:2, 12, 16; Exod 4:22).[240]

(2) The explicit quotation of Ps 2:7 in other parts of the NT (cf. Acts 13:33; Heb 1:5; 5:5; Lk 3:22 *v.l.*) seems to support this connection too.

(3) While the unique word order (cf. Ps 2:7 LXX; Acts 13:33; Heb 1:5; Lk 3:22 *v.l.*) and the absence of further parallels between Ps 2:7 and the baptismal saying are sometimes seen as evidence against the presence of an allusion to Ps 2:7,[241] they are in fact to be taken as evidence in favour of it. The change in word order from υἱός μου εἶ σύ (Ps 2:7 LXX) to σὺ εἶ ὁ υἱός μου in Mk 1:11 can well be explained as a deliberate shift in emphasis

---

[235] See Marshall, "Son or Servant," 125-26. ὁ ἀγαπητός μου in Mt 12:18 probably echoes the baptismal voice rather than vice versa.

[236] Guelich, *Mark*, 33; see Marshall, "Son or Servant,"121-33, for a thorough critique of the view represented by J. Jeremias.

[237] Lk 9:35 has ὁ ἐκλελεγμένος in place of ὁ ἀγαπητός found in Mk 9:7 and Jn 1:34 has a variant reading of ἐκλεκτός instead of υἱός.

[238] Marshall, "Son or Servant," 123.

[239] *Tg. Isa* 41:8-9 renders the MT in the second person form, but it has "servant" instead of "son."

[240] Compare also with 2 Sam 7:14; Mk 12:6.

[241] C. R. Kazmierski, *Jesus the Son of God: a Study of the Markan Tradition and its Redaction by the Evangelist* (Würzburg: Echter, 1979), 38, denies an allusion to Ps 2:7 in Mark 1:11 because the explicit quotations of Ps 2:7 in the NT still keep the word order of the psalm, which has the emphasis on adoption and enthronement. However, Gundry, *Mark*, 52, rightly observes that "divergence is to be expected in allusive quotations. It is explicit quotations of the OT in the NT that are more notable for sticking close to the LXX." Moreover, this change in word order from the LXX is not of any great importance if the text is not dependent upon the LXX.

from the adoption or enthronement motifs of the psalm to the identification of the addressee as God's Son.[242] There is a shift in emphasis from "A son of mine (are) you" to *"You* are my son."[243] It also partly explains the omission of the clause ἐγὼ σήμερον γεγέννηκά σε. Moreover, this change in emphasis is very likely to be responsible for the third person construction of Mt 3:17 (Οὗτός ἐστιν ὁ υἱός μου) and the transfiguration accounts (Mk 9:7; Mt 17:5; Lk 9:35; cf. 2 Pet 1:17), where the emphasis lies on the identification of Jesus as the Son rather than on the Father's role.[244]

Now let us to turn to the possible meaning of the term ἀγαπητός. In Mt 12:18, where Isa 42:1 is quoted, it is the term ἀγαπητός rather than the LXX's ἐκλεκτός that is used. Therefore ἀγαπητός can be taken as evidence of alluding to this OT text. However, other possibilities have also been suggested. One possibility is that the choice of this word was influenced by the Targum on Psalm 2:7 ("Beloved as a son to his father you are to me"),[245] but "its removal of the direct statement of sonship found in the MT makes it most unlikely that it is a source for ἀγαπητός in the baptismal saying."[246] Another possibility is an allusion to Genesis 22, especially in the LXX, where the genitive of the possessive pronoun appears twice[247] thus providing a close verbal connection to the first line of the heavenly voice.[248] While Gen 22 cannot explain the baptismal saying in its entirety,

---

[242] Guelich, *Mark*, 34. In addition to a christological emphasis, a stylistic reason behind the change in word order was suggested by Gundry, *Mark*, 51-52: Unlike the other NT quotations of Ps 2:7 (Acts 13:33; Heb 1:5; 5:5), where the second half of Mark 1:11 (ἐν σοὶ εὐδόκησα) does not follow, the emphatic σὺ εἶ ὁ υἱός μου has the advantage of avoiding an ugly construction of σύ, ἐν σοὶ (you, in you). However, see H.-J. Steichele, *Der leidende Sohn Gottes: eine Untersuchung einiger alttestamentlicher Motive in der Christologie des Markusevangeliums* (Regensburg: Pustet, 1980), 136-37 n. 104, who dismisses the significance of this change, by pointing to Mark 8:29 σὺ εἶ ὁ Χριστός, where the emphasis is on Χριστός, despite its placement at the end of the identification; also Marcus, *The Way*, 51; idem, *Mark*, 162.

[243] This shift in emphasis suggests the priority of Jesus' self-consciousness of divine sonship over his messiahship.

[244] *Contra* Bretscher, "Exodus," 302-03.

[245] Lövestam, *Son*, 96; Schweizer, *TDNT* 8.368, n.240; R. H. Gundry, *The Use of the Old Testament in St. Matthew's Gospel: With Special Reference to the Messianic Hope* (NovTSup 18; Leiden: Brill, 1967), 30f.

[246] Marshall, "Son or Servant," 127-8. Compare with the Targum on 2 Sam 7:14 ("I shall be to him *as a father, and he shall be to me as* a son"), where the relationship of the Messiah to God as his Son is clearly weakened, possibly in reaction to Christian claims. Cf. Lövestam, *Son*, 89.

[247] Cf. vv.12 and 16 τοῦ υἱοῦ σου τοῦ ἀγαπητοῦ.

[248] A. M. Hunter, *The Work and Words of Jesus* (Philadelphia: Westminster, 1973), 43. However, Marshall, "Son or Servant," 128, is more hesitant of its direct presence here.

at least it offers a significant clue towards the meaning of the saying.[249] It is important to observe that the word ἀγαπητός never renders בחיר ("chosen" or ἐκλεκτός) of Isa 42:1 anywhere in the LXX.[250] In the LXX ἀγαπητός can be translated as "beloved" or as "only," but the latter is the most probable meaning when used of a son or daughter.[251] Thus Gen 22:2, 12, 16 provides an important parallel when this term designates Isaac as Abraham's "only" son.[252] This motif seems to be further developed by the writer of the Fourth Gospel when the term μονογενής is used (cf. 1:14, 18; 3:16, 18). And if this lexical possibility is most likely, then we are in a position to claim that "the heavenly voice identifies Jesus as one having a special relationship with the Father."[253] Thus the personal relationship expressed in Genesis 22 becomes important for our understanding of the baptismal saying. In the light of the examination of evidence adduced above we conclude with Marshall that,

it is impossible to say with absolute certainty that the baptismal saying directly reflects Psalm 2:7, Genesis 22:2 and Isaiah 42:1 in its three main components, but it can be claimed with a fair degree of probability that these three passages must be regarded as the background for its interpretation, and that a denial of the presence of ideas from either Psalm 2.7 or Isaiah 42.1 is to be rejected.[254]

The foregoing discussion leads us to conclude that the heavenly voice addressing Jesus as ὁ υἱός μου ὁ ἀγαπητός gives support to our case that Jesus had a self-consciousness of a unique personal relationship to God as his Father and of himself as his Son. Some scholars, however, claim that the heavenly voice only reflects a messianic understanding of him and the title "Son of God" was given to him in the light of his messianic consciousness. In other words, Jesus received the messianic title of Son because he was the Messiah.[255] As the Davidic king in the last days, Jesus is installed as God's Son. The title "Son of God" was first understood in a

---

[249] Marshall, "Son or Servant," 128.
[250] The presence of ἀγαπητός in Matthew's rendering of Isa 42:1 in 12:18 is more likely to reflect the influence of the baptismal narrative rather than a free translation of it.
[251] C. H. Turner, "ὁ υἱός μου ὁ ἀγαπητός" JTS 27 (1925), 113-29 (cf. idem in JTS 28 [1926-7], 362, and A. Souter in JTS 28, 59f.); Kazmierski, Jesus the Son of God, 54-55.
[252] In about half the texts in which ἀγαπητός occurs, it renders the Hebrew word יחיד ("only"). The parallels in Gen 22 make it doubtful that ὁ ἀγαπητός is an independent title; cf. G. D. Kilpatrick, "The Order of Some Noun and Adjective Phrases in the New Testament" NovT 5 (1962), 111-14.
[253] Guelich, Mark, 34.
[254] Marshall, "Son or Servant," 129.
[255] Schweizer, TDNT 8.356-57. However, see Marshall, "Divine Sonship," 134-49, Cullmann, Christology, 275-81.

purely functional sense, and only at a later stage was it filled with a fuller content (i.e., a more personal or metaphysical relationship to God).

However, as Marshall rightly pointed out, "there is little stress, if any, on the thought of Jesus as the Messiah in the baptismal story. If messiahship is a thought present in the story at all, it would appear that Jesus is the Messiah because he is the Son of God rather than vice versa."[256] In short, the baptismal saying "goes beyond a purely functional or messianic use of the title by the use of the qualifying adjective ἀγαπητός which indicates the unique relationship of Jesus to his Father."[257] The allusion to Ps 2:7 in the baptismal account has as its main purpose to declare Jesus as God's Son rather than simply the messiah.

From a more exegetical basis J. Marcus argued that an allusion to Ps 2:7 in Mk 1:11 is part of Mark's own redactional activity, given that the fusion of two or more biblical passages into one conflated citation is "a typical Markan strategy."[258] So such a conflation of OT texts is visible from the introduction of Ps 2:7 into the context otherwise provided by Isa 42:1.[259] Not only does Marcus take the allusion to Ps 2:7 as Markan redaction, but he goes on to argue that in the original form of the tradition Jesus was probably spoken of in the third person (οὗτός ἐστιν) rather than being addressed in the second person (σὺ εἶ).[260]

Marcus supports his view by taking John 1:34 as reflecting an independent form of the baptismal tradition, a form that was known to

---

[256] Marshall, "Divine Sonship," 143. With regard to the priority of Jesus' filial relationship to God over his messianic consciousness Marshall elucidates: "What is of especial importance is that this use of the category of Sonship would be based upon Jesus' consciousness of a unique filial relationship to God rather than upon the conviction that as the Messiah he was the Son of God. The evidence strongly suggests that the fundamental point in Jesus' self-understanding was his filial relationship to God and that it was from this basic conviction that he undertook the tasks variously assigned to the Messiah, Son of man and Servant of Yahweh, rather than that the basic datum was consciousness of being the Messiah. If this is so, the argument that 'the Son' was not a current messianic title becomes irrelevant. In any case, the Synoptic Gospels indicate that Jesus used this title only in his private teaching to his disciples, so that the question whether the people at large would have understood him to be using a current messianic title is further shown to be an irrelevant one" (pp.138-39).

[257] Marshall, "Son or Servant," 130.

[258] On Mark's technique of conflation, see Marcus, *The Way*, 15. Steichele, *Der leidende Sohn*, 125, discounts the evidence that Ps 2:7 and Isa 42:1 were already linked in Judaism by contending that in *Midr. Psalms* 2, par. 9 [14b], both passages are merely part of a list of scriptural texts used to show that Israel is God's son. However, cf. Jeremias, *TDNT* 5.693 (and n.292), 695-7; Lövestam, *Son*, 95f.

[259] Marcus, *The Way*, 54.

[260] See also Bretscher, "Exodus," 302-3, for the argument that the third person form may represent the original tradition and thus the connection with Ps 2:7 is a later development.

Matthew and Luke, though they also knew Mark's edited version of it.[261] Thus, in this form of tradition, Jesus was probably referred to as God's ἐκλεκτός rather than as his υἱός. According to this reconstruction, Mark is said to have brought two changes:

(1) the change to a second person address, which was motivated by his desire to restrict the vision only to Jesus as part of his messianic secret motif: "until Jesus' death on the cross, no human being may know his true identity as Son of God"[262] and

(2) the substitution of the title ὁ υἱός μου ὁ ἀγαπητός for ὁ ἐκλεκτός τοῦ θεοῦ, which brings Ps 2:7 into the picture and thus stresses the importance of the title "Son of God" in his overall story.[263]

The theory of Markan redaction advanced by Marcus has its own weaknesses, however. It is heavily dependent on two assumptions, namely that the third person form of address and the title "chosen one" belong to the original saying. Thus, if the second person form of address is proved to be part of the original tradition, then this theory loses much of its ground. In addition, if υἱός belongs to the original saying, then the entire theory falls to the ground.

Those who take the third person form (οὗτός ἐστιν)[264] as original provide the following evidence: (1) The σὺ εἶ in Mark and Luke already betrays a process of interpretation in the direction of the messianic sonship of the psalm, a development consummated in a variant reading of Lk 3:22.[265] (2) The private nature of the vision in Mark coheres with his messianic secret motif.[266] (3) If Q contained the baptismal narrative it is

---

[261] Brown, *John*, 1.65-66.

[262] Marcus, *The Way*, 54-55. However, see B. Witherington, *The Gospel of Mark: A Socio-Rhetorical Commentary* (Grand Rapids: Eerdmans, 2001), 40-42, for critical comments on Mark's messianic secret: ". . . there is no unified messianic secret motif in Mark" (40); "It is still easier to believe that because of the volatility of Jesus' environment, he might silence or reject certain kinds of acclamations of him to prevent misunderstanding without this implying that he had no messianic self-understanding" (42).

[263] Marcus, *The Way*, 54-55, notes that besides its possible use in the superscription to the Gospel and its use by the demons in 3:11, the title appears in 14:61-64 and in three revelatory scenes, which are strategically placed at the beginning, middle, and end of the Gospel (1:11; 9:7; 15:39).

[264] Found in Mt 3:17; John 1:34 and the Transfiguration narrative (Mk 9:7 and pars.; 2 Pet 1:17).

[265] Bretscher, "Exodus," 302. However, even if this text is secondary, which is likely to be the case, it only shows that the baptismal saying was very early connected with Ps 2:7.

[266] Marcus, *The Way*, 54-55; also J. Marcus, *Mark: a New Translation with Introduction and Commentary* (AB 27; New York: Doubleday, 2000), 164.

more likely that the third person form was older and the Markan private vision a later redaction.[267]

However, the argument for the original third person form is problematic. The baptismal account is recorded in all three Synoptic Gospels (Mk 1:9-11; Mt 3:13-17; Lk 3:21-22) and two pieces of evidence seem to be in favour of its presence in Q:

(1) At a few points Matthew and Luke agree with each other against Mark and make similar changes to Mark (including suppression of the same words, addition of the same words, change of grammatical forms, and change of word order), although the way they change the text is not identical;[268] and

(2) from a narrative perspective of Q, a baptismal narrative seems necessary as the immediately preceding pericope and the succeeding one seem to make better sense with it.[269]

While it seems probable that Q contained the account of Jesus' baptism, it cannot be used as an argument for the originality of the third person form for the following reasons:[270]

---

[267] Marcus, *Mark*, 164, however, admits that "unfortunately . . . the question of whether or not Q included the baptism is quite controversial." See J. S. Kloppenborg, *Q Parallels: Synopsis, Critical Notes & Concordance* (Sonoma: Polebridge, 1988), for bibliographic references for both sides of the argument.

[268] Webb, "Baptism," 264: (1) Both drop the reference to John and the Jordan (Matthew does use it earlier in 3:13). (2) Both after Mark's aorist indicative use of the verb βαπτίζω to an aorist participial form (Matthew used the nominative, while Luke uses the genitive). (3) Both include the name Ἰησοῦς in the statement about Jesus' being baptized, whereas Mark had the name earlier in v. 9. (4) Both change Mark's use of the verb σκίζω ("to tear") to the verb ἀνοίγω ("to open"), but they use different forms of the verb: Matthew uses the aorist passive indicative form (ἠνεώχθησαν), while Luke uses the aorist passive infinitive (ἀνεῳχθῆναι). (5) Both change Mark's prepositional phrase εἰς αὐτόν ("on him") to ἐπ' αὐτόν ("onto him"). (6) Both alter Mark's word order τὸ πνεῦμα ὡς περιστερὰν καταβαῖνον ("the Spirit like a dove descended") by shifting the verb καταβαίνω ("to descend") to precede the phrase ὡς(εἰ) περιστερὰν ("like a dove").

[269] Webb, "Baptism," 264-65.

[270] Cf. von Harnack, *Sayings of Jesus*, 310-14; and B. H. Streeter, *The Four Gospels* (London: Macmillan, 1924), 188, championed the view that Q contained a baptismal account. Recent advocates of this view include W. Grundmann, *Das Evangelium nach Lukas* (THKNT 3; Berlin: Evangelische Verlagsanstalt, 1966), 106f.; H. Schürmann, *Das Lukasevangelium* (HTKNT 3; Freiburg: Herder, 1969), 1.197, 218; P. Hoffmann, *Studien zur Theologie der Logienquelle* (Münster: Aschendorff, 1972), 4, 39; A. D. Jacobson, *Wisdom Christology in Q* (Diss. Claremont, 1978) 35-36. Marcus, *Mark*, 164, notes that "The choice between these two alternatives would be easier if it were certain that Q had a baptismal narrative, because this would increase the likelihood that the public form was older and the Markan private vision a later redaction; unfortunately, however, the question of whether or not Q included the baptism is quite controversial." See Kloppenborg, *Q Parallels*, for a summary of the arguments.

(1) The above evidence is not conclusive; (2) it is quite clear that Matthew and Luke also used Mark in constructing their own baptismal accounts; and (3) Luke is almost identical with Mark in the theophany portion of the text, with the second person form over against Matthew's third person form.

It is therefore safer to conclude that the baptismal account had at least two independent sources, and it is almost impossible to reconstruct the Q text because of the fragmentary nature of the evidence.

Furthermore, even if Mark's messianic secret motif is granted, Luke's choice of the second person form is difficult to explain, unless he had a similar motivation as Mark. Luke's use of the second person form is best explained if he followed Mark and Matthew redacted Mark for his own purpose (e.g., to make it a public declaration).[271]

Moreover, if the theophany was Jesus' private experience rather than a public declaration, the second person form fits very well with what Jesus himself saw and heard, and thus the more public form of the baptismal tradition could well reflect an apologetic desire of the later Gospels (Mt 3:17; Jn 1:34) to emphasize the objective truth of the baptismal events.[272] Since the Matthean version includes conversation between John and Jesus it may be that Matthew is suggesting that John, and possibly the crowds, also heard the voice.[273] Moreover, the fact that the dialogue is reported only in Matthew could well suggest that Jesus' baptism by John has become a matter of embarrassment to the early church by this time. Not only that; the fact that Jesus received a baptism by John – and none other than a baptism of repentance for the forgiveness of sins – might have caused a clash with the belief in Jesus' sinlessness. However, despite all these potential problems, the fact that Matthew chooses to make use of this tradition – rather than suppressing it – is of great significance. Not only does it provide support for its authenticity, but it also strongly suggests that the personal experience of Jesus at his baptism was of supreme significance for the self-understanding of his person and mission![274]

As we will see later in Chapter 7, it is true that there was a wide range of evidence supporting the pre-Christian messianic interpretation of Psalm 2:7, but the foregoing discussion of Mk 1:11 has suggested a number of significant reasons for interpreting the allusion to Ps 2:7 in terms of Jesus'

---

[271] To contend that Matthew and Luke also knew Mark's edited version seems to me a sheer speculation!

[272] Gundry, *Matthew*, 52.

[273] Cf. D. Hill, *The Gospel of Matthew* (NCBC; London: Oliphants, 1972), 97; Davies and Allison, *Matthew*, 1.330.

[274] R. L. Webb, *John the Baptizer and Prophet: a Socio-Historical Study* (JSNTSup 62; Sheffield: JSOT Press, 1991), 57f. Cf. the denial that Jesus was baptized by John in the *Gospel of the Nazareans* (§3.7.3).

sonship to God as we have been trying to show in this chapter, rather than merely messianic sonship.

First, we have seen the change in word order as a deliberate shift in emphasis from the traditional Jewish motif of adoption or enthronement of the psalm to the specific identification of Jesus as God's Son.

Second, despite a possible embarrassment to the early church, the fact that Matthew did make use of the baptismal tradition rather than suppressing it strongly suggests that the personal experience of Jesus at his baptism, in which the emphasis is placed on his unique relationship to God, was of supreme significance for his self-understanding as God's Son.

Third, the fact that the original scene of the baptismal theophany is to be seen as a private experience rather than a public declaration also suggests that Jesus has become fully conscious of his unique sonship to God from the moment of his baptism. In other words, if this experience did not initiate Jesus' self-consciousness of divine sonship, it confirmed and informed it.

Fourth, the word ἀγαπητός is not without significance. It emphasizes a unique personal relationship between Jesus and God.

Fifth, the baptismal narratives (Mk 1:9-11//Mt 3:13-17//Lk 3:21-22), though stylised and adapted to the didactic needs of first-century churches, are intended to reflect an authentic feature of Jesus' self-understanding as God's Son.

Sixth, this view coheres with the special sense of sonship to God reflected in his address to God as *abba*. Thus the dominant category in Jesus' own ministry and mission was probably not messiahship but sonship to God, and from this "his other basic convictions about himself and his mission arose."[275]

4.4. Conclusion

A review of the contemporary debate over Jesus' use of *abba* and the discussion of authenticity and exegesis of his various sayings have led us to the following conclusions:

With regard to Jesus' use of *abba*, we have drawn the following conclusions:

(1) There is overwhelming evidence that Jesus prayed to God and addressed him as *abba* or Father reflecting the intimacy of his relationship with God.

---

[275] Dunn, *Spirit*, 39.

(2) While the fact that the very word *abba* that Jesus himself used was also used by the early church might suggest that Jesus' use of it as an address to God is nothing unique in itself, we have suggested several reasons to think otherwise and concluded that it provides support to his unique sonship to God.

(3) Although we may not be able to talk about Jesus' *subjective* experience of God in Schleiermacherian terms, the Gethsemane narrative and Jesus' prayer of thanksgiving preserved in Q 10:21-22 clearly suggest that Jesus had an intimate and special *relationship* with God. Such a relationship with God enabled him to ask God to let him bypass the cross and to claim for himself exclusive mutuality with God.

(4) The best explanation for the nature and frequency of Father language in the NT is that this phenomenon reflects the impact of Jesus' God language, Jesus' relationship with God, and the way Jesus instructed his disciples to speak about and relate to God.

(5) It is therefore fully warranted to conclude that the prevalence of the use of Father language for God in the early church can only be adequately explained from Jesus' own use of such language and, more importantly, from Jesus' own intimate and special relationship with the Father, which set him apart from other early Jews in important ways. Thus, while an attempt to place Jesus' view of God and his relationship to him within the framework of the OT and early Judaism is understandable, we are not convinced by the view that "Jesus understood God first as father of the people of Israel, and his own relationship to God in and from that framework."[276]

Having evaluated critically the authenticity of these sayings (Mt 11:27; Mk 13:32; Mt 16:17; Lk 22:29; Mk 12:1-12) we have come to the conclusion that the probability of each one of these sayings going back to a *Sitz im Leben Jesu* remains strong. Moreover, our exegesis of the saying in Mt 11:27 has suggested that Jesus was conscious of being God's unique agent who alone mediated the final revelation of God, and thus as God's unique Son. Furthermore, his "divine sonship" sayings in Mk 13:32, Mt 16:17, Lk 22:29, Mk 12:1-12 give cumulative evidence for his self-consciousness of divine sonship.

Besides providing cumulative evidence for Jesus' self-consciousness of divine sonship, our discussion about the parable of the wicked tenants also suggested that there may be strong grounds for connecting the parable with the so-called "pre-Pauline 'sending' formula" embedded in the NT documents when speaking about Jesus' pre-existence ("God sent his Son"; cf. Gal 4:4; Rom 8:3; Jn 3:17; 1 Jn 4:9, 10, 14). Given that Jesus' dominant category of self-understanding was his self-consciousness of divine

---

[276] Quotation from Thompson, *Promise*, 79.

sonship, the bigger the impact of the parable made upon the early Christian understanding of Jesus, the greater role the parable played in the development of the early Christian understanding of Jesus as the pre-existent Son *sent* by the Father. The fact that all three Synoptic evangelists – including the author of *Gos. Thom.* – preserved and made use of the parable strongly suggests that it had left a big impact upon the earliest Christians.

Our critical examination of evidence from the baptismal narrative (Mk 1:11 pars.) has led us to conclude that it is much more likely that Jesus experienced at some point a prophetic call-vision, if not the baptismal theophany, which included the elements of divine sonship and spirit anointing. Moreover, the heavenly voice addressing Jesus as ὁ υἱός μου ὁ ἀγαπητός has strengthened our thesis that Jesus was conscious of a unique personal relationship to God as his Father and regarded himself as his Son.[277]

In response to a widespread view that the baptismal account only reflects a messianic understanding of him and that the title "Son of God" was given to him in the light of his messianic consciousness, we have argued that the use of Ps 2:7 in Mk 1:11 gives support to our view that Jesus was the Messiah because he was the Son of God rather than vice versa. The priority of his divine sonship over his messiahship can be drawn from his self-consciousness of a unique personal relationship to the Father, as we have demonstrated in this chapter. The title "Son" is therefore not merely a way of expressing God's particular care and his promise of victory to a messianic king, but it entails a unique personal relationship to God as his Father.

We thus conclude our discussion by suggesting that Jesus' self-consciousness of divine sonship has a great potential of playing the most significant part in the development of early christology and of serving as the basic foundation for the early Christian understanding of Jesus as the pre-existent Son of God.

---

[277] L. Schenke, "Gibt es im Markusevangelium eine Präexistenzchristologie?" *ZNW* 91 (2000), 45-71, presents an interesting argument that the baptismal saying in Mk 1:11 shares the same form as the "prophetic dialogue" in Mk 1:2-3. Schenke sees Mark pairing these two divine addresses to the Son.

Chapter 5

Jesus' Self-Consciousness of Divine Mission

In the previous chapter we have seen that Jesus was conscious of a unique and personal relationship to God as his Father and of himself as his Son. In this chapter we will examine those sayings of Jesus in which he speaks of himself as having "come" and been "sent" from God (Mk 1:38 par.; Mk 2:17 par.; Mk 10:45; Lk 12:49, 51) and been "sent" by God (Mk 9:37 par.; Mt 15:24). As we have seen in the previous chapter, Jesus also told a parable where he seems to make reference to himself, though very subtle and implicit, as God's only Son sent by him (Mk 12:1-12 pars.). One of the central questions in this chapter is whether Jesus was conscious of his divine and transcendent origin when he spoke of himself as having "come" and been "sent" from/by God. In other words, what was implied about his origin when he spoke in this way? Do these statements imply his divine and transcendent origin or simply his self-consciousness of divine mission, a consciousness of a God-given mission to carry out in this world?

In this chapter we will (1) examine whether those "I have come" and "I was sent" sayings of Jesus as they are preserved in the Synoptics can be regarded as his authentic utterances; (2) discuss the meaning that Jesus wished to convey with these logia; and (3) draw out some of the christological implications of these statements for our overall understanding of Jesus' self-consciousness of divine sonship and divine mission as well as for the early Christian understanding of him as the pre-existent Son of God.

When we discuss Jesus' "I have come" or "I was sent" sayings we need to be aware of different meanings these terms may convey. We need to distinguish, for example, between (1) a local coming/sending, a movement from one place on earth to another and (2) a coming/sending in the theological sense. Within the latter category a further distinction can be made between (a) an immanent coming/sending in the sense of commissioning someone for a particular office (e.g., a prophet) and (b) a transcendent coming/sending of a pre-existent being, such as an angel and the like.

5.1. "I Have Come" Sayings

5.1.1. Different Views about "I Have Come" Sayings

Jesus' ἦλθον sayings have been interpreted by scholars in three ways: (1) simply as an idiom for conveying one's intention or purpose; (2) as indicative of a God-given mission or office, such as messianic, prophetic, and so on; and (3) as also indicative of his pre-existence.

5.1.1.1. Idiomatic Interpretation

First, the *idiomatic interpretation* of the ἦλθον sayings was first suggested by Jeremias and developed in a full scale monograph by Arens.[1] The basic argument of this view is that the original meaning of ἦλθον "can best be expressed as 'my purpose is to . . . ,' 'my Lebensberuf is to . . . ,' for which ἦλθον + inf. may be a circumloquium [*sic*]."[2] Arens argues that the verb acquired a nuance it hardly had before, viz. that of a God-given mission, only when the saying was inserted in its present context. Arens tries to make his case by drawing analogies from the Rabbinic writings. He finds "a number of examples where 'to come' + inf. was used as an idiomatic expression, meaning 'to have the intention, or purpose to . . .' as well as others meaning 'to have as a task, or mission to . . . .'"[3] In light of this evidence and the absence of such examples in Greek literature he concludes that ἦλθον + inf. is likely to be "a Greek rendering of a Palestinian idiom."[4]

---

[1] E. Arens, *The HΛΘON-Sayings in the Synoptic Tradition: a Historico-Critical Investigation* (Freiburg: Universitätsverlag Freiburg, 1976); J. Jeremias, "Die älteste Schicht der Menschensohn-Logien" *ZNW* 58 (1967), 166-67. One of the major problems in assessing Jesus' christological statements in the study of NT christology has been the apparent tension between the high christology in these sayings and their authenticity. The central question is whether such a high christology can be assigned to Jesus himself while maintaining its authenticity. In the past, some scholars (e.g., Bultmann and others) thought that this was hardly possible; any sayings of Jesus that show such a high estimate of himself cannot go back but to the early church. On the other hand, others (e.g., Jeremias) stood against this stream of opinion by defending the authenticity of these sayings while ascribing a somewhat lower christology. In other words, while the former group sacrificed both the authenticity of these sayings and their high christology, the latter sacrificed high christology as the cost of its authenticity. Although current scholarship does not follow either stream of opinion to the extreme, we believe that it still suffers from the same legacy.

[2] Arens, *HΛΘON-Sayings*, 54-55, 62-63. Cf. Jeremias, "älteste Schicht," 166-67 for rabbinic evidence, which in our opinion does not support Jeremias's case.

[3] Arens, *HΛΘON-Sayings*, 270.

[4] Arens, *HΛΘON-Sayings*, 270 (emphasis removed).

However, it is one thing to say that there was an idiomatic expression for ἦλθον sayings in a Semitic language and another thing to say that Jesus' usage of ἦλθον sayings comes from the same idiomatic expression. In our opinion, Arens has not proved the latter.

Arens finds four examples of non-idiomatic use of "to come" (בוא) + inf. of purpose in the Mishnaic texts:

Shabbat 16.6 "If a gentile came to put out (בא לכבות) the fire they may not say to him, 'Put it out', or 'Do not put it out', since they are not answerable for his keeping the Sabbath. But if it was a minor that came to put it out (בא לכבות) they may not permit him, since they are answerable for his keeping the Sabbath."

Sukkah 2.9 "If rain fell, when may he empty out [the Sukkah]? When the porridge would spoil. They propounded a parable: To what can it be compared? to a slave who came to fill the cup (בא למזוג לקוניו) for his master and he poured the pitcher over his [the slave's] face."

Sotah 1.6 "If she bore ornaments of gold and chains and nose-rings and finger-rings, they were taken from her to shame her. He then brought an Egyptian rope and tied it above her breasts. Any that wished to behold came and beheld (כל הרוצה לראות בא לראות), excepting her bondmen . . . ."

Edduyoth 8.7 "R. Joshua said: I have received as a tradition from Rabban Johanan b. Zakkai, who heard from his teacher, and his teacher from his teacher, as a Halakah given to Moses from Sinai, that Elijah will not come to declare unclean or clean, to remove afar or to bring nigh . . . (. . . . אליהו אב לטמא ולטהר, לרחק ולקרב)."

Arens then observes:

In this last text, בוא is to be taken literally, as in the preceding ones, i.e., it indicates a deplacement. However, the statement, taken as a whole, has the implied meaning of 'to have as a purpose to . . . ,' as is clear from the citation of Mal. 3,22f which then follows. Thus, Ed. 8,7 is to be understood as saying that Elijah will come 'not for the purpose of ... [but] to turn the hearts of the fathers etc.' (Mal. 3,22f, which echoes Mt. 10,35 par.).

On the other hand, Arens finds other Mishnaic texts in which an idiomatic expression of "to come" + inf. is used. He gives examples from the following texts: Ned. 10.7[5] uses בא לכלל in the sense of "to fulfil, keep a

---

[5] "If a man said to his wife, 'Let every vow be established that thou shalt vow from this time forth until I return from such-a-place', he has said nothing at all; but if [he said], 'Let them be void', R. Eliezer says: They are made void. But the Sages say: They are not made void. R. Eliezer said: If he can make void vows which already had the force of a prohibition, can he not also make void vows which have not yet the force of a prohibition? They answered: It is written, *Her husband may establish it or her husband may make it void* – such a vow as he may establish, such a vow he may make void; but such a vow as he may not establish, such a vow he may not make void."

vow"; in Sanh. 8.1, Demai 2.3, and Hul. 9.5 it is used in the sense of "to come within the scope of (a given prescription or law)." Maas. 5.5, Hallah 3.4 and Peah 4.8 have the expression בא לעונת המעשרות meaning "the time for tithing"; and R.Sh. 2.9 has "If we come to inquire (אמ באין אנו לדון) [into] the lawfulness of the decisions of the court . . . ," meaning "if we wish, or decide, to . . . ."

Arens concludes that the idiomatic uses of בוא + inf. in Ed. 8.7 and R.Sh. 2.9 support his contention that originally ἦλθον + inf. meant "I have the purpose/intention to . . . ." However, in our opinion, neither Ed. 8.7 nor R.Sh. 2.9 supports his case. The former text lends support for the non-idiomatic use of the expression because it should be interpreted literally. Even though Arens insists on reading this text as having "the implied meaning of 'to have as a purpose to . . . ,'" this is true for any statement constructed with the verb "to come" plus infinitive, viz., it conveys intention and purpose. R.Sh. 2.9 is not a good parallel to Jesus' use of ἦλθον sayings because the expression is used in a different context and with a different meaning. Two different uses should not be confused only because they are constructed with similar forms.

In his examples from Mekhilta, Arens cites only texts related to the Scriptures' coming, i.e., the Scriptures come to teach, to set a limit, to equalize, to forbid, to divide or distinguish. He is right to understand these references in the sense of "Scripture has the function, task, to . . . ," or "serves the purpose of . . . ."[6] However, these texts cannot be used as parallels to Jesus' use of ἦλθον sayings because the criticism applied to R.Sh. 2.9 also applies here. The Scripture as immaterial can only have a function or task to do something or serve the purpose of doing something, whereas a person's "coming" – i.e., Jesus' coming – cannot be limited to having the function or serving the purpose of doing. These two distinct entities should not be confused.

Neither are Arens's examples from the Talmud convincing. While Shab. 18b is an idiomatic usage of "I come + infinitive," it is not a good example to illustrate Jesus' use because the criticism applied to R.Sh. 2.9 and Mekhilta also applies here.[7] Although it is used for a person's coming (i.e., R. Akiba's coming), his "coming," unlike Jesus' coming, only represents a particular interpretation (i.e., of the school of Hillel). In other words, the expression is used in a different context and with a different meaning.

Shab. 18b "Said R. Jose son of R. Judah: The words of R. Akiba are the very words of Beth Hillel: R. Akiba comes only to explain the words of Beth Hillel."

---

[6] Arens, *HΛΘON-Sayings*, 267-68.
[7] Shab. 18b: "R. Akiba comes only to explain the words of Beth Hillel."

The case of Berak 58a is quite ambiguous; "if a man comes to kill you . . ." may be interpreted either idiomatic or non-idiomatic ways.

Berak 58a "R. Shila administered lashes to a man who had intercourse with an Egyptian woman. The man went and informed against him to the Government, saying: There is a man among the Jews who passes judgment without the permission of the Government. An official was sent to [summon] him. When he came he was asked: Why did you flog that man? He replied: Because he had intercourse with a she-ass. They said to him: Have you witnesses? He replied: I have. Elijah thereupon came in the form of a man and gave evidence. They said to him: If that is the case he ought to be put to death! He replied: Since we have been exiled from our land, we have no authority to put to death; do you [*sic*] do with him what you please. While they were considering his case, R. Shila exclaimed, *Thine, Oh Lord, is the greatness and the power.* What are you saying? they asked him. He replied: What I am saying is this: Blessed is the All-Merciful who has made the earthly royalty on the model of the heavenly, and has invested you with dominion, and made you lovers of justice. They said to him: Are you so solicitous for the honour of the Government? They handed him a staff and said to him: You may act as judge. When he went out that man said to him: Does the All-Merciful perform miracles for liars? He replied: Wretch! Are they not called asses? For it is written: *Whose flesh is as the flesh of asses.* He noticed that the man was about to inform them that he had called them asses. He said: This man is a persecutor, and the Torah has said: *If a man comes to kill you, rise early and kill him first.* So he struck him with the staff and killed him. He then said: Since a miracle has been wrought for me through this verse, I will expound it."

Shab. 116ab seems to support a non-idiomatic rather than idiomatic use of "coming," and more so if the speaker refers to what Jesus said:

Shab. 116ab "Imma Shalom, R. Eliezer's wife, was R. Gamaliel's sister. Now, a certain philosopher lived in his vicinity, and he bore a reputation that he did not accept bribes. They wished to expose him, so she brought him a golden lamp, went before him, [and] said to him, 'I desire that a share be given me in my [deceased] father's estate.' 'Divide,' ordered he. Said he [R. Gamaliel] to him, 'It is decreed for us, Where there is a son, a daughter does not inherit.' [He replied], 'Since the day that you were exiled from your land the Law of Moses has been superseded and another book given, wherein it is written, 'A son and a daughter inherit equally.' The next day, he [R. Gamaliel] brought him a Lybian ass. Said he to them, 'Look at the end of the book, wherein it is written, *I came not to destroy the Law of Moses nor to add to the Law of Moses* (לאוספי על אורייתא), (רמשה אתית לא למיפחת מן אורייתא דמשה אתית אלא), and it is written therein, A daughter does not inherit where there is a son.' Said she to him, 'Let thy light shine forth like a lamp.' Said R. Gamaliel to him, 'An ass came and knocked the lamp over!'"

In our opinion, to conclude from the above evidence that originally ἦλθον + inf. probably came from a Semitic manner of locution and meant simply "I have the purpose/intention to . . ." is an arbitrary decision. Even though there were two different meanings from similar expressions, Arens arbitrarily takes the idiomatic usage rather than the non-idiomatic one as the only linguistic parallel for Jesus' use of ἦλθον + inf. We would rather take the examples in Sukkah 2.9 and Ed. 8.7 as the closest examples for Jesus' ἦλθον sayings. Arens has not proved that Jesus' expression of ἦλθον + inf. should be degraded into a simple idiomatic expression. For Arens's case to be convincing there should be stronger evidence that shows a more direct relationship between Jesus' ἦλθον sayings and the idiomatic use of "to come" (בוא) + inf. of purpose in Jewish texts.[8] Obviously, if this interpretation is taken, the "coming" does not involve a movement from one place to another, but merely an idiomatic expression to convey one's intention and purpose.

5.1.1.2. Indicative of Pre-existence

Second, Jesus' ἦλθον sayings have been interpreted as indicative of Jesus' *pre-existence*. With this interpretation we are talking about a transcendent coming that involves a movement from heaven to earth. Lagrange, for example, argued that Jesus' ἦλθον sayings in absolute sense without any local marker are pointers to his pre-existence: "comme il n'y a pas 'je suis venu parmi vous', mais je suis venu tout court, on peut suppléer par la pensée 'dans le monde' et il est probable que Jésus fait ainsi allusion à sa propre pre-existence."[9] However, this interpretation was criticized by Gathercole. He points out that "coming" without local specification is attested not only in the Qumran literature in reference to Messiahs (CD-B 19:10-11; 1QS 9:11; 1QSa 2:14), prophets (1QS 9:11), and other figures, but also in the Synoptic Gospels, where John the Baptist is said to have "come" (Mk 9:12-13; Mt 21:32) without any local reference.[10] Instead, Gathercole regards Jesus' coming as *a voluntary act* with *a specific task* as the crucial indication of his pre-existence:

what these sayings have in common is that the construction ἦλθον + infinitive attests to the coming of Jesus as a voluntary act, which the Son of God has undertaken with a specific intended goal, the goal being expressed by the infinitive construction which follows the statement of the coming. It is, then, not only the fact of the reference to "coming" but the form in which this is expressed in connection with a specific task which points to pre-existence.[11]

---

[8] See also S. J. Gathercole, "On the Alleged Aramaic Idiom behind the Synoptic ἦλθον-sayings" *JTS* 55 (2004), 94-91.

[9] M.-J. Lagrange, *Évangile selon Saint Marc* (EBib; Paris: Lecoffre, 1947), *ad loc.*

[10] S. J. Gathercole, "The Advent of Jesus in the Synoptic Gospels" *an unpublished paper read at Aberdeen University NT Seminar* (2002), 2.

[11] Gathercole, "Advent of Jesus," 3. He then uses this criterion for his exegesis of ten individual sayings (Mk 1:24; Mt 8:29; Mk 1:38; Mk 2:17; Mt 5:17; Lk 12:49; Lk 12:51//Mt 10:34; Mt 10:35; Mk 10:45; Lk 19:10).

However, we wonder whether "coming" as a voluntary act with a specific intention could be sufficient evidence or a crucial indicator of Jesus' transcendent coming and/or his pre-existence. It neither does point to nor reject Jesus' transcendent origin or his pre-existence. On the contrary, a statement of Jesus' prophetic or God-given mission can equally be expressed as a voluntary act with a specific task. The meaning of the saying is therefore hardly determined by the form of the same!

5.1.1.3. Indicative of God-given Mission

Third, the majority of scholars interpret the ἦλθον sayings in connection with a *God-given mission*. Although these sayings were occasionally associated with Jesus' messiahship or more generally with the role of a messenger,[12] the most common view links these sayings with Jesus' prophetic or divine mission.[13] If this interpretation is taken, Jesus' coming should be understood as an immanent coming rather than a transcendent coming.

5.1.2. Mk 2:17

Jesus' response to the Pharisees comes in two parallel sayings. They are reported *verbatim* in all three gospels, with a change in verb tense by Luke in the second saying (ἐλήλυθα)[14] and a reference to Hos 6:6 in Matthew. The first half is the proverbial form of a metaphor involving the healthy and the sick, while the second is an "I have come" saying in the form of a "dialectical negation" about the righteous and the sinners.[15] Bultmann denied the authenticity of the latter saying because the aorist tense in Mark suggests that such a saying had the flavour of retrospective assessments of the life and ministry of Jesus in its totality.[16] However, this is not a necessary conclusion and there is no solid basis for denying its authenticity:[17] (1) the content is congruent with Jesus' ministry as

---

[12] J.-A. Bühner, *Der Gesandte und sein Weg im 4. Evangelium: die kultur- und religionsgeschichtlichen Grundlagen der johanneischen Sendungschristologie sowie ihre traditionsgeschichtliche Entwicklung* (WUNT 2/2; Tübingen: Mohr Siebeck, 1977).

[13] So R. Bultmann, *The History of the Synoptic Tradition* (Oxford: Blackwell, 1963), 152ff.

[14] Luke's change of tense expresses more exactly that Jesus' mission was still in progress.

[15] R. Pesch, *Das Markusevangelium* (HTKNT 2; Freiburg: Herder, 1977), 1.166.

[16] Bultmann, *Synoptic Tradition*, 152-56.

[17] C. E. Carlston, *The Parables of the Triple Tradition* (Philadelphia: Fortress, 1975), 114-15.

consistently portrayed throughout the Synoptic tradition;[18] (2) its structure as a "dialectical negation" is Semitic in keeping with OT counterparts as is the contrast "righteous" and "sinners;"[19] (3) the verb translates the Aramaic form ל (בא) אתא;[20] (4) v.17b has a very close parallel in Lk 12:51, whose authenticity should be accepted;[21] and (5) since early Christians called themselves "the righteous," it is highly unlikely that – according to the criterion of embarrassment – they would have created a saying in which the righteous are excluded from Jesus' mission (cf. Mt 10:41; 13:43, 49; Lk 14:14; Rom 1:17; Jas 5:16; 1 Jn 3:7).[22] Based on the above evidence we conclude that it is most likely that the saying in v.17b goes back to Jesus.[23]

C. E. B. Cranfield notes in his commentary that "The verb is often used of Jesus, particularly by himself, and expresses his consciousness of his mission," but he goes on to suggest that Jesus' use of it "is perhaps a pointer to his consciousness of pre-existence."[24] E. Arens, drawing a distinction between the original statement of the saying and the final setting in Mark, argues that in its original form the saying carried no hint of pre-existence, but something of that sense was acquired through Markan redaction. However, one needs not to posit a distinction between Jesus' original saying and the Markan form because such a distinction is based on the idiomatic interpretation of the original form of the ἦλθον sayings, a theory which we have already rejected. S. Gathercole also finds a pointer

---

[18] Cf. W. D. Davies and D. C. Allison, *A Critical and Exegetical Commentary on the Gospel According to Saint Matthew* (ICC; Edinburgh: T & T Clark, 1988, 1991, 1997), 2.106: "Jesus' fellowship with outcasts, with those who were regarded by many Jews as 'sinners', belongs to the bedrock of the tradition."

[19] H. Kruse, "Die 'dialektische Negation' als semitisches Idiom" *VT* 4 (1954), 385-400. In dialectical negation one statement, often the first, is placed in the negative in order to stress the other. Cf. the antithesis δίκαιος/ἁμαρτωλός with *saddîq/rāšā'*; G. Schrenk, *TWNT* 2.191.

[20] Jeremias, "älteste Schicht," 166-67.

[21] "Think not that I came to cast peace on earth; I came not to cast peace but a sword" is formally very similar to "I came not to call the righteous but sinners."

[22] Cf. Davies and Allison, *Matthew*, 2.106.

[23] Arens, *HΛΘON-Sayings*, 41-43, regards v.17b from the point of view of content as an introduction by association of ideas in the pre-Markan stage, but after applying different criteria of authenticity (i.e., criteria of multiple attestation, language, coherence and discontinuity) to the saying comes to the conclusion that Mk 2:17b "is a very ancient logion, the idea therein expressed having originated in Jesus himself" (pp.47-51, quotation from p.51).

[24] C. E. B. Cranfield, *The Gospel According to Saint Mark* (Cambridge Greek Testament Commentary; Cambridge: CUP, 1963), 106. Cf. Lagrange, *Marc*, 45; E. Lohmeyer, *Das Evangelium des Markus* (Göttingen: Vandenhoeck & Ruprecht, 1951), *ad loc.*

to Jesus' pre-existence in Jesus' *voluntary act* of coming: "While the content of Jesus' mission here (calling sinners) fits prophetic categories, the form of the saying, which emphasises Jesus' voluntary advent with the intent to call sinners, points away from a prophetic coming and toward a coming from heaven."[25] However, we only need to point out that Jesus' voluntary advent can hardly be seen as the crucial evidence for his transcendent origin. Rather, as Gathercole himself admits, Jesus' mission of calling sinners best fits his consciousness of "prophetic" or God-given mission.

5.1.3. Mk 10:45/Mt 20:28

The authenticity of this saying has been denied because it is regarded as a later Christian formulation originating either from Pauline circles,[26] Hellenistic-Jewish Christianity,[27] or the early Jewish community.[28] These objections against the authenticity of this logion can be summed up as follows: (1) it is out of harmony with its context, which focuses on service; (2) the use of ἦλθεν suggests a date after the lifetime of Jesus looking back on it as a whole; (3) λύτρον and the ideas associated with it are found nowhere else in Jesus' teaching; and (4) the original form of the saying is found in Lk 22:27, and Mk 10:45 is a "dogmatic recast" of it, perhaps under Pauline influence. These objections, however, have been effectively answered by a number of scholars.[29]

Against the first objection S. H. T. Page argues that the concepts of service and redemption are hardly mutually exclusive: "To argue that Jesus could not have made the transition from one to the other is pedantic, and in effect assumes that He was incapable of using synthetic parallelism. As a matter of fact such a transition is neither unusual nor inappropriate."[30]

---

[25] Gathercole, "Advent of Jesus," 6.

[26] B. H. Branscomb, *The Gospel of Mark* (MNTC; London: Hodder, 1937), 190-91; D. E. Nineham, *The Gospel of St Mark* (New York: Penguin, 1963), 280-81.

[27] Bultmann, *Synoptic Tradition*, 144, 155, who regards it as deriving "from the redemption theories of Hellenistic Christianity."

[28] E. Lohse, *Märtyrer und Gottesknecht: Untersuchungen zur urchristlichen Verkündigung vom Sühntod Jesu Christi* (FRLANT 64; Göttingen: Vandenhoeck & Ruprecht, 1955), 117-22.

[29] J. Jeremias, *TDNT* 5.706-15; S. H. T. Page, "The Authenticity of the Ransom Logion (Mark 10:45b)" in *Gospel Perspectives: Studies of History and Tradition in the Four Gospels* (eds. R. T. France *et al.*; Sheffield: JSOT Press, 1980), 137-61; P. Stuhlmacher, "Vicariously Giving His Life for Many, Mark 10:45 (Matt. 20:28)" in *Reconciliation, Law, and Righteousness: Essays in Biblical Theology* (Philadelphia: Fortress, 1986), 16-29; R. H. Gundry, *Mark: A Commentary on His Apology for the Cross* (Grand Rapids: Eerdmans, 1993), 587-90.

[30] Page, "Ransom Logion," 139.

Moreover, "since Mark saw no difficulty in the transition from one thought to the other, it is difficult to see how the argument that such a transition would have been impossible for Jesus can be sustained."[31] Page points to two other factors that support its authenticity: (1) these two ideas are found together elsewhere (Jn 12 and 13; 1 Pet 2:21-24); and (2) it can plausibly be argued that the ransom saying was formed in conscious dependence on the Suffering Servant in Isa 53 and Jesus saw himself in the role of this Servant.[32]

Against the second objection we have already demonstrated that ἦλθον sayings cannot be rejected *a priori* as inauthentic. Page rightly points out that the aorist tense does not necessarily imply a creation by the early church:

> the Greek tenses primarily express the kind of action rather than the time of the action, and it is hard to imagine how Jesus could have made a statement about His mission without using the aorist tense. Certainly the tense does not necessarily imply that Jesus' entire life is viewed as being in the past. In fact there is reason to think it should not be understood in this way. Apparently, Mark did not think that the aorist tense suggested that Jesus' life was over, for, if he did, he could have altered it in the interests of verisimilitude. By placing the saying on the lips of Jesus in its present form, Mark indicates that he saw no difficulty with Jesus making such a statement.[33]

Moreover, besides Mk 10:45 there are a substantial number of sayings attributed to Jesus in the Synoptics which speak of his having come and been sent. These sayings show that Jesus was conscious of his divine mission. The fact that Jesus' consciousness of divine mission is found not only in all of the Gospels but is embedded in all strata of the gospel tradition strongly suggests that Jesus spoke of his coming as a past event. C. H. Dodd observed that "The form of pronouncement, ἦλθεν with the infinitive of purpose or an equivalent ἵνα-clause, is one of the most widely established forms in which the sayings of Jesus are transmitted."[34]

With regard to the third objection one can make the following points: (1) although λύτρον occurs only here in the Gospels, some of the ideas associated with it seem to be present in Mk 14:24 ("This is my blood of the covenant, which is poured out for many");[35] (2) the idea of a ransom or of

---

[31] Page, "Ransom Logion," 139.

[32] Page, "Ransom Logion," 140-41. Cf. B. Witherington, *The Christology of Jesus* (Minneapolis: Fortress, 1990), 252: "The literature dealing with the Maccabees makes it clear that some Jews believed the ultimate form of service to and for one's people was to give one's life for them."

[33] Page, "Ransom Logion," 141-42.

[34] C. H. Dodd, *Historical Tradition in the Fourth Gospel* (Cambridge: CUP, 1963), 355.

[35] Witherington, *Christology*, 253.

ransoming life back is a familiar Old Testament concept;[36] (3) although there is an undeniable similarity of thought (which is expected probably in the light of the widespread belief in the redeeming value of Christ's death in the early church), there is little verbal similarity between Mk 10:45 and Paul's redemptive significance of Jesus' death;[37] and (4) in addition to the designation "Son of man," the negative-positive parallelism of οὐκ ἦλθεν διακονηθῆναι ἀλλὰ διακονῆσαι, epexegetical use of καὶ, the phrase δοῦναι τὴν ψυχὴν, the use of ψυχὴν instead of the reflexive pronoun, the use of πολλῶν, and the way λύτρον is used here all point to the typically Semitic features of the saying.[38]

Lastly, the similarities between Mk 10:42-45 and Lk 22:24-27 led scholars like Bultmann and Schürmann to suggest that Mk 10:45a is a theological expansion of an authentic saying about service, which is preserved more accurately in Luke.[39] However, this view is more than doubtful: (1) in terms of linguistic analysis, Mk 10:45 exhibits striking Semitic features as we have seen above, which leads one to conclude that "linguistically, at least, the Lucan account gives evidence of Gentile Christian influence from which Mark is free";[40] (2) not only does Mark appear to be more primitive,[41] it is also possible that both Mark and Luke represent independent traditions because there are striking dissimilarities between them;[42] (3) the settings are also different; in light of Lucan editorial technique, the absence of the saying from Luke can be explained as his decision to use material from another source that was similar to Mk 10:35-45;[43] and (4) the parallel statement in 1 Tim 2:5-6 (εἷς καὶ μεσίτης θεοῦ καὶ ἀνθρώπων, ἄνθρωπος Χριστὸς Ἰησοῦς, ὁ δοὺς ἑαυτὸν ἀντίλυτρον ὑπὲρ πάντων, "and there is one mediator between God and humans, the human being Christ Jesus, who gave himself a ransom for

---

[36] Cf. Ex 30:12; 21:30; Num 18:15; Lev 25:51-52.

[37] Page, "Ransom Logion," 143: "The designation of Jesus as 'the Son of man' finds no parallel in Paul at all, and when Paul speaks of the self-giving of Christ, he uses the reflexive pronoun ἑαυτοῦ rather than using the noun ψυχή. The noun λύτρον is also absent from the Pauline corpus, though ἀντίλυτρον is used in 1 Tim 2:6 and λυτρόω, in Titus 2:14. In addition, there is no exact parallel to ἀντὶ πολλῶν in Paul's writings. Paul never uses ἀντί when speaking of Christ's death, preferring ὑπέρ instead, and he uses πολλοί of the beneficiaries of Christ's death only in Rom 5:15,19."

[38] Page, "Ransom Logion," 148.

[39] Bultmann, *Synoptic Tradition*, 144; H. Schürmann, *Quellenkritische Untersuchung des lukanischen Abendmahlsberichtes Lk. 22,7-38* (Münster: Aschendorff, 1953-1957), 79-92.

[40] Page, "Ransom Logion," 14-49.

[41] Cf. Marshall, *Luke*, 813-4.

[42] Cf. Page, "Ransom Logion," 149.

[43] Page, "Ransom Logion," 149-50.

all") most likely represents a later, hellenized version of Jesus' ransom saying where ἄνθρωπος, "human being," replaces the odd-sounding, Semitizing ὁ υἱὸς τοῦ ἀνθρώπου; ὁ δοὺς ἑαυτὸν, "who gave himself," replaces δοῦναι τὴν ψυχὴν αὐτοῦ, "to give his life"; the hellenizing ἀντίλυτρον, "ransom," replaces λύτρον, "ransom"; and ὑπὲρ πάντων, "for all," replaces the Semitizing ἀντὶ πολλῶν, "for many."[44]

As far as the meaning of the ransom saying is concerned, it is important to recognize that the saying is best understood in terms of themes and images drawn from two OT passages: (1) Second Isaiah, particularly the Suffering Servant Song; and (2) Isa 43:3-4.

As far as the Suffering Servant Song is concerned, despite some opinions to the contrary,[45] there is an increasing recognition that linguistic overlap between the two supports the claim that the concept of the Suffering Servant may lie behind our logion:[46] (1) the verb διακονῆσαι alludes to the Servant of Isa 52:13; 53:11; (2) the clause δοῦναι τὴν ψυχὴν αὐτου closely parallels part of Isa 53:10 ("when you place his life as a guilt offering") and 53:12 ("he poured out his life to death"), or *Tg.* Isa 53:12 ("he delivered up his soul to death"); (3) although λύτρον ἀντι never translates אשם "guilt offering" in the LXX, our logion is to be viewed as a summary of the task of the Suffering Servant rather than a translation of any portion of Isa 52:53-12;[47] and (4) πολλῶν is probably an allusion to לרבים "for the many" in Isa 53:11 (LXX: πολλοῖς, "many") and 12 (LXX: πολλῶν, "of many") "to describe the beneficiaries of the Servant's service" (cf. Mk 14:24 for a possible allusion to לרבים).[48]

Our logion seems also to reflect the language of Isa 43:3-4 ("For I am the Lord your God, the Holy One of Israel, your Saviour. I give [נתתי] Egypt as your ransom [כפרך], Ethiopia and Seba in exchange for you [תחתיך]. Because you are precious in my eyes, and honoured, and I love you, I give man in return for you [ואתן אדם תחתיך], peoples in exchange for

---

[44] J. Jeremias, *Abba: Studien zur neutestamentlichen Theologie und Zeitgeschichte* (Göttingen: Vandenhoeck & Ruprecht, 1966), 216-29; also Stuhlmacher, "Vicariously Giving," 17-18.

[45] Cf. Barrett, "Background of Mark 10:45," 1-18; and M. D. Hooker, *Jesus and the Servant: the Influence of the Servant Concept of Deutero-Isaiah in the New Testament* (London: SPCK, 1959).

[46] Cf. France, *Jesus and the Old Testament*, 116-21; M. Hengel, *The Atonement: a Study of the Origins of the Doctrine in the New Testament* (London: SCM Press, 1981), 49-65; Pesch, *Markusevangelium*, 2.163-64; Stuhlmacher, "Vicariously Giving," 16-29; Davies and Allison, *Matthew*, 3.95-100; D. A. Hagner, *Matthew 14-28* (WBC 33; Dallas: Word Books, 1995), 582-83.

[47] Davies and Allison, *Matthew*, 3.96.

[48] France, *Jesus and the Old Testament*, 120.

your life [נפשׁך תחת]").[49] If this suggestion is correct, then both Isa 53 and Isa 43-3-4 are to be seen as complementing rather than competing "sources out of which Jesus' mission, message, and self-understanding could be informed."[50]

If we interpret the ransom saying in the light of this composite "prophetic" background, the sense of Jesus' "coming" in our logion is related more closely to his God-given mission than his transcendent origin. His God-given mission, one of service and sacrifice for the sake of others, makes perfect sense with the Suffering Servant. In other words, Jesus came to serve, even suffer and die, as the Servant of the Lord.

5.1.4. Lk 19:10

This saying is to some extent similar to the ransom saying preserved in Mk 10:45. The authenticity of this Lukan saying is sometimes questioned due to its use of the title "Son of Man," but if this title is removed from the text, as it is a circumlocution for "I" in this case, there are no compelling reasons to reject its authenticity.[51] Rather, there are good arguments for its authenticity which can be summed up as follows: (1) the shepherd imagery is strongly anchored in the teaching of Jesus; (2) 1 Tim 1:15 is what the saying would have looked like, if it had been derived from a Hellenistic source; and (3) the idea of present salvation as the purpose of Jesus' earthly ministry is already present in Jesus' "realized eschatology."[52]

If our saying goes back most likely to Jesus, then in what sense did he utter this saying? Was it spoken to convey his self-consciousness of his transcendent origin and/or pre-existence? Most commentators have rightly noted that Lk 19:10 is closely connected to the saying preserved in Mk 2:17//Lk 5:32 and the OT imagery found in Ezek 34, where God himself and David gather the scattered sheep of Israel.[53] Nolland's emphasis on the role of David rather than God himself is, however, rightly criticized by Gathercole, who points out that David plays a comparatively minor role in Ezek 34 and the description of Jesus' action in the saying actually

---

[49] Grimm, *Weil ich dich liebe*, 231-77; Stuhlmacher, "Vicariously Giving," 22-26.

[50] C. A. Evans, *Mark 8:27-16:20* (WBC 34B; Dallas: Word Books, 2001), 123.

[51] I. H. Marshall, *The Origins of New Testament Christology* (Downers Grove: Inter-Varsity, 1976, 1990), 74.

[52] I. H. Marshall, *The Gospel of Luke: a Commentary on the Greek Text* (NIGTC; Grand Rapids: Eerdmans, 1978), 698-99; also J. A. Fitzmyer, *The Gospel According to Luke* (AB 28; New York: Doubleday, 1991, 1985), 1226. *Contra* F. Hahn, *Christologische Hoheitstitel* (Göttingen: Vandenhoeck & Ruprecht, 1964), 45.

[53] Cf. Marshall, *Luke*, 698; J. Nolland, *Luke* (WBC 35; Dallas: Word Books, 1993), 906; Fitzmyer, *Luke*, 2.1226: "the Lucan Jesus is depicted as one sent . . . even to act as Yahweh told Ezekiel he would act toward his scattered people as a shepherd."

resembles the work of *God*.[54] This makes the connection between the coming of Jesus in Lk 19:10 and the coming of a Davidic Messiah in Ezek 34:23-24 rather weak.

If the saying is not likely to be interpreted in terms of Jesus' messianic consciousness, in what sense did Jesus utter this saying? While we agree with Gathercole's suggestion that "The intention of his coming implied in the saying seems to go beyond what was expected from a prophet," we need to part company when he suggests that the saying implies Jesus' consciousness of pre-existence by asserting that "interpreting the coming here as 'coming on the scene', or as 'having a specific task' does not do justice to the dynamism expressed in the seeking."[55]

While it is true that we find in this saying a self-understanding of Jesus as highly elevated as in Mt 15:24, where Jesus speaks of himself as one who undertakes a task previously attributed to God, we should be cautious about over-reading the imagery, when interpreting our saying. The task previously attributed to God himself that is now given to Jesus does not necessarily suggest that he came from heaven or that he is to be identified with God. Rather, the key point of the saying is still on the fact that "Jesus viewed himself as Israel's shepherd, which implies he believed he was called to lead, oversee, and even rescue God's people."[56] We conclude therefore that as an authentic utterance of Jesus Lk 19:10 expresses Jesus' self-consciousness of a God-given mission to shepherd the lost sheep of Israel.

5.1.5. Lk 12:49-51/Mt 10:34

The sayings preserved in Lk 12:49-50 are peculiar to Luke, although a somewhat similar saying to v.50 is found in Mk 10:38b, a saying recorded in a section which Luke chose to omit. This led some scholars to regard vv.49-50 as a Lukan creation, but it has been argued that the Semitic nature of v.49 and the lack of linguistic features specific to Luke militate

---

[54] Gathercole, "Advent of Jesus," 9. He points out the correspondence between the two elements in Lk 19:10 and the two declarations by God himself in Ezekiel passage: "'I myself, I, will search for my sheep, and will *seek* them out' (34.11) and 'Therefore will I *save* my flock, and they shall no more be attacked' (34.22)."

[55] Gathercole, "Advent of Jesus," 9.

[56] Witherington, *Christology*, 126. Such a high self-understanding can be also seen in Lk 19:10, about which Fitzmyer, *Luke*, 1226, observes: "Thus the Lucan Jesus is depicted as one sent . . . even to act as Yahweh told Ezekiel he would act toward his scattered people as a shepherd."

against such possibility.[57] If Lk 12:49-50 are more likely to be pre-Lukan, then one may ask whether these sayings were part of Q or Luke's special source material. In view of the verbal link between Lk 12:49 and Mt 10:34 (βάλλω), however, the first option becomes more likely,[58] although it is hard to claim any original unity between the two.[59]

März proposed a case for attributing Lk 12:49 to a (late) Q editing process,[60] but a case for going back to Jesus himself is preferred on the basis of the following points: (1) the phrase πῦρ βάλλειν may be a literal translation of an Aramaic phrase meaning "to kindle fire,"[61] although "it would appear to be tolerable Greek in a metaphorical saying"[62]; (2) the use of τί is more clearly Semitic (2 Sam 6:20; Mt 7:14) in the sense of "how (much)" and similar to מה introducing a rhetorical question;[63] (3) similarly, θέλω εἰ "I wish that" is likely to be Semitic (Isa 9:5; Sir 23:14);[64] (4) the expression βαλεῖν εἰρήνην in Mt 10:34b appears to be a Semitism;[65] (5) the οὐκ . . . ἀλλά structure seems to be the earlier form of Lk 12:51, which can be translated back into Aramaic; and (6) Mt 10:34b makes sense in a setting later in Jesus' ministry when hostility was reaching its climax.[66] Thus, the authenticity of both Lk 12:49 and Mt 10:34b (multiple attestation, if they were independent each other) is much strengthened by the Semitic elements in the language and the dissimilarity from the early church formulations and interests as well as from prevailing Jewish sentiments (criteria of Semitisms and dissimilarity).[67]

---

[57] Marshall, *Luke*, 548; S. J. Patterson, "Fire and Dissension: Ipsissima Vox Jesus in Q 12:49, 51-53?" *Forum* 5.2 (1989), 121-39, argues for the authenticity of this saying on the basis of a less than convincing claim for the greater originality of the form of the saying in *Gos. Thom.* 10. Cf. Arens, *HΛΘON-Sayings*, 64-65.

[58] Cf. T. W. Manson, *The Sayings of Jesus* (London: SCM, 1949), 120; H. Schürmann, *Traditionsgeschichtliche Untersuchungen zu den synoptischen Evangelien* (KBANT; Düseldorf: Patmos, 1968), 213 and n.24; *contra* G. Klein, "Die Prüfung der Zeit (Lukas 12, 54-56)" *ZTK* 61 (1964), 374 n.4.

[59] Nolland, *Luke*, 707.

[60] C. P. März, "'Feuer auf die Erde zu werfen, bin ich gekommen . . .': Zum Verständnis und zur Entstehung von Lk 12, 49" in *A cause de l'Evangile* (ed. F. Refoulé; Paris: Cerf, 1985), 493-501, argues for this case by establishing a thematic connection with 3:16.

[61] J. Jeremias, *The Parables of Jesus* (Göttingen: Vandenhoeck & Ruprecht, 1972), 163.

[62] Marshall, *Luke*, 546. Cf. Mt 10:34; Jos. *Ant.* 1:98; *BD* 299 § 4.

[63] Arens, *HΛΘON-Sayings*, 64ff.

[64] See, however, Herodotus 6:52; 9:44.

[65] Cf. *Lev. R.* 9 [111b], *Mekilta to Exod.* 20,25; *Sifre Num.* 16.

[66] Arens, *HΛΘON-Sayings*, 86.

[67] It is also significant that Lk 12:49 is considered to be an authentic saying by so sceptical a scholar as Arens.

If these sayings are authentic, what insight would we gain regarding the sense in which Jesus' logia were uttered? The crucial element to unlock the sense of the passage is the definition of the fire. As A. von Harnack pointed out, when used in a religious sense "fire" can have either a positive or a negative connotation.[68] It can refer to the fire of judgment (Lk 9:54; Mt 13:30), or to a cleansing or purifying force, or to the cleansing action of God's Holy Spirit, rather than a purely destructive one (1 Cor 3:13). Marshall is certainly correct that "the saying in its present context should be understood with reference to judgment."[69]

Again, Gathercole claims to find in Lk 12:49-51 a pointer to Jesus' claim to his pre-existence.[70] He argues that, unlike Elijah's prayer to call down fire from heaven, Jesus' claim "to be able to bring fire to the earth is an implicit claim to divine identity" because the fire comes from heaven, that is, from God himself. He then concludes that "if Jesus' intention in coming included the intention of bringing fire to the earth, this more clearly than anything thus far identifies him as having come from heaven."[71]

However, there are a number of important points that are worth considering: (1) both Lk 12:49 and 50, in contrast perhaps to Mt 10:34, refer to an activity which, though imminent, will happen in the *future*.[72] (2) While the saying in v.49 seems to refer to an activity that Jesus himself will perform, the baptismal saying in v.50 specifically refers to *something that must happen to him*, although this could be a means by which he fulfils his purpose;[73] these points, which suggest that Jesus is not in complete control of the event to come, make Jesus' "coming" as pointing to his transcendent origin less likely. And (3) the use of the sword metaphor in Mt 10:34 seems to point to the inbreaking of eschatological times and particularly *eschatological judgment*.[74] Thus, together with the fire as a reference to imminent judgment, the above points suggest that the passage in question is "a prophetic judgment oracle," in which Jesus' coming is expressed in terms of bringing God's eschatological judgment upon the land. In other words, Jesus saw his ministry as no more than God-given mission to bring in the eschatological judgment.

---

[68] A. von Harnack, "'Ich bin gekommen': Die ausdrücklichen Selbstzeugnisse Jesu über den Zweck seiner Sendung und seines Kommens" *ZTK* 22 (1912), 12.

[69] Marshall, *Luke*, 547; cf. Acts 2:19; Rev 8:5, 7; 20:9.

[70] Gathercole, "Advent of Jesus," 6.

[71] Gathercole, "Advent of Jesus," 7.

[72] Witherington, *Christology*, 121.

[73] Manson, *Sayings*, 120-21; W. G. Kümmel, *Promise and Fulfilment: the Eschatological Message of Jesus* (SBT 23; London: SCM, 1957), 70 and n.168.

[74] Cf. Isa 34:5; 66:16; Ezek 21; *1 Enoch* 63:11, 91:12, 100:1-2; *2 Bar* 70:6.

5.2. "I Was Sent" Sayings

Jesus' self-consciousness of a God-given mission is perhaps best encapsulated in his "I was sent" sayings preserved in Mt 15:24 par. and Mk 9:37 pars.

5.2.1. Mt 15:24

The authenticity of the saying is often denied because Mt 15:24 and 10:6 are taken to reflect early Palestinian Christian missionary preaching.[75] This suggestion, however, seems doubtful because, while Mt 10:6 seems to limit their mission to the Jews, there is no clear evidence that such early Jewish Christian preaching prohibited going to the Gentiles, although a positive Gentile mission was not openly encouraged.[76] Indeed, it is very unlikely that such particularistic sayings would arise after the early, even pre-Pauline, establishment of the mission to Gentiles. Furthermore, this apparent particularism in Mt 15:24 and 10:6 seems to be in contradiction with the universalistic thrust of Matthew (cf. Mt 2:1ff.; 4:15; 12:18:21; 8:11ff.; 15:21ff.; and esp. 28:19).[77]

The authenticity of the saying can also be defended from a linguistic point of view. That the saying goes back to an Aramaic original is likely because (1) οὐκ . . . εἰ μή reflects אֶלָּא . . . לֹא (i.e., "only"); (2) the divine passive ἀπεστάλην is characteristic of the early tradition; (3) the word εἰς, which is a rendering of the Hebrew ב, is a Semitism; and (4) οἶκος in the sense of "tribe," "lineage," or "community" is Hebraic, and the phrase οἴκου Ἰσραήλ with οἶκος without the definite article reflects the construct state in Hebrew.[78]

Moreover, the essential authenticity of these verses is further supported by other layers of tradition found elsewhere, including Lk 19:9-10, whose authenticity has been already demonstrated earlier.[79] We conclude

---

[75] Cf. F. W. Beare, *The Gospel According to Matthew: a Commentary* (Oxford: Blackwell, 1981), 341-42.

[76] Witherington, *Christology*, 124. There is some evidence that early Judaism was opposed to proselytism (cf. Mt 23:15; *Ant.* 20.38-48), although a massive effort to make Gentile converts is doubtful.

[77] D. Hill, *The Gospel of Matthew* (NCBC; London: Oliphants, 1972), 185; E. Schweizer, *The Good News According to Matthew* (Atlanta: John Knox, 1975), 238.

[78] J. Jeremias, *Jesus' Promise to the Nations* (SBT 24; London: SCM, 1958), 26-27 and n.2: "Matthew's only reason for preserving the logion in spite of its repellent implication was that it bore the stamp of the Lord's authority."

[79] See §5.1.4.

therefore that there is no compelling reason to deny that the saying in Mt 15:24 goes back to Jesus himself.[80]

What implications can be drawn from Mt 15:24 for Jesus' self-understanding? The present saying is in fact about the purpose of his mission. The image of Israel as sheep is attested in various places in the OT (e.g., Ps 23; Ezek 34), and the image of Israel as a nation of lost sheep is also well attested (e.g., Ezek 34 and Jer 50:6). The fact that Jesus uses the image of Israel as a nation of lost sheep to describe his mission suggests that Jesus saw himself "as taking on a task that Yahweh is said to undertake in Ezekiel 34."[81] In other words, "Jesus viewed himself as Israel's shepherd, which implies he believed he was called to lead, oversee, and even rescue God's people."[82] Since this idea is independently attested in Mt 15:24 and Lk 19:10, it is much more likely that this motif goes back to Jesus rather than the Gospel writers' redactional activity. Thus Mt 15:24, together with Lk 19:10, gives us a very important insight into Jesus' self-consciousness of divine mission, i.e., his sense of God-given mission to undertake a task previously attributed to Yahweh.

5.2.2. Mk 9:37/Mt 10:40/Lk 9:48

Mark 9:37b is a saying about the equivalence of receiving Jesus and the one who sent him. This saying as it stands may envisage a post-Easter situation, but this is by no means a basis for doubting that the saying itself goes back to Jesus. On the contrary, the Gospel evidence suggests that the present saying with small variations was readily available in the oral tradition (a very good sign of its authenticity).[83] The saying is not only preserved in Mt 10:40b,[84] Lk 9:48b (with slight variations), and in Lk 10:16c (in a negative statement), but is also independently attested in Jn 13:20 (with the major difference being the use of λαμβάνων instead of δεχόμενος). As both Mk 9:37b and Lk 9:48b occur in connection with the saying about receiving a little child in the name of Jesus, which Matthew

---

[80] So Witherington, *Christology*, 125; Marshall, *Luke*, 698-99; Fitzmyer, *Luke*, 1226.

[81] Witherington, *Christology*, 126.

[82] Witherington, *Christology*, 126. Such a high self-understanding can be also seen in Lk 19:10, about which Fitzmyer, *Luke*, 1226, observes: "Thus the Lucan Jesus is depicted as one sent . . . even to act as Yahweh told Ezekiel he would act toward his scattered people as a shepherd."

[83] So D. A. Hagner, *Matthew 1-13* (WBC 33; Dallas: Word Books, 1993), 294-95.

[84] H. Fleddermann, "The Discipleship Discourse (Mark 9:33-50)" *CBQ* 43 (1981), 62-63, argues for a Q-saying represented by Mt 10:40 and redaction represented by Mk 9:37, for example, by a change to "whoever" clauses. However, according to Gundry, *Mark*, 519, since such clauses are more Semitic than Greek (though not un-Greek) they are less likely to come from Markan redaction.

places in 18:5, it is possible that an original saying about welcoming children has been enlarged by a clause from a separate saying about receiving Jesus and the one who sent him.[85] Although the precise wording of the saying may be uncertain, the present saying and its pars. most likely go back to a *Sitz im Leben Jesu* rather than reflecting later church concerns.

At first glance, the equivalence of receiving Jesus and the one who sent him might be understood as supporting the view that Jesus was sent by God from heaven, i.e., Jesus' claim to his transcendent origin. However, the Jewish idea of *shaliach* found in the latter half of the saying strongly suggests otherwise. This idea of *shaliach* can be summed up in the oft-quoted statement, "the one sent by a man [שלוחו] is like the man himself" (*m. Ber.* 5.5, cf. *Mek. Exod.* 14:31; 18:12).[86] Read in this light, the saying shows that Jesus regarded himself as the messenger of God, the one who was sent by the Father (cf. Lk 10:16; Jn 12:44-45; 13:20; cf. 5:23) and that he was conscious of a God-given mission.

To sum up, the two "I was sent" sayings of Jesus found in Mt 15:24 par. and Mk 9:37 pars. express his self-consciousness of a God-given mission.

5.3. Christological Implications of Jesus' Self-Consciousness

Our discussion of "I have come" and "I was sent" sayings of Jesus has demonstrated that by uttering these logia Jesus revealed himself as one who was conscious of his God-given mission to carry out in this world.

We have clearly demonstrated that the idiomatic interpretation of "I have come" sayings of Jesus ("I have the purpose/intention to . . .") lacks clear evidence and is far from convincing. Moreover, contrary to the view that suggests Jesus' pre-existence, all of the ἦλθον sayings that were under examination have clearly demonstrated that in these sayings the emphasis falls on his God-given *mission* rather than on his transcendent *origin*, even though the idiomatic interpretation was clearly shown to be faulty. In short, Jesus' "coming" is best understood as synonymous to his God-given mission rather than his advent from heaven.

We have come to a similar conclusion with regard to the "I was sent" sayings preserved in Mt 15:24 and Mk 9:37. However, we have found that there is an important distinction between these sayings and the parable of the wicked tenants that we discussed in Chapter 4. With the parable of the wicked tenants we are somewhat more confident than with these "I was

---

[85] Marshall, *Luke*, 395.

[86] For this idea of *shaliach* see esp. K. H. Rengstorf, *TDNT* 1.414-20; cf. Marshall, *Luke*, 397; Hagner, *Matthew*, 295.

sent" sayings. We have recognized that in telling the parable Jesus expressed implicitly – but in a quite subtle manner – his self-consciousness of his divine sonship as well as his divine or transcendent origin.[87] Although these "I was sent" sayings and the parable of the wicked tenants have as a common denominator the motif of being *sent* from/by God, one major difference between the two is that, unlike the "sent" sayings, in his parable Jesus refers to himself as God's *Son* as well as one *sent* by God. The combination of these two elements in the parabolic setting seems to have a stronger implication for christology: it implies that Jesus is *God's Son sent* into this world!

Throughout our examination of the evidence for Jesus' self-consciousness of divine sonship and divine mission we have often been tempted to bring into the discussion some of the christological implications of his self-consciousness in the whole context of his life and teaching, but we have deliberately avoided discussing them. Now it is time to do so.

One might ask the question whether Jesus' self-consciousness of divine sonship and divine mission would imply his consciousness of pre-existence as well. In our discussion of Synoptic evidence for Jesus' self-consciousness of divine sonship and divine mission we have shown that Jesus was conscious of a unique personal relationship to God as his Father and of himself as his Son; in the same way, we have also shown that he was conscious of his divine mission, i.e., a God-given mission to carry out in this world. Such a self-understanding of divine sonship and divine mission on its own right during his earthly ministry can hardly be said to have played a significant role in understanding him as pre-existent. However, if his self-consciousness of divine sonship and divine mission is recalled and re-examined at a later stage by early Christians in view of his resurrection event and the whole context of his life and teaching, such a self-understanding was probably open to interpretation in terms of his pre-existence. In other words, if his self-understanding is re-interpreted retrospectively, such an interpretation is hardly out of question but a real probability. It is at this precise point that the early Christian exegesis of Ps 110:1 and Ps 2:7 comes in and plays a central role.

In this regard, one may legitimately question whether it is reasonable to draw a clear-cut line between Jesus' self-consciousness of divine sonship

---

[87] In support of such a reading of evidence we could point out Jesus' own use of Ps 110:1 in Mk 12:35-37 and 14:62, which seems to be also compatible with his consciousness of pre-existence. An important christological implication from Mk 12:35-37 is that by a way of subtle allusions to himself Jesus wished his audience to consider the possibility that he might be David's Lord who stands and exists before David himself. It thus provides us with a glimpse of his self-understanding which is compatible with his consciousness of pre-existence and supported by his statement before the Sanhedrin in Mk 14:62. For a detailed discussion of Mk 12:35-37 and 14:62 see § 6.2.5.

and divine mission, on the one hand, and his self-consciousness of divinity and pre-existence, on the other. Such a clear distinction between the two could be problematic, if such a self-understanding of himself in terms of his divine sonship and divine mission is retrospectively reflected from a post-resurrection point of view. In that sense, one may speak of his self-understanding as compatible with his self-consciousness of divinity and pre-existence; and in this very sense, Jesus' use of *abba* and his logia about his divine sonship and divine mission as a whole could be said to imply his pre-existence.

As far as we know from the Gospels, Jesus' disciples never fully understood about the person of Jesus before Easter. It was not only because he chose not to reveal himself in an explicit manner but also because of their spiritual blindness. It is therefore important for us to recognize that there was a significant gap between what Jesus really was conscious of himself and what his disciples really understood of him. As we will argue later in our study, this "gap" was later filled by the early Christian exegesis of Ps 110:1 and Ps 2:7, a process through which early Christian exegetes were able to draw out the fuller implications of Jesus' self-revelatory statements in terms of his pre-existence.

Our discussion of Jesus' self-consciousness of divine sonship and divine mission, therefore, leads us to the conclusion that there was a solid foundation upon which the early church was able to build their fuller understanding of Jesus as the pre-existent Son of God. At first glance, there appears to be a significant gap between how Jesus conceived of himself (the christology of Jesus) and what the early church came to believe (the christology of the early church). It was such a big gap – or even for some an apparently "irreconcilable" gap – between the two that led many scholars to place the development of early christology and Jesus' pre-existence in other areas than Jesus himself (e.g., Jewish wisdom tradition, a pre-existent messiah tradition in Second Temple Judaism, Jewish "angelomorphic" divine agent tradition, etc.).

In the following two chapters we will examine how the early church used and interpreted Ps 110:1 and Ps 2:7 and how the "gap" between what Jesus claimed to be and what the early church came to believe was successfully "filled" by their exegesis of the two messianic texts most cherished in the early church. We will argue that through their exegesis of these two psalms they were able to confirm what they were already beginning to believe in the light of Jesus' resurrection and his self-revelatory statements about his divine sonship and divine mission as well as to deepen their understanding of him as the pre-existent Son of God enthroned at his right hand. To this "filling" process we now turn.

Chapter 6

Early Christian Exegesis of Psalm 110:1

Like their Jewish contemporaries, early Christians revered the Old Testament as their sacred writings. It is hardly surprising that Jesus' early followers should turn to the OT scriptures for language to speak about Jesus' death and resurrection. They were, after all, Jews, and like their contemporaries they believed it was in the sacred writings that God's will was to be found.

Despite some contrary opinions, there is evidence for Jewish interpretation of some OT texts in a messianic sense prior to Christianity. Once convinced that Jesus was the long awaited Messiah, they began to focus their attention on those portions of the scriptures which could be interpreted messianically. Their messianic exegesis of the OT provided answers to their search for who Jesus really is.

In the following two chapters we will be arguing that the earliest Christians found two very important psalms in the Scriptures which were vital for their understanding of Jesus as pre-existent Lord and Son of God. We refer to Ps 110:1 and Ps 2:7.[1] The former text was crucial for interpreting Jesus' resurrection as his exaltation to the right hand of God. It was interpreted not only as a prophecy about his "literal" exaltation,[2] but also as a statement of God speaking to one who was already Lord in his sight. In a parallel line of thought, starting from Jesus' claim to be the Son of God early Christians interpreted Ps 2:7 not only as a prophecy about his divine sonship (which was decisively demonstrated through the resurrection), but also as a statement of God speaking to one who was already Son in his sight. In this way, both Ps 110:1 and Ps 2:7 became key texts for their belief that Jesus was already pre-existent Lord and Son of God during and before his earthly life. Thus, the early Christian exegesis

---

[1] The importance of these psalms is also noted by H.-J. Kraus, *Theology of the Psalms* (Minneapolis: Fortress, 1992), 180-88: "It is clear that in early Christianity several Old Testament psalms were extremely important. They were quoted again and again and cited as 'star witnesses' in the proclamation that the promises of God has been fulfilled. . . . Psalms 2 and 110, 'two royal psalms,' . . . stand at the center of the messianic message of the New Testament and are used as witnesses to the messiahship of Jesus of Nazareth" (p.180).

[2] See further §7.3.

of these two messianic psalms is to be given one of the most significant places in the development of Jesus' pre-existence in the early church.

The emergence of Christianity is hardly conceivable without the belief of the disciples that Jesus had risen from the dead and had appeared to them. In the New Testament there is ample evidence that the disciples understood the resurrection of Jesus not just as his coming back to life and raising up to heaven, but especially as his exaltation to and/or enthronement at the right hand of God. Where did they get this idea? The most plausible answer to this question would be that the idea of "sitting" at the right hand of God in Ps 110:1 was crucial for their interpretation of Jesus' resurrection as his exaltation to the right hand of God, since this idea as such is found nowhere else other than in this verse.[3] Hence, the importance of Ps 110:1 in the development of early christology can hardly be overestimated.

The importance of Ps 110:1 for the early church can be clearly seen in the fact that this text is one of the Old Testament texts most often quoted or alluded to in the New Testament.[4] It is generally accepted that all statements about the exalted Christ sitting at the right hand of God directly or indirectly depend on this text. How widespread and early was the use of Ps 110:1 in the early church? Did the disciples come to think of Jesus as Lord when they applied Ps 110:1 to him? If not, what led them to think of Jesus as Lord? Was Jesus already Lord in God's sight before the resurrection, or was his Lordship conferred upon him only at that point? More specifically, was Ps 110:1 understood as showing that Jesus became Lord at his resurrection, or was it interpreted as God speaking to one who was already Lord? How significant and relevant is the Gospel evidence where Ps 110:1 is not only cited by Jesus as he teaches in the temple court

---

[3] For the importance of Ps 2:6 as Jesus' exaltation which, through a cross-reference reading of Pss 110 and 2, would have given further support to the idea in Ps 110:1 see §7.2.1.2.

[4] For secondary literature dealing with this topic see D. M. Hay, *Glory at the Right Hand: Psalm 110 in Early Christianity* (SBLMS 18; Nashville: Abingdon, 1973); M. Gourgues, *A la droite de Dieu: resurrection de Jesus et actualisation du psaume 110, 1 dans le Nouveau Testament* (Paris: J. Gabalda, 1978); T. Callan, "Ps. 110:1 and the Origin of the Expectation That Jesus Will Come Again" *CBQ* 44 (1982), 622-35; W. R. G. Loader, "Christ at the Right Hand - Ps. CX in the New Testament" *NTS* 24 (1978), 199-217; W. R. G. Loader, *Sohn und Hoherpriester: eine traditionsgeschichtliche Untersuchung zur Christologie des Hebraerbriefes* (WMANT 53; Neukirchen-Vluyn: Neukirchener Verlag, 1981) 15-29, 275; J. Dupont, "'Assis à la droite de Dieu' L'interpretation du Ps 110,1 dans le Nouveau Testament" in *Resurrexit: actes du Symposium international sur la resurrection de Jesus, Rome 1970* (eds. B. M. Ahern *et al.*; Citta del Vaticano: Libreria editrice vaticana, 1974), 340-422; M. Hengel, "'Sit at My Right Hand!' The Enthronement of Christ at the Right Hand of God and Psalm 110:1" in *Studies in Early Christology* (Edinburgh: T & T Clark, 1995), 119-225.

(Mk 12:35-37), but also referred to during his trial as he foretells that the Son of Man will sit at the right hand of God and come with the clouds of heaven (Mk 14:62)? Are the Gospel passages authentic and therefore could they have initiated the process? What were the christological implications drawn by the early church when they juxtaposed Ps 110:1 and Ps 8:6? How significant was it for their understanding of Jesus as pre-existent Lord? In the following pages we will attempt to answer all these questions.

First, we will briefly discuss how Ps 110:1 was used and interpreted in pre-Christian Judaism. *Second*, we will examine how the earliest Christians interpreted and made use of this psalm. *Third*, we will argue that this text was first interpreted as a prophecy about Jesus' exaltation to the right hand of God and quickly became part of the early church confessions from an early date. *Finally*, we will also argue that the Gospel passages dealing with Jesus' own use of Ps 110:1 during his ministry (Mk 12:35-37; 14:62) are most likely to be authentic and initiated the process of interpreting Ps 110:1 as a prophecy about his exaltation to the right hand of God. The Gospels tell us that Jesus understood the psalm to refer to himself as David's Lord and the Son of Man seated at the right hand of God who will return to judge. If this is correct, Jesus' understanding of the psalm is surely significant for our enquiry and should not be treated merely as an early Christian understanding of the psalm in a strict sense but as a possible influence of Jesus upon his followers.

6.1. Pre-Christian Interpretation of Psalm 110

6.1.1. Original Setting and Subsequent Function of the Psalm

It is widely agreed among OT scholars that, as one of the royal psalms, Psalm 110 was originally composed for the enthronement of a king in the Davidic dynasty in order to express metaphorically the honour and authority given to him by God.[5] It has also been suggested that the psalm was subsequently used in an annual New Year festival, a real battle, or a

---

[5] The precise date and the original setting of the psalm has been a matter of debate among OT scholars. Attempts to date the psalm vary from pre-exilic to Maccabean periods. Although it has often been claimed to be of Maccabean date, more recent scholarship tends to attribute it to the beginning of the first millennium BC. See, e.g., A. Weiser, *The Psalms: a Commentary* (Göttingen: Vandenhoeck & Ruprecht, 1962), 693; S. H. Hooke, *Alpha and Omega: a Study in the Pattern of Revelation* (Welwyn: J. Nisbet, 1961), 106; R. de Vaux, *Ancient Israel: Its Life and Institutions* (New York: McGraw-Hill, 1961), 402; H.-J. Kraus, *Psalmen* (BKAT 15/1; Neukirchen-Vluyn: Neukirchener Verlag, 1960), 775f.; L. C. Allen, *Psalms 101-150* (WBC 21; Dallas: Word Books, 1983), 83-86.

pre-battle ritual as a promise of victory,[6] but those who were not convinced of a link with any activity of the human Davidic king have regarded the psalm as eschatological and messianic from the outset.[7]

6.1.2. Later Jewish Interpretation of the Psalm

Psalm 110 was not widely used in intertestamental or rabbinic literature. Whether it was given a messianic interpretation by Jews before Christianity is not entirely clear. Hay's survey of the pre-Christian evidence produces scant results.[8] For instance, there is no clear hint of a messianic interpretation in *T. Job* 33:3,[9] 1 Macc 14:41,[10] or Dan 7:9-14;[11] nor is it clearly attested in rabbinic sources before the second half of the third century AD.[12] The available rabbinic evidence shows that c. 130-150 AD the psalm was applied to a historical person such as Abraham, David or Hezekiah.[13] Such evidence seems to suggest that Ps 110:1 was not an established Jewish messianic text.

However, it has been suggested that an earlier Jewish messianic interpretation of the psalm might have been suppressed by some Jews for the purpose of removing a debating weapon from the Christians.[14] By contrast, labelling the arguments for the currency of a messianic interpretation of the psalm based on the Synoptic evidence and the Jewish anti-Christian polemic as "a gratuitous assertion" Fitzmyer argued that the messianic interpretation of the psalm was not current in pre-Christian Jewish circles but may have begun with Jesus himself (Mk 12:35-37//Lk

---

[6] See Allen, *Psalms*, 83, for bibliography.

[7] Cf. E. J. Kissane, "The Interpretation of Psalm 110" *ITQ* 21 (1954), 106; M. Rehm, *Der königliche Messias im Licht der Immanuel-Weissagungen des Buches Jesaja* (Kevelaer: Butzon und Bercker, 1968), 329-31; D. Kidner, *Psalms 73-150: A Commentary on Books 3-6 of the Psalms* (TOTC; London: Inter-Varsity, 1975), 392.

[8] Hay, *Glory*, 21-33.

[9] *Testament of Job* is dated between 1st century BC and 1st century AD.

[10] A possible use of the psalm by Hasmonean rulers.

[11] Hay, *Glory*, 26, proposes that the seer who composed Daniel constructed his vision of the divine throne room, which includes a place for a humanlike figure enthroned in God's presence, with an eye to Ps 110:1, the "only scriptural text which explicitly speaks of someone enthroned beside God."

[12] Cf. H. L. Strack and P. Billerbeck, *Kommentar zum Neuen Testament aus Talmud und Midrasch* (München: Beck, 1956), 4.452-65.

[13] The earliest discussion of Ps 110 in rabbinic literature is credited to Rabbi Ishmael (d. 135 AD). Although his interpretation may have been intended to undercut Christian interpretations, the application to Abraham is attested in other sources (*b. Sanhedrin* 32b; *Midrash Tehillim* on Ps 110).

[14] Strack and Billerbeck, *Kommentar*, 4.452-65; similarly Hay, *Glory*, 33; Hengel, "Right Hand," 178-79.

20:41-44) and was continued by early Christians after him.[15] However, there are some other considerations that, if taken into account, make such a view not so convincing.

First, after the return from the exile, when there was a new temple under the religious and political leadership of the Aaronide priests – without the ark of the covenant and without any king in Jerusalem – the original meaning of Ps 110 (i.e., the king ruling with the honour and authority given by God) would have been lost with time.[16] In later times the Jews would have been left with only two possibilities: a figurative application of the psalm either to a historical person such as Abraham and Hezekiah, or to an eschatological-messianic figure. The evidence from Second Temple Judaism and the New Testament period suggests that the latter possibility was the most likely.[17] If this is correct, the argument that anti-Christian polemic led to non-messianic interpretations in rabbinic sources, especially those in Tannaitic period, gains force.

Second, the idea that the Son of Man/Messiah's enthronement in the *Parables of Enoch* may have been influenced by Ps 110 has been suggested by J. Theisohn, who points out a close connection between the Enochic Son of Man and Psalm 110:

> Ps. 110:1, 5f. (contains) . . . all of the elements (idea of enthronement, element of judgement, element of polarization) which are necessary for the transference of the formula of sitting on the throne of glory and thus on the throne of Yahweh to the elect one. Ps. 110:1, 5f. is . . . the only passage in the Old Testament period which fulfils these conditions; one can conclude that the elect one – as the one who sits as judge on the throne of Yahweh – . . . is to be related to the theme 'kingdom' and is significantly influenced by the peculiar form of royal ideas which are present in Ps. 110.[18]

---

[15] J. A. Fitzmyer, *The Gospel According to Luke* (AB 28; New York: Doubleday, 1991, 1985), 1311; also E. Schweizer, *Das Evangelium nach Markus* (Göttingen: Vandenhoeck & Ruprecht, 1967), 145-46, who notes the lack of messianic use in the Qumran and other early Jewish writings.

[16] Hengel, "Right Hand," 178.

[17] I. H. Marshall, "The Messiah in the First Century: A Review Article" *Criswell Theological Review* 7 (1993), 67-83.

[18] J. Theisohn, *Der auserwählte Richter: Untersuchungen zum traditionsgeschichtlichem Ort der Menschensohngestalt der Bilderreden des Äthiopischen Henoch* (StUNT 12; Göttingen: Vandenhoeck & Ruprecht, 1975), 98 (ET from Hengel, "Right Hand," 186). Hengel maintains that the similarity between Ps 110 and the figure of the son of man is not only alluded to for the first time in Dan 7:13 and broadly developed in 1 Enoch, but also present in the answer of Jesus to the priest in Mk 14:62. For the date of the Parables of 1 Enoch, see J. H. Charlesworth, ed., The Old Testament Pseudepigrapha (London: Darton, Longman & Todd, 1983-85), 1.7.

Third, J. Schaper has recently argued for a messianic interpretation of the psalm in the LXX.[19] He claims that this verse is "One of the most remarkable messianic interpretations in the Greek Psalter."[20] He interprets v.3 as a reference to a pre-existent messiah, by paying particular attention to the overall context of the psalm and the translators' deliberate choice of words such as ἑωσφόρος, δύναμις, λαμπρότης, and ῥάβδος. Although we disagree with his understanding of the messiah as a pre-existent being, we agree with his interpretation of the psalm as messianic.[21]

Fourth, there is evidence that some of the Psalms were already interpreted messianically by the time the Psalter was collected and that, if so, Ps 110 was so interpreted.[22] David's psalms were meant to be read "in the knowledge that God has chosen a messiah and surely keeps God's promises." As J. L. Mays explains,

> The Davidic relation brings out the prophetic potential in the psalms. David is the king whose throne has an everlasting future based on the promise of God. The songs he sponsored and spoke are to be read in the context of that promise. They are "messianic," not because all of them are about the anointed of Israel, but rather in the sense that they are language to be spoken in the knowledge that God has chosen a messiah and surely keeps God's promises.[23]

Finally, Jesus' question about the Son of David in Mk 12:35-37 makes better sense if the messianic understanding of Ps 110:1 is presupposed in its original life-setting, as we will show when we discuss the authenticity question in detail below (§6.2.5.1).

While the data available to us does not allow us to be certain how widely a messianic interpretation of the psalm was accepted prior to

---

[19] J. Schaper, *Eschatology in the Greek Psalter* (WUNT 2/76; Tübingen: Mohr Siebeck, 1995), 101-7. He built his case on the view of P. Volz, *Die Eschatologie der jüdischen Gemeinde im neutestamentlichen Zeitalter nach den Quellen der rabbinischen, apokalyptischen und apokryphen Literatur* (Tübingen: Mohr Siebeck, 1934), 205 and W. Bousset, *Die Religion des Judentums im späthellenistischen Zeitalter* (HNT 21; Tübingen: Mohr Siebeck, 1926), 265.

[20] Schaper, *Eschatology*, 101.

[21] For our critical assessment of Schaper's view see §3.2.6.

[22] Cf. J. L. Mays, *The Lord Reigns: a Theological Handbook to the Psalms* (Louisville: Westminister John Knox, 1994), 94-98, 119-27; see also Hengel, "Right Hand," 179, for a comment made by Klaus Koch in a similar fashion: "The messianic interpretation of the royal psalms appears to be presupposed by the redaction of the Psalter. How would you otherwise explain that the relevant texts are either at the beginning of a David-Psalter, such as Pss. 2 and 107, or at the end of one, such as 72 and 110? Psalm 89 concludes the third Psalter. For those who composed the collection of psalms in the post-exilic period these psalms apparently had programmatic character, and that can only be a messianic one."

[23] Mays, *The Lord Reigns*, 98.

Christianity, the view that it was current in pre-Christian Judaism receives strong support from the arguments put forward above.

We have suggested earlier that the Enochic Son of Man sitting on the throne seems to provide an important precedent for the early Christian understanding of Jesus' sitting at the right hand of God. In Ps 110:1 the one who sits at the right hand of God participates directly in God's reign. The sitting at the right hand of God means the transference of divine authority and judgement. Similarly, in LXX Dan 7:9-11 the dominion of God and of the "one like a son of man" becomes one in its execution. Over against the MT and Theodotion, the mysterious figure in the LXX version of Dan 7 is connected even more closely to the Ancient of Days.[24] The "one like a son of man" almost takes the place of God and his authority thus becomes identical to the authority of God and his dominion identical to God's dominion.

The similarity of expressions and ideas between Ps 110:1 and Dan 7:9-14 becomes clearer in *1 Enoch*, where the Son of Man/the Messiah will sit on the throne of God passing judgement upon all mortal and spiritual beings at the end of days.[25] In *1 Enoch* the Son of Man is further depicted as a pre-existent heavenly being who possesses all dominion.[26] The following extracts from the *Parables of Enoch* will make clear the similarity between both texts:[27]

51:3 "In those days, (the Elect One) shall sit on my throne, and from the conscience of his mouth shall come out all the secrets of wisdom, for the Lord of the Spirits has given them to him and glorified him."
55:4 "Kings, potentates, dwellers upon the earth: You would have to see my Elect One, how he sits in the throne of glory and judges Azaz'el and all his company, and his army, in the name of the Lord of the Spirits!"

---

[24] The LXX does not envision the identity of these two figures, as some think, but rather expresses the similarity of the Son of Man to the Ancient of Days; cf. S. Kim, *"The 'Son of Man'" as the Son of God* (WUNT 30; Tübingen: Mohr Siebeck, 1983), 22-24.

[25] Hengel, "Right Hand,"185-89. We will closely follow his arguments.

[26] The *Parables of Enoch* are not Jewish-Christian work and should be dated no later than early Christianity. According to Hengel, "Right Hand," 185-86, "they originated in a Jewish group – which possibly existed at the same time as the Jerusalem congregation – that was dedicated to the traditions of Enoch and comes from the time between approximately 40 BC and AD 70." For the date of the *Parables* see E. Isaac, "1 (Ethiopic Apocalypse of) Enoch" in *The Old Testament Pseudepigrapha* (ed. J. H. Charlesworth; London: Darton, Longman & Todd, 1983), 7. He regards *1 Enoch* "as dependent upon the Old Testament as it is influential upon the New Testament and later extracanonical literature. During the exilic and post-exilic periods, apocalyptic became a major trend in Jewish thought. It was inherited by Christianity and remains an element in it to the present" (p.9).

[27] Translations are taken from Charlesworth, *OTP*.

61:8 "He placed the Elect One on the throne of glory; and he shall judge all the works of the holy ones in heaven above, weighing in the balance their deeds."

62:2 "The Lord of the Spirits has sat down on the throne of his glory, and the spirit of righteousness has been poured out upon him. The word of his mouth will do the sinners in; and all the oppressors shall be eliminated from before his face."

The resemblance between Ps 110 and the "one like a son of man" in Dan 7:13 is not only broadly developed in the *Parables of Enoch*, but is also present in Jesus' confession to the high priest about the Messiah in Mk 14:62.

Ἐγώ εἰμι,
καὶ ὄψεσθε τὸν υἱὸν τοῦ ἀνθρώπου
ἐκ δεξιῶν καθήμενον τῆς δυνάμεως
καὶ ἐρχόμενον μετὰ τῶν νεφελῶν τοῦ οὐρανοῦ.
I am,
and you will see the Son of Man
seated at the right hand of the Power,
and coming with the clouds of heaven.

This christological statement of high voltage spoken by Jesus at his trial does not derive from the creativity of the gospel writer but exhibits an early Christian tradition that connects Jesus' exaltation to the right hand of God and his return. Although we cannot prove whether Jesus indeed spoke to the high priest and the members of the Sanhedrin in this way or in a similar fashion, our detailed examination of the trial scene (§6.2.5.2) strongly suggests that with such a claim to authority Jesus caused a severe threat to the religious authority of the day which eventually led to his charge of blasphemy. "The age of this tradition is indicated not only by the Jewish circumlocution for the name of God (cf. 14:61) but also by the fact that in this statement . . . the members of the Sanhedrin are threatened that they will *see* Jesus as the coming Judge. Around the year 70 that was no longer possible."[28]

In the *Parables of Enoch* the kings and the mighty ones are also similarly addressed:

55:4   . . . you will see my Elect One sitting on the throne of glory . . .
62:3   and they shall see and recognize him sitting on the throne of his glory (cf. v.5)

However, the sitting at the right hand of God, which so clearly expresses the communion with God, is missing in the *Parables*. Nevertheless, it is possible to infer from these texts that the Son of Man was enthroned by the

---

[28] Hengel, "Right Hand," 187.

Lord of Spirits on the "throne of (his) glory" (61:8; cf. 62:3, 5), that is, the throne of God himself (51:3), and as the representative of God carries out the judgement over the kings and mighty ones. In other words, the throne of God becomes the throne of the Elect One/the Son of Man and can even appear as the "throne of his (that is, the Son of Man's) glory" (cf. 63:5; 69:27, 29).

According to Hengel, similar pictures are also found in the NT documents: (1) the Gospel of Matthew mentions twice that the Son of Man will sits ἐπὶ θρόνου δόξης αὐτοῦ (19:28; 25:31), acting as the representative of God with God's authority; (2) the Sibylline Oracles also show acquaintance with the language of the *Parables of Enoch* (6 Sib 1f.); and (3) in 2 Cor 5:10 Paul speaks of all Christians appearing before the βῆμα τοῦ Χριστοῦ as the throne of the eschatological judge, while in Rom 14:10 he says that "we will all stand before the βῆμα τοῦ θεοῦ."

We can therefore safely conclude that the Enochic Son of Man sitting on the throne probably provided an important precedent for the early Christian understanding of Jesus as a pre-existent being exalted and enthroned at the right hand of God.

6.2. Early Christian Interpretation of Psalm 110:1

6.2.1. Psalm 110:1 in Early Christian Literature

Ps 110:1 is the scriptural passage with the greatest number of citations or definite allusions in the NT. The 27th edition of Nestle-Aland identifies seven quotations (Mt 22:44; Mk 12:36; Lk 20:42-43; Acts 2:34-35; 1 Cor 15:25; Heb 1:13; 8:1) and nine allusions to Ps 110:1 (Mt 26:64; Mk 14:62; Mk 16:19; Lk 22:69; Rom 8:34; Eph 1:20; Col 3:1; Heb 1:3; 10:12-13), adding up sixteen passages in total. If we include all the passages referring to the exaltation of Jesus and/or "sitting" at the right hand of God (Acts 2:33; 5:31; 7:55-56; Heb 12:2; 1 Pet 3:22; Rev 3:21) the number goes up to twenty two.[29]

David M. Hay has done a comprehensive study of the early Christian use of Psalm 110 in his *Glory at the Right Hand*.[30] Another detailed survey of the topic would have little to add to his study. Nevertheless, a summary of his main findings on the opening verse of the psalm would be useful.

---

[29] Cf. Hay, *Glory*, 15, 155, found some thirty-three quotations and allusions to the vv.1 and 4 of Psalm 110 scattered throughout the NT and seven more in other Christian writings produced before the middle of the second century.

[30] Hay, *Glory*.

The opening verse of Psalm 110 can be divided into three basic parts: (a) introduction (εἶπεν ὁ κύριος τῷ κυρίῳ μου "The Lord said to my Lord"); (b) the exaltation/enthronement (κάθου ἐκ δεξιῶν μου "Sit at my right hand"); and (c) the subjection of the powers (ἕως ἂν θῶ τοὺς ἐχθρούς σου ὑποπόδιον τῶν ποδῶν σου "until I make your enemies your footstool").

The following is a table of thirty references to Ps 110:1 in early Christian literature before Justin with quotations (Q) or allusions (A) to different parts of the verse.[31]

Text	Ref.	Function	"right hand"
Mk 12:36	Q 1a-c	proves that Christ should be called "Lord" and not "son of David" (spoken by Jesus)	ἐκ δεξιῶν
Mt 22:44	Q 1a-c	Same	ἐκ δεξιῶν
Lk 20:42	Q 1a-c	Same	ἐκ δεξιῶν
Mk 14:62	A 1b	describes Jesus' (= Son of Man's) future vindication (spoken by Jesus)	ἐκ δεξιῶν
Mt 26:64	A 1b	Same	ἐκ δεξιῶν
Lk 22:69	A 1b	Same	ἐκ δεξιῶν
Mk 16:19	A 1b	describes Jesus' ascension	ἐκ δεξιῶν
Acts 2:33-36	Q 1a-c	proves that Jesus, not David, was exalted as Lord and Christ; from here Christ pours out the Pentecost gifts of the Spirit	τῇ δεξιᾷ (v.33) ἐκ δεξιῶν (v.35)
Acts 5:31	A 1b	describes how God exalted Jesus as leader and saviour	τῇ δεξιᾷ
Acts 7:55-56	A 1b	describes Jesus as the exalted Son of Man (Stephen's vision)	ἐκ δεξιῶν
Rom 8:34	A 1b	describes how the exalted Christ Jesus intercedes for the faithful	ἐν δεξιᾷ
1 Cor 15:25	A 1c	proves that Christ must reign until his enemies are subjected	-
Eph 1:20-22	A 1bc	describes God's exaltation of Jesus over other powers as head of the church	ἐν δεξιᾷ
Eph 2:6[32]	A 1b	describes believers' raising and exaltation with Christ	-
Col 3:1	A 1b	describes Christ's exaltation, in which believers share	ἐν δεξιᾷ
Heb 1:3	A 1b	describes the exaltation of Jesus after he made purification for sins	ἐν δεξιᾷ

---

[31] This is an adaptation of the table by M. C. Albl, 'And Scripture Cannot Be Broken': the Form and Function of the Early Christian Testimonia Collections (NovTSup 96; Leiden: Brill, 1999), 217-19, which is based on Hay's tabular summary. Albl added one more reference to Ps 110:1 from Ascension of Isaiah.

[32] This passage lacks the characteristic "right hand" terminology, but the verb "seated" and the association with Eph 1:20-22 ensure that an allusion to Ps 110:1 is intended.

Heb 1:13	Q 1bc	proves the superiority of Christ over the angels	ἐκ δεξιῶν
Heb 8:1	A 1b	describes Jesus as high priest in glory	ἐν δεξιᾷ
Heb 10:12-13	A 1bc	describes the exaltation of the high priest Jesus after his sacrifice; his waiting for the subjection of his enemies	ἐν δεξιᾷ
Heb 12:2	A 1b	describes Jesus' vindication and exaltation after suffering	ἐν δεξιᾷ
1 Pet 3:22	A 1bc	describes exaltation of Christ and subjection of powers in context of believers' salvation through baptism	ἐν δεξιᾷ
Rev 3:21[33]	A 1b	describes exaltation to the heavenly throne of believers who "conquer," just as Christ was exalted to God's throne	-
1 Clem. 36:5-6	Q 1bc	proves the superiority of Christ over the angels	ἐκ δεξιῶν
Polycarp *Phil.* 2:1	A 1bc	describes Christ's exaltation and subjection of powers in context of exhorting believers – they too will be raised	ἐκ δεξιῶν
Barn. 12:10-11	Q 1a-c	proves that Christ is Son of God and not David's Son	ἐκ δεξιῶν
Sib. Or. 2.241-45	A 1b	describes Christ as judge; conflation with Dan 7:13	ἐπὶ δεξιᾷ
Apoc. Peter 6	A 1b	Same	"at the right hand"[34]
Asc. Isaiah 10:14; 11:32	A 1b	describes glorious ascension of Christ after judgement	
Apoc. Jas. 14:30-31	A 1b	describes Jesus' imminent ascension to glory	"(the) right side"[35]
Excerpt of Theodotus 62.1-2	Q 1b	describes the "psychic" (ψυχικός) Christ sitting at the right hand of the Demiurge until the consummation	

As we can see from the table, the importance of Ps 110:1 for the early church is evident not only from the number of its references but also from its widespread attestation in NT and post-NT literature. The most common feature of all these references is that Ps 110:1 is linked to the idea of Jesus' exaltation or vindication after his death and resurrection. Many of these references clearly testify that early Christians understood Jesus' resurrection as his exaltation to the right hand of God (Acts 2:32-35; Rom 8:34; Eph 1:20; 1 Pet 3:22).[36] The widespread use and familiarity with the

---

[33] Again the "right hand" terminology is lacking, but the reference to "sitting" on the throne with Christ and God in exaltation is a strong indication that Ps 110:1 is intended.

[34] Translation from Ethiopic.

[35] English translation from Coptic.

[36] Such an understanding is implied in Acts 5:31; 7:55-56; 1Cor 15:25; Col 3:1; Heb 1:3; 10:12; 12:2.

pictorial expression of Jesus' exaltation as *sitting* or simply *being* at "the right hand of God" strongly suggests that such a picture of Jesus was very significant for early Christian understanding of Jesus.

6.2.2. Indirect Sources of Psalm 110:1

Another interesting feature of the early Christian use of Ps 110:1 can be seen when one compares the exact wording of these references. When Ps 110:1 is explicitly quoted, the LXX reading of ἐν δεξιῶν is always used; however, the majority of the allusions use constructions with δεξιᾷ: ἐν δεξιᾷ (Rom 8:34; Col 3:1; Eph 1:20; 1 Pet 3:22; Heb 1:3; 8:1; 10:12; 12:2); τῇ δεξιᾷ (Acts 2:33; 5:31); ἐπὶ δεξιᾷ (*Sib. Or.* 2.243).[37] Especially striking is the use of Ps 110:1 in the Epistle to the Hebrews: when the writer quotes Ps 110:1 in 1:13, he follows the LXX in reading the genitive ἐν δεξιῶν, but when he alludes to this passage in 1:3 he writes the dative ἐν δεξιᾷ. All the other allusions to the session at the right hand in Hebrews (8:1; 10:12; 12:2) agree with v.3 in using the dative ἐν δεξιᾷ rather than the genitive ἐν δεξιῶν. Moreover, Rom 8:34, 1 Pet 3:22, and the quotations in Acts merely speak of "being" at the right hand of God without a specific reference to the "sitting."

The above evidence strongly suggests that these allusions are drawn from indirect sources other than the LXX itself.[38] Hay draws two important implications of indirect sources for Ps 110:1: (1) the person who makes an allusion to the psalm does not necessarily show direct acquaintance with the original psalm but simply the intermediary sources (*Vorlagen*); and (2) those *Vorlagen* not only provided early Christians their phrasing, but they also conditioned their interpretation of the psalm.[39]

6.2.3. Psalm 110:1 in a Pre-Pauline Confession

How widespread and early was the belief in Jesus' exaltation to the right hand of God established in the early church? The idea of Jesus' sitting at God's right hand occurs only twice in the early letters of Paul (Rom 8:34; 1 Cor 15:25, 28). Does such scanty evidence suggest that the idea of Jesus'

---

[37] The allusions are clearly to Ps 110:1, as shown by verbal parallels (esp. "sitting" or "right hand") or other clues in the context (e.g., earlier references to Ps 110). Other scriptural references to the right hand of God (e.g., Ps 80:17; *Test. Job* 33) are most likely not in view (see Hay, *Glory*, 17 n.9).

[38] It is theoretically possible that the allusions are based on another Greek translation or on direct access to the Hebrew (ἐν δεξιᾷ is in fact a natural translation of the MT). Nevertheless, we have no scriptural manuscript evidence for such a reading.

[39] Hay, *Glory*, 38-43.

exaltation was not important to Paul and his readers when he wrote these letters? M. Hengel argues that the opposite was the case:

The time of its effectiveness in forming and influencing christology was already past. Romans was written presumably in the winter of 56/57 as Paul resided in Corinth and 1 Corinthians about one and a half years earlier. By this time the basic aspects of christology had long been established. Paul presupposes that in the congregations in Corinth and Rome a knowledge of the christological concepts that were connected with Ps 110:1 – concepts to which he only alludes – was unquestionably present. He can use these formulas because he knows that the congregations understand them. In the manifold quotations and allusions in the New Testament only after-effects of the original meaning of Ps. 110:1 for the beginnings of christology are visible.[40]

6.2.3.1. *Rom 8:34 (cf. 1 Pet 3:22; Col 3:1)*

Rom 8:34 is the earliest datable witness available in the NT about Jesus' exaltation at the right hand of God and the existence of a pre-Pauline kerygmatic formula behind this verse has been persuasively argued by Hengel.[41]

First, a fourfold confession-like formulation can be identified in Rom 8:34:[42]

1) Christ Jesus, who died (ὁ ἀποθανών);
2) who was raised (ἐγερθείς);
3) who is at the right hand of God (ὅς καί ἐστιν ἐν δεξιᾷ τοῦ θεοῦ);
4) who intercedes for us (ὅς καὶ ἐντυγχάνει ὑπὲρ ἡμῶν).

---

[40] Hengel, "Right Hand," 137-38. See also M. Hengel, "Christology and New Testament Chronology" in *Between Jesus and Paul: Studies in the Earliest History of Christianity* (Philadelphia: Fortress, 1983), 30-47; M. Hengel, *The Son of God: the Origin of Christology and the History of Jewish-Hellenistic Religion* (London: SCM, 1976), 80-83. Cf. Gourgues, *droite de Dieu*, 55: "recourant à un formulaire déjà fixé, connue de la communauté" "resorting to an already fixed form, known to the community"; 56 "Le fait que ni Paul ni 1 P(etr) ne sentent le besoin d'expliquer la formule qu'ils emploient, ni d'en expliciter le rattachement au psaume . . . indiquerait également que cette formule était déja familière aux lecteurs."

[41] Hengel, "Right Hand," 137-63.

[42] Hengel, "Right Hand," 139. See also E. Fuchs, *Die Freiheit des Glaubens: Römer 5-8 ausgelegt* (BEvT 14; München: Kaiser, 1949), 117-21; R. Zorn, *Die Fürbitte im Spätjudentum und im Neuen Testament* (Unpub. Diss., University of Göttingen, 1957), 147-52. The clause ὅς καί ἐστιν ἐν δεξιᾷ τοῦ θεοῦ has already been separated from the LXX text of Ps 110:1 and is completely integrated into the context, bearing witness to an earlier development of that tradition. *Contra* G. Lohfink, *Die Himmelfahrt Jesu: Untersuchungen zu den Himmelfahrts- und Erhöhungstexten bei Lukas* (SANT 26; München: Kosel, 1971), 84f., who regards the third and fourth clauses as explanatory of the statement about the resurrection and v.34 as a rhetorical question.

Second, Paul probably knew that the formula was highly esteemed in the congregation in Rome (cf. Hebrews; 1 Peter; *1 Clem.* 36:5) and wanted to emphasize the common belief he shares with them.[43]

Third, there are a considerable number of allusions to Ps 110:1 in the NT which do not appear to be derived directly from the psalm but from early church confessions or hymns.[44] God's invitation to sit has been simplified into a statement of the place where Christ is now (κάθου ἐκ δεξιῶν μου → ὅς καί ἐστιν ἐν δεξιᾷ τοῦ θεοῦ).[45] A good example of this is the three NT passages with clear allusions to Ps 110:1b that are almost identical with one another:

Rom 8:34   ὅς καί ἐστιν ἐν δεξιᾷ τοῦ θεου
1 Pet 3:22   ὅς ἐστιν ἐν δεξιᾷ [τοῦ] θεοῦ
Col 3:1   ὁ Χριστός ἐστιν ἐν δεξιᾷ τοῦ θεοῦ καθήμενος

Fourth, significant pieces of evidence are in support of this view:[46] (1) none of the three texts in question has a single word in common with the LXX;[47] (2) both Rom 8:34 and 1 Pet 3:22 include a more extensive listing of the salvific events than the other passages referring to Jesus' exaltation;[48] (3) the intercession of the Exalted One (the fourth component in Rom 8:34) appears also in Hebrews;[49] (4) certain allusions to Ps 110:1 seem to add little or nothing to the texts in which they occur (Col 3:1; cf.

---

[43] M. Hengel, "Hymns and Christology" in *Between Jesus and Paul: Studies in the Earliest History of Christianity* (Philadelphia: Fortress, 1983), 87. In his letters to the Romans Paul makes use of several other christological formulas which are unique to this letter (cf. 1:3f.; 3:25; 4:25; 8:32; 14:9).

[44] Hay, *Glory*, 39, speaks of "indirect sources."

[45] Hengel, "Right Hand," 141.

[46] Hengel, "Right Hand," 145. Hay, *Glory*, 40-41, cites scholars who maintain that Eph 1:20-23; 2:4-10; and 1 Pet 3:18-22 are of hymnic origin with a baptismal *Sitz im Leben*. However, in our opinion, their arguments seem inconclusive.

[47] This phenomenon cannot be adequately otherwise explained unless we imagine that the writer to the Colossians was deliberately copying the statement from Romans or the writer of 1 Peter was dependent on Romans, for which there is no conclusive evidence. Cf. Hay, *Glory*, 39-40. Hengel, "Right Hand," 141-45, suggests that the use of is an indication of a variant translation of the Hebrew text which was independent of the LXX and is a proof that the form preserved in Rom 8:34 is of old age.

[48] While Rom 8:34 has four elements (death, resurrection, exaltation at the right hand, and intercession), 1 Pet 3:22 has three (sitting at the right hand, ascension and victory over the powers). But, if 3:18 is included, with three more elements (suffering, death and resurrection) 1 Pet 3:18-22 has six christological components.

[49] Hengel, "Right Hand," 145-47, suggests that the connection between the first and the fourth verse of Ps 110 was not first made by the writer of this relatively later letter to the Hebrews, but more probably goes back to a much earlier stage and was already known to Paul.

Pol *Phil* 2:1), suggesting that the idea was already well known to the writer and his readers;[50] and (5) a number of allusions appear in contexts suggestive of hymnic or church confessional origin (Eph 1:20-22; 2:4-10; Heb 1:2-3; Pol *Phil* 2:1), although the evidence might not be entirely conclusive.[51]

6.2.3.2. Conclusion

That there were traditional formulas behind the NT allusions to Ps 110:1, whether they be church confessions, hymns or liturgical material, is probable. We can almost be certain that the theme of Christ sitting at the right hand of God was widespread in the early church and is pre-Pauline in character.

6.2.4. Christological Fusion of Psalm 110:1 and Psalm 8:6

Another important aspect of the early Christian use of Ps 110:1 is the fusion of the second half of this verse with the second half of Ps 8:6 (LXX 8:7): πάντα ὑπέταξας ὑποκάτω τῶν ποδῶν αὐτοῦ.[52] The fusion of these two psalms is clearly attested in 1 Cor 15:25-27; Eph 1:20-22; 1 Pet 3:22; and

---

[50] Hay, *Glory*, 40, states: "The less essential to its context an allusion is, the more we must be ready to regard it as a stereotyped truism, quite possibly inserted by the writer without much thought just because it was so familiar to himself and his readers."

[51] See Hay, *Glory*, 40-43 and references cited there. Cf. J. Frankowski, "Early Christian Hymns Recorded in the New Testament: A Reconsideration of the Question in Light of Heb 1.3" *BZ* 27 (1983), 183-94; J. F. Balchin, "Colossians 1:15-20: an Early Christological Hymn? The Arguments from Style" *Vox Evangelica* 15 (1985), 65-94. They are more inclined to see a common theme or tradition rather than church confessions or hymns behind these texts.

[52] Psalm 8 is a prominent christological text in the New Testament. It is quoted three times (1 Cor 15:27, Heb 2:6-8, Matt 21:16), clearly alluded to three times (Phil 3:21, Eph 1:22, 1 Pet 3:22), and may be echoed in other places as well (e.g., Rom 8:20-21, Phil 2:6-11, Mark 12:36). By joining these two verses, the early church expressed the victory and dominion of the messiah over the angelic powers. Cf. M. S. Kinzer, *'All Things Under His Feet': Psalm 8 in the New Testament and in Other Jewish Literature of Late Antiquity* (PhD dissertation; University of Michigan, 1995), who, through an analysis of rabbinic, pseudepigraphic, Samaritan, and Gnostic texts, attempts to show that Ps 8 was already understood in many first-century Jewish circles to speak of an individual (e.g., Adam, Enoch, Abraham, Moses) and his exaltation above the angels. According to him, the New Testament appropriation of the psalm was thus based on an already existing exegetical tradition. Though the similarity of v.6b to Ps 110:1 may have facilitated the New Testament's Christological reading of Ps 8, the primary impulse came from this pre-existing exegetical tradition. As a result of this, he argues that, we can better appreciate how the relevant New Testament texts present Jesus as a new Adam, who is greater than Enoch and Moses.

the letter of Polycarp to the Philippians 2:1-2, but is also evident in Mk 12:36.[53]

M. Hengel argued that at the root of the fusion of these psalms in 1 Cor 15:25-27; Eph 1:20-22 and 1 Peter 3:22 lies an early Christian use of "messianic hymns" of the two related motifs of exaltation and subjugation of the powers.[54] Both psalms, included in the hymnbook of the Jewish congregation, were sung in Jerusalem as messianic hymns, which were mutually interpreted one another and at the same time exerted a significant influence upon the origin of early christology. Early Christian exegetes could bring together and meaningfully interpret Ps 110:1 and Ps 8:6 as speaking about Jesus' exaltation and his subjugation of the powers. The similarity in words most probably led the early church to interpret both texts in terms of one another.[55] A christological-soteriological interpretation of Ps 8 was therefore a legitimate possibility from the beginning.[56]

6.2.4.1. 1 Cor 15:25-27

The earliest available evidence of such an interpretation of Ps 110:1 and Ps 8:6 is attested in 1 Cor 15:25-27. Here we find Paul's brief description of the dramatic course of the end of history: there will be first the resurrection of Christ, then at his return the resurrection of the believers, and then the real end will come, when Christ will hand over the kingdom of God "after he has destroyed every rule and every authority and power" (v.24).

The fusion of Ps 110:1b and Ps 8:6b takes place in v.25. The statement δεῖ γὰρ αὐτὸν βασιλεύειν ἄχρι οὗ θῇ πάντας τοὺς ἐχθροὺς ὑπὸ τοὺς πόδας αὐτοῦ is clearly an allusion to Ps 110:1 and Ps 8:6. These verses are not cited directly but woven together into the narrative. Already in v.24c,

---

[53] Hengel, "Right Hand," 163-72.

[54] Hengel, "Hymns," 78-96, esp. 84-88.

[55] Hay, *Glory*, 44-45, notes that "The passage most often linked with it [Ps. 110.1], Ps. 8:7, might have been connected with it independently by various Christians because of the similarity of the two psalms texts." Here we may see a deliberate connection of the two psalms with two different "titles": κύριος and υἱὸς (τοῦ) ἀνθρώπου.

[56] Hengel, "Right Hand," 168-69: "Whereas Ps. 110 contains the title κύριος (and in the second line ἀρχιερεύς), Ps. 8 has υἱὸς ἀνθρώπου ('son of man') and ἄνθρωπος. The Targum of Psalms translates in both cases with *bar nāšā*, the Peshitta with *gbr'* and *br'nš*. Hebrews subordinates both texts – Ps. 110:1 and 8:7 – to the title υἱὸς which is for the author definitive and which in 1:2 establishes the general theme of the letter. In other words, these texts that described the exaltation of the Resurrected One were not associated with specific titles; they supported the variation and interchangeability of titles." Hay, *Glory*, 44-45.

before the actual citation, the last part of Ps 110:1 was paraphrased.[57] Several changes are to be noted: (a) the "sitting at the right hand of God" in heaven is interpreted by Paul as Christ's active reigning: δεῖ . . . αὐτὸν βασιλεύειν (cf. βασιλεία in v.24); (b) a first person direct discourse with God as speaker is transformed into a third person narrative, introduced by the subordinate conjunction γάρ; (c) the ἕως ἂν of Ps 110:1 is replaced with ἄχρι οὗ, emphasizing the temporal limitation of the kingship;[58] (d) πάντας (equivalent to the πάντα of Ps 8:7) is inserted and the clause ὑπὸ τοὺς πόδας αὐτου is replaced with ὑποπόδιον τῶν ποδῶν, most likely due to the influence of Ps 8:7;[59] (e) however, the most significant change is the christological transposition of subject by which, instead of God, Christ becomes the subject of the action (cf. Phil 3:21).[60] For the psalmist the grammatical subject of θῶ (first person) is God, but for Paul the subject of θῇ (third person) is Christ.[61]

Paul then quotes Ps 8:6 in v.27 to reinforce the point. While Paul states πάντα γὰρ ὑπέταξεν ὑπὸ τοὺς πόδας αὐτοῦ, the LXX text reads πάντα ὑπέταξας ὑποκάτω τῶν ποδῶν αὐτοῦ. Again Paul edits the psalm text to suit his purpose: (a) as in v.25 γάρ is added and the direct discourse is avoided (change from second person to third); (b) the ὑποκάτω plus genitive becomes ὑπό plus accusative; (c) as many commentators agree, a double transposition should be assumed here: "In the psalm it was *God* who subjected all things under the feet of *man in general*. For Paul,

---

[57] Hay, *Glory*, 36 n.6: "Rather than simply being an 'introduction' to the allusion to vs 1c, this clause may be an allusion to, or paraphrase of, vs 1b of the psalm: 'Sit at the right hand' is interpreted as a commission to reign."

[58] Cf. J. Lambrecht, "Paul's Christological Use of Scripture in 1-Corinthians 15.20-28" *NTS* 28 (1982), 505. Paul also prefers this phrase (cf. Rom 11:25; 1Cor 11:26; Gal 3:19).

[59] So Lambrecht, "Christological Use," 506.

[60] In Phil 3:21, where Christ is clearly the subject, Paul writes . . . τοῦ δύνασθαι αὐτὸν καὶ ὑποτάξαι αὐτῷ τὰ πάντα employing the same psalm verse.

[61] The exegesis of this passage has been controversial since the times of the early church. For Christ as subject, see Becker Jürgen, *Auferstehung Der Toten Im Urchristentum* (Stuttgart: KBW Verlag, 1976), 86; H. Conzelmann, *1 Corinthians: a Commentary on the First Epistle to the Corinthians* (Hermeneia; Philadelphia: Fortress, 1975), op. cit.; Dupont, "Assisa à la droite de Dieu," 390-91; and others. For God as subject argue among others Beza, Grotius, Bengel, Wettstein, Rosenmüller, Godet, U. Luz, *Das Geschichtsverständnis des Paulus* (BEvTh 49; München: Kaiser, 1968), 86; and T. Aono, *Die Entwicklung des paulinischen Gerichtsgedankens bei den Apostolischen Vätern* (Europäische Hochschulschriften, XXIII, 137; Bern: P. Lang, 1979), 26-28. For a detailed defence of the christocentric reading of vv.23-28, see Lambrecht, "Christological Use," 508-11, who argues against the theocentric reading proposed by Aono, *Entwicklung*, 26-28, who suggests that already in v.24c, the second ὅταν-clause, God is the subject.

because of the parallelism with v. 25, it is most probably *Christ* who subjects all things under *his own* feet."[62] In the quotation, the πάντα is certainly stressed, but the idea of destroying (vv.26 and 24) and "putting under the feet" (v.25) is also taken up: "he subjected under his feet."

Is Paul here quoting psalms or is he making free use of scripture? One may assume that Paul is here *quoting* psalms as proof texts, but the evidence seems to suggest that Paul is using scriptural language to express his own ideas: (1) there are no introductory formulas in vv.25-28; and (2) if "the expression ὅταν δὲ εἴπῃ, itself loaded with problems, is disregarded," there is no clear indication that Paul intended to "cite" scripture here.[63]

Lastly, we need to ask whether such a combination of psalms is Paul's own. However, since these two psalms are fused together also in Eph 1:20-22; 1 Pet 3:22 and, although separated by some verses, in Heb 1:13 and 2:6-9, it seems to confirm our view that these psalms were already combined before Paul as "messianic psalms," although the Ephesians passage could at least be dependent on 1 Cor 15:25-27.[64] Furthermore, the fact that Paul presupposes that his use of psalms will be readily understood by the Corinthians also supports our view.

The above evidence then clearly suggests that in vv.25-28 Paul understands both psalms as referring to the same eschatological event with two related motifs: Christ's active reigning (βασιλεία) since his resurrection/exaltation and his subjugation of the powers.[65] In short, Paul brings out the christological and eschatological dimensions of Ps 110 and Ps 8 by bringing together psalms already used and combined before him.

6.2.4.2. Eph 1:20-22

The fusion of Ps 110:1 and Ps 8:6 occurs also in Eph 1:20-22. The writer states first that God raised Christ from the dead, and then God made him to sit at his right hand in the heavenly places far above all rule and authority and power and dominion; and then the theme of Jesus' subjection of the powers follows: καὶ πάντα ὑπέταξεν ὑπὸ τοὺς πόδας αὐτοῦ. Here we find two identical changes to the statement in 1 Cor 15:25, 27 over against Ps

---

[62] Lambrecht, "Christological Use," 507.

[63] Lambrecht, "Christological Use," 508. This point is not without bearing on the christocentric exegesis of the passage.

[64] For the possibility of Eph 1:20-22 being dependent on 1 Cor 15, see Lambrecht, "Christological Use," 520 n.33. For a pre-Pauline liturgical origin of the combination, see Luz, *Geschichtsverständnis*, 344.

[65] Hengel, "Right Hand," 165. He adds that "Because in v.27 God is the subject of ὑπέταξεν and in v.28 God is designated as ὑποτάξας, the θῇ πάντας ... in v.25 also has to be attributed to him."

8:6 LXX (ὑπέταξας to ὑπέταξεν and ὑποκάτω to ὑπό). Thus, the passage shows the continued use of the fusion between Ps 110:1 and Ps 8:6 in Pauline circles.

6.2.4.3. 1 Pet 3:22

Similarly, in 1 Pet 3:22 a statement of Jesus' exaltation (ὅς ἐστιν ἐν δεξιᾷ [τοῦ] θεοῦ) is followed by a statement of the subjugation of powers ὑποταγέντων αὐτῷ ἀγγέλων καὶ ἐξουσιῶν καὶ δυνάμεων, which reminds us of πάντα ὑπέταξας in Ps 8:6. According to Achtemeier, the passage reflects "early creedal material" and shares traditions with other NT passages but does not show literary dependence on them; however, with his use of ἐν δεξιᾷ, the writer indicates "his dependence on tradition rather than on the psalm directly."[66] In short, the writer is dependent on indirect sources where both Ps 110:1 and Ps 8:6 were already combined.

6.2.4.4. Polycarp Phil. 2.1

πιστεύσαντες εἰς
τὸν ἐγείραντα τὸν κύριον ἡμῶν Ἰησοῦν Χριστὸν ἐκ νεκρῶν
καὶ δόντα αὐτῷ δόξαν καὶ θρόνον ἐκ δεξιῶν αὐτοῦ·
ᾧ ὑπετάγη τὰ πάντα ἐπουράνια καὶ ἐπίγεια,
ᾧ πᾶσα πνοὴ λατρεύει
ὃς ἔρχεται κριτὴς ζώντων καὶ νεκρῶν.

In a letter of Polycarp written probably between 115 and 120, the fusion of "the sitting at the right hand of God" and the subjection of the powers occurs again as part of the five-fold formulaic statement of salvific events, similar to 1 Pet 3:18-22. The divine passive of the aorist ὑπετάγη and the aorist participle δόντα shows that the exaltation to the right hand and the handing over of power are fused together and become a single event of the past.[67] The creed-like form and the lengthy adjectival statement without direct relevant to the context strongly suggest that the statement is much older than the date of the composition of the letter.[68]

---

[66] P. J. Achtemeier, *A Commentary on First Peter* (Hermeneia; Minneapolis: Fortress, 1996), 273.

[67] Hengel, "Right Hand," 167.

[68] See Hay, *Glory*, 40; also H. Paulsen and W. Bauer, *Die Briefe des Ignatius von Antiochia und der Brief des Polykarp von Smyrna* (HNT 18; Die Apostolischen Väter II; Tübingen: Mohr (Paul Siebeck), 1985), 115, who speak of Polycarp's use of "traditional christological statements."

6.2.4.5. Hebrews 2:8-9

How does the fusion of Ps 110:1 and Ps 8:6 affect the early Christian understanding of Jesus, particularly in reference to Ps 110:1? Dunn insists that Heb 2:8-9 should be seen as the most effective use of Ps 8:5-6 for Adam christology, where Jesus is said to fulfil God's original intention for man.[69] But was this the implication early Christians drew from the juxtaposition of these two psalms? Is Dunn's interpretation of Ps 8:4-6 in Heb 2:8:9 justified? Scholars are sharply divided between an anthropological (Jesus as representative of humanity) and a christological interpretation (Jesus as the heavenly Son of Man).

Arguments for the former view can be summed up as follows:[70] (1) Ps 8 was understood as speaking of man in early Christianity; (2) there is no firm evidence for a messianic interpretation of the psalm in rabbinic literature; (3) "son of man" in the OT is generally synonymous for man and this usage is reflected in the NT; and (4) τὸν δὲ 'Ιησοῦν strongly suggest a contrast with some other figure, namely "man." One can paraphrase vv. 8-9 as follows: "Ps. 8 speaks of man's complete authority over the universe. But we see no sign of this at present. What we do see is Jesus, abased for a time, but now exalted in glory."[71]

On the other hand, the following arguments are generally proposed for a christological interpretation of the psalm: (1) some of the arguments for an anthropological interpretation supported by Christian writers after NT times and by modern scholars are less important by comparison with the evidence of Hebrews itself, whose author exhibits a quality of being a creative exegete;[72] (2) "Although the phrase υἱὸς ἀνθρώπου is not part of the author's own vocabulary, the use of ὁ υἱὸς τοῦ ἀνθρώπου in the Gospels is so frequent, and so closely associated with Jesus, that it may well have led the author of Hebrews to read Ps. 8 in a christological sense";[73] (3) even if the writer saw "son of man" as synonymous with "man," it does not necessarily follow that he assimilated the meaning of "son of man" to that of "man," or vice versa; (4) there were speculations in

---

[69] J. D. G. Dunn, *Christology in the Making: a New Testament Inquiry into the Origins of the Doctrine of the Incarnation* (London: SCM, 1980, 1989), 109: that is: "The risen Jesus is crowned with the glory that Adam failed to reach by virtue of his sin."

[70] The summaries of both arguments are from P. Ellingworth, *The Epistle to the Hebrews: a Commentary on the Greek Text* (NIGTC; Grand Rapids: Eerdmans, 1993), 150-51.

[71] Ellingworth, *Hebrews*, 150.

[72] That the psalm originally referred to man is, though probable, "hardly relevant." See J. C. Adams, *The Epistle to the Hebrews with Special Reference to the Problem of Apostasy in the Church to which it was Addressed* (M.A. Thesis, Leeds, 1964), 305.

[73] P. Giles, *Jesus the High Priest in the Epistle to the Hebrews and in the Fourth Gospel* (M.A. Thesis, Manchester, 1973), 3-10.

Jewish apocalyptic and in Christianized gnosticism about a figure known as the Son of Man, the first or perfect man, or simply as (the) man; (5) the ὄνομα κυρίου in Heb 1:2, 4 (cf. Ps 8:1, 9) would mean primarily Jesus' title of "Son"; (6) vv.10ff. are based on πάντα in the last line of the quotation rather than its first two lines, thereby suggesting that there is no previous reference to humanity in general in Hebrews; (7) the best explanation for the contrast implied in τὸν δὲ . . . 'Ιησοῦν lies in the author's difficulty in applying the quotation consistently to Christ;[74] and (8) both the context in Hebrews and the fusion of Pss 110:1 and 8:6-8 elsewhere in the NT suggest that ὑποκάτω τῶν ποδῶν αὐτοῦ in 2:8a should be understood in the same way as ὑποπόδιον τῶν ποδῶν σου in 1:13.

While both sides of the argument appear to stand in a stark contrast, an attempt to deny the christological reading of the passage is not convincing. In Heb 2:9 the status of Jesus during his earthly life is expressed with the aid of Ps 8:6: "we see Jesus who for a little while was made lower than the angels." The author of Hebrews interprets the two lines of Ps 8:6 without reference to the synonymous parallelism of the original text. From the perspective of the psalmist, to be made "little lower" than heavenly beings is to be "crowned with glory and honour," but according to our author the two members of the parallelism represent two stages in the life of Jesus: the first line concerns Jesus' temporary abasement, while the second speaks of his subsequent exaltation and glorification. This christological reading of the text explains the omission of the first member of the following parallelism (Ps 8:7a). Our author's understanding of the eternal sonship of Jesus is therefore supported by his conscious departure from the original Semitic parallelism which produces a distinctly confessional understanding of the quotation.[75] As W. L. Lane succinctly puts it,

> The three lines reproduced by the writer combine to form a confession of faith that celebrates the three successive moments in the drama of redemption, i.e., the incarnation, the exaltation, and the final victory of Jesus, the first pertaining to the past, the second to the present, and the third to the future.[76]

Our author, therefore, applies the quotation from Ps 8:6 not to the first Adam but to Christ as the last Adam, the head of the new creation and

---

[74] This can be paraphrase in the following manner: "Ps 8:6b speaks of the universal Lordship of Christ, but, as Ps. 110:1b shows, this has not yet been fully manifested. What we do see is Jesus now exalted in glory."

[75] Cf. O. Linton, "Le *Parallelismus Membrorum* dans le Nouveau Testament: Simple remarques" in *Mélanges bibliques: en hommage au R. P. Beda Rigaux* (eds. A.-L. Descamps *et al.*; Gembloux: Duculot, 1970), 495-96; cf. Delling, *TDNT* 8.42.

[76] W. L. Lane, *Hebrews* (WBC 47; Dallas: Word Books, 1991), 48.

ruler of the world to come. We probably have here a tacit identification of "the son of man" in Ps 8:4 with the "one like a son of man" in Dan 7:13, who receives "an everlasting dominion" from the Ancient Days. It is true that in Ps 8:4 "the son of man" stands in a synonymous parallelism with "man" in the preceding line, but it is equally true that "one like a son of man" in Dan 7:13 simply means "one like a human being." As F. F. Bruce concludes, "The fact remains that, ever since Jesus spoke of himself as the Son of Man, this expression has had for Christians a connotation beyond its etymological force, and it had this connotation for the writer to the Hebrews."[77] Moreover, it is significant that Heb 2:8-9 shares common features with the other two Pauline passages, such as a note of unrealised eschatology, the focus on Ps 8:6b (especially on [τὰ] πάντα), a reference to the relation of believers to Christ, and the application of the psalm to Christ.[78] It is therefore most likely that Ps 110:1 and Ps 8:6 were for christological reasons early connected to one another and the latter was interpreted in the light of the former (cf. 1 Cor 15:25-27 and Eph 1:20-22).[79]

6.2.4.6. Conclusion

Evidence from 1 Cor 15:25-27; Eph 1:20-22; 1 Pet 3:22; Polycarp *Phil.* 2.1; and Heb 2:8-9 suggests that a christological-soteriological combination of Ps 110:1 and Ps 8:6 as "messianic psalms" was already known to Paul and it was meant to speak about Jesus' exaltation and his subjugation of all his enemies. The strong influence of these psalms in the early church can be seen in a clear quotation of Ps 110:1 in Mk 12:36 and Mt 22:44 where the last line is contaminated under the influence of Ps 8:6. Only Lk 20:42-43, which explicitly states that David said it ἐν βίβλῳ ψαλμῶν, corrects the citation as does the Byzantine text and the Old Latin version of Mk. Since this combination is not only attested widely but also as early as the first letter to the Corinthians, we can safely conclude that such an interpretation of the psalms was widespread among early Christian pre-Pauline congregations.[80]

---

[77] F. F. Bruce, *The Epistle to the Hebrews* (NICNT; Grand Rapids: Eerdmans, 1990), 73; G. W. Buchanan, *To the Hebrews* (AB 36; Garden City: Doubleday, 1972), 38-51; P. Giles, "The Son of Man in the Epistle to the Hebrews" *ExpT* 86 (1974-1975), 328-32.

[78] Ellingworth, *Hebrews*, 151; for a thorough discussion of the reasons for taking the quotation of Ps 8 to refer to Christ, see Adams, *Epistle to the Hebrews*, 304-323.

[79] Ellingworth, *Hebrews*, 151, notes that "In 1 Cor. 15:25-27, Paul's main point is that πάντα ὑπέταξεν in Ps. 8:6b does not exclude Christ's own final submission to the Father. In Eph. 1:20-23, the πάντα is taken to be the Church as the body of Christ and the true πλήρωμα." Cf. Hengel, "Right Hand," 165.

[80] Hengel, "Right Hand," 172-75.

6.2.5. Jesus' Use of Psalm 110:1

We have seen that the use of Ps 110:1 for interpreting Jesus' resurrection as his exaltation to the right hand of God was widespread and early. How early can this belief go back in time? Is there any evidence that Jesus himself would have suggested such an understanding during his earthly ministry? In what follows, we attempt to answer these questions.

W. Bousset championed the view that it was the influence of the Hellenistic world that led the early Christians to regard Jesus as the Lord. He claimed that they began to see Jesus in the light of the pagan cults from which some of them had been converted. The person who had originally been revered simply as a teacher and prophet was increasingly assimilated to a deity worshipped in pagan cults and so began to be seen as spiritually present with his worshippers and as someone worthy of worship (1 Cor 8:5-6). Thus, the recognition of Jesus as Lord belongs to a second stage in the development of early christology.[81]

One of the long-recognized problems of Bousset's theory is that it cannot account satisfactorily for the early Christian cry *maranatha* recorded in 1 Cor 16:22. This cry has been preserved in Aramaic, and it was evidently used in a Greek-speaking church in that language. This evidence suggests that it is much more likely that Jesus was regarded as the coming Lord in a church that normally spoke Aramaic and where the decisive theological development took place in an Aramaic-speaking culture.[82]

In a similar vein, F. Hahn argued from the evidence of phrases like *maranatha* that the early Christians saw Jesus as Lord first of all in the context of his parousia. He pointed to various Synoptic texts which indicate the use of *kyrios* in relation to the last judgement (Mt 7:21, 22; 25:11, 37, 44). He also argued that Ps 110:1 was originally applied to Jesus' future coming (Mk 14:61-62). At first, the resurrection was seen merely as a withdrawal or translation to a state of inactivity (Mk 2:18-20; Acts 1:9-11; 3:20-21). Then, as the parousia was delayed, the early church began to recognize that he was not merely the Lord-designate, but already the Lord. This recognition, in Hahn's view, led the early church to apply the title of "Lord" to the risen Jesus, and then to the earthly life of Jesus.[83]

---

[81] W. Bousset, *Kyrios Christos: a History of the Belief in Christ From the Beginnings of Christianity to Irenaeus* (Nashville: Abingdon, 1970).

[82] I. H. Marshall, "Jesus as Lord: the Development of the Concept" in *Jesus the Saviour: Studies in New Testament Theology* (Downers Grove: Inter-Varsity, 1990), 202. For a critique of Bousset's view see I. H. Marshall, *The Origins of New Testament Christology* (Downers Grove: Inter-Varsity, 1976, 1990), 104-7.

[83] F. Hahn, *The Titles of Jesus in Christology* (London: Lutterworth, 1969), 89-103.

Hahn's view is also far from satisfactory, however. It does not explain how the title Lord came to be applied to *Jesus* as the coming Son of man and Lord in the first place, a question all the more pressing for those who deny that Jesus spoke of himself as the coming Son of man.[84] But if there is no good explanation of what prompted the early Christians to proceed from the future coming of Jesus to applying the title of "Lord" to him, it is much more plausible that they began by believing that Jesus was Lord and then prophesied that the Lord would come.[85]

A critical assessment of the theories put forward by Bousset and Hahn suggests that the root of Jesus' Lordship lies somewhere else. While Ps 110:1 was clearly applied by the NT writers to the post-resurrection exaltation of Jesus, the Synoptic Gospels unanimously report that Jesus used this text not only to challenge the traditional scribal understanding of the messiah as a mere human descendant of David (Mk 12:35-37 pars.), but also to answer the high priest's question during his trial before the Sanhedrin (Mk 14:62 pars.). The use of Ps 110:1 by Jesus himself could provide us with an avenue to explore the possible root of Jesus' Lordship. The significance of these accounts for our enquiry, however, will only become apparent, if we can refute the view of those who reject the authenticity of the Gospel passages.

6.2.5.1. Mk 12:35-37

In this passage Jesus asks how it is possible that the messiah can be called David's son when David himself speaks of the messiah as his lord in Ps 110:1. The use of this text by Jesus, however, has been much questioned by NT scholars.[86]

Several arguments have been proposed against the authenticity of this saying:[87] (1) The lack of speculation about the messiah based on Ps 110:1 in early Jewish literature and the frequent use of this text in the NT for such discussion suggest that it was a creation by the early church. (2) The

---

[84] We will argue later that Jesus' self-reference as the coming Son of man goes back to himself (see §6.2.5). In addition to this criticism, Hahn's view on Jesus' Lordship is part of a larger theory that cannot offer a satisfactory explanation at many points.

[85] Marshall, *Origins*, 101-4. For a criticism of Hahn's view see P. Vielhauer, "Erwägungen zur Christologie des Markusevangeliums" in *Aufsätze zum Neuen Testament* (Munich: Kaiser, 1965), 167-75, who noted that in the OT it is living people, not dead people, who are translated to heaven.

[86] See G. Schneider, "Die Davidssohnfrage (Mk. 12, 35-37)" *Bib* 53 (1972), 66-81, for the survey of modern exegesis.

[87] One of the most prominent proponents of this view is Hahn, *Titles of Jesus*, 103-5, 251-54, who detects a two-stage christology in which Jesus was regarded as "Son of David" during his earthly life and "David's lord" after his exaltation.

passage shows a pronounced christological interest, making use of Christian christological titles. (3) The wordplay involving the title "Lord" does not exist in the Hebrew but is only possible in the LXX. (4) There seems to be an attempt to replace the Son of David messianism with a Son of man or Son of God one. (5) Jesus takes the initiative in a discussion which is about Jewish messianic teaching.[88]

However, a careful assessment of the evidence renders these arguments doubtful. First, it is true that there was no known speculation about the messiah based on Ps 110:1 in early Judaism, but we have earlier suggested that there was a messianic interpretation of the psalm in pre-Christian Judaism (§6.1.2) and, even if we were wrong, there is no reason why this should prevent Jesus from introducing this text into the discussion, and this would then explain its later use in the early church.[89] The passage in question suggests that Jesus is introducing a novel point that seemingly conflicts with the traditional scribal understanding of the messiah as Son of David. Moreover, the fact that the use of Ps 110:1 here is somewhat different from its use elsewhere in the NT argues against the early church's creation.[90] Furthermore, evidence from a separate tradition (Mark 14:62 pars.), if authentic, increases the probability that it has a *Sitz im Leben Jesu*.[91]

Second, the passage lacks a clear Christian interest.[92] Jesus does not use this text to directly refer to himself; in fact, his allusive use of Ps 110:1 could even lead to the conclusion that he was referring to someone other than himself. It is also a mistake to assume that Jesus totally ignored the titles used in Jewish messianology.[93] The Davidic origin of the messiah was too well established for Jesus to dispute such a matter. No evidence of such a dispute is attested elsewhere in the Gospel tradition. Rather, the tradition about the Davidic descent of the messiah was so clearly attested in the OT and Judaism that it is inconceivable that Jesus or the early church could ever have denied it. The idea of a Davidic messiah begins from 2 Sam 7, which had undergone significant modifications by the time of the Chronicler in 1 Chr 17:11, 14 where a collective reference to "your

---

[88] R. W. Funk, *The Gospel of Mark: Red Letter Edition* (Sonoma: Polebridge, 1991), 187-88.

[89] B. Witherington, *The Christology of Jesus* (Minneapolis: Fortress, 1990), 190.

[90] Cf. B. M. F. van Iersel, *'Der Sohn' in den synoptischen Jesusworten* (Leiden: Brill, 1961) 171-73, esp. n.3.

[91] See our discussion of this passage later.

[92] E. Lohmeyer, *Das Evangelium des Markus* (Göttingen: Vandenhoeck & Ruprecht, 1951), 263; V. Taylor, *The Gospel According to St. Mark: the Greek Text* (London: Macmillan, 1952), 492-3.

[93] I. H. Marshall, *The Gospel of Luke: a Commentary on the Greek Text* (NIGTC; Grand Rapids: Eerdmans, 1978), 746-47.

offspring" became a specific reference to "one who shall be from among your sons."[94] Later it appears more often in the prophetic books (Isa 9:2-7; 11:1-9; Jer 23:5-6; 30:9; 33:15, 22; Ezek 34:23-24; 37:24; Hos 3:5; and Amos 9:11), although the precise terminology "son of David" is not attested before *Pss. Sol.* 17:23. It seems thereafter to have become a common expression in rabbinic texts.[95] It is also important to note the Qumran evidence in 4QFlor 1:11-13, where the promise to David is interpreted in the light of Amos 9:11,[96] and to various Midrashim on 2 Sam 7:1.[97] Moreover, the fact that the Synoptic writers show no embarrassment in combining this narrative with an affirmation of the Davidic descent of the messiah favours the view that from the beginning there was no denial of Davidic descent.[98] Therefore, in Mk 12:35-37 Jesus is showing the inadequacy, not the inaccuracy, of the traditional understanding of the messiah.[99] The point Jesus intends to drive home is that the messiah is more than a Son of David, not that he is other than a Son of David. Further, it is unlikely that the church would create a text that could lead to the conjecture, presently made by various scholars, that Jesus disputed the Davidic origins of the messiah.[100]

Third, since Jesus is citing Ps 110:1 from memory and not reading from the Hebrew scroll, it is possible that he quoted this text in the Aramaic that he was doubtless speaking at the time. J. A. Fitzmyer has shown that the wordplay would have been perfectly possible even in Aramaic, where the title *mare* could have stood behind both uses of κύριος: *amar marya le mari*,[101] However, the wordplay is not necessary for the saying to be authentic. The text obviously is to be interpreted as: "God says to 'my Lord' (i.e., David's descendant), Sit at my right hand." The question Jesus poses is "how the messiah can be called David's Lord when he is David's son" rather than "how the messiah can be called David's God." There is no likelihood of confusion between "God" and "my Lord" despite the same

---

[94] J. A. Fitzmyer, "Son of David and Mt. 22:41-46" in *Essays on the Semitic Background of the New Testament* (London: G. Chapman, 1971), 118-19.

[95] Cf. b. Sanh 98a; y. Ta'an. 4.8.68d; b. Sanh. 97a.

[96] Cf. C.D. 7.16; *b. Sanh.* 96b.

[97] D. Flusser, "Two Notes on the Midrash on 2 Sam. 7:1" *IEJ* 9 (1959), 99-109.

[98] J. Nolland, *Luke* (WBC 35; Dallas: Word Books, 1993), 971.

[99] Witherington, *Christology*, 190.

[100] Cf. C. A. Evans, "Recent Development in Jesus Research: Presuppositions, Criteria, and Sources" in *Jesus and His Contemporaries: Comparative Studies* (Leiden: Brill, 1995), 19.

[101] J. A. Fitzmyer, "The Contribution of Qumran Aramaic to the Study of the New Testament" *NTS* 20 (1973-1974), 389f. Fitzmyer, *Luke*, 1312. See D. L. Bock, *Luke* (BECNT; Grand Rapids: Baker Books, 1996), 1630-41, for a detailed treatment of Ps 110:1 and its suitability to this setting.

Greek (or Aramaic) word being used. Moreover, there is a clear distinction between the two uses of "lord" in Ps 110:1, especially in the Hebrew, and there is no danger of אֲדֹנִי being taken in a divine sense.

Fourth, evidence is lacking for any alleged attempt to reject the Son of David tradition in favour of a Son of man or a Son of God messianism. The former case requires reading Mk 14:62 into our text, whereas the latter case ignores the fact that the point at issue is not the messiah being God's Son but David's *kyrios*.[102]

Fifth, to argue that Jesus never takes the initiative in a discussion is a misuse of form criticism. We have evidence of Jesus taking the initiative (Mk 8:27, 34; 9:16, 33; 10:33; 12:43) and the allusive character of his teaching to make his point (cf. Luke 7:22ff.).[103] As Taylor says, "The allusive character of the saying favours the view that it is an original utterance; it half conceals, half reveals the 'Messianic Secret.'"[104]

Sixth, one of the strongest arguments in favour of its authenticity, however, comes from its allusive character and the christological ambiguities of the account, well reflected in the multiplicity of interpretations concerning its function and sense.[105] It is the very ambiguity and Jewishness of the way Jesus makes his point that speaks for the authenticity of Jesus' use of Ps 110:1. The playing down of the Davidic sonship of the messianic figure militates against the normal post-Easter emphasis (cf. Acts 2:30-36; 13:23-39; Rom 1:2-4; and Heb 1:3-14).

The above evidence therefore leads to the conclusion that "it is far more likely that Ps 110:1 goes back to a period when the issues surrounding Jesus' identity were surfacing than to roots in a community that was openly confessing him in the midst of dispute," and that "the roots of the well attested NT use of Ps 110:1 go back, in all likelihood, to Jesus himself."[106]

---

[102] Witherington, *Christology*, 190. Cf. Marshall, *Luke*, 746-47; Fitzmyer, *Luke*, 1312-13; Taylor, *Mark*, 491-93.

[103] Cf. A. M. Ramsey, "History and the Gospel" in *Studia evangelica* (ed. Cross F. L.; Berlin: Akademie-Verlag, 1968), 75-85, see p. 78, cited by I. H. Marshall, *I Believe in the Historical Jesus* (London: Hodder & Stoughton, 1977), 170-71; Witherington, *Christology*, 191.

[104] Taylor, *Mark*, 493.

[105] Taylor, *Mark*, 493: "the allusive character of the saying favours the view that it is an original utterance; it half conceals and half reveals the 'Messianic secret'. . . . It is difficult to think that the doctrinal beliefs of a community could be expressed in this allusive manner." So also Nolland, *Luke*, 971. See further Hay, *Glory*, 26, 110, 114, 158-59.

[106] D. L. Bock, Blasphemy and Exaltation in Judaism and the Final Examination of Jesus: a Philological-Historical Study of the Key Jewish Themes Impacting Mark 14:61-64 (WUNT 2/106; Tübingen: Mohr Siebeck, 1998), 222.

On the other hand, some scholars argued that the saying was meant to reject the traditional scribal understanding of the messiah as a human descendant of David. J. Klausner thought that Jesus was calling into question the Davidic origin of the messiah,[107] whereas C. Burger held that, since Jesus was thought not to be a descendant of David, the early Christians wanted to defend Jesus' messiahship by denying the messiah's Davidic lineage.[108] However, as we have seen, there is no evidence that Jesus' Davidic descent was in doubt or not known in the early church.[109]

Other scholars regarded the present saying as a qualification of the expectation of the Davidic messiah. O. Cullmann suggested that Jesus' intention was not to deny the Davidic descent itself, but the understanding of it in terms of political kingship.[110] However, the inadequacy of this view is shown by the fact that the very quotation of Ps 110:1 also speaks in politico-royal terms.[111]

Dismissing all the above explanations as "beside Jesus' point," R. Gundry insisted that the real point of Jesus' question was about the scribes' designation of the messiah as "Son of David."[112] In other words, the *source* of the designation "Son of David" is what precisely Jesus asks for: "So whence (καὶ πόθεν) [do the scribes get it that the Christ] is his son?" He contended that

In view of Jesus' noting the divine inspiration of David and citing of Ps 110:1, the question asks for an inspired scriptural source. There is none. So the scribes stand exposed: they pass for experts in Scripture, but their designation of the Christ does not even come from it. The placement of αὐτοῦ, "his," before ἐστιν υἱός, "is he son," does not emphasize whose son the Christ is not, but makes emphasis fall on the refusal of the OT to use the word "son" for the relationship of the Christ to David . . . and therefore on

---

[107] J. Klausner, *Jesus of Nazareth: His Life, Times, and Teaching* (New York: Macmillan, 1926), 320: "Jesus had already declared himself Messiah. But the Messiah was to be the *Son of David*, whereas Jesus was a Galilaean and the son of Joseph the carpenter! How could he be the Messiah? To evade this serious difficulty Jesus must find a passage of Scripture according to which the Messiah need not necessarily be the Son of David; and like an expert Pharisee he finds it."

[108] C. Burger, *Jesus als Davidssohn: eine traditionsgeschichtliche Untersuchung* (Göttingen: Vandenhoeck & Ruprecht, 1970), 52-59; cf. Schneider, "Davidssohnfrage," 83.

[109] *Contra* B. Lindars, *New Testament Apologetic: the Doctrinal Significance of the Old Testament Quotations* (London: SCM, 1961), 47, who thinks that the synoptic passage about David's son represents a slightly later stage, when the Davidic controversy has arisen.

[110] O. Cullmann, *The Christology of the New Testament* (London: SCM, 1963), 130-33.

[111] Marshall, *Luke*, 744-45.

[112] R. H. Gundry, *Mark: A Commentary on His Apology for the Cross* (Grand Rapids: Eerdmans, 1993), 718-9, 722-23.

the contrast between David's calling the Christ "my Lord" and the absence from the OT of "Son of David" for the Christ.[113]

According to this interpretation, πόθεν in the NT does not mean "from what standpoint?" or "in what way?" but rather "from where?" This interpretation, however, seems to depend heavily on a titular understanding of the phrase υἱὸς Δαυίδ (v.35). As Nolland rightly pointed out, "The limited early use of a titular 'Son of David,' along with the use of 'my lord' in the Psalm quotation, and 'his son' in Mark 12:37 tip the scales in the direction of reading 'son of David' primarily in terms of Davidic descent rather than a titular 'Son of David.'"[114]

Approaching from a different perspective, D. Daube proposed that the saying of Jesus is part of a fourfold scheme in rabbinic discussion in which an apparent contradiction between two verses is brought to light and the difficulty is resolved by showing that each verse is right in its own context.[115] Thus the question was intended to qualify the characterisation of the messiah as a son of David.[116]

From Mk 12:35-37 Marshall draws a number of important clues for Jesus' understanding of Ps 110:1 and the lordship of the messiah. First, Jesus here declares that the messiah carries the title of "Lord." Second, Jesus finds the evidence for this title in Ps 110:1. Third, Jesus holds that Ps 110:1 must be regarded as a prophecy about the messiah awaiting to be fulfilled.[117]

What then was the primary intention of Jesus in asking the question? In the first place, Jesus was challenging the scribal understanding of the messiah as simply a descendant of David. In so doing Jesus may also have expressed criticism against the Davidic expectation documented in *Ps. Sol.* 17 and elsewhere in which the messiah is portrayed as a political figure, casting off foreign rule.[118]

---

[113] Gundry, *Mark*, 718-9, 722-23. See J. Marcus, "Mark 14:61: 'Are You the Messiah-Son-of-God?'" *NovT* 31 (1989), 135-36, for the emphatic position of αὐτοῦ.

[114] Nolland, *Luke*, 971.

[115] D. Daube, "Four Types of Questions" *JTS* 2 (1951), 45-48; D. Daube, *The New Testament and Rabbinic Judaism* (London: University of London, 1956), 158-63.

[116] This view is rejected by Schneider, "Davidssohnfrage," 83-85, who contended that the question as haggadic in character arises only in Mark's context, and the two texts contrasted are not really in conflict if Ps 110:1 is not given a messianic interpretation. However, as Prof. Marshall rightly pointed out, the question can still be haggadic in character when taken on its own, and it is probable that the Jews understood Ps 110:1 messianically.

[117] Marshall, "Jesus as Lord," 205.

[118] Witherington, *Christology*, 191, pointed out that "Jesus did in fact contest the alien rule of Satan over human spirits, but did not directly confront Caesar."

However, the form of Jesus' teaching registered in the passage suggests that his intention was more than that; for Jesus, the messiah must be a person who embraces within himself the characteristics of being both an exalted figure and the Son of David. Indeed the pericope reflects precisely the sort of allusive, or indirect, manner that Jesus seems to have used in public to indicate how he viewed himself (cf. Mk 12:1-12).[119] His method was to make subtle allusions to himself in such a way as to entice his audience into careful and deep reflection on the person of himself. In Mk 12:35-37 Jesus appears to suggest that the messiah is David's Lord, and as such he stands above and exists prior to David. Jesus leaves open the possibility that he might be David's Lord, and thus supernatural in dignity and origin.[120] His teaching on the real identity of the Son of David thus provides us with a glimpse of how he viewed himself. This implication is enforced, as we will see below, with his pronouncement in Mk 14:62 where he uses this same text together with Dan 7:13 to suggest that he will be invested with divine authority.

The evidence thus suggests that the early Christian belief in Jesus as Lord – if not pre-existent Lord – ultimately goes back to something Jesus himself suggested during his earthly ministry in such a way that the question would probably arise for his audience, especially his disciples, as they pondered on what he had said. It is then not entirely out of question that Jesus could have alluded to himself not only as the long-awaited messiah but even as pre-existent Lord, although at that time they would not have picked it up.

6.2.5.2. Mk 14:62

During the trial before the Sanhedrin Jesus replies to the question of the high priest with a combined allusion to Ps 110:1 and Dan 7:13. However, the authenticity of his reply has often been seriously doubted due to its high christology and the allegedly post-Easter setting. The authenticity of this saying is in fact closely connected to the question whether the trial scene itself goes back to a *Sitz im Leben Jesu*. A number of reasons for questioning the authenticity of the trial scene have been adduced.

First, it is argued that the basic setting of the trial reflects Mark's own work, especially since the transition from the temple charge to the christological issue is too abrupt to be plausible.[121]

---

[119] For our discussion of Mk 12:1-12 see § 4.3.5.

[120] Cf. Taylor, *Mark*, 493; Marshall, *Luke*, 746-49.

[121] Cf. H. Anderson, *Mark*, 330-31, who suggests that the temple charge goes back to the trial scene, but the combination of temple and christology is not credible.

Second, it is disputed whether the circumlocutions used for God such as εὐλογητός and δύναμις reflect an authentic tradition. The authenticity of these circumlocutions is questioned for two reasons: (i) the term εὐλογητός "as a circumlocution for the name of God is almost completely unattested," and (ii) the title "'Son of God' is rarely used as a messianic designation in extant Jewish literature."[122]

Third, Jesus' use of Ps 110:1 and Dan 7:13 requires a post-Easter scenario. Not only that; N. Perrin claimed that the conflation of Ps 110:1 and Dan 7:13 (read with Zech 12:10) is the result of the merging of two Christian *pesher* traditions which employed Jewish "messianic" interpretations of Dan 7:13. Mk 14:62 is thus a result of the "historicization" of these traditions, i.e., placing later formulations on the lips of Jesus.[123]

Fourth, the question whether Jesus referred himself as the apocalyptic Son of Man has been the focus of intense debate among scholars, with no signs of abating.

Fifth, it has been claimed that the stacking up of christological titles in Mark 14:61-62 is an argument against authenticity.

Recently D. L. Bock considered each of these objections to see whether the saying is likely to go back to Jesus or to the early church.[124]

First, W. Reinbold has recently made an attempt to demonstrate that the basic setting of the trial comes from Mark. He rejects the entire work by O. Betz and A. Strobel by questioning Betz's view that a morning trial took place in its traditional temple locale and by arguing against Strobel that the charge of deception does not apply to Jesus nor is it raised in the NT tradition.[125] However, the criticism by Reinbold is to be rejected as inadequate for the following reasons:[126] (i) there are several NT texts indicating that Jesus was seen as a deceiver by explicitly using terms like

---

[122] D. H. Juel, *Messiah and Temple: the Trial of Jesus in the Gospel of Mark* (SBLDS 31; Missoula: Scholars Press, 1977), 78-79, thinks that "the best explanation of the phrase in Mark is that it is a pseudo-Jewish expression created by the author as appropriate in the mouth of the high priest." Cf. Anderson, *Mark*, 331.

[123] N. Perrin, "Mark XIV. 62: The End Product of a Christian Pesher Tradition?" *NTS* 13 (1965-1966), 150-55. See also N. Perrin, *Rediscovering the Teaching of Jesus* (New Testament Library; London: SCM, 1967), 172-85.

[124] Here we will follow closely the discussion by Bock, *Blasphemy*, 209-33.

[125] W. Reinbold, *Der älteste Bericht über den Tod Jesu: literarische Analyse und historische Kritik der Passionsdarstellungen der Evangelien* (BZNW 69; Berlin: Walter de Gruyter, 1994), 256ff. Cf. O. Betz, "Probleme des Prozesses Jesu" in *Aufstieg und Niedergang der römischen Welt* (eds. H. Temporini *et al.*; Berlin: Gruyter, 1982), 565-647; and A. Strobel, *Die Stunde der Wahrheit: Untersuchungen zum Strafverfahren gegen Jesus* (WUNT 21; Tübingen: Mohr Siebeck, 1980), 46-61, who regarded Deut 13:1-13 as a key text for a deceiver charge and idolatry.

[126] Bock, *Blasphemy*, 211-13.

πλάνος and πλανᾷ (Mt 27:63-64; Jn 7:12, 47); (ii) there is consistent testimony from Christian and Jewish sources that Jesus was put to death, in part, for deceiving Israel (cf. *b. Sanh.* 43a; *m. Sanh.* 7.4; 4Q375; 4Q376; *Dial. Trypho* 69.7; 108.2; *Contra Celsus* 1.68; 1.71; *Demonstratio Evangelica* 3, 3, 1-4; 3, 6, 1); (iii) it ignores the important observation made by Bock that "In Judaism, idolatry and blasphemy were comparable and sometimes were seen as interrelated offenses, but they did not have to be such";[127] (iv) it fails to deal adequately with Betz who showed how the temple threat could have been interpreted as putting the nation at risk before Rome in a way that demanded response; and finally (v) Reinbold does not give a careful assessment of the overall arguments from an historical background but merely criticizes some specific points of minor importance made by some scholars.

Second, after surveying the key linguistic data for both εὐλογητός and δύναμις in Jewish literature (for the expression "the blessed One" and for the reference to power) Bock draws two conclusions. Concerning the expression εὐλογητός he concludes that "Even the fragmentary nature of our sources shows a series of examples that are quite similar to what we have in Mark" (*m. Ber.* 7.3; *1 Enoch* 77:2).[128] Concerning the expression "the Power" (*1 Enoch* 62:7; *SifNum* 112; *b. 'Erub.* 54b; *b. Yebam.* 105b; *Tg. Job* 5:8; *b. Šabb.* 88b; *b. Meg.* 31b *et al.*) he concludes that

> to invoke 'the Power' is to speak of the God of the nation who speaks with authority, The expression is so widely attested in the early midrashim that it has a good claim to early roots. The consistency of the usage shows that the expression is full of subtlety and significance. Jesus claims he will sit next to the Almighty, serving beside the true God with full authority as his unique representative. . . . This kind of involved Jewish expression is unlikely to have its origin in the early church, particularly in a gospel that is written with Gentile concerns in mind.[129]

Moreover, Bock summarises arguments for the probability that Mark did not create these circumlocutions: (i) Mark has no hesitation in using "Son of God" (cf. 1:1; 3:11; 5:7; 15:39), so it would be unusual for him to use an expression that has no direct reference to God;[130] (ii) the very

---

[127] Bock, *Blasphemy*, 212; see also chapter 2 for the distinction between acts of blasphemy, which can be idolatrous acts and/or acts of arrogance, and the category of blasphemous utterances.

[128] Bock, *Blasphemy*, 217.

[129] Bock, *Blasphemy*, 218-19.

[130] Cf. C. R. Kazmierski, *Jesus the Son of God: a Study of the Markan Tradition and its Redaction by the Evangelist* (Würzburg: Echter, 1979), 171, who notes that to attribute the circumlocution to Mark "would be strange in light of his redactional interest in the Hellenistic form of the confession of Sonship." He argues instead that Mark got it from Jewish Christian tradition.

dissimilarity of the expression from Christian titles speaks for "Son of the blessed One" as a non-Christian use; (iii) the expression "Power" is not a substitute for God elsewhere in the NT, despite the numerous uses of Ps 110:1 in these texts (Acts 2:34-35; Rom 8:34; Eph 1:20; Col 3:1; Heb 1:3; 13; 8:1; 10:12; 12:2). He therefore comes to the conclusion that

> The respect shown to God by the high priest in asking his key question in this sensitive trial setting and the reciprocal response by Jesus are very appropriate for this setting. It is a subtle touch that by its unique character points to authenticity at the root of the trial tradition.[131]

Third, we have already discussed authenticity issues connected to Jesus' use of Ps 110:1 when we discussed Mk 12:35-37.[132] There we concluded that the roots of the well attested NT use of Ps 110:1 are most likely to go back to Jesus himself. We also suggested that it may imply that Jesus wished his audience to consider the possibility that he might be David's Lord, and thus supernatural in dignity and origin. But what about the use of Dan 7:13-14? While there has been in the past an intense debate as to whether it is possible to speak of a Son of man figure in Judaism, more recently there is an increasing recognition that there existed in Judaism speculations about an exalted figure whose roots lie in Dan 7.[133] Scholars cite evidence from Jewish sources such as 11QMel 2.18; *EzeTra*; 1En 46:2-4; 48:2; 62:5, 7, 9, 14; 63:11; 69:27, 29; 70:1; 71:14, 17; 4Ezra 13; *b. Hag.* 14a; *b. Sanh.* 38b; 4Q491. Evidence from a variety of sources thus suggests that nothing requires a post-Easter scenario.[134]

On the other hand, Perrin's suggestion about the *pesher* traditions remains speculative. His use of late midrashic collections as evidence for pre-Christian Jewish messianic readings is unacceptable, although his use of Enoch traditions is on firmer ground. His view on the "historicization" of the *pesher* rules out the possibility that these traditions began in the teachings of Jesus – an unnecessarily sceptical exclusion. At the same time, Perrin is right to bring out the close connections between established Jewish traditions, Christian exegetical activity in combining testimonia,

---

[131] Bock, *Blasphemy*, 220.

[132] See above our discussion on the use of Ps 110:1 in Mk 12:35-37 and its implications. See Bock, *Luke*, 1630-41, for a detailed treatment of Ps 110:1 and its suitability to this setting.

[133] J. J. Collins, "The Son of Man in First-Century Judaism" *NTS* 38 (1992), 448-66; W. Horbury, "The Messianic Associations of 'the Son of Man'" *JTS* 36 (1985), 34-55.

[134] Bock, *Blasphemy*, 223-24: "Dan 7 imagery was a part of first century Jewish eschatological and apocalyptic speculation, apart from the question of the presence of a defined Son of Man figure. This means that Dan 7 was a text that was present in the theologically reflective thinking of Judaism and was quite available to Jesus once he started thinking in eschatological-vindication terms."

and the influence of this activity on christology. As Albl rightly concludes, in Mk 14:62 we have

a compositional use of Ps 110:1 and Dan 7:13. The conflation of texts is hardly due to an *ad hoc* inspiration of the evangelists; rather it points to an earlier stage of exegetical activity in which the image of Jesus' exaltation (Ps 110:1) is combined with the image of the eschatological Son of Man from Daniel. Psalm 110:1 can be used as an implicit *testimonium*, showing that the "Son of Man" will be exalted, because its meaning has been established by this earlier exegetical activity.[135]

Fourth, the evidence from the Gospels raises two important questions that renders the view of the title "Son of man" as a creation by the early church doubtful:[136] (i) the title is massively placed on Jesus' lips unlike any other major christological title like "Lord," "Son of God," and "Messiah"; and (ii) if the title was created by the early church as the self-designation of Jesus, why has it left almost no trace of it in NT writings other than the Gospels, also unlike the other titles?[137] Moreover, the fact that the Jewish leaders are threatened that they will *see* Jesus as the coming Judge renders the early church creation theory most unlikely.[138] Around AD 70 that was no longer possible. The evidence leads us to conclude that "Dan 7 not only would have been available for Jesus' use, but that the evidence suggests that this text was a significant feature of his thinking by the end of his ministry, as most of the explicit references to Dan 7 appear as Jesus drew near to Jerusalem."[139]

Fifth, Bock counters on both formal and conceptual grounds the objection that the piling up of christological titles is an argument against

---

[135] Albl, *Scripture*, 230.

[136] *Contra* M. Casey, *Son of Man: the Interpretation and Influence of Daniel 7* (London: SPCK, 1979), who contended that the Aramaic phrase for Son of man could not be a title. We can counter Casey by saying that Jesus is simply citing Dan 7:13, where the text refers to "a figure like a man" here called simply "the Son of man," and it was possible for him to do so, regardless of the existence of the Aramaic idiom that meant "a human being like me" or something of the kind. The existence of the idiom does not exclude the possibility of other usages. The Targum of Ps 8, for example, demonstrates that it was possible to translate a non-idiomatic occurrence of the Son of man. While Ps. 8 LXX has υἱὸς ἀνθρώπου ('son of man') and ἄνθρωπος, the Targum translates in both cases with *bar nāšā*.

[137] These two penetrating questions were raised by R. E. Brown, *The Death of the Messiah: From Gethsemane to the Grave: a Commentary on the Passion Narratives in the Four Gospels* (London: G. Chapman, 1994), 507.

[138] Hengel, "Right Hand," 187.

[139] Bock, *Blasphemy*, 227. Bock also deals with the formal question whether Jesus would have combined OT texts in a way like that found in Mk 14:62 and points to Mk 7:6-10/Mt 15:4-9 (Isa 29:13; Exod 20:12 [Deut 5:16]; Exod 21:17 [Lev 20:9]) and Mt 22:33-39 (Deut 6:4-5; Lev 19:18) as evidence.

authenticity. On formal ground he points out that "it is not unusual in Judaism for titles to be piled on one another when one is emphasizing a point," especially when something solemn is being said.[140] If this is correct, nothing is formally unusual for the high priest's questioning Jesus with a combined set of titles or descriptions which is in accord with the seriousness of the moment.

Nor is there any difficulty on conceptual grounds. Read in this light, it appears that the high priest is asking Jesus to confirm his messianic status. Scholars in the past expressed doubt on this point because they pointed out that the messianic claim itself was not a capital crime in Judaism, that is, it was not blasphemy. According to Bock, however, this criticism makes an incorrect assumption about the relationship between the question asked and the reply Jesus formulated.[141] In other words, "what the examination was seeking and what resulted from the examination were exactly the same thing."[142] However, the way Ps 110:1 and Dan 7:13 are woven together strongly suggests that the trial which began as an examination about a messianic claim ended up as more than that. The juxtaposition of these two texts by Jesus was so provocative for the Jewish leadership that he deserved to be charged with "the highest of religious offenses possible, namely, blasphemy." Bock explains two reasons behind that charge:

First, the reply speaks for an exalted Jesus who sees himself as too close to God in the leadership's view. Second, he makes claims as a judge who one day will render a verdict and/or experience a vindication against the very leadership that sees itself as appointed by God.[143]

Our discussion of Mk 14:62 leads us to conclude that it is highly probable that during the trial before the Sanhedrin (i) Jesus uttered the saying combining both Ps 110:1 and Dan 7:13; and (ii) his reply caused a severe threat to the Jewish leaders that eventually led to his charge of blasphemy.

6.2.5.3. Conclusion

We have provided reasons for rejecting the arguments of many scholars who, in a variety of ways, reject the authenticity of Mk 12:35-37 and 14:62. Evidence from Jesus' own use of Ps 110:1 in two Markan passages

---

[140] Bock, *Blasphemy*, 230, cites evidence from *1 Enoch* 77:2 ("Most High" and "eternally Blessed"); *1 Enoch* 48:2 ("the Lord of Spirits, the Before-time"); *Ps. Sol.* 17:21 ("their king, the son of David"); and Isa 9:6.

[141] As the study of Bock, *Blasphemy*, showed, the observation that the messianic claim is not inherently blasphemous is correct.

[142] Bock, *Blasphemy*, 231.

[143] Bock, *Blasphemy*, 231.

allows us to conclude that (1) Jesus did not only suggest that the messiah is David's Lord, but that he also spoke of the exaltation of the Son of Man to the right hand of God; and (2) the early church interpreted his exaltation as having taken place at the resurrection and continued to use Ps 110:1 that he had cited as expressing this belief.[144]

6.2.6. Psalm 110:1 as Confirmation of Jesus' Lordship

The remaining question is whether Jesus was seen as being already Lord before he was risen from the dead, or Lordship was conferred upon him only at that point. More specifically, was Ps 110:1 understood to refer to Jesus becoming Lord at his resurrection, or was it seen as a reference to his Lordship being confirmed by the resurrection? A casual reading of Acts 2 appears to support the first view because Jesus is said to be *made* Lord and Christ (v.36).[145] Similarly, Phil 2:9-11 could also suggest that the name of "Lord" was conferred on Jesus at his exaltation.[146] A more careful exegesis of the texts, however, gives support to the view that early Christians saw Jesus' resurrection as essentially the confirming of a status rather than the conferral of a new status.

When Peter concludes his sermon with the statement "God has made this Jesus, whom you crucified, both Lord and Christ" (Acts 2:36), does he mean that this act of appointment by God took place after the crucifixion? The immediately preceding mention of the resurrection (vv.34-35) may well lead us into thinking in that direction. If so, Peter is pointing to the guilt of the Jews who crucified the One whom God had already made Lord and Christ after the crucifixion. However "if, as is more probable, the resurrection be regarded here as the point at which this act of exaltation took place (see Phil. 2.9-11), there is no suggestion that this in any way

---

[144] As additional evidence supporting our view that Jesus' own use of Ps 110 lies at the root of the early Christian belief in his Lordship we can point out his own teaching about the Sabbath in Mk 2:28 and a number of parables in which he makes reference to an absent master who may come back unexpectedly and find his servants either doing their duty faithfully or taking advantage of his absence (cf. Lk 12:35-48; Mt 25:14-30; Mk 13:35; Mt 24:42). Cf. Witherington, "Lord," *DJG* 485. Also Marshall, "Jesus as Lord," 203.

[145] Cf. Dunn, *Christology*, 181, who thinks that the early Christians generally understood that Jesus received the title "Lord" on his exaltation, by virtue of his resurrection (Acts 2.36; Phil. 2.9-11; cf. Rom. 10.9f.; 1 Cor. 16.22). However, we will question his view that seems to equate Jesus' receiving the title "Lord" with his becoming Lord.

[146] But alongside these we must put verses like 1 Cor 9:5 and 11:23, which see Jesus as lord in his earthly life.

denied his previous status."[147] Neither does the immediate context suggest that Jesus became Lord at his resurrection. Peter's concluding statement derives from what he has just been arguing for. He has been trying to prove Jesus' Lordship (vv.34-35) and his Messiahship (vv.25-32).[148] As Marshall correctly pointed out, "it was because he was the Messiah (*cf.* 2:22; 10:38ff.) that Jesus was raised from the dead, and it was one who was already called Lord who was summoned to sit at God's right hand."[149] Therefore, Peter's final "punch" was not concerned with the appointment of Jesus as Lord and Messiah, but to point out the terrible atrocity committed by the Jews to one who was already their Lord and Messiah. The titles "Lord" and "Christ" are concerned with function and status.[150] The resurrection confirms and manifests an existing position.

A similar line of thought is found in Phil 2:9-11. Along with the statement that "God highly exalted Christ," we find the parallel assertion that God "gave him the name that is above every name." Although there has been considerable debate as to the precise name given to the exalted One, it is now widely accepted that it refers to the name of "Lord."[151] What this second clause does is not to describe a further or separate stage in the exaltation, but, as the parallel statement to the first, it amplifies its meaning and indicates its nature.[152] It needs to be understood in the context of the hymn as a whole, where exaltation and pre-existence are not exclusive concepts.[153]

---

[147] I. H. Marshall, "The Divine Sonship of Jesus" in *Jesus the Saviour: Studies in New Testament Theology* (Downers Grove: Inter-Varsity, 1990), 145.

[148] I. H. Marshall, *The Acts of the Apostles: an Introduction and Commentary* (TNTC; Grand Rapids: Eerdmans, 1980), 76-80; similarly, G. Schneider, *Die Apostelgeschichte* (HTKNT 5; Freiburg: Herder, 1980), 1.276-77, although he regards it as the work of Luke; R. Pesch, *Die Apostelgeschichte* (EKKNT 5; Zürich: Benziger Verlag, 1986), 1.126-28, seems to be in agreement with our view that the resurrection coupled with Scripture led to christology.

[149] Marshall, *Acts*, 80.

[150] Marshall, "Divine Sonship," 145.

[151] So the majority of scholars, except C. F. D. Moule, "Further Reflexions on Philippians 2.5-11" in *Apostolic History and the Gospel: Biblical and Historical Essays Presented to F. F. Bruce on His 60th Birthday* (eds. W. W. Gasque *et al.*; Exeter: Paternoster, 1970), 270, who contends that it is the name "Jesus."

[152] P. T. O'Brien, *The Epistle to the Philippians: a Commentary on the Greek Text* (NIGTC; Grand Rapids: Eerdmans, 1991), 237. Hence, the two aorists ὑπερύψωσεν and ἐχαρίσατο are coincident.

[153] We are aware of those scholars who deny the idea of pre-existence in this hymn. Cf. Dunn, *Christology*, 114-21. See a critique of Dunn's view in I. H. Marshall, "Incarnational Christology in the New Testament" in *Jesus the Saviour: Studies in New Testament Theology* (Downers Grove: Inter-Varsity, 1990), 169-70. Also N. T. Wright, Review of Dunn's *Christology in the Making*, *Churchman* 95 (1981), 170-72; I. H. Marshall, Review of Dunn's *Christology in the Making*, *TJ* 2 (1981), 241-45.

6.3. Conclusion

Our discussion of the use of Ps 110:1 in the NT has made clear that this messianic text was uniformly applied to Jesus' resurrection as his exaltation to the right hand of God. We have noted that a cursory reading of the evidence may suggest that Ps 110:1 was first applied to Jesus' resurrection and interpreted by the early church as his becoming Lord at that time by being exalted to the right hand of God.

Our examination of evidence, however, has shown the inadequacy of this line of reasoning. As we have already said, the emergence of the Christian faith is unthinkable without Jesus' resurrection being interpreted as his exaltation to the right hand of God and we have shown that this belief was part of the earliest confessions of the early church. In this respect, an early connection of Ps 8:6 to Ps 110:1 strongly suggests that Christ's cosmic Lordship was recognized at an early stage. Moreover, we have argued that Ps 110:1 was understood by the early church not only as a prophecy about his exaltation to the right hand of God, but also as a statement of God speaking to one who was already Lord in his sight. In this way, the early Christians interpreted Jesus' resurrection as essentially confirming his existing status rather than conferring a new status.

We have also argued that the early Christian understanding of Jesus as Lord is ultimately rooted in his allusive reference to Ps 110:1 as a prophecy about the messiah awaiting to be fulfilled (Mk 12:35-37) and his understanding of this divine oracle as a prophecy about his own exaltation to the right hand of God (Mk 14:62). Moreover, the evidence from Mk 12:35-37 has suggested that by way of subtle allusions to himself the text leaves open the possibility that he might be David's Lord who stands and exists before David himself and thus provides us with a glimpse of his self-understanding which seems compatible with his pre-existence, an implication supported by his statement before the Sanhedrin later in Mk 14:62.

We arrive therefore at the conclusion that one of the most significant christological implications from the early Christian messianic exegesis of Ps 110:1 was that they came to interpret Jesus' resurrection as his exaltation to God's right hand, through which his status as the pre-existent Lord saw its confirmation.

Since the early Christian exegesis of Ps 110 was highly unlikely to have been done in isolation from that of Ps 2, further christological implications of the interpretation of both psalms in the early church will be drawn at the end of the next chapter. Now it is time to turn to an examination of how the early church interpreted Ps 2:7 in their attempt to get a fuller understanding of who Jesus really was.

Chapter 7

Early Christian Exegesis of Psalm 2:7

Psalm 2:7, understood as a messianic text in the NT, was highly significant for early Christian understanding of the person of Jesus. Perhaps, together with Psalm 110:1, this messianic text was among the most important messianic texts that helped early Christians to deepen their understanding of Jesus. The present chapter will examine how Ps 2:7 was understood and used within the development of early christology.

It is a common view among NT scholars that the earliest application of Ps 2:7 to Jesus was in reference to his resurrection and from that time onward he was regarded as God's son. This view therefore insists that Jesus *became* Son by being raised from the dead. Moreover, scholars who hold such a view are also sceptical about the authenticity of the theophany at Jesus' baptism, particularly the divine voice coming from heaven (Mk 1:11). It is often argued that the baptismal accounts recorded in the Gospels are to be understood as theological constructions of the evangelists about the person of Jesus rather than as historically reliable records of early Christian traditions about Jesus' baptism. However, we will challenge this commonly-held view by discussing the place and significance of Ps 2:7 in the development of early christology.

During the course of our discussion we will be asking a number of questions which will serve as guide to our own understanding of the early Christian use and interpretation of Ps 2:7. Did the early church already think of Jesus as God's son when they applied Ps 2:7 to him? If not, what prompted them to think of Jesus as God's son? Was Ps 2:7 seen as scriptural proof that Jesus became God's son at his resurrection, or was it seen as a prophecy about his divine sonship (i.e., God speaking to one who was already his Son) fulfilled at the resurrection? Was Jesus' divine sonship conferred upon him only at the resurrection or was he already God's son during and before his earth life? How significant and relevant was the theophany experienced by Jesus at his baptism for the early Christian use of Ps 2:7? If this baptismal narrative is authentic, could it have initiated the process? How significant was it for the early Christian understanding of Jesus as the pre-existent Son of God? We hope that by answering these questions we will be able to present our arguments as follows.

First, we will argue that Ps 2:7 was first seen as a prophecy about Jesus' divine sonship decisively fulfilled at the resurrection and quickly became part of the early church confessions from an early date (cf. Rom 1:3-4). It is highly likely that the early church saw Jesus' resurrection as essentially the confirming of his status as God's son rather than the conferral of a new status.

Second, we will also argue that the theophany experienced by Jesus at his baptism would have initiated the process of interpreting Ps 2:7 as a prophecy about his divine sonship, in which God speaks to one who was already his Son. The baptismal narrative that speaks about Jesus' personal experience of the divine declaration from heaven echoing the words of Ps 2:7 is to be understood as a confirmation of his self-consciousness of divine sonship and its significance for the early Christian understanding of him as God's Son should not be undermined.

Finally, the discussion will lead to the conclusion that one of the most significant christological implications from the early Christian messianic exegesis of Ps 2:7 was that Jesus was already God's Son during and before his earthly life.

7.1. Pre-Christian Interpretation of Psalm 2

7.1.1. Original Setting and Subsequent Function of the Psalm

Psalm 2 is generally known as a royal psalm. Although OT scholarship has proposed a variety of hypotheses about the original setting of the psalm, the majority of scholars think that the psalm was composed for the occasion of the enthronement of a Davidic king.[1]

The recognition that Psalm 2 may have been preserved to be used repeatedly for some aspect of ancient Israel's life has produced a number of proposals for the subsequent function of the psalm.

1) *Coronation Ceremony*: it has been proposed that Ps 2 originated in the cultic setting and in particular that it functioned as part of a cult drama connected with the coronation ceremony and enthronement of a newly installed king.[2] The literary form and liturgical dimensions of the psalm seem to be in accord with the features of a coronation ceremony: anointing

---

[1] P. C. Craigie, *Psalms 1-50* (WBC 19; Waco: Word Books, 1983), 64; J. W. McKay and J. Rogerson, *Psalms* (CBC; Cambridge: CUP, 1977), 1.19-20. Proposals about the original composition of the psalm range from the pre-exilic to Maccabean periods.

[2] This view, following the seminal work of H. Gunkel, *Die Psalmen* (Göttingen: Vanderhoeck & Ruprecht, 1968), 5; and S. Mowinckel, *The Psalms in Israel's Worship* (Oxford: Blackwell, 1982), 61-65, has many followers.

(v.2); installation (v.6); legitimation (v.7) and empowering (v.9).[3] The psalm was thus sung in Jerusalem on the occasion of the king's enthronement festival when God installed the king upon Zion (Ps 2:6).

2) *Annual Enthronement Ritual*: having observed the investiture imagery of enthronement, it has been suggested that the psalm was used each year, not only on the occasion of the coronation of a new king, but on the occasion of an annual enthronement ritual, something comparable to ancient Near Eastern practices.[4]

3) *New Year or Autumnal Festival*: as a variant of the previous view, it has been suggested that the psalm belongs to the final stage of a dramatic cultic ritual at a New Year or an Autumnal Festival.[5] According to this view, the enemies in the psalm are not an actual and imminent threat, but a personification of all enemies to thwart Yahweh's plans or chaos powers or shadow figures which belong to the cult drama.

4) *Military Ritual*: still others contend that the psalm was used repeatedly as a cult ritual before battle. This view stresses the sense of urgency reflected in the psalm and regards it as a response to a current and actual threat.[6]

5) *Eschatological Function*: the psalm has also been viewed solely as an eschatological composition which announces the coming of Messiah and his kingship over the world.[7] This view often places the psalm in a post-exilic setting, but the composition is understood to have been fully eschatological from the beginning. The proponents of this view rely on a number of considerations: (1) the universal perspective of the psalm (since worldwide domination was never a reality for an earthly king of Israel or Judah); (2) Ps 2:7 is understood literally as a physical begetting and birth;

---

[3] Craigie, *Psalms*, 62-69.

[4] H.-J. Kraus, *Psalms 1-59: a Commentary* (Minneapolis: Augsburg, 1988), 126, compared the enthronement imagery of the psalm with the "Sed" festival celebrated in Egypt or to a "royal Zion festival." Similarly, H. Schmidt, *Die Psalmen* (HAT 1/15; Tübingen: Mohr Siebeck, 1934), 5-6, suggested that the psalm was recited each year at the anniversary of the enthronement of the reigning king.

[5] A. R. Johnson, *Sacral Kingship in Ancient Israel* (Cardiff: University of Wales Press, 1955), 128-29. Similarly, J. H. Eaton, *Kingship and the Psalms* (Sheffield: JSOT Press, 1986), 111-13.

[6] A. Bentzen, *King and Messiah* (London: Lutterworth, 1955), 16-17; J. Willis, "A Cry of Defiance: Psalm 2" *JSOT* 47 (1990), 33-50, regards the language of the psalm as a cry of defiance prior to either a single combat of individuals or an actual battle involving the army of ancient Israel.

[7] See C. A. Briggs, *A Critical and Exegetical Commentary on the Book of Psalms* (ICC; Edinburgh: T & T Clark, 1906), 12-14; P. P. Saydon, "The Divine Sonship of Christ in Psalm II" *Script* 3 (1948), 32-35; A. Deissler, "Zum Problem der Messianität von Psalm 2" in *De la Tôrah au Messie* (eds. J. Doré *et al.*; Paris: Brouwer, 1981), 287-91.

(3) there is no known historical setting for the scene portrayed in the psalm; and (4) the psalm is applied to the messiah in the NT.

How the psalm may have been used in ancient Israel, however, depends very much on how we interpret the statement of sonship in v.7, "You are my son, today have I begotten you." The relationship of God and the king of ancient Israel is described in Ps 2 in terms of sonship. As the Lord's "anointed," the relationship between the king and Yahweh was intimate.

The view that the psalm was composed with an exclusively eschatological or messianic outlook from the beginning, therefore, loses its justification. Although the psalm was clearly used as referring to the messiah by the NT writers, it does not necessarily warrant such a conclusion. The perspective of the psalm does not relate to events in the distant future but to an impending political crisis. Those who interpret Ps 2 as a messianic psalm from the beginning fail to appreciate the diverse ways the OT texts were used by the NT writers.[8]

It has been suggested that the statement about divine sonship (Ps 2:7) refers to a literal divine birth either in the same way that other surrounding nations regarded their kings as divine or in the sense of the begetting of an eschatological messiah. Ancient Jews, however, would not have accepted the notion of the physical divine sonship of the king.[9] Rather, it is highly more likely that the king was seen as God's "son" through adoption at his accession to the throne rather than through an actual physical birth.[10] As the heir of God and a universal ruler the king is considered the "son" of Yahweh, the creator and ruler of the whole universe.[11]

7.1.2. Later Jewish Interpretation of the Psalm

Although our knowledge about the original composition and its functions of Psalm 2 in ancient Israel is very limited, how Second Temple Jews interpreted the psalm can be known from LXX and Targumic translations of the psalm, its place in the canonical Psalter, and various references to it in the OT Pseudepigrapha, Qumran documents and rabbinic literature.[12]

---

[8] Willis, "A Cry of Defiance," 34-36.

[9] Such a view would not be supported by the theology of kingship in the Old Testament.

[10] Cf. A. Weiser, *The Psalms: a Commentary* (Göttingen: Vandenhoeck & Ruprecht, 1962), 113; Kraus, *Psalms 1-59*, 130-31.

[11] Cf. Pss 24:1-2; 47:2, 7, 8; 89:11; Isa 6:3.

[12] For a survey of the messianic use of Ps in early Judaism see E. Lövestam, *Son and Saviour: A Study of Acts 13, 32-37* (Lund: Gleerup, 1961), 15-23.

7.1.2.1. LXX and Targumic Translations

The LXX version of Psalm 2 can be regarded as one of the earliest extant Jewish interpretations of the psalm. While the LXX translation still maintains most of the formal elements of the MT, there are some significant differences. One of the most remarkable differences between the two is that, while in the LXX the king alone is the speaker throughout the psalm, in the MT the speech alternates between Yahweh and the king.[13]

Is there any evidence of messianic interpretation in the LXX version of the psalm? By pointing to a number of textual similarities between *Pss. Sol.* and the LXX Psalm 2, J. Schaper has recently argued that by the time of the psalm's translation into Greek "a pre-exilic royal psalm had, through a long-going process of reinterpretation, become a messianic hymn."[14] He also suggests that the authors or translators of *Pss. Sol.* 17 and 18 used imagery which they borrowed from Ps 2 for the purpose of writing messianic psalms. This proposal seems to be well-founded and adds support to the messianic interpretation of the psalm in pre-Christian Judaism.

We have criticized the proposal by Horbury and Schaper that the LXX translator(s) of Ps 110:3 referred to a pre-existent messianic figure, but our objection did not rule out that the referent could be a messianic/eschatological figure (§3.2.6). On the contrary, it is quite plausible that Ps 110:3 would have been read in the light of Ps 2:7 or vice versa as referring to the "birth" of one single figure as a close verbal correspondence between the two verses suggest:

μετὰ σοῦ ἡ ἀρχὴ ἐν ἡμέρᾳ τῆς δυνάμεώς σου ἐν ταῖς λαμπρότησιν τῶν ἁγίων ἐκ γαστρὸς πρὸ ἑωσφόρου ἐξεγέννησά σε (Ps 110:3)

διαγγέλλων τὸ πρόσταγμα κυρίου κύριος εἶπεν πρός με υἱός μου εἶ σύ ἐγὼ σήμερον γεγέννηκά σε (Ps 2:7)

The Targum, on the other hand, renders Ps 2:7 in a peculiar way: "You are as dear to Me as a son is to a father; you are as meritorious as though I had created you this day."[15] Such a Targumic rendering of the psalm could well

---

[13] In the LXX the king speaks in 2:6-7 and remains as the uninterrupted speaker as he addresses the enemies. Moreover, there is no allusion in the LXX to "son" in v.12.

[14] J. Schaper, *Eschatology in the Greek Psalter* (WUNT 2/76; Tübingen: Mohr Siebeck, 1995), 72-76.

[15] *Tg.* Ps 2:7 is probably not messianic. See S. H. Levey, *The Messiah: an Aramaic Interpretation: the Messianic Exegesis of the Targum* (Cincinnati: Hebrew Union College-Jewish Institute of Religion, 1974), 105.

be taken as showing a caution concerning the nature of "sonship" and a reluctance to identify the person as divine or messianic.[16]

7.1.2.2. Canonical Placement

The precise location of Psalm 2 in the first section of the canonical Psalter is also significant.[17] It tells us something about the process through which the Psalter were being shaped into its final form. J. L. Mays argues that some of the psalms were already interpreted messianically by the time the Psalter was collected.[18] According to Mays, there is some evidence in both early Jewish and Christian traditions that the first and the second psalms were joined together, and the two psalms as a whole were considered to be the opening psalm of the Psalter.

In Jewish tradition, Rabbi Johanan is credited with the following words in the Babylonian Talmud: "Every chapter that was particularly dear to David he commented with 'Happy' and terminated with 'Happy.' He began with 'Happy,' as it is written, '*Happy is the man,*' and he terminated with 'Happy,' as it is written, '*Happy are all they that take refuge in him*'" (*b.Ber.* 9b). Within the early Christian tradition the evidence is found in Acts 13:33, where the Western text reads "in the first psalm."[19] If these two psalms were originally joined in the Psalter (despite being independent compositions prior to their incorporation in the Book of Psalms), it suggests that their original intention was to provide the reader a double perspective as the opening psalm: Psalm 1 as an introduction from the perspective of wisdom, while Psalm 2 as a prophetic approach to the

---

[16] J. W. Watts, "Psalm 2 in the Context of Biblical Theology" *HBT* 12 (1990), 80. The complexity of the textual tradition, which suggests that it evolved over a considerable period of time, means that little can be said with certainty about the date of *Tg. Ps.* There are non-Masoretic readings implied at a number of points (e.g., Pss 97:11; 22:1), which are a sign of early material, but one cannot make too much of this. Cf. Alexander, "Targum, Targumim," *ABD* 320-31.

[17] It has been noted that Ps 2 is often linked with Ps 1 by some verbal similarities, leading some to postulate that the two psalms originally formed a literary unit. The verbal connections include the word אשרי "blessed" in 1:1 and 2:12 forming an *inclusio*; the verb "הגה" in 1:2 ("he meditates") and 2:1 ("scheme, plot"); and the combination of "way" and "perish" in 1:6 and 2:12. See W. H. Brownlee, "Psalms 1-2 as a Coronation Liturgy" *Bib* 52 (1971), 321-36, who defends the literary unity of both psalms; and J. Willis, "Psalm 1: an Entity" *ZATW* 91 (1979), 381-401, for a critique of this view. On the whole, the original unity of the psalms is unlikely.

[18] Cf. J. L. Mays, *The Lord Reigns: a Theological Handbook to the Psalms* (Louisville: Westminster John Knox, 1994), 94-98, and our discussion in §6.1.2.

[19] Origen says that he has seen two Hebrew manuscripts in which the first two psalms were joined as one. Justin, Tertullian, Cyprian, Eusebius, and Hilary also testify more or less explicitly to the practice of regarding these two psalms as one.

book.[20] In other words, as an introduction to the whole book, the first psalm calls for the *individual* to follow the path of life, whereas the second psalm urges *nations* to make the same choice. If so, it suggests that Psalm 2 was taken to have broader applications to Jewish faith than the coronation of an ancient Davidic king or the infusion of courage prior to an impending military confrontation.[21]

7.1.2.3. OT Pseudepigraphic Literature

Allusions to Psalm 2 in the OT Pseudepigrapha are scant. We have already noted some possible references to the psalm in the *Psalms of Solomon*.[22] In 17:21-24 the psalmist speaks of the coming king as "the son of David" who is to rule in justice and to "smash the arrogance of sinners like a potter's jar; to shatter all their substance with an iron rod" (cf. Ps 2:9). Furthermore, the king is to purge Jerusalem so that nations may come "from the ends of the earth to see his glory" (v.30-31; cf. Ps 2:8). Such a description of the coming king shortly before the Christian era well illustrates how Psalm 2 was used not only to reinforce hope in the midst of foreign invasion, but also, by some Jews, to portray the future universal rule of the messiah.[23]

Allusions to Psalm 2 may also be found in the *Similitudes of Enoch*,[24] where the Son of Man's judgement over the kings is prompted by the fact that "they do not extol and glorify him, and neither do they obey him" (*1 En.* 46:5; cf. Ps 2:11-12). Another possible allusion to Psalm 2 occurs in 48:10, where the rulers of the world are said to be judged because they "have denied the Lord of the Spirits and his Messiah" (cf. Ps 2:2).

7.1.2.4. Qumran Documents

Among the Qumran documents, allusions to Psalm 2 are found in 4QFlor 1:10-12 and 1QSa 2:11-12.

---

[20] Craigie, *Psalms*, 60.

[21] W. H. Bellinger, "The Psalms and Acts: Reading and Rereading" in *With Steadfast Purpose* (ed. N. H. Keathley; Waco: Baylor University, 1990), 138.

[22] It is dated between 70 and 45 BC. For a translation and introduction, see R. Wright, "Psalms of Solomon" in *The Old Testament Pseudepigrapha* (ed. J. H. Charlesworth; London: Darton, Longman & Todd, 1983), 2.639-70.

[23] D. P. Wallace, *Texts in Tandem: the Coalescent Usage of Psalm 2 and Psalm 110 in Early Christianity* (PhD dissertation; Baylor University, 1995), 115.

[24] For a translation and introduction see E. Isaac, "1 (Ethiopic Apocalypse of) Enoch" in *The Old Testament Pseudepigrapha* (ed. J. H. Charlesworth; London: Darton, Longman & Todd, 1983), 1.5-89.

The fragmentary text of 4QFlor 1:7-13, 18-19[25] is a pesher commentary on 2 Sam 7:10-14; Ps 1:1; and Ps 2:1-2. Unfortunately the remainder of the scroll is missing at the end of the citation of Ps 2:1-2 and its interpretation.

In 4QFlor we find explicit messianic exegesis of 2 Sam 7:11-14. Nathan's oracle is eschatologized and directly applied to the "branch of David [צמח דויד] who will stand with the interpreter of Torah, who will sit on the throne in Zion at the end of days" (11-12). Although the interpretation alludes to Jer 33:15-17 ("In those days and at that time I cause a righteous branch [צמח] to spring forth for David [דויד] . . . David shall never lack a man to sit on the throne"), it is applied to the fulfilment of Amos 9:11: "I will raise up the tent of David which is fallen."[26]

Referring to Ps 2 the Qumran midrash says, "Why do the nations rage and the peoples meditate vanity, the kings of the earth rise up, and the princes take counsel together against the Lord and His Messiah? Interpreted, this saying concerns the kings of the nations who shall rage against the elect of Israel in the last days."[27] Although little of the interpretation has survived, Ps 2:1-2 is interpreted as the persecution of the community by the wicked kings in an eschatological battle.

According to D. Goldsmith and G. J. Brooke, 4QFlor is a pesher that has in mind not only 2 Sam 7 but also Ps 2:7.[28] Linking passages on the basis of their verbal similarities was common in Judaism. Such a combination also occurs in the New Testament. Heb 1:5 brings together both Ps 2:7 and 2 Sam 7:14 as the first members of a long christological catena and Acts 13:32-33 documents a more intricate interweaving of these oracles.[29]

---

[25] For the text see J. M. Allegro, "Further Messianic References" *JBL* 75 (1956), 176-77; J. M. Allegro, *Qumran Cave 4 I (4Q158-4Q186)* (DJD 5; Oxford: Clarendon, 1968), 53-57; E. Lohse, *Die Texte aus Qumran: Hebräisch und Deutsch* (München: Kösel, 1981), 256-58. 4QFlor, dated to the first century BC, proclaims the coming of two Messiah, a Davidic or kingly Messiah and an Aaronic or priestly Messiah.

[26] C. A. Evans, "Jesus and the Messianic Texts from Qumran: A Preliminary Assessment of the Recently Published Materials" in *Jesus and His Contemporaries: Comparative Studies* (Leiden: Brill, 1995), 105. Amos 9:11 is a text which Christians understood as fulfilled in the inclusion of Gentiles into the Church (cf. Acts 15:14-18); it is also understood messianically in later rabbinic (*b. Sanh.* 96b-97a) and targumic sources.

[27] G. Vermes, *The Dead Sea Scrolls in English* (London: Penguin Books, 1987), 293-94.

[28] D. Goldsmith, "Acts 13:33-37: A *Pesher* on 2 Samuel 7" *JBL* 87 (1968), 321-24; G. J. Brooke, *Exegesis at Qumran: 4Q Florilegium in its Jewish Context* (JSOTSS 29; Sheffield: JSOT Press, 1985), 209; Cf. D. H. Juel, *Messianic Exegesis*, 62-77.

[29] The importance of these two texts as messianic oracles and as background for their use in the NT has long been recognized. See, for example, J. A. Fitzmyer, "4Q Testimonia and the New Testament" *TS* 18 (1967), 513-15.

Despite some difficulty in restoring the text, many scholars agree that
1QSa 2:11-12 should read "when God will have begotten [יוליד] the
Messiah among them."[30] C. A. Evans gives three reasons in support of this
restoration:

(1) in the photograph the last letter seems to be a daleth (in any event, it is too short to be
a final kaph); (2) most of the scholars who studied the scroll in the early 1950s (when the
leather text was in better condition than it is today) were convinced that יוליד was the
correct reading; and (3) the controversial restoration is completely in step with Ps 2:2, 7:
"The kings of the earth set themselves, and the rulers take counsel together, against the
Lord and his Messiah [מְשִׁיחוֹ] . . . He said to me: "You are My son, today I have
begotten [יְלִדְתִּיךָ] you." Given the language of Ps 2:2, 7 there is nothing unusual or
unexpected in restoring 1QSa 2:11-12 to read: "when God will have begotten the
Messiah.[31]

However, how was the "begotten" language interpreted by the Qumran
covenanters? Was it interpreted literally or metaphorically? The restoration
of the obscure word as יוליד does not necessarily suggest a literal
interpretation. Evans thinks that it was interpreted metaphorically as "the
confidence that someday God will raise up a messianic figure,"[32] although
Sigal argued too confidently for the literal interpretation that it attests "the
notion of a divine concept of the Messiah."[33] The following evidence,
however, suggests the metaphorical understanding was in view:

1) The original setting of the psalm suggests that it should be
understood metaphorically. The adoption of David as God's son is clearly
stated in 2 Sam 7:14 and in Ps 89:26-27. In Ps 2:7 this relationship is

---

[30] This restoration was first made by Barthélemy in D. Barthélemy and J. T. Milik,
Qumran Cave I (DJD 1; Oxford: Clarendon, 1955), 117. Similarly, J. A. Fitzmyer, "The
Aramaic 'Elect of God' Text From Qumran Cave IV" *CBQ* 27 (1965), 348-72; J. J.
Collins, "The *Son of God* Text from Qumran" in *From Jesus to John: Essays on Jesus
and New Testament Christology in Honour of Marinus de Jonge* (ed. M. C. de Boer;
Sheffield: Sheffield Academic Press, 1993), 65-82; and accepted by M. Hengel, *The Son
of God: the Origin of Christology and the History of Jewish-Hellenistic Religion*
(London: SCM, 1976), 44. Alternative readings include: Barthélemy and Milik, *Qumran
Cave I*, 117: "when God will have brought [יוליך] the Messiah"; Vermes, *Dead Sea
Scrolls in English*, 102: "when the (Priest) Messiah shall summon [יועיש] them"; H. N.
Richardson, "Some Notes on 1QSa" *JBL* 76 (1957), 108-22, esp. 116-17.

[31] Evans, "Jesus and the Messianic Texts," 96. Cf. R. Gordis, "The 'Begotten'
Messiah in the Qumran Scrolls" *VT* 7 (1957), 191-94, who thinks that the most probable
background for 1QSa is Ezek 36:12 וְהוֹלַכְתִּי עֲלֵיכֶם אָדָם, as suggested by the reading
presupposed by the LXX: καὶ γεννήσω ἐφ' ὑμᾶς ἀνθρώπους.

[32] Evans, "Jesus and the Messianic Texts," 97-98. This question will be of crucial
importance when we discuss later the use of Ps 2:7 in Acts 13:33.

[33] P. Sigal, "Further Reflections on the 'Begotten' Messiah" *HAR* 7 (1983), 221-33.
His article is broadly concerned with the question of whether there was a pre-Christian
concept of a divinely conceived Messiah.

expressed in more mythological terms: "I will tell of the decree of the Lord: he said to me, 'You are my son; today I have begotten you.'"

2) 4QFlor is applied to the fulfilment of Amos 9:11.[34] The text reads: "This is the 'branch of David' [צמח דויד] who will stand with the interpreter of Law, who will sit on the throne in Zion at the end of days; as it is written, 'I will raise up [והקימותי] the tent of David which is fallen' [Amos 9:11]. This is the 'fallen tent of David' who will stand to save Israel." (11-13). The verb קום ("to raise up") used in the citation of Amos 9:11 is translated in the LXX with ἀναστήσω "to raise up," the same verb used in Acts 13:33. There is also an allusion to Jer 33:15-17 ("In those days and at that time I cause a righteous branch [צמח] to spring forth for David [דויד] ... David shall never lack a man to sit on the throne"), where the verb "to spring forth" [צמח] is used. This evidence adds support for the metaphorical interpretation.

To sum up, the Qumran texts provide evidence for the view that Ps 2:7 was already connected to 2 Sam 7 and interpreted metaphorically to have messianic significance at Qumran.[35]

7.1.2.5. Rabbinic Sources

Allusions to Ps 2 in rabbinic sources are usually associated with the idea of opposition, rebellion, and hostile attack upon God, the messiah, and Israel.[36] The rebellion of nations against Yahweh and his anointed one was variously interpreted as the rebellion of Korah against Aaron and the rebellion of Gog and Magog against the children of Israel in time to come.[37] The rabbinic literature also made use of Ps 2:1-2 in the context of opposition as a source of security and assurance in the face of future difficulty. Moreover, Ps 2:7 was applied both to the children of Israel as

---

[34] Evans, "Jesus and the Messianic Texts," 105. Amos 9:11 is a text which Christians understood as fulfilled in the inclusion of Gentiles into the Church (cf. Acts 15:14-18); it is also understood messianically in later rabbinic (*b. Sanh.* 96b-97a) and targumic sources.

[35] Cf. E. E. Ellis, *The Gospel of Luke* (London: Oliphants, 1974), 91-92, who argued that 4 Ezra 7:28-29 may also provide evidence for a messianic interpretation of Ps 2:7 as early as the first century, if the references to "my son the Messiah" allude to this psalm. However, we think that the references are too vague to be convincing.

[36] Cf. *Midrash* on Ps 2.

[37] With regard to Gog and Magog see H. L. Strack and P. Billerbeck, *Kommentar zum Neuen Testament aus Talmud und Midrasch* (München: Beck, 1956), 3.831-40.

sons of God and to the messiah, but the aspect of divine sonship for the messiah is not emphasized.[38]

As far as the rabbinic literature is concerned, the messianic interpretation of Ps 2:7 is quite clear.[39] Although the rabbis were against the Christian claim of Jesus' divine sonship,[40] they by no means rejected the messianic application of Ps 2:7. The lack of emphasis on 2:7 and divine sonship could well be explained as a reaction against the Christian use of the verse for Jesus' divine sonship and as an intimation that a "richer messianic application of the God's son proclamation existed in early Judaism before Christ."[41]

7.1.2.6. Conclusion

In view of a wide range of evidence for the psalm's messianic significance (especially 4QFlor and in 1QSa), we can be fairly confident that there was messianic interpretation of Ps 2:7 prior to Christianity. Nevertheless, this conclusion does not necessarily suggest that when Ps 2:7 was used by early Christian exegetes for their understanding of Jesus, it was only interpreted as a messianic proof text. In fact, a further christological significance was found in the text when it was read in connection with other texts: i.e., the christological exegesis of messianic texts in the fullest sense. In order to fully and properly understand how this messianic psalm was re-interpreted by early Christian exegetes we need to turn to the early Christian use of Ps 2:7 in the NT.

7.2. Early Christian Interpretation of Psalm 2:7

While there are plenty of references to Ps 110:1 throughout the NT, references to Ps 2:7 are less widespread. It is quoted in Acts 13:33, Heb

---

[38] Cf. *Midr.* Ps 2.9: "Another comment on 'You are my son': God does not say 'I have a son,' but 'You are my son,' as when a master wishing to give pleasure to his slave, says to him, 'You are as dear to me as a son.'"

[39] Cf. *b. Sukk.* 52a; *Midr.* Ps 2.9 (on 2:7). In the latter passage Isa 42:1; 52:13; Ps 110:1; and Dan 7:13-14 are also cited and interpreted messianically.

[40] See for example *Exod. Rab.* 29.5 [on 20:1]. Commenting on Exod 20:1 Rabbi Abbahu (ca. 300) is reported to have said, "A human king may rule, but he has a father and a brother; but God said: 'I am not thus; I am the first, for I have no father, and I am the last, for I have no brother, and besides me there is no God, *for I have no son.*'" See also *y. Ta'an.* 2:1.

[41] Lövestam, *Son*, 23; cf. Watts, "Psalm 2," 80; E. Huntress, "'Son of God' in Jewish Writings Prior to the Christian Era" *JBL* (1935), 117-23, who argued that the reluctance of Jews to use the title "son of God" was a pre-Christian phenomenon.

1:5 and 5:5 and alluded to in Rom 1:3-4, and in the Gospel accounts of Jesus' baptism and transfiguration (Mk 1:11 pars. and Mk 9:7 pars.). As in the case of Ps 110:1, all quotations and allusions to Ps 2:7 – with the two Gospel narratives as an exception – appear at first glance to be associated with Jesus' resurrection and/or exaltation.

Such evidence led the majority of scholars to conclude that the earliest Christian use of Ps 2:7 was in reference to Jesus' resurrection along the line of Acts 13:33.[42] J. D. G. Dunn, for example, asserts that "the first Christians thought of Jesus' divine sonship principally as a role and status he had entered upon, been appointed to, at his resurrection."[43] According to this view, Jesus was not regarded as God's Son during or prior to his earthly life but *became* Son at the resurrection and the early church subsequently read this title back into his earthly life, his conception and eventually his pre-existence.[44]

However, we question (i) whether the earliest use of Ps 2:7 was in reference to Jesus' resurrection; and (ii) whether such an adoptionist interpretation of Jesus' divine sonship can be supported by the evidence.

It will be argued that Ps 2:7 was first used as scriptural proof for Jesus' divine sonship, a prophecy decisively fulfilled at his resurrection. It will also be argued that Ps 2:7 was first connected with Jesus' baptism. At his baptism, Jesus' self-consciousness of divine sonship received the final confirmation (Mk 1:11), while the prophecy about his divine sonship (Ps 2:7) was fully demonstrated through the resurrection. The resurrection was never thought to be the moment that Jesus became God's Son. Rather, his resurrection was seen as the full manifestation of his real, existing status as God's Son. In other words, the early church interpreted Ps 2:7 as a prophecy about Jesus' divine sonship decisively demonstrated at his resurrection and regarded him as already God's Son during and before his earthly life.

---

[42] Those who hold this view also point to Heb 1:5; 5:5 and Rom 1:3-4 as supporting evidence. Cf. J. D. G. Dunn, *Christology in the Making: a New Testament Inquiry into the Origins of the Doctrine of the Incarnation* (London: SCM, 1980, 1989), 35-36; B. Lindars, *New Testament Apologetic: the Doctrinal Significance of the Old Testament Quotations* (London: SCM, 1961), 140-3; Lövestam, *Son*, 23-48; B. M. F. van Iersel, *'Der Sohn' in den synoptischen Jesusworten* (Leiden: Brill, 1961), 66-73, 83, 174f.; Schweizer, "υἱός," *TDNT* 8.367; R. E. Brown, *The Birth of the Messiah: a Commentary on the Infancy Narratives in the Gospels of Matthew and Luke* (New York: Doubleday, 1993), 29f., 136.

[43] Dunn, *Christology*, 36. He also wrote that "The language of the earliest post-Easter confession of Jesus' sonship and the earliest use of Ps. 2:7 certainly seem to have placed the decisive moment of 'becoming' quite clearly in the resurrection of Jesus" (p.46).

[44] Brown, *Birth*, 29-32.

7.2.1. *Psalm 2:7 in Acts 13:33*

Acts 13:16-41 records Paul's sermon preached at Pisidian Antioch.[45] As part of his sermon Paul explicitly quotes Ps 2:7 in v.33.[46] The quotation follows immediately after the expression ἀναστήσας 'Ιησοῦν in the same verse: "what God promised to the fathers, he has fulfilled to us, their children, by raising Jesus (ἀναστήσας 'Ιησοῦν); as also it is written in the second psalm, 'You are my Son; today I have begotten you.'"

Since Ps 2:7 is explicitly quoted here, the passage could provide us with crucial evidence of how this messianic text was understood in the early church. The interpretation of the passage, however, is surrounded with much controversy.

7.2.1.1. *Meaning of* ἀναστήσας 'Ιησοῦν

The first problem we face when we exegete the passage is the meaning of ἀναστήσας 'Ιησοῦν. Does it refer to Jesus' resurrection from the dead? Or

---

[45] The speeches in Acts are a matter of controversy, but this is not the right place to discuss the issue at length. While the majority of scholars hold that these speeches are likely to be Luke's free compositions, we agree with a minority view that by and large the contents of the speeches preserve early Christian traditions. For a concise defence of the latter view see B. Witherington, *The Acts of the Apostles: a Socio-Rhetorical Commentary* (Grand Rapids: Eerdmans, 1998), 117-20, who states that "there is good reason to think that Luke is using sources for his speeches, but presenting summaries of the speeches, editing them according to his own agendas, and sometimes rendering portions in his own words for stylistic purposes" (p.120); cf. an apt characterization of the speeches in Acts by F. J. Foakes-Jackson, *The Acts of the Apostles* (London: Macmillan, 1933), xvi: "Whatever these speeches may be, it cannot be disputed that they are wonderfully varied as to their character, and as a rule admirably suited to the occasion on which they were delivered. Luke seemed to have been able to give us an extraordinarily accurate picture of the undeveloped theology of the earliest Christians, and enables us to determine the character of the most primitive presentation of the Gospel. However produced, the speeches in Acts are masterpieces, and deserve the most careful attention." Also G. N. Stanton, *Jesus of Nazareth in New Testament Preaching* (SNTSMS 27; London: CUP, 1974), 67-85. Cf. S. Walton, *Leadership and lifestyle: the portrait of Paul in the Miletus speech and 1 Thessalonians* (SNTSMS 108; Cambridge: CUP, 2000); W. Barclay, "A Comparison of Paul's Missionary Preaching and Preaching to the Church" in *Apostolic History and the Gospel* (eds. W. W. Gasque *et al.*; Exeter: Paternoster, 1970), 165-75; M. L. Soards, *The Speeches in Acts: Their Content, Context, and Concerns* (Louisville: Westminster/John Knox, 1994).

[46] Ps 2:7 is quoted in exact agreement with both the LXX and the Masoretic text. This agreement extends even down to the word order of the text. The text also agrees with the other citations of this passage in Heb 1:5 and 5:5. This is the first time that Ps 2:7 is explicitly cited in Luke-Acts, although it has been alluded to in the baptismal narrative and in the transfiguration scene.

does it refer to Jesus' coming onto the scene of history?[47] The answer to this question is not straightforward because elsewhere in Acts the verb ἀνίστημι is used with two different meanings: God's raising up Jesus from the dead (2:24, 32; 13:34; 17:31) as well as his raising up of a prophet like Moses (3:22; 7:37).

While a minority of scholars take ἀναστήσας Ἰησοῦν as a reference to Jesus' historical appearance,[48] the majority of scholars maintain that it refers to his resurrection.[49]

In favour of the historical appearance view the following arguments have been proposed: (1) the absence in v.33 (in contrast to vv.30 and 34) of the qualifier ἐκ νεκρῶν is significant; (2) set in the larger context, the use of ἐγείρω in v.33 is a conceptual parallel to vv.22-23, which supports the historical appearance view; (3) the reference is a summary of the section 13:23-31; and (4) the use of ἀναστήσας for a historical appearance is found in Acts 3:22, 26 and 7:37.

According to this view, Acts 13:32-33 refer to the historical appearance of Jesus, with scriptural proof from Ps 2:7, and vv.34-37 move on to the theme of the resurrection, with proof texts from Isa 55:3 and Ps 16:10. Not only did God fulfil his promise to the fathers by "raising" Jesus onto the scene of history (v.33: ἀναστήσας Ἰησοῦν), but he also confirmed the fulfilment of that promise by "raising" him up from the dead (v.34: ἀνέστησεν αὐτὸν ἐκ νεκρῶν).

In support of this view, M. L. Strauss suggests that the quotation of Ps 2:7 has a *twofold* purpose: while Ps 2:7 is cited as a prophecy fulfilled at the resurrection, its main purpose is to prove that Jesus is the Son of God, and hence the messiah.[50] Thus, ἀναστήσας does not simply refer to Jesus' coming on to the scene of history, but his whole career (i.e., his whole life,

---

[47] For a detailed examination of this question see M. Rese, *Alttestamentliche Motive in der Christologie des Lukas* (SNT 1; Gütersloh: Mohn, 1969), 82-86, who assembles both sides of the argument.

[48] The whole life of Jesus view is taken by Rese, *Alttestamentliche Motive*, 82-86; F. F. Bruce, *Acts*, 309; *idem*, "The Davidic Messiah," 12; C. K. Barrett, *Acts*, 645ff.; R. N. Longenecker, *Acts*, 428; H. H. Wendt, *Apostelgeschichte*, 213; M. L. Strauss, *The Davidic Messiah in Luke-Acts*, 164-66.

[49] The resurrection view is held by most scholars, including J. Dupont, "Filius meus es tu," 522-43, esp. 528-35; Lövestam, *Son*, 8-11; E. Haenchen, *Acts*, 411; U. Wilckens, *Missionsreden*, 51 n.3; E. Schweizer, "The Concept of the Davidic 'Son of God'," 190; M. F.-J. Buss, *Missionspredigt,* 89; C. Burger, *Jesus als Davidssohn*, 140; G. Schneider, *Apostelgeschichte*, 2.137; R. Pesch, *Apostelgeschichte*, 2.38; D. L. Bock, *Proclamation*, 244-49; J. Jervell, *Apostelgeschichte*, 359; J. Jervell, *Theology*, 32; K. Anderson, *The Resurrection of Jesus in Luke-Acts* (PhD. dissertation, Brunel University, 2000), 245-50.

[50] Strauss, *Messiah*, 164.

death, and resurrection).[51] In this way, the citation of Ps 2:7b (υἱός μου εἶ
σύ) provides scriptural proof for the claim that Jesus is the messiah raised
up from David's seed in fulfilment of God's promise to the fathers (vv.23
and 33), while the second part of the citation (ἐγὼ σήμερον γεγέννηκά σε)
"moves the argument forward by setting the stage for the statement of the
resurrection (v.34a) and its scriptural proofs from Isa 55.3 and Ps 16.10
(vv.34b, 35)."[52] He then interprets σήμερον as the day of the resurrection
and the birth imagery as referring to "the new resurrection life bestowed
on Jesus by the Father."[53]

On the other hand, the resurrection view appeals: (1) to the near context
(vv.31, 34); (2) to the precedent of use of the verb without a qualifier in
Acts 2:24, 32; (3) to the combination of ἀνίστημι (or ἐγείρω) with Jesus
(of Nazareth), which occurs frequently in Luke-Acts with reference to the
resurrection (Acts 2:24, 32; 4:10; 5:30; 10:40; 13:30); and (4) to the
unlikelihood that ἀναστήσας would change meanings twice between vv.31
and 34. If this is the case, God fulfils his promise to David by raising up
Jesus from the dead, Ps 2:7 serving as scriptural proof for the resurrection.

In support of the resurrection view, E. Lövestam has made an attempt to
link the psalm's birth motif to the resurrection.[54] He argued that the birth
motif in Ps 2:7c "today I have begotten you" was already linked to the
resurrection in the early church. He brought forward four texts in support
of his case: (1) the image of the birth pangs of death from Acts 2:24; (2)
the image of the underworld and the travail of birth in 4 Ezra 4:40-42; (3)
the image of "the first-born from the dead" in Col 1:18 and Rev 1:5; and
(4) the statement about the Son of God in power by the resurrection in
Rom 1:4. His suggestion, however, seems dubious, since the link between
the texts in question and the birth imagery and/or the resurrection is not as
strong as one would expect.[55]

D. L. Bock makes a fresh attempt to argue for the resurrection view. He
notes that the introductory phrase in vv.32-33 neatly breaks down into
three parts, with three subsequent citations referring back to each one in
the same order: (1) the citation of Ps 2:7 (v.33b) referring back to the
proclamation of the *promise* to the Fathers (v.32a); (2) the citation of Isa
55:3 (v.34b) referring back to its *fulfilment* to their children, to us (v.33a);

---

[51] Cf. K. Lake and H. J. Cadbury, *The Beginnings of Christianity* (London:
Macmillan, 1920), 4.154-55.

[52] Strauss, *Messiah*, 164.

[53] Strauss, *Messiah*, 164.

[54] Lövestam, *Son*, 43-47.

[55] For a criticism of Lövestam's proposal, see Bock, *Proclamation*, 246-48, who
categorically concludes that "the evidence for birth imagery linked to the resurrection in
the NT does not exist" (p.248). Cf. Strauss, *Messiah*, 165 n.1.

and (3) the citation of Ps 16:10 (v.35b) referring back to the disputed reference to the *raising up* of Jesus (v.33b). According to this view, (1) the citation of Ps 2:7 refers to the promise made to the king as an ideal Davidic ruler; (2) Isa 55:3 contributes to the fact that these Davidic τὰ ὅσια τὰ πιστά are promised ὑμῖν; and (3) the citation of Ps 16:10 contributes the point that the resurrection establishes the incorruptibility of the Holy One.[56]

Bock contends that the quotation of Ps 2:7 forms "part of the chain of texts to point to the fulfilment of the Davidic promise in Jesus (vv.22-23) as that fulfilment is demonstrated through his resurrection."[57] Bock tries to show that Ps 2:7 is used "to designate Jesus as God's son," a designation decisively demonstrated by the resurrection because "the resurrection proves publicly his unalterable and exalted position before God, as well as revealing him clearly to be the promised Son."[58] So, according to Bock, the primary function of the citation of Ps 2:7 in v.33 is to confirm the promise of divine sonship, while the relationship between Ps 2:7 and the resurrection, though present, is indirect.

7.2.1.2. Evaluation

As we have seen, the arguments for either view of the meaning of ἀναστήσας are evenly balanced. While Bock and Strauss argued for opposite views, their fresh exegeses of the passage came to a similar conclusion with regard to the primary use of the psalm. They agree that Ps 2:7 is cited as scriptural proof for Jesus' divine sonship, which was fulfilled at the resurrection. However, none of them has provided the so-called missing link between the psalm and the resurrection. At this point, we introduce our suggestion that the missing link is to be found in Ps 2:6, which probably was already understood by the early church as a prophecy about Jesus' exaltation to the right hand of God.

While Lövestam's attempt to find a specific and direct link between the psalm's birth motif to the resurrection was not convincing, we propose that another possible link between the psalm and the resurrection may be found in Ps 2:6, although it is not specifically quoted here. In Ps 2:6 God addresses the kings of the earth saying: "I have set my king on Zion, my holy hill." Since the psalm was understood messianically and applied to

---

[56] Bock, *Proclamation*, 244-45. What we witness here is not an exaltation theology as elsewhere in Acts, but "the indestructibility of Jesus as the one able to bring the promise to the nation."

[57] Bock, *Proclamation*, 248.

[58] Bock, *Proclamation*, 245-56 (quotation from p.249); cf. Bellinger, "Psalms and Acts," 140-41.

Jesus by the early church, this divine statement too was most likely interpreted as applying to Jesus. It is also conceivable that in the early church Zion was understood as the heavenly Jerusalem, where God is, and so he takes Jesus and sets him up there as King. If so, the early church would have been led to interpret the verse 6 as a messianic prophecy about Jesus being exalted by God. Then the promise in vv.7-8 was understood as a reference to the messiah's heavenly reign till his enemies are defeated (cf. 1 Cor 15:24-28; Ps 110:1; Ps 8:6). In support of our proposal that there was such messianic interpretation going on in the early church we provide the following lines of evidence.

First, as we have seen above, while Ps 2 was originally connected with the coronation of a Davidic king, it was subsequently sung in Jerusalem at the occasion of the king's enthronement festival when God installed the king upon Zion (Ps 2:6).[59] Such use of the psalm may have been the starting point for the messianic interpretation of v.6 as the messiah being enthroned or exalted by God at the heavenly Jerusalem, where he is.

Second, in Gal 4:26 we find the idea of a "heavenly Jerusalem" ("Jerusalem above") in contrast to "the present Jerusalem."[60] This idea of the earthly and the heavenly Jerusalem, however, was not peculiar to Paul because the way he introduces the idea suggests that he and his audience already knew about this idea.[61] Paul's use of the idea here is probably the earliest literary reference to it. We find the same idea in Hebrews and Revelation.[62] In Heb 12:22 the actual expression "heavenly Jerusalem" occurs, while in Rev 14:1 the seer sees the Lamb standing on Mount Zion.

Third, this idea of a "heavenly Jerusalem" has a rich Jewish background.[63] The concept has to do with the culmination of God's

---

[59] Cf. Gunkel, *Psalmen*, 5; Mowinckel, *Psalms in Israel's Worship*, 61-65 and many others.

[60] "Jerusalem above" stands as the antithesis to "the present Jerusalem." Although no explicit antithesis to Mount Sinai is mentioned here, it is quite clear that "Jerusalem above" serves as the antithesis to "the present Jerusalem." On the other hand, the reference to "Jerusalem above" as being "our mother" (Gal 4:26) also draws on a rich Jewish background. Ps 87 is a song that praises Jerusalem (Zion) as the mother of God's own; Isa 66:7-11 describes Jerusalem (Zion) as a mother in labour bringing forth a son; and 4 Ezra 10:7 depicts Zion symbolically as "the mother of us all."

[61] F. F. Bruce, *The Epistle of Paul to the Galatians: a Commentary on the Greek Text* (NIGTC; Exeter: Paternoster, 1982), 221.

[62] Bruce, *Galatians*, 220-21; R. N. Longenecker, *Galatians* (WBC 41; Dallas: Word Books, 1990), 213-14. Cf. Heb 12:22, with 11:10, 14-16; Rev 3:12; 21:2, 9ff., where the full realization of God's kingdom and Christ's reign is set out in terms of a "heavenly" or "new" Jerusalem that was looked forward to by the patriarchs and is now experienced by Christians in inaugurated fashion.

[63] Cf. T. L. Donaldson, *Jesus on the Mountain: a Study in Matthean Theology* (JSNTSup 8; Sheffield: JSOT Press, 1985), 30-83.

redemptive purposes in human history, the realization of God's reign in its totality. As such, it is an eschatological concept that describes Jerusalem as it will be at the end of time, often in contrast to what the city is at present. References to a "heavenly Jerusalem" were still in embryonic form in the OT (cf. Ps 87:3; Isa 54; Ezek 40-48) and Jewish wisdom literature (cf. Sir 36:13ff.; Tob 13), but the idea in more developed form is found in the apocalyptic writings of Second Temple Judaism.[64] This suggests that, although the expression "heavenly Jerusalem" is found only in Heb 12:22 and nowhere else in the NT nor in Jewish apocalyptic literature, there can be no doubt that the metaphor was derived from the apocalyptic tradition.[65] The idea of a "heavenly Jerusalem" in contrast to the present Jerusalem is also attested in rabbinic literature, although without reflecting negatively on Judaism itself.[66]

Fourth, there is also evidence for an increasing interest in Second Temple Judaism in the contrast between Mt. Sinai as the mountain of revelation and Mt. Zion as the mountain of eschatological redemption.[67] The linking of eschatological redemption with Mt. Zion symbolism in Heb 12:22 and Matthew probably reflects an established Christian tradition that builds on a developed "mountain theology" in Second Temple Judaism.[68]

Fifth, a connection between the messiah and the throne in Zion at the end of days is also attested in the Qumran document (4QFlor 11-13).[69]

Sixth, we have already seen in the previous chapter that the early church regarded Jesus' resurrection as his exaltation to the right hand of God, i.e., where God is, mainly on the basis of Ps 110:1.[70] The conviction that Jesus

---

[64] Cf. *1 En* 53.6; 90.28-29; *2 En* 55.2; *Ps. Sol.* 17.33; 4 Ezra 7:26; 8:52; 10:25-28, 38-59; *2 Apoc. Bar.* 4.2-6; 32.2; 59.4; also 1QM 12.1-2; and 4QShirShab, which speak of angelic ministry in a heavenly temple. For discussions of the development of this tradition, see K. L. Schmidt, "Jerusalem als Urbild und Abbild," *ErJb* 18 (1950) 207-48; R. E. Clements, *God and Temple: the Idea of the Divine Presence in Ancient Israel* (Oxford: Blackwell, 1965), 126-27; R. J. McKelvey, *The New Temple: the Church in the New Testament* (London: OUP, 1968), 25-41; D. Flusser, "Two Notes on the Midrash on 2 Sam. 7:1" *IEJ* 9 (1959), 99-109.

[65] Cf. H. Bietenhard, *Die himmlische Welt im Urchristentum und Spätjudentum* (WUNT 2; Tübingen: Mohr Siebeck, 1951), 192-204; Lohse, *TDNT*, 7.337, esp. n.287.

[66] Cf. *b.Ta'an.* 6a; *b.Hag.* 12b; *Gen. Rab.* 55.7; 69.7; *Num. Rab.*4.13; *Midr. Pss.* 30.1; 122.4; *Cant. Rab.* 3.10; 4.4; *Pesiq. R.* 40.6.

[67] Donaldson, *Mountain*, 30-83.

[68] Donaldson, *Mountain*, 87-213.

[69] 4QFlor 11-13: "This is the 'branch of David' [צמח דויד] who will stand with the interpreter of Law, who will sit on *the throne in Zion* at the end of days; as it is written, 'I will raise up [והקימותי] the tent of David which is fallen' [Amos 9:11]. This is the 'fallen tent of David' who will stand to save Israel."

[70] Such an understanding is clearly attested in Acts 2:32-35; Rom 8:34; Eph 1:20; 1 Pet 3:22 and implied in Acts 5:31; 7:55-56; 1Cor 15:25; Col 3:1; Heb 1:3; 10:12; 12:2.

is enthroned/exalted beside God may have found further scriptural support
from Ps 2:6. Thus it is highly likely that the early church took the idea of
Jesus' exaltation to God's right hand not only from Ps 110:1 but also from
Ps 2:6. Since the early church regarded both psalms (Ps 110 and Ps 2) as
two of the most important messianic psalms for their understanding of who
Jesus really was, a cross-reference reading of these two psalms is highly
likely.

Seventh, such a cross-reference reading of the psalms may be supported
by the evidence that the images from Ps 2 are often linked with Ps 110: (i)
in 1 Cor 15:24-28 the subjection of the power and the theocentric
conclusion in Paul's argument (supported by references to Ps 110:1 and Ps
8:6) are thematically connected to the imagery of Ps 2:7-8; in Ps 2:7-8, it is
God and his decree that ultimately give the Son authority over the enemy
powers; (ii) the usage of the title "the Son" in 15:28, following the
allusions to Ps 110 and Ps 8, may be an echo of Ps 2:7; and (3) both psalms
equally speak about the "birth" of the messiah (cf. Ps 110:3 "ἐκ γαστρὸς
πρὸ ἑωσφόρου ἐξεγέννησά σε"; Ps 2:7 "υἱός μου εἶ σύ ἐγὼ σήμερον
γεγέννηκά σε").

Eighth, our suggestion also fits in with the temporal order of the
prophetic psalm as suggested by Acts 4:25-26. Ps 2:1-2 was fulfilled when
Jesus was put to death by the Gentiles and the people of Israel (vv.25-28),
while   Ps   2:6-8   was   fulfilled   when   he   was   vindicated   at   his
resurrection/exaltation as the Son of God enthroned at his right hand.[71]

Ninth, wide attestations of "heavenly Jerusalem," "mountain theology"
and "throne in Zion" in Jewish sources, especially in the apocalyptic
writings of Second Temple Judaism, strongly suggest that the idea about
Mt. Zion as "heavenly Jerusalem" was taken up by the early church when
they read Ps 2 together with Ps 110 as applying to Jesus.

If our suggestion that the Jewish tradition about Mt. Zion as the
heavenly Jerusalem was taken up by the early church and led them to see
Ps 2:6 as a prophecy about Jesus' exaltation/enthronement to the right
hand of God is convincing, then it provides not only the missing link
between the psalm and the resurrection and/or exaltation in the NT (cf.
Rom 1:3-4; Heb 1:5; 5:5), but also the crucial evidence for the view that in
Acts 13:33 Ps 2:7 was cited not only as scriptural proof for Jesus' divine
sonship but also as an indirect reference to the resurrection.[72] Once Ps 2:6
together with Ps 110:1 was interpreted as a prophecy about Jesus'
exaltation at God's right hand, the early church began to interpret the
"today" as the day of the resurrection and/or exaltation, the day when God

---

[71] So Strauss, *Messiah*, 165.

[72] The lack of evidence for the resurrection being linked to the begetting language of
v.7c in the early church renders our suggestion more convincing.

decisively fulfilled his prophecy about Jesus' divine sonship. The absence of Ps 2:6 as a reference to Jesus' exaltation in the NT may seem striking, but it can be explained by the high popularity of Ps 110:1 among early Christians, a text which succinctly proves the ideas of his exaltation and/or enthronement to God's right hand and the subjection of powers during his heavenly reign. It is also conceivable that the early church wanted to reserve Ps 2 as a scriptural text for Jesus' divine sonship and Ps 110 for his exaltation.

At this point, we would like to make some critical comments on the arguments brought forward by Bock and Strauss.

First, while Bock's rebuttal of Lövestam's attempt to relate the psalm's birth motif directly and specifically to the resurrection is sound, his suggestion that the citation of Ps 2:7 in Heb 1:5 and 5:5 is not connected to the resurrection event alone, but always with reference to the concept of exaltation seems ill-founded. His distinction between the resurrection event and exaltation in Hebrews is somewhat artificial because the writer of Hebrews never refers to Jesus' resurrection by name except in the closing doxology, but operates in terms of his exaltation. As we will see below, in Hebrews the resurrection is always included in the exaltation. The early church regarded the resurrection and the exaltation as two aspects of the same event.

Second, Strauss is right to see a connection between the allusion to Ps 2:7 in Luke's baptismal narrative (Lk 3:22; cf. 9:35) and the citation of the same in v.33. If Luke has already linked it to the baptism, it is very unlikely that he has forgotten about it by the time he wrote Acts 13! However, his suggestion that the role of the psalm in both passages is to confirm Jesus' messianic identity is unlikely. As we have already argued, the main purpose of the baptismal narrative, including an allusion to Ps 2:7, is to declare Jesus not only as the messiah but also as God's Son.[73] It is certainly plausible that divine sonship was merely understood in terms of messiahship,[74] but our discussion of Jesus' self-consciousness of divine sonship strongly suggests that the early church drew important implications from his claim to be God's Son during his earthly life and applied Ps 2:7 to him rather than making a simple equation between the divine sonship and the messiahship. It is also significant that the theophany experienced by Jesus at his baptism represents a final confirmation of his divine sonship rather than merely his messiahship.

---

[73] See further §4.3.6.

[74] Cf. N. T. Wright, *The Letter to the Romans* (The New Interpreter's Bible; Nashville: Abingdon, 2002), 417, thinks that at this early stage and even in Rom 1:3-4 the sonship of Jesus is to be understood in terms of messiahship rather than a declaration of divine nature.

Third, as far as we can see from what Strauss has written, he seems to suggest that Luke probably interpreted the "today" as the day of the resurrection and the begetting language as a reference to the new resurrection life bestowed on Jesus by God because he was aware of "the early Christian application of the psalm to the resurrection and/or exaltation" in the light of the Davidic promise tradition.[75] If his basic argument is correct,[76] then such an application of the psalm is most likely to come from what the early church saw in Ps 2:6, a prophecy about Jesus' exaltation to the right hand of God.

Fourth, with regard to Strauss's suggestion that Ps 2:7b refers to Jesus as God's Son and v.7c to "the new resurrection life," we need to point out that these two clauses are in parallel structure and thus are likely to be understood as one single statement about the messiah's divine sonship, rather than as two separate units with two different meanings, unless there are good reasons to think otherwise.[77] This point renders our suggestion that Ps 2:6 as understood as a prophecy about the exaltation provides the missing link between the psalm and the resurrection.

7.2.1.3. Conclusion

Our discussion of Ps 2:7 in Acts 13:33 leads us to conclude that, while there is no explicit link between the begetting language of Ps 2:7c and the resurrection in the early church, the missing link between the psalm and the resurrection is to be found in an early Christian tradition about Jesus' resurrection and/or exaltation rooted in Ps 2:6. If the evidence adduced so far is correct, ἀναστήσας Ἰησοῦν does not only refer to Jesus' entrance to the scene of history as God's Son (or more specifically, his earthly ministry as such at the baptism), but also includes an indirect reference to God's "raising" him up from the dead. The citation of Ps 2:7 as a whole served as scriptural proof for Jesus' divine sonship which was seen as decisively demonstrated through the resurrection. That is, the early church interpreted the resurrection as the moment when Jesus' existing status as God's Son was fully manifested as the Son of God "in power" (Rom 1:4). So the use of Ps 2:7 in Acts 13 provides us with crucial evidence that the earliest Christians saw Jesus' resurrection as a confirmation of his existing position and status as God's Son. As we will see, this is in line with other instances of Ps 2:7 being linked to the resurrection and/or exaltation in the

---

[75] Strauss, *Messiah*, 164-65, also 57-67.

[76] Cf. Strauss, *Messiah*, who contends that "The earliest evidence that Jesus' resurrection was linked to the Davidic promise tradition appears in Rom. 1.3-4" (p.60).

[77] This point also renders Lövestam's suggestion that the birth motif was understood as the resurrection in the early church less attractive.

NT (Rom 1:3-4; Heb 1:5, 5:5). Though Ps 2:6 is not explicitly quoted in Acts 13:33, an early interpretation of it as Jesus' exaltation explains why Ps 2:7 is linked with the resurrection and/or exaltation in the NT.

	ἀναστήσας	Ps 2:7
The Historical Appearance View		
Standard View	Raising up Jesus onto the scene of history	Scriptural proof for Jesus' coming onto the scene of history
Strauss's View	Raising up Jesus onto the scene of history, including the resurrection	Scriptural proof for Jesus' messianic identity and the resurrection; Ps 2:7c moves the argument forward by setting the stage for the statement of the resurrection (v.34a) and its proof texts from Is 55:3 and Ps 16:10 (vv.34b, 35).
My View	Raising up Jesus onto the scene of history, including the resurrection	Here Ps 2:7 is used as scriptural proof for Jesus' divine sonship (his coming onto the scene of history as God's Son) and as an indirect reference to the resurrection. The two parallel clauses of Ps 2:7 form a single statement about divine sonship; they are not to be separated. The missing link between Ps 2 and the resurrection is found in v.6. Pre-Christian Jewish tradition of Mt. Zion as "heavenly Jerusalem" coupled with Ps 110:1 and 8:6 led to an early Christian interpretation of Ps 2:6 as Jesus' exaltation beside God.
The Resurrection View		
Standard View	Raising up Jesus from the dead	Scriptural proof for the resurrection
Lövestam's View	Raising up Jesus from the dead	Scriptural proof for the resurrection With a specific link between the birth motif (Ps 2:7c) and the resurrection
Bock's View	Raising up Jesus from the dead, referring to Ps 16:10 (v.35b)	Scriptural proof for Jesus' divine sonship referring back to the *promise* to the fathers (v.32a)
My 2nd Option	Raising up Jesus from the dead	Here Ps 2:7 is used as scriptural text about what happens at the resurrection, that is, the early church interpreted the resurrection as the moment when Jesus' divine sonship was fully manifested. The missing link is found in pre-Christian Jewish tradition of Mt. Zion as "heavenly Jerusalem," which together with Pss 110:1 and 8:6 led to an early Christian interpretation of Ps 2:6 as Jesus' exaltation beside God.

7.2.2. Psalm 2:7 in Rom 1:3-4

7.2.2.1. Original Form of the Formula

It is generally accepted among scholars that, despite considerable degree of disagreement as to the original form, in Rom 1:3-4 Paul is quoting an early Christian confession or creed in order to establish a point of theological contact between himself and his Roman readers. The following arguments for a pre-Pauline tradition have been suggested:[78] (1) the formulation of the verses in parallel participial clauses, which are characteristic of fixed formulas; (2) the dichotomy of σάρξ and πνεῦμα in a non-Pauline way; (3) the mention of the Davidic descent of Jesus, which plays no role in Paul; (4) the "adoptionist" christology, rather than pre-existence christology, implied in ὁρισθέντος υἱοῦ θεοῦ; (5) the absence of Jesus' crucifixion, which Paul would not have missed if it came from him; (6) unusual or unique expressions like ὁρισθέντος υἱοῦ θεοῦ and πνεῦμα ἁγιωσύνης; (7) the formula as Paul's summary of the εὐαγγέλιον θεοῦ leads us to expect something traditional (cf. 1 Cor 15:1-4; 2 Tim 2:8; 1 Tim 3:15-16).

Recent scholarship, however, tends to be more sceptical about its pre-Pauline origin. This tendency is partly due to the lack of confidence in the criteria used to identify and to reconstruct old traditions. As early as 1975 V. S. Poythress already expressed reservation about the pre-Pauline origin of the formula by postulating a mediating view that Rom 1:3-4 is Paul's "free composition using a number of traditional expressions and ideas," in order to give "a decidedly traditional flavour to it."[79] About two decades later, J. M. Scott, mounting an impressive rebuttal of each of the common arguments for a traditional formula, concluded that "it is in no way certain that Rom. 1:3b-4 contains a pre-Pauline creed."[80] More recently, C. G.

---

[78] Cf. J. D. G. Dunn, *Romans* (WBC 38; Dallas: Word Books, 1988), 5; R. Jewett, "The Redaction and Use of an Early Christian Confession in Romans 1:3-4" in *The Living Text: Essays in Honor of Ernest W. Saunders* (eds. D. E. Groh *et al.*; Lanham: University Press of America, 1985), 100-02, who lists twelve possible indications of confessional material in Rom 1:3-4; E. Käsemann, *Commentary on Romans* (London: SCM, 1980), 10-13. Here we follow the concise summary by V. S. Poythress, "Is Romans 1:3-4 a Pauline Confession after All?" *ExpTim* 87 (1975-1976), 180.

[79] Poythress, "Confession," 181-82, provides point-by-point objections against pre-Pauline origin of Rom 1:3-4, although he professed agnosticism on the subject.

[80] J. M. Scott, *Adoption as Sons of God: an Exegetical Investigation into the Background of huiothesia in the Pauline Corpus* (WUNT 2/48; Tübingen: Mohr Siebeck, 1992), 227-36 (quotation from p.236). He rejects arguments based on vocabulary (non-Pauline), style (participial parallelism), theology (no role playing in Paul of the Davidic descent of Jesus; the adoptionistic language vs. Paul's pre-existence of the Son of God), argument from silence (the absence of the suffering an death of Christ in these lines), and 2 Tim 2:8.

Whitsett has argued that in this Romans passage Paul "makes his own conscious and distinctive use of an early conventional exegesis of 2 Sam 7 and Ps 2."[81]

Recent scholarship on Rom 1:3-4 suggests that there is reason to be somewhat sceptical about the fragment as a whole being a pre-Pauline "fixed" confessional formula.[82] However, to argue that Paul is *either* quoting a traditional creed-like formula *or* making a free composition of his own is a false dichotomy, and the answer lies somewhere in between. While it is true that earlier arguments for its pre-Pauline origin seem to have relied too heavily on form-critical observations, failing to make sufficient efforts to understand the text as it stands,[83] it is, at the same time, difficult to dismiss the evidence for Paul's use of the traditional elements in its entirety.

Most scholars seem to agree that it is at least possible to find some traces of Paul's use of traditional material here, despite their discrepancies over its real extent. It would therefore be advisable to use form-criticism with greater care, taking only as pre-Pauline those expressions that can be assigned with a high degree of certainty as early traditional elements. In our opinion, among the seven pieces of evidence listed above for pre-Pauline tradition only points 2, 6, and 7 are compelling:[84]

With regard to the unusual expressions like ὁρισθέντος υἱοῦ θεοῦ and πνεῦμα ἁγιωσύνης (point 6), they are very unlikely to be Paul's own words.[85] (1) As Leslie C. Allen has shown, ὁρίζειν in Rom 1:4 and προορίζειν in the NT conventionally refer to the royal decree language of

---

[81] C. G. Whitsett, "Son of God, Seed of David: Paul's Messianic Exegesis in Romans 1:3-4" *JBL* 119 (2000), 661-81 (quotation from p.661). Whitsett attempts to demonstrate that "Paul joins these two conspicuous christological prophecies by their common theme of divine sonship and interprets them as mirroring his own twofold confession of Christ as the instrument of God's faithfulness to Israel and mercy to Gentiles," a particular theme also found in Rom 15:7-13. He claims that it is possible to find an exegetical connection between the two Roman passages (p.662). Cf. Poythress, "Confession," 182, who has already made a suggestion that the creed-like formula is too well adapted to the recurring theme of Jew and Gentile throughout the rest of Romans.

[82] Cf. Poythress, "Confession," 182.

[83] J. D. G. Dunn, "Jesus - Flesh and Spirit: an Exposition of Romans 1.3-4" *JTS* 24 (1973), 42-43, rightly pointed out that the first task of the exegete is to determine the meaning of the passage in its present context which "must serve as a control for and test of the more speculative hypotheses aimed at uncovering the earlier form and its significance."

[84] The rest of the evidence can be equally explained either way.

[85] Even Scott, *Adoption*, 232, admits that they are not from Paul, although he argues strongly for the Pauline statement.

Ps 2:7.[86] (2) Since this verb is found nowhere else in Paul, it is much more likely that it formed part of an early Christian confession. Even if ὁρισθέντος resulted from Paul's own allusive use of Ps 2:7,[87] it seems more likely that he is indebted to his predecessors rather than his own creative use. (3) Similarly, the fact that the expression πνεῦμα ἁγιωσύνης is also uncharacteristic of Paul makes it more likely that it derived from a traditional formula rather than Paul's own composition. (4) The adjectival genitive, ἁγιωσύνης, could be an indication that we have here an Hebraic idiom rather than the simple adjective "holy."

Regarding the two κατά phrases, their origin has also been the focus of much debate. While some scholars take them to be Pauline insertions,[88] an increasingly large majority attribute them to the original creed.[89]

It is therefore fair to conclude that, despite some valid points in recent attempts to undermine the arguments for the pre-Pauline origin, there seems to be some compelling evidence for pre-Pauline material and this makes it still highly likely that Rom 1:3-4 preserves traces of pre-Pauline material which could provide us with a glimpse of an early Christian confession about Jesus.

7.2.2.2. Is the Formula Adoptionistic?

It is also often claimed that the original formula lacked the phrase "in power," and thus signified that Jesus became Son of God at the resurrection (the so-called adoptionist christology). By adding this phrase

---

[86] L. C. Allen, "The Old Testament Background of (ΠΡΟ)ΟΡΙΖΕΙΝ in the New Testament" *NTS* 17 (1970-1971), 104-08: "the accompanying verb ὁρισθέντος and indeed most of the instances of (προ)ὁρίζειν in the New Testament come from the same source. 'You are my son' was the coronation 'decree' (חק) of Yahweh: Christ was '*decreed* to be Son of God'. In each case . . . the verb occurs in a context from which Ps. ii and/or Christ' sonship is not far removed" (p.104).

[87] So Whitsett, "Son of God," 676.

[88] E.g., N. A. Dahl, *The Crucified Messiah: and Other Essays* (Minneapolis: Augsburg, 1974), 43; O. Betz, *What Do We Know About Jesus?* (London: SCM, 1968), 96 n.17; K. Wengst, *Christologische Formeln und Lieder des Urchristentums* (SNT 7; Gütersloh: Mohn, 1972), 112-14. E. Linnemann, "Tradition und Interpretation in Röm. 1,3 f." *EvT* 31 (1971), 275, thinks that only the second κατά and not the rest of the prepositional phrase was inserted by Paul.

[89] See esp. E. Schweizer, "Röm 1,3f, und der Gegensatz von Fleisch und Geist vor und bei Paulus" in *Neotestamentica* (Zürich: Zwingli Verlag, 1963), 180f.; Dunn, "Flesh and Spirit," 60; Scott, *Adoption*, 231f. R. Jewett, *Paul's Anthropological Terms: a Study of Their Use in Conflict Settings* (AGAJU 10; Leiden: Brill, 1971), 136-38; Jewett, "Romans 1:3-4," 99-122, postulates a three-stage development, with the κατά phrases being added in a second, but still pre-Pauline, stage (see pp.102-13 for a summary of earlier discussions of the passage).

Paul has transformed the meaning of the statement so as to imply that Jesus had been Son of God all along, and that at the resurrection he became Son in a new sense.[90] Those who take this view tend to see a dichotomy between the earthly Jesus as Son of David and his post-resurrection status as Son of God. However, this view is open to considerable question.

First, it is much more likely that Paul agrees with the description of the Son in vv.3-4. (1) it is quite unthinkable that Paul would give his tacit approval to an aberrant christology as part of the content of his gospel, especially in so prominent a position as the superscription, for that would impugn his gospel and his apostleship. (2) While one may argue that Paul subtly "expands" the adoptionistic fragment by setting it within the framework of his own pre-existence christology,[91] it can be answered that Paul does not use περὶ τοῦ υἱοῦ αὐτοῦ to expand vv.3b-4, but rather he uses vv.3b-4 to expand περὶ τοῦ υἱοῦ αὐτου.[92] (3) although it is not impossible that Paul might have re-interpreted the traditional formula to suit his purpose, the evidence is far more likely that Paul is quoting what he himself affirms.[93]

Second, the exegesis of the passage will show that the argument for an adoptionistic christology is difficult, if not impossible, to sustain.

7.2.2.3. *2 Sam 7:12-14 and Psalm 2:7 as Background of Rom 1:3-4*

Scott argued that the traditional background of Rom 1:3-4 is likely to be found in 2 Sam 7:12-14, where God makes a promise to David that the messiah from his "seed" (σπέρμα) would be adopted as Son of God.[94] Hence, Scott takes τοῦ ὁρισθέντος υἱοῦ θεοῦ in Rom 1:4a as "a

---

[90] So Dunn, *Romans*, 14: "According to this creedal formula, then Jesus became something he was not before, or took on a role which was not previously his before." Also among others, W. R. Kramer, *Christ, Lord and Son of God* (London: SCM, 1966), 108-26; Wengst, *Formeln*, 116; Käsemann, *Romans*, 13.

[91] Cf. S. Kim, *The Origin of Paul's Gospel* (WUNT 2/4; Tübingen: Mohr Siebeck, 1981), 111; Burger, *Jesus als Davidssohn*, 31-32; Wengst, *Formeln*, 112; E. Käsemann, *An die Römer* (HNT 8a; Tübingen: Mohr Siebeck, 1973), 11Jewett, "Romans 1:3-4," 119.

[92] So Scott, *Adoption*, 235; Linnemann, "Röm. 1,3 f.," 271; C. A. Wanamaker, *The Son and the sons of God: a Study in Elements of Paul's Christological and Soteriological Thought* (Ph.D diss. University of Durham, 1980), 93-95.

[93] Dunn, *Romans*, 5: "the more redaction argued for, the less fitted would the formula be to serve its most obvious function of assuring the Roman addressees that Paul fully shared their common faith." See also Wright, *Romans*, 416-17.

[94] Cf. also 4QPB 4; *Ps. Sol.* 17:4; 4QFlor 1:10-11.

circumlocution for the Adoption Formula in 2 Sam 7:14a."[95] This view, however, was criticized by Whitsett as one-sided.

Whitsett finds in this Romans passage an early conventional exegesis that combined 2 Sam 7:12-14 with Ps 2:7-8.[96] According to Whitsett, Paul is here doing his own conscious messianic exegesis, in which both God's promise to David (the Jews) and his faithfulness to the seed of Abraham (the nations) are confirmed by Jesus' Davidic descent. Moreover, if one reads Rom 1:3-4 together with 15:8-9a and 15:12, it is possible to see that Paul is in fact alluding to two aspects of Jesus' messiahship: confirming God's faithfulness to Israel and glorifying God among the nations.[97] The conflation of 2 Sam 7:12-14 and Ps 2:7 was wholly a part of the rhetoric of Romans, and the allusive character of this juxtaposition suggests that Paul's audience already knew the conflation of these two passages.

With regard to an allusion to Ps 2:7 in Rom 1:4, several pieces of evidence can be suggested:[98] (1) early Christians believed that God's promise to David was fulfilled when Jesus' resurrection was regarded as his royal investiture;[99] (2) Jesus' divine sonship and his resurrection/exaltation are encapsulated by ὁρισθέντος, a verb found

---

[95] Scott, *Adoption*, 241-42. Cf. those who recognize the relevance of 2 Sam 7:12 for Rom 1:3-4 in securing that Jesus is born of the "seed" of David: D. C. Duling, "The Promises to David and Their Entrance into Christianity: Nailing Down a Likely Hypothesis" *NTS* 19 (1973-1974), 73; E. Schweizer, "Review of E. Linnemann's 'Tradition and Interpretation in Röm. 1,3f.'" *EvT* 31 (1971), 276; N. A. Dahl, "Promise and Fulfillment" in *Studies in Paul: Theology for the Early Christian Mission* (Minneapolis: Augsburg, 1977), 128; Betz, *What Do We Know*, 96; Kim, *Origin*, 109.

[96] Whitsett, "Son of God," 661-81: "Scott's explanation does not finally agree with the numerous authors he cites supporting the influence of Ps 2:7 in Rom 1:4; consequently, his construal of the confession does not reproduce the twofold christological pattern which we have seen repeatedly and which fits the overriding Jew/Gentile concern of Romans" (p.677 n.65). Other scholars seeing Ps 2:7 as providing the background of Rom 1:4 are, Allen, "Background," 104-8; Schweizer, "Review of E. Linnemann," 276; Burger, *Jesus als Davidssohn*, 28; W. R. Kramer, *Christos, Kyrios, Gottessohn: Untersuchungen zu Gebrauch und Bedeutung der christologischen Bezeichnungen bei Paulus und den vorpaulinischen Gemeinden* (ATANT 44; Zürich: Zwingli Verlag, 1963), 106; F. Hahn, *Christologische Hoheitstitel* (Göttingen: Vandenhoeck & Ruprecht, 1964), 254; Jewett, "Romans 1:3-4," 114.

[97] This view is to be differentiated from Strauss's "two-step proof of Jesus' Davidic messiahship" (*Davidic Messiah*, p.63).

[98] Whitsett, "Son of God," 676-78. For the view that Ps 2:7 provides the background for Rom 1:4 see Allen, "Background," 104-8; Schweizer, "Review of E. Linnemann," 276; Jewett, "Romans 1:3-4," 114; Burger, *Jesus als Davidssohn*, 28; Kramer, *Christos*, 106; Hahn, *Hoheitstitel*, 254.

[99] Duling, "Promises to David," 70.

nowhere else in Paul;[100] and (3) pre-Christian Jewish messianic exegetes had long combined 2 Sam 7 and Ps 2 (4QFlor 1:10-13, 18-19; *Ps. Sol.* 17:4, 23), and the same combination occurs in Heb 1:5.

The presence of an allusion to Ps 2:7 in Rom 1:4, however, does not necessarily tell us about how the early church interpreted this psalm in relation to Jesus' divine sonship and/or his resurrection.

7.2.2.4. *Exegesis of Rom 1:3-4*

The first participial clause τοῦ γενομένου ἐκ σπέρματος Δαυὶδ "born of the seed of David"[101] is a clear assertion that Jesus was the anointed Son of David, the royal Messiah, the fulfillment of prophetic hopes long cherished among the people of Israel for the age to come.[102] In other words, it speaks about Jesus' earthly appearance in fulfillment of the Jewish messianic expectation. According to Jewish tradition stemming from 2 Sam 7:12, the Messiah was expected to come from the "seed" of David.[103] That Jesus was descended from David's line is a common assertion in the NT, including the tradition lying behind the different birth narratives of Matthew and Luke and the older formulations quoted here and in 2 Tim 2:8.[104] It follows that the clause "must have been a messianic expression from the beginning

---

[100] Whitsett, "Son of God," 676, thinks that, particularly associated with language of resurrection and divine sonship, ὁρίζειν points to Paul's allusive use of Ps 2. Cf. Allen, "Background," 104-08. Particularly in the messianic sermons in Acts, these verbs are regularly joined to the theme of Jesus' resurrection as his "appointment" (e.g., Acts 10:42). Moreover, Paul's use of προορίζειν in 1 Cor 2:7 (the only other use of either verb by Paul outside Romans) as part of an interpretation of Ps 2 increases the probability of its use here in Rom 1:4. Cf. J. Marcus, *The Way of the Lord: Christological Exegesis of the Old Testament in the Gospel of Mark* (Louisville: Westminster/John Knox, 1992), 63, also finds an allusion to Ps 2 in the "rulers of this age" of 1 Cor 2:8.

[101] The use of γενέσθαι here is synonymous with γεννᾶσθαι, but Paul does not choose the former because it better expresses Jesus' virginal conception, i.e., that Jesus "came into being" rather than "was born." So correctly, R. E. Brown and P. J. Achtemeier, eds., *Mary in the New Testament: a Collaborative Assessment by Protestant and Roman Catholic Scholars* (Philadelphia: Fortress Press, 1978), 37-38; Scott, *Adoption*, 237. Yet this does not exclude the possibility that Paul knew the virgin birth tradition, since Matthew and Luke trace Jesus' lineage through Joseph, while maintaining that Jesus was born of Virgin Mary. The use of the similar expression γενέσθαι ἐκ γυναικός in Gal 4:4 reopens the possibility that Paul presupposes Jesus was born (to God) of a particular woman (Mary).

[102] See Isa 11; Jer 23:5-6; 33:14-18; Ezek 34:23-31; 37: 24-28; *Pss. Sol.* 17:23-51; 4QFlor 1:10-13; 4QpGen 49; 4QpIsaᵃ 2:21-28; *Shemoneh Esreh* 14-15.

[103] Cf. 4QPB 4; *Pss. Sol.* 17:4; 4QFlor 1:10-13.

[104] See also Acts 2:30; Rev 5:5; 22:16 and regularly in Mt (1:1; 9:27; 12:23; 15:22; 20:30-31; 21:9, 15).

– for a statement that Jesus was simply a man descended from David is too banal to have formed part of a confessional formula."[105]

The second participial clause contains an unusual number of elements the interpretation of which is disputed. There is not much doubt that the Greek verb ὁρισθέντος should be taken to mean "appointed" rather than "declared" or "shown to be," since no clear example of its use in the latter sense either earlier than, or contemporary with, the NT has been adduced. This led some scholars to claim that the use of this verb here supports the adoptionistic view. However, although Paul retained the verb when he make use of the ancient formula here, he himself does not understand this verb in this way.[106] The second clause does not stand, as most scholars assume,[107] in antithetical parallelism to the first, but rather in climactic or progressive parallelism. While the first clause describes the Son by reference to his human birth, singling out for special mention the relationship to David, the second clause describes Jesus by reference to another event, namely, his resurrection, though in this case the event itself as such is specified not by the verb but by a dependent phrase ἐξ ἀναστάσεως νεκρῶν. It is also significant that all the NT quotations and allusions to Ps 2:7 understand it as a confirmation, vindication or glorification of an already existing status (Acts 13:33; Heb 1:5; 5:5; Mk 1:11 pars.; 9:7 pars.), rather than as an adoption to sonship.

With regard to the phrase ἐν δυνάμει, it seems better to connect it with υἱοῦ θεοῦ than with the verb. In support of this it may be said that the sense which results from taking "in power" with "Son of God" accords well, while the sense which results from taking it with ὁρισθέντος, accords ill, not only with Paul's teaching elsewhere but also with the presence of "his Son" at the beginning of v.3. We understand the first part of the clause to mean "who was appointed Son-of-God-in-power," that is, in contrast with his being Son of God in apparent weakness and poverty during his earthly existence.

With regard to ἐξ ἀναστάσεως νεκρῶν, the preposition ἐξ is to be interpreted in the sense of "from the time of" or "since" rather than "on the ground of" or "because of." Jesus' resurrection was scarcely the ground of his glorification, but it was the event which was the beginning of his glorified life as Son of God in power.

As we have pointed out, the relationship between the two participial clauses is important for the understanding of Jesus' sonship in the early

---

[105] Marshall, "Divine Sonship," 145.

[106] Cf. Gal 4:4; Rom 8:3.

[107] It is often thought that the two parallel participial clauses are to be taken as directly contrasting each other: σπέρματος Δαυίδ contrasted with υἱοῦ θεοῦ, and κατὰ σάρκα in contrast with κατὰ πνεῦμα ἁγιωσύνης.

church. It is often thought that the two parallel participial clauses are to be taken as directly contrasting each other: σπέρματος Δαυὶδ contrasted with υἱοῦ θεοῦ, and κατὰ σάρκα in contrast with κατὰ πνεῦμα ἁγιωσύνης. Dunn, for example, refers to the two christological statements as "in antithetical parallelism."[108] It is true there is a measure of contrast, but "antithetical" seems to exaggerate or even distort it. Jesus' Davidic descent is not the final thing to be said about him, but neither is it to be taken here as in any way negative, as if σπέρματος Δαυὶδ were something untrue or misleading. In Rom 15:7-9 Paul positively refers to Jesus' Jewish descent and ministry-orbit, making it all part of the divine plan both for fulfilment of "promises of the fathers" and the salvation of Gentiles. Moreover, κατὰ σάρκα is best understood as a neutral reference to Jesus' birth "according to the flesh," i.e., "according to his human descent" (cf. Rom 4:1; 9:3) rather than anything particularly negative or critical.[109] Thus, the relationship between the two lines in vv.3-4 is not to be taken as antithetical, that is, to *contrast* who Jesus was and who he became at the resurrection, or between "seed of David" and "Son of God," but as climactic or progressive parallelism.[110] Read in this light, what Paul is affirming here is that the one who has always been God's Son (cf. "his Son" at the beginning of v.3), but was brought by his human birth into a relationship with David as far as his human nature is concerned, was appointed the glorious Son-of-God-in-power from the time of his resurrection.

How then is Ps 2:7 related to Jesus' divine sonship and his resurrection in Rom 1:4? If we are correct to argue that the early church interpreted Ps 2:6 as Jesus' exaltation to the right hand of God in the light of an

---

[108] Dunn, *Romans*, 5, 12, for example, refers to the two christological statements as "in antithetical parallelism," but he does express caution about "interpreting the formula itself in a rigidly antithetical way . . ." (p.23).

[109] The closest parallel to here is in 9:5. So correctly C. E. B. Cranfield, *A Critical and Exegetical Commentary on the Epistle to the Romans* (ICC; Edinburgh: T & T Clark, 1982), 1.59; Brown and Achtemeier, *Mary*, 35-36; Wengst, *Formeln*, 113; Wanamaker, *Son*, 97-98; *contra* Dunn, *Romans*, 13, who suggests that "Paul read the formula he quotes here with at least some negative connotation attaching to κατὰ σάρκα: that so far as Jesus' role in God's saving purpose through the gospel was concerned, Jesus' physical descent, however integral to that role, was not so decisive as his status κατὰ πνεῦμα." The emphasis on the human descent of Jesus in Rom 1:3, however, is in accord with the Jewish messianic expectation.

[110] So L. W. Hurtado, "Jesus' Divine Sonship in Paul's Epistle to the Romans" in *Romans and the People of God* (eds. N. T. Wright *et al.*; Grand Rapids: Eerdmans, 1999), 227, who notes that "had Paul intended the two lines to be antithetical, we should have expected the particle *de*, which usually implies contrast" (e.g., Rom 8:5-6, 9, 13); Scott, *Adoption*, 239-42; Linnemann, "Röm. 1,3 f.," 275 n.31, who speaks of "rhetorical parallelism."

understanding of Mt. Zion as the heavenly Jerusalem, then the allusion to
Ps 2:7 here would provide the earliest evidence that the early church saw
Jesus' resurrection as the decisive moment that his divine sonship was
fully demonstrated in the light of Ps 2:6 (in a similar line of thought as in
Acts 13:33). The pre-Pauline formula in Rom 1:3-4, as it is endorsed by
Paul, thus speaks about the two stages in the same person's (Jesus')
existence: the first clause describes Jesus as the promised Davidic Messiah
during his earthly life, while the second one speaks about Jesus as the
heavenly Son of God, who is now exalted and enthroned at the right hand
of God. If the words ἐν δυνάμει belong to the original formula, as we
think, the second clause clearly refers to his heavenly reign as the
enthroned Son of God.[111] As we have seen, ὁρισθέντος means "appointed"
or "designated" (cf. Acts 10:42; 17:31) rather than simply "declared," but
if the original formula has already referred to the Son-of-God-in-power, it
cannot have meant that the one who was David's descendant during his
earthly life only became Son of God when he was raised from the dead.[112]

Our answer to those who insist that Paul added the phrase words ἐν
δυνάμει in order to bring the original formula in line with his conviction
that Jesus was God's Son from the beginning (cf. vv.1-3 εὐαγγέλιον θεοῦ
... περὶ τοῦ υἱοῦ αὐτοῦ)[113] would be that already in the tradition before
Paul the designation "Son of God" was connected not only with the texts
concerning David, but also with a pre-Pauline "sending" formula (cf. Gal
4:4; Rom 8:3-4; Jn 3:16, 17; 1 Jn 4:9; cf. Mk 12:1-9).[114] This evidence
suggests that the conviction about Jesus as God's Son "in power"
developed early and not just when Paul incorporated an ancient formula in
his letter to the Romans.

The traditional background for Rom 1:3-4 does not merely lie in a
Jewish messianic juxtaposition of 2 Sam 7:12-14 and Ps 2:7 but in the
early Christian exegesis of Ps 110:1 and Ps 2:7 – perhaps two most
significant messianic and/or christological psalms in the NT – through
which Jesus' divine sonship saw its scriptural confirmation. Rom 1:3-4 is
neither about "the Messiah from the "seed" (σπέρμα) of David . . . [being]

---

[111] So M. de Jonge, "Jesus, Son of David and Son of God" in *Intertextuality in
Biblical Writings: Essays in Honour of Bas van Iersel* (ed. S. Draisma; Kampen: J. H.
Kok, 1989), 102-3.

[112] Against adoptionistic christology Marshall, "Divine Sonship," 145 writes that
"there is no Jewish evidence which would lead us to suppose that the early Church could
have conceived of the Messiah as being adopted by God at some stage after the
completion of his earthly work." For a fuller argumentation against an adoptionistic
view, with relevant bibliographies, see Scott, *Adoption*, 234-36.

[113] See Whitsett, "Son of God," 674-75, for an attempt to link περὶ τοῦ υἱοῦ αὐτοῦ.
with ἐν γραφαῖς ἁγίαις.

[114] See further in Ch.8.

adopted as Son of God," nor about "two aspects . . . of Jesus' messiahship."[115] The two balanced clauses are not merely a twofold formulation about Jesus' messiahship but a climactic parallelism about Jesus, both the Davidic Messiah and the heavenly Son of God, whose root lies most probably in the early Christian exegesis of Ps 110:1 and Ps 2:7 in the light of their reinterpretation of Jesus' self-consciousness of divine sonship.[116]

We thus come to the conclusion that Rom 1:3-4 is a confessional formula dealing with the two stages of the same person's career. Jesus is Son of David and Son of God all along. His being υἱοῦ θεοῦ ἐν δυνάμει became fully manifested by being raised from the dead. The "decree" (ὁρισθέντος) of Yahweh declaring the messiah as his Son was understood by the earliest Christians as a prophecy about Jesus' divine sonship fulfilled ἐξ ἀναστάσεως νεκρῶν. Thus, the first clause is to be understood as a statement about Jesus as the earthly messiah and the second as a statement about him as the Son of God enthroned at his right hand.

7.2.3. Psalm 2:7 in Heb 1:5 and 5:5

In the letter to the Hebrews, Ps 2:7 is explicitly quoted twice. One is in the context of asserting Jesus' superiority over the angels as the Son (1:5) and the other is in the context of showing Jesus' superiority over Aaron as the great High Priest (5:5).

In the opening chapter of Hebrews, Ps 2:7 is cited as the first in the series of scriptural quotations. Having declared that the exalted Son received a more excellent name than the angels (v.4), the writer identifies that name as υἱός (v.5). Here he quotes both Ps 2:7 and 2 Sam 7:14 from the LXX. Both texts were familiar messianic texts that had already been brought together in early Jewish tradition. By joining these two texts the writer provides strong biblical support for the assertion that the position of the angels is subordinate to the status of the Son. The writer declares at the same time that Jesus alone enjoys the unique relationship with the Father which finds its expression in the designation "my Son."[117]

---

[115] Cf. Scott, *Adoption*, 241-42; and Whitsett, "Son of God," 681.

[116] Marshall, "Development," 158: it "is most plausibly understood as a statement about the nature of Jesus. . . . An ontological understanding of the person of Jesus is surely implicit here." Similarly, Bock, *Proclamation*, 247-48.

[117] Thus, the messianic application of Ps 2:7 to Jesus was not a radical break with Jewish exegetical tradition, but rather a natural continuation of a process which had already begun in pre-Christian Judaism. Cf. 4QFlor 1:10-13, 18-19; Goldsmith, "Acts 13," 321-23.

7.2.3.1. Adoptionist Christology?

Scholarly opinions are sharply divided on the issue of Hebrews' christology. While some maintain that Jesus is portrayed as a heavenly being throughout,[118] others contend that he is seen as essentially human who became "son by appointment" (1:2).[119]

Those who argue for the latter view often link the writer's designation of Jesus as Son in Hebrews 1 to the earthly Jesus who was later exalted by God to his right hand to become his Son. G. B. Caird, for example, argued that our writer "does not begin with a reference to the eternal Son," but "begins with a contrast between what God has said in the past through the prophets and what he has now, in these last days, said through Jesus."[120] L. D. Hurst supported his teacher's view in the following terms: (1) v.2 is mainly about the historical Jesus, and "in the last days" clearly points to the work of the Jesus of history and not of the pre-existent Logos; (2) the Son is said to have been *appointed* "heir of all things" (v.2b), to have *become* "greater than the angels" (v.4), and to have *inherited* "a name more excellent than theirs" (v.4); (3) the opening paragraph ends with a reference again to the work of the historical Jesus: "purification for sins" (v.3c).[121]

Furthermore, according to these scholars, the evidence that the psalm verse is explicitly cited in the context of Jesus' resurrection and/or exaltation, while it is only alluded to in the account of his baptism suggests that the former context was probably the most primitive, and such an application of the psalm should be regarded as the one originally intended in the compilation of the scriptural catena in vv.5-13.

7.2.3.2. Christology of the Exordium

The first four verses consist of one long, well elaborated sentence with alliteration and rhythm that encapsulates many of the key themes that will

---

[118] E. F. Scott, *The Epistle to the Hebrews: Its Doctrine and Significance* (Edinburgh: T & T Clark, 1922), 152.

[119] Cf. Dunn, *Christology*, 52-56. G. B. Caird, "Son by Appointment" in *The New Testament Age* (ed. W. C. Weinrich; Macon: Mercer U.P., 1984), 73-81; L. D. Hurst, "The Christology of Hebrews 1 and 2" in *The Glory of Christ in the New Testament: Studies in Christology* (eds. L. D. Hurst et al.; Oxford: Clarendon, 1987), 151-64; J. A. T. Robinson, *The Human Face of God* (London: SCM, 1972), 156.

[120] Caird, "Son by Appointment," 74. Cf. Dunn, *Christology*, 52-56; Hurst, "Christology of Hebrews," 151-64; Robinson, *Human Face*, 156.

[121] Hurst, "Christology of Hebrews," 155-56.

develop in the following chapters.[122] The literary structure of the exordium can be divided into three carefully balanced segments:[123]

(1) The first segment (vv.1-2) contrasts the former and final addresses by God (vv.1-2a), with two relative clauses specifying two important characteristics of the Son (v.2bc).

(2) The second (v.3) contrasts between eschatological and protological aspects of the Son's activity, with two assertions about the Son's role in creation (v.3ab) and then reference to his salvific work and exaltation.

(3) The final segment (v.4) draws an inference from the exalted status of the Son in two balanced clauses.

God's final address comes not through prophets (ἐν τοῖς προφήταις) but "through a Son" (ἐν υἱῷ). The anarthrous use of υἱός does not imply that there are many sons whom God could have chosen as agents of revelation, but it rather emphasizes the exalted status of that final agent.[124] The affirmation that God ἔθηκεν the Son "heir of all things" (κληρονόμον πάντων) introduces the theme of inheritance that will also conclude the exordium. In the affirmation that the Son and heir is also the protological agent "through whom" (δι' οὗ) God created the universe, the influence of the wisdom tradition becomes more prominent. In the juxtaposition of the protological and eschatological perspectives a tension begins to emerge that will continue through the exordium and the following scriptural catena: "Christ was made heir of that which he, as God's agent, created."[125]

The language used of the Son's superiority, *become* (γενόμενος) and *inherited* (κεκλητονόμηκεν), appears somewhat odd, given the preceding remarks about the Son's primordial relationship with the Father.[126] Yet the possible implication that Christ became the Son at some point should not be pressed, for the focus, here as regularly in Hebrews, is not on the

---

[122] On the programmatic significance of the opening verses, see esp. A. Vanhoye, *Situation du Christ: Hébreux 1-2* (LD 58; Paris: Cerf, 1969), 1-117; E. Grässer, "Hebräer 1,1-4: ein exegetischer Versuch" *EKKNTV* 3 (1971), 55-91; and W. R. G. Loader, *Sohn und Hoherpriester: eine traditionsgeschichtliche Untersuchung zur Christologie des Hebraerbriefes* (WMANT 53; Neukirchen-Vluyn: Neukirchener Verlag, 1981), 68-80.

[123] See H. W. Attridge, *The Epistle to the Hebrews: a Commentary on the Epistle to the Hebrews* (Hermeneia; Philadelphia: Fortress, 1989), 36.

[124] For a similar use of υἱός without a definite article, see 1:5; 3:6; 5:8; and 7:28.

[125] Attridge, *Hebrews*, 41.

[126] J. P. Meier, "Structure and Theology in Heb 1.1-14" *Bib* 66 (1985), 168-89, particularly emphasizes that the passage is in the form of a ring and makes too much of the fact that the hymn begins with an eschatological word about the Son. However, our author views both the person and work of Christ from the eschatological perspective throughout the letter, and even protology is seen in the light of eschatology.

inauguration of Christ's new status, but on his superiority.[127] Moreover, the nuance of the perfect tense in κεκληρονόμηκεν is that he is already in possession of that special *name*. That this unspecified name refers to "Son" can be clearly seen from the emphatic introduction of the title in v.2 and the focus of the first quotation of the following scriptural catena (Ps 2:7).

7.2.3.3. Function of Psalm 2:7 in Hebrews

We have seen that the exordium clearly speaks about Christ in terms of his eternal sonship and primordial significance. However, the function of Ps 2:7 in the scriptural catena in Heb 1:5-13 is often thought to stand in tension with such a high christology and the language of the psalm about Christ *becoming* Son. Since the patristic period, the apparent tension has led interpreters to variously assign the decisive moment of Christ *becoming* Son either at the creation or some event at the beginning,[128] at his incarnation,[129] at his baptism,[130] at his exaltation,[131] or even timeless?[132]

Assigning the moment of becoming Son to Christ's exaltation seems to fit in well with the original function of the scriptural catena and the emphasis on the exaltation motif of the letter, but this view has also difficulty with later passages which speak of Jesus as the Son during his earthly life (cf. 5:8, also 2:11-13). To deal with this difficulty and the apparent tension between the catena and the exordium a number of different solutions have been proposed.

---

[127] Attridge, *Hebrews*, 47.

[128] So some patristic interpreters such as Origen *In. Joh.* 1.1, and Augustine *In Ps. 2.7,* as well as modern commentators such as E. Ménégoz, *La théologie de l'Épitre aux Hébreux* (Paris: Fischbacher, 1894), 82; O. Michel, *Der Brief an die Hebräer* (Göttingen: Vandenhoeck & Ruprecht, 1949), 110.

[129] So most patristic interpreters; and E. Riggenbach, *Der Brief an die Hebraer* (Leipzig: A. Deichert, 1913), 18-19, who also sees the baptism as a possibility; also C. Spicq, *L'Épître aux Hébreux* (EBib; Paris: Gabalda, 1953), 2.16.

[130] So H. Strathmann, *Der Brief an die Hebräer* (NTD 9; Göttingen: Vandenhoeck & Ruprecht, 1963), 77.

[131] Most recent commentators favour this option. See F. Büchsel, *Die Christologie des Hebräerbriefs* (BFCT 27.2; Gütersloh: Bertelsmann, 1922), 7; E. Käsemann, *The Wandering People of God: an Investigation of the Letter to the Hebrews* (Minneapolis: Augsburg Pub. House, 1984), 97-98; F. J. Schierse, *Verheissung und Heilsvollendung: zur theologischen Grundfrage des Hebräerbriefes* (München: Karl Zink, 1955), 95; Vanhoye, *Situation*, 139; D. Peterson, *Hebrews and Perfection: an Examination of the Concept of Perfection in the Epistle to the Hebrews* (SNTSMS 47; Cambridge: CUP, 1982), 85.

[132] R. M. Wilson, *Hebrews* (NCBC; Grand Rapids: Eerdmans, 1987), 38; J. Moffatt, *A Critical and Exegetical Commentary on the Epistle to the Hebrews* (ICC 40; Edinburgh: T & T Clark, 1924).

Those who contend that Jesus became Son at some point (e.g., resurrection/ exaltation) have maintained that, while the term "Son" is applied to Jesus at the point of his exaltation, it is used proleptically in other contexts. Thus, the use of the term to the pre-existent or incarnate Christ should be understood to mean "he who will become son."[133] Other commentators insisted that since no reconciliation is offered in the text we should not attempt to provide one but let two very different traditions stand together unreconciled.[134] Still others suggested that the solution lies in understanding the language of Ps 2:7 ("today") in a metaphorical or allegorical sense to mean the eternal sonship of Christ, and to recognize that the author may be operating basically with the pre-existence christology of the exordium.[135]

The most plausible solution to the problem is, however, to reconcile the two christological perspectives while recognizing the primary focus on the exaltation.[136] According to this view, the author understands the word "today" in the quotation as the day when Jesus was vested with his royal dignity as Son of God, the occasion of his exaltation and enthronement.[137] This view, as we have seen, is consistent with Rom 1:4, where the second participial clause "designated Son of God in power . . . by the resurrection from the dead" has reference to that "particular event in the history of the Son of God incarnate by which he was *instated* in a position of sovereignty and invested with power, an event which in respect of investiture with power surpassed everything that could previously be ascribed to him in his incarnate state."[138] A conscious attempt to associate the divine acclamation of Christ as God's Son (Ps 2:7) with the divine acclamation of him as high priest (Ps 110:4) in the psalm quotations in Heb 5:5-6 strongly suggests that both are referring to the same occasion. However, it needs to be

---

[133] This reconciliation of Käsemann, *Wandering People*, 99, finds numerous echoes in subsequent literature. See Grässer, "Hebräer 1,1-4," 81; and J. W. Thompson, *The Beginnings of Christian Philosophy: the Epistle to the Hebrews* (CBQMS 13; Washington: Catholic Biblical Association of America, 1982), 131.

[134] Cf. H. L. MacNeill, *The Christology of the Epistle to the Hebrews: Including its Relation to the Developing Christology of the Primitive Church* (Chicago: University of Chicago Press, 1914); Büchsel, *Christologie des Hebräerbriefs*, 7-9; and Dunn, *Christology*, 53; Attridge, *Hebrews*, 54-55, who points out a similar phenomenon in Philo, who often leaves different, and sometimes contradictory, exegetical traditions without any attempt to reconcile them, and similar combinations in the *Parables of Enoch* (48:2 and 71:14-17) and in Paul (Rom 1:3 and 1 Cor 8:6).

[135] A parallel is found in Philo, who often interprets temporal language about God as a reference to God's unchanging eternal being.

[136] Cf. F. F. Bruce, *The Epistle to the Hebrews* (NICNT; Grand Rapids: Eerdmans, 1990), 54; and Peterson, *Hebrews and Perfection*, 85; Lövestam, *Son*, 27-37.

[137] Bruce, *Hebrews*, 54.

[138] J. Murray, *The Epistle to the Romans* (NICNT; Gran Rapids: Eerdmans, 1968), 10.

emphasized that this solution does not undermine Jesus' eternal sonship at all. On the contrary, it indicates that the precise relationship of Jesus' exaltation and his divine sonship is that of a confirmation of his existing position and status, rather than conferral of a new status. As F. F. Bruce puts it:

he who was the Son of God from everlasting entered into the full exercise of all the prerogatives implied by his Sonship when, after his suffering had proved the completeness of his obedience, he was raised to the Father's right hand.[139]

The main focus of the scriptural exposition in Heb 1:4-2:9 is to emphasize Jesus' supremacy over the angels, and the first two texts quoted at the beginning of the catena (Ps 2:7 and 2 Sam 7:14) provide a scriptural validation of the title "Son" used in the exordium. As we have seen in the previous chapter (§6.2.4.5), the status of Jesus during his earthly life is stated in 2:9 with the aid of Ps 8:6, where our author interprets the two members of the synonymous parallelism of the psalm as representing two stages in the life of Jesus: after his temporary abasement, Jesus is exalted and glorified. Such an understanding of the parallelism with his conscious omission of the first line of the following parallelism (Ps 8:7a) produces a distinctly confessional understanding of the quotation and supports our author's understanding of the eternal sonship of Jesus.

Our discussion of both the exordium and the scriptural catena in Hebrews suggests that the arguments put forward for an adoptionist christology (e.g., that Jesus *became* Son at his resurrection and/or exaltation) in Hebrews are hardly convincing. Such a conclusion is also corroborated by a number of other observations.

First, it is important to point out that, when Jesus is said to have "inherited" the name of Son in v.4, it does not mean that the name was not his before his exaltation. That the name of "Son" belonged to him during his earthly life is clear from Heb 5:8: "Son though he was, he learned obedience by what he suffered." Even it belonged to him ages before his incarnation as it is implied in 1:2. He inherits the title "Son," as he inherits all things (v.2), by the Father's eternal appointment.[140]

Second, the clause δι' οὗ καὶ ἐποίησεν τοὺς αἰῶνας (v.2c) is consistent with other statements in the NT about Jesus' pre-existence (cf. Jn 1:3; Col 1:16), which can be traced back to the language of a primitive Christian hymn describing him as the Father's agent in the work of creation.[141]

---

[139] Bruce, *Hebrews*, 54. Also P. Ellingworth, *The Epistle to the Hebrews: a Commentary on the Greek Text* (NIGTC; Grand Rapids: Eerdmans, 1993), 113.

[140] Bruce, *Hebrews*, 50-51.

[141] Cf. E. Percy, *Probleme der Kolosser- und Epheserbriefe* (Lund, 1946), 38-39.

Third, many scholars today recognize a divine Wisdom christology in Heb 1:2b-3.[142] Although the writer never speaks of Jesus as "the Wisdom of God," there is strong justification for detecting a divine Wisdom christology here. The writer introduces Jesus as the divine Son (1:2), but his functions belong to the divine Wisdom: he is the mediator of revelation, the agent and sustainer of creation, and the reconciler of human beings to God (1:2b-3). Moreover, the writer makes use of rare and unusual vocabulary in a single statement to describe the relationship of the Son to God: "he is the radiance of the divine glory (ἀπαύγασμα τῆς δόξης) and an exact representation of the divine nature (χαρακτὴρ τῆς ὑποστάσεως)."[143]

Fourth, in Heb 5 Jesus is clearly seen as God's Son during his earthly existence. The references to ἐν ταῖς ἡμέραις τῆς σαρκὸς αὐτοῦ (v.7) – an expression which emphasizes the conditions of human weakness of which he partook during his earthly existence – and to καίπερ ὢν υἱός[144] (v.8) meaning "Son though he was" strongly suggests that Jesus, being already God's Son, performed the role of a priest during his earthly life as he does now as the heavenly priest.

7.2.3.4. Conclusion

Although the proclamation of Jesus' divine sonship from Ps 2:7 in Heb 1:5 and 5:5 points to Jesus' exaltation, this occasion is seen as the day when Jesus was vested with his royal dignity as Son of God. As we have seen above, the precise relationship of Jesus' exaltation to his divine sonship is that of confirmation of his existing position and status, rather than conferral of a new status. While Hebrews does not help us to get back to an

---

[142] F. F. Bruce, *Commentary on the Epistle to the Hebrews: the English Text With Introduction, Exposition and Notes* (London: Marshall, Morgan & Scott, 1974), 4-6; and many others.

[143] W. L. Lane, "Detecting Divine Wisdom Christology in Hebrews 1:1-4" *New Testament Student* 5 (1982), 151-53, disagreeing with Spicq, *Hébreux*, 1.49, contends that "the writer borrowed a word employed in the Septuagint to describe the relationship between Wisdom and the eternal, divine light, and used it, not because of its associations in the context from which he took it, but simply because it seemed to him an appropriate word to express the relationship which he believed existed between the Father and the Son." Cf. R. Williamson, *Philo and the Epistle to the Hebrews* (Leiden: Brill, 1970), 36-41.

[144] This expression is commonly translated "though he was a son" because of the absence of the definite article before the substantive "Son." However, it should be rendered as "Son though he was," if we were to bring out the full force of the clause. So Bruce, *Hebrews*, 130.

earlier usage of Ps 2:7, at least it does not suggest that there was an earlier usage which was different from the writer's use.

7.2.4. Psalm 2:7 in Mk 1:11

In Chapter 4 we have already discussed the baptismal narrative in connection with Jesus' self-consciousness of divine sonship (§4.3.6). There we have argued that (1) the evidence for the authenticity of the baptismal narrative, including the theophany, is strong; and (2) Jesus was conscious of a unique personal relationship to God as his Father.

At this point, we only need to draw out some further implications for the place of Ps 2:7 within the development of the early christology. If, as we have seen, the baptismal theophany, including the divine voice from heaven, is likely to be an authentic representation of what happened rather than a creative reconstruction by the early church,[145] the subsequent interpretations of Ps 2:7 in the NT too were probably based on Jesus' relating of this experience to his disciples. And if this is the case, the possible link between the theophany experienced by Jesus at his baptism and his self-consciousness of divine sonship cannot be undermined.[146] That is, the baptismal voice preserved in Mk 1:11 not only provides an important piece of historical evidence that Jesus probably had a special experience which led to an increase in, if not a confirmation of, his self-awareness of his sonship during his baptism, but it also suggests that this baptismal experience of Jesus lies behind, or prompts to, the subsequent use of this messianic text by early Christians. Ps 2:7 is therefore to be viewed as one of the most important texts for the early Christian understanding of Jesus as the Son of God and the subsequent use of it in the early church.

7.2.5. Conclusion

Our discussion of the use of Ps 2:7 in the NT leads us to the following conclusions.

First, we proposed that there was probably an early Christian interpretation of Ps 2:6 as a prophecy about Jesus' exaltation in the light of

---

[145] It has been variously argued that the early church created the tradition with an apologetic purpose of dealing with the problems of Jesus' baptism by John or to provide a first interpretation of who Jesus was or even to set Jesus' sonship and messianic role at the beginning of his ministry. For a discussion of this topic see §4.3.6.

[146] Such reasoning compels us to place a greater deal of emphasis on Jesus' divine sonship for the development of early christology.

a widespread pre-Christian Jewish tradition about Mt. Zion as the heavenly Jerusalem.

Second, such an interpretation of Ps 2:6 helps us to understand why Ps 2:7 is often linked to the resurrection/exaltation in the NT. Once Ps 2:6 was interpreted as Jesus' exaltation, the early church began to interpret Ps 2:7 as a prophecy about Jesus' divine sonship being decisively demonstrated through his resurrection. This explains the "missing" link between Ps 2 and the resurrection/exaltation in the NT.

Third, we suggested how Ps 2:7 came to be linked both to Jesus' divine sonship and his resurrection. In the first place, it was because the early church remembered Jesus' claim to be God's Son that they applied Ps 2:7 to him. Then, a cross reading of Pss 2 and 110 together with the pre-Christian Jewish tradition of Mt. Zion as the heavenly Jerusalem, where God himself resides, led them to see Ps 2:6 as Jesus' exaltation to the right hand of God. Finally, when asked when Jesus' divine sonship was fully manifested their answer was that his divine sonship was decisively demonstrated at the resurrection. Thus, Ps 2:7 began to be understood by the early church as a prophecy about Jesus' divine sonship decisively fulfilled at his resurrection/exaltation.

Fourth, one of the most significant christological implications from the early Christian messianic exegesis of Ps 2:7 is that in God's sight Jesus was already his Son during and before his earthly existence. Early Christians saw Jesus' resurrection as confirmation of his existing position and status as God's Son and therefore the view that the early church held that Jesus *became* God's Son at the resurrection is to be abandoned.

Fifth, a widely accepted view among NT scholars is that Jesus' divine sonship was first understood merely as messianic sonship and only later was it filled with fuller content. That is, the primary factor in regarding Jesus as the Son of God was his status as the messiah. It is certainly plausible that the first Christians might have understood the messiahship itself in terms of divine sonship, but the evidence strongly suggests that it is much more likely that they drew deeper implications from Jesus' filial consciousness than a simple equation between the divine sonship and the messiahship.

7.3. Early Christian Exegesis of Ps 110:1 and Ps 2:7 and Jesus' Pre-existence

Our discussion of the early Christian exegesis of Ps 110:1 and Ps 2:7 has a very significant christological implication on the emergence of the early Christian conviction about Jesus' pre-existence.

In his *Christology in the Making* Dunn insists more than once that there would be no difficulty in believing in Jesus' exaltation without also believing in his pre-existence or at any rate, that such an asymmetry did, in fact, exist.[147] By emphasizing the familiarity of the ancient world with the translation, ascension, apotheosis or deification of an individual and that of Jewish readers with speculation regarding Moses, Elijah, and Enoch, Dunn declares categorically that "We cannot therefore assume that in the context of first-century thought the development [of pre-existence] . . . was simply the outworking of the inherent logic of the initial belief in Christ's resurrection and exaltation."[148] However, this assertion seems problematic for the following reasons.

First, if our attempt to uncover how early Christians interpreted Pss 110 and 2 in the light of Jesus' self-consciousness of divine sonship is convincing, they would most likely have discovered the powerful picture of the risen Jesus "literally" enthroned to the right hand of God as the divine Lord and the pre-existent Son of God.[149] Their cross-reference reading of these messianic psalms in the light of Jesus' self-consciousness of divine sonship and divine mission would have helped them see that Jesus is now "literally" exalted and enthroned at the right hand of God from the resurrection onwards (Ps 110:1; Ps 2:6) as opposed to a metaphorical statement of God's bestowal of honour and authority to the king. In the same way, Jesus' claim to be God's son would have been confirmed and interpreted by the early Christian exegesis of these messianic psalms as a "real" sonship as opposed to a metaphorical statement of God's care and promise of victory to the messiah/king. It is therefore highly likely that such a novel understanding of the psalms and of the risen Jesus would have led the early church to see him as divine and pre-existent Lord and Son.

Second, Dunn seems to suggest that at the least wisdom christology (embracing either ideal pre-existence or real pre-existence) is necessary for the doctrine of pre-existence to emerge in the early church and because the

---

[147] Dunn, *Christology*, 63, 163, 205, 260. For example, he asserts that "It is often assumed that the thought of Christ's pre-existence emerged as a natural and inevitable corollary to belief in Christ's exaltation" (p. 63); also "where it was taken for granted that belief in Christ's exaltation to Lordship after death would inevitably have carried with it the corollary of his pre-existence for the first Christians, there was no need to look for an explanation of this corollary in a specific Wisdom christology" (p.163).

[148] Dunn, *Christology*, 63 (his emphasis removed).

[149] Jews and early Christians no doubt envisaged the heavenly sphere in which God is in the same way as the earthly sphere, so that for them it would not be unfair to say that he *literally* sits on a throne. By contrast, when a human being (e.g., a king) is said to share God's throne, this is metaphorical language for God giving him dominion and victory.

Jews were already familiar with the translation of Moses, Elijah and Enoch the early Christian belief in Jesus' exaltation to the right hand of God was not enough for them to see him as divine and pre-existent Lord and Son. Dunn's view, however, seems to undervalue the significance of the early Christian belief in Jesus' divine sonship, a conviction based on his self-consciousness of a unique personal relationship to God as Father and confirmed by the early Christian exegesis of Ps 2:7, and his "literal" exaltation to the right hand of God for the development of early christology. First of all, we need to recognize that the translation of Moses and Elijah is something very different from Jesus' exaltation, although the description of the Son of Man/Messiah in *1 Enoch* as a pre-existent being enthroned at the right hand of God set a real precedent for Jesus' exaltation and/or enthronement and thus viewing him as pre-existent.[150] As C. F. D. Moule rightly pointed out:

A polytheist can accommodate the apotheosis of a Heracles. Can a monotheist rank Jesus in a transcendental category (very different from that of a translated Moses or Elijah) and still manage not to perceive that this must imply eternal existence?[151]

Moule's observation has great significance because it opens the door which the mainstream of recent scholarship on early christology has declared to be a blind alley.[152] Our study, however, strongly suggests that this point still stands and, to the best of our knowledge, no convincing arguments have been brought against it. As we have argued so far, the early Christian messianic exegesis of Ps 110 and Ps 2 in the light of Jesus' self-consciousness of divine sonship and divine mission led them to grasp firmly who Jesus really was. The tremendous impact left by the resurrection event and the striking picture of Jesus "literally" enthroned to God's right hand can hardly be dismissed as insignificant for the early Christian understanding of him as divine and pre-existent Lord and Son.

---

[150] See above §6.1.2.

[151] C. F. D. Moule, Review of Dunn's *Christology in the Making*, *JTS* 33 (1982), 262. C. F. D. Moule, *The Origin of Christology* (Cambridge: CUP, 1977), 139, is well aware that the majority of modern christologies have abandoned such a notion altogether.

[152] Modern discussions of the emergence of the doctrine of Jesus' pre-existence in the early church tend to think of his divinity and pre-existence as two clearly distinguishable ideas/entities. It is commonly accepted that it is because he was first seen as divine that the idea of his pre-existence arose as a subsequent development from his divinity. For those who see a correlation between Jesus' exaltation and his pre-existence see J. Knox, *The Humanity and Divinity of Christ: a Study of Pattern in Christology* (Cambridge: CUP, 1967), 11; Pannenberg, *Jesus*, 153-54; and the more carefully formulated arguments of O. Cullmann, *The Christology of the New Testament* (London: SCM, 1963), 321, and Moule, *Origin*, 135-41.

Third, our view is demanded by the early Christian devotion to Jesus which Hurtado regards as a significant mutation in the Jewish monotheistic tradition.[153] According to Hurtado, six features of the mutation can be traced back into the earliest years of Christianity: (1) hymnic practices, (2) prayer and related practices, (3) use of the name of Christ, (4) the Lord's Supper, (5) confession of faith in Jesus, and (6) prophetic pronouncements of the risen Christ.[154] With regard to the first point, there is no indication of "any awareness by Paul that the worship practices in his churches were essentially different from what was familiar among Jewish churches, including those in Palestine."[155] Concerning the prayer practices, while "early Christian prayer is characteristically directed to God 'the Father,'" we find indications that the heavenly Christ was also addressed directly in prayer (cf. Acts 7:59-60; 1:24; 2 Cor 12:2-10; prayer-like expressions such as "grace and peace," a fragment of Aramaic prayer addressed to Christ such as *maranatha*). With regard to the third point, one can point out the early Christian practice of baptism done "in the name" of Jesus and its related references to calling "upon the name" of Jesus the Lord (Acts 9:14, 21; 22:16; 1 Cor 1:2; Rom 10:13), which is apparently derived originally from OT passages that refer to calling "upon the Lord [Yahweh]."[156]

Fourth, although we have dismissed the theory about the concept of a pre-existent messiah in Second Temple Judaism advanced by Horbury and Schaper as too speculative (§3.2), we have left open the possibility that, in view of the peculiar translation in the LXX, Ps 110:3 could still be understood by early Christians as pointing to Christ's pre-existence. While this possibility cannot be proved or disproved due to the lack of evidence of such an interpretation before second century AD, a cross-reference reading of Pss 110 and 2 would have encouraged Christian exegetes to read Ps 110:3 as a reference to the Messiah's supernatural origin and hence Jesus' pre-existence. However, the absence of any reference to this verse in that direction in the NT cannot be brought against this possibility, for its applicability as a reference to Christ's pre-existence might well have been soon superseded by other types of language, such as "God *sent* his Son" or simply by the pictorial expression of Jesus as God's Son being enthroned

---

[153] See L. W. Hurtado, *One God, One Lord: Early Christian Devotion and Ancient Jewish Monotheism* (London: SCM, 1988, 1998); R. Bauckham, "The Worship of Jesus in Apocalyptic Christianity" *NTS* 27 (1981), 322-41.

[154] Hurtado, *One God*, 100-14. Cf. D. E. Aune, *The Cultic Setting of Realized Eschatology in Early Christianity* (NovTSup 28; Leiden: Brill, 1972), 5: "Perhaps the single most important historical development within the early church was the rise of the cultic worship of the exalted Jesus within the primitive Palestinian church."

[155] Hurtado, *One God*, 102.

[156] Cf. C. J. Davis, *The Name and Way of the Lord: Old Testament Themes, New Testament Christology* (JSOTSS 129; Sheffield: Sheffield Academic Press, 1996).

at the right hand of God. At any rate, if Ps 110:3 was understood as pointing to Jesus' pre-existence, it would provide further support for our view.

Fifth, it is also significant that Paul, the writer of Hebrews and John show their awareness of Jesus' pre-existence. The identity of Jesus as God's Son is taken for granted throughout Paul's letters and it exists alongside the use of *Kyrios* and the attribution of divine functions to Jesus.[157] It must therefore have been widely present in the early church. In the case of Luke-Acts, while the idea of Jesus' pre-existence does not arise explicitly in Acts 13:33ff. nor in Acts as a whole, it does not preclude that Luke was aware of it or that it was compatible with his christology. His account of Jesus' birth with his conception by the Holy Spirit (Lk 1-2) certainly suggests it. Moreover, Luke's main concern in writing Acts was to give an account of the birth of Christianity, which, from the eschatological perspective, begins with God sending Jesus as the messiah.

Against Dunn's view, therefore, the foregoing arguments strongly suggest that the early Christian exegesis of Ps 110:1 and Ps 2 in the light of Jesus' self-consciousness of divine sonship and divine mission led them to see Jesus as the pre-existent Lord and Son of God enthroned to his right hand.

A final comment needs to be made here. Those who have been following our discussion of the early Christian exegesis of Ps 110:1 and Ps 2:7 might be asking the question whether we can locate this early Christian exegetical activity to a specific individual, location or date. The fragmentariness of the evidence, however, makes such an attempt too speculative, if not impossible. Since our evidence comes from various sources almost throughout the NT (e.g., Paul, Acts, Hebrews, Gospels, etc.), it is difficult to assign this exegetical activity to a particular individual or place. Nevertheless, we suggest that those responsible for this exegesis should probably be identified as pre-Pauline Christians, since the use of Ps 110:1 and Ps 2:7 can be traced back to pre-Pauline confession-like formulas such as Rom 8:34 and 1:3-4. Paul presupposes that his allusions and quotations to Ps 110:1 in Rom 8:34 and 1 Cor 15:25-27 will be immediately understood by Christians in Rome. Moreover, there is strong evidence that in Rom 1:3-4 Paul uses a fragment of an early Christian confession.

---

[157] See further in the next chapter.

Chapter 8

"God Sent His Son"

Now one task remains to be done. In our detailed investigation into Jewish wisdom language in the OT and Second Temple Judaism (§2.2) we came to the conclusion that wisdom language was used as no more than a literary personification of God's presence and action for his people in this world without compromising his transcendence and uniqueness. We also concluded that personified Wisdom was not a ready-made category of pre-existence into which Jesus could be placed by early Christians in their understanding of him as a pre-existent being. However, such conclusions do not necessarily preclude the possibility that Jewish wisdom speculations might have exercised – in one way or the other – influence upon the early Christian understanding of Jesus. On the contrary, the majority of scholars today maintain that the Jewish wisdom tradition has exerted great influence upon the thinking of early Christians, as evidenced by the pre-Pauline "sending" formula, and in particular upon the Apostle Paul. It is commonly supposed that the pre-Pauline 'sending' formula, "God sent his Son" (Gal 4:4-5; Rom 8:3-4; Jn 3:17; 1 Jn 4:9), was developed on the basis of a divine wisdom christology. If this were the case, it would be a serious objection to our view that the earliest christology was a christology of divine sonship. In this chapter we will endeavour to argue that the sending formula is in fact rooted in the pre-existent Son christology developed from the early Christian exegesis of messianic psalms (Ps110:1 and Ps 2:7) in the light of Jesus' self-consciousness of divine sonship and divine mission.

In the first part of the chapter we will attempt to argue that, contrary to the current tendency in NT scholarship, Paul's wisdom christology is neither so pervasive in his writings nor is it so clearly attested in some of those traditional wisdom texts. We will concentrate on those passages where Paul's wisdom christology is often argued or assumed by scholars. Once the presence of Paul's wisdom christology is rejected in these passages, we will propose a more plausible alternative for the emergence of Jesus' pre-existence in Paul's christology.

8.1. Wisdom Christology in Paul

In what follows we will attempt to show that wisdom christology was not so pervasive in Paul's theology as some scholars have argued for or simply assumed. In other words, wisdom christology was not yet fully developed in Paul. In order to assess the degree of its pervasiveness in Paul's thinking, we will examine some of the texts invoked for wisdom christology.

8.1.1. 1 Cor 1:24, 30

It is true that in 1 Cor 1:24, 30 Christ is clearly and explicitly linked with θεοῦ σοφία and σοφία ἀπὸ θεοῦ. Such a link between Christ and wisdom has prompted some scholars to argue for wisdom christology behind these statements. As we have seen in our survey, however, what Paul would have meant with these statements is far from clear. Although the majority of scholars today seem to agree at least that Paul's first Corinthian correspondence should be interpreted in terms of Jewish wisdom theology rather than a Gnostic background of Paul's opponents, the nature of the conflict and divisions in the Corinthian church is still much debated.[1] Moreover, while the problem of the divisions in Corinth is closely related to the issue of wisdom and folly in 1 Cor 1-4, the complex question of whether or to what extent Paul took up – or was influenced by – the terminology of his opponents, and if so how much he modified the meaning of their key terms is still much debated.[2] Although there is still much uncertainty regarding the term and concept of σοφία,[3] scholars seem to agree that σοφία in 1 Cor 1-4 is not to be understood as a pre-existent

---

[1] The amount of discussion of the wisdom content of 1 Cor 1-4 among scholars since Conzelmann's article in 1965 has been overwhelming. H. Conzelmann, "Paulus und die Weisheit" *NTS* 12 (1965-1966), 231-44. For a list of the secondary literature on the related topic, see B. Witherington, *Jesus the Sage: the Pilgrimage of Wisdom* (Minneapolis: Fortress, 1994), 299 n.12.

[2] Cf. J. M. Reese, "Paul Proclaims the Wisdom of the Cross: Scandal and Foolishness" *BTB* 9 (1979), 149.

[3] Scholars interpret the term σοφία (1) on the basis of the Greek philosophical tradition; (2) as esoteric truth revealed in the utterances of the pneumatics; or (3) as related to Jewish wisdom speculation. Cf. E. Best, "The Power and the Wisdom of God: 1 Corinthians 1:18-25" in *Paolo a una chiesa divisa* (ed. L. de Lorenzi; Roma: Abbazia, 1980), 19-22. Regarding the term σοφία λόγου (1:17) see R. A. Horsley, "Wisdom of Word and Words of Wisdom in Corinth" *CBQ* 39 (1977), 224-39; U. Wilckens, "Das Kreuz Christi als die Tiefe der Weisheit Gottes: zu 1. Kor 2,1-16" in *Paolo a una chiesa divisa* (ed. L. de Lorenzi; Roma: Abbazia, 1980), 59-67.

divine being or divine hypostasis.[4] However, many scholars still today
acknowledge that in these statements Jesus is credited with the function of
salvation which the Jewish wisdom tradition ascribed to wisdom.[5]

However, the suggestion for Paul's wisdom christology in these
statements is far from persuasive. It is important to realize that the
statements in vv. 24 and 30 are soteriological statements, rather than
christological statements. In v.24 Paul is concerned not so much their [on
the Corinthians] being able to *perceive* the cross as wisdom (that will be
explained in 2:6-16), but on the actual *effective work* of the cross in the
world."[6] Paul "is not using philosophical categories, nor is he personifying
wisdom in Christ; rather, this is an evangelical statement . . . . Christ is the
'wisdom of God' precisely because he is 'the power of God for the
salvation of everyone who believes.'"[7] After all, the statement begins with
Χριστὸν θεοῦ δύναμιν, in direct response to the quest of the Jews in vv.22-
23. If it were a christological statement, one may as well argue for a
personified dynamis christology behind this statement.

Likewise, when Paul says that Christ ἐγενήθη σοφία ἡμῖν ἀπὸ θεοῦ
("was made [or became] our Wisdom from God"), he is not referring
Christ as God's pre-existent Wisdom. Rather, Paul's point is
soteriological. Paul wishes to explain that as the result of Christ's death on
the cross, all human wisdom is of no use and only God's wisdom as
expressed and embodied in the crucified Christ has the power to save. We
can therefore safely conclude that the view that in 1 Cor 1:24, 30 lies
Paul's wisdom christology is not so compelling.

---

[4] Cf. Conzelmann, "Weisheit," 183; Best, "Power and Wisdom," 35; J. D. G. Dunn, *Christology in the Making: a New Testament Inquiry into the Origins of the Doctrine of the Incarnation* (London: SCM, 1980, 1989), 178; H. Weder, *Das Kreuz Jesu bei Paulus: ein Versuch, über den Geschichtsbezug des christlichen Glaubens nachzudenken* (FRLANT 125; Göttingen: Vandenhoeck & Ruprecht, 1981), 155 n.124. *Contra* C. A. Gieschen, *Angelomorphic Christology: Antecedents and Early Evidence* (AGAJU 42; Leiden: Brill, 1998), 332.

[5] Cf. W. D. Davies, *Paul and Rabbinic Judaism: Some Rabbinic Elements in Pauline Theology* (London: SPCK, 1948, 1970), 154-55; M. Hengel, *The Son of God: the Origin of Christology and the History of Jewish-Hellenistic Religion* (London: SCM, 1976), 74; S. Kim, *The Origin of Paul's Gospel* (WUNT 2/4; Tübingen: Mohr Siebeck, 1981), 117; C. M. Pate, *The Reverse of the Curse: Paul, Wisdom, and the Law* (WUNT 2/114; Tübingen: Mohr Siebeck, 2000), 278. While the above scholars find pre-existence in these statements, it is denied by Dunn, *Christology*, 167, 177-79. who thinks that Paul thought of the crucified Christ as the wisdom of God, "the embodiment of God's plan of salvation and the measure and fullest expression of God's continuing wisdom and power" (p.179).

[6] G. D. Fee, *The First Epistle to the Corinthians* (NICNT; Grand Rapids: Eerdmans, 1987), 77.

[7] Rom 1:16; cf. v.30 below. Fee, *1 Corinthians*, 77.

8.1.2. 1 Cor 8:6

This verse comes in the midst of an argument about food offered to idols and is one of four expressly monotheistic texts in Paul where he makes use of the traditional formula "one God."[8] Some scholars detect Jewish wisdom background to this formula. They usually point to many references of the ideas of creator and redeemer to wisdom (Wis 7:26; 8:1, 4, 7; Sir 1:4) and connections between knowledge and wisdom (Wis 7:15-17; 10:10; 15:3) in Jewish wisdom literature.[9] Witherington suggests that in this passage Paul "is reading the Shema through the later sapiential reflections on monotheism, wisdom, and idolatry . . . Paul is taking what was formerly said of God the *Father*, and *Sophia*, and now saying the same of the Father and Jesus Christ."[10]

On the other hand, the rhythmic character of the formula and its parallel statements both in Hellenism and in Hellenistic Judaism[11] led some

---

[8] Cf. Gal 3:20; Rom 3:29-30; 1 Tim 2:5 and the thorough discussion of these texts (excepting 1 Tim 2:5) in C. H. Giblin, "Three Monotheistic Texts in Paul" *CBQ* 37 (1975), 527-47.

[9] Cf. Witherington, *Sage*, 315-16; cf. N. T. Wright, *The Climax of the Covenant: Christ and the Law in Pauline Theology* (Edinburgh: T & T Clark, 1991), 120-36; Pate, *Reverse*, 278-79.

[10] Witherington, *Sage*, 316; most scholars agree that Paul describes Christ in terms of the Jewish wisdom theology; cf. E. Schweizer, "Zur Herkunft der Präexistenzvorstellung bei Paulus" in *Neotestamentica* (Zürich: Zwingli Verlag, 1963), 106; A. Feuillet, *Le Christ, sagesse de Dieu: d'apres les épitres pauliniennes* (Paris: Lecoffre, 1966), 78-82; H. Conzelmann, *1 Corinthians: a Commentary on the First Epistle to the Corinthians* (Hermeneia; Philadelphia: Fortress, 1975); P. Stuhlmacher, "Zur paulinischen Christologie" in *Versöhnung, Gesetz und Gerechtigkeit: Aufsätze zur biblischen Theologie* (Göttingen: Vandenhoeck & Ruprecht, 1981), 213; H. Gese, "Wisdom, Son of Man, and the Origins of Christology: The Consistent Development of Biblical Theology" *HBT* 3 (1981), 46; J. M. Reese, "Christ As Wisdom Incarnate: Wise Than Solomon, Loftier Than Lady Wisdom" *BTB* 11 (1982), 45-46; cf. E. J. Schnabel, *Law and Wisdom From Ben Sira to Paul* (WUNT 2/16; Tübingen: Mohr Siebeck, 1985), 245-46: "It appears to be beyond doubt that Paul consciously describes Christ in wisdom language: Christ, as is divine wisdom in the Jewish sapiential theology, is the creative and salvational power and action of God. The description of Christ as mediator of creation which seems to be the natural consequence from his identification with wisdom implies or presupposes a pre-existence christology."

[11] In Hellenism see *Marc. Aur. Ant.* 4.23, speaking of Nature, "of you are all things, in you are all things, unto you are all things." In Hellenistic Judaism see Philo, who thinks of God as the origin of all things, which he brought into being through the Logos (*Cher.* 127: "we shall see that its [the universe's] cause is God, by whom it has come into being, . . . its instrument the word of God, through which it was framed"; cf. *Leg. All.* 3.96; *Op. Mund.* 24-25). Cf. the discussion in R. A. Horsley, "The Background of the Confessional Formula in 1 Kor. 8.6" *ZNW* 69 (1978), 130-35, who dismisses the possible Stoic influences altogether.

scholars to suggest that the statement is a pre-Pauline creedal formulation which originated from Hellenistic Jewish Christianity.[12] While the stylistic considerations discussed by Murphy-O'Connor in favour of viewing it as pre-Pauline are significant, there is no decisive evidence to prove or to disprove, as he himself admits.[13] Rather, as G. Fee suggested, it is most likely to be "a Pauline construct, created *ad hoc* in the present argument."[14] While admitting that it has a creedal ring and reflects language found elsewhere in religious texts, Fee thinks that "none of this means that it did not originate here with Paul," since the statement so thoroughly fits the present argument that makes better sense if Paul is making use of language common to Hellenistic Judaism rather than taking over an existing formula.[15] If Fee's view is correct, the question of origin or background of this allegedly pre-Pauline statement becomes irrelevant, although one cannot dismiss altogether the possibility that Paul might have reflected on wisdom language while writing this Christianized monotheistic formula.

It is important to note several remarkable features from the formula. First, the two parts of the formula are in perfect parallel. The formulae "one God" and "one Lord" are followed by the personal designations "the Father" and "Jesus Christ," in which the appellation "Son" is implied by the use of "Father" as the personal designation of God. Second, Paul picks up the language of Jesus himself, the personal image of "Father," to set forth the Christian understanding of God. As we have seen in Chapter 4, such a designation existed in early Judaism before him, but it was Jesus who expressly taught his followers to understand God in this way. Third, Paul places the work of Christ in the closest kind of relationship to God. He can assert that there is only one God and at the same time he can also assign the designation "Lord," which in the OT belongs to the one God, to the "Son." The formula is so constructed that its Trinitarian implications are hardly deniable.[16] In short, the formula is more closely connected to pre-existent Son christology than wisdom christology.

8.1.3. 1 Cor 10:4

In this verse Paul identifies the rock with Christ (ἡ πέτρα δὲ ἦν ὁ Χριστός). In this identification many commentators find the influence of

---

[12] Cf. Conzelmann, *Corinthians*, 144 n.38. See J. Murphy-O'Connor, "1 Cor. 8:6: Cosmology or Soteriology?" *RB* 85 (1978), 254-55, for an overview of different opinions on this issue.

[13] Murphy-O'Connor, "Cosmology," 254-55.

[14] Fee, *1 Corinthians*, 374.

[15] Fee, *1 Corinthians*, 374.

[16] Fee, *1 Corinthians*, 375.

Hellenistic Judaism, especially from Philo and *Wisdom of Solomon*.[17] *Wisdom* 10:17-18 and 11:4 describe σοφία as the one who guided and protected the Israelites in the wilderness who drank from the "flinty rock" (πέτρα ἀκρότομος), while Philo (*Leg. All.* 2.86; *Det* 115-8) explicitly equates ἀκρότομος πέτρα with σοφία (and λόγος). According to this view, what Paul is saying in this verse is that Christ, the Wisdom of God, provided both physical and spiritual sustenance for the wandering Israelites. The identification of Christ with Wisdom is based in part on the misunderstanding that Paul has already identified Christ with Wisdom in 1:24-30.

However, such a contact with Philo is quite unlikely.[18] The parallels between Paul and Philo are of different kind. While Philo is engaging in pure allegory, Paul is most likely making an actual claim about a historical situation.[19] According to Fee, it is far more likely that "Paul has made a simple transfer of images from the rock at Horeb to such passages as the Songs of Moses in Deut. 32 (vv.4, 15, 18, 30, 31), where the God of Israel is identified as *the* Rock, whose ways are just and perfect, yet who was rejected by them in the wilderness (see esp. vv.15, 18)."[20] The fact that the language "provoking the Lord to jealousy" and their "sacrificing to demons" in vv.16-17 of the Song are reflected by Paul in 10:21-22 makes this suggestion much more plausible. Thus, by this identification Paul is about to make a point similar to that in the Songs of Moses: that even

---

[17] Cf. R. Hamerton-Kelly, *Pre-Existence, Wisdom, and the Son of Man: a Study of the Idea of Pre-Existence in the New Testament* (SNTSMS; Cambridge: CUP, 1973), 131-32; Davies, *Paul*, 153; Schnabel, *Law*, 246-47; Hengel, *Son of God*, 15, 72-73 attributes the exegesis of 10:1-4 to non-Pauline Greek speaking Jewish Christians since it is not typically Pauline, but cf. W. P. Brown, Review of Witherington's *Jesus the Sage: the Pilgrimage of Wisdom*, *Int* 50 (1996), 318 n.91, who suggests that in view of 1 Cor 1-4 "it was Paul himself who conjured this up, especially in the light of the way he is able to handle the promise to Abraham and the Sarah and Hagar stories in Galatians 3-4." Those who take 1 Cor 10 to belong to the Corinthians' exegesis and theology generally regard 10:4b as Pauline; cf. U. Luz, *Das Geschichtsverständnis des Paulus* (BEvTh 49; München: Kaiser, 1968), 118-19; R. L. Jeske, "The Rock was Christ: the Ecclesiology of 1 Corinthians 10" in *Kirche: Festschrift für Günther Bornkamm zum 75. Geburtstag* (eds. D. Lührmann *et al.*; Tübingen: Mohr Siebeck, 1980), 246.

[18] Fee, *1 Corinthians*, 449.

[19] Witherington, *Sage*, 317; Schnabel, *Law*, 247. Both scholars point out that the combination of interesting parallels and notable differences between Paul's and his predecessors' interpretation shows that there was a common sapiential tradition that all three writers were drawing on and modifying to suit their own purposes.

[20] Fee, *1 Corinthians*, 449. Cf. A. van Roon, "The Relationship between Christ and the Wisdom of God according to Paul" *NovT* 16 (1974), 228-30, also rejects wisdom christology here; in his view, it is "a reapplication of the identification between God and the rock to Christ" by implicitly applying a divine predicate to him.

though God gave them "spiritual food," they rejected him for their idols. The identification between the rock and Christ serves to stress not only the typological character of Israel's experience (that they were being nourished in the wilderness by Christ himself), but also the continuity between Israel and the Corinthians (that the Corinthians are in danger of experiencing the same judgement).[21]

Is then the idea of Christ's pre-existence present here? The past tense of the verb in the statement ἡ πέτρα δὲ ἦν ὁ Χριστός seems significant. Dunn rejects the importance of the verb ἦν and suggests that Paul "is not talking about Christ's pre-existence here."[22] However, it is important to note the following point: when Paul identifies or interprets an element from a prior quotation or biblical allusion elsewhere he uses the present tense of εἰμί, but in each of these cases the word being interpreted is always given a contemporary application (cf. 2 Cor 3:17; Gal 4:25; Eph 4:9). The fact that Paul deliberately uses the verb in past tense "was" makes far more likely that he intended to point the reality of Christ's presence in the OT events than that he sees him there simply in a figurative way."[23] Therefore, we find more compelling the suggestion that this verse is to be understood in the light of the Songs of Moses in Deut 32 than the Hellenistic Jewish wisdom tradition.

8.1.4. Rom 10:5-8

Romans 10:5-8 is another Pauline passage commonly thought to be influenced by wisdom tradition. Here Paul is contrasting Moses with "the righteousness by faith" with a quotation taken from Deut 30:12-14. That Paul makes use of Deut 30:11-14 should not be surprising, for this passage was the subject of considerable reflection among Jews both in Palestine and in the diaspora.[24] Moreover, a literary connection between Rom 10:6-8 and Baruch 3:29-30 has been recognized by many commentators.[25]

---

[21] Fee, *1 Corinthians*, 449.

[22] J. D. G. Dunn, Baptism in the Holy Spirit: a Re-Examination of the New Testament Teaching on the Gift of the Spirit in Relation to Pentecostalism Today (SBT 2/15; London: SCM Press, 1970), 125.

[23] Fee, *1 Corinthians*, 449.

[24] Cf. J. D. G. Dunn, *Romans* (WBC 38; Dallas: Word Books, 1988), 604-5.

[25] It was first pointed out by H. Windisch, "Die göttliche Weisheit der Juden und die paulinische Christologie" in *Neutestamentliche Studien: Georg Heinrici zu seinem 70. Geburtstag* (ed. A. Deissmann; Leipzig: Hinrichs, 1914), 224, and then further developed by M. J. Suggs, "'The Word is Near You': Rom 10:6-10 within the Purpose of the Letter" in *Christian History and Interpretation: Studies Presented to John Knox* (eds. W. R. Farmer *et al.*; Cambridge: CUP, 1967), 40. Cf. also E. Käsemann, *Commentary on Romans* (London: SCM, 1980), 289 and Dunn, *Romans*, 603-9.

Deut 30:12-14	Baruch 3:29-30	Rom 10:6-8
¹² τίς ἀναβήσεται ἡμῖν εἰς τὸν οὐρανὸν καὶ	²⁹ τίς ἀνέβη εἰς τὸν οὐρανὸν καὶ	⁶ Τίς ἀναβήσεται εἰς τὸν οὐρανόν; τοῦτ' ἔστιν Χριστὸν
λήμψεται αὐτὴν ἡμῖν καὶ ἀκούσαντες αὐτὴν ποιήσομεν. ¹³ οὐδὲ πέραν τῆς θαλάσσης ἐστὶν λέγων Τίς διαπεράσει ἡμῖν εἰς τὸ πέραν τῆς θαλάσσης καὶ	ἔλαβεν αὐτὴν καὶ κατεβίβασεν αὐτὴν ἐκ τῶν νεφελῶν; ³⁰ τίς διέβη πέραν τῆς θαλάσσης καὶ	καταγαγεῖν· ⁷ ἤ, τίς καταβήσεται εἰς τὴν ἄβυσσον; τοῦτ' ἔστιν Χριστὸν ἐκ νεκρῶν ἀναγαγεῖν.
λήμψεται ἡμῖν αὐτήν καὶ ἀκουστὴν ἡμῖν ποιήσει αὐτήν καὶ ποιήσομεν	εὖρεν αὐτὴν καὶ οἴσει αὐτὴν χρυσίου ἐκλεκτοῦ	
¹⁴ ἔστιν σου ἐγγὺς τὸ ῥῆμα σφόδρα ἐν τῷ στόματί σου καὶ ἐν τῇ καρδίᾳ σου καὶ ἐν ταῖς χερσίν σου αὐτὸ ποιεῖν		⁸ ἀλλὰ τί λέγει; ἐγγύς σου τὸ ῥῆμά ἐστιν ἐν τῷ στόματί σου καὶ ἐν τῇ καρδίᾳ σου, τοῦτ' ἔστιν τὸ ῥῆμα τῆς πίστεως ὃ κηρύσσομεν.

Baruch's poem to wisdom (3:9-4:4), similar in many ways to Job 28:12-28, declares that among the nations only Israel has been given Wisdom in the form of the Torah.[26] Baruch quotes from Deut 30:12-13 to contrast human inability to find or gain Wisdom with the Creator's omniscience and provision of Torah to Jacob. While Deuteronomy passage commands Israel to hear and keep the requirement of the law, Baruch's poem claims that Israel enjoys a privileged status vis-à-vis the nations in having access to the law.[27] How then does Paul interpret the same passage in Rom 10:5-8?

As the above chart shows,[28] the parallel with Bar 3:29-30 is quite striking. Both Baruch and Paul quote Deut 30:12a almost *verbatim* and,

---

[26] See our discussion of Baruch as part of Jewish speculations about wisdom language to speak about God's presence and action in this world in §2.2.4.

[27] Suggs, "Word," 309.

[28] The chart is taken from E. E. Johnson, *The Function of Apocalyptic and Wisdom Traditions in Romans 9-11* (SBLDS 109; Atlanta: Scholars Press, 1989), 133-34.

omitting v.13a, both pick up with the second rhetorical question in Deut 30:13b. A comparison between Baruch and Paul indicates that Paul's exegesis of Deut 30:12-14 was probably influenced by Baruch's:[29] (1) Paul's interpretation (Χριστὸν καταγαγεῖν) seems to follow Baruch's alteration of καὶ κατεβίβασεν αὐτὴν ἐκ τῶν νεφελῶν for καὶ ἀκούσαντες αὐτὴν ποιήσομεν; (2) Baruch's preference for διαβαίνω to διαπεράω seems to account for Paul's use of καταβήσεται in v.7; (3) following Baruch's poem about Wisdom is the traditional promise set out at the end of Baruch's poem that life awaits those who take hold of wisdom (4:1), Paul too sets Lev 18:5 beside Deut 30:12-14 and interprets the ζήσεται of the former passage by means of the latter one. Moreover, further wisdom texts call for attention, such as Prov 30:3-4 and Sir 24:5. The indebtedness of Paul to Baruch's wisdom poem led some scholars to conclude that behind Rom 10:6-8 stands "hypostatic" wisdom christology.[30] However, such a conclusion seems to go beyond what the passage intends to convey.

As we have seen earlier, in Baruch Torah is already seen as the locus where Wisdom has manifested herself (§2.2.4). By way of parallel, Paul seems to affirm that Christ as the true embodiment of Wisdom has manifested himself or made himself available in the word of faith "that we proclaim." That is, the parallels between Baruch and Paul can be expressed as what Baruch affirmed of Wisdom as it is embodied in Torah is what Paul affirms either about Christ, or Christ as he is conveyed through the word of faith. If this is correct, the primary meaning Paul wants to convey by the statement of Rom 10:4 is that Christ is the goal or aim of Torah, although the implication that Christ and his work bring to an end to seeking righteousness by means of the law cannot be entirely dismissed. While for non-Christian Jews of Paul's day, Wisdom can only be found in Torah, as is clearly taught by sages like Sirach and Baruch, Paul wants to say that she is now found in Christ alone. R. B. Hays is right when he writes that "The conjunction *gar* (for) in 10:4 is the crucial logical connective. This sentence explains what was said in the foregoing sentence: the real aim of the Law, the righteousness of God, *is* Jesus Christ."[31] So what we have here is not the equation Torah = Wisdom = Christ,[32] but Torah pointing forward to Christ, for "*he* rather than Torah is the incarnation or full embodiment of Wisdom."[33] This interpretation is consistent not only with the contrast between the righteousness that comes

---

[29] Suggs, "Word," 308-11; Johnson, *Function*, 133-35.

[30] Windisch, "göttliche Weisheit," 223; Kim, *Origin*, 117, 130.

[31] R. B. Hays, *Echoes of the Scriptures in the Letters of Paul* (New Haven: Yale University Press, 1989), 75-76.

[32] *Pace* Suggs, "Word," 311-12.

[33] Witherington, *Sage*, 327.

from the law and the righteousness that comes from faith in v.5, but also with the close association of Christ and Torah in v.4.

Witherington goes further to suggest that the personification of "the righteousness that comes from faith" (v.6) refers to Christ speaking as pre-existent Wisdom.[34] However, in our view, he seems to press his argument too far. Bearing in mind that Paul is here contrasting between the righteousness that comes from the law and the righteousness comes from faith by means of a literary device called *personification*, one ought not to place to much weight on Christ *personified*, as Witherington himself admits. Moreover, Paul concludes his argument by contrasting the word of faith that is near to you with the Law (cf. 10:8ff.). While Johnson concludes that "the *gospel* is itself the wisdom of God, near to all, able to save all,"[35] Witherington thinks that "*Christ* is the embodiment of God's Wisdom and righteousness and he is made available through the preaching of the Gospel."[36] Although we fully agree with Witherington's interpretation, we think that it is important to stress that there is a distinction between Christ as the embodiment of God's Wisdom and righteousness and Christ as pre-existent heavenly Wisdom. We can therefore conclude that Paul's use of wisdom tradition in Rom 10 is to be classified as his "personified" wisdom christology.

8.1.5. Rom 11:33-36

It has long been recognized that Rom 11:33-36 contain traditional elements with parallels in both Jewish and Greco-Roman sources and that the passage has poetic or hymnic structure.[37] A good number of indications for its hymnic composition can be adduced: (1) a strophic structure of nine lines; (2) the repetition of triads (three genitives dependent on v.33a; three

---

[34] Witherington, *Sage*, 327.

[35] Johnson, *Function*, 137.

[36] Witherington, *Sage*, 327, who rightly criticizes Johnson for failing "to grasp the subtlety of Paul's argument. Paul clearly says in his commentary in Rom. 10:6-8a that he is speaking about Christ in the same way Baruch and Ben Sira were speaking about Wisdom. The Wisdom that is near the believer is Christ who they must confess, not merely the preached word which is only the vehicle for making Christ accessible. Only in a derivative sense is Paul suggesting that the Gospel is God's Wisdom here, and only because its content is Christ. Torah and Gospel are the instruments, but Wisdom and Christ are the key focal points of the discussion in Baruch and Romans respectively."

[37] E. Norden, *Agnostos Theos*, 240-50; G. Bornkamm, "The Praise of God," 105-11; Käsemann, *Romans*, 318; U. Wilckens, *Der Brief an Die Römer* (EKKNT 6/1-3; Koln: Benziger, 1980), 2.269; R. Deichgräber, *Gotteshymnus und Christushymnus in der frühen Christenheit: Untersuchungen zu Form, Sprache und Stil der frühchristlichen Hymnen* (Göttingen: Vandenhoeck & Ruprecht, 1967), 60-64. R. P. Martin, *Worship in the Early Church* (London: Marshall, Morgan and Scott, 1974), 36-37. Johnson, *Function*, 164-73.

parallel rhetorical questions each beginning with τίς, vv.34-35a; three prepositions of the τὰ πάντα formula, v.36a); (3) a chiastic structure forging a relationship between the divine attributes and the rhetorical questions; (4) nine references to God using the typical hymnic pronoun αὐτός; and (5) a concluding doxology in v.36b which parallels numerous doxologies (e.g., Sir 39:14-16; *1 Enoch* 22:14; 1QS 11:15; 4 Macc 18:24; cf. Phil 2:11b).[38] A strophic arrangement of a parallel construction of nine lines can be set out as follows:

Ὦ βάθος πλούτου καὶ σοφίας καὶ γνώσεως θεοῦ·
ὡς ἀνεξεραύνητα τὰ κρίματα αὐτοῦ
καὶ ἀνεξιχνίαστοι αἱ ὁδοὶ αὐτοῦ.
Τίς γὰρ ἔγνω νοῦν κυρίου;
ἢ τίς σύμβουλος αὐτοῦ ἐγένετο;
ἢ τίς προέδωκεν αὐτῷ,
καὶ ἀνταποδοθήσεται αὐτῷ;
ὅτι ἐξ αὐτοῦ καὶ δι' αὐτοῦ καὶ εἰς αὐτὸν τὰ πάντα·
αὐτῷ ἡ δόξα εἰς τοὺς αἰῶνας, ἀμήν.

That this "hymn" is likely to have had a life of its own before Romans is argued by E. E. Johnson. She suggests the following evidence: (1) "the interweaving of customarily 'Jewish' and 'Hellenistic' words and ideas," such as the βάθος of God, the α-privative verbal adjectives ἀνεξεραύνητα and ἀνεξιχνίαστοι in v.33, and the double quotation in vv.34-35; (2) similarity in language and function of the three rhetorical questions about God's wisdom to those in 2 Bar 75:1-5; 1 *En* 93:11-14; 1QH 7:26-33; 10:3-7; (3) the τὰ πάντα formula in v.36 bears striking resemblance to the "Bekenntnisformel der stoischen Theologie";[39] and (4) the presence of four Pauline *hapax legomena* in vv.33-35 (ἀνεξεραύνητα, ἀνεξιχνίαστοι, σύμβουλος, προέδωκεν) suggests the use of a source, although the latter two derive from the scripture quotations. Johnson concludes:

This abundance of unusual vocabulary and vocabulary used in uncharacteristic ways provides the final piece of evidence that Rom 11:33-36 has traditional origins. The intricacy of the hymn's structure and content fuels the suspicion that it had a life of its own prior to Romans. This is by no means to assert that Paul is incapable of rhetorical elegance: the preceding paragraph (vv 28-32) attests his skill. But the abundance of non-

---

[38] Cf. the bibliography listed in the preceding note, and J. H. Charlesworth, *The Old Testament Pseudepigrapha and the New Testament: Prolegomena for the Study of Christian Origins* (SNTSMS 54; Cambridge: CUP, 1985), 266-72, 281-83.

[39] The formula is found in Marcus Aurelius and elsewhere. Cf. Norden, *Agnostos Theos*, 240, n.1, gives credit to T. Gataker for the observation.

Pauline words and concepts, coupled with the self-contained character of the hymn tip the scales in favor of a pre-Pauline origin.[40]

In short, the argument for a pre-Pauline Jewish origin of the hymn is compelling.

8.1.5.1. Hymn to God's Wisdom or to Christ as Wisdom?

The fact that the hymn contains words and ideas closely related to wisdom raises an important question: Who is the object of praise in the hymn? Despite the absence of the name of Christ, some scholars detected in Rom 11:33-36 Paul's identification of Christ with pre-existent wisdom and argued that the passage is a hymn directed to Christ as God's wisdom rather than God or God's wisdom itself. A. T. Hanson argued that the combined quotation of Isa 40:13 and Job 41:3 in Rom 11:34-35 is a christological proof text referring to Christ as the pre-existent wisdom of God:[41]

the combined citation in Romans 11:34-35 is in fact an implicitly Christological statement. Paul has ended his exposition of the whole design of God, and exclaims with admiration at the depth and unexpectedness of that design. But, far from suggesting that God's intention has always been inscrutable, he implies by his two citations that it has always been known to God's counsellor, the pre-existent Christ, or Son, to whom God disclosed his whole mind and in whom his whole plan for the redemption and justification has been carried out.[42]

Similarly, Schnabel attempted to define God's wisdom in christological terms. According to Schnabel, σοφία (θεοῦ) and γνῶσις θεοῦ are "incomprehensible since nobody has been his 'counsellor'" or "has 'known' (ἔγνω) his 'mind' (νοῦς, v.34a)" except Christ, and it is in him this wisdom or knowledge is found.[43]

However, these conclusions are far from convincing and rightly criticized by Johnson. She rejects the line of argument suggested by Hanson and Schnabel on the basis of the following evidence:[44] (1) "it presupposes a great deal of second-guessing on the part of Paul's readers

---

[40] Johnson, *Function*, 172-73. She conjectures that Paul appropriated this Jewish hymn to God's wisdom in use in synagogue for the conclusion of his whole argument.

[41] A. T. Hanson, *The New Testament Interpretation of Scripture* (London: SPCK, 1980), 86-93. The combined use of these two texts in rabbinic sources (e.g., *Pesikta Rabbati* 25.2; *Pesikta de Rab Kahana* 9.2) and here in Romans led Hanson to conclude that such a combination in Jewish tradition predates Paul's.

[42] Hanson, *Interpretation*, 85.

[43] Schnabel, *Law*, 249-50 and the footnotes there. Cf. Wilckens, *Römer*, 2.272.

[44] Johnson, *Function*, 168.

who would presumably be expected to detect a most subtle christological reference"; (2) "it assigns to vv 33-36 a completely different role in their context and attributes to Paul another agenda than are otherwise evident"; (3) "God is clearly the subject of the preceding discussion, the source of the mystery of salvation (11:21-32)"; (4) the association of Isa 40 and Job 41 in later Jewish tradition and with God's wisdom does not make the "hymn" christological, but provides another indication of its traditional origins; and (5) as Paul's doxological response to 11:28-32,[45] the hymn "expresses Paul's awe and wonder at the miracle of God's redemption of the world," which is consistent with God's dealings with the world by means of Israel.[46]

Although we are not trying to deny the presence of any Jewish wisdom motifs in this hymn, since there is no christological reference in the hymn, it is safer to conclude that the hymn in 11:33-36, far from providing evidence for Paul's wisdom christology, should be regarded as a hymn to God or, more precisely, to God's wise ordering of history and redemption.

8.1.6. Conclusion

Our discussion of the so-called Pauline wisdom passages suggests that Paul's understanding of Jesus as pre-existent Wisdom is not as clearly attested as some scholars have argued or assumed. This is an important conclusion for our argument that Paul's understanding of Jesus as pre-existent is more likely based on the early Christian understanding of him as the pre-existent Son of God in the light of their exegesis of two messianic psalms and the re-interpretation of Jesus' self-understanding of himself as God's Son.

8.2. Pre-Pauline Sending Formula

The present section will attempt to demonstrate that wisdom christology was not the starting point for the early Christian conviction about Jesus' pre-existence, but a further development from the conception of Jesus as the pre-existent Son of God, an understanding developed from the early Christian exegesis of Ps 110:1 and Ps 2:7 in the light of Jesus' self-consciousness of divine sonship and divine mission. Although the so-called pre-Pauline "sending" formula embedded in a number of NT texts

---

[45] According to Johnson, 11:28-32 are not only the conclusion of chapters 9-11, but the whole of Rom 1:16-11:27 and the hymn in 11:33-36 serves as the "liturgical" conclusion to the argument, just as 11:28-32 serves as the "logical" conclusion.

[46] Johnson, *Function*, 174.

(Gal 4:4; Rom 8:3; Jn 3:17; and 1 Jn 4:9) is compatible with divine wisdom christology, its root seems to go back to pre-existent Son christology.

We propose that the formula "God sent his Son" in Gal 4:4-5 is best understood if it is read against the background of the early Christian understanding of Jesus as the pre-existent Son of God who was exalted and "literally" enthroned at the right hand of God, an understanding developed from the early Christian exegesis of Ps 110:1 and Ps 2:7 in the light of Jesus' self-consciousness of divine sonship and divine mission.

8.2.1. Different Interpretations

There have been different proposals about the possible traditional background behind Gal 4:4-5. Each proposal has its own view about the presence or absence of a "sending" formula, pre-Pauline or Pauline character of the formula, specific parallels to certain texts or traditions, and the consequent presence or absence of the concept of Jesus' pre-existence. What follows is a brief review of recent scholarship on this specific topic.

E. Schweizer argued that the clauses "God sent his Son" (ἐξαπέστειλεν ὁ θεὸς τὸν υἱὸν αὐτοῦ) and "in order to redeem" (ἵνα . . . ἐξαγοράσῃ) in Gal 4:4 together made up an early Christian "sending formula" that arose within the Torah-Wisdom-Logos speculations of Alexandrian Judaism and was taken over by Hellenistic Christians in application to Christ as God's Son.[47] According to Schweizer, the original formula was twofold: (1) God sending his pre-existent Wisdom (this can also be ὁ λόγος or ὁ υἱὸς) for the purpose of (2) redeeming or saving humanity. He suggests that the *Sitz im Leben* of Gal 4:4 may be Alexandrian Judaism because "sending by God and the Son of God title are combined only in the realm of Egyptian Judaism."[48]

Schweizer finds parallels between Wis 9:10-17 and Gal 4:4-7 in the verb ἐξαποστέλλειν (a *hapax legomenon* in Paul) employed for the sending of both Wisdom and the Son and in the fact that the sending of Wisdom and Son in both passages is followed by the sending of the Holy Spirit.[49]

---

[47] E. Schweizer, "Zum religionsgeschichtlichen Hintergrund der 'Sendungsformel' Gal. 4,4f., Rö. 8,3f., Jn 3,16f., 1Jn 4,9" *ZNW* 57 (1966), 199-210; Schweizer, "υἱός," *TDNT* 8.354-57; E. Schweizer, "Paul's Christology and Gnosticism" in *Paul and Paulinism: Essays in Honour of C. K. Barrett* (eds. M. D. Hooker *et al.*; London: SPCK, 1982), esp. 118-19.

[48] Schweizer, *TDNT* 8.375.

[49] Wis 9:17; Gal 4:7; though Wis 9:17 also uses the verb πέμπειν.

He also finds parallels from Philo.[50] His thesis has had a great influence on the exegesis of Gal 4:4-5, with many scholars accepting it without reservations. There are, however, a few exceptions.

James D. G. Dunn denies the parallelism between Wis 9:10-17 and Gal 4:4-5 and the presence of a pre-Pauline sending formula, and finds the linguistic background of the statement in "the more specific Christian tradition that Jesus both thought of himself as God's son and spoke of himself as 'sent' by God (Mark 9.37 pars.; 12.6 pars.; Matt 15.24; Luke 4.18; 10.16)."[51] In particular, the parable of the wicked tenants of Mk 12:6 would be the most probable background for Gal 4:4-7 because:

> Here we have the father sending his son in what can fairly be called an eschatological act – Mark 12.6; last of all . . . (ἔσχατον) – just as in Gal. 4.4 God sends his son 'at the fullness of time'. Moreover, at the same point in the parable . . . we have a close conjunction of the ideas of sonship and inheritance – again just as in Gal 4.4-7.[52]

Dunn denies that the sending of the Son implies his pre-existence because in his view it is Adam christology-soteriology, rather than Wisdom language, that is present in Gal 4:4-5.[53] Thus, the Galatians passage is indebted to two distinct Christian traditions about Jesus as the sent Son and the Last Adam. Dunn insists that Paul and his readers thought of Jesus simply in terms of divine commission rather than divine incarnation in the fullest sense.[54]

Dunn also rejects a link between Gal 4:4-6 and Wis 9:10-17, on the following three grounds: (1) Paul's references elsewhere to Jesus' identification with wisdom are linked to a cosmic rather than soteriological context (1 Cor 8:6; Col 1:15-17); (2) the identification of Wisdom as God's son would not be a natural inference for Paul's readers since *sophia* is a female figure and was never called God's 'son' in pre-Pauline

---

[50] Schweizer, *TDNT* 8.355-56. His assertion that in Philo we find a verb of sending with its object being the "son (of God)" (e.g., *Agr.* 51) and the idea that *the* Son creates other sons (e.g., *Conf.* 145-48) are not quite right; cf. his other references, such as *Her.* 205 (Word is "chief messenger"); *Cher.* 35; *Qu. Ex.* 2.13; *Som.* 1.103 are all metaphorical of some kind of divine communications to mind. There is nothing like the incarnation of God's son.
[51] Dunn, *Christology*, 38-43 (quotation from p.40).
[52] Dunn, *Christology*, 40, denies also the presence of pre-existence in early Christian tradition about Jesus' divine sonship and divine mission. Moreover, the connections he suggests between the two texts are somewhat strained.
[53] So R. N. Longenecker, *Galatians* (WBC 41; Dallas: Word Books, 1990), 168-69, following Dunn, concludes that "Jesus in his earthly life was God's Son not because of his preexistence but by virtue of his commissioning by God, which is what Paul learned from the early church and what he formulated in what we now have as Gal 4:4-5."
[54] Dunn, *Christology*, 46.

literature; (3) Adam christology, rather than wisdom christology, fits better as the background of Gal 4:4-6.[55]

Seyoon Kim, like Dunn, also disagrees with Schweizer that Wis 9:10-17 parallels Gal 4:4-5 or that it is a basis for Paul's reflection on Christ, but does accept the presence of a sending formula in Gal 4:4-5 and its possible parallelism with Jewish Torah-Wisdom-Logos speculations.[56] However, he rejects the pre-Pauline character of the formula and argues that it was Paul who drew the connection between Wisdom-Logos and the Son. According to Kim, the formula in Gal 4:4-5 (and Rom 8:3-4) was composed by Paul himself based on the insight obtained from his encounter with Christ on his way to Damascus; in the Damascus-road Christophany, Jesus of Nazareth "was revealed to him as the exalted and enthroned Son of God."[57] As a rabbi, Paul already knew that the Torah is to be equated with Wisdom. However, in his encounter with Christ at Damascus Paul realized that:

Christ superseded the Torah . . . [and that] Wisdom, the revelation of God, is found in him, and not in the Torah as the Jews thought. . . . So Paul began to ascribe all the attributes and functions of the divine Wisdom to Christ: pre-existence and mediatorship in creation, revelation and salvation. Paul expressed these attributes and functions especially clearly through the formula of God's sending his Son into the world to save mankind (Rom 8.3; Gal 4.4).[58]

---

[55] Dunn, *Christology*, 39. While we agree with Dunn's rejection of the parallelism between Gal 4 and Wis 9, his reasons for doing so are not entirely convincing. His first two objections were rightly countered by Schnabel, *Law*, 242: "[1] It should be noted . . . that 1 Cor 1,24.30 where Paul explicitly identifies Christ with God's wisdom belongs to a definitely soteriological context (as Gal 4.4!). The fact that 1 Cor was written after Gal does not prove that the equation was made for the first time by Paul in 1 Cor 1,24.30. [2] And, further, the argument of the feminine character of 'wisdom' carries no decisive weight since Paul describes Christ in terms of (still fem.) wisdom in many other passages. This suggests that the correlation of wisdom and Christ does by no means necessitate the total formal identification of these two 'entities', especially since *sophia* is not a genuine hypostasis or distinctive heavenly being, but rather a conception or way of theologizing." Cf. A. T. Hanson, *The Image of the Invisible God* (London: SCM, 1982), 60, gives evidence from Philo (*Fug.* 51:3 and *Abr.* 100-2) and shows that for Philo "the gender of an abstract noun at least gives no clue as to its real meaning." Also Witherington, *Sage*, 293. For a critical assessment on the third point see below §8.2.3.1.

[56] Kim, *Origin*, 117-19, dismisses the parallel to Wis 9 in one sweeping statement without any substantiations: "these parallels are not close enough or substantial enough for us to suppose that Paul was consciously dependent upon Wis. 9.10-17" (*ibid.*, 118).

[57] Kim, *Origin*, 126. See the critique of Kim's thesis in J. D. G. Dunn, "'A Light to the Gentiles': the Significance of the Damascus Road Christophany for Paul" in *The Glory of Christ in the New Testament: Studies in Christology* (eds. L. D. Hurst *et al.*; Oxford: Clarendon, 1987), 251-66, esp. 256-62. Also P. A. Rainbow, "Jewish Monotheism As the Matrix for New Testament Christology, a Review Article" *NovT* 33 (1991), 87 n. 21.

[58] Kim, *Origin*, 258.

For Kim, the early church first thought of Jesus taking the place of the Law as the means of salvation and only consequently was prompted to think of him in terms of divine Wisdom.[59] He adduces three pieces of evidence: (1) Jesus attacked the contemporary expositions of the Law and claimed to be the fulfilment of the Law (Mt 5:17; 11:13/Lk 16:16); (2) his death was pronounced by the Law as God's curse; and (3) Greek-speaking Christians were persecuted because they were critical of the Temple-cult and the contemporary expositions of the Law.[60]

However, the precise relationship between the evidence and the possible line of christological development that Kim adduces seems more than dubious and misleading. Since we are talking about a historical figure, it is unlikely that Jesus was seen as taking the place of an abstract entity (the Law), then thought of in terms of another abstract figure (divine Wisdom) and then all the predicates of this abstract figure were transferred to him who walked on earth not more than a decade ago. Rather, it is much more plausible and straightforward that it is because Jesus was first seen as the pre-existent Son (as a result of the early Christian exegesis of Ps 110:1 and Ps 2:7 in the light of Jesus' self-consciousness of divine sonship and divine mission, as we would argue) that he was then spoken of in terms of divine Wisdom, a very useful imagery for the early church to reflect upon the full significance of Christ (including his activity at creation).[61] More importantly, it is most unlikely whether an understanding of Jesus as the means of salvation would have come from the Law vis-à-vis Christ rather than from the soteriological significance derived from Jesus' own proclamation of his saving mission (cf. Mk 10:45, *et al.*). If so, Wisdom christology is not to be seen as the starting point but the "last runner" in the relay race for early "high" christology.

James M. Scott, in a fresh approach to the possible background for the "sending of God's Son," postulates the new Exodus motif as the background for Gal 4:1-7.[62] Scott argues against the common interpretation of Gal 4:1-7 which finds "considerable discontinuity between an idiosyncratic 'legal illustration' (vv 1-2) and its 'application' (vv 3-7)."[63] Rather, according to his view, a basic harmony exists between Israel's redemption to a divine adoptive sonship at the foreordained time of the

---

[59] Cf. Hengel, *Son of God*, 72-73, who suggests that the early church thought of Jesus first in terms of Wisdom and transferred the all-embracing functions of Wisdom to him before it was led to reflect upon his relationship to the Law.

[60] Kim, *Origin*, 44-50, 126-27.

[61] Nevertheless, we are doubtful that the wisdom motif is present in Gal 4:4-5.

[62] J. M. Scott, *Adoption as Sons of God: an Exegetical Investigation into the Background of huiothesia in the Pauline Corpus* (WUNT 2/48; Tübingen: Mohr Siebeck, 1992), 121-86.

[63] Scott, *Adoption*, 186.

exodus from Egypt (Gal 4:1-2) and the believers' redemption to a divine adoptive sonship at the foreordained time of the second exodus (Gal 4:3-7). He then concludes that *huiotheisia* in Gal 4:5 "refers to a specific Old Testament/Jewish background, even though the term is not found in either the Septuagint or any other Jewish literature of the period."[64] In this way, Scott rejects the presence of the "sending" formula as well as its pre-Pauline character in Gal 4:4-5.

Having surveyed different interpretations of Gal 4:4-5, we can draw the following chart for the sake of clarity:

Different Interpretations on Gal 4:4-5

	Schweizer	Dunn	Kim	Scott	My view
Sending Formula	Yes	No	Yes	No	Yes
Pre-Pauline	Yes	-	No	-	Yes
Parallel with Wis 9:10-17	Yes	No	No	No	linguistic parallel only; there is a significant conceptual difference
Parallel with Jesus as God's Son and 'sent' by God	No	Yes + Adam christology	No	No	Yes
Parallel with New Exodus motif	No	No	No	Yes	No
Pre-existence	Yes	No	Yes	-	Yes

What implications or conclusions can we draw from the different proposals about the possible traditional background for Gal 4:4-6?

8.2.2. Our Critical Assessments

8.2.2.1. Pre-Pauline Formula

First, we agree with Schweizer and many other scholars[65] that Gal 4:4 is most likely to contain a pre-Pauline "sending" formula (cf. Rom 8:3-4; Jn 3:16-17; and 1 Jn 4:9). However, Scott rejects the pre-Pauline character of

---

[64] Scott, *Adoption*, 267.

[65] Many scholars assume the pre-Pauline origin of the formula; cf. Schweizer, "Hintergrund," 199-210; L. Goppelt, *Theologie*, 2.400-4; F. Mussner, *Galaterbrief*, 272; H. D. Betz, *Galatians*, 206, and others.

Gal 4:4-5 on the following grounds:[66] (1) the so-called "formula" varies considerably between the Pauline and Johannine literature and even within the latter itself, leaving only the common denominator among the passages mentioned above – "God sent his Son" – insufficient data to establish a formula; (2) there is a chronological problem in using the later Johannine texts to establish a "pre-Pauline" tradition; and (3) the chiastic structure of Galatians 4:4-6 militates against one ἵνα-clause being pre-Pauline (v.5a) and the other not (v.5b).

However, his arguments against the pre-Pauline character are not convincing. First, a closer examination of the four passages that allegedly contain the "sending" formula reveals more commonalities than Scott admits. We find the same syntactical pattern in these passages. God is the subject followed by a verb of sending as predicate. The object is the Son, followed by a final clause introduced by ἵνα, which explains the soteriological significance of the sending (Gal 4:4b-6; Rom 8:3; Jn 3:16-17; 1 Jn 4:9, 10, 14). In fact, all these four texts commonly share two basic elements which are sufficient evidence for the presence of a formulaic statement: (a) God sent his Son; (b) for a salvific purpose.[67] Second, since the sending formula occurs in John independently of Pauline tradition, where both presuppose Jesus' pre-existence, to posit dependence of these two authors on a common "parent tradition" is not methodologically unsound.[68] Third, Paul could perfectly well have incorporated a pre-formed saying ("in order to redeem those under the law") so as to set a parallel with the second statement – his own – "that we might receive adoption," thereby creating a chiasm. These three remarks, then, rightly call into question the force of Scott's arguments.

Moreover, evidence from the structure and content of Gal 4:4-5, coupled with the use of the first person plural in the verb λάβωμεν, suggests pre-Pauline character of the formula.[69] In this regard Longenecker notes the following points: (1) the first person plural "we" in v.3 and v.5 is referring primarily to Jewish believers, while "you" in vv.6-7 is applying the thrust of the confession quoted in vv.4-5 to the Gentile converts; (2) with regard to content, Gal 4:4-5 begin with a *hapax legomenon* in Paul "the fullness of time" and then include another Pauline *hapax legomenon* "born of a woman," with both phrases reflecting the interests of early Jewish Christianity; and (3) only the second of the participial clauses "born

---

[66] Scott, *Adoption*, 169-71.

[67] Cf. Pate, *Reverse*, 140-41, who adds two more elements, i.e., a connection with the role of the Spirit (Gal 4:6; Rom 8:2; John 3:5-8; 1 John 4:13) and the context of the four passages are rooted in *Wis* 9, but they go beyond evidence.

[68] Schweizer, *TDNT* 8.375.

[69] See Longenecker, *Galatians*, 166-67.

under the law" is really relevant to the argument of Galatians, while the first one "born of a woman" is never discussed in the letter.

Furthermore, the apparent close parallelism of Gal 4:4-6 with another widely held pre-Pauline confession-like formula like Rom 1:3-4 strengthens this interpretation.[70]

8.2.2.2. Parallels to Wisdom 9:10-17?

Second, we disagree with Schweizer that the correlation between Jesus and divine Wisdom can be found in Gal 4:4-6. While it is true that the similarity between Gal 4:4-6 and Wis 9:10-17 looks striking and that Paul's extensive use of the book of *Wisdom* elsewhere may increase the probability that he is dependent upon that material here too, we question whether the parallelism between the two is as close as Schweizer and others think. Few scholars, except Scott (and Dunn probably for wrong reasons), seem to be aware of the more striking differences in terms of concepts between the supposed parallel passages.

Against any connection between Gal 4:4-6 and Wis 9:10-17 Scott provides three reasons: (1) *Wisdom* 9 does not identify pre-existent Wisdom as the Son of God; (2) *Wisdom* 9 "does not refer to the sending of Wisdom as generally efficacious and redemptive within Israel's *Heilsgeschichte*, but rather as an answer to Solomon's personal prayer for Wisdom to guide him"; and (3) *Wisdom* 9 speaks of a single sending of Wisdom which is identified with the sending of the Spirit.[71]

While evidence adduced by Scott against wisdom background for Gal 4:4-6 was intended to support his argument for the presence of new Exodus motifs,[72] he made some good observations regarding possible differences between the two passages. However, he fails to bring out the most significant *conceptual* difference between the two passages. While in *Wisdom* the sending of Wisdom is to guide individuals, like the role of the Holy Spirit, in Galatians the sending of the Son is to come into the world and to die as a human actor. Such a difference points to a clear distinction between the concept of inspiration and the concept of incarnation as such. One cannot therefore conclude with Schweizer that Gal 4:4-5 implies a connection with Wis 9:10-17 or that by inserting an already existing "sending" formula Paul intended to identify Jesus with pre-existent Wisdom. Rather, in view of the absence of clear evidence of the identification of Christ in terms of pre-existent Wisdom in Paul's authentic letters, this observation helps us to formulate our own understanding about

---

[70] See below §8.2.3.3.

[71] Scott, *Adoption*, 169.

[72] Pate, *Reverse*, 145.

the priority of Son christology over wisdom christology in the development of pre-existent christology in the early church.

8.2.2.3. Root of the Formula

Third, and most importantly, we differ with Schweizer about the possible root of the "sending" formula.[73] The fact that we can detect Wisdom influence in Gal 4:4-6 does not necessarily lead to the conclusion that the formula should have derived from Hellenistic Jewish Wisdom/Logos speculations as Schweizer argued.[74] As several studies have already shown, a sharp distinction between Palestinian and Hellenistic Christianity is not warranted. As M. Hengel has clearly shown, all Judaism during the period in question was in a sense "Hellenistic Judaism," as there was no Judaism which was not part of the Hellenistic world and influenced in some way by its thought and culture.[75] Surely, the same implication applies to early Christianity. The realization that all Judaism, including that found in Palestine and even that of the Pharisees, was influenced by Hellenism in some way or the other has been accompanied by an awareness of the diversity which existed in early Judaism and around NT times.

Furthermore, while a linguistic parallelism between Gal 4 and Wis 9 cannot be denied altogether, there are also some differences between the two, especially differences in the concepts involved: (1) Whereas Wis 9 speaks of a single sending of Wisdom which is identified with the sending of the Spirit (cf. v.17), Gal 4 speaks of a double sending of the Son and the Spirit (cf. vv.4, 6). (2) In a similar vein, while the emphasis in Wis 9 is on the sending of Wisdom to guide individuals (similar to the sending of the Holy Spirit), in Gal 4 the whole thrust of the christological statement is on sending the Son into the world as a human actor to die for a salvific purpose. The former has more in common with the concept of *inspiration*,

---

[73] Cf. Longenecker, *Galatians*, 167, who also expressed his doubt about the evidence drawn by Schweizer: "one can wonder (1) if the links drawn by Schweizer between Wisdom, Logos, and Son (of God) in Hellenistic Judaism are not somewhat tenuous (see esp. Schweizer's argument in *Jesus*, 81-82), and (2) if the parallels between the NT and Hellenistic Judaism are not somewhat few and disparate."

[74] It is important to note that, while Jewish tradition about Wisdom as the pre-existent agent of God in creation who comes and dwells among men is usually associated with "Hellenistic Jewish" thinking, the clear presence of teaching about the pre-existence of wisdom in Sirach 24 (originally written in Hebrew) calls for a caution. It is certainly not impossible that such a tradition originated among Jewish-Christian Hellenists in Jerusalem like the Stephen party, a group with whom the newly converted Paul came into close contact in Damascus.

[75] Cf. M. Hengel, *Judaism and Hellenism*; I. H. Marshall, "Palestinian and Hellenistic Christianity," 271-87. See now also J. D. G. Dunn, *The Partings of the Ways*, 9-10; J. M. G. Barclay, *Jews in the Meditteranean Diaspora*, 83-91.

whereas in the latter the concept of *incarnation* in its fullest sense is in view! The conceptual dissimilarity between Wis 9 and Gal 4 strongly suggests that the theory of Alexandrian Jewish tradition about wisdom and logos as the root of "God sending his Son" is unlikely. Rather, as we have argued, the idea about God sending his Son was drawn from the early Christian proclamation about Jesus based on their christological exegesis of two messianic psalms (Ps 110:1 and Ps 2:7) in the light of Jesus' divine sonship and divine mission.

8.2.3. Does Gal 4:4-6 Speak of the Son's Pre-existence?

Having discussed various issues related to the background for Gal 4:4-6, we now turn to the key question of our whole discussion: Does Gal 4:4-6 speak about or at least imply the Son's pre-existence? Closely related to this question is, however, whether the passage reflects Paul's Adam christology. This is therefore the right place to deal with Dunn and others who, on the basis of Adam christology, deny Jesus' pre-existence not only in Gal 4:4-5 but also in other Pauline passages, such as Phil 2:6-11, Rom 8:3 and 2 Cor 8:9, where the idea of pre-existence is usually thought to be present or implied.[76]

8.2.3.1. Adam Christology?

Dunn attaches particular importance to the place of Adam in earliest Christianity and thus in Paul's thinking. In Dunn's view, Gal 4:4 and Rom 8:3 are statements merely referring to the oneness of Jesus with the human race so that he might deliver humankind from bondage and sin and grant them his own sonship in exchange.[77] Similarly, 2 Cor 8:9 is to be understood of Jesus giving up the richness of his communion with God for the desolation of the cross.[78] The Philippian hymn is, however, the passage with respect to which Dunn most strongly argues for Adam christology.[79] The hymn speaks about the human Jesus, his life of humility, and his exaltation to an earthly position of glory, not to the pre-existent Christ or his incarnation. The sequence of the hymn's thought is "first Adam/last Adam," as in 1 Cor 15:45-49, without reference "to any particular time

---

[76] Dunn, *Christology*, 39, 114-25. Cf. C. H. Talbert, "The Problem of Pre-Existence in Phil. 2:6-11" *JBL* 86 (1967), 141-53; other important contributions include H. W. Bartsch, *Die konkrete Wahrheit und die Lüge der Spekulation* (Frankfurt: Lang, 1974); J. Murphy-O'Connor, "Christological Anthropology in Phil. 2:6-11" *RB* 83 (1976), 25-50; G. Howard, "Phil. 2:6-11 and the Human Christ" *CBQ* 40 (1978), 368-87.

[77] Dunn, *Christology*, 111-13.

[78] Dunn, *Christology*, 121-23.

[79] Dunn, *Christology*, 39, 114-25.

scale – pre-existence, pre-history or whatever."[80] As the first Adam was in the image (εἰκών) and likeness of God (Gen 1:26-27), so Christ, the second Adam, existed in the form (μορφή = εἰκών) of God (Phil 2:6). While the first Adam wrongly tried to become like God (Gen 3:5), the second Adam did not strive to be equal with God, nor regarded equality with God as something to use for his own advantage.

While the contrast between Adam's arrogance and self-seeking and Jesus' humility and self-humbling is clear in general terms, it becomes doubtful whether the Adam-Christ parallel/contrast was Paul's intention at all when the parallels between Gen 1-3 and Phil 2 are carefully examined.[81] We point out several linguistic, exegetical, and theological shortcomings that seem to play against Adam christology. First, it is questionable whether the terms μορφή and εἰκών are really interchangeable; nowhere in the LXX or the NT is Adam referred to as μορφὴ θεοῦ[82] and it cannot be sustained for its second occurrence, μορφὴν δούλου (v.7).[83] Second, the Adam-Christ parallel does not do justice to the force of the recapitulatory phrase καὶ σχήματι εὑρεθεὶς ὡς ἄνθρωπος "and being found in form as man" (v.7), which is very odd if it refers to a person who had never been anything else but a man. Again, the *contrast* "between 'being in the form of God' and 'becoming in the form of men' is extremely odd if the contrast is only between two stages in the career of a man."[84] Third, on a philological ground the idiomatic expression οὐχ ἁρπαγμὸν ἡγήσατο has also been shown to refer to something that was *already present* and at Christ's *disposal* (i.e., his equality with God, which he did not use to his own advantage).[85] Fourth, Dunn is criticized for failing to "press the hymn's 'logic' to inquire what is behind the first

---

[80] Dunn, *Christology*, 119.

[81] J. M. Furness, "Behind the Philippian Hymn" *ExpTim* 79 (1967-1968), 181.

[82] While the semantic fields of the two terms overlap considerably, there seems to be some difference in nuance between them. See esp. D. H. Wallace, "A Note on Morphé" *TZ* 22 (1966), 19-25; C. Spicq, "Note sur MORPHE dans les papyrus et quelques inscriptions" *RB* 80 (1973), 37-45; cf. N. T. Wright, "ἁρπαγμός and the Meaning of Philippians 2:5-11" *JTS* (1986), 331-32; also Kim, *Origin*, 195-98.

[83] G. F. Hawthorne, *Philippians* (WBC 43; Dallas: Word Books, 1983), 82.

[84] I. H. Marshall, "Incarnational Christology in the New Testament" in *Jesus the Saviour: Studies in New Testament Theology* (Downers Grove: Inter-Varsity, 1990), 170; cf. J. T. Sanders, *The New Testament Christological Hymns: Their Historical Religious Background* (SNTSM 15; Cambridge: CUP, 1971), 66; N. T. Wright, Review of Dunn's *Christology in the Making*, *Churchman* 95 (1981), 170-72; T. Y.-C. Wong, "The Problem of Pre-Existence in Philippians 2, 6-11" *ETL* 62 (1986), 271-73; C. A. Wanamaker, "Philippians 2.6-11: Son of God or Adamic Christology" *NTS* 33 (1987), 181-83.

[85] R. W. Hoover, "The Harpagmos Enigma: A Philological Solution" *HTR* 64 (1971), 118; N. T. Wright, "ἁρπαγμός and the Meaning of Philippians 2:5-11" *JTS* 37 (1986), 339.

Adam's characterization as made in the divine 'likeness.'"[86] Instead, "Pauline theology points to humankind's recovery of the *imago Dei* . . . , which is not what Adam had lost but what the heavenly Christ had" (Rom 8:29; 2 Cor 3:18; Col 3:10; cf. Eph 4:13, 24).[87]

For Dunn, the ultimate source for Adam christology in the early church is Ps 8:6, where a "description of Christ's Lordship . . . was also a description of God's purpose and intention for *adam*/man"; and Heb 2:8-9 (cf. 1 Cor 15:27; Eph 1:22; Phil 3:21) is the passage that expounds the psalm most effectively as an expression of Adam christology.[88] However, as we have already shown (§6.2.4), the fusion between Ps 110:1 and Ps 8:6 in the early church was christologically motivated and Heb 2:8-9 is best understood christologically rather than anthropologically.

As far as Gal 4:4 and Rom 8:3 are concerned, "God *sent* his *Son* raises associations other than those raised in a parable about the owner of a vineyard or in a statement that God sent the prophets."[89] Again, while Dunn interprets "rich" to refer to Christ's spiritual communion with the Father, Marshall offers a more cogent solution:

the verse [is to be understood] in the light of Phil 4:19 where riches and glory are closely associated; the 'becoming poor' is then not a reference merely to incarnation but to the whole process of humiliation and suffering through which Christ brought glory to his people (2 Cor 6:10).[90]

We have thus rejected the presence of Adam christology in Gal 4:4-5 and other Pauline passages, but, as N. T. Wright argues, even if Adam christology is granted we cannot rule out the idea of Jesus' pre-existence in these passages. After all, the Philippian hymn makes better sense, says Wright, "if we see Christ and Adam as contrasted but not in strict parallelism."[91]

Christ's obedience is not simply the replacement of Adam's disobedience. It does not involve merely the substitution of one sort of humanity for another, but the solution of

---

[86] R. P. Martin, *Carmen Christi: Philippians 2:5-11 in Recent Interpretation and in the Setting of Early Christian Worship* (SNTSMS 4; Cambridge: CUP, 1967), xxi.

[87] Martin, *Carmen*, xxi.

[88] Dunn, *Christology*, 109.

[89] I. H. Marshall, Review of Dunn's *Christology in the Making*, *TJ* 2 (1981), 244.

[90] Marshall, Review of Dunn's *Christology in the Making*, 244.

[91] N. T. Wright, "Jesus Christ is Lord: Philippians 2.5-11" in *The Climax of the Covenant: Christ and the Law in Pauline Theology* (Edinburgh: T & T Clark, 1991), 91-92. See also E. Lohmeyer, *Kyrios Jesus: Eine Untersuchung zu Phil. 2, 5-11* (Heidelberg: C. Winter, 1928), 41, who pointed out that only of a divine being can it be said that he was *obedient* unto death, since for all other human beings since Adam death comes as a mere necessity.

the problem now inherent in the first sort, namely, sin. The temptation of Christ was not to snatch at a forbidden equality with God, but to cling to his rights and thereby opt out of the task allotted to him, that he should undo the results of Adam's snatching.

Moreover, as Prof. Marshall has correctly pointed out, vv.6-7 are very odd if the person referred to had never been anything other than a human being.[92]

All the evidence adduced above, therefore, makes it dubious whether Dunn's attempt to interpret the Philippian hymn and other passages in terms of Adam christology is successful. We conclude therefore that the rejection of Jesus' pre-existence on the basis of Adam christology does not stand up to close scrutiny, and even if Adam-Christ contrast is granted we cannot rule out the view that the idea of Jesus' pre-existence is present or implied in these passages.

8.2.3.2. Christ as the Second Moses?

Gal 4:4 can also be understood as God commissioning his Son, without the implication of Son' pre-existence. In an investigation into the background of υἱοθεσία in the Pauline corpus, J. M. Scott stands against the common interpretation of Gal 4:1-7, and argues that it is a typology between Israel's redemption to divine adoptive sonship at the foreordained time of the exodus from Egypt (vv.1-2) and the believers' redemption to divine adoptive sonship at the foreordained time of the second exodus (vv.3-7).[93] Rejecting any use of an image derived from legal immaturity in Paul, Scott argues that the situation of subjection described in vv.1-2 alludes to Israel's 430 years of slavery in Egypt, the liberation from which at the Exodus and its celebration in Hos 11:1 in terms of adoptive sonship, then becomes type of the eschatological adoption received by believers as described in vv.4-5.

In the light of this OT Jewish background he argues that Gal 4:4 is to be understood as speaking of the messianic Son of God in terms of Moses typology (i.e., Christ as the Second Moses).[94] He finds support for his view from (1) 1 Cor 10:1-13, where the typology of Moses/Christ is also present; and (2) the term of sending itself: In the LXX ἀποστέλλειν and ἐξαποστέλλειν are used most frequently of the divine sending of a prophet, especially the sending of Moses, and in a *piyyut* from Egypt (ca. iv-v AD) Moses is referred to as the "sent one" (שליח) of God and as one "born of a woman" (דאשה יליד) and the Israelites are called the "sons" of God.

---

[92] Marshall, "Incarnational," 170.

[93] Scott, *Adoption*, 186.

[94] Scott, *Adoption*, 165-69.

However, Scott's fresh interpretation of Gal 4:1-7 is not persuasive. It is true that Paul makes allusion to the 430 years of Exod 12:40 in 3:17, but his argument across Gal 3 clearly shows that he is interested in the *following* period of captivity and slavery that began with the coming of the law, rather than the Egyptian period of slavery in itself.[95] "If Gal. 4:1-2 contains any anaphoric reference to a period of slavery, it must be to that under the law, described so graphically in 3:23-25 and later (v.3) presented as a subjection under the analogous to the erstwhile pagan bondage of the Gentile Galatians (cf. 4:9)."[96] It is at this point that the entire typology pattern of Scott's interpretation falls apart, rendering unlikely his suggestion of seeing Christ as the Second Moses.

8.2.3.3. Pre-existent Son Christology

As the suggestions that Jesus' pre-existence is absent in Gal 4:4-5 (and other Pauline passages) on the ground of Adam christology and the Second Moses christology are not compelling, we now turn to examine whether Gal 4:4-5 reflect the early Christian understanding of Jesus as the pre-existent Son of God. We have argued in earlier chapters that the early Christian exegesis of Ps 110:1 and Ps 2:7 in the light of Jesus' divine sonship and divine mission led them to the conviction that Jesus is the pre-existent Son sent from heaven by God. We now argue that the pre-Pauline "sending" formula embedded in the christological statement in Gal 4:4 (cf. Rom 8:3 and Johannine parallels) provides evidence for such an understanding apart from wisdom christology prior to Paul writing his letters. Our discussion of the possible background and form of the formula suggested that in Gal 4:4-5 Paul is simply taking over an existing "sending formula" which, without recourse to wisdom christology, has already come to encapsulate the concept of Jesus' pre-existence. If this is correct, then where do we have to turn for a more plausible background for the pre-Pauline "sending" formula than the early Christian understanding of Jesus as the pre-existent Son of God?[97]

Taking E. Schweizer's theory further, R. H. Fuller proposed that we find in Gal 4:4 the beginning of a pre-Pauline summary, perhaps of the kind described as a "baptismal anamnesis" by N. A. Dahl, which Paul

---

[95] B. Byrne, Review of Scott's *Adoption as Sons of God*, *JTS* 44 (1993), 291-92.

[96] Byrne, Review of Scott's *Adoption as Sons of God*, 292.

[97] It is not by chance that we do not find as many traces of wisdom christology in Paul as many scholars have simply assumed.

amplifies in vv.4-6.[98] A tentative form of the summary suggested by Fuller can be reconstructed in six cola as follows:

ἐξαπέστειλεν ὁ θεὸς τὸν υἱὸν	God sent forth his Son,
αὐτοῦ, γενόμενον ἐκ γυναικός,	born of a woman,
ἵνα τὴν υἱοθεσίαν ἀπολάβωμεν	that we might receive our instatement as sons.
Ὅτι δέ ἐστε υἱοί,	Now, because you are sons,
ἐξαπέστειλεν ὁ θεὸς τὸ πνεῦμα . . .	God has sent forth the Spirit . . .
κρᾶζον, Αββα ὁ πατήρ.	crying 'Abba, Father!

The first three cola speak of God's sending of his Son, the second three of his sending of the Spirit. Does the "sending" of the Son imply his pre-existence? The parallel between "sending" of the Son and of the Spirit seems to be crucial. If the Spirit was the Spirit before God sent him, the Son was presumably the Son before God sent *him*. Moreover, it seems clear that Paul believed in Christ's pre-existence (Phil 2:6-11; 2 Cor 8:9; Rom 8:3; 1 Cor 8:6; 10:4; cf. Col 1:15-17). If Paul thought of Christ as pre-existent, then this concept may well have been in his mind when he spoke of God as sending his Son, even if the Son's pre-existence would not be necessarily inferred from this passage. Compare with Rom 8:3, ὁ θεὸς τὸν ἑαυτοῦ υἱὸν πέμψας ἐν ὁμοιώματι σαρκὸς ἁμαρτίας, where the idea of pre-existence seems certainly be present in Paul's mind. But, if we have a pre-Pauline summary here, would pre-existence have been in the minds of those responsible for the summary? We contend that, although pre-existence is irrelevant to the argument of the passage in question, this idea was probably present in the minds of Paul's predecessors.

As we have seen above, in Dunn's view the linguistic and the conceptual backgrounds for the "sending" formula in Gal 4:4-5 are to be found in Jesus' sayings about himself as having been "sent" by God (Mk 9:37; 12:6; Mt 15:24; Lk 4:18; 10:16) and Adam christology respectively. Although we have rightly dismissed the relevance of an Adamic background for Gal 4:4-5, Dunn's suggestion of the linguistic background is much more promising. After all, it is reassuring that our basic argument receives weighty support from someone who largely rejects the idea of Jesus' pre-existence in this and other Pauline passages, although we disagree with him about the full significance of Jesus' statements in the Gospels for his self-understanding. We have argued in Chapters 4 and 5 that Jesus' self-consciousness of divine sonship and divine mission was open to interpretation in terms of his pre-existence if it is seen in the whole context of his teaching and life.

---

[98] R. H. Fuller, "The Conception/Birth of Jesus as a Christological Moment" *JSNT* 1 (1978), 37-52, esp. 40-41; N. A. Dahl, "Anamnesis: Mémoire et commémoration dans le christianisme primitif" *ST* 1 (1947), 69-95, esp. 74-75.

We should not underestimate Paul's understanding of Jesus as the Son of God and the significance of the title in his letters. The statistical evidence of Paul's use of the title "Son" or "Son of God" for Christ is indeed misleading.[99] It is true that Paul seldom talks about the person of Jesus as a topic in itself, but he does "almost casually and implicitly in discussions of other topics."[100] It is equally true that Paul does not use the term υἱός very often, but it is undoubtedly a major christological title for him, as M. Hengel correctly emphasized.[101] Paul uses the term "Son" when he wishes to make important soteriological assertions and to describe the content of his gospel (Rom 1:3, 4, 9; 8:2, 29, 32; Gal 1:15-16, 4:4-5; 2 Cor 1:18-19; 1 Cor 1:9; 15:28; 1 Thess 1:10). Hence, Prof. Marshall's caution about the contrasting views about Jesus between the modern scholarship and the New Testament itself would be a healthy reminder for the students of NT christology:

> Our modern tendency is to insist that Jesus was every bit a man, just the same as one of us. This may perhaps cause us to do less than justice to the New Testament representation of him as primarily the Son of God who took on the form of man. Where modern discussion emphasizes the fullness of his humanity, the New Testament emphasizes the fullness of his divinity.[102]

Moreover, there are a number of important pieces of evidence that provide support for the priority of the pre-existent Son christology over wisdom christology.

First, many scholars find in the so-called Christ Hymn in Phil 2:6-11 not only the idea of Jesus' pre-existence but also his divine sonship. Despite some opinions to the contrary, among all the Pauline passages in which the pre-existence of Jesus is thought to be present or implied, the Philippian hymn is regarded by scholars not only as one of the clearest "pre-existent" passages in Paul, but also as pre-Pauline origin. As some scholars suggest, one possible evidence for Jesus' divine sonship is the reference to "God the Father" in the concluding verse (v.11) which seems to suggest that at the beginning of the hymn (perhaps just before the

---

[99] While Paul uses the title *Kyrios* 184 times, the term υἱὸς θεοῦ is only found 15 times. Statistics are from Hengel, *Son of God*, 7.

[100] Marshall, "Incarnational," 172.

[101] Hengel, *Son of God*, 7-16. *Contra* W. R. Kramer, *Christ, Lord and Son of God* (London: SCM, 1966), 189, who, on the basis of the "statistical" evidence and form-critical analysis, concludes that for Paul "the title Son of God and the ideas associated with it are of relatively minor importance."

[102] Marshall, "Incarnational," 170.

relative pronoun ὅς in v.6) the reference to the "Son" would have stood in a way or other.[103]

Second, and more importantly, some scholars see the idea of Jesus' divine sonship in Phil 2:6-11 because the hymn, both in form and in content, seems to show close resemblance to other texts speaking of Jesus as the Son of God. The content of the first half of the hymn does not only remind us of passages like Gal 4:4-5 and Rom 8:3-4, which speak of the sending of God's Son into the world, but the linguistic parallels between them are also striking. The phrase ἐν ὁμοιώματι ἀνθρώπων γενόμενος is very similar to ἐν ὁμοιώματι σαρκὸς ἁμαρτίας in Rom 8:3 and in a different way to γενόμενον ἐκ γυναικός in Gal 4:4.

Phil 2:7   ἐν ὁμοιώματι ἀνθρώπων γενόμενος
Rom 8:3   ἐν ὁμοιώματι σαρκὸς ἁμαρτίας
Gal 4:4   γενόμενον ἐκ γυναικός

Such similarities led E. Käsemann to suggest that the phrase "in the likeness of sinful flesh" in Rom 8:3 was modelled on "being born in the likeness of men" in Phil 2:7. At the same time, the words "being born of a woman" in Gal 4:4 serve a similar function to the words "born in the likeness of men" in Phil 2.7.[104]

Third, Gal 4:4 also shows some resemblance to Rom 1:3. If we set these two "pre-Pauline" confession-like formulas side by side, linguistic and conceptual parallels are also quite striking:

Gal 4:4	Rom 1:3
4b ἐξαπέστειλεν ὁ θεὸς τὸν υἱὸν αὐτοῦ, 4cd γενόμενον ἐκ γυναικός, γενόμενον ὑπὸ νόμον,	3a περὶ τοῦ υἱοῦ αὐτοῦ 3b τοῦ γενομένου ἐκ σπέρματος Δαυὶδ κατὰ σάρκα,

While "ἐξαπέστειλεν ὁ θεὸς τὸν υἱὸν αὐτου" (Gal 4:4b) corresponds to "περὶ τοῦ υἱοῦ αὐτου" (Rom 1:3a), "γενόμενον ἐκ γυναικός, γενόμενον ὑπὸ νόμον" (Gal 4:4cd) does to "γενομένου ἐκ σπέρματος Δαυὶδ κατὰ σάρκα" (Rom 1:3b). While the first parallel is about the relationship between God and his Son, the second pair speaks about the Son's earthly appearance. Rom 1:3-4 could be understood in terms of messianic

---

[103] Cf. Kramer, *Christ*, 123, maintains that the title Son of God formed the "bracket within which the two parts of the hymn were brought together." Also I. H. Marshall, "The Christ-Hymn in Philippians 2:5-11: a Review Article" *TynBul* 19 (1968), 104-27.

[104] E. Käsemann, *Römer*, 206, claims that "das christologisch angewandte Motiv der Sendung des präexistenten Sohnes . . . begegnet auch in Hymnus Phil 2.6ff."

enthronement only,[105] but the reference to "his Son" in v.3, the emphasis on "in power" and the inclusion of "our Lord" in reference to the Son in v.4 all indicate that Paul is speaking about the exaltation of the pre-existent Son to the status of lordship at the resurrection, which in turn provides a close parallel to the second half of Philippian hymn.[106] Again, it is important to note that this hymn speaks of Jesus' exaltation and pre-existence without recourse to wisdom christology.[107] If we can see parallels between the two passages, then by inference we can also conclude that in Rom 1:3-4 we witness to an instance of pre-existent Son christology without Wisdom influence.

Fourth, the rareness or the infrequent occurrences of God "sending" Jesus into the world in the NT outside John strongly suggests that "God sent his Son" is a christological formula which would naturally be linked to a saving purpose (Gal 4:4; Rom 8:3; Jn 3:17; and 1 Jn 4:9) because the "sending" formula without the latter half would not be complete and would prompt people to ask, "why God sent his Son?" This idea would then be tied in with the idea of God giving or giving up his Son (cf. Rom 8:32; Eph 5:2, 25; Jn 3:16). We have several Son of God texts in Paul which are especially concerned with the death of God's Son (Rom 5:8-11; 8:32; Gal 2:19-20; cf. also Col 1:13-20).

The available evidence thus seems to suggest that, not until the early Christian conviction about Jesus as the pre-existent Son of God had fully developed as a result of their exegesis of Ps 110:1 and Ps 2:7 in the light of Jesus' self-consciousness of divine sonship and divine mission, did wisdom christology play a significant role for the development of the doctrine of Jesus' pre-existence. If Wisdom did contribute to the doctrine at all, it must have done it at some point by adding to the already developed doctrine the significance of Jesus' mediation or active participation in creation, the only element missing from the doctrine of Jesus' pre-existence in the NT.

---

[105] Cf. N. T. Wright, *The Letter to the Romans* (The New Interpreter's Bible; Nashville: Abingdon, 2002) 417, who takes vv.3-4 as "a reasonably straightforward two-part statement of Jesus' Messiahship." Also, M. L. Strauss, *The Davidic Messiah in Luke-Acts: the Promise and Its Fulfillment in Lukan Christology* (JSNTSup 110; Sheffield: Sheffield Academic Press, 1995), 60.

[106] Wanamaker, "Son of God," 184.

[107] Some scholars found wisdom motifs here as well. Cf. D. Georgi, "Der vorpaulinische Hymnus Phil 2,6-11" in *Zeit und Geschichte: Dankesgabe an Rudolf Bultmann zum 80. Geburtstag* (eds. E. Dinkler *et al.*; Tübingen: Mohr Siebeck, 1964), 263-93; Murphy-O'Connor, "Anthropology," 25-50, and the literature cited there. Unlike others who found a wisdom background to the hymn, Georgi insists on the presence of the pre-existence motif by seeing the image of the wise man merged with the idea of transcendent Wisdom.

However, those attributes of divine Wisdom attributed to Jesus' pre-existence in Paul (except participation in creation) could equally well be, if not better, explained in terms of the early Christian understanding of him as the pre-existent Son of God, the responsibility for such an understanding resting on their exegesis of Ps 110:1 and Ps 2:7 in the light of Jesus' divine sonship and divine mission. For example, the sharing of God's throne can be explained by the picture of Jesus' enthronement in Ps 110:1 (cf. Ps 2:6; and other references to "the right hand" of God), which may presuppose his divine identity and pre-existence (§7.3). Moreover, his coming and being sent into the world may well derive from the early Christian *re*-interpretation of his sayings about his divine mission in terms of his transcendent origin when they did the exegesis of Ps 110:1 and 2:7. We should not forget, after all, that Paul never makes an explicit identification of Jesus with Wisdom anywhere[108] or states that "God sent his Wisdom in order to . . ." but he specifically says that "God sent his *Son* in order to . . ."! Moreover, the meaning of salvation ascribed to Jesus is far more closely related to his death and resurrection than his replacement of the Torah in view of Jewish identification of Wisdom and the Torah.

8.3. Conclusion

Our discussion of the possible background for Gal 4:4-6 suggests that New Testament scholars often do not allow enough room for the creative power of early Christians to make use of Jewish traditions, to combine two different strands of traditions and to interpret one in the light of the other as they reflected upon the person of Jesus in the light of the resurrection event. It is therefore highly likely that, rather than being confined to Jewish wisdom tradition alone, Gal 4:4 reflects not only the early Christian conviction about Jesus as the pre-existent Son sent from heaven, but also the subsequent development of the same conviction in terms of the divine Wisdom who was active in creation. Our proposal seems to account best for the explicit reference to his *Son* in the formulation "God sent his Son." With Jewish wisdom tradition alone the christological formula about God sending his *Son* found in Gal 4:4 and elsewhere cannot be adequately explained. Gal 4:4 explicitly states that "God sent his *Son*" not his Wisdom, probably because the early Christian tradition about Jesus' divine sonship and divine provenance already entailing his pre-existence had already been merged with the idea of Jesus as the wisdom of God. The use

---

[108] See above that in 1 Cor 1:24, 30 Paul is not identifying Jesus with personified Wisdom but as an expression of God's plan of salvation being carried out through Christ.

of the title "Son" rather than "Wisdom" must be therefore highly significant.

The sapiential background for Gal 4:4-6 should not be emphasized at the expense of the importance of the early Christian tradition about Jesus' divine sonship and divine mission. Although it is true that wisdom is associated with sonship in *Wisdom*, it does not explain why the christological statement is formulated as "God sent his Son" rather than "God sent his Wisdom." We cannot just be content with an explanation that, because wisdom is associated with sonship in Hellenistic Judaism, Paul or the formulator of this pre-Pauline formula uses the title "Son" for Christ instead of otherwise more expected title "Wisdom" (cf. 1 Cor 1:24, 30).

As we have already demonstrated in Chapter 5, the parable of the wicked tenants in Mk 12:1-12[109] most probably goes back to Jesus and reflects his self-consciousness of a unique personal relationship with God the Father and of his being "sent" from heaven.[110] We have also demonstrated in Chapter 7 that Jesus' self-consciousness of divine sonship and divine provenance being compatible with his pre-existence was confirmed by the early Christian exegesis of Ps 2:7 as entailing his pre-existence.

If our arguments are correct, then it is highly likely that the early Christian exegesis of two messianic psalms in the light of Jesus' own teaching about his divine sonship and divine provenance led them to view Jesus as the pre-existent Son of God and is to be seen as one of the earliest and most significant influences for the development of the NT doctrine of Jesus' pre-existence.

---

[109] E. Schweizer, *Jesus* (London: SCM, 1971), 84 n.42, regards it as "a product of the Christian community, in which the allegorical equation of the vineyard owner with God, the servant with the prophets, and the son with Jesus is already influential."

[110] For our discussion of the authenticity of the parable see §4.3.5.2. *Contra* Schweizer, *Jesus*, 84. His observation that "in all four passages that speak of God's sending his Son, both in Paul and in John, the statement focuses not on Jesus' incarnation, but on his crucifixion" seems to downplay the probability that the sending formula was first formulated to speak about the incarnation of the pre-existent Son and then was later found most appropriate to speak about the crucifixion. Commenting on Rom 8:3, Käsemann, *Romans*, 217, states that "Paul changed the tradition of the sending formula, which stresses the incarnation of the pre-existent Son, in order to draw attention to the act of salvation on which the accent falls in v. 3d. He was no longer concerned with the incarnation as such . . . but with the crucifixion . . . . This could have been the case already in his tradition if a coherent tradition underlies the whole statement up to v. 4a and he does not take up merely individual motifs."

```
┌─────────────────────────┐
│       Pre-Pauline       │
│    "Sending" Formula    │
│   "God sent his Son"    │
│      (the Essence)      │
└─────────────────────────┘
```

```
┌─────────────────────────┐
│     Early Christian     │
│  Understanding of Jesus │
│    as the Pre-existent  │
│       Son of God        │
└─────────────────────────┘
```

```
┌─────────────────────────┐
│  Early Christian Exegesis │
│  of Ps 110:1 and Ps 2:7  │
│      (the Catalyst)      │
└─────────────────────────┘
```

```
┌─────────────────────────┐
│      Jesus' Self-       │
│  consciousness of Divine │
│    Sonship and Divine   │
│         Mission         │
│     (the Foundation)    │
└─────────────────────────┘
```

The Development of the Pre-existent Son Christology

Chapter 9

Conclusion

Having reviewed recent scholarship on the origin and development of pre-existence christology in the early church, with a particular attention to Jewish speculations regarding personified divine attributes and exalted angels in Second Temple period, we proposed that a more cogent explanation for Jesus' pre-existence in early christology is found in the early Christian understanding of Jesus as the pre-existent Son of God as a result of their exegesis of Ps 110:1 and Ps 2:7 in the light of Jesus' self-understanding of himself as God's Son.

In the light of a growing number of studies which explore a possible relationship between early christology and a bifurcation of the Jewish conception of God by an increasing speculation of the so-called "intermediary beings" in Second Temple Judaism we examined whether these intermediaries such as the personified divine attributes, principal angels and a pre-existent messiah ever provided a ready-made category for viewing Jesus as a divine and pre-existent being alongside God.

In *Chapter 2* a detailed examination of the Wisdom of God, the Word of God and the Name of God in early Jewish tradition demonstrated that these personified divine attributes never led to the development of divine hypostases separate from God. We proposed that, rather than leading towards a dual conception of God or providing a ready-made category for viewing Jesus as a divine and pre-existent being alongside God, the vivid descriptions of these divine attributes offered the Second Temple Jews a variety of religious language to speak meaningfully and powerfully about God's presence, manifestation and action in the world without calling into question his transcendence and uniqueness.

In *Chapter 3* we examined the evidence from an increasing interest in exalted angels, including the Angel of the Lord and angelomorphic figures, and the concept of a pre-existent messiah in Second Temple Judaism to see whether a sharp distinction between God and these intermediary beings has been undermined or compromised. However, neither Jewish angelology nor the pre-existent messiah ever exercised sufficient influence on early christology to be seen as a ready-made category for viewing Jesus as a divine and pre-existent being alongside God.

In *Chapter 4* we discussed whether and in what sense Jesus conceived himself to be the Son of God. The investigation was focused on his use of *abba* and other Synoptic texts closely related to his self-consciousness of being uniquely related to God as his Father and conceiving himself as God's Son (Mt 11:27; Mk 13:32; Mt 16:17; Lk 22:29; Mk 12:1-12; Mk 1:9-11). The discussion led us to conclude that Jesus was conscious of a unique personal relationship to God as his Father.

While the fact that the very word *abba* that Jesus himself used was also used by the early church might suggest that Jesus' use of it as an address to God is nothing unique in itself, we suggested several reasons to think otherwise and concluded that it provides support to his self-consciousness of divine sonship.

Having evaluated critically the authenticity of these sayings we concluded that the probability of each one of these sayings going back to a *Sitz im Leben Jesu* remains strong. Moreover, our exegesis of the saying in Mt 11:27 suggested that Jesus was conscious of being God's unique agent who alone mediated the final revelation of God, and thus as God's unique Son. Furthermore, his "divine sonship" sayings in Mk 13:32, Mt 16:17, Lk 22:29, and Mk 12:1-12 give cumulative evidence for his self-consciousness of divine sonship. Again, our discussion about the parable of the wicked tenants also suggested that there may be strong grounds for connecting the parable with the so-called "pre-Pauline 'sending' formula" embedded in the NT documents when speaking about Jesus' pre-existence ("God sent his Son"; cf. Gal 4:4; Rom 8:3; Jn 3:17; 1 Jn 4:9, 10, 14).

Our examination of evidence from the baptismal narrative (Mk 1:11) led us to conclude that it is much more likely that Jesus experienced at some point a prophetic call-vision, if not the baptismal theophany, which included the elements of divine sonship and spirit anointing. Moreover, the heavenly voice addressing Jesus as ὁ υἱός μου ὁ ἀγαπητός strengthened our thesis that Jesus was conscious of a unique personal relationship to God as his Father and regarded himself as his Son.

In response to a widespread view that the baptismal account only reflects a messianic understanding of him and that the title "Son of God" was given to him in the light of his messianic consciousness, we argued that the use of Ps 2:7 in Mk 1:11 supports our view that Jesus was the messiah in that he was the Son of God rather than vice versa. The priority of his divine sonship over his messiahship can be drawn from his self-consciousness of a unique personal relationship to the Father. The title "Son" is therefore not merely a way of expressing God's particular care and his promise of victory to a messianic king, but rather entails a unique personal relationship to God as his Father.

We concluded our discussion by suggesting that Jesus' self-consciousness of divine sonship has the potential of playing one of the most significant roles in the development of early christology and could be seen as the foundation for the early Christian understanding of Jesus as the pre-existent Son of God.

In *Chapter 5* we investigated whether and in what sense Jesus was conscious of having come from and been sent by God. The discussion was concentrated on those sayings that can be broadly grouped as "I have come" sayings (Mk 2:17 pars.; Mk 10:45 par.; Lk 19:19; 12:49, 51 par.) and "I was sent" sayings (Mt 15:24 par.; Mk 9:37 pars.). Our discussion of "I have come" and "I was sent" sayings of Jesus has demonstrated that by uttering these logia Jesus revealed himself as one who was conscious of his God-given mission to carry out in this world. We have demonstrated that the idiomatic interpretation of "I have come" sayings of Jesus ("I have the purpose/intention to . . .") lacks clear evidence and is far from convincing. Moreover, contrary to the view that suggests Jesus' pre-existence, our examination of the ἦλθον sayings have clearly demonstrated that in these sayings the emphasis falls on his God-given *mission* rather than on his transcendent *origin*, even though the idiomatic interpretation was clearly shown to be faulty. In short, Jesus' "coming" is best understood as synonymous to his God-given mission rather than his advent from heaven.

We came to a similar conclusion with regard to the "I was sent" sayings preserved in Mt 15:24 and Mk 9:37. However, we found that there is an important distinction between these sayings and the parable of the wicked tenants that we discussed in Chapter 4. With the parable of the wicked tenants we are somewhat more confident than with these "I was sent" sayings. We have recognized that in telling the parable Jesus expressed implicitly – but in a quite subtle manner – his self-consciousness of his divine sonship as well as his divine or transcendent origin. Although these "I was sent" sayings and the parable of the wicked tenants have as a common denominator the motif of being *sent* from/by God, one major difference between the two is that, unlike the "sent" sayings, in his parable Jesus refers to himself as God's *Son* as well as one *sent* by God. The combination of these two elements in the parabolic setting seems to have a stronger implication for christology: it implies that Jesus is *God's Son sent* into this world!

Having discussed evidence for Jesus' self-consciousness of divine sonship and divine mission, we asked the question whether his self-consciousness implies or amounts to his consciousness of pre-existence. In our discussion of Synoptic evidence for Jesus' self-consciousness of divine sonship and divine mission we have shown that Jesus was conscious of a unique personal relationship to God as his Father and of himself as his

Son; in the same way, we have also shown that he was conscious of his divine mission, i.e., a God-given mission to carry out in this world. Such a self-understanding of divine sonship and divine mission on its own right during his earthly ministry can hardly be said to have played a significant role in understanding him as pre-existent. However, if his self-consciousness of divine sonship and divine mission is recalled and re-examined at a later stage by early Christians in view of his resurrection event and the whole context of his life and teaching, such a self-understanding was probably open to interpretation in terms of his pre-existence.

It is at this precise point that the early Christian exegesis of Ps 110:1 and Ps 2:7 comes in and plays a central role. It is therefore important to recognize a gap between what Jesus claimed and what his disciples really understood. We proposed that this gap was later filled by the early Christian messianic exegesis of Ps 110:1 and Ps 2:7, which played the most significant part in helping them draw out the fuller implications of Jesus' self-revelatory statements about his divine sonship and divine provenance in terms of his divinity and pre-existence.

Our discussion of Jesus' self-consciousness of divine sonship and divine provenance suggested that we have a solid foundation upon which the early church was able to build their understanding of Jesus as the pre-existent Lord and Son of God. At first glance, there appears to be a significant gap between how Jesus conceived of himself (the christology of Jesus) and what the early church came to believe (the christology of the early church). It was the "big" gap or even the seemingly "unbridgeable" gap between the two that led many scholars to find the basis for the development of early christology, and especially of Jesus' pre-existence, in other areas than Jesus' own consciousness (e.g., Jewish wisdom tradition, pre-existent messiah tradition in early Judaism, Jewish "angelomorphic" divine agent traditions).

To fill this seemingly "unbridgeable" gap we turned to examine how the early church interpreted Ps 110:1 and Ps 2:7, the two messianic psalms most cherished in the early church (Chapters 6 and 7). We proposed that through their messianic exegesis of these two psalms they came to confirm what they were already beginning to believe as a result of the impression left by Jesus and his resurrection as well as a deepening of their understanding of him as Lord and Son of God enthroned at his right hand.

In *Chapter 6* the use of Ps 110:1 in the NT clearly showed that this messianic text was uniformly applied to Jesus' resurrection as his exaltation to the right hand of God. We also noted that a cursory reading of the evidence might suggest that Ps 110:1 was first applied to Jesus' resurrection and interpreted by the early church as his becoming Lord at that time by being exalted to the right hand of God. The evidence, however, showed the inadequacy of this line of reasoning. Not only was this belief part of the earliest confessions of the early church, but also the early linking of Ps 8:6 to Ps 110:1 strongly suggested that Christ's cosmic Lordship was recognized at an early stage. We also argued that Ps 110:1 was understood by the early church not only as a prophecy about his exaltation to the right hand of God, but also as a statement of God speaking to one who was already Lord in his sight. In this way, the early Christians interpreted Jesus' resurrection as essentially confirming his existing status rather than conferring a new status.

We also proposed that the early Christian understanding of Jesus as Lord is ultimately rooted in his allusive reference to Ps 110:1 as a prophecy about the messiah awaiting to be fulfilled (Mk 12:35-37) and his understanding of this divine oracle as a prophecy about his own exaltation to the right hand of God (Mk 14:62). Moreover, the evidence from Mk 12:35-37 suggested that by way of subtle allusions to himself the text leaves open the possibility that he might be David's Lord who stands and exists before David himself and thus provides us with a glimpse of his self-understanding which seems compatible with his pre-existence, an implication supported by his statement before the Sanhedrin later in Mk 14:62.

In *Chapter 7* we drew the following conclusions from the early Christian use of Ps 2. First, we proposed that there was probably an early Christian interpretation of Ps 2:6 as a prophecy about Jesus' exaltation in the light of a widespread pre-Christian Jewish tradition about Mt. Zion as the heavenly Jerusalem.

Second, such an interpretation of Ps 2:6 helps us to understand why Ps 2:7 is often linked to the resurrection/exaltation in the NT. Once Ps 2:6 was interpreted as Jesus' exaltation, the early church began to interpret Ps 2:7 as a prophecy about Jesus' divine sonship being decisively demonstrated through his resurrection. Thus the missing link between Ps 2 and the resurrection/exaltation is supplied.

Third, we suggested how Ps 2:7 came to be linked both to Jesus' divine sonship and his resurrection. In the first place, it was because the early church remembered Jesus' claim to be God's Son that they applied Ps 2:7 to him. Then, a cross reading of Pss 2 and 110 together with the pre-Christian Jewish tradition of Mt. Zion as the heavenly Jerusalem, where God himself resides, led them to see Ps 2:6 as Jesus' exaltation to the right hand of God. Finally, when asked when Jesus' divine sonship was fully manifested their answer was that his divine sonship was decisively demonstrated at the resurrection. Thus, Ps 2:7 began to be understood by the early church as a prophecy about Jesus' divine sonship decisively fulfilled at his resurrection/exaltation.

Fourth, our discussion of the use of Ps 2:7 in Acts 13:33, Rom 1:3-4 and Heb 1:5, 5:5 allowed us to conclude that in God's sight Jesus was already his Son during and before his earthly existence. The early Christians saw Jesus' resurrection as confirmation of his existing position and status as God's Son and therefore the view that the early church held that Jesus *became* God's Son at the resurrection is to be abandoned.

Fifth, we confirmed our conclusion in Chapter 4 that it is much more likely that the early church drew deeper implications from Jesus' filial consciousness than a simple equation between the divine sonship and the messiahship.

Our examination of the early Christian use of Pss 110:1 and 2:7 against the background of Jesus' self-consciousness of divine sonship and divine mission in the whole context of his life and teaching led us to conclude that the root of pre-existent Son christology is to be found in the early Christian exegesis of two messianic psalms (the catalyst) in the light of Jesus' self-consciousness of divine sonship and divine mission (the foundation). The tremendous impact left by the resurrection event and the resulting conception of Jesus "literally" enthroned to God's right hand led them to see Jesus as the pre-existent Lord and Son of God.

In *Chapter 8* we concluded that wisdom christology is not clearly attested in Paul's authentic letters. We examined a possible origin of the pre-Pauline 'sending' formula "God sent his Son" (Gal 4:4-5; Rom 8:3-4; Jn 3:16-17; and 1 Jn 4:9) and proposed that this christological formula was most likely derived from an early Christian understanding of Jesus as the pre-existent Son of God rather than from divine wisdom christology. Once Jesus' divinity and pre-existence were confirmed through the exegesis of the psalms, the early church found Jewish wisdom traditions helpful in drawing out the full significance of his pre-existence in terms of his being active in creation and co-eternal with God the Father. Early Christian conviction about Jesus as the pre-existent Son sent by the Father (Gal 4:4; Rom 8:3) should be regarded as the culmination of the early church's desire to know more about one who was crucified, raised from the dead by God and "literally" enthroned to his right hand as Lord and Saviour, and it was done through their exegesis of two of the most important messianic texts in the light of Jesus' self-revelatory statements.

Thus, our study has provided a more cogent explanation of the origin and development of the early Christian understanding of Jesus as the pre-existent Son of God over against the trend in recent scholarship which emphasizes the influences of Jewish angelology on early christology.

Bibliography

Primary Sources

Aland, B., *et al.* (eds.) *The Greek New Testament.* 4th ed. Stuttgart: Deutsche Bibelgesellschaft; United Bible Societies, 1998.

Braude, W. G. (trans.) *The Midrash on Psalms.* Yale Judaica Series Vol. 13 & 14. 2 Vols. New Haven; London: Yale University Press, 1959.

Charles, R. H. (ed.) *The Apocrypha and Pseudepigrapha of the Old Testament in English.* 2 Vols. Oxford: Clarendon, 1913.

Charlesworth, J. H. (ed.) *The Old Testament Pseudepigrapha.* 2 Vols. London: Darton, Longman & Todd, 1983-85.

Colson, F. H. and G. H. Whitaker. *Philo: in Ten Volumes and Two Supplementary Volumes.* The Loeb Classical Library. London: Heinemann, 1929-53.

Danby, H. C. *The Mishnah: Translated from the Hebrew with Introduction and Brief Explanation Notes.* Oxford: OUP, 1933.

Elliger, K. and W. Rudolph. (eds.). *Biblia Hebraica Stuttgartensia.* Stuttgart: Deutsche Bibelgesellschaft, 1984.

Epstein, I. (ed.) *The Babylonian Talmud.* 35 Vols. London: Soncino Press, 1935-48.

Freedman, H. and M. Simon. (eds.). *Midrash Rabbah.* 10 Vols. London: Soncino, 1983.

García Martínez, F. and E. J. C. Tigchelaar. (eds.). *The Dead Sea Scrolls Study Edition.* Leiden: Brill, 1998.

Hengel, M., H. P. Rüger, P. Schäfer, and J. Neusner. (eds.). *Übersetzung des Talmud Yerushalmi.* 16 Vols. Tübingen: Mohr Siebeck, 1975.

Jacobson, H. *The Exagoge of Ezekiel.* Cambridge; New York: Cambridge University Press, 1983.

Nestle, E., *et al.* (eds.) *Novum Testamentum Graece.* 27th ed. Stuttgart: Deutsche Bibelgesellschaft, 1993.

Rahlfs, A. (ed.) *Septuaginta: id est, Vetus Testamentum graece iuxta LXX interpretes.* Stuttgart: Deutsche Bibelgesellschaft, 1949.

Vermes, G. *The Complete Dead Sea Scrolls in English.* London: Allen Lane, 1997.

Yonge, C. D. (trans.) *The Works of Philo: Complete and Unabridged.* New updated ed. Peabody: Hendrickson, 1854-55/1993.

Secondary Sources

Abelson, J. *The Immanence of God in Rabbinical Literature.* London: Macmillan, 1912.

Achtemeier, P. J. *A Commentary on First Peter.* Hermeneia. Minneapolis: Fortress, 1996.

Adams, J. C. *The Epistle to the Hebrews with Special Reference to the Problem of Apostasy in the Church to which it was Addressed.* M.A. Thesis, Leeds, 1964.

Albl, M. C. *'And Scripture Cannot Be Broken': the Form and Function of the Early Christian Testimonia Collections.* NovTSup 96. Leiden: Brill, 1999.

Alexander, P. S. "Targum, Targumim." *ABD* 6.320-31.

Allegro, J. M. "Further Messianic References." *JBL* 75 (1956) 174-87.

___. *Qumran Cave 4 I (4Q158-4Q186).* DJD 5. Oxford: Clarendon, 1968.

Allen, L. C. "The Old Testament Background of (ΠPO)OPIZEIN in the New Testament." *NTS* 17 (1970-1971) 104-08.

___. *Psalms 101-150.* WBC 21. Dallas: Word Books, 1983.

Allison, D. C. "Two Notes on a Key Text: Matthew 11:25-30." *JTS* 39 (1988) 477-85.

Anderson, H. *The Gospel of Mark.* NCBC. London: Oliphants, 1976.

Anderson, K. *The Resurrection of Jesus in Luke-Acts.* PhD. dissertation, Brunel University, 2000.

Aono, T. *Die Entwicklung des paulinischen Gerichtsgedankens bei den Apostolischen Vätern.* Europäische Hochschulschriften, XXIII, 137. Bern: P. Lang, 1979.

Arens, E. *The HΛΘON-Sayings in the Synoptic Tradition: a Historico-Critical Investigation.* Freiburg: Universitätsverlag Freiburg, 1976.

Arvedson, T. *Das Mysterium Christi: eine Studie zu Mt 11:25-30.* Uppsala: Wretmans Boktryckeri, 1937.

Attridge, H. W. *The Epistle to the Hebrews: a Commentary on the Epistle to the Hebrews.* Hermeneia. Philadelphia: Fortress, 1989.

Aune, D. E. *The Cultic Setting of Realized Eschatology in Early Christianity.* NovTSup 28. Leiden: Brill, 1972.

Aus, R. *The Wicked Tenants and Gethsemane: Isaiah in the Wicked Tenants' Vineyard, and Moses and the High Priest in Gethsemane.* Atlanta: Scholars Press, 1996.

Bailey, K. E. "Informal Controlled Oral Tradition and the Synoptic Gospels." *Themelios* 20.2 (1995) 4-11.

___. "Middle Eastern Oral Tradition and the Synoptic Gospels." *ExpTim* 106 (1995) 363-67.

Balchin, J. F. "Paul, Wisdom and Christ." In H. H. Rowdon (ed.), *Christ the Lord: Studies in Christology Presented to Donald Guthrie.* Leicester: Inter-Varsity, 1982: 204-19.

___. "Colossians 1:15-20: an Early Christological Hymn? The Arguments from Style." *Vox Evangelica* 15 (1985) 65-94.

Bammel, E. "Das Gleichnis von bösen Winzern (Mk 12,1-9) und das jüdische Erbrecht." *Revue internationale des droits de l'Antiquité* 3 (1959) 11-17.

Barclay, J. M. G. *Jews in the Mediteranean Diaspora. From Alexander to Trajan (323 BCE-117 CE.)* Edinburgh: T & T Clark, 1996.

Barclay, W. "A Comparison of Paul's Missionary Preaching and Preaching to the Church." In W. W. Gasque and R. P. Martin (eds.), *Apostolic History and the Gospel.* Exeter: Paternoster, 1970: 165-75.

Barker, M. *The Great Angel: a Study of Israel's Second God.* London: SPCK, 1992.

___. "The High Priest and the Worship of Jesus." In C. C. Newman, J. R. Davila, and G. S. Lewis (eds.), *The Jewish Roots of Christological Monotheism: Papers From the St. Andrews Conference on the Historical Origins of the Worship of Jesus.* JSJSup 63. Leiden: Brill, 1999: 93-111.

Barr, J. "Theophany and Anthropomorphism in the Old Testament." In International Organization of Old Testament Scholars *Congress Volume: Oxford, 1959.* VTSup 7. Leiden: Brill, 1960: 31-38.

____. *The Semantics of Biblical Language*. London: OUP, 1961.

____. "Hypostatization of Linguistic Phenomena in Modern Theological Interpretation." *JSS* 7 (1962) 85-92.

____. "'Abba, Father' and the Familiarity of Jesus' Speech." *Theology* 91 (1988) 173-79.

____. "'Abba' Isn't 'Daddy'." *JTS* 39 (1988) 28-47.

Barrett, C. K. "The Background of Mark 10:45." In A. J. B. Higgins (ed.), *New Testament Essays: Studies in Memory of Thomas Walter Manson, 1893-1958*. Manchester: Manchester University Press, 1959: 1-18.

____. "Mark 10:45: a Ransom for Many." In *New Testament Essays*. London: SPCK, 1972: 20-26.

____. *A Critical and Exegetical Commentary on the Acts of the Apostles*. ICC. 2 Vols. Edinburgh: T & T Clark, 1994.

Barthélemy, D. and J. T. Milik. *Qumran Cave I*. DJD 1. Oxford: Clarendon, 1955.

Bartsch, H. W. *Die konkrete Wahrheit und die Lüge der Spekulation: Untersuchung über den vorpaulinischen Christushymnus und seine gnostische Mythisierung*. Frankfurt: Lang, 1974.

Bauckham, R. "The Sonship of the Historical Jesus in Christology." *SJT* 31 (1978) 245-60.

____. "The Worship of Jesus in Apocalyptic Christianity." *NTS* 27 (1981) 322-41.

____. *The Climax of Prophecy: Studies on the Book of Revelation*. Edinburgh: T & T Clark, 1993.

____. *God Crucified: Monotheism and Christology in the New Testament*. Didsbury Lectures 1996. Carlisle: Paternoster, 1998.

____. "The Worship of Jesus in Philippians 2:9-11." In R. P. Martin and B. J. Dodd (eds.), *Where Christology Began: Essays on Philippians 2*. Louisville: Westminster/John Knox, 1998: 128-39.

____. "The Throne of God and the Worship of Jesus." In C. C. Newman, J. R. Davila, and G. S. Lewis (eds.), *The Jewish Roots of Christological Monotheism: Papers From the St. Andrews Conference on the Historical Origins of the Worship of Jesus*. JSJSup 63. Leiden: Brill, 1999: 43-69.

Baumgarten, J. M. "4Q500 and the Ancient Conception of the Lord's Vineyard." *JJS* 40 (1989) 1-6.

Baumgartner, W. "Zum Problem des Jahwe-Engels." In *Zum Alten Testament und seiner Umwelt: Ausgewählte Aufsätze*. Leiden: Brill, 1959: 240-46.

Bayer, H. F. *Jesus' Predictions of Vindication and Resurrection: the Provenance, Meaning, and Correlation of the Synoptic Predictions*. WUNT 2/20. Tübingen: Mohr Siebeck, 1986.

Beare, F. W. *The Earliest Records of Jesus*. Oxford: Blackwell, 1962.

____. *The Gospel According to Matthew: a Commentary*. Oxford: Blackwell, 1981.

Beasley-Murray, G. R. *Jesus and the Kingdom of God*. Grand Rapids: Eerdmans, 1986.

Beasley-Murray, P. "Colossians 1:15-20: an Early Christian Hymn Celebraiting the Lordship of Christ." In D. A. Hagner and M. J. Harris (eds.), *Pauline Studies: Essays Presented to Professor F. F. Bruce on His 70th Birthday*. Exeter: Paternoster, 1980: 169-83.

____. "Romans 1:3f.: An Early Confession of Faith in the Lordship of Jesus." *TynBul* 31 (1980) 147-54.

Becker Jürgen. *Auferstehung der Toten im Urchristentum*. Stuttgart: KBW Verlag, 1976.

Bellinger, W. H. "The Psalms and Acts: Reading and Rereading." In N. H. Keathley (ed.), *With Steadfast Purpose*. Waco: Baylor University, 1990: 127-43.

Benoit, P. "Divinity of Jesus in the Synoptic Gospels." In *Jesus and the Gospel.* London: Darton, Longman & Todd, 1973: 47-70.

Bentzen, A. *Introduction to the Old Testament.* Copenhagen: Gad, 1952.

___. *King and Messiah.* London: Lutterworth, 1955.

Best, E. *The Temptation and the Passion.* Cambridge: CUP, 1965.

___. "The Power and the Wisdom of God: 1 Corinthians 1:18-25." In L. de Lorenzi (ed.), *Paolo a una chiesa divisa.* Roma: Abbazia, 1980: 9-39.

Betz, H. D. *Galatians: a Commentary on Paul's Letter to the Churches in Galatia.* Hermeneia. Philadelphia: Fortress, 1979.

Betz, O. *What Do We Know about Jesus?* London: SCM, 1968.

___. "Probleme des Prozesses Jesu." In H. Temporini and W. Haase (eds.), *Aufstieg und Niedergang der römischen Welt.* Berlin: Gruyter, 1982: 565-647.

Bietenhard, H. *TDNT* 5.242-83.

Black, M. "The Christological Use of the Old Testament in the New Testament." *NTS* 18 (1971) 1-14.

___. (ed.). *The Book of Enoch or I Enoch: a New English Edition.* SVTP 7. Leiden: Brill, 1985.

Blenkinsopp, J. *Wisdom and Law in the Old Testament: the Ordering of Life in Israel and Early Judaism.* New York: OUP, 1995.

Blomberg, C. *Interpreting the Parables.* Downers Grove: Inter-Varsity, 1990.

Bock, D. L. *Proclamation From Prophecy and Pattern: Lucan Old Testament Christology.* JSNTSup 12. Sheffield: JSOT, 1987.

___. *Luke.* BECNT. Grand Rapids: Baker Books, 1996.

___. *Blasphemy and Exaltation in Judaism and the Final Examination of Jesus: a Philological-Historical Study of the Key Jewish Themes Impacting Mark 14:61-64.* WUNT 2/106. Tübingen: Mohr Siebeck, 1998.

Boman, T. *Hebrew Thought Compared with Greek.* London: SCM, 1960.

Bonnard, P. *L'Evangile selon Saint Matthieu.* Neuchatel: Delachaux & Niestle, 1963, 1970.

Borgen, P. "Philo of Alexandria." In M. E. Stone (ed.), *Jewish Writings of the Second Temple Period: Apocrypha, Pseudepigrapha, Qumran, Sectarian Writings, Philo, Josephus.* Philadelphia: Fortress, 1984: 233-82.

___. "Philo of Alexandria: a Critical and Synthetical Survey of Research Since World War II." In H. Temporini and W. Haase (eds.), *Aufstieg und Niedergang der römischen Welt .* Berlin: Gruyter, 1984:

___. *Philo of Alexandria: an Exegete for His Time.* NovTSup 86. Leiden: Brill, 1997.

Bornkamm, G. *Jesus of Nazareth.* London: Hodder & Stoughton, 1960.

___. "The Praise of God (Romans 11:33-36)." In *Early Christian Experience: a Selection of Articles.* NTL. London: SCM, 1969: 105-111.

Boström, G. *Proverbiastudien: die Weisheit und das fremde Weib in Spr. 1-9.* Lund: Gleerup, 1935.

Bousset, W. *Jesu Predigt in ihrem Gegensatz zum Judentum: Ein religionschichtlicher Vergleich.* Göttingen: Vandenhoeck & Ruprecht, 1892.

___. *Kyrios Christos: Geschichte des Christusglaubens von den Anfängen des Christentums bis Irenaeus .* Göttingen: Vandenhoeck & Ruprecht, 1913. English Translation as *Kyrios Christos: a History of the Belief in Christ from the Beginnings of Christianity to Irenaeus* (Nashville: Abingdon, 1970).

Bousset, W. and H. Gressmann. *Die Religion des Judentums im späthellenistischen Zeitalter.* HNT 21. 3rd Ed. Tübingen: Mohr Siebeck, 1926.

Box, G. H. "The Idea of Intermediation in Jewish Theology: A Note on Memra and Shekinah." *JQR* 23 (1933) 103-19.

Bretscher, P. "Exodus 4:22-23 and the Voice from Heaven." *JBL* 87 (1968) 301-11.

Breytenbach, C., H. Paulsen, and C. Gerber. (eds.). *Anfänge der Christologie: Festschrift für Ferdinand Hahn zum 65. Geburtstag.* Göttingen: Vandenhoeck & Ruprecht, 1991.

Briggs, C. A. *A Critical and Exegetical Commentary on the Book of Psalms.* ICC. Edinburgh: T & T Clark, 1906.

Brooke, G. J. *Exegesis at Qumran: 4Q Florilegium in its Jewish Context.* JSOTSS 29. Sheffield: JSOT Press, 1985.

___. "4Q500 1 and the Use of the Scripture in the Parable of the Vineyard." *DSD* 2 (1995) 268-94.

Brown, R. E. *The Gospel According to John.* AB. 2 Vols. London: Chapman, 1971.

___. *The Birth of the Messiah: a Commentary on the Infancy Narratives in the Gospels of Matthew and Luke.* New York: Doubleday, 1993.

___. *The Death of the Messiah: From Gethsemane to the Grave: a Commentary on the Passion Narratives in the Four Gospels.* 2 Vols. London: G. Chapman, 1994.

Brown, R. E. and P. J. Achtemeier. (eds.). *Mary in the New Testament: a Collaborative Assessment by Protestant and Roman Catholic Scholars.* Philadelphia: Fortress Press, 1978.

Brown, W. P. Review of B. Witherington's *Jesus the Sage: the Pilgrimage of Wisdom.* *Int* 50 (1996) 198-199.

Brownlee, W. H. "Psalms 1-2 as a Coronation Liturgy." *Bib* 52 (1971) 321-36.

Bruce, F. F. *Commentary on the Epistle to the Hebrews: the English Text with Introduction, Exposition and Notes.* London: Marshall, Morgan & Scott, 1974.

___. "The Davidic Messiah in Luke-Acts." In G. A. Tuttle (ed.), *Biblical and Near Eastern Studies: Essays in Honor of William Sanford LaSor.* Grand Rapids: Eerdmans, 1978: 7-17.

___. *The Epistle of Paul to the Galatians: a Commentary on the Greek Text.* NIGTC. Exeter: Paternoster, 1982.

___. *The Acts of the Apostles: the Greek Text with Introduction and Commentary.* Grand Rapids: Eerdmans, 1990.

___. *The Epistle to the Hebrews.* NICNT. Grand Rapids: Eerdmans, 1990.

Buchanan, G. W. *To the Hebrews.* AB 36. Garden City: Doubleday, 1972.

Büchsel, F. *Die Christologie des Hebräerbriefs.* BFCT 27.2. Gütersloh: Bertelsmann, 1922.

Bühner, J.-A. *Der Gesandte und sein Weg im 4. Evangelium: die kultur- und religionsgeschichtlichen Grundlagen der johanneischen Sendungschristologie sowie ihre traditionsgeschichtliche Entwicklung.* WUNT 2/2. Tübingen: Mohr Siebeck, 1977.

Bultmann, R. *Theology of the New Testament.* London: SCM, 1952.

___. *Die Geschichte der synoptischen Tradition.* Göttingen: Vandenhoeck & Ruprecht, 1958.

___. *The History of the Synoptic Tradition.* Oxford: Blackwell, 1963. Translation of *Die Geschichte der synoptischen Tradition.* Göttingen: Vandenhoeck & Ruprecht, 1958.

Burger, C. *Jesus als Davidssohn: eine traditionsgeschichtliche Untersuchung.* Göttingen: Vandenhoeck & Ruprecht, 1970.

Buss, M. F.-J. *Die Missionspredigt des Apostels Paulus im Pisidischen Antiochien: Analyse von Apg 13, 16-41 im Hinblick auf die literarische und thematische Einheit der Paulusrede.* FB 38. Stuttgart: Verlag Katholisches Bibelwerk, 1980.

Byrne, B. *"Sons of God - Seed of Abraham": a Study of the Idea of the Sonship of God of All Christians in Paul Against the Jewish Background.* AnBib 83. Rome: Biblical Institute Press, 1979.

___. Review of J. M. Scott's *Adoption As Sons of God. JTS* 44 (1993) 288-294.

Cadoux, A. T. *The Parables of Jesus: Their Art and Use.* New York: Macmillan, 1931.

Caird, G. B. "The Development of the Doctrine of Christ in the New Testament." In W. N. Pittenger (ed.), *Christ for Us Today.* London: SCM, 1968: 66-81.

___. "Son by Appointment." In W. C. Weinrich (ed.), *The New Testament Age.* Macon: Mercer U.P., 1984: 1.73-81.

Caird, G. B. and L. D. Hurst. *New Testament Theology.* Oxford: Clarendon Press, 1994.

Callan, T. "Ps. 110:1 and the Origin of the Expectation that Jesus will Come Again." *CBQ* 44 (1982) 622-36.

Capes, D. B. *Old Testament Yahweh Texts in Paul's Christology.* WUNT 2/47. Tübingen: Mohr Siebeck, 1992.

Carlston, C. E. *The Parables of the Triple Tradition.* Philadelphia: Fortress, 1975.

Carrell, P. R. *Jesus and the Angels: Angelology and the Christology of the Apocalypse of John.* SNTSMS. Cambridge: CUP, 1997.

Casey, M. *Son of Man: the Interpretation and Influence of Daniel 7.* London: SPCK, 1979.

___. *From Jewish Prophet to Gentile God: the Origins and Development of New Testament Christology.* Cambridge: CUP, 1991.

___. *Is John's Gospel True?* London; New York: Routledge, 1996.

Cerfaux, L. *Christ in the Theology of St. Paul.* New York: Herder, 1959.

Charlesworth, J. H. *The Old Testament Pseudepigrapha and the New Testament: Prolegomena for the Study of Christian Origins.* SNTSMS 54. Cambridge: CUP, 1985.

___. "From Jewish Messianology to Christian Christology: Some Caveats and Perspectives." In W. S. Green, E. S. Frerichs, and J. Neusner (eds.), *Judaisms and their Messiahs at the Turn of the Christian Era.* Cambridge: CUP, 1987: 225-64.

___. "Jesus' Concept of God and His Self-Understanding." In *Jesus Within Judaism: New Light From Exciting Archaeological Discoveries.* London: SPCK, 1989: 131-64.

___. (ed.). *The Messiah: Developments in Earliest Judaism and Christianity.* Minneapolis: Fortress, 1992.

Charlesworth, J. H. and C. A. Evans. "Jesus in the Agrapha and Apocryphal Gospels." In B. D. Chilton and C. A. Evans (eds.), *Studying the Historical Jesus: Evaluation of the State of Current Research.* Leiden: Brill, 1994: 479-533.

Chester, A. "Jewish Messianic Expectations and Mediatorial Figures and Pauline Christology." In M. Hengel and U. Heckel (eds.), *Paulus und das antike Judentum.* WUNT 58. Tübingen: Mohr Siebeck, 1991: 17-89.

Chilton, B. D. *The Glory of Israel: the Theology and Provenience of the Isaiah Targum.* JSOTSup 23. Sheffield: JSOT Press, 1982.

___. "Jesus ben David: Reflections on the *Davidssohnfrage.*" *JSNT* 14 (1982) 88-112.

___. *A Galilean Rabbi and His Bible: Jesus' Use of the Interpreted Scripture of His Time.* Wilmington: Michael Glazier, 1984.

Chilton, B. D. and C. A. Evans. "Jesus and Israel's Scriptures." In B. D. Chilton and C. A. Evans (eds.), *Studying the Historical Jesus: Evaluation of the State of Current Research.* Leiden: Brill, 1994: 299-309.

Christ, F. *Jesus Sophia: die Sophia-Christologie bei den Synoptikern.* ATANT 57. Zürich: Zwingli Verlag, 1970.

Clements, R. E. *God and Temple: the Idea of the Divine Presence in Ancient Israel.* Oxford: Blackwell, 1965.

Coggins, R. J. *Sirach.* Guides to Apocrypha and Pseudepigrapha. Sheffield: Sheffield Academic Press, 1998.

Collins, J. J. *The Apocalyptic Vision of the Book of Daniel.* Missoula: Scholars Press, 1977.

____. "The Son of Man in First-Century Judaism." *NTS* 38 (1992) 448-66.

____. "The *Son of God* Text From Qumran." In M. C. de Boer (ed.), *From Jesus to John: Essays on Jesus and New Testament Christology in Honour of Marinus De Jonge.* JSNTSup 84. Sheffield: Sheffield Academic Press, 1993: 65-82.

____. *The Scepter and the Star: the Messiahs of the Dead Sea Scrolls and Other Ancient Literature.* New York: Doubleday, 1995.

____. "The Background of the 'Son of God' Text." *BBR* 7 (1997) 51-62.

____. *Jewish Wisdom in the Hellenistic Age.* Edinburgh: T & T Clark, 1998.

Conzelmann, H. "Paulus und die Weisheit." *NTS* 12 (1965-1966) 231-44.

____. "The Mother of Wisdom." In J. M. Robinson (ed.), *The Future of Our Religious Past: Essays in Honour of Rudolf Bultmann.* London: SCM, 1971: 230-43.

____. *1 Corinthians: a Commentary on the First Epistle to the Corinthians.* Hermeneia. Philadelphia: Fortress, 1975.

Craigie, P. C. *Psalms 1-50.* WBC 19. Waco: Word Books, 1983.

Cranfield, C. E. B. *The Gospel According to Saint Mark.* Cambridge Greek Testament Commentary. Cambridge: CUP, 1963.

____. *A Critical and Exegetical Commentary on the Epistle to the Romans.* ICC. Edinburgh: T & T Clark, 1982.

____. "Some Comments on Professor J. D. G. Dunn's *Christology in the Making* with Special Reference to the Evidence of the Epistle to the Romans." In L. D. Hurst and N. T. Wright (eds.), *The Glory of Christ in the New Testament.* Oxford: Clarendon, 1987: 267-80.

Crossan, J. D. "The Parable of the Wicked Husbandmen." *JBL* 90 (1971) 451-65.

____. *In Parables: the Challenge of the Historical Jesus.* San Francisco; London: Harper & Row, 1973.

____. *The Historical Jesus: the Life of a Mediterranean Jewish Peasant.* Edinburgh; San Francisco: T&T Clark; Harper, 1991.

Cullmann, O. "L'apôtre Pierre instrument du diable et instrument de Dieu." In A. J. B. Higgins (ed.), *New Testament Essays.* Manchester: Manchester University Press, 1959: 94-105.

____. *The Christology of the New Testament.* London: SCM, 1963.

D'Angelo, M. R. "Abba and Father: Imperial Theology and the Jesus Traditions." *JBL* 111 (1992) 611-630.

Dahl, N. A. "Anamnesis: Mémoire et commémoration dans le christianisme primitif." *ST* 1 (1947) 69-95.

____. *The Crucified Messiah: and Other Essays.* Minneapolis: Augsburg, 1974.

____. "Sources of Christological Language." In *The Crucified Messiah: and Other Essays.* Minneapolis: Augsburg, 1974: 10-36.

____. "Promise and Fulfillment." In *Studies in Paul: Theology for the Early Christian Mission.* Minneapolis: Augsburg, 1977: 121-36.

Dalman, G. H. *The Words of Jesus: Considered in the Light of Post-Biblical Jewish Writings and the Aramaic Language.* Vol. 1. Edinburgh: T & T Clark, 1902.

Daly, R. J. "The Soteriological Significance of the Sacrifice of Isaac." *CBQ* 39 (1977) 45-75.

Daube, D. "Four Types of Questions." *JTS* 2 (1951) 45-48.

___. *The New Testament and Rabbinic Judaism*. London: University of London, 1956.

Davies, P. R. and B. D. Chilton. "The Aqedah: a Revised Tradition History." *CBQ* 40 (1978) 514-46.

Davies, W. D. and D. C. Allison. *A Critical and Exegetical Commentary on the Gospel According to Saint Matthew*. ICC. Edinburgh: T & T Clark, 1988, 1991, 1997.

Davies, W. D. *Paul and Rabbinic Judaism: Some Rabbinic Elements in Pauline Theology*. London: SPCK, 1948, 1970.

Davis, C. J. *The Name and Way of the Lord: Old Testament Themes, New Testament Christology*. JSOTSS 129. Sheffield: Sheffield Academic Press, 1996.

Davis, J. A. *Wisdom and Spirit: an Investigation of 1 Corinthians 1.18-3.20 against the Background of Jewish Sapiential Traditions in the Greco-Roman Period*. Lanham; London: University Press of America, 1984.

Davis, P. G. "Divine Agents, Mediators, and New Testament Christology." *JTS* 45 (1994) 479-503.

de Dinechin, O. "καθώς: La similitude dans l'évangile selon saint Jean." *RSR* 58 (1970) 195-236.

de Jonge, M. "The Use of the Word 'Anointed' in the Time of Jesus." *NovT* 8 (1966) 132-48.

___. *Christology in Context: the Earliest Christian Response to Jesus*. Philadelphia: Westminster, 1988.

___. "Jesus, Son of David and Son of God." In S. Draisma (ed.), *Intertextuality in Biblical Writings: Essays in Honour of Bas van Iersel*. Kampen: J. H. Kok, 1989: 95-104.

de Lagarde, P. A. *Hagiographa Chaldaice*. Leipzig: Teubner, 1973.

de Moor, J. C. "The Targumic Background of Mark 12:1-12: The Parable of the Wicked Tenants." *JSJ* 29 (1998) 63-80.

de Vaux, R. *Ancient Israel: Its Life and Institutions*. New York: McGraw-Hill, 1961.

Deichgräber, R. *Gotteshymnus und Christushymnus in der frühen Christenheit: Untersuchungen zu Form, Sprache und Stil der frühchristlichen Hymnen*. Göttingen: Vandenhoeck & Ruprecht, 1967.

Deissler, A. "Zum Problem der Messianität von Psalm 2." In J. Doré, M. Carrez, and P. Grelot (eds.), *De la Tôrah au Messie*. Paris: Brouwer, 1981: 283-92.

Derrett, J. D. M. "Fresh Light on the Parable of the Wicked Vinedressers." *Revue internationale des droits de l'Antiquitè* 10 (1963) 11-42.

___. "Allegory and the Wicked Vinedressers." *JTS* 25 (1974) 426-32.

Deutsch, C. *Hidden Wisdom and the Easy Yoke: Wisdom, Torah and Discipleship in Matthew 11.25-30*. JSNTSup 18. Sheffield: JSOT Press, 1987.

___. "Wisdom in Matthew: Transformation of a Symbol." *NovT* 32 (1990) 13-47.

Dey, L. K. K. *The Intermediary World and Patterns of Perfection in Philo and Hebrews*. SBLDS 25. Missoula: Scholars Press, 1975.

Di Lella, A. A. "Conservative and Progressive Theology: Sirach and Wisdom." *CBQ* 28 (1966) 139-54.

___. "Wisdom of Ben-Sira." *ABD* 6.931-45.

___. "The Meaning of Wisdom in Ben Sira." In L. G. Perdue, B. B. Scott, and W. J. Wiseman (eds.), *In Search of Wisdom*. Louisville: Westminster/John Knox, 1993: 133-48.

Dibelius, M. *From Tradition to Gospel*. Cambridge: CUP, 1971.

Dillon, J. M. *The Middle Platonists: a Study of Platonism, 80 B.C. to A.D. 220.* London: Duckworth, 1977.

Dix, G. "The Heavenly Wisdom and the Divine Logos in Jewish Apocalyptic." *JTS* 26 (1925) 1-12.

Dodd, C. H. *The Apostolic Preaching and Its Developments: Three Lectures With an Appendix on Eschatology and History.* London: Hodder and Stoughton, 1936.

___. *The Johannine Epistles.* MNTC. London: Hodder & Stoughton, 1946.

___. *According to the Scriptures: the Sub-Structure of New Testament Theology.* London: Nisbet, 1952.

___. *The Interpretation of the Fourth Gospel.* Cambridge: CUP, 1953.

___. *The Parables of the Kingdom.* Welwyn: James Nisbet, 1961.

___. *Historical Tradition in the Fourth Gospel.* Cambridge: CUP, 1963.

___. "A Hidden Parable in the Fourth Gospel." In *More New Testament Studies.* Manchester: Manchester University Press, 1968: 30-40.

Donaldson, T. L. *Jesus on the Mountain: a Study in Matthean Theology.* JSNTSup 8. Sheffield: JSOT Press, 1985.

Dormandy, R. "Hebrews 1:1-2 and the Parable of the Wicked Husbandmen." *ExpTim* 100 (1989) 371-75.

Duling, D. C. "The Promises to David and Their Entrance into Christianity: Nailing Down a Likely Hypothesis." *NTS* 19 (1973-1974) 55-77.

Dunn, J. D. G. *Baptism in the Holy Spirit: a Re-Examination of the New Testament Teaching on the Gift of the Spirit in Relation to Pentecostalism Today.* SBT 2/15. London: SCM Press, 1970.

___. "Jesus - Flesh and Spirit: an Exposition of Romans 1.3-4." *JTS* 24 (1973) 40-68.

___. *Jesus and the Spirit: a Study of the Religious and Charismatic Experience of Jesus and the First Christians as Reflected in the New Testament.* London: SCM, 1975.

___. *Christology in the Making: a New Testament Inquiry into the Origins of the Doctrine of the Incarnation.* London: SCM, 1980, 1989.

___. "Was Christianity a Monotheistic Faith From the Beginning?" *SJT* 35 (1982) 303-336.

___. "Let John Be John." In P. Stuhlmacher (ed.), *Das Evangelium und die Evangelien: Vortrage vom Tübinger Symposium 1982.* WUNT 28. Tübingen: Mohr Siebeck, 1983: 309-39.

___. "'A Light to the Gentiles': the Significance of the Damascus Road Christophany for Paul." In L. D. Hurst and N. T. Wright (eds.), *The Glory of Christ in the New Testament: Studies in Christology.* Oxford: Clarendon, 1987: 251-66.

___. *Romans.* WBC 38. Dallas: Word Books, 1988.

___. *The Partings of the Ways: Between Christianity and Judaism, and Their Significance for the Character of Christianity.* London: SCM, 1991.

___. "The Making of Christology: Evolution or Unfolding?" In J. B. Green and M. Turner *Jesus of Nazareth: Lord and Christ: Essays on the Historical Jesus and New Testament Christology.* Grand Rapids: Eerdmans, 1994: 437-52.

___. "'Son of God' as 'Son of Man' in the Dead Sea Scrolls?: a Response to John Collins on 4Q246." In S. E. Porter and C. A. Evans (eds.), *The Scrolls and the Scriptures: Qumran Fifty Years After.* JSPSS 26. Sheffield: Sheffield Academic Press, 1997: 198-210.

___. "Christ, Adam, and Preexistence." In R. P. Martin and B. J. Dodd (eds.), *Where Christology Began: Essays on Philippians 2.* Louisville: Westminster/John Knox, 1998: 74-83.

Dupont, J. "Filius meus es tu: L'interprétation de Ps II,7 dans le Nouveau Testament." *RSR* 35 (1948) 522-43.

___. "'Assis à la droite de Dieu' L'interpretation du Ps 110,1 dans le Nouveau Testament." In B. M. Ahern, E. Dhanis, and G. Ghiberti (eds.), *Resurrexit: actes du Symposium international sur la resurrection de Jesus, Rome 1970*. Citta del Vaticano: Libreria editrice vaticana, 1974: 340-422.

Durham, J. I. *Exodus*. WBC 3. Dallas: Word Books, 1986.

Dürr, L. *Die Wertung des göttlichen Wortes im Alten Testament und im antiken Orient: zugleich ein Beitrag zur Vorgeschichte des neutestamentlichen Logosbegriffes*. Leipzig: J. C. Hinrichs Verlag, 1938.

Eaton, J. H. *Kingship and the Psalms*. Sheffield: JSOT Press, 1986.

Eichrodt, W. *Theology of the Old Testament*. OTL. 2 Vols. London: SCM, 1967.

Ellingworth, P. *The Epistle to the Hebrews: a Commentary on the Greek Text*. NIGTC. Grand Rapids: Eerdmans, 1993.

Ellis, E. E. *Paul's Use of the Old Testament*. Edinburgh; London: Oliver and Boyd, 1957.

___. *The Gospel of Luke* . London: Oliphants, 1974.

___. "'Wisdom' and 'Knowledge' in 1 Corinthians." In *Prophecy and Hermeneutic in Early Christianity*. Grand Rapids: Eerdmans, 1978: 45-62.

Eskola, T. *Messiah and the Throne: Jewish Merkabah Mysticism and Early Christian Exaltation Discourse*. WUNT 2/142. Tübingen: Mohr Siebeck, 2001.

Evans, C. A. "God's Vineyard and Its Caretakers." In *Jesus and His Contemporaries: Comparative Studies*. AGAJU 25. Leiden: Brill, 1995: 381-406.

___. "Jesus and the Messianic Texts From Qumran: A Preliminary Assessment of the Recently Published Materials." In *Jesus and His Contemporaries: Comparative Studies*. AGAJU 25. Leiden: Brill, 1995: 83-154.

___. "Recent Development in Jesus Research: Presuppositions, Criteria, and Sources." In *Jesus and His Contemporaries: Comparative Studies*. AGAJU 25. Leiden: Brill, 1995: 1-49.

___. "Jesus' Parable of the Tenant Farmers in Light of Lease Agreements in Antiquity." *JSP* 14 (1996) 65-83.

Evans, C. A. *Mark 8:27-16:20*. WBC 34B. Dallas: Word Books, 2001.

Evans, C. A. "How Septuagintal Is Isa 5:1-7 in Mark 12:1-9?" *NovT* 45 (2003) 105-10.

Fee, G. D. *The First Epistle to the Corinthians*. NICNT. Grand Rapids: Eerdmans, 1987.

___. "Philippians 2:5-11: Hymn or Exalted Pauline Prose?" *BBR* 2 (1992) 29-46.

Feldmeier, R. "Heil im Unheil: Das Bild Gottes nach der Parabel von den bösen Winzern (Mk. 12,1-12 par)." *TBei* 25 (1994) 5-22.

Festugiere, A. J. "A propos des Arétalogies d'Isis." *HTR* 42 (1949) 209-34.

Feuillet, A. "Jésus et la Sagesse divine d'après les évangiles synoptiques." *RB* 62 (1955) 161-196.

___. *Le Christ, sagesse de Dieu: d'apres les épitres pauliniennes*. Paris: Lecoffre, 1966.

Ficker, R. "מלאך." *THAT* 1.900-908.

Fieger, M. *Das Thomasevangelium: Einleitung Kommentar und Systematik*. Münster: Aschendorff, 1991.

Fitzmyer, J. A. "The Aramaic 'Elect of God' Text From Qumran Cave IV." *CBQ* 27 (1965) 348-72.

___. "4Q Testimonia and the New Testament." *TS* 18 (1967) 513-15.

____. *The Genesis Apocryphon of Cave 1: a Commentary.* Rome: Biblical Institute Press, 1971.

____. "Son of David and Mt. 22:41-46." In *Essays on the Semitic Background of the New Testament.* London: G. Chapman, 1971: 113-26.

____. "The Contribution of Qumran Aramaic to the Study of the New Testament." *NTS* 20 (1973-1974) 382-407.

____. "Methodology in the Study of the Aramaic Substratum of Jesus' Sayings in the New Testament." In J. Dupont (ed.), *Jesus aux origines de la Christologie.* Gembloux: Leuven University Press, 1975: 73-102.

____. "The Contribution of Qumran Aramaic to the Study of the New Testament." In *A Wandering Aramean: Collected Aramaic Essays.* SBLMS 25. Missoula: Scholars Press, 1979: 85-113.

____. "Abba and Jesus' Relation to God." In F. Refoule (ed.), *A cause de l'Evangile: études sur les Synoptiques et les Actes.* Paris: Cerf, 1985: 15-38.

____. *The Gospel According to Luke.* AB 28. New York: Doubleday, 1991, 1985.

____. "4Q246: The 'Son of God' Document From Qumran." *Bib* 74 (1993) 153-174.

____. *The Acts of the Apostles.* AB 31. New York: Doubleday, 1998.

Fleddermann, H. "The Discipleship Discourse (Mark 9:33-50)." *CBQ* 43 (1981) 57-75.

Fletcher-Louis, C. H. T. *Luke-Acts: Angels, Christology and Soteriology.* WUNT 2/94. Tübingen: Mohr Siebeck, 1997.

Flusser, D. "Two Notes on the Midrash on 2 Sam. 7:1." *IEJ* 9 (1959) 99-109.

Foakes-Jackson, F. J. *The Acts of the Apostles.* London: Macmillan, 1933.

Fossum, J. E. *The Name of God and the Angel of the Lord: Samaritan and Jewish Concepts of Intermediation and the Origin of Gnosticism.* WUNT 36. Tübingen: Mohr Siebeck, 1985.

____. *The Image of the Invisible God: Essays on the Influence of Jewish Mysticism on Early Christology.* Göttingen: Vandenhoeck & Ruprecht, 1995.

France, R. T. *Jesus and the Old Testament: His Application of Old Testament Passages to Himself and His Mission.* London: Tyndale, 1971.

____. "The Worship of Jesus: a Neglected Factor in Christological Debate?" In H. H. Rowdon (ed.), *Christ the Lord: Studies in Christology Presented to Donald Guthrie.* Leicester: Inter-Varsity, 1982: 17-36.

____. *The Gospel of Mark: a Commentary on the Greek Text.* NIGTC. Grand Rapids: Eerdmans, 2002.

Frankowski, J. "Early Christian Hymns Recorded in the New Testament: a Reconsideration of the Question in Light of Heb 1.3." *BZ* 27 (1983) 183-94.

Freedman, D. N. and B. E. Willoughby. "מלאך." *TWAT* 4.901.

Fretheim, T. E. "Word of God." *ABD* 6.961-68.

Fuchs, E. *Die Freiheit des Glaubens: Römer 5-8 ausgelegt.* BEvT 14. München: Kaiser, 1949.

Fuller, R. H. *The Foundations of New Testament Christology.* London: Lutterworth, 1965.

____. "The Conception/Birth of Jesus as a Christological Moment." *JSNT* 1 (1978) 37-52.

Funk, R. W. and R. W. Hoover. *The Five Gospels: the Search for the Authentic Words of Jesus: New Translation and Commentary.* New York; Oxford: Macmillan, 1993.

Funk, R. W. *The Gospel of Mark: Red Letter Edition.* Sonoma: Polebridge, 1991.

Furness, J. M. "Behind the Philippian Hymn." *ExpTim* 79 (1967-1968) 178-82.

García Martínez, F. "The Eschatological Figure of 4Q246." In *Qumran and Apocalyptic: Studies on the Aramaic Texts from Qumran*. Leiden: Brill, 1992: 162-79.

Gärtner, B. "שׁלב als Messiasbezeichnung." *SEÅ* 18-19 (1953-1954) 98-108.

Gathercole, S. J. "On the Alleged Aramaic Idiom behind the Synoptic ἦλθον-sayings." *JTS* 55 (2004) 84-91.

___. "The Advent of Jesus in the Synoptic Gospels." *an unpublished paper read at Aberdeen University NT Seminar* (2002) 1-16.

___. "Is Wisdom Christology a way into the Pre-existence of Christ?: Matthew 11.16-30 and 23.34-24-1 as Test Cases." *an unpublished paper read at Aberdeen University NT Seminar* (2002) 1-7.

___. "Pre-existence in the Synoptic Gospels: the Evidence of Mark 1-2." *an unpublished paper read at Aberdeen University NT Seminar* (2002) 1-9.

Georgi, D. "Der vorpaulinische Hymnus Phil 2,6-11." In E. Dinkler and H. Thyen (eds.), *Zeit und Geschichte: Dankesgabe an Rudolf Bultmann zum 80. Geburtstag*. Tübingen: Mohr Siebeck, 1964: 263-93.

Gerhardsson, B. *The Reliability of the Gospel Tradition*. Peabody: Hendrickson, 2001.

Gese, H. *Zur biblischen Theologie*. München: Kaiser, 1977.

___. "Wisdom, Son of Man, and the Origins of Christology: The Consistent Development of Biblical Theology." *HBT* 3 (1981) 23-58.

Giblin, C. H. "Three Monotheistic Texts in Paul." *CBQ* 37 (1975) 527-47.

Gibson, A. *Biblical Semantic Logic: a Preliminary Analysis*. Oxford: Blackwell, 1981.

Gieschen, C. A. *Angelomorphic Christology: Antecedents and Early Evidence*. AGAJU 42. Leiden: Brill, 1998.

Giles, P. *Jesus the High Priest in the Epistle to the Hebrews and in the Fourth Gospel*. M.A. Thesis, Manchester, 1973.

___. "The Son of Man in the Epistle to the Hebrews." *ExpT* 86 (1974-1975) 328-32.

Glasson, T. F. *Jesus and the End of the World*. Edinburgh: Saint Andrew, 1980.

Gnilka, J. *Das Evangelium nach Markus*. EKKNT 2. 2 Vols. Einsiedeln: Benziger Verlag, 1978-79.

Goetz, S. C. and C. L. Blomberg. "The Burden of Proof." *JSNT* 11 (1981) 39-63.

Goldberg, A. *Untersuchungen über die Vorstellung von der Schekhinah in der frühen rabbinischen Literatur (Talmud und Midrasch)*. Berlin: Walter de Gruyter, 1969.

___. *Erlösung durch Leiden. Drei rabbinische Homilien über die Trauernden Zions und den leidenden Messias Ephraim, PesR 34. 36. 37*. FJS 4. Frankfurt: Lang, 1978.

___. "Die Namen des Messias in der rabbinischen Traditionsliteratur. Ein Beitrag zur Messiaslehre des rabbinischen Judentums." *Frankfurter Judaistische Beiträge* 7 (1979) 1-93.

Goldsmith, D. "Acts 13:33-37: a *Pesher* on 2 Samuel 7." *JBL* 87 (1968) 321-24.

Goodenough, E. R. *An Introduction to Philo Judaeus*. Oxford: Blackwell, 1962.

Gordis, R. "The 'Begotten' Messiah in the Qumran Scrolls." *VT* 7 (1957) 191-94.

Goulder, M. D. *Midrash and Lection in Matthew*. London: SPCK, 1974.

___. "Psalm 8 and the Son of Man." *NTS* 48 (2002) 18-29.

Gourgues, M. *A la droite de Dieu: resurrection de Jesus et actualisation du psaume 110, 1 dans le Nouveau Testament*. Paris: J. Gabalda, 1978.

Grässer, E. "Hebräer 1,1-4: ein exegetischer Versuch." *EKKNTV* 3 (1971) 55-91.

Green, J. B., S. McKnight, and I. H. Marshall. (eds.). *Dictionary of Jesus and the Gospels*. Downers Grove: Inter-Varsity, 1992.

Grether, O. *Name und Wort Gottes im Alten Testament*. ZAW 64. Giessen: A. Topelmann, 1934.

Grundmann, W. *Das Evangelium nach Lukas.* THKNT 3. Berlin: Evangelische Verlagsanstalt, 1966.

Guelich, R. A. *Mark 1-8:26.* WBC 34A. Dallas: Word Books, 1989.

Guillet, J. "Luc 22,29: une formule johannique dans l'évangile de Luc." *RSR* 69 (1981) 113-22.

Gundry, R. H. "The Narrative Framework of Matthew XVI.17-19." *NovT* 7 (1964) 1-9.

___. *The Use of the Old Testament in St. Matthew's Gospel: with Special Reference to the Messianic Hope.* NovTSup 18. Leiden: Brill, 1967.

___. *Mark: a Commentary on His Apology for the Cross.* Grand Rapids: Eerdmans, 1993.

___. *Matthew: a Commentary on his Handbook for a Mixed Church under Persecution.* Grand Rapids: Eerdmans, 1994.

Gunkel, H. *Die Psalmen.* Göttingen: Vanderhoeck & Ruprecht, 1968.

Habermann, J. *Präexistenzaussagen im Neuen Testament.* Europäische Hochschulschriften 23/362. Frankfurt: Lang, 1990.

Haenchen, E. *Der Weg Jesu: Eine Erklärung des Markus-Evangeliums und der kanonischen Parallelen.* Berlin: Topelmann, 1966.

___. *The Acts of the Apostles.* Philadelphia: Westminster, 1971.

Hagner, D. A. "Paul's Christology and Jewish Monotheism." In P. K. Jewett, R. A. Muller, and M. Shuster (eds.), *Perspectives on Christology.* Grand Rapids: Zondervan, 1991: 19-38.

___. *Matthew 1-13.* WBC 33. Dallas: Word Books, 1993.

___. *Matthew 14-28.* WBC 33. Dallas: Word Books, 1995.

Hahn, F. *Christologische Hoheitstitel.* Göttingen: Vandenhoeck & Ruprecht, 1964.

___. *The Titles of Jesus in Christology.* London: Lutterworth, 1969.

Hall, D. R. *The Gospel Framework: Fiction or Fact?: a Critical Evaluation of Der Rahmen der Geschichte Jesu by Karl Ludwig Schmidt.* Carlisle: Paternoster, 1998.

Hamerton-Kelly, R. *Pre-Existence, Wisdom, and the Son of Man: a Study of the Idea of Pre-Existence in the New Testament.* SNTSMS. Cambridge: CUP, 1973.

___. "God the Father in the Bible." In J. B. Metz, E. Schillebeeckx, and M. Lefébure (eds.), *God As Father?* Concilium 143. Edinburgh: T. & T. Clark; New York: Seabury Press, 1981:

Hamp, V. *Der Begriff 'Wort' in den aramäischen Bibelübersetzungen: Ein exegetischer Beitrag zur Hypostasen-Frage und zur Geschichte der Logos-Spekulation.* München: Filser, 1938.

Hannah, D. D. *Michael and Christ: Michael Traditions and Angel Christology in Early Christianity.* WUNT 2/109. Tübingen: Mohr Siebeck, 1999.

Hanson, A. T. *Jesus Christ in the Old Testament.* London: SPCK, 1965.

___. *The New Testament Interpretation of Scripture.* London: SPCK, 1980.

___. *The Image of the Invisible God.* London: SCM, 1982.

Harris, J. R. *Testimonies.* Cambridge: CUP, 1916-20.

___. *The Origin of the Prologue to St John's Gospel.* Cambridge: CUP, 1917.

Hawthorne, G. F. *Philippians.* WBC 43. Dallas: Word Books, 1983.

Hay, D. M. *Glory at the Right Hand: Psalm 110 in Early Christianity.* SBLMS 18. Nashville: Abingdon, 1973.

Hayman, P. "Monotheism: a Missued Word in Jewish Studies?" *JJS* 42 (1991) 1-15.

Hays, R. B. *Echoes of the Scriptures in the Letters of Paul.* New Haven: Yale University Press, 1989.

Hayward, R. *Divine Name and Presence: the Memra.* Totowa: Allanheld, 1981.

Heidt, W. G. *Angelology of the Old Testament: a Study in Biblical Theology.* Washington: The Catholic University of America Press, 1949.

Heinisch, P. *Personifikationen und Hypostasen im Alten Testament und im Alten Orient.* BZ 9.10/12. Münster: Aschendorff, 1921.

Hengel, M. "Das Gleichnis von den Weingärtnern Mc 12,1-12 im Lichte der Zenonpapyri und der rabbinischen Gleichnisse." *ZNW* 59 (1968) 1-39.

___. *Judaism and Hellenism: Studies in Their Encounter in Palestine During the Early Hellenistic Period.* 2 Vols. London: SCM, 1974.

___. *The Son of God: the Origin of Christology and the History of Jewish-Hellenistic Religion.* London: SCM, 1976.

___. *The Atonement: a Study of the Origins of the Doctrine in the New Testament.* London: SCM Press, 1981.

___. "Christology and New Testament Chronology." In *Between Jesus and Paul: Studies in the Earliest History of Christianity.* Philadelphia: Fortress, 1983: 30-47.

___. "Hymns and Christology." In *Between Jesus and Paul: Studies in the Earliest History of Christianity.* Philadelphia: Fortress, 1983: 78-96.

___. *The 'Hellenization' of Judaea in the First Century After Christ.* London: SCM, 1990.

___. "'Sit at My Right Hand!' The Enthronement of Christ at the Right Hand of God and Psalm 110:1." In *Studies in Early Christology.* Edinburgh: T & T Clark, 1995: 119-225.

Herzog, W. R. *Parables as Subversive Speech: Jesus as Pedagogue of the Oppressed.* Louisville: Westminster/John Knox, 1994.

Hester, J. D. "Socio-Rhetorical Criticism and the Parable of the Wicked Tenants." *JSNT* 45 (1992) 27-57.

Hill, D. *The Gospel of Matthew.* NCBC. London: Oliphants, 1972.

Hingle, N. N. *Jesus, a Divine Agent: Three Christological Comparisons Between the Gospels of Matthew and John.* Aberdeen Univ. Ph.D. dissertation, 1995.

Hirth, V. *Gottes Boten im Alten Testament: die alttestamentliche Mal'ak-Vorstellung unter besonderer Berücksichtigung des Mal'ak-Jahwe-Problems.* ThA 32. Berlin: Evang. Verlagsanst, 1975.

Hoffmann, P. *Studien zur Theologie der Logienquelle.* Münster: Aschendorff, 1972.

Hooke, S. H. *Alpha and Omega: a Study in the Pattern of Revelation.* Welwyn: J. Nisbet, 1961.

Hooker, M. D. *Jesus and the Servant: the Influence of the Servant Concept of Deutero-Isaiah in the New Testament.* London: SPCK, 1959.

___. *The Son of Man in Mark.* London: SPCK, 1967.

___. "On Using the Wrong Tool." *Theology* 75 (1972) 570-81.

Hoover, R. W. "The Harpagmos Enigma: A Philological Solution." *HTR* 64 (1971) 95-119.

Horbury, W. "The Messianic Associations of 'the Son of Man'." *JTS* 36 (1985) 34-55.

___. "The Christian Use and the Jewish Origins of the Wisdom of Solomon." In H. G. M. Williamson, R. P. Gordon, J. A. Emerton, and Day John (eds.), *Wisdom in Ancient Israel: Essays in Honour of J. A. Emerton.* Cambridge: CUP, 1995: 183-85.

___. *Jewish Messianism and the Cult of Christ.* London: SCM, 1998.

___. "Jewish Messianism and Early Christology." *an unpublished paper presented at H. H. Bingham NT Colloquium* (2001) 1-20.

Horsley, R. A. "Wisdom of Word and Words of Wisdom in Corinth." *CBQ* 39 (1977) 224-39.

____. "The Background of the Confessional Formula in 1 Kor. 8.6." *ZNW* 69 (1978) 130-5.

Howard, G. "Phil. 2:6-11 and the Human Christ." *CBQ* 40 (1978) 368-87.

Huffmon, H. B. "Name." *DDD* 1148-51.

Hultgren, A. J. *The Parables of Jesus: a Commentary.* Grand Rapids: Eerdmans, 2000.

Hunter, A. M. "Crux Criticorum - Matt. 11:25-30 - a Reappraisal." *NTS* 3 (1961-1962) 241-49.

____. *The Work and Words of Jesus.* Philadelphia: Westminster, 1973.

Huntress, E. "'Son of God' in Jewish Writings Prior to the Christian Era." *JBL* (1935) 117-23.

Hurst, L. D. "Re-Enter the Pre-Existent Christ in Philippians 2.5-11?" *NTS* 32 (1986) 449-57.

____. "The Christology of Hebrews 1 and 2." In L. D. Hurst and N. T. Wright (eds.), *The Glory of Christ in the New Testament: Studies in Christology.* Oxford: Clarendon, 1987: 151-64.

____. "Christ, Adam, and Preexistence Revisited." In R. P. Martin and B. J. Dodd (eds.), *Where Christology Began: Essays on Philippians 2.* Louisville: Westminster/John Knox, 1998: 84-95.

Hurtado, L. W. *One God, One Lord: Early Christian Devotion and Ancient Jewish Monotheism.* London: SCM, 1988, 1998.

____. "What Do We Mean by 'First-Century Jewish Monotheism'?" In D. Lull (ed.), *SBLSP.* Atlanta: Scholars Press, 1993: 348-68.

____. "Christ-Devotion in the First Two Centuries: Reflections and a Proposal." *Toronto Journal of Theology* 12 (1996) 17-33.

____. "First-Century Jewish Monotheism." *JSNT* 71 (1998) 3-26.

____. "Jesus' Divine Sonship in Paul's Epistle to the Romans." In N. T. Wright and S. Soderlund (eds.), *Romans and the People of God.* Grand Rapids: Eerdmans, 1999: 217-33.

____. "Pre-70 CE Jewish Opposition to Christ-Devotion." *JTS* 50 (1999) 35-58.

____. "Religious Experience and Religious Innovation in the New Testament." *JR* 80 (2000) 183-205.

____. *Lord Jesus Christ: Devotion to Jesus in Earliest Christianity.* Grand Rapids: Eerdmans, 2003.

Hyatt, J. P. *Commentary on Exodus.* NCBC. London: Oliphants, 1971.

Isaac, E. "1 (Ethiopic Apocalypse of) Enoch." In J. H. Charlesworth (ed.), *The Old Testament Pseudepigrapha.* London: Darton, Longman & Todd, 1983: 1.5-89.

Jacob, E. *Theology of the Old Testament.* London: Hodder and Stoughton, 1958.

Jacobson, A. D. *Wisdom Christology in Q.* Diss. Claremont, 1978.

Jeremias, J. *Jesus' Promise to the Nations.* SBT 24. London: SCM, 1958.

____. "Theophany in the OT." *IDBSup* 896-98.

____. "παῖς θεοῦ." *TDNT* 5.677-717.

____. *Abba: Studien zur neutestamentlichen Theologie und Zeitgeschichte.* Göttingen: Vandenhoeck & Ruprecht, 1966.

____. "Die älteste Schicht der Menschensohn-Logien." *ZNW* 58 (1967) 159-72.

____. *The Prayers of Jesus.* SBT 2/6. London: SCM, 1967.

____. *New Testament Theology.* London: SCM, 1971.

____. *The Parables of Jesus.* Göttingen: Vandenhoeck & Ruprecht, 1972.

Jervell, J. *The Theology of the Acts of the Apostles.* New Testament Theology. Cambridge: CUP, 1996.

____. *Die Apostelgeschichte.* KEKNT 3. Göttingen: Vandenhoeck & Ruprecht, 1998.

Jeske, R. L. "The Rock was Christ: the Ecclesiology of 1 Corinthians 10." In D. Lührmann and G. Strecker (eds.), *Kirche: Festschrift für Günther Bornkamm zum 75. Geburtstag.* Tübingen: Mohr Siebeck, 1980: 245-55.

Jewett, R. *Paul's Anthropological Terms: a Study of their Use in Conflict Settings.* AGAJU 10. Leiden: Brill, 1971.

___. "The Redaction and Use of an Early Christian Confession in Romans 1:3-4." In D. E. Groh and R. Jewett (eds.), *The Living Text: Essays in Honor of Ernest W. Saunders.* Lanham: University Press of America, 1985: 99-122.

Johnson, A. R. *Sacral Kingship in Ancient Israel.* Cardiff: University of Wales Press, 1955.

___. *The One and the Many in the Israelite Conception of God.* Cardiff: University of Wales Press, 1961.

Johnson, E. E. *The Function of Apocalyptic and Wisdom Traditions in Romans 9-11.* SBLDS 109. Atlanta: Scholars Press, 1989.

Johnson, L. T. *Religious Experience in Earliest Christianity.* Minneapolis: Fortress, 1998.

Johnson, M. D. "Reflections on a Wisdom Approach to Matthew's Christology." *CBQ* 36 (1974) 44-64.

Juel, D. H. *Messiah and Temple: the Trial of Jesus in the Gospel of Mark.* SBLDS 31. Missoula: Scholars Press, 1977.

___. *Messianic Exegesis: Christological Interpretation of the Old Testament in Early Christianity.* Philadelphia: Fortress, 1988.

Jülicher, A. *Die Gleichnisreden Jesu.* Tübingen: Mohr Siebeck, 1899. Reprinted, Darmstadt: Wissenschaftliche Buchgesellschaft, 1963.

Kaiser, W. C. *Exodus. The Expositor's Bible Commentary.* F. E. Gaebelein and R. P. Polcyn. (eds.) Grand Rapids: Regency Reference, 1990.

Karrer, M. *Der Gesalbte: die Grundlagen des Christustitels.* Göttingen: Vandenhoeck & Ruprecht, 1990.

Käsemann, E. "The Problem of the Historical Jesus." In *Essays on New Testament Themes.* SBT 41. London: SCM, 1964: 15-47.

___. *An die Römer.* HNT 8a. Tübingen: Mohr Siebeck, 1973.

___. *Commentary on Romans.* London: SCM, 1980.

___. *The Wandering People of God: an Investigation of the Letter to the Hebrews.* Minneapolis: Augsburg Pub. House, 1984.

Kayatz, C. *Studien zu Proverbien 1-9: eine form- und motivgeschichtliche Untersuchung unter Einbeziehung ägyptischen Vergleichsmaterials.* WMANT 22. Neukirchen-Vluyn: Neukirchener Verlag, 1966.

Kazmierski, C. R. *Jesus the Son of God: a Study of the Markan Tradition and its Redaction by the Evangelist.* Würzburg: Echter, 1979.

Kidner, D. *Psalms 73-150: a Commentary on Books 3-6 of the Psalms.* TOTC. London: Inter-Varsity, 1975.

Kilpatrick, G. D. "The Order of Some Noun and Adjective Phrases in the New Testament." *NovT* 5 (1962) 111-14.

Kim, S. *The Origin of Paul's Gospel.* WUNT 2/4. Tübingen: Mohr Siebeck, 1981.

___. *"The 'Son of Man'" as the Son of God.* WUNT 30. Tübingen: Mohr Siebeck, 1983.

Kimball, C. A. "Jesus' Exposition of Scripture in Luke (20:9-19): an Inquiry in Light of Jewish Hermeneutics." *BBR* 3 (1993) 77-92.

Kingsbury, J. D. "The Parable of the Wicked Husbandmen and the Secret of Jesus' Divine Sonship in Matthew: Some Literary-Critical Observations." *JBL* 105 (1986) 643-55.

Kinzer, M. S. *'All Things Under His Feet': Psalm 8 in the New Testament and in Other Jewish Literature of Late Antiquity.* PhD dissertation; University of Michigan, 1995.

Kissane, E. J. "The Interpretation of Psalm 110." *ITQ* 21 (1954) 103-14.

Klausner, J. *Jesus of Nazareth: His Life, Times, and Teaching.* New York: Macmillan, 1926.

___. *The Messianic Idea in Israel.* London: Allen and Unwin, 1956.

Klein, G. "Die Prüfung der Zeit (Lukas 12, 54-56)." *ZTK* 61 (1964) 373-90.

Kloppenborg [Verbin], J. S. "Wisdom Christology in Q." *LTP* 34 (1978) 129-47.

___. "Isis and Sophia in the Book of Wisdom." *HTR* 75 (1982) 57-84.

___. *Q Parallels: Synopsis, Critical Notes & Concordance.* Sonoma: Polebridge, 1988.

___. "Egyptian Viticultural Practices and the Citation of Isa 5:1-7 in Mark 12:1-9." *NovT* 44 (2002) 134-59.

Klostermann, E. *Das Lukasevangelium.* HNT. Tübingen: Mohr Siebeck, 1929.

___. *Das Matthäusevangelium.* HNT 4. Tübingen: Mohr Siebeck, 1971.

Knight, G. A. F. *A Christian Theology of the Old Testament.* London: SCM, 1959.

Knox, J. *The Humanity and Divinity of Christ: a Study of Pattern in Christology.* Cambridge: CUP, 1967.

Knox, W. L. "The Divine Wisdom." *JTS* 38 (1937) 230-7.

___. *St Paul and the Church of the Gentiles.* Cambridge: CUP, 1939.

Kramer, W. R. *Christos, Kyrios, Gottessohn: Untersuchungen zu Gebrauch und Bedeutung der christologischen Bezeichnungen bei Paulus und den vorpaulinischen Gemeinden.* ATANT 44. Zürich: Zwingli Verlag, 1963.

___. *Christ, Lord and Son of God.* London: SCM, 1966.

Kraus, H.-J. *Psalmen.* BKAT 15/1. Neukirchen-Vluyn: Neukirchener Verlag, 1960.

___. *Psalms 1-59: a Commentary.* Minneapolis: Augsburg, 1988.

___. *Theology of the Psalms.* Minneapolis: Fortress, 1992.

Kruse, H. "Die 'dialektische Negation' als semitisches Idiom." *VT* 4 (1954) 385-400.

Kuhn, H. B. "The Angelology of the Non-Canonical Jewish Apocalypses." *JBL* 67 (1947) 217-32.

Kümmel, W. G. *Promise and Fulfilment: the Eschatological Message of Jesus.* SBT 23. London: SCM, 1957.

___. "Das Gleichnis von den bösen Weingärtnern (Mk 12:1-9)." In *Heilsgeschehen und Geschichte: Gesammelte Aufsätze 1933-64.* MGT 3. Marburg: N. G. Elwert Verlag, 1965: 207-17.

___. *The Theology of the New Testament: according to its Major Witnesses, Jesus, Paul, John.* Nashville: Abingdon, 1973.

Ladd, G. E. *A Theology of the New Testament.* Grand Rapids: Eerdmans, 1974.

Lagrange, M.-J. *Évangile selon St Luc.* EBib. Paris: Gabalda, 1941.

___. *Évangile selon Saint Marc.* EBib. Paris: Lecoffre, 1947.

___. *Évangile selon saint Matthieu.* EBib. Paris: Gabalda, 1948.

Lake, K. and H. J. Cadbury. *The Beginnings of Christianity.* 5 Vols. London: Macmillan, 1920.

Lambrecht, J. "Paul's Christological Use of Scripture in 1-Corinthians 15.20-28." *NTS* 28 (1982) 502-527.

___. *Out of the Treasure: the Parables in the Gospel of Matthew.* Louvain: Peeters, 1992.

Lane, W. L. "Detecting Divine Wisdom Christology in Hebrews 1:1-4." *New Testament Student* 5 (1982) 150-58.
___. *Hebrews*. WBC 47. Dallas: Word Books, 1991.
Larcher, C. *Études sur le livre de la Sagesse*. EBib. Paris: Lecoffre, 1969.
Leaney, A. R. C. "The Gospels as Evidence for First-Century Judaism." In D. E. Nineham (ed.), *Historicity and Chronology in the New Testament*. London: SPCK, 1965: 28-45.
Lentzen-Deis, F. *Die Taufe Jesu nach den Synoptikern: literarkritische und gattungsgeschichtliche Untersuchungen*. Frankfurt: Knecht, 1970.
Levenson, J. D. *The Death and Resurrection of the Beloved Son: the Transformation of Child Sacrifice in Judaism and Christianity*. New Haven: Yale University Press, 1993.
Levey, S. H. *The Messiah: an Aramaic Interpretation: the Messianic Exegesis of the Targum*. Cincinnati: Hebrew Union College-Jewish Institute of Religion, 1974.
Lindars, B. *New Testament Apologetic: the Doctrinal Significance of the Old Testament Quotations*. London: SCM, 1961.
___. *Jesus Son of Man: a Fresh Examination of the Son of Man Sayings in the Gospels in the Light of Recent Research*. London: SPCK, 1983.
Linnemann, E. *Studien zur Passionsgeschichte*. FRLANT 102. Göttingen: Vandenhoeck & Ruprecht, 1970.
___. "Tradition und Interpretation in Röm. 1,3 f." *EvT* 31 (1971) 264-76.
Linton, O. "Le *Parallelismus Membrorum* dans le Nouveau Testament: Simple remarques." In A.-L. Descamps and A. de Halleux (eds.), *Mélanges bibliques: en hommage au R. P. Beda Rigaux*. Gembloux: Duculot, 1970: 488-507.
Llewelyn, S. R. "Self-Help and Legal Redress: The Parable of the Wicked Tenants." In R. A. Kearsley and S. R. Llewelyn (eds.), *New Documents Illustrating Early Christianity*. North Ryde: Macquarie University, 1992: 86-105.
Loader, W. R. G. "Christ at the Right Hand - Ps. CX in the New Testament." *NTS* 24 (1978) 199-217.
___. *Sohn und Hoherpriester: eine traditionsgeschichtliche Untersuchung zur Christologie des Hebraerbriefes*. WMANT 53. Neukirchen-Vluyn: Neukirchener Verlag, 1981.
Lods, A. "L'Ange de Yahvé et l'âme extérieure." *BZAW* (1913) 259-78.
Lohfink, G. *Die Himmelfahrt Jesu: Untersuchungen zu den Himmelfahrts- und Erhöhungstexten bei Lukas*. SANT 26. München: Kosel, 1971.
Lohmeyer, E. *Kyrios Jesus: eine untersuchung zu Phil. 2, 5-11*. Heidelberg: C. Winter, 1928.
___. *Das Evangelium des Markus*. Göttingen: Vandenhoeck & Ruprecht, 1951.
Lohse, E. *Märtyrer und Gottesknecht: Untersuchungen zur urchristlichen Verkündigung vom Sühntod Jesu Christi*. FRLANT 64. Göttingen: Vandenhoeck & Ruprecht, 1955.
___. *Der Prozeß Jesu Christi. Die Einheit des Neuen Testaments Exegetische Studien zur Theologie des Neuen Testaments*. ESTNT 1. Göttingen: Vandenhoeck & Ruprecht, 1973.
___. *Die Texte aus Qumran: Hebräisch und Deutsch*. München: Kösel, 1981.
Longenecker, R. N. *Galatians*. WBC 41. Dallas: Word Books, 1990.
___. *Acts*. Grand Rapids: Zondervan, 1995.
Lövestam, E. *Son and Saviour: a Study of Acts 13, 32-37*. Lund: Gleerup, 1961.
Lowe, M. "From the Parable of the Vineyard to a Pre-Synoptic Source." *NTS* 28 (1982) 257-63.

Lührmann, D. *Die Redaktion der Logienquelle.* WMANT 33. Neukirchen-Vluyn: Neukirchener Verlag, 1969.

___. *Das Markusevangelium.* HNT 3. Tübingen: Mohr Siebeck, 1987.

Luz, U. *Das Geschichtsverständnis des Paulus.* BEvTh 49. München: Kaiser, 1968.

___. *Matthew 1-7.* Edinburgh: T & T Clark, 1990.

___. *Matthew 8-20.* Hermeneia. Minneapolis: Fortress, 2001.

Mach, M. *Entwicklungsstadien des jüdischen Engelglaubens in vorrabbinischer Zeit.* TSAJ 34. Tübingen: Mohr Siebeck, 1992.

Mack, B. L. "Wisdom Myth and Mythology." *Int* 24 (1970) 46-60.

___. *Logos und Sophia: Untersuchungen zur Weisheitstheologie im hellenistischen Judentum.* Göttingen: Vandenhoeck & Ruprecht, 1973.

Macleod, D. *The Person of Christ.* Contours of Christian Theology. Leicester: Inter-Varsity, 1998.

MacNeill, H. L. *The Christology of the Epistle to the Hebrews: Including its Relation to the Developing Christology of the Primitive Church.* Chicago: University of Chicago Press, 1914.

Maloney, E. C. *Semitic Interference in Marcan Syntax.* SBLDS 51. Missoula: Scholars Press, 1980.

Mann, C. S. *Mark: a New Translation with Introduction and Commentary.* AB 27. New York: Doubleday, 1986.

Manson, T. W. *The Teaching of Jesus.* Cambridge: CUP, 1935.

___. *The Sayings of Jesus.* London: SCM, 1949.

Marböck, J. *Weisheit im Wandel: Untersuchungen zur Weisheitstheologie bei Ben Sira.* BBB 37. Bonn: Hanstein, 1971.

Marcus, J. "Mark 14:61: 'Are You the Messiah-Son-of-God?'." *NovT* 31 (1989) 125-141.

___. *The Way of the Lord: Christological Exegesis of the Old Testament in the Gospel of Mark.* Louisville: Westminster/John Knox, 1992.

___. *Mark: a New Translation with Introduction and Commentary.* AB 27. New York: Doubleday, 2000.

Marcus, R. "On Biblical Hypostases of Wisdom." *HUCA* 23 (1950-1951) 157-171.

Marshall, I. H. "The Christ-Hymn in Philippians 2:5-11: a Review Article." *TynBul* 19 (1968) 104-27.

___. "Palestinian and Hellenistic Christianity: Some Critical Comments." *NTS* 19 (1972-1973) 271-87.

___. *The Origins of New Testament Christology.* Downers Grove: Inter-Varsity, 1976, 1990.

___. *I Believe in the Historical Jesus.* London: Hodder & Stoughton, 1977.

___. *The Gospel of Luke: a Commentary on the Greek Text.* NIGTC. Grand Rapids: Eerdmans, 1978.

___. *The Acts of the Apostles: an Introduction and Commentary.* TNTC. Grand Rapids: Eerdmans, 1980.

___. Review of J. D. G. Dunn's *Christology in the Making.* *TJ* 2 (1981) 241-45.

___. "The Development of Christology in the Early Church." In *Jesus the Saviour: Studies in New Testament Theology.* Downers Grove: Inter-Varsity, 1990: 150-64. Originally published in *TynBul* 18 (1967), 77-93.

___. "The Divine Sonship of Jesus." In *Jesus the Saviour: Studies in New Testament Theology.* Downers Grove: Inter-Varsity, 1990: 134-49. Originally published in *Int* 21 (1967), 87-103.

___. "Incarnational Christology in the New Testament." In *Jesus the Saviour: Studies in New Testament Theology*. Downers Grove: Inter-Varsity, 1990: 165-80. Originally published in H. H. Rowdon. (ed.) *Christ the Lord: Studies in Christology Presented to Donald Guthrie*. Leicester: Inter-Varsity Press, 1982, 1-16.

___. "Jesus as Lord: the Development of the Concept." In *Jesus the Saviour: Studies in New Testament Theology*. Downers Grove: Inter-Varsity, 1990: 197-210.

___. "Son of God or Servant of Yahweh?: a Reconsideration of Mark 1.11." In *Jesus the Saviour: Studies in New Testament Theology*. Downers Grove: Inter-Varsity, 1990: 121-133. Originally published in *NTS* 15 (1968-9), 326-36.

___. "The Messiah in the First Century: A Review Article." *Criswell Theological Review* 7 (1993) 67-83.

Martin, R. P. *Carmen Christi: Philippians 2:5-11 in Recent Interpretation and in the Setting of Early Christian Worship*. SNTSMS 4. Cambridge: CUP, 1967.

___. *Worship in the Early Church*. London: Marshall, Morgan and Scott, 1974.

Martin, R. P. and B. J. Dodd. *Where Christology Began: Essays on Philippians 2*. Louisville: Westminster/John Knox, 1998.

März, C. P. "'Feuer auf die Erde zu werfen, bin ich gekommen . . .': Zum Verständnis und zur Entstehung von Lk 12, 49." In F. Refoulé (ed.), *A cause de l'Evangile*. LD 123. Paris: Cerf, 1985: 479-512.

Mays, J. L. *The Lord Reigns: a Theological Handbook to the Psalms*. Louisville: Westminister John Knox, 1994.

McBride, S. D. *The Deuteronomic Name Theology*. Cambridge: CUP, 1969.

McConville, J. G. "God's 'Name' and God's 'Glory'." *TynBul* 30 (1979) 149-63.

McKay, J. W. and J. Rogerson. *Psalms*. CBC. 3 Vols. Cambridge: CUP, 1977.

McKelvey, R. J. *The New Temple: the Church in the New Testament*. London: OUP, 1968.

McKnight, S. *A New Vision for Israel: the Teachings of Jesus in National Context*. Studying the Historical Jesus. Grand Rapids: Eerdmans, 1999.

Mealand, D. L. "Dissimilarity Test." *SJT* 31 (1978) 41-50.

Meier, J. P. "Structure and Theology in Heb 1.1-14." *Bib* 66 (1985) 168-89.

___. *A Marginal Jew: Rethinking the Historical Jesus*. 3 Vols. New York: Doubleday, 1991-2001.

Meier, S. A. "Angel of Yahweh." *DDD* 96-108.

Mell, U. *Die 'anderen' Winzer: eine exegetische Studie zur Vollmacht Jesu Christi nach Markus 11,27-12,34*. WUNT 77. Tübingen: Mohr Siebeck, 1994.

Ménégoz, E. *La théologie de l'Épitre aux Hébreux*. Paris: Fischbacher, 1894.

Mettinger, T. N. D. *The Dethronement of Sabaoth: Studies in the Shem and Kabod Theologies*. Lund: Gleerup, 1982.

Metzger, B. M. *A Textual Commentary on the Greek New Testament: a Companion Volume to the United Bible Societies' Greek New Testament*. London: UBS, 1975.

Michel, O. *Der Brief an die Hebräer*. Göttingen: Vandenhoeck & Ruprecht, 1949.

Milavec, A. "A Fresh Analysis of the Parable of the Wicked Husbandmen in the Light of Jewish-Christian Dialogue." In C. Thoma and M. Wyschogrod (eds.), *Parable and Story in Judaism and Christianity*. New York: Paulist, 1989: 81-117.

___. "Mark's Parable of the Wicked Husbandmen As Reaffirming God's Predilection for Israel." *JES* 26 (1989) 289-312.

___. "The Identity of 'The Son' and 'The Others': Mark's Parable of the Wicked Husbandmen Reconsidered." *BTB* 20 (1990) 30-37.

Moffatt, J. *A Critical and Exegetical Commentary on the Epistle to the Hebrews*. ICC 40. Edinburgh: T & T Clark, 1924.

Moore, G. F. "Christian Writers on Judaism." *HTR* 14 (1921) 197-254.
___. "Intermediaries in Jewish Theology: Memra, Shekinah, Metatron." *HTR* 15 (1922) 41-85.
___. *Judaism in the First Centuries of the Christian Era: the Age of the Tannaim.* 3 Vols. Cambridge: CUP, 1930.
Morrice, W. G. "The Parable of the Tenants and the Gospel of Thomas." *ExpTim* 98 (1987) 104-7.
Morris, L. Review of J. D. G. Dunn's *Christology in the Making. Themelios* 8 (1982) 15-19.
Moule, C. F. D. "Further Reflexions on Philippians 2.5-11." In W. W. Gasque and R. P. Martin (eds.), *Apostolic History and the Gospel: Biblical and Historical Essays Presented to F. F. Bruce on His 60th Birthday.* Exeter: Paternoster, 1970: 264-76.
___. *The Origin of Christology.* Cambridge: CUP, 1977.
___. Review of J. D. G. Dunn's *Christology in the Making. JTS* 33 (1982) 259-63.
Mowinckel, S. *He That Cometh.* Nashville: Abingdon, 1956.
___. *The Psalms in Israel's Worship.* Oxford: Blackwell, 1982.
Muñoz Leon, D. *Dios-Palabra: Memrá en los Targumim del Pentateuco.* Granada: Institutión San Jerónomo, 1974.
Murphy-O'Connor, J. "Christological Anthropology in Phil. 2:6-11." *RB* 83 (1976) 25-50.
___. "1 Cor. 8:6: Cosmology or Soteriology?" *RB* 85 (1978) 253-67.
Murphy, R. E. "The Personification of Wisdom." In H. G. M. Williamson, R. P. Gordon, J. A. Emerton, and J. Day (eds.), *Wisdom in Ancient Israel: Essays in Honour of J.A. Emerton.* Cambridge: CUP, 1995: 222-33.
___. *The Tree of Life: an Exploration of Biblical Wisdom Literature.* New York: Doubleday, 1996.
Murray, J. *The Epistle to the Romans.* NICNT. Gran Rapids: Eerdmans, 1968.
Mussner, F. *Der Galaterbrief.* HTKNT 9. Freiburg: Herder, 1974.
Newman, C. C. *Paul's Glory-Christology: Tradition and Rhetoric.* NovTSup 69. Leiden: Brill, 1992.
Newman, C. C., J. R. Davila, and G. S. Lewis. *The Jewish Roots of Christological Monotheism: Papers from the St. Andrews Conference on the Historical Origins of the Worship of Jesus .* JSJSup 63. Leiden: Brill, 1999.
Newsom, C. A. "Woman and the Discourse of Patriarchal Wisdom: a Study of Proverbs 1-9." In P. L. Day (ed.), *Gender and Difference in Ancient Israel.* Minneapolis: Fortress, 1989: 142-60.
___. "Angels." *ABD* 1.248-53.
Nicholson, E. W. *Deuteronomy and Tradition.* Oxford: Blackwell, 1967.
Nickelsburg, G. W. E. "Enoch, Levi, and Peter: Recipients of Revelation in Upper Galilee." *JBL* 100 (1981) 575-600.
Nikiprowetzky, V. *Le commentaire de l'Ecriture chez Philon d'Alexandrie, son caractere et sa portee: observations philologiques.* ALGHJ 11. Leiden: Brill, 1977.
Nolland, J. *Luke.* WBC 35. Dallas: Word Books, 1993.
Norden, E. *Agnostos Theos: Untersuchungen zur Formengeschichte religiöser Rede.* Leipzig: Teubner, 1956.
North, R. "Separated Spiritual Substances in the Old Testament." *CBQ* 29 (1967) 419-449.
O'Brien, P. T. *The Epistle to the Philippians: a Commentary on the Greek Text.* NIGTC. Grand Rapids: Eerdmans, 1991.

O'Neill, J. C. Review of C. H. T. Fletcher-Louis's *Luke-Acts: Angels, Christology and Soteriology*. *JTS* 50 (1999) 225-230.

Oehler, G. Fr. *Theologie des Alten Testaments*. Stuttgart: J. F. Steinkopf, 1882.

Oesterley, W. O. E. and G. H. Box. *The Religion and Worship of the Synagogue: an Introduction to the Study of Judaism from the New Testament Period*. London: I. Pitman, 1911.

Olyan, S. M. *A Thousand Thousands Served Him: Exegesis and the Naming of Angels in Ancient Judaism*. TSAJ 36. Tübingen: Mohr Siebeck, 1993.

Page, S. H. T. "The Authenticity of the Ransom Logion (Mark 10:45b)." In R. T. France and D. Wenham (eds.), *Gospel Perspectives: Studies of History and Tradition in the Four Gospels*. Sheffield: JSOT Press, 1980: 137-61.

Pate, C. M. *The Reverse of the Curse: Paul, Wisdom, and the Law*. WUNT 2/114. Tübingen: Mohr Siebeck, 2000.

Patterson, S. J. "Fire and Dissension: Ipsissima Vox Jesus in Q 12:49, 51-53?" *Forum* 5.2 (1989) 121-39.

___. *The Gospel of Thomas and Jesus*. Sonoma: Polebridge, 1993.

Perdue, L. G. *Wisdom and Creation: the Theology of Wisdom Literature*. Nashville: Abingdon, 1994.

Perrin, N. "Mark XIV. 62: The End Product of a Christian Pesher Tradition?" *NTS* 13 (1965-1966) 150-55.

___. *Rediscovering the Teaching of Jesus*. New Testament Library. London: SCM, 1967.

___. *What Is Redaction Criticism?* Guides to Biblical Scholarship. Philadelphia: Fortress Press, 1969.

Pesch, R. *Das Markusevangelium*. HTKNT 2. Freiburg: Herder, 1977, 1991.

___. *Die Apostelgeschichte*. EKKNT 5. Zürich: Benziger Verlag, 1986.

Peterson, D. *Hebrews and Perfection: an Examination of the Concept of Perfection in the Epistle to the Hebrews*. SNTSMS 47. Cambridge: CUP, 1982.

Petzoldt, M. *Gleichnisse Jesu und christliche Dogmatik*. Göttingen: Vandenhoeck & Ruprecht, 1984.

Pfeifer, G. *Ursprung und Wesen der Hypostasenvorstellungen im Judentum*. ArbT 1/31. Stuttgart: Calwer, 1967.

Philonenko, M. *Le Trône de Dieu*. WUNT 69. Tübingen: Mohr Siebeck, 1993.

Polkow, D. "Method and Criteria for Historical Jesus Research." In D. J. Lull (ed.), *Society of Biblical Literature Seminar Papers*. Atlanta: Scholars Press, 1987: 336-356.

Poythress, V. S. "Is Romans 1:3-4 a Pauline Confession after All?" *ExpTim* 87 (1975-1976) 180-83.

Procksch, O. *TDNT* 4.89-100.

Puech, É. "Fragment d'une apocalypse en araméen (4Q246=ps Dan d) et le 'royaume de Dieu'." *RB* 99 (1992) 98-131.

Rainbow, P. A. *Monotheism and Christology in I Corinthians 8. 4-6*. D.Phil. Dissertation, Oxford University, 1987.

___. "Jewish Monotheism As the Matrix for New Testament Christology, a Review Article." *NovT* 33 (1991) 78-91.

Ramsey, A. M. "History and the Gospel." In Cross F. L. (ed.), *Studia Evangelica*. TUGAL 102. Berlin: Akademie-Verlag, 1968: 75-85.

Rankin, O. S. *Israel's Wisdom Literature: its Bearing on Theology and the History of Religion*. Edinburgh: T & T Clark, 1936.

Reese, J. M. *Hellenistic Influence on the Book of Wisdom and its Consequences.* AnBib 41. Rome: Biblical Institute Press, 1970.

___. "Paul Proclaims the Wisdom of the Cross: Scandal and Foolishness." *BTB* 9 (1979) 147-53.

___. "Christ As Wisdom Incarnate: Wise Than Solomon, Loftier Than Lady Wisdom." *BTB* 11 (1982) 44-47.

Rehm, M. *Der königliche Messias im Licht der Immanuel-Weissagungen des Buches Jesaja.* Kevelaer: Butzon und Bercker, 1968.

Reid, D. G., R. P. Martin, and G. F. Hawthorne. (eds.). *Dictionary of Paul and His Letters.* Downers Grove: Inter-Varsity, 1993.

Reinbold, W. *Der älteste Bericht über den Tod Jesu: literarische Analyse und historische Kritik der Passionsdarstellungen der Evangelien.* BZNW 69. Berlin: Walter de Gruyter, 1994.

Rese, M. *Alttestamentliche Motive in der Christologie des Lukas.* SNT 1. Gütersloh: Mohn, 1969.

Richardson, H. N. "Some Notes on 1QSa." *JBL* 76 (1957) 108-22.

Richardson, N. *Paul's Language About God.* JSNTSup 99. Sheffield: Sheffield Academic Press, 1994.

Riesner, R. *Jesus als Lehrer: eine Untersuchung zum Ursprung der Evangelien-Überlieferung.* WUNT 2/7. Tübingen: Mohr Siebeck, 1981.

___. "Präexistenz und Jungfrauengeburt." *TBei* 12 (1981) 177-87.

Riggenbach, E. *Der Brief an die Hebraer.* Leipzig: A. Deichert, 1913.

Ringgren, H. *Word and Wisdom: Studies in the Hypostatization of Divine Qualities and Functions in the Ancient Near East.* Lund: Ohlsson, 1947.

___. "Geister, Dämonen, Engel." *RGG* 2.1301-2.

___. "Hypostasen." *RGG* 3.503-506.

Robinson, B. P. "Peter and his Successors: Tradition and Redaction in Matthew 16.17-19." *JSNT* 21 (1984) 85-104.

Robinson, J. M. *A New Quest of the Historical Jesus.* Studies in Biblical Theology 25. London: SCM, 1959.

___. "Jesus as Sophos and Sophia." In R. L. Wilken (ed.), *Aspects of Wisdom in Judaism and Early Christianity.* Notre Dame: University of Notre Dame Press, 1975: 1-16.

Robinson, J. A. T. *The Human Face of God.* London: SCM, 1972.

___. "The Parable of the Wicked Husbandmen: a Test of Synoptic Relationships." *NTS* 21 (1975) 443-61.

Rohling, A. "Über den Jehovaengel des AT." *TQ* 48 (1866) 431.

Röttger, H. *Mal'ak Jahwe, Bote von Gott: die Vorstellung von Gottes Boten im hebräischen Alten Testament.* Frankfurt: Lang, 1978.

Rowland, C. "The Vision of the Risen Christ in Rev. 1.13ff: the Debt of an Early Christology to an Aspect of Jewish Angelology." *JTS* 31 (1980) 1-11.

___. *The Open Heaven: a Study of Apocalyptic in Judaism and Early Christianity.* London: SPCK, 1982.

Rowlandson, J. *Landowners and Tenants in Roman Egypt: the Social Relations of Agriculture in the Oxyrhynchite Nome.* Oxford: Clarendon, 1996.

Ruck-Schröder, A. *Der Name Gottes und der Name Jesu: eine neutestamentliche Studie.* WMANT 80. Neukirchen-Vluyn: Neukirchener Verlag, 1999.

Runia, D. T. *Philo of Alexandria and the Timaeus of Plato.* Leiden: Brill, 1986.

Rylaarsdam, J. C. *Exodus. Interpreter's Bible.* G. A. Buttrick. (ed.) New York: Abingdon, 1952.

Sanders, E. P. *Paul and Palestinian Judaism: a Comparison of Patterns of Religion.* London: SCM, 1977.

Sanders, J. T. *The New Testament Christological Hymns: their Historical Religious Background.* SNTSM 15. Cambridge: CUP, 1971.

———. *Ben Sira and Demotic Wisdom.* SBLMS 28. Chico: Scholars Press, 1983.

Sandmel, S. *Philo of Alexandria: an Introduction.* New York; Oxford: OUP, 1979.

Saydon, P. P. "The Divine Sonship of Christ in Psalm II." *Script* 3 (1948) 32-35.

Schaper, J. *Eschatology in the Greek Psalter.* WUNT 2/76. Tübingen: Mohr Siebeck, 1995.

Schelbert, G. "Sprachgeschichtliches zu 'Abba'." In P. Casetti, O. Keel, and A. Schenker (eds.), *Mélanges Dominique Barthélemy.* OBO 38. Fribourg: Éditions universitaires, 1981: 395-447.

Schencke, W. *Die Chokma (Sophia) in der jüdischen Hypostasenspekulation: ein Beitrag zur Geschichte der religiösen Ideen im Zeitalter des Hellenismus.* Kristiania: Utgit, 1913.

Schenke, L. "Gibt es im Markusevangelium eine Präexistenzchristologie?" *ZNW* 91 (2000) 45-71.

Schierse, F. J. *Verheissung und Heilsvollendung: zur theologischen Grundfrage des Hebräerbriefes.* München: Karl Zink, 1955.

Schimanowski, G. *Weisheit und Messias: die jüdischen Voraussetzungen der urchristlichen Präexistenzchristologie.* WUNT 2/17. Tübingen: Mohr Siebeck, 1985.

Schmidt, H. *Die Psalmen.* HAT 1/15. Tübingen: Mohr Siebeck, 1934.

Schmidt, K. L. *Der Rahmen der Geschichte Jesu: literarkritische Untersuchungen zur ältesten Jesusüberlieferung.* Berlin: Trowitzsch, 1919.

Schnabel, E. J. *Law and Wisdom From Ben Sira to Paul.* WUNT 2/16. Tübingen: Mohr Siebeck, 1985.

Schnackenburg, R. *God's Rule and Kingdom.* Freiburg: Herder, 1963.

Schneider, G. "Die Davidssohnfrage (Mk. 12, 35-37)." *Bib* 53 (1972) 65-90.

———. *Die Apostelgeschichte.* HTKNT 5. Freiburg: Herder, 1980.

Schrage, W. *Das Verhältnis des Thomas-Evangeliums zur synoptischen Tradition und zu den koptischen Evangelien-übersetzungen.* BZNWAK 29. Berlin: A. Töpelmann, 1964.

Schramm, T. *Der Markus-Stoff bei Lukas: eine literarkritische und redaktionsgeschichtliche Untersuchung.* SNTSMS 14. Cambridge: CUP, 1971.

Schuller, E. M. "4Q372 1: a Text about Joseph." *RQ* 14/55 (1990) 349-76.

———. "The Psalm of 4Q372.1 Within the Context of 2nd Temple Prayer: Genre and Prosody of Jewish and Christian Piety in Psalmody." *CBQ* 54 (1992) 67-79.

Schulz, S. *Q: die Spruchquelle der Evangelisten.* Zürich: Theologischer Verlag, 1972.

Schürmann, H. *Quellenkritische Untersuchung des lukanischen Abendmahlsberichtes Lk. 22,7-38.* Münster: Aschendorff, 1953-57.

———. *Traditionsgeschichtliche Untersuchungen zu den synoptischen Evangelien.* KBANT. Düseldorf: Patmos, 1968.

———. *Das Lukasevangelium.* HTKNT 3. Freiburg: Herder, 1969, 1994.

Schüssler Fiorenza, E. "Wisdom Mythology and the Christological Hymns of the New Testament." In R. L. Wilken (ed.), *Aspects of Wisdom in Judaism and Early Christianity.* Notre Dame: University of Notre Dame Press, 1975: 17-41.

Schwartz, D. R. "Two Pauline Allusions to the Redemptive Mechanism of the Crucifixion." *JBL* 102 (1983) 259-268.

Schweizer, E. "Zur Herkunft der Präexistenzvorstellung bei Paulus." *EvT* 19 (1959) 65-70.

___. "Röm 1,3f, und der Gegensatz von Fleisch und Geist vor und bei Paulus." In *Neotestamentica*. Zürich: Zwingli Verlag, 1963: 180-89.

___. "Zur Herkunft der Präexistenzvorstellung bei Paulus." In *Neotestamentica*. Zürich: Zwingli Verlag, 1963: 105-09.

___. "υἱός." *TDNT* 8.340-392.

___. "The Concept of the Davidic 'Son of God' in Acts and its Old Testament Background." In L. E. Keck and J. L. Martyn (eds.), *Studies in Luke-Acts: Essays Presented in Honor of Paul Schubert*. Nashville: Abingdon, 1966: 186-93.

___. "Zum religionsgeschichtlichen Hintergrund der 'Sendungsformel' Gal. 4,4f., Rö. 8,3f., Jn 3,16f., 1Jn 4,9." *ZNW* 57 (1966) 199-210.

___. *Das Evangelium nach Markus*. Göttingen: Vandenhoeck & Ruprecht, 1967.

___. *Beiträge zur Theologie des Neuen Testaments: Neutestamentliche Aufsätze (1955-1970)*. Zürich: Zwingli-Verlag, 1970.

___. *Jesus*. London: SCM, 1971.

___. "Review of E. Linnemann's 'Tradition und Interpretation in Röm. 1,3f.'." *EvT* 31 (1971) 275-76.

___. *Das Evangelium nach Matthäus*. Göttingen: Vandenhoeck & Ruprecht, 1973.

___. *The Good News According to Matthew*. Atlanta: John Knox, 1975.

___. "Paul's Christology and Gnosticism." In M. D. Hooker and S. G. Wilson (eds.), *Paul and Paulinism: Essays in Honour of C. K. Barrett*. London: SPCK, 1982: 115-23.

___. "What Do We Really Mean When We Say, 'God Sent His Son'?" In J. T. Carroll, C. H. Cosgrove, and E. E. Johnson (eds.), *Faith and History: Essays in Honor of Paul W. Meyer*. Atlanta: Scholars Press, 1990: 298-312.

Scott, B. B. *Hear Then the Parable: a Commentary on the Parables of Jesus*. Minneapolis: Fortress, 1989.

Scott, E. F. *The Epistle to the Hebrews: its Doctrine and Significance*. Edinburgh: T & T Clark, 1922.

Scott, J. M. *Adoption as Sons of God: an Exegetical Investigation into the Background of huiothesia in the Pauline Corpus*. WUNT 2/48. Tübingen: Mohr Siebeck, 1992.

Scott, R. B. Y. "Wisdom in Creation: the 'Amon of Proverbs 8.30." *VT* 10 (1960) 213-23.

Scroggs, R. "Paul: ΣΟΦΟΣ and ΠΝΕΥΜΑΤΙΚΟΣ." *NTS* 14 (1967-1968) 33-55.

Segal, A. F. *Two Powers in Heaven: Early Rabbinic Reports about Christianity and Gnosticism*. SJLA 25. Leiden: Brill, 1977.

___. "The Risen Christ and the Angelic Mediator Figures in Light of Qumran." In J. H. Charlesworth *Jesus and the Dead Sea Scrolls*. New York: Doubleday, 1992: 302-29.

Seitz, C. R. *Word Without End: the Old Testament as Abiding Theological Witness*. Grand Rapids: Eerdmans, 1998.

Sevrin, J.-M. "Un groupement de trois paraboles contre les richesses dans L'Evangile selon Thomas: EvTh 63, 64, 65." In J. Delorme (ed.), *Les paraboles évangéliques: perspectives nouvelles*. LD 135. Paris: Editions du Cerf, 1989: 425-39.

Sheppard, G. T. *Wisdom as a Hermeneutical Construct: a Study in the Sapientializing of the Old Testament*. BZAW 151. Berlin: Walter de Gruyter, 1980.

Sibinga, J. S. Review of K. R. Snodgrass's *The Parable of the Wicked Tenants: an Inquiry into Parable Interpretation*. *NovT* 26 (1984) 383-384.

Sigal, P. "Further Reflections on the 'Begotten' Messiah." *HAR* 7 (1983) 221-33.

Skarsaune, O. *The Proof from Prophecy, a Study in Justin Martyr's Proof-Text Tradition: Text-Type, Provenance, Theological Profile*. NovTSup 56. Leiden: Brill, 1987.

Snodgrass, K. R. *The Parable of the Wicked Tenants: an Inquiry into Parable Interpretation.* WUNT 27. Tübingen: Mohr Siebeck, 1983.
___. "The Gospel of Thomas: a Secondary Gospel." *SecCent* 7 (1989) 19-38.
___. "Recent Research on the Parable of the Wicked Tenants." *BBR* 8 (1998) 187-215.
Soards, M. L. *The Speeches in Acts: their Content, Context, and Concerns.* Louisville: Westminster/John Knox, 1994.
Speiser, E. A. *Genesis.* AB. New York: Doubleday, 1964.
Spicq, C. *L'Épître aux Hébreux.* EBib. Paris: Gabalda, 1953.
___. "Note sur MORPHE dans les papyrus et quelques inscriptions." *RB* 80 (1973) 37-45.
Stanton, G. N. "On the Christology of Q." In S. S. Smalley and B. Lindars (eds.), *Christ and Spirit in the New Testament.* Cambridge: CUP, 1973: 27-42.
___. *Jesus of Nazareth in New Testament Preaching.* SNTSMS 27. London: CUP, 1974.
Stauffer, E. "Zur Vor - und Frühgeschichte des Primatus Petri." *ZKG* 62 (1943) 3-34.
Steichele, H.-J. *Der leidende Sohn Gottes: eine Untersuchung einiger alttestamentlicher Motive in der Christologie des Markusevangeliums.* Regensburg: Pustet, 1980.
Stein, R. H. "The 'Criteria' for Authenticity." In R. T. France and D. Wenham (eds.), *Studies of History and Tradition in the Four Gospels.* Gospel Perspectives 2. Sheffield: JSOT Press, 1980: 225-63.
___. *Luke.* NAC 24. Nashville: Broadman, 1992.
Stern, D. "Jesus' Parables From the Perspective of Rabbinic Literature: The Example of the Wicked Husbandmen." In C. Thoma and M. Wyschogrod (eds.), *Parable and Story in Judaism and Christianity.* New York: Paulist, 1989: 42-80.
___. *Parables in Midrash: Narrative and Exegesis in Rabbinic Literature.* Cambridge: CUP, 1991.
Stier, F. *Gott und sein Engel im alten Testament.* Münster: Aschendorff, 1934.
Strack, H. L. and P. Billerbeck. *Kommentar zum Neuen Testament aus Talmud und Midrasch.* München: Beck, 1956.
Strathmann, H. *Der Brief an die Hebräer.* NTD 9. Göttingen: Vandenhoeck & Ruprecht, 1963.
Strauss, M. L. *The Davidic Messiah in Luke-Acts: the Promise and its Fulfillment in Lukan Christology.* JSNTSup 110. Sheffield: Sheffield Academic Press, 1995.
Strobel, A. *Die Stunde der Wahrheit: Untersuchungen zum Strafverfahren gegen Jesus.* WUNT 21. Tübingen: Mohr Siebeck, 1980.
Stuckenbruck, L. T. "An Angelic Refusal of Worship: the Tradition and its Function in the Apocalypse of John." In E. H. Lovering (ed.), *SBLSP 33.* Atlanta: Scholars Press, 1994: 679-96.
___. *Angel Veneration and Christology: a Study in Early Judaism and in the Christology of the Apocalypse of John.* WUNT 2/70. Tübingen: Mohr Siebeck, 1995.
Stuhlmacher, P. "Zur paulinischen Christologie." In *Versöhnung, Gesetz und Gerechtigkeit: Aufsätze zur biblischen Theologie.* Göttingen: Vandenhoeck & Ruprecht, 1981: 209-23.
___. "Vicariously Giving His Life for Many, Mark 10:45 (Matt. 20:28)." In *Reconciliation, Law, and Righteousness: Essays in Biblical Theology.* Philadelphia: Fortress, 1986: 16-29.
Suggs, M. J. "'The Word Is Near You': Rom 10:6-10 Within the Purpose of the Letter." In W. R. Farmer, C. F. D. Moule, and R. R. Niebuhr (eds.), *Christian History and Interpretation: Studies Presented to John Knox.* Cambridge: CUP, 1967: 289-312.
___. *Wisdom, Christology, and Law in Matthew's Gospel.* Cambridge: CUP, 1970.

Talbert, C. H. "The Problem of Pre-Existence in Phil. 2:6-11." *JBL* 86 (1967) 141-53.
___. "The Myth of a Descending-Ascending Redeemer in Mediterranean Antiquity." *NTS* 22 (1976) 418-40.
Taylor, V. *The Gospel According to St. Mark: the Greek Text.* London: Macmillan, 1952.
Theisohn, J. *Der auserwählte Richter: Untersuchungen zum traditionsgeschichtlichem Ort der Menschensohngestalt der Bilderreden des Äthiopischen Henoch.* StUNT 12. Göttingen: Vandenhoeck & Ruprecht, 1975.
Theissen, G. and A. Merz. *The Historical Jesus: a Comprehensive Guide.* London: SCM, 1998.
Thiselton, A. C. "The Supposed Power of Words." *JTS* 25 (1974) 283-99.
___. *The First Epistle to the Corinthians: a Commentary on the Greek Text.* NIGTC. Grand Rapids: Eerdmans, 2000.
Thompson, J. W. *The Beginnings of Christian Philosophy: the Epistle to the Hebrews.* CBQMS 13. Washington: Catholic Biblical Association of America, 1982.
Thompson, M. M. *The Promise of the Father: Jesus and God in the New Testament.* Louisville: Westminster/John Knox, 2000.
Tobin, T. H. *The Creation of Man: Philo and the History of Interpretation.* CBQMS 14. Washington, DC: Catholic Biblical Association of America, 1983.
Tournay, R. J. *Voir et entendre Dieu avec les Psaumes ou La liturgie prophétique du Second Temple à Jerusalem.* CRB 24. Paris: Gabalda, 1988.
Turner, C. H. "ὁ υἱός μου ὁ ἀγαπητός." *JTS* 27 (1925) 113-29.
Urassa, W. M. *Psalm 8 and its Christological Re-interpretations in the New Testament Context: an Inter-Contextual Study in Biblical Hermeneutics.* European University Studies 23. Frankfurt: Lang, 1998.
van der Woude, A. S. "De *Mal'ak Jahweh*: Een Godsbode." *NedTTs* 18 (1963-1964) 1-13.
___. "Name." *THAT* 935-963.
van Iersel, B. M. F. *'Der Sohn' in den synoptischen Jesusworten.* Leiden: Brill, 1961, 1964.
van Roon, A. "The Relationship between Christ and the Wisdom of God according to Paul." *NovT* 16 (1974) 207-39.
VanderKam, J. C. "Righteous One, Messiah, Chosen One, and Son of Man in 1 Enoch 3-71." In J. H. Charlesworth (ed.), *The Messiah: Developments in Earliest Judaism and Christianity*. Minneapolis: Fortress, 1992: 169-91.
Vanhoye, A. *Situation du Christ: Hébreux 1-2.* LD 58. Paris: Cerf, 1969.
Vermes, G. *Scripture and Tradition in Judaism: Haggadic Studies.* Leiden: Brill, 1961, 1973.
___. *Jesus the Jew: a Historian's Reading of the Gospels.* London: Collins, 1973.
Vielhauer, P. "Erwägungen zur Christologie des Markusevangeliums." In *Aufsätze zum Neuen Testament.* TBü 31. Munich: Kaiser, 1965: 199-215.
Vögtle, A. *Offenbarungsgeschehen und Wirkungsgeschichte: Neutestamentliche Beiträge.* Freiburg: Herder, 1985.
Volz, P. *Die Eschatologie der jüdischen Gemeinde im neutestamentlichen Zeitalter nach den Quellen der rabbinischen, apokalyptischen und apokryphen Literatur.* Tübingen: Mohr Siebeck, 1934.
von Harnack, A. *The Sayings of Jesus: the Second Source of St. Matthew and St. Luke.* London: Williams & Norgate, 1908.
___. "'Ich bin gekommen': Die ausdrücklichen Selbstzeugnisse Jesu über den Zweck seiner Sendung and seines Kommens." *ZTK* 22 (1912) 1-30.

von Rad, G. *Studies in Deuteronomy*. SBT 9. London: SCM, 1953.
___. *Old Testament Theology*. 2 Vols. Edinburgh: Oliver & Boyd, 1965.
___. *Genesis*. OTL. London: SCM, 1972.
___. *Wisdom in Israel*. Nashville: Abingdon, 1972.
Wallace, D. H. "A Note on Morphé." *TZ* 22 (1966) 19-25.
Wallace, D. P. *Texts in Tandem: the Coalescent Usage of Psalm 2 and Psalm 110 in Early Christianity*. PhD dissertation; Baylor University, 1995.
Walton, S. *Leadership and lifestyle: the portrait of Paul in the Miletus Speech and 1 Thessalonians*. SNTSMS 108. Cambridge: CUP, 2000.
Wanamaker, C. A. *The Son and the Sons of God: a Study in Elements of Paul's Christological and Soteriological Thought*. Ph.D diss. University of Durham, 1980.
___. "Christ As Divine Agent in Paul." *SJT* 39 (1986) 517-28.
___. "Philippians 2.6-11: Son of God or Adamic Christology." *NTS* 33 (1987) 179-93.
Watson, F. B. "The Triune Divine Identity: Reflections on Pauline God Language, in Disagreement with J.D.G. Dunn." *JSNT* 80 (2000) 99-124.
Watts, J. W. "Psalm 2 in the Context of Biblical Theology." *HBT* 12 (1990) 73-91.
Webb, R. L. *John the Baptizer and Prophet: a Socio-Historical Study*. JSNTSup 62. Sheffield: JSOT Press, 1991.
___. "Jesus' Baptism: its Historicity and Implications." *BBR* 10 (2000) 261-309.
Weder, H. *Das Kreuz Jesu bei Paulus: ein Versuch, über den Geschichtsbezug des christlichen Glaubens nachzudenken*. FRLANT 125. Göttingen: Vandenhoeck & Ruprecht, 1981.
Weinfeld, M. *Deuteronomy and the Deuteronomic School*. Oxford: Clarendon, 1972.
Weiser, A. *The Psalms: a Commentary*. Göttingen: Vandenhoeck & Ruprecht, 1962.
Weiss, H.-F. *Untersuchungen zur Kosmologie des hellenistischen und palästinischen Judentums*. TUGAL 97. Berlin: Akademie-Verlag, 1966.
Weiss, J. *Der erste Korintherbrief*. Göttingen: Vandenhoeck & Ruprecht, 1910.
Wendt, H. H. *Die Apostelgeschichte*. Göttingen: Vandenhoeck & Ruprecht, 1913.
Wengst, K. *Christologische Formeln und Lieder des Urchristentums*. SNT 7. Gütersloh: Mohn, 1972.
Wenham, G. J. *Genesis 16-50*. WBC 2. Dallas: Word Books, 1994.
Weren, W. J. C. "Psalm 2 in Luke-Acts: An Intertextual Study." In S. Draisma (ed.), *Intertextuality in Biblical Writings: Essays in Honour of Bas van Iersel*. Kampen: J. H. Kok, 1989: 189-203.
Werner, M. *Die Entstehung des christlichen Dogmas: problemgeschichtlich dargestellt*. Bern-Leipzig: Haupt, 1941.
Westerholm, S. *Jesus and Scribal Authority*. Coniectanea Biblica: New Testament Series 10. Lund: Gleerup, 1978.
Westermann, C. *Genesis 12-36: a Commentary*. Minneapolis: Augsburg, 1985.
Whitsett, C. G. "Son of God, Seed of David: Paul's Messianic Exegesis in Romans 1:3-4." *JBL* 119 (2000) 661-81.
Whybray, R. N. *Wisdom in Proverbs: the Concept of Wisdom in Proverbs 1-9*. SBT 45. London: SCM, 1965.
Wicks, H. J. *The Doctrine of God in the Jewish Apocryphal and Apocalyptic Literature*. London: Hunter & Longhurst, 1915.
Wilckens, U. *Weisheit und Torheit: eine exegetisch-religionsgeschichtliche Untersuchung zu 1. Kor. 1 und 2*. BHT 26. Tübingen: Mohr Siebeck, 1959.
___. *Die Missionsreden der Apostelgeschichte*. WMANT 5. Neukirchen-Vluyn: Neukirchener Verlag, 1961.
___. "σοφία." *TDNT* 7.465-67, 496-529.

___. "Das Kreuz Christi als die Tiefe der Weisheit Gottes: zu 1. Kor 2,1-16." In L. de Lorenzi (ed.), *Paolo a una chiesa divisa*. Roma: Abbazia, 1980: 43-81.

___. *Der Brief an Die Römer*. EKKNT 6/1-3. Koln: Benziger, 1980.

Williamson, R. *Philo and the Epistle to the Hebrews*. Leiden: Brill, 1970.

___. *Jews in the Hellenistic World: Philo*. Cambridge: CUP, 1989.

Willis, J. "Psalm 1: an Entity." *ZATW* 91 (1979) 381-401.

___. "A Cry of Defiance: Psalm 2." *JSOT* 47 (1990) 33-50.

Wilson, I. *Out of the Midst of the Fire: Divine Presence in Deuteronomy*. SBLDS 151. Atlanta: Scholars Press, 1995.

Wilson, R. M. *Hebrews*. NCBC. Grand Rapids: Eerdmans, 1987.

Windisch, H. "Die göttliche Weisheit der Juden und die paulinische Christologie." In A. Deissmann (ed.), *Neutestamentliche Studien: Georg Heinrici zu seinem 70. Geburtstag*. Untersuchungen zum Neuen Testament 6. Leipzig: Hinrichs, 1914: 220-234.

Winston, D. *The Wisdom of Solomon: a New Translation with Introduction and Commentary*. AB 43. New York: Doubleday, 1979.

___. *Logos and Mystical Theology in Philo of Alexandria*. Cincinnati; Hoboken, N.J: Hebrew Union College Press, 1985.

Witherington, B. *The Christology of Jesus*. Minneapolis: Fortress, 1990.

___. "Lord." *DJG* 484-92.

___. *Jesus the Sage: the Pilgrimage of Wisdom*. Minneapolis: Fortress, 1994.

___. *The Acts of the Apostles: a Socio-Rhetorical Commentary*. Grand Rapids: Eerdmans, 1998.

___. *The Gospel of Mark: a Socio-Rhetorical Commentary*. Grand Rapids: Eerdmans, 2001.

Witherington, B. and L. M. Ice. *The Shadow of the Almighty*. Grand Rapids: Eerdmans, 2002.

Wolfson, H. A. *Philo: Foundations of Religious Philosophy in Judaism, Christianity, and Islam*. 2 Vols. Cambridge: CUP, 1947.

Wong, T. Y.-C. "The Problem of Pre-Existence in Philippians 2, 6-11." *ETL* 62 (1986) 267-82.

Wright, G. E. "God Amidst His People: the Story of the Temple." In *The Rule of God: Essays in Biblical Theology*. New York: Doubleday, 1960: 55-76.

Wright, N. T. *The Messiah and the People of God: a Study of Pauline Theology with Particular Reference to the Argument of the Epistle to the Romans*. D.Phil. Diss., Oxford University, 1980.

___. Review of J. D. G. Dunn's *Christology in the Making*. *Churchman* 95 (1981) 170-72.

___. "ἁρπαγμός and the Meaning of Philippians 2:5-11." *JTS* 37 (1986) 321-52.

___. "Adam, Israel and the Messiah." In *The Climax of the Covenant: Christ and the Law in Pauline Theology*. Edinburgh: T & T Clark, 1991: 18-40.

___. *The Climax of the Covenant: Christ and the Law in Pauline Theology*. Edinburgh: T & T Clark, 1991.

___. "Jesus Christ Is Lord: Philippians 2.5-11." In *The Climax of the Covenant: Christ and the Law in Pauline Theology*. Edinburgh: T & T Clark, 1991: 56-98.

___. *The New Testament and the People of God*. London: SPCK, 1992.

___. *Jesus and the Victory of God*. London: SPCK, 1996.

___. "Jesus and the Identity of God." *Ex Auditu* 14 (1999) 42-56.

___. *The Letter to the Romans*. The New Interpreter's Bible. Vol. X. Nashville: Abingdon, 2002.

Wright, R. "Psalms of Solomon." In J. H. Charlesworth (ed.), *The Old Testament Pseudepigrapha*. London: Darton, Longman & Todd, 1983: 2.639-70.

Young, B. H. *Jesus the Jewish Theologian*. Peabody: Hendrickson Publishers, 1995.

Zimmerli, W. *Gottes Offenbarung: gesammelte Aufsatze zum Alten Testament*. TBü 19. München: Kaiser, 1963.

Zimmermann, J. "Observations on 4Q246: the 'Son of God'." In J. H. Charlesworth, G. S. Oegema, and H. Lichtenberger (eds.), *Qumran-Messianism: Studies on the Messianic Expectations in the Dead Sea Scrolls*. Tübingen: Mohr Siebeck, 1998: 175-90.

Zorn, R. *Die Fürbitte im Spätjudentum und im Neuen Testament*. Unpub. Diss., University of Göttingen, 1957.

Index of Authors

Index of References

Index of Subjects

Abba, 28, 29, 35, 116, 122, 123, 124, 125, 126, 127, 128, 129, 130, 131, 132, 133, 134, 135, 136, 139, 142, 146, 178, 179, 201, 318
Adam christology, 221, 298, 299, 301, 305, 306, 307, 308, 309, 310
Adoptionist christology, 264, 276
Angel of the Lord, 16, 17, 43, 87, 90, 95, 317
Angelomorphic christology, 2, 18, 45

Baptismal theophany, 136, 168, 178, 180, 278, 318
Blasphemy, 209, 233, 236

Confessional formula, 263, 268, 271
Criteria of authenticity, 118, 188

Deuteronomistic History, 80
Divine agency, 2, 8, 13, 14, 18, 47, 201, 320
Divine hypostasis, 37, 39, 40, 44, 45, 46, 48, 50, 51, 53, 54, 55, 58, 59, 61, 62, 68, 69, 72, 75, 77, 82, 95, 286
Divine identity, 2, 13, 25, 196, 314
Divine mission, 34, 35, 36, 115, 165, 181, 187, 190, 198, 200, 201, 280, 281, 283, 284, 296, 297, 298, 300, 305, 309, 310, 313, 314, 315, 319, 322
Divine Name, 16, 42, 82, 90
Divine sonship, 25, 26, 27, 28, 29, 30, 34, 35, 36, 115, 117, 120, 146, 151, 155, 165, 167, 168, 172, 178, 179, 180, 181, 200, 201, 202, 240, 241, 243, 250, 251, 255, 258, 259, 260, 261, 263, 266, 267, 269, 270, 271, 276, 277, 278, 279, 280, 281, 283, 284, 296, 297, 298, 300, 305, 309,

310, 311, 312, 313, 314, 315, 318, 319, 320, 321, 322
Divine Wisdom, 2, 3, 41, 42, 277, 299, 300, 303, 314

Enochic Son of Man, 24, 206, 208, 210
Enthronement, 14, 24, 34, 46, 171, 172, 178, 203, 204, 206, 211, 241, 242, 256, 258, 275, 281, 313, 314
Exaltation, 3, 4, 10, 21, 24, 32, 202, 203, 204, 209, 210, 211, 212, 213, 214, 215, 216, 217, 219, 220, 222, 223, 224, 225, 235, 237, 238, 239, 251, 255, 257, 258, 259, 260, 261, 266, 269, 272, 273, 274, 275, 276, 277, 278, 279, 280, 281, 305, 313, 320, 321
Exalted angels, 15, 24, 35, 85, 99, 115, 317

Father language, 29, 127, 130, 131, 132, 133, 134, 136, 179

God as Father, 29, 30, 122, 127, 128, 129, 130, 131, 132, 133, 135, 142, 281
God-given mission, 181, 182, 187, 189, 193, 194, 196, 197, 198, 199, 200, 319, 320

Heavenly Jerusalem, 6, 256, 258, 261, 270, 279, 321
Hypostasis, 9, 13, 22, 35, 38, 39, 41, 42, 43, 48, 53, 54, 58, 62, 67, 75, 76, 78, 80, 82, 83, 84, 88, 299, 317

Incarnation, 10, 11, 42, 99, 222, 274, 276, 292, 298, 303, 305, 307, 315
Inspiration, 65, 103, 229, 235, 303, 304

Wissenschaftliche Untersuchungen zum Neuen Testament
Alphabetical Index of the First and Second Series

Bolyki, János: Jesu Tischgemeinschaften. 1997. *Volume II/96.*

Bosman, Philip: Conscience in Philo and Paul. 2003. *Volume II/166.*

Bovon, François: Studies in Early Christianity. 2003. *Volume 161.*

Brocke, Christoph vom: Thessaloniki – Stadt des Kassander und Gemeinde des Paulus. 2001. *Volume II/125.*

Brunson, Andrew: Psalm 118 in the Gospel of John. 2003. *Volume II/158.*

Büchli, Jörg: Der Poimandres – ein paganisiertes Evangelium. 1987. *Volume II/27.*

Bühner, Jan A.: Der Gesandte und sein Weg im 4. Evangelium. 1977. *Volume II/2.*

Burchard, Christoph: Untersuchungen zu Joseph und Aseneth. 1965. *Volume 8.*

– Studien zur Theologie, Sprache und Umwelt des Neuen Testaments. Ed. von D. Sänger. 1998. *Volume 107.*

Burnett, Richard: Karl Barth's Theological Exegesis. 2001. *Volume II/145.*

Byron, John: Slavery Metaphors in Early Judaism and Pauline Christianity. 2003. *Volume II/162.*

Byrskog, Samuel: Story as History – History as Story. 2000. *Volume 123.*

Cancik, Hubert (Ed.): Markus-Philologie. 1984. *Volume 33.*

Capes, David B.: Old Testament Yaweh Texts in Paul's Christology. 1992. *Volume II/47.*

Caragounis, Chrys C.: The Development of Greek and the New Testament. 2004. *Volume 167.*

– The Son of Man. 1986. *Volume 38.*

– see *Fridrichsen, Anton.*

Carleton Paget, James: The Epistle of Barnabas. 1994. *Volume II/64.*

Carson, D.A., O'Brien, Peter T. and *Mark Seifrid* (Ed.): Justification and Variegated Nomism.
Volume 1: The Complexities of Second Temple Judaism. 2001. *Volume II/140.*
Volume 2: The Paradoxes of Paul. 2004. *Volume II/181.*

Ciampa, Roy E.: The Presence and Function of Scripture in Galatians 1 and 2. 1998. *Volume II/102.*

Classen, Carl Joachim: Rhetorical Criticsm of the New Testament. 2000. *Volume 128.*

Colpe, Carsten: Iranier – Aramäer – Hebräer – Hellenen. 2003. *Volume 154.*

Crump, David: Jesus the Intercessor. 1992. *Volume II/49.*

Dahl, Nils Alstrup: Studies in Ephesians. 2000. *Volume 131.*

Deines, Roland: Die Gerechtigkeit der Tora im Reich des Messias. 2004. *Volume 177.*

– Jüdische Steingefäße und pharisäische Frömmigkeit. 1993. *Volume II/52.*

– Die Pharisäer. 1997. *Volume 101.*

– and *Karl-Wilhelm Niebuhr (Ed.):* Philo und das Neue Testament. 2004. *Volume 172.*

Dettwiler, Andreas and *Jean Zumstein (Ed.):* Kreuzestheologie im Neuen Testament. 2002. *Volume 151.*

Dickson, John P.: Mission-Commitment in Ancient Judaism and in the Pauline Communities. 2003. *Volume II/159.*

Dietzfelbinger, Christian: Der Abschied des Kommenden. 1997. *Volume 95.*

Dimitrov, Ivan Z., James D.G. Dunn, Ulrich Luz and *Karl-Wilhelm Niebuhr* (Ed.): Das Alte Testament als christliche Bibel in orthodoxer und westlicher Sicht. 2004. *Volume 174.*

Dobbeler, Axel von: Glaube als Teilhabe. 1987. *Volume II/22.*

Du Toit, David S.: Theios Anthropos. 1997. *Volume II/91*

Dübbers, Michael: Christologie und Existenz im Kolosserbrief. 2005. *Volume II/191.*

Dunn, James D.G. (Ed.): Jews and Christians. 1992. *Volume 66.*

– Paul and the Mosaic Law. 1996. *Volume 89.*

– see *Dimitrov, Ivan Z.*

Dunn, James D.G., Hans Klein, Ulrich Luz and *Vasile Mihoc* (Ed.): Auslegung der Bibel in orthodoxer und westlicher Perspektive. 2000. *Volume 130.*

Ebel, Eva: Die Attraktivität früher christlicher Gemeinden. 2004. *Volume II/178.*

Ebertz, Michael N.: Das Charisma des Gekreuzigten. 1987. *Volume 45.*

Eckstein, Hans-Joachim: Der Begriff Syneidesis bei Paulus. 1983. *Volume II/10.*

– Verheißung und Gesetz. 1996. *Volume 86.*

Ego, Beate: Im Himmel wie auf Erden. 1989. *Volume II/34*

Ego, Beate, Armin Lange and *Peter Pilhofer (Ed.):* Gemeinde ohne Tempel – Community without Temple. 1999. *Volume 118.*

Eisen, Ute E.: see *Paulsen, Henning.*

Ellis, E. Earle: Prophecy and Hermeneutic in Early Christianity. 1978. *Volume 18.*

– The Old Testament in Early Christianity. 1991. *Volume 54.*

Endo, Masanobu: Creation and Christology. 2002. *Volume 149.*

Ennulat, Andreas: Die 'Minor Agreements'. 1994. *Volume II/62.*

Ensor, Peter W.: Jesus and His 'Works'. 1996. *Volume II/85.*

Eskola, Timo: Messiah and the Throne. 2001. *Volume II/142.*
– Theodicy and Predestination in Pauline Soteriology. 1998. *Volume II/100.*
Fatehi, Mehrdad: The Spirit's Relation to the Risen Lord in Paul. 2000. *Volume II/128.*
Feldmeier, Reinhard: Die Krisis des Gottessohnes. 1987. *Volume II/21.*
– Die Christen als Fremde. 1992. *Volume 64.*
Feldmeier, Reinhard and *Ulrich Heckel* (Ed.): Die Heiden. 1994. *Volume 70.*
Fletcher-Louis, Crispin H.T.: Luke-Acts: Angels, Christology and Soteriology. 1997. *Volume II/94.*
Förster, Niclas: Marcus Magus. 1999. *Volume 114.*
Forbes, Christopher Brian: Prophecy and Inspired Speech in Early Christianity and its Hellenistic Environment. 1995. *Volume II/75.*
Fornberg, Tord: see *Fridrichsen, Anton.*
Fossum, Jarl E.: The Name of God and the Angel of the Lord. 1985. *Volume 36.*
Foster, Paul: Community, Law and Mission in Matthew's Gospel. *Volume II/177.*
Fotopoulos, John: Food Offered to Idols in Roman Corinth. 2003. *Volume II/151.*
Frenschkowski, Marco: Offenbarung und Epiphanie. Volume 1 1995. *Volume II/79 –* Volume 2 1997. *Volume II/80.*
Frey, Jörg: Eugen Drewermann und die biblische Exegese. 1995. *Volume II/71.*
– Die johanneische Eschatologie. Volume I. 1997. *Volume 96.* – Volume II. 1998. *Volume 110.*
– Volume III. 2000. *Volume 117.*
Frey, Jörg and *Udo Schnelle (Ed.):* Kontexte des Johannesevangeliums. 2004. *Volume 175.*
Freyne, Sean: Galilee and Gospel. 2000. *Volume 125.*
Fridrichsen, Anton: Exegetical Writings. Edited by C.C. Caragounis and T. Fornberg. 1994. *Volume 76.*
Garlington, Don B.: 'The Obedience of Faith'. 1991. *Volume II/38.*
– Faith, Obedience, and Perseverance. 1994. *Volume 79.*
Garnet, Paul: Salvation and Atonement in the Qumran Scrolls. 1977. *Volume II/3.*
Gese, Michael: Das Vermächtnis des Apostels. 1997. *Volume II/99.*
Gheorghita, Radu: The Role of the Septuagint in Hebrews. 2003. *Volume II/160.*
Gräbe, Petrus J.: The Power of God in Paul's Letters. 2000. *Volume II/123.*

Gräßer, Erich: Der Alte Bund im Neuen. 1985. *Volume 35.*
– Forschungen zur Apostelgeschichte. 2001. *Volume 137.*
Green, Joel B.: The Death of Jesus. 1988. *Volume II/33.*
Gregory, Andrew: The Reception of Luke and Acts in the Period before Irenaeus. 2003. *Volume II/169.*
Gundry, Robert H.: The Old is Better. 2005. *Volume 178.*
Gundry Volf, Judith M.: Paul and Perseverance. 1990. *Volume II/37.*
Hafemann, Scott J.: Suffering and the Spirit. 1986. *Volume II/19.*
– Paul, Moses, and the History of Israel. 1995. *Volume 81.*
Hahn, Johannes (Ed.): Zerstörungen des Jerusalemer Tempels. 2002. *Volume 147.*
Hannah, Darrel D.: Michael and Christ. 1999. *Volume II/109.*
Hamid-Khani, Saeed: Relevation and Concealment of Christ. 2000. *Volume II/120.*
Harrison; James R.: Paul's Language of Grace in Its Graeco-Roman Context. 2003. *Volume II/172.*
Hartman, Lars: Text-Centered New Testament Studies. Ed. von D. Hellholm. 1997. *Volume 102.*
Hartog, Paul: Polycarp and the New Testament. 2001. *Volume II/134.*
Heckel, Theo K.: Der Innere Mensch. 1993. *Volume II/53.*
– Vom Evangelium des Markus zum viergestaltigen Evangelium. 1999. *Volume 120.*
Heckel, Ulrich: Kraft in Schwachheit. 1993. *Volume II/56.*
– Der Segen im Neuen Testament. 2002. *Volume 150.*
– see *Feldmeier, Reinhard.*
– see *Hengel, Martin.*
Heiligenthal, Roman: Werke als Zeichen. 1983. *Volume II/9.*
Hellholm, D.: see *Hartman, Lars.*
Hemer, Colin J.: The Book of Acts in the Setting of Hellenistic History. 1989. *Volume 49.*
Hengel, Martin: Judentum und Hellenismus. 1969, ³1988. *Volume 10.*
– Die johanneische Frage. 1993. *Volume 67.*
– Judaica et Hellenistica. Kleine Schriften I. 1996. *Volume 90.*
– Judaica, Hellenistica et Christiana. Kleine Schriften II. 1999. *Volume 109.*
– Paulus und Jakobus. Kleine Schriften III. 2002. *Volume 141.*

Hengel, Martin and *Ulrich Heckel* (Ed.): Paulus und das antike Judentum. 1991. *Volume 58.*

Hengel, Martin and *Hermut Löhr* (Ed.): Schriftauslegung im antiken Judentum und im Urchristentum. 1994. *Volume 73.*

Hengel, Martin and *Anna Maria Schwemer:* Paulus zwischen Damaskus und Antiochien. 1998. *Volume 108.*

– Der messianische Anspruch Jesu und die Anfänge der Christologie. 2001. *Volume 138.*

Hengel, Martin and *Anna Maria Schwemer* (Ed.): Königsherrschaft Gottes und himmlischer Kult. 1991. *Volume 55.*

– Die Septuaginta. 1994. *Volume 72.*

Hengel, Martin; Siegfried Mittmann and *Anna Maria Schwemer* (Ed.): La Cité de Dieu / Die Stadt Gottes. 2000. *Volume 129.*

Herrenbrück, Fritz: Jesus und die Zöllner. 1990. *Volume II/41.*

Herzer, Jens: Paulus oder Petrus? 1998. *Volume 103.*

Hoegen-Rohls, Christina: Der nachösterliche Johannes. 1996. *Volume II/84.*

Hofius, Otfried: Katapausis. 1970. *Volume 11.*

– Der Vorhang vor dem Thron Gottes. 1972. *Volume 14.*

– Der Christushymnus Philipper 2,6-11. 1976, ²1991. *Volume 17.*

– Paulusstudien. 1989, ²1994. *Volume 51.*

– Neutestamentliche Studien. 2000. *Volume 132.*

– Paulusstudien II. 2002. *Volume 143.*

Hofius, Otfried and *Hans-Christian Kammler:* Johannesstudien. 1996. *Volume 88.*

Holtz, Traugott: Geschichte und Theologie des Urchristentums. 1991. *Volume 57.*

Hommel, Hildebrecht: Sebasmata. Volume 1 1983. *Volume 31* – Volume 2 1984. *Volume 32.*

Hvalvik, Reidar: The Struggle for Scripture and Covenant. 1996. *Volume II/82.*

Johns, Loren L.: The Lamb Christology of the Apocalypse of John. 2003. *Volume II/167.*

Joubert, Stephan: Paul as Benefactor. 2000. *Volume II/124.*

Jungbauer, Harry: „Ehre Vater und Mutter". 2002. *Volume II/146.*

Kähler, Christoph: Jesu Gleichnisse als Poesie und Therapie. 1995. *Volume 78.*

Kamlah, Ehrhard: Die Form der katalogischen Paränese im Neuen Testament. 1964. *Volume 7.*

Kammler, Hans-Christian: Christologie und Eschatologie. 2000. *Volume 126.*

– Kreuz und Weisheit. 2003. *Volume 159.*

– see *Hofius, Otfried.*

Kelhoffer, James A.: The Diet of John the Baptist. 2005. *Volume 176.*

– Miracle and Mission. 1999. *Volume II/112.*

Kieffer, René and *Jan Bergman (Ed.):* La Main de Dieu / Die Hand Gottes. 1997. *Volume 94.*

Kim, Seyoon: The Origin of Paul's Gospel. 1981, ²1984. *Volume II/4.*

– Paul and the New Perspective. 2002. *Volume 140.*

– "The 'Son of Man'" as the Son of God. 1983. *Volume 30.*

Klauck, Hans-Josef: Religion und Gesellschaft im frühen Christentum. 2003. *Volume 152.*

Klein, Hans: see *Dunn, James D.G..*

Kleinknecht, Karl Th.: Der leidende Gerechtfertigte. 1984, ²1988. *Volume II/13.*

Klinghardt, Matthias: Gesetz und Volk Gottes. 1988. *Volume II/32.*

Koch, Michael: Drachenkampf und Sonnenfrau. 2004. *Volume II/184.*

Koch, Stefan: Rechtliche Regelung von Konflikten im frühen Christentum. 2004. *Volume II/174.*

Köhler, Wolf-Dietrich: Rezeption des Matthäusevangeliums in der Zeit vor Irenäus. 1987. *Volume II/24.*

Köhn, Andreas: Der Neutestamentler Ernst Lohmeyer. 2004. *Volume II/180.*

Kooten, George H. van: Cosmic Christology in Paul and the Pauline School. 2003. *Volume II/171.*

Korn, Manfred: Die Geschichte Jesu in veränderter Zeit. 1993. *Volume II/51.*

Koskenniemi, Erkki: Apollonios von Tyana in der neutestamentlichen Exegese. 1994. *Volume II/61.*

Kraus, Thomas J.: Sprache, Stil und historischer Ort des zweiten Petrusbriefes. 2001. *Volume II/136.*

Kraus, Wolfgang: Das Volk Gottes. 1996. *Volume 85.*

– and *Karl-Wilhelm Niebuhr* (Ed.): Frühjudentum und Neues Testament im Horizont Biblischer Theologie. 2003. *Volume 162.*

– see *Walter, Nikolaus.*

Kreplin, Matthias: Das Selbstverständnis Jesu. 2001. *Volume II/141.*

Kuhn, Karl G.: Achtzehngebet und Vaterunser und der Reim. 1950. *Volume 1.*

Kvalbein, Hans: see *Ådna, Jostein.*

Kwon, Yon-Gyong: Eschatology in Galatians. 2004. *Volume II/183.*

Laansma, Jon: I Will Give You Rest. 1997. *Volume II/98.*

Labahn, Michael: Offenbarung in Zeichen und Wort. 2000. *Volume II/117.*

Lambers-Petry, Doris: see *Tomson, Peter J.*

Lange, Armin: see *Ego, Beate.*

Lampe, Peter: Die stadtrömischen Christen in den ersten beiden Jahrhunderten. 1987, ²1989. *Volume II/18.*

Landmesser, Christof: Wahrheit als Grundbegriff neutestamentlicher Wissenschaft. 1999. *Volume 113.*

– Jüngerberufung und Zuwendung zu Gott. 2000. *Volume 133.*

Lau, Andrew: Manifest in Flesh. 1996. *Volume II/86.*

Lawrence, Louise: An Ethnography of the Gospel of Matthew. 2003. *Volume II/165.*

Lee, Aquila H.I.: From Messiah to Preexistent Son. 2005. *Volume II/192.*

Lee, Pilchan: The New Jerusalem in the Book of Relevation. 2000. *Volume II/129.*

Lichtenberger, Hermann: see *Avemarie, Friedrich.*

Lichtenberger, Hermann: Das Ich Adams und das Ich der Menschheit. 2004. *Volume 164.*

Lierman, John: The New Testament Moses. 2004. *Volume II/173.*

Lieu, Samuel N.C.: Manichaeism in the Later Roman Empire and Medieval China. ²1992. *Volume 63.*

Lindgård, Fredrik: Paul's Line of Thought in 2 Corinthians 4:16-5:10. 2004. *Volume II/189.*

Loader, William R.G.: Jesus' Attitude Towards the Law. 1997. *Volume II/97.*

Löhr, Gebhard: Verherrlichung Gottes durch Philosophie. 1997. *Volume 97.*

Löhr, Hermut: Studien zum frühchristlichen und frühjüdischen Gebet. 2003. *Volume160.*

– *:* see *Hengel, Martin.*

Löhr, Winrich Alfried: Basilides und seine Schule. 1995. *Volume 83.*

Luomanen, Petri: Entering the Kingdom of Heaven. 1998. *Volume II/101.*

Luz, Ulrich: see *Dunn, James D.G.*

Mackay, Ian D.: John's Raltionship with Mark. 2004. *Volume II/182.*

Maier, Gerhard: Mensch und freier Wille. 1971. *Volume 12.*

– Die Johannesoffenbarung und die Kirche. 1981. *Volume 25.*

Markschies, Christoph: Valentinus Gnosticus? 1992. *Volume 65.*

Marshall, Peter: Enmity in Corinth: Social Conventions in Paul's Relations with the Corinthians. 1987. *Volume II/23.*

Mayer, Annemarie: Sprache der Einheit im Epheserbrief und in der Ökumene. 2002. *Volume II/150.*

McDonough, Sean M.: YHWH at Patmos: Rev. 1:4 in its Hellenistic and Early Jewish Setting. 1999. *Volume II/107.*

McGlynn, Moyna: Divine Judgement and Divine Benevolence in the Book of Wisdom. 2001. *Volume II/139.*

Meade, David G.: Pseudonymity and Canon. 1986. *Volume 39.*

Meadors, Edward P.: Jesus the Messianic Herald of Salvation. 1995. *Volume II/72.*

Meißner, Stefan: Die Heimholung des Ketzers. 1996. *Volume II/87.*

Mell, Ulrich: Die „anderen" Winzer. 1994. *Volume 77.*

Mengel, Berthold: Studien zum Philipperbrief. 1982. *Volume II/8.*

Merkel, Helmut: Die Widersprüche zwischen den Evangelien. 1971. *Volume 13.*

Merklein, Helmut: Studien zu Jesus und Paulus. Volume 1 1987. *Volume 43.* – Volume 2 1998. *Volume 105.*

Metzdorf, Christina: Die Tempelaktion Jesu. 2003. *Volume II/168.*

Metzler, Karin: Der griechische Begriff des Verzeihens. 1991. *Volume II/44.*

Metzner, Rainer: Die Rezeption des Matthäusevangeliums im 1. Petrusbrief. 1995. *Volume II/74.*

– Das Verständnis der Sünde im Johannesevangelium. 2000. *Volume 122.*

Mihoc, Vasile: see *Dunn, James D.G..*

Mineshige, Kiyoshi: Besitzverzicht und Almosen bei Lukas. 2003. *Volume II/163.*

Mittmann, Siegfried: see *Hengel, Martin.*

Mittmann-Richert, Ulrike: Magnifikat und Benediktus. 1996. *Volume II/90.*

Mußner, Franz: Jesus von Nazareth im Umfeld Israels und der Urkirche. Ed. von M. Theobald. 1998. *Volume 111.*

Niebuhr, Karl-Wilhelm: Gesetz und Paränese. 1987. *Volume II/28.*

– Heidenapostel aus Israel. 1992. *Volume 62.*

– see *Deines, Roland*

– see *Dimitrov, Ivan Z.*

– see *Kraus, Wolfgang*

Nielsen, Anders E.: "Until it is Fullfilled". 2000. *Volume II/126.*

Nissen, Andreas: Gott und der Nächste im antiken Judentum. 1974. *Volume 15.*

Noack, Christian: Gottesbewußtsein. 2000. *Volume II/116.*

Noormann, Rolf: Irenäus als Paulusinterpret. 1994. *Volume II/66.*

Novakovic, Lidija: Messiah, the Healer of the Sick. 2003. *Volume II/170.*

Obermann, Andreas: Die christologische Erfüllung der Schrift im Johannesevangelium. 1996. *Volume II/83.*

Öhler, Markus: Barnabas. 2003. *Volume 156.*

Okure, Teresa: The Johannine Approach to Mission. 1988. *Volume II/31.*
Onuki, Takashi: Heil und Erlösung. 2004. *Volume 165.*
Oropeza, B. J.: Paul and Apostasy. 2000. *Volume II/115.*
Ostmeyer, Karl-Heinrich: Taufe und Typos. 2000. *Volume II/118.*
Paulsen, Henning: Studien zur Literatur und Geschichte des frühen Christentums. Ed. von Ute E. Eisen. 1997. *Volume 99.*
Pao, David W.: Acts and the Isaianic New Exodus. 2000. *Volume II/130.*
Park, Eung Chun: The Mission Discourse in Matthew's Interpretation. 1995. *Volume II/81.*
Park, Joseph S.: Conceptions of Afterlife in Jewish Insriptions. 2000. *Volume II/121.*
Pate, C. Marvin: The Reverse of the Curse. 2000. *Volume II/114.*
Peres, Imre: Griechische Grabinschriften und neutestamentliche Eschatologie. 2003. *Volume 157.*
Philonenko, Marc (Ed.): Le Trône de Dieu. 1993. *Volume 69.*
Pilhofer, Peter: Presbyteron Kreitton. 1990. *Volume II/39.*
– Philippi. Volume 1 1995. *Volume 87.* – Volume 2 2000. *Volume 119.*
– Die frühen Christen und ihre Welt. 2002. *Volume 145.*
– see *Ego, Beate.*
Plümacher, Eckhard: Geschichte und Geschichten. Aufsätze zur Apostelgeschichte und zu den Johannesakten. Herausgegeben von Jens Schröter und Ralph Brucker. 2004. *Volume 170.*
Pöhlmann, Wolfgang: Der Verlorene Sohn und das Haus. 1993. *Volume 68.*
Pokorný, Petr and *Josef B. Souček:* Bibelauslegung als Theologie. 1997. *Volume 100.*
Pokorný, Petr and *Jan Roskovec* (Ed.): Philosophical Hermeneutics and Biblical Exegesis. 2002. *Volume 153.*
Porter, Stanley E.: The Paul of Acts. 1999. *Volume 115.*
Prieur, Alexander: Die Verkündigung der Gottesherrschaft. 1996. *Volume II/89.*
Probst, Hermann: Paulus und der Brief. 1991. *Volume II/45.*
Räisänen, Heikki: Paul and the Law. 1983, ²1987. *Volume 29.*
Rehkopf, Friedrich: Die lukanische Sonderquelle. 1959. *Volume 5.*
Rein, Matthias: Die Heilung des Blindgeborenen (Joh 9). 1995. *Volume II/73.*

Reinmuth, Eckart: Pseudo-Philo und Lukas. 1994. *Volume 74.*
Reiser, Marius: Syntax und Stil des Markusevangeliums. 1984. *Volume II/11.*
Rhodes, James N.: The Epistle of Barnabas and the Deuteronomic Tradition. 2004. *Volume II/188.*
Richards, E. Randolph: The Secretary in the Letters of Paul. 1991. *Volume II/42.*
Riesner, Rainer: Jesus als Lehrer. 1981, ³1988. *Volume II/7.*
– Die Frühzeit des Apostels Paulus. 1994. *Volume 71.*
Rissi, Mathias: Die Theologie des Hebräerbriefs. 1987. *Volume 41.*
Roskovec, Jan: see *Pokorný, Petr.*
Röhser, Günter: Metaphorik und Personifikation der Sünde. 1987. *Volume II/25.*
Rose, Christian: Die Wolke der Zeugen. 1994. *Volume II/60.*
Rothschild, Clare K.: Luke Acts and the Rhetoric of History. 2004. *Volume II/175.*
Rüegger, Hans-Ulrich: Verstehen, was Markus erzählt. 2002. *Volume II/155.*
Rüger, Hans Peter: Die Weisheitsschrift aus der Kairoer Geniza. 1991. *Volume 53.*
Sänger, Dieter: Antikes Judentum und die Mysterien. 1980. *Volume II/5.*
– Die Verkündigung des Gekreuzigten und Israel. 1994. *Volume 75.*
– see *Burchard, Christoph*
Salier, Willis Hedley: The Rhetorical Impact of the Sēmeia in the Gospel of John. 2004. *Volume II/186.*
Salzmann, Jorg Christian: Lehren und Ermahnen. 1994. *Volume II/59.*
Sandnes, Karl Olav: Paul – One of the Prophets? 1991. *Volume II/43.*
Sato, Migaku: Q und Prophetie. 1988. *Volume II/29.*
Schäfer, Ruth: Paulus bis zum Apostelkonzil. 2004. *Volume II/179.*
Schaper, Joachim: Eschatology in the Greek Psalter. 1995. *Volume II/76.*
Schimanowski, Gottfried: Die himmlische Liturgie in der Apokalypse des Johannes. 2002. *Volume II/154.*
– Weisheit und Messias. 1985. *Volume II/17.*
Schlichting, Günter: Ein jüdisches Leben Jesu. 1982. *Volume 24.*
Schnabel, Eckhard J.: Law and Wisdom from Ben Sira to Paul. 1985. *Volume II/16.*
Schnelle, Udo: see *Frey, Jörg.*
Schutter, William L.: Hermeneutic and Composition in I Peter. 1989. *Volume II/30.*

Schwartz, Daniel R.: Studies in the Jewish Background of Christianity. 1992. *Volume 60.*

Schwemer, Anna Maria: see *Hengel, Martin*

Scott, James M.: Adoption as Sons of God. 1992. *Volume II/48.*

– Paul and the Nations. 1995. *Volume 84.*

Shum, Shiu-Lun: Paul's Use of Isaiah in Romans. 2002. *Volume II/156.*

Siegert, Folker: Drei hellenistisch-jüdische Predigten. Teil I 1980. *Volume 20* – Teil II 1992. *Volume 61.*

– Nag-Hammadi-Register. 1982. *Volume 26.*

– Argumentation bei Paulus. 1985. *Volume 34.*

– Philon von Alexandrien. 1988. *Volume 46.*

Simon, Marcel: Le christianisme antique et son contexte religieux I/II. 1981. *Volume 23.*

Snodgrass, Klyne: The Parable of the Wicked Tenants. 1983. *Volume 27.*

Söding, Thomas: Das Wort vom Kreuz. 1997. *Volume 93.*

– see *Thüsing, Wilhelm.*

Sommer, Urs: Die Passionsgeschichte des Markusevangeliums. 1993. *Volume II/58.*

Souček, Josef B.: see *Pokorný, Petr.*

Spangenberg, Volker: Herrlichkeit des Neuen Bundes. 1993. *Volume II/55.*

Spanje, T.E. van: Inconsistency in Paul? 1999. *Volume II/110.*

Speyer, Wolfgang: Frühes Christentum im antiken Strahlungsfeld. Volume I: 1989. *Volume 50.*

– Volume II: 1999. *Volume 116.*

Stadelmann, Helge: Ben Sira als Schriftgelehrter. 1980. *Volume II/6.*

Stenschke, Christoph W.: Luke's Portrait of Gentiles Prior to Their Coming to Faith. *Volume II/108.*

Sterck-Degueldre, Jean-Pierre: Eine Frau namens Lydia. 2004. *Volume II/176.*

Stettler, Christian: Der Kolosserhymnus. 2000. *Volume II/131.*

Stettler, Hanna: Die Christologie der Pastoralbriefe. 1998. *Volume II/105.*

Stökl Ben Ezra, Daniel: The Impact of Yom Kippur on Early Christianity. 2003. *Volume 163.*

Strobel, August: Die Stunde der Wahrheit. 1980. *Volume 21.*

Stroumsa, Guy G.: Barbarian Philosophy. 1999. *Volume 112.*

Stuckenbruck, Loren T.: Angel Veneration and Christology. 1995. *Volume II/70.*

Stuhlmacher, Peter (Ed.): Das Evangelium und die Evangelien. 1983. *Volume 28.*

– Biblische Theologie und Evangelium. 2002. *Volume 146.*

Sung, Chong-Hyon: Vergebung der Sünden. 1993. *Volume II/57.*

Tajra, Harry W.: The Trial of St. Paul. 1989. *Volume II/35.*

– The Martyrdom of St.Paul. 1994. *Volume II/67.*

Theißen, Gerd: Studien zur Soziologie des Urchristentums. 1979, ³1989. *Volume 19.*

Theobald, Michael: Studien zum Römerbrief. 2001. *Volume 136.*

Theobald, Michael: see *Mußner, Franz.*

Thornton, Claus-Jürgen: Der Zeuge des Zeugen. 1991. *Volume 56.*

Thüsing, Wilhelm: Studien zur neutestamentlichen Theologie. Ed. von Thomas Söding. 1995. *Volume 82.*

Thurén, Lauri: Derhethorizing Paul. 2000. *Volume 124.*

Tolmie, D. Francois: Persuading the Galatians. 2005. *Volume II/190.*

Tomson, Peter J. and *Doris Lambers-Petry* (Ed.): The Image of the Judaeo-Christians in Ancient Jewish and Christian Literature. 2003. *Volume 158.*

Trebilco, Paul: The Early Christians in Ephesus from Paul to Ignatius. 2004. *Volume 166.*

Treloar, Geoffrey R.: Lightfoot the Historian. 1998. *Volume II/103.*

Tsuji, Manabu: Glaube zwischen Vollkommenheit und Verweltlichung. 1997. *Volume II/93.*

Twelftree, Graham H.: Jesus the Exorcist. 1993. *Volume II/54.*

Urban, Christina: Das Menschenbild nach dem Johannesevangelium. 2001. *Volume II/137.*

Visotzky, Burton L.: Fathers of the World. 1995. *Volume 80.*

Vollenweider, Samuel: Horizonte neutestamentlicher Christologie. 2002. *Volume 144.*

Vos, Johan S.: Die Kunst der Argumentation bei Paulus. 2002. *Volume 149.*

Wagener, Ulrike: Die Ordnung des „Hauses Gottes". 1994. *Volume II/65.*

Wahlen, Clinton: Jesus and the Impurity of Spirits in the Synoptic Gospels. 2004. *Volume II/185.*

Walker, Donald D.: Paul's Offer of Leniency (2 Cor 10:1). 2002. *Volume II/152.*

Walter, Nikolaus: Praeparatio Evangelica. Ed. von Wolfgang Kraus und Florian Wilk. 1997. *Volume 98.*

Wander, Bernd: Gottesfürchtige und Sympathisanten. 1998. *Volume 104.*

Watts, Rikki: Isaiah's New Exodus and Mark. 1997. *Volume II/88.*

Wedderburn, A.J.M.: Baptism and Resurrection. 1987. *Volume 44.*

Wegner, Uwe: Der Hauptmann von Kafarnaum. 1985. *Volume II/14.*

Weissenrieder, Annette: Images of Illness in the Gospel of Luke. 2003. Volume II/164.

Welck, Christian: Erzählte ‚Zeichen‘. 1994. *Volume II/69.*

Wiarda, Timothy: Peter in the Gospels . 2000. *Volume II/127.*

Wilk, Florian: see *Walter, Nikolaus.*

Williams, Catrin H.: I am He. 2000. *Volume II/113.*

Wilson, Walter T.: Love without Pretense. 1991. *Volume II/46.*

Wischmeyer, Oda: Von Ben Sira zu Paulus. 2004. *Volume 173.*

Wisdom, Jeffrey: Blessing for the Nations and the Curse of the Law. 2001. *Volume II/133.*

Wucherpfennig, Ansgar: Heracleon Philologus. 2002. *Volume 142.*

Yeung, Maureen: Faith in Jesus and Paul. 2002. *Volume II/147.*

Zimmermann, Alfred E.: Die urchristlichen Lehrer. 1984, ²1988. *Volume II/12.*

Zimmermann, Johannes: Messianische Texte aus Qumran. 1998. *Volume II/104.*

Zimmermann, Ruben: Christologie der Bilder im Johannesevangelium. 2004. *Volume 171.*

– Geschlechtermetaphorik und Gottesverhältnis. 2001. *Volume II/122.*

Zumstein, Jean: see *Dettwiler, Andreas*

Zwiep, Arie W.: Judas and the Choice of Matthias. 2004. *Volume II/187.*

For a complete catalogue please write to the publisher
Mohr Siebeck • P.O. Box 2030 • D–72010 Tübingen/Germany
Up-to-date information on the internet at www.mohr.de